MILESTONES
IN
GLASNOST
AND
PERESTROYKA
POLITICS AND PEOPLE

MILESTONES

IN GLASNOST AND PERESTROYKA

POLITICS AND PEOPLE

ED A. HEWETT and VICTOR H. WINSTON

Editors

THE BROOKINGS INSTITUTION
Washington, D.C.

Copyright © 1991

THE BROOKINGS INSTITUTION

1775 Massachusets Avenue, N.W., Washington, D.C. 20036

Library of Congress Cataloging-in-Publication Data:
Milestones in glasnost and perestroyka / Ed A. Hewett and
　Victor H. Winston, editors.
　　　　p.　　cm.
　　Readings based on contributions to Soviet economy 1985–1991.
　　Includes bibliographical references and indexes.
　　Contents: v. 1. The economy—v. 2. Politics and people.
　　ISBN 0-8157-3622-3 (v. 1 : alk. paper)—ISBN 0-8157-3621-5 (v. 1 : pbk. :
alk. paper)—ISBN 0-8157-3624-x (v. 2 : alk. paper)—ISBN 0-8157-3623-1 (v. 2:
pbk. : alk. paper)
　　　1. Soviet Union—Economic policy—1986–　. 2. Soviet Union—Economic
conditions—1985–　. 3. Glasnost. 4. Perestroîka. I. Hewett, Edward A.
II. Winston, Victor H., 1925–　.
HC336.26.M555　　1991
338.947′009′048—dc20　　　　　　　　　　　　　　　　　　　　91-15304
　　　　　　　　　　　　　　　　　　　　　　　　　　　　　　CIP

9 8 7 6 5 4 3 2 1

The paper used in this publication meets the minimum requirements of the American National Standard for Information Sciences—Permanence of paper for Printed Library Materials, ANSI Z39.48-1984

Set in Linotron Times Roman
Composition by Harper Graphics
　Waldorf, Maryland
Printed by R.R. Donnelley and Sons Co.
　Harrisonburg, Virginia

Foreword

IN MARCH 1985 Mikhail Gorbachev became General Secretary of the Communist Party and set in motion efforts to open up and restructure Soviet society. *Glasnost'* and *perestroyka* have clearly brought profound changes to the Soviet Union and to the international community. But because of their dizzying pace and uncertain course, these changes have often been as bewildering as they have been dramatic.

Fortunately, also in the spring of 1985 the journal *Soviet Economy* was launched. Introducing the initial volume, the editors recognized that the Soviet economy was "in the early stages of an important transitional period in which the leadership will (and must) introduce significant changes in economic policies and possibly in the fundamentals of the system." They pledged that their journal would present research results and analytic observations concerning those changes as well as essays placing them in historical context. In 1987, when the nexus between economics and politics became the focus of very interesting research, *Soviet Economy* began to publish seminal papers in political science and contemporary history. Since then, the journal has consistently offered important research and analysis by Western political scientists and historians along with contributions from key participants in the reform process in the Soviet Union.

This book on Soviet politics and people, and its companion volume on the Soviet economy, present articles drawn largely from *Soviet Economy*. These readings are intended to offer a valuable chronicle and analysis of the milestones in the reform process. Because *Soviet Economy*, which is published in association with the Joint Committee on Soviet Studies of the American Council of Learned Societies and the Social Science Research Council, is not a Brookings publication, formal review and verification procedures established for the Institution's publications have not been applied in this case.

Ed A. Hewett, founding editor of *Soviet Economy* and a former senior fellow in the Brookings Foreign Policy Studies program, is now Special Assistant to the President on National Security Affairs and Senior Director of Soviet Affairs at the National Security Council. Hewett's work on this book was completed before he joined the National Security Council staff. Accordingly, the views he expressed here are his own and not necessarily those of the U.S. Government. Victor H. Winston, coeditor of *Soviet Economy* and a former head of research at the Mid-European Studies Center of Radio Free Europe, is an adjunct professor of international affairs at George Mason University.

The editors are indebted to all the contributors to this volume, but wish to express their particular appreciation to George W. Breslauer, professor of political science and chairman of the Center for Slavic and East European Studies, University of California, Berkeley, whose suggestions and comments were of great value. Professional courtesies were also extended by William G. Hyland, editor, *Foreign Affairs*; James H. Noren, senior economist, Office of Soviet Analysis, Central Intelligence Agency; Blair A. Ruble, director, Kennan Institute for Advanced Russian Studies; David R. Marples, associate professor of Russian and Soviet history at the University of Alberta; as well as by *Soviet Economy's* coeditors Timothy J. Colton, Morris and Ann Feldburg Professor of Government and Russian Studies at Harvard University, and Gertrude E. Schroeder, professor of economics, University of Virginia. The editors also acknowledge William E. Pomeranz of the Kennan Institute for Advanced Russian Studies and Brian W. Hayman, operations manager in the publishing house responsible for *Soviet Economy*, for their outstanding support in the compilation of indexes; and Drew Portocarrero and Elisa Barsoum for their assistance in verifying and processing selected information. Finally, the editors wish to express their deep appreciation to Robert L. Faherty, Norman Turpin, and all the participants in the publishing effort at Brookings.

The views expressed in this book are those of the individual authors and should not be ascribed to the trustees, officers, or staff members of the Brookings Institution.

BRUCE K. MAC LAURY
President

July 1991
Washington, D.C.

Contents

Part I THE EARLY YEARS OF THE GORBACHEV ERA

The Early Years of the Gorbachev Era: An Introduction   3
Victor H. Winston

1. The Gorbachev Succession   11
   William G. Hyland
   Before the Succession   *12*
   The Emerging Change   *13*
   The Soviet Union and the West   *15*
   Doing Business with Gorbachev   *17*
   References   *18*

2. Chernobyl': A Catalyst for Change   19
   Zhores Medvedev
   The Accident   *19*
   Official Reaction   *23*
   Evacuation and Contamination   *26*
   Political Repercussions and Reverberations   *28*
   References   *30*

3. Gorbachev's Social Contract   31
   Peter A. Hauslohner
   The First Post-Stalin Social Contract   *33*
   "De-Alignment"   *37*
   Gorbachev's Program   *42*
   Institutionalizing the New Order   *50*
   Conclusions   *57*
   References   *60*

4. The Politics of Systemic Economic Reform   65
   Timothy J. Colton
   The Gorbachev Record   *65*

What Is There to Explain?   *67*
Levels of Analysis   *68*
Level I: The Top Leader   *69*
Level II: The Political Leadership   *74*
Level III: The Bureaucracy   *78*
Level IV: The Knowledge Specialists   *82*
Level V: The Population   *85*
Looking Forward   *88*
References   *89*

5. The Social Dimensions of *Perestroyka*   91
   Blair A. Ruble
   Social Transformation   *92*
   New Social Groups   *95*
   Shifting Authority Relations   *99*
   Policy Consequences: Can Gorbachev Catch Up?   *101*
   References   *101*

**Part II   THE POLITICS AND ADVERSITIES
           OF CHANGE**

The Politics and Adversities of Change: An Introduction   107
Timothy J. Colton

6. The 19th Party Conference   112
   Ed A. Hewett with Thane Gustafson and
   Victor H. Winston
   The Elections   *112*
   Compromises on the Agenda   *117*
   Opponents of *Perestroyka*   *118*
   Basic Themes of the Conference   *124*
   Concluding Comments   *128*
   References   *130*

7. The Politics of the 19th Party Conference   132
   Jerry F. Hough
   Identifying What Is Important   *132*
   What Was Accomplished   *133*
   Interpreting the Results   *135*
   References   *138*

8. Interpretations and Perceptions of *Perestroyka*   139
   Andrey Sakharov with Yelena Bonner, Stephen F.
   Cohen, Ed A. Hewett, and Victor H. Winston
   The Political Alternatives and Conceptions   *140*

The Radical *Perestroyka* *141*
The Politics of Constitutional Change *143*
The Survival of *Perestroyka* *145*
American Perceptions of *Perestroyka* *148*
Concluding Comments *150*
References *151*

9. The Heralds of Opposition to *Perestroyka*　　153
   Yitzhak M. Brudny
   The Tradition of the "Thick Journal" *153*
   Russian Nationalism in *Novvy Mir* and *Molodaya
   Gvardiya*, 1956–1970 *155*
   Nash Sovremennik, 1970–1985 *157*
   Nash Sovremennik and *Molodaya Gvardiya* under
   　Gorbachev *159*
   Popularity of Russian Nationalist Appeal *177*
   References *183*

10. Gorbachev and the "National Question"　　190
    Gail W. Lapidus
    Six Varieties of National Self-Assertion *191*
    Emerging Policy Debates *193*
    "New Political Thinking" on National Relations *197*
    Our Common Home: Restructuring the Federal System *199*
    The Economics of Federalism: Republic Economic
    　Sovereignty *206*
    Language Policy *212*
    Nationality and the Soviet Armed Forces *216*
    National Minorities: The Revenge of Otto Bauer *219*
    The Problem of Party Fragmentation *223*
    Power and Politics *227*
    The Central Committee Plenum *229*
    Concluding Remarks *232*
    References *234*

Part III　THE STIRRINGS OF DEMOCRATIZATION
The Stirrings of Democratization: An Introduction　　241
George W. Breslauer

11. The Politics of Successful Economic Reform　　246
    Jerry F. Hough
    How Gorbachev Consolidated Power *247*
    The Elections to the Congress of People's Deputies *256*

The Congress of People's Deputies and the Supreme Soviet *266*
A Threat from the Left? *276*
Gorbachev's Calculations *280*
References *286*

12. Labor Unrest and Movements in 1989 and 1990   287
    Peter Rutland
    Soviet Industrial Relations before *Perestroyka* *288*
    Background of the Coal Miners' Strikes *291*
    The Events of July 1989 *294*
    The Aftermath of the Strikes *301*
    Preliminary Assessment *315*
    Four Scenarios for the Future *320*
    Concluding Comments *322*
    References *324*

13. The Moscow Election of 1990   326
    Timothy J. Colton
    Formal Organization of Nominations and Campaigning *328*
    Voting and Winning *335*
    The Candidates *338*
    The Party That Wasn't *343*
    Thunder on the Left *346*
    The Spoiler Slates *354*
    The Voters Speak *361*
    The Correlates of Success *369*
    Conclusions *378*
    References *380*

Part IV   MIKHAIL GORBACHEV AS LEADER
Mikhail Gorbachev as Leader: An Introduction   385
Peter H. Solomon, Jr.

14. Evaluating Gorbachev as Leader   390
    George W. Breslauer
    The Normative versus the Analytic *390*
    Establishing Baselines for Evaluation *391*
    Gorbachev: Event-Making Man? *395*
    Missed Opportunities? *397*
    Transformational Leadership *403*
    Gorbachev as Transformational Leader *407*
    Transitions to Democracy *410*
    Gorbachev's Contribution: Tragic or Transformational? *417*

Conclusion: In Praise of Gorbachev's Leadership Strategy   *422*
Afterword: The 28th Congress of the CPSU   *424*
References   *426*

15. The Quality of Gorbachev's Leadership   431
Peter Reddaway
Gorbachev in Historical Perspective   *431*
Gorbachev's Vision: A Critical Appraisal   *433*
A Comment on Migranyan   *436*
Gorbachev's Evaporating Support   *436*
Mounting Pressures from the Right   *438*
The Uneasy Left   *441*
Gorbachev's Options   *442*
Concluding Note   *444*
References   *445*

16. Gorbachev's Leadership: Another View   446
Archie Brown
Pressure from the "Right"   *448*
The Challenge from the "Left"   *450*
Gorbachev's Politics   *453*
Modernization or Transformation   *454*
Institutional Innovation   *456*
New Complexities   *457*
References   *458*

17. Gorbachev's Leadership: A Soviet View   460
Andranik Migranyan
The Collapse of Authority   *461*
Gorbachev's Options   *462*
References   *464*

18. Understanding Gorbachev: The Importance of Politics   465
Jerry F. Hough
Recognizing the Existence of Politics   *466*
The Consolidation of Power   *469*
Changing the Mechanisms of Power   *472*
1917 or 1929?   *475*
The Young and the Military   *478*
Conclusion   *482*
References   *483*

19. Gorbachev: Diverse Perspectives   485
George W. Breslauer
Jerry Hough's Critique   *487*
The State of the Art   *488*
Gorbachev's Values and Strategy   *489*

On the Effectiveness of Gorbachev's Strategy   *490*
On the Use of Comparative Analysis   *491*
On Leadership Evaluation   *492*
Conclusion   *494*
References   *495*

Part V   EPILOGUE

Half Measures   497
Yevgeniy Yevtushenko

Chronology of Events, March 11, 1985–July 11, 1991   499

Name Index   537

Subject Index   547

Tables

Chapter 4
1. Political Factors Promoting and Inhibiting Economic Reform in a
    Soviet-Type Society   70

Chapter 5
1. Percentage of Total American, Italian, and Soviet Populations in
    Urban Areas, 1940–1981   92
2. Size Category of Large American and Soviet Cities, 1939/40–1979/80 93
3. Educational Level of the Soviet Population, 1939–1986   93
4. Educational Level of Urban and Rural Populations of the Soviet Union,
    1939–1986   94
5. Employment Structure of the Soviet Economy by Sector, 1940–1985   95

Chapter 10
1. National Composition of Soviet Union Republics, 1979 and 1989   220
2. Political Attitudes in Lithuania, March 1990   226

Chapter 11
1. Results of March 1989 Elections in the RSFSR, by Occupation   263
2. The USSR Council of Ministers   272

Chapter 13
1. Distribution of Candidates for the Moscow Soviet across Electoral
    Districts   332
2. Outcomes for Candidates in First Round (March 4, 1990)   337
3. Outcomes for Candidates in Runoff Vote (March 18, 1990)   338

4. Characteristics of Registered and Winning Candidates   339
5. Selected Characteristics of Candidates by Slate   352
6. Selected Parameters of Election Returns   361
7. Distrubution of Votes by Slate   362
8. Regression Coefficients for Left Slate's Percentage of Valid
    First-Round Votes   371

Chapter 14
1. Images of the Soviet Future (to the Year 2010)   418

Figures

Chapter 2
1. Site Map of the Chernobyl' Atomic Power Station   20
2. Area Near the Chernobyl' Reactor Site   25

Chapter 13
 1. Moscow Rayons   329
 2. Average Number of Candidates per Electoral District   333
 3. Average Number of Left Candidates per Electoral District   351
 4. Average Number of Right Candidates per Electoral District 358
 5. Average Number of Center Candidates per Electoral District 360
 6. Left Candidates' Share of Popular Vote in First Round   363
 7. Right Candidates' Share of Popular Vote in First Round   364
 8. Center Candidates' Share of Popular Vote in First Round   365
 9. Unendorsed Candidates' Share of Popular Vote in First Round 366
10. Left Candidates' Share of Popular Vote in Runoff   367

Contributors

Yelena G. Bonner Author

George W. Breslauer Professor of Political Science and Chairman of the Center for Slavic and East European Studies, University of California, Berkeley

Archie Brown Professor of Politics, Oxford University, and Fellow of St. Anthony's College, Oxford

Yitzhak M. Brudny Assistant Professor, Department of Political Science, Yale University

Stephen F. Cohen Professor, Department of Politics, Princeton University

Timothy J. Colton Morris and Anna Feldburg Professor of Government and Russian Studies, Harvard University, and coeditor of *Soviet Economy*

Thane Gustafson Associate Professor, Department of Government, Georgetown University

Peter A. Hauslohner Policy Planning Staff, U.S. Department of State

Ed A. Hewett Special Assistant to the President on National Security Affairs, Senior Director of Soviet Affairs at the National Security Council, and founding editor of *Soviet Economy*

Jerry F. Hough Professor of Political Science and Director of the Center on East-West Trade, Investment, and Communications, Duke University, and Senior Fellow, Brookings Institution

William G. Hyland Editor, *Foreign Affairs*

Gail W. Lapidus Professor of Political Science, University of California, Berkeley, and Chair, Berkeley, Stanford Program in Soviet Studies

Zhores A. Medvedev Senior Research Scientist, National Institute for Medical Research, London

Andranik Migranyan Senior Researcher, Institute of International Economic and Political Research, USSR Academy of Sciences

Peter Reddaway   Professor of Political Science and International Affairs, George Washington University

Blair A. Ruble   Director, Kennan Institute for Advanced Russian Studies

Peter Rutland   Assistant Professor of Government, Wesleyan University

Andrey D. Sakharov   Nobel Prize Laureate

Peter H. Solomon, Jr.   Professor of Political Science, University of Toronto

Victor H. Winston   Adjunct Professor of International Affairs, George Mason University, and coeditor of *Soviet Economy*

Yevgeniy Yevtushenko   Poet

MILESTONES
IN
GLASNOST
AND
PERESTROYKA

POLITICS AND PEOPLE

Part I

The Early Years of the Gorbachev Era

The Early Years of the Gorbachev Era: An Introduction

Victor H. Winston

MIKHAIL GORBACHEV'S reputation as a committed innovator began to crystallize only after he had been in power for nearly two years. During the early years of his era, Gorbachev's policies did not challenge the fundamentals of the Marxist-Leninist system or openly assault the tenets of the prescribed struggle to accelerate the "inevitable collapse of capitalism." Like some of his predecessors, the man who later accelerated the collapse of communism by allowing democracy to replace it in Eastern Europe began his early reign by devising goals and assigning priorities to efforts that were neither atypical nor unexpected. His conduct of foreign affairs gave little indication of the changes that came years later, and on the home front Gorbachev's first years in power were marked by drives to strengthen socialist discipline and measures to eliminate alcoholism. His slogan of choice was *uskoreniye* (acceleration)—an emphasis on enhanced productivity to attain higher plan targets. And the beginnings of real democracy in politics, of the kind never experienced by the Soviet populace, were not advanced by Gorbachev beyond the level of discussion until January 1987.[1] Accordingly, the early years of the Gorbachev era can stand apart from the years that followed.

Strictly speaking, March 11, 1985, the day when the media announced that Mikhail Gorbachev had become General Secretary of the Communist Party of the Soviet Union, may not be the day when his remarkable impact on world history began. Several years earlier Jerry Hough had called attention to Gorbachev as a leader with "all the appearance of an eventual general secretary" and one that "would almost surely initiate a reform" (Hough, 1982, p. 43). Later, in February 1984, the future recipient of the Nobel Peace Prize appeared on the front pages after the death of Yuriy Andropov. Expected to head the CPSU by defeating the ailing Konstantin Chernenko, this energetic and per-

---

1. It should be noted that this was within a month after Andrey Sakharov returned to Moscow.

sonable party politician groomed by Andropov began to be perceived, at home and abroad, as a harbinger of beneficial change. Still, though the uninspiring Chernenko lacked the attributes of leadership, the majority of the Politburo were not prepared to cope with Gorbachev's commitment to oppose corruption in the upper echelons of the society. And then, as nearly always thereafter, his inability to manage the economic domain may have been, at the least, unhelpful to his supporters.[2] So in the end, the arguments of Gorbachev's detractors at the Politburo caused the scale to be tipped in favor of one additional year of gerontocratic governance in Moscow. But the spotlight on Gorbachev and his future remained in place. Moreover, a different relationship between East and West was anticipated, and that anticipation heightened after his trip to London in December 1984, when Margaret Thatcher declared "we can do business." So the *early years* of the era may have several milestones to mark the beginning, but none as distinct as the day in March 1985 when the tired old guard at the Kremlin yielded to a man born after the Bolshevik revolution.

The media and academia reacted to the news about Gorbachev's ascent with a flood of predictions ranging from renewed fear of the visibly strengthened superpower to exuberant optimism guided by wishful thinking and emotion. Out of this mountain of journalistic and academic writings comes Chapter 1 of this volume—a succinct and cautious reaction by William Hyland, the editor of *Foreign Affairs*.

After noting that power had finally moved to a man of a new generation— at last a partner the United States could deal with—Hyland quickly raises the point of Gorbachev's formidable political skills. "Now the Gorbachev era begins" and the new leader of the Soviet Union will be "forced to carry out the careful maneuvers, strike the political bargains," and engage in expedient shifts in policy. To those who study Gorbachev's later interaction with Boris Yel'tsin or his orchestration of subordinates like Leonid Abalkin, these astute observations may reverberate as understatements. Indeed, in the aftermath of the early years, Gorbachev played the political game and shifted political gears with intensity and within a range that was no longer typical of the system or reminiscent of any of his predecessors. And as time went on, the intervals between his policy shifts began to shrink, so that hardly a day could be expected to pass without some news portending political drama.[3] But in March 1985, when "The Gorbachev Succession" was written for publication, Hyland's analysis and perception of the emerging era of change were clearly on target.

Hyland also did not disappoint in suggesting that it would be "rash to conclude that activism means genuine reform." On the economic front, the activism has proved much less substantive than intended, yielding results that

2. At the time, Mikhail Gorbachev was in charge of the country's crisis-ridden agricultural sector.

3. For example, during the week of April 22, 1991, when the draft of this introduction was being completed, Gorbachev managed to strike yet another political bargain with Yel'tsin, deflect the challenge of the restive "Soyuz" faction on the right, and retain the leadership of the CPSU—all amidst near chaotic conditions in the economy and decline in popular support to an embarrassing 15 percent.

are obstructing a genuine reform. Although Hyland did not anticipate in 1985 the dramatic political events that were in evidence two years thereafter, Chapter 1 exhibits the sobering caution that guided Soviet-American relations through the early years of the era and again in the early 1990s.

The first calendar year of Gorbachev's governance was hardly a remarkable period; it was not dramatically different from similar ones in the days of Khrushchev, Brezhnev, Andropov, or Chernenko. There was a relatively benign *chistka* (purge) at the top, which elbowed out the former contenders and brought in new faces. Most if not all observers in the Soviet studies community expected Gorbachev to devote some time to the consolidation of his newly acquired power. The first move came within six weeks of his "coronation" in March, when the Central Committee of the CPSU promoted its Secretaries Yegor Ligachev and Nikolay Ryzhkov to full membership in the Politburo. The former, also Andropov's protégé (though Gorbachev's nemesis in the not too distant future), assumed the position of second-in-command by ascending to the stewardship of ideology, while the latter replaced Nikolay Tikhonov as Prime Minister roughly six months thereafter. No less important, however, were the promotions to full membership in the Politburo of Eduard Shevardnadze and Boris Yel'stin, who established Moscow as his power base around the end of the year. Shevardnadze and Yel'stin replaced Grigoriy Romanov and Viktor Grishin.[4] Quite likely, Romanov and Grishin would have changed the course of history had either succeeded in blocking Gorbachev's rise to power during the second week of March following the death of Chernenko.

The first clear marker to indicate that revolutionary events would follow might have been found at the 27th Congress of the CPSU, which convened on the last day of February 1986. Reinforcing earlier commitments to *uskoreniye* and measures such as his hapless campaign against alcoholism, Gorbachev issued a clarion call for sweeping economic reform. His aspirations for the Soviet Union now embraced not only the country's economy but also its society. They were to be realized by living up to familiar slogans and, significantly, by changing the mentality of the populace as well. But like the scope of personnel changes at the Central Committee, the Politburo, and elsewhere to solidify Gorbachev's power, the outcome of the 27th Congress was not unexpected. Accordingly, not many eyebrows were raised when the Twelfth Five-Year Plan, which is identified with the Congress, included targets that were at best reasonably beyond reach and at worst carelessly out of range. Except

---

4. Shevardnadze's promotion in July coincided with Romanov's removal, while Yel'tsin became First Secretary of the Moscow Gorkom of the CPSU in December after Grishin's departure. Gorbachev's *chistkas* during the early years of his reign prompted the removal from the Politburo of eight full members of the nine who, together with Gorbachev, constituted that body on the day he acceded to power. Grigoriy Romanov was the first to leave in July 1985, followed by Nikolay Tikhonov in October 1985, Viktor Grishin in February 1986, and Dinmukhamed Kunayev in January 1987. Four members, Geydar Aliyev, Mikhail Solomentsev, Andrey Gromyko, and Vladimir Shcherbitskiy, respectively, were forced out in 1987, 1988, 1988, and 1989. Vitaliy Vorotnikov, one of Andropov's protégés, managed to be the last survivor. He retired in July 1990 when the Politburo was reorganized and left without effective power for the first time in 70 years. Andrey Gromyko died in office.

for a demonstration in Yakutia in April 1986—the first of the ethnic disorders Gorbachev would face—there were no developments of worldwide significance in the economy or polity until the last week of that month.[5]

Shortly after midnight on Saturday, April 26, 1986, a poorly designed reactor at the Chernobyl' power plant complex exploded in the world's worst and by far most consequential nuclear accident. The disaster, frequently identified as a catalyst for change in the Soviet Union, shook the orthodox foundation of Marxism and Leninism by expanding the limits of, and introducing momentous substance to, *glasnost'*.[6]

The word *glasnost'* rose from relative obscurity to attain universal significance as a symbol of free speech. Mentioned by Andropov and later by Gorbachev (in a eulogy at Chernenko's funeral), the word must have been elevated by someone to the level of a CPSU slogan prior to the Gorbachev era. But since investigators attempting to identify the circumstances may have to await the publication of Gorbachev's (or perhaps Aleksandr Yakovlev's) memoirs, most of the generalizations linking the prominence of *glasnost'* to the Chernobyl' disaster appear reasonable, even if not absolutely precise.

Chapter 2 was selected from the growing collection of writings about Chernobyl'.[7] Written in early 1987, the essay attracted our attention because the author's early insights and perceptive observations capture the spirit of the first year of the Gorbachev era.[8] The author, Zhores Medvedev, is a research biochemist on the staff of the National Institute for Medical Research in London. Exiled from the Soviet Union in 1973, he later wrote one of the best-received books on the Chernobyl' disaster (Medvedev, 1990) and continued to participate in the worldwide effort to probe the circumstances and consequences of the event.[9]

Medvedev tells us that Gorbachev was informed about the explosion within five hours after it occurred. At that time, the local authorities were still reporting to Moscow that the reactor was intact and that radiation was at normal levels. When Swedish media reported the accident and called for immediate answers, only a brief four-line reference appeared in Soviet newspapers, published two days thereafter. Two weeks went by before Gorbachev finally spoke up. Medvedev, who watched his speech on television, concluded that it was disappointingly vague and neither informative nor candid. At an emergency meeting of the Politburo said to have been convened on April 28, the two overruled voices advocating more *glasnost'* were reportedly those of Gorbachev and

5. Arguably, some events in cultural life (e.g., Khrushchev's reappearance on television in July 1985) and diplomacy (e.g., the release of Natan Sharansky in February 1986) may be interpreted as clear signs of a change to come.

6. *Glasnost'* gradually began to overcome censorship, but not before it failed the test in the immediate aftermath of Chernobyl'.

7. *Soviet Economy* convened a panel to discuss the implications within two months after the event. Chaired by Ed Hewett, the panel included the late Theodore Shabad and eight other American specialists (Panel, 1986).

8. The essay was actually an addendum to a book (Medvedev, 1987, pp. 259–269).

9. Zhores Medvedev visited the vicinity of Chernobyl' on April 25, 1991, during the course of the commemorative gathering to mark the fifth anniversary of the disaster.

Vitaliy Vorotnikov. At some future date we may reliably find out what actually occurred at that meeting—who voted against the proposed cancellation of the May Day parade in Kiev (just 75 miles south of the source of contaminating radiation) and who was concerned solely about the country's nuclear power capacity. But while Gorbachev and the other members of the Politburo may have had an idea of the awesome dimensions of the disaster, the truth was not allowed to be told to the Soviet people.

Interestingly, the cover-up ensnared Andrey Sakharov, who was led to believe that Chernobyl' was "an accident, not a catastrophe"—a casual remark over a wiretapped telephone eagerly exploited by the authorities to pacify public opinion (Sakharov, 1990, p. 608). Was Zhores Medvedev on target with regard to assessments of the damage in the aftermath of the explosion? An answer came from David Marples, a Canadian Sovietologist who visited the vicinity of Chernobyl' on April 26, 1991, and interviewed officials and survivors to verify data for an article in *Soviet Economy* (Marples, 1991a). Whereas Medvedev relied on the report submitted by Soviet specialists to the International Atomic Energy Agency in Vienna, the republican authorities and investigators in the Ukraine and Belorussia generally regard that organization as an ally of the much distrusted federal Ministry of Atomic Power and Industry. Accordingly, most studies based on information of republican origin view the levels of damage reported in Chapter 2 as serious understatements devised to facilitate a cover-up. The conflict of governance between the center and the republics may be present here. Or more likely, as Marples readily admits, no one has all the answers or a monopoly on truth to assess the mounting health crisis, the contamination of land, the dislocation of evacuees, or the potential energy crisis exacerbated by the coal strikes of 1991.[10]

The world's worst nuclear accident, which gave rise to numerous inquiries and studies both in the Soviet Union and abroad, will undoubtedly be remembered as the catalyst for formidable change in the awareness of the Soviet people. We are yet to find out whether it served as a traumatic event in the life of Mikhail Gorbachev, prompting him to think of *glasnost'* more as a genuine symbol of free speech than, as some say, a tactic to intimidate officials who impeded the consolidation of his power.

Roughly six months before the Chernobyl' disaster, Peter Hauslohner, then a young scholar on the Yale University faculty, was invited by the USSR Academy of Sciences' Institute of State and Law to use its research resources in Moscow. He began to structure his study of the ways in which both the Soviet regime and the population coexisted by contributing to each other's quest for survival. The tacit set of understandings between the passive citizenry, which acknowledged the legitimacy of the CPSU and the governing bureau-

---

10. The supply of electric power was to have been augmented by reliance on added nuclear power plant capacity. While the 27th Congress of the CPSU expected the share of nuclear power to reach 40 percent by the year 2000, in April 1991 only 45 nuclear reactors were in operation. The total closures and abandonments of planned facilities was at the level of about 60 in May 1991 (Marples, 1991b).

cracy, and the ruling elite, which reciprocally protected that citizenry, is the subject of Chapter 3. Hauslohner's analysis of Gorbachev's "social contract," defined as a set of norms, constituency benefits, and political-economic institutions that the elite and public have regarded as legitimate means of regulating their interaction and relations, suggested that prospects for radical reform were beginning to increase. One of Gorbachev's targets was the social policy that prevailed throughout the Brezhnev era. It rewarded workers regardless of their performance and held wage differentials to very low levels—a major roadblock to productivity and accomplishment, especially among the energetic, young, and skilled. Hauslohner shows that Gorbachev's new social policies would come to favor precisely these strata of the population. Although he was pursuing his objectives primarily at the level of rhetoric, a major realignment of incomes to spur efficiency and achievement among the "yuppies" of Soviet society would progress beyond the stage of tinkering with ideas in the not-too-distant future. Indeed, soon after the system experienced the lasting shock waves emanating from Chernobyl', the early perceptions of reform based on enhanced motivation quickly began to merge with reality.

No single factor, of course, allowed Gorbachev to begin to restructure his society during the early years of his reign. Incidents and accidents intervened to allow him to manipulate the elite and impress the West for the benefit of his *perestroyka*, which he defined as "a carefully prepared program rather than a pompous declaration" (Gorbachev, 1988, p. 13). Observers who, at the time, interpreted Gorbachev's definitions with great hope and little distrust are now, of course, more cautious. But neither Blair Ruble nor Timothy Colton,[11] respectively the authors of Chapters 4 and 5, deviated from sober analysis to satisfy, even in part, the currents of wishful thinking that were slowly permeating academia in the West. Both evaluated Gorbachev's early years shortly after the June 1987 Plenum of the Central Committee of the CPSU. That plenum left few doubts about the direction of *perestroyka*, especially after Gorbachev finally managed to promote Aleksandr Yakovlev to full membership in the Politburo. Colton assesses the prospects for implementing the economic reform by considering five different levels of analysis: the top leader, the collective leadership, the bureaucracy, the intelligentsia, and the population. He identifies five political litmus tests to gauge the chances of systemic economic reform that began to evolve into a visible force. Colton avoids the temptation to predict the course and limits his careful assessment to a set of astute questions that demonstrate a firm grasp of the problems confronting the leadership and the populace of the Soviet Union.

Blair Ruble extends Colton's analysis by exploring one of his levels, the population, in greater depth. He examines the new groups that have emerged

---

11. At the time professor of political science at the University of Toronto, Timothy J. Colton is now Morris and Anna Feldberg Professor of Government and Russian Studies at Harvard University. Blair A. Ruble, currently director of the Kennan Institute of Advanced Russian Studies of the Woodrow Wilson Center for Scholars, was at the time director of the Soviet Program at the Social Science Research Council.

within the Soviet social hierarchy. He relates effective management of antic-ipated social conflicts, one of Gorbachev's major challenges, to the sensitivities of the working class, the young professionals, the professional and paraprofes-sional women, and the committed national elites. Just as clearly as Colton, Ruble shies away from predictions. But he reaches several prudent conclusions by identifying fissures that separate each stratum from the other (and many within themselves) and by indicating that Gorbachev will face decisions that would benefit some social groups at the expense of others.

A definite milestone ending the period of the early years and beginning a new era is difficult to establish. Different observers will point to different significant events, depending on their focus. Thus, in the cultural arena, the transition event may be when Elem Klimov became first secretary of the Film-makers Union in May 1986. On the front involving nationalities, the chrono-logical milestone is likely to be the rioting in Alma-Ata in December 1986. With regard to the economy, major events occurred in late 1986 and early 1987—a turning point when Gorbachev was driven to reconsider the roots of Soviet socialism. The stirrings were evident at two historic plenums of the Central Committee of the CPSU. The one on January 16, 1987, outlined reforms in the choice of personnel; the other on June 25, 1987, spelled out the measures embodying Gorbachev's new concept of radical reform.[12] In foreign affairs, the milestone may well be Gorbachev's first visit to the United States on December 8, 1987, though some may point back to January 1987 when the first law on joint ventures was adopted. The plenum of the Central Committee of the CPSU in January 1987 brought a dramatic change in political life when it reformed the electoral system, establishing a secret ballot and multicandidate elections.

But in my opinion, shared undoubtedly by many Western observers of Soviet affairs, the major watershed demarcating the early years from the subsequent era was on December 23, 1986, the day Andrey Sakharov stepped off the train after Gorbachev invited him to return to Moscow. On that day, the early era ended, and the period of seemingly irreversible transformation began.

---

12. These developments are discussed in considerable detail in the first part of *Milestones in Glasnost' and Perestroyka: The Economy*.

REFERENCES

Gorbachev, Mikhail S., *Perestroika*. New York: Harper & Row, 1988.

Hough, Jerry F., "Changes in Soviet Elite Composition," in Seweryn Bialer and Thane Gustafson, eds., *Russia at the Crossroads*. London: George Allen & Unwin, 1982.

Marples, David R., "Chernobyl': Observations on the Fifth Anniversary," *Soviet Economy*, 7, 2:175–188, April–June 1991a.

———, "Chernobyl': Five Years Later," *Soviet Geography*, 32, 5:291–313, April 1991b.

Medvedev, Zhores, *Gorbachev*. Oxford: Basil Blackwell, 1987.

————, *The Legacy of Chernobyl'*. New York: W. W. Norton, 1990.

"Panel on the Economic and Political Consequences of Chernobyl'," *Soviet Economy*, 2, 2:97–130, April–June 1986.

Sakharov, Andrei, *Memoirs*. New York: Alfred A. Knopf, 1990.

CHAPTER 1

The Gorbachev Succession

William G. Hyland

TWO TRENDLINES suddenly intersected in March 1985. The arms control negotiations between the two superpowers resumed, after a long break that had threatened to become a permanent breakdown. As the delegations were arriving in Geneva, Konstantin Chernenko died in Moscow, and Mikhail S. Gorbachev was quickly named the new general secretary of the Communist Party of the Soviet Union. The succession to Leonid Brezhnev had at last been completed.

The new talks in Geneva are indeed new: they begin against the backdrop of a threat of a revolutionary upheaval in the superpowers' strategic competition. For the first time in the nuclear age, the possibility of strategic defense is being taken seriously: at issue is whether this prospect will prove to be the cause of a truly dangerous confrontation between Moscow and Washington, or the source of new common ground and even a political breakthrough.

In Moscow, for the first time, the leadership of the Soviet party has passed to a man born after the Bolshevik revolution. Change is in the air. A new generation is taking power. In his initial public remarks, however, the new general secretary elaborated on old and familiar themes: prosperity and reform at home, and peace and security abroad. He promised both, of course. But it was not a bad platform.

It is fashionable in the West to dismiss, with some contempt, the idea of any major changes in Soviet foreign policy simply because of new personalities. Nevertheless, the reelected President of the United States finally had a partner to deal with; a man who could easily survive well beyond the end of President Reagan's second term. So the President extended an invitation for an early summit meeting. And the atmosphere of Soviet-American relations began to clear.

Much will depend on Geneva, and whether an acceptable resolution can be found to what looked like an immediate stalemate over American plans to

First published in *Foreign Affairs*, 63, 4, pp. 800–809, Spring 1985. © 1985 by the Council on Foreign Relations, Inc. [Eds.]

proceed with a Star Wars defense and Soviet determination to block it. The resolution of this confrontation, in turn, will depend in some measure on whether Mikhail Gorbachev is a man who would be willing and able to challenge the Soviet system and change it.

BEFORE THE SUCCESSION

The Soviet state and party form a massive bulwark against change. It is largely the same system as that created by Josef Stalin, though without his personal insanities. It is a heavy bureaucracy, bound by a stultifying ideology and administered by careerists, whose vested interests are in maintaining the status quo, perhaps occasionally permitting just enough change to mollify the forces of discontent. Only strong leaders have affected this mass inertia: Stalin by terror, Khrushchev by surprise attack. Stalin, of course, succeeded all too well; Nikita Khrushchev eventually faltered and suffered the fate of innovators—in October 1964 he was the victim of a coup staged by his loyal lieutenants, Leonid Brezhnev, Aleksey Kosygin, and Mikhail Suslov. (Mikhail Gorbachev at the time was a minor functionary in the town of Stavropol in the Caucasus.)

There were flickers of change in the wake of the anti-Khrushchev coup. A reform program was sponsored by Kosygin in 1965. But the Brezhnev era was not to be a time of change. Rather, it was a time for the system to settle down after the tumult of Khrushchev. For a decade the Soviet leadership was virtually unchanged. Reform was quietly dropped, as was de-Stalinization. Party morale was repaired, the split with China became definitive, and Russia massively rearmed.

Leonid Brezhnev made the Soviet Union a true superpower. But there was a price. Stability became stagnation: the economy ran down; the leadership began to atrophy. And superpower status, once earned, could not be maintained without aggressive foreign and defense policies that eventually clashed with the main line of Brezhnev's détente policies. By the early 1980s, the necessary flexibility and dexterity required to deal with growing problems abroad were beyond the capacity of the ailing and aging Brezhnev. It seemed to outsiders that it was time for a change.

But Soviet politics does not change much. There are rules of engagement. One of them is that seniority counts; that was Brezhnev's contribution. Thus the succession progressed first to the reliable Yuriy Andropov and then to the tried and true Konstantin Chernenko. It remains one of the Kremlin's many mysteries why Chernenko, whom Brezhnev had anointed as the crown prince, was denied the succession in the first round after Brezhnev died in November 1982. It is also something of a mystery why, given his health, he was granted a second chance when Andropov died in February 1984.

In any case, Andropov proved to be something of a surprise. Thought to be the representative of the old orthodoxy by virtue of his service in the dreaded

KGB, he loomed as a potentially disruptive force—but as a reformer. His campaign against corruption seemed to herald more sweeping changes, perhaps even a shift to the liberal economic reforms of Hungary, where Andropov had served in the 1950s. It was against this background that Mikhail Gorbachev emerged as the nominal second in command and a potential successor; thus, Gorbachev came to be closely identified with the reform faction.

To be designated as the successor is a dubious and dangerous honor. The position has been occupied by many Soviet leaders who then passed into oblivion (Kirichenko, Kozlov, Kirilenko). Gorbachev's success in surviving the change from Andropov to Chernenko, and then assuming power so smoothly, suggests he has formidable political skills, a conclusion that seems borne out by the firsthand testimony of his British interlocutors during his visit to London last December.

Yet the transfer of power from Chernenko to Gorbachev was the tip of the iceberg. Below the waterline, Soviet politics was marked by the clash between the forces of continuity and the imperative of change. The tendencies toward reform that began under Andropov (presumably supported by Gorbachev) were stifled under Chernenko's brief reign. Indeed, some advocates of economic reform were officially chastised in one of those Aesopian pronouncements that signal major controversy in Soviet politics. The magazine that had sponsored some suggestions of change was forced to apologize for its errors (Stern, 1984).

The strength of the old guard was also dramatically demonstrated in September 1984, when the chief of the general staff, Marshal Nikolay Ogarkov, was summarily dismissed, and sent to the military equivalent of Siberia. His ostensible error was that he complained too publicly about the economic inefficiencies that were blocking the kind of military progress necessary if the Soviet Union was to adjust to an era of nuclear stalemate. One suspects that he was removed less for his heretical views than for his boldness in challenging the aging political coalition in the Politburo. It is intriguing to speculate about the military's position in politics, now that Chernenko has departed. Could there be a comeback for professional officers such as Ogarkov? One thinks of Marshal Zhukov's career. It was this general atmosphere of reaction under Chernenko that led to speculation that the new successor would not be Gorbachev, but the more conservative Grigoriy Romanov. One can wonder whether this would have been the outcome had Chernenko lingered on.

THE EMERGING CHANGE

Now the Gorbachev era begins. The conventional wisdom in the West is that we should not expect much change until Gorbachev has consolidated his position. It took Khrushchev a full three years to defeat his rivals for Stalin's mantle. It took Brezhnev about four to five years to emerge from the group that overthrew Khrushchev. One would expect a younger, less experienced leader to take even longer. Moreover, Soviet history suggests that succession struggles lead to strange turns in policy. Stalin vilified Trotsky, drove him out of the Soviet Union in 1929, but then adopted his economic program. Khrushchev attacked Malenkov for his heretical departures from Stalinism, then used de-Stalinization to drive out Molotov. In the Khrushchev era it was Frol Kozlov, the potential successor, who was portrayed as the Stalinist (in a famous poem by Yevtushenko), but it was Kozlov's rival, Brezhnev, who prevailed and then halted the attacks on the memory of the dead dictator in the name of restoring stability.

Thus it is conceivable—indeed consistent with Soviet history—that Gorbachev too will be forced to carry out the careful maneuvers, strike the political bargains, and engage in the shifts of policy that the system requires if he is to hold on to power in the Kremlin. But there is also reason to believe that this will not prove to be the case this time. Gorbachev's position as second in command was only mildly challenged when Chernenko was in office in the summer and fall of last year (1984). He has been presiding over the Politburo for some time, and the circumstances of his accession to Chernenko's position suggest a prior decision, one dating back perhaps several months. And most important, he does not assume power as only the first among equals, as was the case with Andropov and Chernenko.

The Gorbachev Politburo, which shrank to only ten members when Chernenko died, is not a collection of powerful contenders as was the case when Stalin died or when Khrushchev was overthrown. The Gorbachev Politburo has two tiers: the remainder of the old guard (Andrey Gromyko, Nikolay Tikhonov, Viktor Grishin, Mikhail Solomentsev, and Vladimir Shcherbitskiy) and several younger members. His rivals are not particularly impressive. It is difficult to put Grishin, the longtime leader of the party *gorkom* in Moscow, in the same category as Molotov in 1953 or Kosygin in 1964. This does not mean that Gorbachev's power approaches that of Brezhnev in his prime. The old guard, especially the durable Prime Minister Tikhonov and the redoubtable foreign minister, Gromyko, clearly will influence politics and policy. Moreover, Grigoriy Romanov, who might have succeeded Chernenko, remains a potential rival for Gorbachev.

Politics in the Kremlin does not stop simply because of a change in generations. Nevertheless, the position of general secretary carries with it enormous power and wide prerogatives. And there is ample room on the Politburo for Gorbachev to build up his own base of power. He acts like a man in charge, and there may be good reason for his self-confidence. We may well be spared the dreary process of Kremlin infighting.

Gorbachev's emergence as a reformer seems now to be taken for granted—at least in the West. "Impatient Seeker of Economic Change," ran one headline in an American newspaper. His most frequently quoted statement has been: "We will have to carry out profound transformations in the economy and in the entire system of social relations." Yet the Soviet Union is not China, where a nearly magical transformation could take hold because Mao's system had made only a scratch on an ancient society.

This is not true of the Soviet Union. The Stalinist system has been maturing for decades. It cannot be easily reshaped. Soviet officials, with some indignation, insist that the USSR is not Hungary, that reforms that are possible in a small economy are not applicable to the vast machinery of the Soviet Union. And, even if Gorbachev is determined to make significant changes, what would be their essence? Will a tired party apparatus be able to institute a dynamic economic reform program that would threaten that party's very legitimacy? Or will the party have to be shaken and reformed as well? But this was Khrushchev's downfall—an example Gorbachev surely must remember.

Nonetheless, we must be prepared for a period in which the Soviet Union does attempt to throw off some of the dead weight of the past. Gorbachev seems likely to be a vigorous leader, forceful and dynamic. Is this in the Western interest?

THE SOVIET UNION AND THE WEST

Strange as it may seem, a healthy, self-confident Soviet Union may now be more in the Western interest than an adversary that is brooding and snarling to cover its fears and weaknesses. Some observers believe that only when the domestic crisis deepens will we witness any genuine reforms or shifts in Soviet foreign policy. But one aspect of that crisis may now be over, with the change in leadership. At this stage in the nuclear era, the President of the United States needs a reliable counterpart in the Kremlin who can commit the USSR beyond the next change in the old guard. The United States needs to negotiate with a leadership that is not cowed by the fear of compromise. And the United States should want a leadership that will recognize that the Soviet Union needs to put its own house in order instead of taking refuge in a bombastic and dangerous foreign policy.

This does not mean that the Gorbachev succession is all to the good. He is an untested and, to a large extent, unknown quantity. He could even prove a short-term leader. His road to power has been almost effortless—and, to a degree, fortuitous. It remains to be seen whether he has the ruthlessness that is a prerequisite for ruling in the Kremlin.

It would also be rash to conclude that activism means genuine reform. A shrewd Soviet leader can operate for a long time by treating the symptoms of the USSR's problems rather than attacking the structural base. Nor can we assume that liberal economic reforms mean conciliatory foreign policies. It is much too early to diagram a Soviet game plan. But we have to take careful note of certain objective factors that operate on Soviet foreign policy.

Gorbachev inherits a foreign policy that recently suffered a major failure, which has been only partially repaired. During the interregnum since Brezhnev, the USSR met with one of its worst and most significant defeats: failing utterly to prevent the U.S. deployment of missiles in Western Europe. This failure may have occurred partly because, as the confrontation over the missiles unfolded, Brezhnev was no longer up to the challenge. As usual, the Soviets relied too heavily on the "peace forces" in Europe and on German politics to head off the U.S. deployments. Moreover, while Brezhnev was ailing, major diplomatic openings were missed. Andropov ran to catch up, turning out proposals almost every month; but he fell seriously ill, and a possible slight turn in tactics was snuffed out by the Korean airline disaster in September 1983, which coincided with the beginning of his final illness. It is still fascinating to speculate about who made the ghastly decisions during this crisis. What was Gorbachev's role? He was, after all, thought to be Andropov's second in command at that time. If so, he did not suffer from the crisis, whereas the chief Soviet public spokesman, Marshal Ogarkov, was removed from office a year later.

It was left to Konstantin Chernenko to salvage what he could. A Brezhnev protégé who had advanced in the years of détente, Chernenko apparently fell back on that experience—creating an opening to the Americans. His initial instinct was to shift away from the harshness of superpower relations. His first major speech on March 2, 1984, seemed to move in this direction. He laid out several measures that could be taken to rebuild confidence. It seemed like the beginning of a new dialogue (Horelick, 1985). But something or someone interfered (perhaps the old guard could not agree). Relations worsened when the Soviet Union pulled out of the Los Angeles Olympics. But a sudden turnaround began shortly thereafter, when on June 29, 1984, the Chernenko administration invited the United States to new arms control talks, thus refuting the conventional wisdom that the Soviets would not do business with Ronald Reagan. Despite the failure of that particular exchange, by the early fall Gromyko was in Washington chatting with the very man who had written off the Soviet Union as an "evil empire."

The new line was shored up in innumerable statements and interviews attributed to Chernenko, thus suggesting that he had played an important role in initiating the turn toward the United States. Even when he was taken ill, the new line was not abandoned, suggesting collective support of the Politburo. By then, however, the Soviet leadership was under the nominal control of Gorbachev, who for his part took a rather conciliatory position during his visit to the United Kingdom. And the Soviets nailed down the opening of new arms control talks. In his initial address to the Central Committee after taking power, Gorbachev confirmed that there was indeed a new line, when he fondly recalled the détente of the 1970s in terms reminiscent of Brezhnev. And the Soviet delegation in Geneva ostentatiously revealed that Gorbachev had presided over the Politburo meeting of March 7 that authorized their negotiating instructions.

It is easy to dismiss Gorbachev's early statements as campaign rhetoric. After all, one would not expect the new general secretary to start his career by frightening his audiences with threats of war. Yet it was only a year ago that the Soviet Union was warning of the danger of a new war. The late minister of defense, Marshal Dimitriy Ustinov, was one of the most strident voices; Gromyko, with some reluctance, seemed to fall into line. Romanov lacerated the United States: "The American reactionaries are ready to commit any crime, even the vilest one, to incite tensions." And Gorbachev echoed some of the same language in December 1983:

> Not we but capitalism has to maneuver, camouflage its actions and resort to wars, terror, falsification and subversion in an effort to hold back the inexorable advance of time. . . . In terms of its intensity, content and methods, the "psychological warfare" that imperialism is currently waging constitutes a special variety of aggression that flouts the sovereignty of countries.

Within a year, by the time of his visit to the United Kingdom, he was taking a more conciliatory line, thus supporting Chernenko—to the point that Prime Minister Thatcher said that he was a man she could do business with.

DOING BUSINESS WITH GORBACHEV

If the West can do business with Gorbachev, it will have to be on new terms worked out by both sides. If Gorbachev intends to consolidate the current turn in Soviet-American relations, the focal point has to be the arms negotiations in Geneva. He will have to address the issues without too much delay and, in particular, decide how to cope with the famous Star Wars defense. The United States is not likely to yield to the blandishments and threats of the Soviet negotiators. Good atmospherics, an affable manner, and clever tactics will not charm the United States under Ronald Reagan—though in the age of television and instant global communications Gorbachev may be a formidable public rival. The new Soviet leader will be challenged at some point to offer a realistic basis for compromise.

If and when such a Soviet offer is made, the United States will then be challenged to find a response, rather than rigidly insisting on its own proposals. A failure in Geneva this time could have vastly more serious consequences than the last breakdown, when the Soviets walked out in December 1983. This time we cannot simply wait for another turn in the Soviet leadership. The structure of the superpower relationship could collapse. This is a heavy burden on both leaders.

The shifts in superpower relations cannot be attributed only to the changes from Brezhnev to Andropov to Chernenko. The clash between the United States and the Soviet Union has deep roots in the conflicting national interests of each side—from Afghanistan to Poland to Nicaragua—to say nothing of the fierce strategic competition and the failures in arms control. In this broad sense, personalities are not overly important.

But it would be foolish to take a pseudo-Marxist view and dismiss the human factor altogether. Stalin made a difference. So did Khrushchev and Brezhnev. Now Mikhail Sergeyevich Gorbachev takes their place. He is reported to be highly intelligent, quite capable, and bristling with energy. If so, then he should understand that at some point he will have to grapple with strategic realities. One of those realities is that the Soviet Union finds itself beset with problems: a potential explosion in its decaying East European empire; an endless war in Afghanistan; infectious religious fanaticism along its southern borders; vibrant adversaries in China and Japan. Above all, its main enemy (to borrow a phrase from Mao)—the United States—has proven its amazing resilience, ten years after the debacles of Vietnam and Watergate.

It may not be that the Soviet Union is headed for a historical decline, as some Americans have been too eager to predict. For Moscow still has opportunities for strategic gains in Europe, perhaps in China, and even in Central America. But the new leaders in Moscow should also recognize that the "correlation of forces" that they so carefully assess is no longer favorable to the Soviet Union. Thus, it may be an opportune moment for a new leader to establish an equilibrium with the United States. It would not be a bad policy for Gorbachev to consider as he prepares for the next Party Congress, which should be held late this year. The new Five-Year Plan should be adopted at that time, and Gorbachev will have an opportunity to shore up his political leadership.

Perhaps the most that can be said at this very early point is that vitality seems to be the watchword of the Gorbachev succession. There are certainly dangers in a Soviet Union that is pressing outward, under new and more dynamic leadership. (A "Soviet Kennedy" has been a recurring Western nightmare.) But belligerence is not Gorbachev's only option; he may choose to tend to the malaise in Soviet society. His first pronouncements point in that direction.

The United States, in the Bush mission to Chernenko's funeral and the Reagan invitation to Gorbachev, seems to be extending its hand. A summit meeting seems likely. There is always the risk of another "peace offensive" designed to buy time for a new Soviet leadership, as was the case of the Geneva Summit of 1955. Nevertheless, there are some grounds for optimism at this critical juncture in the relations between the two superpowers.

REFERENCES

Horelick, Arnold, "The Return of Arms Control," *Foreign Affairs* (America and the World Issue 1984/1985), 63, 3:511–537, 1985.
"Stern Rebuke for Advocate of Economic Reform," *Radio Liberty Research Bulletin*, No. RL 476/84, December 19, 1984.

CHAPTER 2

Chernobyl': A Catalyst for Change

Zhores Medvedev

THE NUCLEAR disaster at Chernobyl' in April 1986 suddenly shattered not only Soviet hopes of doubling the internal production of nuclear generated energy by 1990, but the whole basis of the nuclear concept of scientific and technical progress. The dream of the comprehensive use of nuclear generated electricity and heat from "nuclear-industrial complexes"[1] exploded together with reactor No. 4 at the Chernobyl' power station. The Chernobyl' nuclear energy plant was one of the showpieces of Soviet technology. With four 1,000 megawatt (MW) operational reactors in one plant, it was at 4,000 MW the largest generator of nuclear produced electricity in the USSR. Two more reactors (each of 1,000 MW capacity) were under construction on the same site (Figure 1). At the end of the new Five-Year Plan, the power station was expected to produce 6,000 MW of electricity, and to be the main source of energy for the industrial heartland of the Ukraine. The importance of Chernobyl' for Soviet industry is best illustrated by comparing it to the key energy project of Stalin's industrialization, the famous Dnieper hydroelectric station, completed in 1932. The largest European hydroelectric station of its time, it had a capacity of 560 MW. Four more hydroelectric stations were built on the Dnieper between 1955 and 1967 and the total capacity of the Dnieper cascade grew to 2,000 MW, half the power of the Chernobyl' nuclear plant in 1986.

THE ACCIDENT

Only one power unit exploded at 1:23 a.m. on Saturday, April 26, but the other three had to be shut down immediately and for a long period.[2] The loss

First published in Medvedev (1986, pp. 259–269). The annotations in this chapter are by the author [ZhM], David R. Marples [DRM], and the editors. [Eds.]

1. In which the hot water from reactor cooling systems would no longer be wasted but would be used for central heating, heating greenhouses, and providing warm water ponds for fish breeding before being used for irrigation. [ZhM.]

2. It later transpired that the shutdown of the other three reactors took place less quickly. Unit three continued to operate for several hours after the explosion at unit four, while units one and two were not switched off until the following day. Moreover, the shutdowns were short-lived. By November 1986, the first two units had been

Figure 1. *Site Map of the Chernobyl' Atomic Power Station*

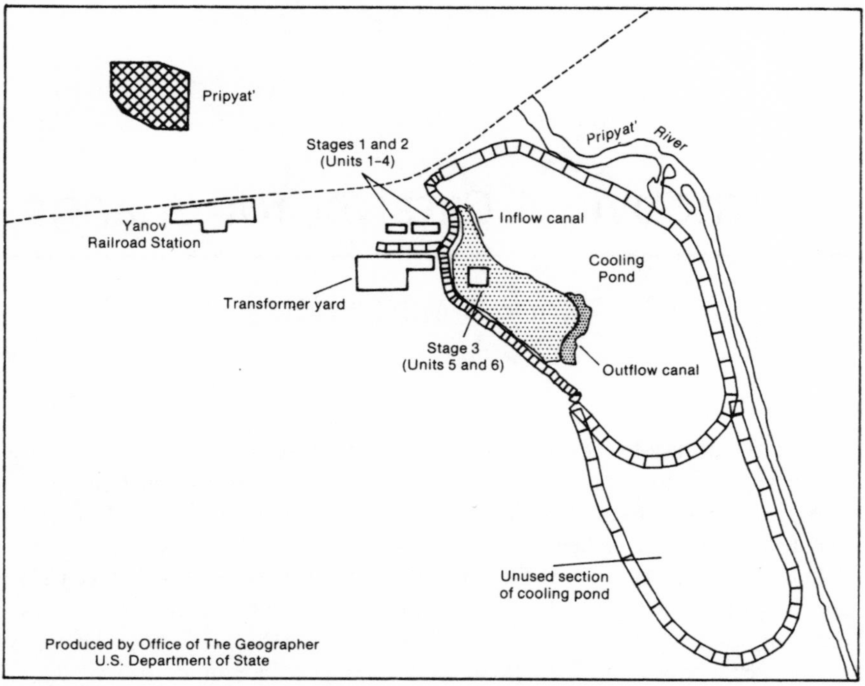

Source: Drafted for *Soviet Ecomony*; reproduced from Thornton (1986a, p. 132).

of 4,000,000 kilowatts of electric power capacity was a great blow to the economy; but a much larger human and ecological disaster developed rapidly. The human population and agriculture around Chernobyl' were in acute danger and there was a threat to the water supply of almost one third of the Ukraine.

As far as is now known, Gorbachev and other members of the Politburo were informed about the disaster five hours after it occurred, when local and Kiev firemen had failed to extinguish the fire. The graphite in the core of the reactor was on fire and it was too hot and burning too fiercely to be extinguished with water. If a similar accident had happened during Khrushchev's time, he would have flown to Kiev immediately and taken charge of the emergency. In April 1986 not even the political bosses of the Ukraine (First Secretary Vladimir Shcherbitskiy and Prime Minister Aleksandr Lyashko) arrived at Chernobyl' until six days later. A fairly low level Government Commission under a Deputy Prime Minister, Boris Shcherbina,[3] was appointed to investigate the cause of

---

returned to the grid system, only six months after the accident. Unit three was returned to service, despite public protests, in December 1987 (see Marples, 1988, pp. 207–08). In February 1990, the Ukrainian parliament resolved to close the Chernobyl' station permanently by 1995, a decision that has met with strong resistance at the plant itself (see Marples, 1991a). [DRM]

3. Shcherbina died after a long illness on August 22, 1990, at the age of seventy-one (*Tass*, August 22,

the accident and the remedies. A news blackout was imposed, probably in the hope that the accident could be contained. The real scale of the tragedy was not immediately clear even to the Soviet government.

It had not yet been realized in Moscow that an enormous amount of airborne radioactivity had been released which could hardly be hidden from neighboring countries. Monitoring the level of radioactivity in the air is the responsibility of a special secret department of the State Committee for Meteorology which, like other similar "civilian" establishments, is in fact operated by the military. The system consists of a network of towers containing special counters for measuring radioactivity and autoradiographic facilities to estimate the level of radioactivity and the nature of radioactive particles. But nobody knows how the system really works. It is quite possible that no one could make a projection of the formation of the radioactive cloud because it was too high in the air. The population of towns quite close to the burning reactor was not evacuated immediately, nor even instructed to remain indoors.

For the first six or seven hours after this worst post-war nuclear accident the people who dealt with the emergency were the commander of the small local fire brigade, Major Leonid P. Telyatnikov, and his 15 men. Telyatnikov soon realized that he could not stop the reactor fire and decided to concentrate on preventing it spreading to the other reactors. His decision saved the country from a much larger disaster. The roof of the burning reactor (No. 4, the newest reactor, which had been in operation since 1983) had collapsed and the roofs of the other three were in danger. The roof of No. 3, the nearest reactor to No. 4, had already caught fire, and there was also a danger that the blaze would spread to the machine and turbine sections of the complex. All the buildings were linked in one complex and their roofs were made of bitumen, an inflammable material (which was a violation of fire regulations). Moreover, the fire was spreading rapidly through the complex via the inflammable plastic which isolated the electric cables. It had clearly been a grave mistake to build four reactors in a single operational complex so close together. Telyatnikov decided that he could prevent the fire from spreading to the other reactors and the machine and turbine unit by using water and the other fire extinguishing material available. But the local fire brigade was far too small and a call was made to Kiev for help in the emergency. Kiev, however, is 120 km away and the extra firemen arrived too late to save the lives of many of Telyatnikov's heroic men. It was estimated later that some of them received more than 5,000 rads of radiation each, almost 20 times the lethal dose. They had absorbed so much radioactive smoke in their lungs that some of the doctors who treated them in the emergency units in Chernobyl and Kiev developed radiation sickness later.[4]

The other three reactors were shut down, but control teams had to remain

---

1990). It is not known whether his death was related to his exposure to very high levels of radiation at Chernobyl'. [DRM]

4. The most detailed account of the firefighters' struggle against the elements is that of Grigoriy Medvedev (1991). [DRM]

in the operational rooms to supervise the work of the cooling systems. Shutting down the reactor stops the fission process, but the core elements remain highly radioactive and generate up to 5–7 percent of their total thermal power for weeks. If permanent cooling does not continue the uranium rods begin to overheat and can melt the zirconium alloy cladding of the fuel and the steel of the pressurized tubes.

Graphite moderated reactors of the Chernobyl' type (RBMK)[5] produce large amounts of plutonium and were originally designed for purely military purposes. The civilian model consists of obsolete 1950s technology. It does not have a single large pressurized vessel, like most Western models. Instead there are more than 1,600 separate pressure tubes and water boils under pressure in each of them. This means that there are more than 1,600 control elements. Steam from the reactor core and turbines are in the same circuit. This makes it difficult to prevent radioactive contamination of the machine hall in the case of an accident. At Chernobyl' servicing the other three reactors presented a problem—a routine shift system could not be used, because in conditions of very high radiation, each shift can only work for a few minutes at the controls. Engineers from other nuclear power stations were flown to Chernobyl' to help.

Around Soviet "atomic towns" there is a health protection zone with a radius of about 2 km. Most of the families of staff and construction workers live nearby. Although Chernobyl' power station is named after the old town of Chernobyl' located about 15 km south of the reactors, with a population of about 30,000, most of the workers lived in the newly built modern town of Pripyat, only 3 km north of the burning plant. In 1986 Pripyat had a population of more than 40,000. These were the people who were in most danger after the accident, as the wind was blowing the radioactivity toward them.[6] Emergency evacuation was required, but officials in Kiev and Moscow were not yet ready to order it. Assessment of the situation took more than 30 hours. Perhaps a military emergency would produce a different response, but in the civilian sector of the nuclear industry there were no contingency plans for a reactor fire and the spread of radioactivity on that scale. Bureaucratic confusion reigned. The medical system of the power station complex was the responsibility of a special secret department of the USSR Ministry of Health, while the medical services in the nearest towns fell under the local Ukrainian health network. Dosimetric control was under different commands inside and outside the station. Moreover, responsibility for the operation of the power station was entrusted to the Ministry of Power and Electrification, whereas the fuel cycles and the problems of the reactor core were within the competence of the Ministry of Medium Machine Building, the euphemism for the military branch of the atomic

5. RBMK is the Russian acronym for a reactor that uses a graphite moderator and is cooled by water. The prototype was the nuclear power plant constructed just outside Leningrad. [DRM]

6. According to a Chernobyl' official, radiation levels on the bridge approaching Pripyat on the day after the accident were around 80 rems per hour, i.e., potentially lethal for anyone outdoors within a matter of hours. (cited in Marples, 1991b; see also Medvedev, 1990). [DRM]

industry.[7] Soviet paranoia and secretiveness about anything to do with industrial accidents, military matters, and nuclear power made the confusion worse. There was no local radio or television broadcast to advise people what to do and about staying indoors. Instead, thousands of militiamen cordoned off the station, keeping stray tourists from the danger zone. It was Saturday, and the large Pripyat-Kiev artificial reservoir was a favorite recreation and fishing spot.

OFFICIAL REACTION

On April 27 the government ordered the army to take over the emergency. Military helicopters began to fly over the burning reactor, dropping sand, clay, lead, and boron (which absorbs neutrons). Thirty-six hours after the initial explosion 49,000 people from Pripyat and two smaller settlements nearby were evacuated; 1,100 buses had been commandeered from Kiev to help with the task. It took several days and hundreds of helicopter sorties to extinguish the fire. More than 5,000 tons of sand and other material were dropped. But the hot molten mass of the reactor core was still in danger of melting down, the ultimate nightmare known as the "China syndrome." The very thin concrete foundations of the Chernobyl' reactors and the pool of cooling water under them made the danger worse. Miners and Moscow and Kiev metro construction workers were sent in urgently with equipment to dig an underground tunnel, pump out the water, and strengthen the reactor foundations. Thousands of tons of concrete were pumped into the foundation, beginning the process of entombing the whole reactor in thick concrete.

The release of radioactivity was decreased, but not entirely halted. A week later another 50,000 people were evacuated because the wind had changed direction. This was done only after Ryzhkov and Ligachev visited the disaster area on May 2. Shcherbitskiy also finally arrived. Gorbachev was apparently kept informed of developments, but remained silent. The Kremlin routine went on as usual: the May Day demonstrations took place (in Kiev, as in other towns), there were meetings with foreigners, awards were presented, and congratulations received. The Chernobyl' accident was mentioned briefly on Moscow television news on Monday evening, April 28, after Sweden had reported a major reactor accident in the Soviet Union and urgently asked for information. A brief, four-line report was published in Soviet newspapers for the first time on April 30. Similar brief daily reports were the only information about the disaster for nearly a week. It was only on May 6 that Shcherbina, chairman of the government commission, was allowed to break the silence and hold a brief press conference in Moscow. After the conference, the Soviet press began

7. In July 1986, a new Ministry of Atomic Energy was created to oversee the industry. In 1990, its functions were amalgamated with those of the USSR Ministry of Medium Machine Building cited by Medvedev and it was renamed the Ministry of Atomic Energy and Industry. In 1991, the ministry's jurisdiction over the Chernobyl' area was challenged by the Ukrainian government, which published two new laws on the status of the Chernobyl'-affected territories and that of those living in contaminated areas. Marples (1991). [DRM]

publishing reports from special correspondents in the disaster areas (or the "battle area," as Soviet newspaper language dubbed it). The main theme of these reports was the heroism and courage which had been demonstrated: there was no word yet about responsibility or negligence. The disaster was treated as if it had been the eruption of a volcano, a natural force out of control.

The international dimensions of the disaster were increasing. It was calculated later in the West that about 50 million curies of radioactive iodine and about 6 million curies of radioactive caesium, the two most volatile radioactive products, were released during the first week after the disaster. About 6 million curies of less volatile radioactive strontium were released within the borders of the Soviet Union.[8] By way of comparison, the 1957 Windscale reactor fire in Britain released 80,000 curies of iodine and 20 curies of caesium. The U.S. Three Mile Island accident of March 1979 released hardly any radioactivity into the environment (a total of only about 15 curies of radioactive iodine escaped from the striken reactor). The largest post-war contamination of a geographically significant area before Chernobyl' was also in the Soviet Union, where a nuclear waste disposal site exploded in the Kyshtym district of the Urals in 1958. Iodine, a short-lived isotope, was no longer present in the stored and reprocessed spent nuclear fuel. But between 1 and 3 million curies of strontium and more than 100,000 curies of caesium contaminated the surrounding areas (Medvedev, 1979).

An "exclusion zone" with a radius of 30 km around the damaged nuclear reactor at Chernobyl' had to be isolated and protected (Figure 2). Guarded by the army, all farms and livestock in the area were evacuated. More than 300,000 hectares of agricultural land were abandoned, probably for many years, and even more land needs to be kept under strict control.[9] The most serious damage to soil comes from radioactive strontium, which binds strongly with soil particles. Caesium is more easily leached by water. Both isotopes have a half-life of more than 30 years and contaminate the environment for centuries.

After two weeks Gorbachev's silence had become unnatural. The enormous scale of the disaster was obvious to everyone and the leader needed to address the nation and offer some kind of explanation. This was a serious test for Gorbachev. I watched his televised address live, via satellite, and found it disappointing. He was less self-confident than usual, and his speech was neither candid nor informative. His proposal for an urgent meeting with Reagan in Hiroshima to discuss a nuclear test ban was pure propaganda, unworthy of a statesman at a time like this. He explained very little about the possible cause of the accident, merely saying that "the reactor capacity suddenly increased during a scheduled shut-down . . . the considerable emission of steam and subsequent reaction resulted in the formation of hydrogen, its explosion, dam-

---

8. As reported in *Nature*, Vol. 221, 1986, p. 187. [ZhM]

9. By 1991, the figure for contaminated farmland was around 12 million hectares. In Ukraine, an area affected less than Byelorussia, it is estimated that about 37,000 square kilometers have been contaminated by significant amounts of cesium (*Radyans'ka Ukraina*, February 14, 1991). [DRM]

Figure 2. *Area Near the Chernobyl' Reactor Site*

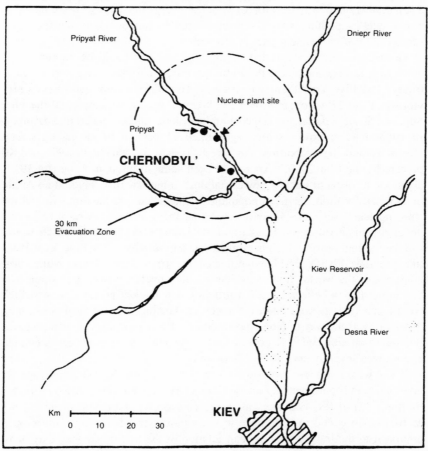

Source: Marples (1988, p. 2), courtesy of the University of Alberta Press.

age to the reactor and the associated radioactive release.'' He made a vague
promise to take proper corrective action in future, saying that ''all aspects of
the problem—design, projecting, technical, and operational—are under the
close scrutiny of the commission.''[10] The coordination of all efforts at the
national level was given to a special Politburo group headed by Nikolay Ryzhkov. He gave higher casualty figures than had previously been admitted. This
was not surprising, since radiation sickness often develops slowly. But he did
not say a word about the long-term effects of the radiation and the resultant
health hazards. Nor did he promise to reconsider the practice of locating nuclear

10. Gorbachev's speech on Soviet television on May 14 was reported in the news media (e.g., *Pravda*,
May 15, 1986); an official translation was issued by the Embassy of the USSR in London. [ZhM]

power plants near cities.[11] Ryzhkov treated the whole accident as if it had been a natural disaster ("a sinister force of nuclear energy that has escaped control"), rather than something which was connected to human plans for the rapid acceleration of the nuclear energy programme.

Gorbachev carefully avoided saying anything that could be interpreted as expressing reservations about the ambitious program for nuclear-generated electricity. The Five-Year Plan, which had been endorsed only two months previously at the 27th Congress of the CPSU and was to be adopted at the June Supreme Soviet session, envisaged doubling Soviet nuclear generating capacity. In 1985, nuclear power stations generated 11 percent of the nation's total electricity and the proportion was due to rise to 22 percent in 1990 and 40 percent by the year 2000.[12] There had been some discussion in the late 1970s about the location of nuclear power stations. Some scientists favored an Arctic or Siberian location, far from population centers, but the government and the "pro-nuclear" scientists supported locating them in the centers of industrial development in European Russia and the Urals, close to cities which would use the thermal power which is produced as a by-product. The Five-Year Plan, like previous Five-Year Plans, reflected the latter view. Thus, while most countries of the world were reconsidering their nuclear power development,[13] the Soviet Union believed that constructing new nuclear power stations which would generate thermal energy for central heating and for heat-consuming industries was the way to future development. These projects had been accepted without discussion and were now in doubt. The public faith in nuclear-generated energy was severely shaken by Chernobyl'.

There were rumors in Moscow later (which were probably true) that a special emergency Politburo meeting on the Chernobyl' disaster took place on Monday morning, April 28, two days after the catastrophe. Gorbachev and Vitaliy Vorotnikov are said to have been in the minority in advocating a more open approach to the tragedy and the cancellation of the traditional May Day demonstrations in Kiev, Gomel', and other towns close to Chernobyl', where radioactive dust in the air made it dangerous (particularly for children) to stay outdoors. The majority favored a news blackout, making it impossible for Gorbachev to make a public announcement sooner. Later that day, when the radioactive cloud reached Sweden, a compromise four-sentence statement was all that the Politburo authorized.

EVACUATION AND CONTAMINATION

When more open reporting was authorized by the Politburo after May 6, Ryzhkov, Chebrikov, Ligachev, and Shcherbitskiy continued resisting the

---

11. Or even within cities as envisaged in the new Five-Year Plan and the plan for long-term cooperation with CMEA countries. [ZhM]

12. Accounts of the Soviet nuclear energy program in 1985–1986 are to be found in Thornton (1986; 1986a) and Panel (1986, pp. 102–110 and 114–121). [Eds.]

13. For example, no new nuclear power plants had been built or projected in the United States since 1979. [ZhM]

extension of the danger zone beyond the 30 km radius, despite the obvious health hazards. It took over three weeks for the radiological services to make a more precise map of the radioactive contamination which represented a danger to the population; and this map was not made public. The contamination was, in fact, related to the pattern of rainfall during the period when there was a massive release of radioactive isotopes, from April 25 to May 5. In some districts of Belorussia well outside the exclusion zone, the contamination level was so high that the medical authorities requested the government to evacuate the population. The extent of the contamination was only revealed in June, when medical tests were ordered for people in towns and villages up to 100 km west, north, and east of the original exclusion zone.[14]

The Ministry of Health has the power to order the evacuation of children to sanatoria and summer camps and this was done. More than a million children from the Kiev region and from Belorussia were evacuated, often with their mothers. But permanent resettlement of the population is a more difficult problem and it affected 140,000 people, mostly from the exclusion zone. The decision was made to decontaminate many other towns and villages without resettling the local population. The way in which it was done in one rural town, Bragino, with a population of about 7,000 and situated about 80 km north of Chernobyl', was described in *Izvestiya* (June 15, 1986). A layer of topsoil and vegetation up to 10 cm in depth had to be removed from the streets, gardens, and surrounding areas and the streets covered in new, "washable" asphalt. Many thousands of tons of contaminated soil had to be buried somewhere. In June the area in which agriculture was banned was increased dramatically, but without evacuating peasants or livestock. Although the "permissible" level of radiation in agricultural produce and in the environment was raised arbitrarily,[15] an area of 20,000 sq km north and east of Chernobyl' (which included towns such as Bragino, Yel'sk, and Mozyr') had to be abandoned for normal agricultural use, probably for many years.

The contamination of at least one million hectares of agricultural land was a severe blow to the plan for agricultural production. Moreover, it was obvious that the scale of the damage to agriculture was actually much greater than that. By the beginning of June it became clear that 1986 was not expected to be a success in other agricultural regions either. The unfulfilled winter crop plans and the delayed sowing made it unlikely that the total grain harvest would exceed the poor level of 1985. But radioactive contamination of such a large area posed an even greater longer term danger. If the Soviet government had followed Western safety standards, the agricultural produce of about half of Byelorussia and a third of the Ukraine would have been considered unsuitable

14. Today, areas as far east as the city of Kursk, and west to the Polish border are officially acknowledged to have been seriously irradiated. Residents of the Belorussian capital of Minsk are reportedly suffering from thyroid problems incurred after the Chernobyl' accident. Detailed maps of the fallout region are finally being printed in the press (e.g., see *Radyans'ka Ukraina*, February 23, 1991). [DRM]

15. In Kiev the "permissible" annual dose of radiation was increased from the international top level of 0.5 rems per annum to 10 rems. [ZhM]

for consumption, at least in 1986. However, the actual levels of contamination of soil, water, and agricultural produce expressed in physical units were kept secret. It was also decided that contaminated milk could be processed into butter and cheese and kept in store until the level of radioactivity had declined to the level where it could be safely consumed.

POLITICAL REPERCUSSIONS AND REVERBERATIONS

Everyone expected that Shcherbitskiy would be retired at the Central Committee plenum, which took place just before the Supreme Soviet session on June 18. His reputation in the Ukraine was extremely poor, since the Ukrainian people knew that their leadership was misleading them. Paradoxically, however, Gorbachev could not afford to dismiss him. There was no suitable party figure in the Ukraine to replace him and the Chernobyl' disaster had given rise to an increase in nationalist feelings. The very fact that news of the disaster had been suppressed for so long and that the evacuation had been delayed, as well as the contrast between the Ukrainian names of those who died in the weeks after the accident and the Russian names of the administrators of the Chernobyl' power station who were accused of negligence and dismissed, all contributed to this nationalism.[16] The choice of Shcherbitskiy's successor was extremely delicate. His predecessor, Pyotr Shêlest, had been a fervent nationalist, who had resisted the blatant Russification of the Ukraine, making his important local speeches in Ukrainian rather than Russian, and pressing for more independent decision-making power for the Ukraine. But he had gone too far in his conflict with Brezhnev and had been dismissed. When Shcherbitskiy, a more Russified Ukrainian, took over, he spoke Russian at party gatherings and reduced the role of the Ukrainian language in schools and universities. It would have been relatively easy to retire Shcherbitskiy, but Gorbachev did not yet know how to deal with the problem of preventing a resurgence of nationalism.[17]

16. Viktor Bryukhanov, the Chernobyl' atomic power station's director, was expelled from the CPSU. Initially, the Politburo censored and subjected to rigorous party penalties the following ranking officials: Yevgeniy G. Kulov, the former deputy minister of Medium Machine Building (the secretive nuclear fuel and nuclear weapons agency) who assumed the chairmanship of the State Committee for Safety in the nuclear power industry upon its creation in August 1983; Gennadiy A. Shasharin, a first deputy minister of Electric Power responsible for the construction and operation of the Soviet nuclear power industry; Ivan Y. Yemel'yanov, an electric power engineer and corresponding member of the USSR Academy of Sciences since 1974; and A. G. Meshkov, a first deputy minister of Medium Machine Building. On August 14, 1986, *Pravda* reported that six other high officials had been held responsible for the Chernobyl' accident and penalized by the CPSU. Expelled from party membership were Gennadiy A. Yeretennikov, who at the time of the Chernobyl' disaster was deputy minister of Electric Power in charge of all Soviet nuclear power stations, and Ye. V. Kulikov, a department head at the Ministry of Medium Machine Building (Special, 1986, pp. 181–182); the connection between that military-oriented ministry and the commercial Chernobyl' power station had not been officially explained at the time. [Eds.]

17. Shcherbitskiy was retired in September 1989 and died in January 1990. He was replaced by Vladimir Ivashko, but in July 1990, the latter took up a position as deputy general secretary of the CPSU in Moscow. Since this date, the Ukrainian party leader has been Stanislav Hurenko, whose political views are not dissimilar to those of the late Shcherbitskiy (see Solchanyk, 1989, and Mihalisko, 1990). [DRM]

A full report about the Chernobyl' disaster was prepared in August and presented at a special meeting of the International Atomic Energy Agency in Vienna. The Western press correctly praised it as frank and comprehensive. It was an impressive two-volume technical document which explained how local engineers and operators had decided to carry out an unauthorized experimental test of the reactor which violated many safety regulations. The Soviet delegation in Vienna presented a long catalogue of almost incomprehensible errors which led to the accident. They identified the main cause of the disaster as "human error," or a strange sequence of errors. In the discussions they acknowledged that the technical defects in the reactor design were contributing factors, but this was not stated in the official report.[18]

Western commentators who praised the Chernobyl' report for its frankness missed an important point: it was made public in the West, but not in the Soviet Union. The Soviet government had no objections to the effect of the report in raising anti-nuclear feelings in the West, but considered it vital to prevent similar fears at home. Accordingly, the report was not made available to the Soviet press. Soviet newspapers published only a brief account of the press conference in Moscow on August 21, 1986, at which foreign journalists were given detailed information about the sequence of events. The Soviet media stressed that the error of the operators in carrying out the experimental test with the emergency cooling system switched off was the main cause of the disaster (*Izvestiya*, August 23, 1986). The week-long discussion in Vienna by nuclear energy experts from more than 50 countries was not covered in the Soviet press. Foreign scientific journals such as *Science, Nature,* and *New Scientist* which published detailed analyses of the Chernobyl' report did not reach the open shelves of Soviet research libraries.

Although Western experts praised the frankness of the report, they criticized the design of the RBMK reactor (which is unique to the Soviet Union). It was clear even to non-experts that the design was obsolete. But that particular design represents about 60 percent of Soviet nuclear-generated energy capacity and many more similar reactors are under construction. Modifications were clearly essential and in Vienna the head of the Soviet team, Academician Valeriy Legasov,[19] admitted that technical changes were being considered and that the total planned volume of electricity from RBMK reactors in 1987 had been reduced by 10 percent to allow time for their safety features to be improved.

The Chernobyl' accident provoked considerable anti-nuclear sentiment in

18. In January 1991, a commission from the USSR State Industrial Atomic Inspectorate issued a new report of the causes of the Chernobyl' disaster that contradicted the general tenor of the 1986 version in that it attributed the accident almost entirely to the design of the reactor and its control rods in particular (see Marples, 1991). [DRM]

19. Legasov committed suicide on April 27, 1988. At that time it was speculated that he was suffering from depression or from radiation sickness (Marples, 1988). In 1991, a prominent Ukrainian scientist working with the USSR State Industrial Inspectorate Commission implied strongly that Legasov could no longer live with "the deception" carried out in the report delivered by the Soviet delegation to the International Atomic Energy Agency in Vienna. In other words, Legasov, like other scientists at the Kurchatov Institute of Atomic Energy, was well aware of the design flaws in the Chernobyl' reactor (Marples, 1991a). [DRM]

the Soviet population, particularly in the Ukraine, Byelorussia, and the Baltic republics. However, the Soviet press did not publish a single anti-nuclear article or statement. Criticism was levelled against Brezhnev, but not against the new programs. For example, the selection of Chernobyl' for a giant nuclear power station was said to have been a mistake. The area is ecologically unsuitable, since it is close to the Pripyat marshes and to the Dnieper, which provides water to Kiev and many other large cities. It was also said that the construction of nuclear power stations had deviated from the original project. Putting the blame on Brezhnev, however, did not prevent damage to Gorbachev's reputation as a result of the Chernobyl' disaster. His "honeymoon" with the Soviet public was now distinctly over. The development of nuclear power as a top priority has been a cornerstone of Soviet technological achievement. The collapse of this vision would have lasting effects.

REFERENCES

Marples, David R., *The Social Impact of the Chernobyl Disaster.* New York: St. Martin's Press, 1988.

———, "Chernobyl': Observations on the Fifth Anniversary," *Soviet Economy,* 7, 2:175–188, April–June 1991a (forthcoming).

———, *Ukraine Under Perestroika.* New York: St. Martin's Press, 1991b (forthcoming).

Medvedev, Grigoriy, *The Truth About Chernobyl.* New York: Basic Books, 1991.

Medvedev, Zhores A., *Nuclear Disaster in the Urals.* New York: Norton, 1979.

———, *Gorbachev.* Oxford: Basil Blackwell, Ltd., 1986.

———, *The Legacy of Chernobyl.* London: Basil Blackwell, Ltd., 1990.

Mihalisko, Kathleen, "Volodymyr Ivashko and Ukraine," *RFE/RL Research Institute Report on the USSR,* 2, 29, July 20, 1990.

"Panel on the Economic and Political Consequences of Chernobyl'," *Soviet Economy,* 2, 2:97–130, April–June 1986.

Solchanyk, Roman, "Shcherbitsky Leaves the Political Arena: The End of an Era?" *RFE/RL Research Institute Report on the USSR,* 1, 40, October 6, 1989.

"Special Politburo Meeting on Chernobyl'", *Soviet Economy.* 2, 2:180–185, April–June 1986.

Thornton, Judith, "Soviet Electric Power after Chernobyl': Economic Consequences and Options," *Soviet Economy,* 2, 2:131–179, April–June 1986a.

———, "Chernobyl' and Soviet Energy," *Problems of Communism,* 35, 6:1–17, November–December 1986.

CHAPTER 3

Gorbachev's Social Contract

Peter A. Hauslohner

THE LONG-TERM decline in the Soviet economy's growth performance typically is attributed to certain characteristics of the economic system itself. At the same time, the transition to a new, more effective system is thought to be significantly inhibited by (among other things) Soviet leaders' fear of a potentially explosive public reaction to the growth of inequality, instability, and insecurity—outcomes which many think are likely to follow reforms of a decentralizing and/or marketizing sort. Yet one might invert this argument and, putting politics squarely ahead of economics, suggest that some of the most important "defects" of the economic system are better viewed as the consequences of a particular method of legitimating political authority which emphasizes egalitarianism, stability, and security.[1] One might then argue that were Soviet leaders ever to alter (or be forced to alter) their approach to legitimation, the probability of fundamental economic reforms would rise significantly. In practice, we need not choose between these formulations. On the contrary, what's important to recognize is that any state's economic development strategy, as embodied in the institutional economy, and its legitimation strategy are mutually constraining and that the relative effectiveness of one is liable to depend partly on its "fit" with the other.

The purpose of this chapter is to explore some of these constraints and the implications for the prospects of Soviet economic reform. I make two principal arguments: (1) that the marked deterioration in Soviet economic performance during the past fifteen years can be partly and significantly

First published in *Soviet Economy*, 1987, 3, 1, pp. 54–89. This paper was based partly on research conducted in Moscow, where the author was a guest of the USSR Academy of Sciences' Institute of State and Law during September–October 1985, and at the Center for Slavic and East European Studies of the University of California at Berkeley, under an Andrew W. Mellon postdoctoral fellowship. For these opportunities, he wishes to thank the International Research and Exchanges Board, which also helped to make possible an earlier research trip to the Soviet Union (April 1981), and the staff of the Center at Berkeley and its director, George W. Breslauer. Expert research assistance was provided by Brian Carter of Yale. For comments on earlier drafts, he would like to thank David R. Cameron, Miriam Golden, and Blair Ruble. [Eds.]
  1. David Granick (1987) takes this approach in his book on the Soviet labor market.

explained by the rising costs and declining effectiveness of those mechanisms on which the Soviet state has relied in recent decades to maintain social peace—a development of which Mikhail Gorbachev and the present Soviet leadership seem not unmindful; and (2) that Gorbachev and his fellow leaders have, in the last two years, begun to assemble new mechanisms of legitimation which appear compatible with "radical" economic reform, and which may even require it.

By radical reform I mean what I believe most scholars who use the term mean, namely, changes that would effect a substantially more decentralized, deregulated, and market-reliant economy than exists at present. Such changes, it should be emphasized, do not necessarily mean a retreat from socialism, an outcome better described as revolution than reform. As a way of distinguishing between the two, I suggest that the following could serve as a minimum list of conditions which will not be surrendered voluntarily in the foreseeable future: public ownership of the overwhelming preponderance of the means of production; severe limits on non-labor income; and state direction of the economy which goes far beyond what the most ambitious government has ever attempted in a capitalist system.

If this is an acceptable minimalist definition of centrally managed socialism, it is also a socialism which can accommodate a variety of policies and institutions. Publicly owned property might be managed by state agencies or leased to state-charted cooperatives. Non-labor income might be limited by proscribing individual employment or by permitting it and applying a highly progressive tax on various forms of economic rent. Steering the economy might be accomplished directly, through detailed production planning and the allocation of supplies, or indirectly, through the aggressive use of taxes, investment subsidies, and stricter enforcement of the law. There is little doubt but that since the early 1930s, Soviet policymakers have leaned heavily and consistently toward the first of these poles—that is, toward statism, proscription, and direct regulation. Reform might thus be defined as movement toward the other pole, with the difference between "moderate" and "radical" involving some measure of the distance traveled.

The overarching political monopoly of the Communist Party is, I assume, another frontier which reform cannot, by definition, violate and remain reform. I stress "overarching," because here, too, there is room for variation in the way in which the Party's leading role might be defined and maintained. There is a tendency in the West to assume a particularly stringent definition of the Party's need for control, and then to argue that such a political monopoly and radical economic reform are incompatible. This, I believe, is a mistake. Political hegemony can be exercised indirectly as well as directly, and what counts as "political" has always been a variable. We should not be so blinded by the preferences which Soviet leaders have exhibited in the past that we are unable to imagine a new leadership opting for a smaller political sphere and a lighter hand at the controls. There is, in particular, no obvious or logical reason why party hegemony must inevitably be threatened by a partial reduction in the party's day-to-day control over the economy and by a transfer of the control given up to more democratic institutions.[2]

There are also no good grounds for simply assuming the party, or the party apparatus, to be anything like a monolithic opponent of reform. On the contrary, one might expect *apparatchiki* to vary in their responses both to the prospect and to the fact of reform, depending on their individual talent for thriving in a deregulated environment, their position in the current economy, and what they are offered in the way of enhanced political rights in exchange for the loss of economic rights. In any event, we possess very little systematic evidence regarding party officials' attitudes toward reform. What meager evidence there is (e.g., Dzhafarli et al., 1983; Beissinger, 1986) suggests a diversity of attitudes, including some support for far-reaching systemic change. That suggests that the primary challenge facing would-be Soviet reformers is to mobilize a coalition of supporters within the party and to *de*mobilize opponents, rather than to overcome the opposition of the Party *qua* institution.[3]

THE FIRST POST-STALIN SOCIAL CONTRACT

To an economist, probably the most striking features of Soviet economic performance for the last thirty years have been the dramatic declines in GNP and productivity growth and the unusually small contribution to growth from gains in factor productivity. To a political economist, however, Soviet performance stands out for somewhat different reasons: (1) the large and persisting *imbalances* in growth; and (2) the remarkably high levels of *political and social order*. The puzzle for a political economist is how both were accomplished simultaneously.

The most important imbalances have been characteristic of the comparatively developed East European socialist economies as a group; i.e., relatively high shares (of GNP) and rapid rates of growth in investment and goods production; and relatively low shares and slow rates of growth in consumption and services. The maintenance of such imbalances over time is a sign of the state's enormous power in a centrally planned economy. But it is also the mark of a particular, and until recently basically successful, economic development strategy. High levels of investment and the concentration of resources in goods production, where productivity has risen faster than in services, evidently have enabled the

2. This doesn't mean that Soviet party leaders will not themselves continue to prefer a stringent conception of their need for control, which might indeed preclude radical reform as I have defined it.

3. Several prominent Soviet reform sympathizers insisted to me privately that this is the case; and Academician Zaslavskaya (1985, pp. 20–22) has argued as much in print.

socialist economies to compensate for the effects of lower rates of factor productivity growth in individual sectors, as compared to capitalist economies (Pryor, 1985). Because of this "composition effect," the European socialist economies' long-term aggregate growth performance has been no worse on average than that of their capitalist competitors.[4]

This strategy has had its costs, however. One is a living standard which remains well below that found in the developed capitalist world. Another, from the public's standpoint, is that implementation of this strategy has required institutions which permit ordinary individuals in these countries virtually no political or economic power. Finally and most importantly, the emphasis on rapid rates of industrial growth has meant, particularly in those countries that were least developed when the Communists took power, far-reaching transformations of the social structure, involving the vast uprooting of peoples and cultures and the weakening, if not destruction, of many of the traditional sources of social order and cohesion. The question thus arises: how have socialist governments managed to keep the peace? Or, more specifically, how should one explain the Soviet state's great success, comparatively speaking, in maintaining social and political order and the extreme rarity in that country of serious political and economic violence?

Part of the answer clearly has to do with the government's repression of open dissent and, more broadly, its reliance on a vast infrastructure of hierarchical political controls to inhibit the mobilization of opposition. But coercion cannot be the whole of the story or even, arguably, its largest part. Popular protest, particularly of an economic sort, has never been stilled altogether. At the same time, the state's coercive apparatus has become significantly less harsh and less visible over the past three decades, especially compared to the period before. Lacking a good alternative explanation, growing numbers of Western specialists have concluded that the degree of social and political order observed in the Soviet Union, and in the developed socialist world generally, must be due to volunteered (rather than coerced) compliance and, more particularly, a result of the high-stability, high-security, egalitarian, and libertarian elements of an otherwise austere and illiberal social policy. Domestic peace has been maintained, it is argued: (1) because consumption has improved steadily, if slowly; (2) because the risks of growth to individuals have been minimized through high levels of job security and stable prices for most basic consumption items; (3) because the benefits of growth have been widely and relatively evenly shared through a steady expansion of the social wage and a generally egalitarian incomes policy; and (4) because despite being given virtually no power over key political and economic decisions, most citizens have been allowed considerable personal freedom as workers and consumers. In a

---

4. Nor has the rate of decline in their growth as a group been any greater, although in this particular respect the Soviet Union is an outlier. The Soviet economy was throughout the period an average performer by most measures. But even before the pronounced stagnation of 1979–1982, the "retardation" of Soviet aggregate growth was much greater than predicted by Pryor's model (1985, p. 233).

phrase, social peace and order have been preserved partly, and perhaps largely, thanks to an implicit "social contract" between the regime and society.[5]

This formulation has become quite widely shared (e.g., White, 1986). Indirect empirical support for the hypothesis can be found in the rough correlation which seems to exist between the care with which the regime has upheld its side of this putative bargain over time and the incidence and severity of popular economic protest (Hauslohner, 1984, pp. 148–158 and 425–445; and, indirectly, Pravda, 1979). Of course, "contract" is somewhat of a misnomer, for the deliberations which led to these policies were conducted on one side only. Soviet society may effectively accept or reject what the regime has to offer, but it has no power to haggle over details. On the other hand, the historical evidence suggests that one side's welshing has prompted the other side to renege; this implies the presence of something of a *quid pro quo* element which perhaps makes contract a not entirely inappropriate label.

However, if the hypothesis is right, it needs to be elaborated in several crucial respects. First, the social contract must be understood not only as a set of desirable material benefits, but as norms—implicit conventions which have been widely accepted by the public and by the elite as expected and fair rules of the economic game. Although there is, to my knowledge, no good systematic evidence of this, all of the policies and policy outcomes listed above are routinely described as norms both in the media and in private conversation (e.g., Rimashevskaya, 1986b).[6] It is true that such statements may coincide with, or even mask, the material self-interests of particular groups that stand to gain from these policies. Nevertheless, the norms themselves appear to exist independently of, and on a different plane from, their associated material advantages. Indeed—and this is the point—it is difficult to imagine the social contract inspiring much compliance for very long unless it was regarded as "just" by the possibly many persons to whom these policies have given little, if any, practical benefit.

Secondly, the benefits of the social contract have *not* been distributed equally, which is to say that social policy has produced both "winners" and "losers." The comprehensive wage reforms of both Khrushchev and Brezhnev, for example, tended to favor blue collar workers over white collar workers and persons employed in goods production over those in services.[7] Similarly, most blue

5. This particular specification is my own. For somewhat different versions, see Pravda (1981), Breslauer (1978), Bialer (1980, Ch. 8), and Lapidus (1983). One of the first statements of the general proposition was Connor (1975).

6. A leading Moscow sociologist once insisted to me privately that the powerful tendency among ordinary Soviet citizens to equate "justice" (*spravedlivost'*) with "equality" (*ravenstvo*) has become the single greatest obstacle to accelerated economic growth.

7. The declining earnings gap between white collar professionals and blue collar workers is well known; however, the more poorly paid nonprofessional white collars (*sluzhashchiye*) have also been losers, comparatively speaking. Service employees, meanwhile, make about 30 percent less on average than persons working in goods production; and although that is about the same as in the mid-1950s, the gap has increased significantly since the huge minimum wage increase of 1968. More importantly, both the Khrushchev and Brezhnev wage rounds (1956–1965, 1972–1979) gave service workers their wage hikes last, several years *after* many of those working in goods production received them, which resulted in a sizable comparative income loss for service workers by

collar workers have, since the mid-1950s, enjoyed strong legal job rights; but these were never extended to large numbers of management personnel, and the number who lack protection has been growing (Nikitinskiy and Rozovskiy, 1977).

To be sure, deciding who wins and who loses as a result of any one policy, let alone from all state policies taken together, is exceedingly difficult and perhaps even impossible. Nevertheless, one can make a case, as numerous Soviet commentators have recently been arguing, that the social policies of the past 30 years have been biased against certain groups (white collar professionals, service workers) and that persons with assets, such as exceptional talent, skill, education, energy, or simply money to spend, on the whole did worse than they might otherwise have expected to do, compared to those without. Such inequalities (or society's perception of them) must have played a role in helping to preserve the social contract over time. Widely shared norms may have encouraged *compliance* with policy. But the regime's *de facto* preference for certain groups' interests over others' can plausibly be assumed to have aroused *positive support* among the former both for the policies and for the regime. Support, more than compliance, implies a willingness to fight to preserve one's advantages and to actively oppose their withdrawal—a prospect which must have helped to deter policymakers whenever they considered changing course.

Lastly, for the social contract to have worked, either as a set of norms or as a package of real benefits, it had to be *institutionalized*; people had to be able to count on these policies being delivered in practice day after day. This meant that the regime had not only to enact the necessary laws and decrees, it had to empower or create anew specific organizations whose mission it was to implement and defend these policies on a regular basis. Concretely, it meant having to reestablish a labor ministry (Goskomtrud) to design national wage and income policies.[8] It also meant revitalizing the trade unions, both as defender of the new social policies in decision-making arenas at the Center, and as key agents behind the implementation and oversight of social policy generally at the grass-roots level (e.g., Ruble, 1981). Ultimately, the social contract almost certainly could not have survived had it not come to rest on a solid institutional base: a dense edifice of organizations and officials for whom defending the social contract became both goal and standard operating procedure.

---

the time the reforms were completed.

Needless to say, earnings differences are themselves not policy, but outcomes. Distinguishing the separate impacts of the market and policy on final earnings is a complicated matter, and some economists (Western *and* Soviet) have argued that the forces of supply and demand are chiefly to blame for the declining blue collar-white collar earnings gap. Among Soviet writers, however, most opinion seems to give policy an equal, if not larger, share of the blame, and this is my judgment as well.

8. The first Soviet labor ministry, Narkomtrud, lasted from 1917 until 1933. The founding and subsequent history of Goskomtrud, established in 1955, are discussed in detail elsewhere (Hauslohner, 1984).

"DE-ALIGNMENT"

The social contract did survive, and for a long time it worked tolerably well. At least that is the judgment of many Western specialists, and it is one which General Secretary Gorbachev and other top party leaders have themselves echoed (e.g., Gorbachev, 1985a, p. 27; *Materialy*, 1985, p. 7; and Ligachev at the 27th CPSU Congress, in *Pravda*, February 28, 1986, p. 4). Yet, there are numerous signs that this bargain between the regime and the society has now come undone, and Gorbachev has seemed to acknowledge this as well (e.g., Gorbachev, 1987).

The evidence of an unraveling social contract is striking. For one thing, the direct economic costs of maintaining the social contract have been soaring. Included here are the huge sums of scarce hard currency spent on food imports (Treml, 1986); the already enormous yet still growing domestic budget subsidies allocated to food, housing, transportation, and other basic consumption items (Treml, 1983); and even, one might argue, the excessive wage increases allowed at the time of the 1979–1982 "recession," when the leadership proved unwilling to force workers to absorb the full effects of the rapid falloff in GNP and productivity growth (Grossman, 1983; Hauslohner, 1984, p. 428). Less easily measured but probably more important have been the indirect costs in forgone GNP, resulting from the negative effects of immobile labor and small interpersonal wage differentials on the growth of productivity, and as reflected in the rising stock of underutilized capital and a supply of labor for the flourishing second economy (e.g., Granick, 1987, Ch. 6; Zaslavskaya, 1980).

As dramatic as the escalating costs has been the unmistakable erosion of the social contract's purported benefits to the regime. Statistics on liquor sales and adult mortality imply a steady and significant rise in the extent of drunkenness and alcoholism during the past two decades (e.g., Treml, 1982; Feshbach, 1983). Although there appear to be no aggregate data to substantiate the charge, numerous reports have claimed that labor discipline declined markedly in the last years of the Brezhnev administration (Teague, 1985, pp. 4–5, 10–12). Some Western observers have described a growing pessimism for the future, concentrated especially among the rapidly expanding professional class (Bushnell, 1979). All these data convey a deepening demoralization and spreading anomie in the society at large. At the same time, direct and undisguised social protest also has increased. One recent Soviet source reports a rise in the number of formal complaints about management-inspired and/or tolerated labor law violations, sent by disgruntled workers to authorities at the Center (Livshits and Nikitinskiy, 1985, p. 103). And, the end of the Brezhnev period saw a resurgence of worker militancy, including several small-scale attempts, albeit quickly suppressed, to establish independent trade unions (Gidwitz, 1982).

Most telling, however, are the signs of deepening conflict among the political and intellectual elite. Since approximately the mid-1970s, every element of the social contract has been subjected to increasingly pointed criticism (e.g., Haus-lohner, 1984, pp. 435ff). Wage egalitarianism has probably been the most popular target.[9] Perhaps more significant have been the multiplying attacks on full employment and job security, which have been blamed openly for en-couraging sloth, indiscipline, and excessive labor turnover.[10] While there was relatively little substantive change in social policy before Brezhnev's death, there is reason to think that whatever elite consensus once existed in support of the social contract had, by that point, largely disintegrated.

What has gone wrong? Slow growth is surely part of the problem. A smaller pie has squeezed everyone, and elite tension and popular unhappiness can be said to have increased on this account alone.[11] On the other hand, the broad-ranging critiques of contemporary Soviet society which have begun to circulate among the establishment (including the Gorbachev-endorsed claim that a gap has opened between "production forces" and "production relations") diagnose a social crisis which is far more complex and deeply rooted than could rea-sonably be attributed to unwanted austerity alone (e.g., Gorbachev, 1985a, pp. 12–13; and 1987).[12] At the same time, there is evidence that at all three of the levels just discussed (normative, constituency, and institutional) support for the social contract has been declining.

It appears, for example, that not just the elite but large segments of the public have grown deeply dissatisfied with the current distribution system. When legitimately earned rubles cannot be turned promptly and easily into consumption except through luck or connections, and when illegitimately earned fortunes make hardworking, law-abiding souls look like fools, it should not be surprising to find people turning cynical toward egalitarian distribution and the rules which extend welfare state protections to everyone, slackers and all.[13] Since Gorbachev's election as General Secretary, a wide-ranging public debate has erupted over the meaning of "social justice" and the degree to which justice has—or, more often, has not—been served (e.g., Trehub, 1986). Mean-while, academic sociology has shown a growing interest in recent years in trying to understand the role that social norms play in establishing social cohe-sion, and in learning concretely what distributive principles the public regards as fair and why (e.g., Rogovin, 1982). All this suggests that the normative

9. On the change in mainstream elite attitudes toward the wage system and distributive policy generally, see Kapustin and Vikhlyayev (1985), a product of a massive conference organized by the USSR Academy of Sciences' Institute of Economics in Moscow shortly after Brezhnev's death.

10. Thus, some critics have argued openly for "the creation of a modest shortage of jobs, so as to interest people, to make them value work" (Distsiplina, 1981, p. 41). For a particularly outspoken and widely noted example of this argument, see Popov (1980).

11. This is what most Western scholars have emphasized (e.g., White, 1986).

12. A well-known example of such a diagnosis is contained in Tat'yana Zaslavskaya's "Novosibirsk Memorandum" (Doklad, 1983).

13. "Confidence in the progressive character and justice of the social system," according to Zaslavskaya (1986a), "is a most important source of the masses' creative energy, labor effort, and economic initiative, and of the acceleration of socio-economic development. On the other hand, frequent encounters with injustice, the divergence of word and deed, the lack of defense of good and the lack of punishment of evil breed indifference and [promote] an escape into one's private interests. In the best circumstances, it ends up as social passivity, and in the worst—cynicism and anti-social behavior."

consensus underpinning the existing rules on distribution and burden-sharing has diminished and that public compliance with those rules probably has been weakening.

There also has been a major shift in the relative weights in the population of social policy's traditional winners and losers, implying a decline in "constituency" support for the social contract. Specifically, the supply of college-educated professionals and the proportion of the labor force employed in service both have increased substantially in the past three decades. Also, the economic importance of the technical intelligentsia and of services, and the critical role played by mid-level management, have become much more evident, as the economy has moved, albeit slowly, into its post-industrial development phase. And yet, the old wage and employment policies, with their bias in favor of blue-collar production workers, until recently remained largely unchanged. In the meantime, society as a whole has become dramatically better educated, more affluent, and more complex. Traditional class distinctions have become increasingly blurred, while intraclass differentiation has grown (e.g., Pravda, 1982). In the 1950s, in the context of a much "simpler" society, it probably made political and economic sense to consolidate wage scales, reduce wage differentiation, impose uniform work rules, and so forth—but no longer. Today, one can fairly say that increasing numbers of citizens have found themselves poorly served by, or even excluded from, the benefits of a social bargain assembled thirty years ago when social, economic, and political conditions were very different. In the language of American electoral politics, one can imagine a kind of social "de-alignment" taking shape, as the number of partisans of the old order declines, relatively speaking, and the number of dissatisfied "independents" grows, waiting to be mobilized behind a new program.[14]

Finally, the institutions in charge of implementing the social contract merit some of the blame as well. Thus, while it is likely that Soviet trade unions have never enjoyed extensive loyalty from ordinary workers, things evidently got worse in the 1970s, as union organs at all levels grew even less responsive and less democratic than before.[15] Wage administration also deteriorated, and Goskomtrud became one of the most frequently and sharply criticized of all central agencies (e.g., Hauslohner, 1984, pp. 318–323, 398, 436–437, 598–599, and 728–730). As a result, both the unions and the labor bureaucracy

14. This is suggested indirectly by the government's willingness to grant legitimacy and some material support to the study of Western-style political economy. After the June 1983 Central Committee plenum of ideology, Academician Zaslavskaya was placed in charge of a journal on "economic sociology," for which she had long been lobbying. In the journal's first issue, she and a coauthor defined their subject as, among other things, "analysis of the development of the economy as a social process representing the specific behavior and interaction of classes, strata, and groups in Soviet society" (Zaslavskaya and Ryvkina, 1984, p. 11). Gorbachev (1985a, pp. 15–16) also has expressed sympathy for a more behavioral "interest group" analysis of Soviet society.

15. This judgment is based on: (1) my interviews with leading Soviet labor specialists in Moscow in September–October 1985; (2) some evidence on internal union deliberations (stenographic reports of most Central Trade Union Council (VTsSPS) plenums held between 1955 and 1965 and of two more held in early 1984) in which discussions grew considerably less open and critical (more formal and ritualistic) over time, and in which participation by lower-ranking union officials and the flow of information both diminished markedly; and (3) the tone of the Soviet secondary literature published in the late 1970s and early 1980s (e.g., *Profsoyuzy*, 1979).

grew less able to defuse the conflicts which arose during the application of policy and, by implication, less able to ensure discipline and compliance with the rules.[16] At the same time and just as important, the unions and Goskomtrud continued to defend most traditional social policies and, more covertly, helped to undermine even relatively modest attempts at change. Whether this was out of loyalty to old constituencies or because their own organizational interests were best served in this way is less significant than the fact that the process of economic adjustment was seriously obstructed as a result.[17]

Together, these facts suggest a somewhat different interpretation of the recent deterioration in Soviet economic performance than the "economic system" explanation favored by so many in the West and, increasingly, in the Soviet Union as well. This view contends that present Soviet economic difficulties are largely "structural" in origin, and that long-term decline is an inevitable consequence of the enduring Stalinist economic system. It is argued that methods and institutions which may have worked well in the early stages of industrialization, when there were abundant unemployed resources lying about ready to be mobilized, do not suit the needs of a post-industrial economy when unemployed resources have largely disappeared and growth depends increasingly on improved utilization of the resources (including the so-called human factor) already at work. Moreover, it is not just growth *per se*, but a different kind of growth—growth that puts a premium on quality and the aesthetic side of things—which is required today and which Stalinist institutions seem particularly incapable of delivering.

There are two problems with this analysis, however. One is that it obscures the differences between structure and strategy. Thus, even if the standard diagnosis is right in a narrow sense, it ultimately is not directive planning or administered pricing that is to blame, but the belief that a method which specializes in mobilizing and concentrating production factors can still be an effective way of producing growth in today's conditions. Two corollaries flow from this. On the one hand, changes in political-economic structure could not have been expected to occur without significant delay: a) because the signs of weakness in Soviet performance were for a long time ambiguous; and b) because deep-seated beliefs never change quickly regardless of the circumstances. On the other hand, when those beliefs do change and a consensus has crystalized behind some new strategy, then major structural changes are almost certain to follow. The transition may be slowed by bureaucratic resistance, but not stopped, for the Soviet Union is still a highly centralized, one-party dictatorship.

16. For example, while workers were directing an increasing number of complaints about labor law violations to central authorities, the number of grievances examined by the enterprises' union-run disputes' commissions remained the same—an average 1–2 per commission per year (Livshits and Nikitinskiy, 1985, p. 103).

17. Even minor innovations suffered in the face of resistance (or a lack of support) from the unions and the labor bureaucracy (e.g., the Shchekino chemical combine's labor-shedding experiment, development of the labor exchanges, and efforts to organize effective retraining and reemployment programs for displaced workers), although these would have required no basic institutional reforms nor repudiation of the regime's prevailing economic strategy and might have reduced at least the steepness of the decline in overall performance. See the discussion in Hauslohner (1984, pp. 198–201, 286–287, 500–501, and 514–520).

The standard view also ignores the reciprocal relationship that exists between economic development strategy and social policy. The Stalinist developmental strategy, as previously noted, has exacted a large price from the population in the form of depressed living standards, the public's exclusion from the arenas of political-economic power, and the inevitable turmoil accompanying rapid socioeconomic change. Since the 1950s, the social unrest which these costs might have been expected to arouse has been kept in check, in significant part because of the provisions of an implicit social contract.[18] But the social contract had its own costs. Egalitarianism required that the surplus created at relatively profitable enterprises had to be reallocated to less profitable ones, which weakened the incentive to produce at both. The promise of security and fairness required uniform rules and a powerful, supervisory Center; but that meant severe restrictions on the flexibility and initiative of producers at the grass roots. New institutions, which had to be established in order to design and oversee implementation of the rules, developed their own stake in protecting the policies which mandated those rules. In recent years, the social contract has evidently taken an even larger share of the economy's surplus. It has led to growing inefficiencies on account of its inability to accommodate the increasing differentiation of the economy and society. And it has obstructed or prevented the kinds of economic adjustment which might have slowed the rate of decline, or even allowed for a smoother, less traumatic transition to a new growth strategy.

In short, the alternative interpretation does not contradict the standard view of the Soviet economy's ills so much as it argues that that view is incomplete and misleading, especially in its narrow focus on structural flaws. Declining performance is better seen as partly a problem of strategy and partly a consequence of the effort to maintain popular consent, the latter because the mechanisms which Soviet leaders have depended on to keep the peace the last thirty years have become significantly more expensive and less effective. An obsolete development strategy is undeniably a major cause of the deterioration in economic performance, and the slowdown in growth has doubtless helped to undermine the social contract. Yet, the reverse effect—the unraveling social contract's contribution to economic decline—may have been just as great.

This interpretation also suggests that crafting a new social contract is probably imperative, whatever Gorbachev's economic program turns out to be. However, if radical economic reform is on the agenda, then this new social contract will have to be compatible with it. This means: (1) that the normative underpinnings of a new social policy will have to be consistent with the prin-

18. While Stalin himself was alive, domestic peace was kept (though in the beginning not very well) largely through coercion, good prospects of upward mobility for the obedient and hardworking, and a special "deal" (enhanced material advantages and unquestioned authority over subordinates) for the tiny but rapidly growing, home-grown technical intelligentsia. But with the dispensing of terror and the slowing of upward mobility in the 1950s, and in the context of a dramatically transformed social structure, the regime's social peacekeeping formula stood in obvious need of reform.

ciples and logic of a decentralized, deregulated economy; (2) that the material benefits of policy will have to arouse a socio-political base for which radical reform is congenial or at least acceptable; and (3) that policy will have to be institutionalized in such a way so as not to impair the operations of the new economic mechanism. One way to test whether radical reform is in fact on the agenda is to see whether an effort to remake social policy in the manner just prescribed is now under way.

GORBACHEV'S PROGRAM

At least provisionally, the test is positive: a new social policy is being constructed, of a sort which suggests that radical economic reform *is* on Gorbachev's agenda. This does not mean that Gorbachev is following a detailed blueprint, or that he necessarily understands the requisite architecture of the social contract in the same way that I do. Nor does it mean that the new policies which have been introduced or promised will be fully implemented. On the other hand, they appear to be the kinds of policies needed for a significantly more decentralized, deregulated, and market-reliant socialism to endure. And, insofar as they are implemented, the pressures in favor of radical reform are likely to grow.

Policies

Gorbachev's rhetoric and the changes announced thus far (including some enacted before his election as General Secretary but after Brezhnev's death in 1982) describe a social policy comprised of three, unequally sized parts.[19] The largest and most important part has to do with distribution broadly defined. First, Gorbachev has promised a substantial improvement in living standards: in the next 15 years, real incomes are to rise by more than half, and the output of consumer goods and services is to double. At the same time, consumption will probably include fewer "entitlements," inasmuch as certain basic consumer prices (for food, housing, and high quality services) seem destined to rise.[20] Distribution also is to become more meritocratic: earnings from work are to be linked more closely to performance, there are to be steeper barriers to non-labor incomes, and consumer purchasing power is to be strengthened by increasing the supply of goods and services relative to the quantity of rubles

19. Although the following is my own synthesis of Gorbachev's program, it is similar in most respects to accounts by other Western scholars: e.g., Connor (1986) and Teague (1987).

20. This is my judgment based on the following factors: Gorbachev's own, sometimes vague remarks at various times; the considerable attention given to (and open advocacy of) consumer price reform in the last several years (e.g., Kazakevich, 1986; and, especially, Zaslavskaya, 1986c, pp. 71–72); the decision to raise state housing rents (*Pravda*, April 17, 1986, p. 1); and, finally, the logic of the current situation. As Natal'ya Rimashevskaya, the noted welfare economist, has argued in the specific case of housing (1986a, p. 66), unbalanced commodity and service markets are likely never to be brought into equilibrium so long as policymakers concentrate solely on the supply side and make no effort to curtail demand. For further discussion, see Hauslohner (1987).

in circulation. Finally, overall inequality is likely to rise, perhaps significantly, in part because of fewer entitlements and a more meritocratic distribution of goods, but mainly on account of far-reaching changes in wage policy.[21]

A second part of Gorbachev's program implies a significant reallocation of economic security. In effect, the General Secretary has promised greater security for those who cannot work (a stronger safety net for young children, their mothers, and the disabled), while threatening less security for everyone else. Thus, child payments and pensions are being raised and new socio-political institutions are being established (or their status enhanced), in order to better articulate and defend the interests of women and the elderly.[22] On the other hand, Gorbachev appears committed to bringing an end to the regime of overfull employment and extraordinary job security. Labor-shedding experiments are multiplying, wage and other incentive policies are being redrawn so as to greatly increase enterprises' interest in laying off workers, and even legal job protections have been marginally weakened.[23]

A third component of this social policy consists of a dramatically altered mix of political rights and personal liberties. Some individual freedoms are being curtailed, as has happened already with respect to the consumption of alcohol. Freedom of choice in education also seems likely to be narrowed, in the wake of the vocational emphasis of the school reforms announced so far. And, it is possible that mobility between jobs and occupations will become marginally more difficult, if the restrictive powers of the local labor organs are expanded in the manner some experts have been advocating. In other respects, however, individuals are being promised more economic freedom and, potentially, some modicum of power. The cooperative sector is to be expanded, and restrictions on individual and family employment are to be relaxed. Most importantly, ordinary citizens are being promised substantially wider opportunities to participate in and influence the management of their

---

21. Wage and salary differentials are to be widened, formal ceilings on earnings are to be sharply relaxed, and the minimum wage will probably be held down—in every respect the opposite of policy under Khrushchev and Brezhnev. See the more detailed discussion below in the section on "winners and losers."

22. Gorbachev, in his report to the 27th Congress (1986a, p. 6), proposed that formal organizations be established for seniors and women. The decision to create the All-Union Organization of Veterans of War and Labor was taken six months later (*Pravda*, September 27, 1986); its head is former Politburo member, K. T. Mazurov. The development of women's councils (*zhensovety*) has been slower, and the former chair of the Soviet Women's Committee, Tereshkova, has said that no "deadlines" were planned in this respect (*Izvestiya*, February 1, 1987, p. 4).

23. The most important labor-shedding experiment so far was conducted on the Belorussian railroad and resulted in layoffs of more than 10 percent of the workforce (Vaganov and Shcherbachenko, 1986). At the start of 1986 similar rules were extended to ten other railroad lines. Goskomtrud officials recently estimated that perhaps 4 percent of total employment in the production branches may be displaced during the 12th Five-Year Plan (Afanas'yev and Medvedeva, 1987, p. 68), but that appears to be a rather smaller figure than the 13–19 million *absolute decline* in employment in goods production that Gosplan economist Kostakov is predicting by the end of the century (1986). In April 1984, the USSR Supreme Court "clarified" the law, ruling that employers' "reemployment" obligations, in the case of workers dismissed for other than disciplinary reasons, no longer extended beyond the enterprise. Employers are required to offer dismissed employees vacant jobs that exist within their enterprises (providing the former are sufficiently qualified) but are not required to seek such jobs outside (Sokrashcheniye, 1985). Meanwhile, reformers are continuing to urge, as they have for many years, that *all* responsibility for finding displaced workers new jobs be transferred from employers to the job placement bureaus.

workplaces and residences. It is almost as if Gorbachev is proposing to compensate the public for its loss of economic rights and security with a large dose of democratization.

This is Gorbachev's vision. To assess the possibility that these policies will become the core of a new social contract, we need to examine them in the same terms used to analyze the first post-Stalin social contract: as a set of norms; as a package of benefits to prospective constituents; and as a potential edifice of concrete laws, institutions, and officials.

Norms

There is no doubt that Gorbachev is aware of the need to give his social policy a durable normative foundation, as evidenced by his repeated stress on the need for "psychological restructuring" throughout society (e.g., 1986b). His chief tactics include the aforementioned debate about social justice and the campaign for "openness" (*glasnost'*). At one level, of course, these activities have nothing at all to do with building new norms. Their purpose is to arouse popular support for Gorbachev's leadership and to make it easier for his supporters to attack the old regime. But Gorbachev's motives run deeper than this.

For example, Gorbachev clearly wants to legitimize large material rewards for effort, skill, and risk-taking. Unlike Khrushchev, Gorbachev is never heard arguing that earnings differences are too wide; on the contrary, existing differences are too small and, more importantly, too loosely correlated with job performance. The General Secretary is an avowed proponent of "pay-by-results," as opposed to pay according to the amount of time worked or the skill and intensity of the worker and/or job (e.g., 1985b, p. 28).[24] At the same time, Gorbachev is proposing a far-reaching revision of what constitutes "results" in this connection. At the 27th Congress, he at one point asked the audience rhetorically: why should we pay workers to produce goods which then sit on the shelves unused and unwanted (1986a, p. 5)?[25] There are answers to that question. One can imagine the ideologists in the audience replying: "because labor inputs are the source of value, and because it is the state's responsibility to determine the value of goods produced and labor expended." Or, one can imagine workers thinking: "because we have no control over what we produce why should we suffer the mistakes of others?" Still Gorbachev has persisted. His answer to workers is to promise them greater say over what gets produced and how. His answer to the ideologists, however, is less compromising, for he has argued, at times quite explicitly, that labor inputs should

24. A recent *Pravda* editorial (March 16, 1987) declared: "it should not be feared that the elimination of leveling (*uravnilovka*) will lead to something 'unanticipated.' Pay for excellent, correctly-normed work, however excessive such pay may seem to some, is always moral."

25. In the speech as given, Gorbachev interrupted his prepared text a few moments later to reiterate the point, this time eliciting applause which before had eluded him—a difference he himself noted dryly.

not be the only determinant of value and that the state should *not* be wholly responsible for establishing the value of goods or the measure of labor. Gorbachev has suggested that use value, the value to consumers, ought to play a larger role than it has both in pricing goods and in determining enterprise revenues and workers' earnings.

Gorbachev also has urged the public to show greater intolerance of nonlabor incomes, and he has called for stricter prosecution of those who profit from the black market, the misuse of state property, and all forms of official corruption. But he has tried to do this while, at the same time, redefining nonlabor income so as to allow much greater practical scope and heightened political legitimacy for various forms of personal employment.[26] More broadly, Gorbachev has been promoting a reexamination of socialist property relations in a related effort to provide greater practical scope and political legitimacy for cooperative forms of economic organization, not just in agriculture but in services and even small-scale industry. In effect, Gorbachev has joined the attack on the arguments advanced by leading ideologists in the late Brezhnev era, who contended that cooperative organization is inherently inferior to state organization and that inasmuch as Soviet society was already well along the path to communism, one could begin to think of eliminating those cooperatives which remained. The counter-argument, which has now won Gorbachev's support, is that cooperatives are not inferior but, rather, just as progressive and that Soviet society is, in any case, much further away from communism than Brezhnev's optimists had imagined (Gorbachev, 1987; Teague, 1986a).

Finally, Gorbachev and his allies have tried to give legitimacy to the very idea of "reform"—a concept which some of Gorbachev's ideological opponents have evidently declared to be alien to socialism. They have also attempted to gain support for judging prospective reforms (and perhaps socialism itself) more on the basis of substance and results. In an oft-quoted passage to the 27th Party Congress, Gorbachev criticized those who opposed change for fear of departing from socialism (1986a, p. 5). That argument is overused, Gorbachev said in effect, but also misused. The true measure of the appropriateness or desirability of change, he said to the audience's applause, should be whether or not it works—whether it gets the country closer to socialism in practice.

Needless to say, the inculcation of new norms is a long-term and highly uncertain project, the full effects of which will not be known for years to come. Yet, without prejudging the ultimate impact of this effort, it is useful to consider what has been accomplished so far and some of the more striking problems. On the positive side, there has been a remarkable expansion of debate, both in public and among the elite, about all of the issues just listed and more coverage in the press of genuinely reformist ideas and experiments than at any

26. In his speech to the Congress (1986a, p. 6), he immediately followed his attack on non-labor incomes with this caveat: "But, while eliminating unearned incomes, it is impermissable to allow a shadow to fall on those who receive additional earnings through honest labor. . . . It is necessary to look attentively on suggestions concerning the improved regulation of individual employment." Recent articles in *Kommunist* have taken an even bolder line in arguing for greater legitimacy for the private sector (Trud, 1986; Latsis, 1987).

time since the 1920s.[27] Such "morally questionable" things as migrant labor brigades (*shabashniki*), family farming, and independent service cooperatives have received considerable attention, much (but not all) of it laudatory. These ideas are not new, of course, and there is no evidence that the population's thinking has changed much as a result of the greater attention now being paid to them. But the amount of coverage has grown enormously, and the public's broad exposure to controversial ideas is surely the only way to make them acceptable on a large scale.

Even more important is the different treatment that is now being given to particularly difficult issues like inequality and unemployment. The discussion of redundancy (*vysvobozhdeniye*) is a good example. The mere fact that public debate about this issue has become easier and less risky is, by itself, a measure of the fundamental shift that has occurred in the attitudes of the elite.[28] Also different, however, is the way in which redundancy is being presented to the public. Twenty years ago, when redundancy first became an important subject in connection with the Kosygin reform, most commentators emphasized ways to lessen, if not to eliminate entirely, the personal and social costs of redundancy, as if it were possible to reduce those costs nearly to zero. Today, experts are much more forthright in stating that individuals will have to get used to the idea that being without a job temporarily is sometimes an inevitable concomitant of a rapidly growing, modern economy—even a socialist economy (Kostakov, 1986a, 1986b, 1987).[29] Again, simply saying this is no guarantee that the public will come to accept it as a normal and "fair" rule of life. But not saying it (or saying the opposite) will just as surely postpone the day when massive, covert opposition to redundancy no longer is the major obstacle to technological progress that it is alleged to be at present.

On the negative side, it is clear that freer debate has permitted the airing of a substantial amount of opposition to Gorbachev's proposals, and there is some evidence that he has been unable (or perhaps unwilling) to closely control this debate or its impact on policy. Thus, a gathering attack on the inviolability of the party-state apparatus, in the weeks just prior to the 27th Congress, ended up provoking much resentment and criticism, even from persons whom Gorbachev might otherwise be expected to count as allies.[30] Meanwhile, despite

27. Particularly important and illuminating is the discussion elicited by the editors of *Kommunist*, following a particularly forthright pro-reform article by Zaslavskaya (1986c). See, especially, the excerpts from replies reported in No. 17, 1986, pp. 61–68; and a preliminary summary of the discussion in No. 3, 1987, pp. 97–108.

28. The difficulties encountered by some of the specialists who raised the redundancy issue in the mid-1960s are described in Hauslohner (1984, pp. 209–210).

29. At the 27th Party Congress, Party Second Secretary Yegor Ligachev called for "rebuilding" a government retraining system and vowed: "Socialism cannot permit and will not permit, as a result of scientific-technical progress, significant groups of working people—and their numbers may reach into the millions—to become superfluous people in society, [to be] unprepared for work in the new conditions" (*Pravda*, February 28, 1986, p. 4). The message, of course, was double-edged.

30. At the Congress, Vladimir Kalashnikov, party first secretary in Volgograd province, made a forceful plea for consumer price reform, an unusually bold move for such a prominent politician, and then turned around and criticized *Pravda* for unwarranted sensationalism in its criticism of party and state officials, even more explicitly than Ligachev had done earlier (*Pravda*, March 2, 1986, p. 3). In the West, these events were generally

the effort to protect individual employment from the assault launched against nonlabor incomes, legislation on the latter preceded that on the former, and the first effects of the new measures evidently strengthened the pressures and penalties leveled against perfectly legal individual activities of the sort Gorbachev wants to give broader scope to (e.g., Vo imya, 1986).[31] Finally, the most recent and perhaps most dramatic example was the Central Committee's apparent unwillingness, at its January 1987 plenum, to take the democratization of government and the Party nearly as far as Gorbachev had proposed in his opening speech to that meeting (see below).

We must be careful, however, not to exaggerate the negative connotations of this. If the internalization of revised norms is required for new social policies to endure, then narrowing the public debate prematurely or simply denying the floor to the opponents of change would almost certainly be a strategic mistake. On the contrary, a skillful reformist leadership, whether it believes it or not, has a powerful interest in not concealing what others in the elite and the public as a whole are really thinking and doing in response to changes as they are introduced.

Winners and Losers

Gorbachev's social policy implies a markedly different set of prospective winners and losers than obtained under the rule of his predecessors. Speaking very broadly, college-educated professionals and especially those who are young (the Soviet equivalent of "yuppies") are likely to gain from Gorbachev's policies, while the traditional working class (blue collar workers employed in goods production) seems destined to lose, relatively speaking if not absolutely. So far this has been true both symbolically and substantively.

In his speeches, Gorbachev has often emphasized the crucial role of the scientific-technical intelligentsia in promoting the acceleration of economic growth and technological progress. On several occasions he has agreed that the incomes and social status of professionals such as scientists, engineers, and designers (but also teachers and health care workers) must and will be raised (e.g., Gorbachev, 1985b, pp. 19–22). By comparison, he has been conspicuously inattentive to the role and importance of the working class as a separate category. In fact, on those occasions when a kind word for the working class

interpreted as a failed attempt to put the issue of elite privilege on the agenda. My view is that what may initially have been designed as such an effort got out of hand. What Ligachev and Kalashnikov really were denouncing, I think, was the publication of criticisms depicting *apparatchiki* as somehow equivalent to a ruling stratum which opposed changes beneficial to society for fear of losing its hegemony and implying, more generally, that the troubles besetting society might ultimately be the result of "Soviet power" itself. For a particularly explicit example of the latter, see the first of the three articles by T. Samolis, the series evidently responsible for the backlash (*Pravda*, December 5 and 27, 1985; February 13, 1986, p. 3).

31. Of course, from a tactical standpoint, it may have been better for the cause of individual employment that this was the sequence of events rather than the reverse. Now that some of the unwanted consequences of a more punitive approach to regulating private employment have been demonstrated, it may be easier to quell the protests over "obscene" incomes, which are bound to arise once other restrictions are liberalized and regulation becomes more economic in character.

has seemed to be in order, Gorbachev has made what almost seems like a calculated snub. At a meeting commemorating the 50th anniversary of the Stakhanovite movement (*Pravda*, September 21, 1985, pp. 1–2), the General Secretary criticized extensively the way "socialist competitions" have been run and then went on to lavish extravagant praise on two young Leningrad automobile designers who had recently won a national competition for innovative design. Rather than extol the merits of shock work as one might have expected, Gorbachev instead chose to emphasize the obsolescence of much of the traditional practice of worker mobilization and the need to give youth in particular more freedom and opportunity—all to an audience composed mostly of veteran manual workers and rate-busters in their forties, fifties, and sixties!

Substantive policy changes have generally reflected these same priorities. The first major wage reform announced after Gorbachev's election as General Secretary was the decision in May 1985 to raise the salaries of scientists, other professionals employed in research institutes, and industrial designers and technicians.[32] Teachers' salaries were already going up as part of the 1984 Education reform, and a schedule of salary increases in the health professions has since been announced as well (*Pravda*, October 17, 1986, p. 1).[33] Meanwhile, a major wage reform in goods-production branches, adopted in mid-September 1986, is explicitly less favorable to blue collar workers as a class than to professionals and clericals.[34] It is likely to be even more unfavorable to blue collar workers in the course of implementation, since wage hikes are to be almost wholly financed out of enterprise profits and are to be introduced factory-by-factory as the necessary resources are accumulated. This procedure stands in sharp contrast to the practice under Khrushchev and Brezhnev of introducing wage reforms across all factories in an industry or region simultaneously, and of financing most of the wage reform directly out of the state budget.

Other indicators tell much the same story. While some intellectuals are reportedly distressed with the anti-alcohol campaign, the effects of that campaign probably fall most heavily on workers. On the other hand, if the regime wanted seriously to improve the consumption opportunities of workers, an obvious way to do so would be to increase significantly the production of inexpensive cars which a fairly high proportion of the professional class already seems to own. Yet, car production is hardly increasing at all (*Pravda*, January 26, 1986, and January 18, 1987). Moreover, in his speech to Tol'yatti's autoworkers, the General Secretary concentrated instead on the importance of

32. The decree was signed on May 22, 1985, but not announced until July (*Sbornik postanovleniy pravitel'stva SSSR*, 1985, No. 21, Art. 104).

33. Also worth noting are the effects of the 1982 Food Program which Gorbachev played a significant role in designing. In 1982–1984, average earnings for professionals in agriculture went up 22 percent (42 rubles/month); those for nonprofessional white collars rose 33 percent (42 rubles); while the earnings of ordinary workers increased by only 10 percent (16 rubles) (*Narkhoz.*, 1985, p. 417).

34. The reform specifies higher formal raises for professionals and personnel in management than for manual workers, plus a unified bonus fund which, based on previous experience, is also likely to prove unfavorable to workers. The reform, dated September 17, 1986, is described in detail in a series of articles in *Sotsialisticheskiy trud*, No. 1, 1987, pp. 1–82.

producing state-of-the art vehicles suitable for export (*Pravda*, April 9, 1986). Meanwhile, the government has decided in highly publicized fashion to expand the production and sale of personal computers and video recorders and to make more land available to the urban population for summer gardens and dachas. Both price and planned output levels make it clear the "high-tech" consumption goods will for a long time be primarily the province of the affluent and well-connected. Less obvious, perhaps, the increased supply of land for dachas also is likely to benefit mainly the middle class, insofar as possession of a car may in many cases be necessary for one to make any practical use of this land (often located far from city centers).[35] Finally, if one views more "hard" news and higher quality culture as middle class consumption goods, then the *glasnost'* campaign and the remarkable liberalization in culture now occurring also ought to be regarded as components of a new distribution policy which grants its biggest favors to college-educated, middle-class professionals.

The foregoing are broad generalizations, and there will naturally be exceptions. Many highly skilled manual workers can be expected to do quite well under these policies, while white collar professionals who will not (or cannot) step up the pace may be forced out of their occupations entirely.[36] Another complicating factor involves democratization and its effects on interclass relations within the enterprise. For example, a key issue in the ongoing debate over the role of brigades in the nonfarm economy is whether to include engineers and technicians (ITR) in enlarged brigades and, more specifically, whether to give blue collar workers a role in determining ITR earnings. The prospect, not surprisingly, seems to arouse a certain amount of anxiety among white collar workers. And, where enlarged brigades have been tried experimentally (the "Novosibirsk experiment"), the level of conflict between the two groups has risen noticeably (e.g., Kutyryev, 1986, pp. 97–100).[37] In other words, depending on how far democratization proceeds, the net effects of Gorbachev's social policy on professionals as a class are obviously going to be more mixed than is suggested by the changes in wage and consumption measures alone.

Gorbachev would doubtless use very different language to describe the groups to which his policies are intended to appeal. Academician Zaslavskaya has identified radical reform's natural constituency as comprised of the "skilled and energetic" (Vybor, 1985), and Gorbachev's program could be fairly described as an effort to mobilize a coalition of interests cutting across traditional class lines (e.g., Popov, 1987). In light of our earlier discussion of changes

35. A secretary in Moscow told me that her husband, an engineer, had turned down the offer of a plot of land from his employer for precisely this reason.

36. A Goskomtrud official estimated (*Literaturnaya gazeta*, January 15, 1986, p. 12) that 6–10 percent of those covered by the May 1985 wage measures will probably lose their jobs. In the experiment conducted in Leningrad, which served as prototype for the May reform, women were considerably more likely to complain than men, on the unsurprising and understanding grounds that an intensified work regime is often impossible to reconcile with existing family responsibilities (Parfenov in *Pravda*, May 20, 1985, p. 3).

37. Elsewhere, however, Kutyryev (1985) suggests that enlarged brigades working on contract—in which blue collar workers are given an opportunity to see for themselves how much genuinely skilled engineering work (and good white collar work generally) is really worth—may be an important and even necessary means of overcoming popular resistance to substantially increasing the white collar-blue collar earnings gap.

in Soviet social structure, such an approach may well be more effective a strategy than one based on more conventional social categories. The crucial question, however, is what will happen in practice. Will the "skilled and energetic" members of Soviet society perceive themselves to be at the center of Gorbachev's coalition? If so, will their perceptions and consequent expectations be attached by equivalent gains in consumption, status, and power? The answer, as suggested by our previous discussion, is likely to depend substantially on the way in which Gorbachev's proposed new norms and policies are given concrete institutional expression.

INSTITUTIONALIZING THE NEW ORDER

Any new social contract must be institutionalized, and it is in this connection that one can see the most serious pitfalls lurking ahead. The problem of institution-building exists at the grass-roots level and at the Center.

The main issue at the grass-roots level is democratization. Gorbachev has voiced consistent support for increasing public participation "in all spheres of public life," even from before his election as General Secretary (1985a, 28ff), although his recent proposals (1987) for overhauling the Soviet electoral system and for a substantial deepening of intra-party democracy are easily the most far-reaching. The rest of the elite, however, has lagged behind. At the January 1987 Central Committee Plenum, only those proposals for democratizing the workplace received clearcut endorsement (*Pravda*, January 29, 1987, pp. 1–2). On the other hand, Gorbachev himself has given first priority to reform at the workplace, where change is probably most necessary if a new social contract is to be securely anchored.

At first, the new General Secretary pushed the cause of workplace democratization, by attaching his name and prestige to a series of measures inherited from or originally conceived under, his predecessors. He spoke out strongly in favor of the broader use of brigades throughout the economy, especially those thought to be the most "progressive": economic-accounting (*khozraschetnyy*) and contract brigades (*brigadnyy podryad*), as well as enlarged brigades operating at the level of whole shops and sections (the "Novosibirsk experiment").[38] He also endorsed the introduction of formal, routinized procedures of job certification (*atestatsiya rabochikh mest*) for both blue-collar and white-collar workers.[39] And he gave special attention to the idea of strength-

---

38. The "economic" purpose of brigades is to rationalize members' incentives by making a substantial portion of each individual's earnings dependent on the collective result broadly defined. The "social" purpose is to give brigade members a greater voice in organizing their work and in determining their own and other members' earnings. For background on recent experiments with brigades and related legislative changes, see Slider (1986) and Heinemeier (1987).

39. Provisions for the periodic certification of specialists were included in the May 1985 pay reform, while a subsequent decree mandated the periodic certification of jobs in production branches (*Sbornik postanovleniy pravitel'stva SSSR*, 1985, No. 21, Art. 104, and No. 28, Art. 141). The purpose of the latter decree is to involve workers directly in decisions regarding the decommissioning of old and/or primitive equipment and jobs and the consequent displacement of labor and capital for reallocation to more productive uses elsewhere.

ening the much-maligned 1983 Law on Laboring Collectives.[40] Most of the time, Gorbachev has justified increased participation, at the workplace and elsewhere, as a way to mobilize popular interest and effort—to exploit more fully the "human factor," thereby unleashing great pent-up reserves of innovation and productivity.[41] Less explicitly, workplace democratization has been presented as an integral part of an entire social policy package—in effect, a "good" which the new leadership is offering in exchange for other goods to be taken away, in the hope of diffusing whatever protest these take-backs may arouse. Thus, while a pronounced aim of Gorbachev's policies is to make able-bodied workers' welfare more tightly dependent on individual and enterprise performance, serious efforts to realize that aim are liable to provoke acute popular discontent, if workers' control over the determinants of performance remains as limited as it is now. It should be said, however, that the logic of such an "exchange" is questionable: one can imagine democratic institutions absorbing protest—or, protestors using those institutions to magnify their voice. More recently, as we'll see below, Gorbachev has suggested a rather different rationale for democratization.

Meanwhile, even as Gorbachev was arguing the merits of brigades and the potential of the Law on Laboring Collectives, it was becoming obvious to sympathetic specialists that such measures were far too modest to have any significant effect by themselves. At bottom, the problem was the failure to deal seriously with the two most important obstacles to workplace democratization: (1) the paucity of workers' rights and resources vis-à-vis management and, relatedly, resistance from the enterprise trade unions, which stand to lose resources and influence in the event real democratization goes forward (e.g., Tsepin, 1981, pp. 52–53; and Slider, 1986); and (2) the enterprise's extremely limited authority vis-à-vis other organizational actors, particularly its ministerial supervisors (Central Committee Secretary Zaykov in *Pravda*, October 30, 1986, p. 2; Zakon, 1985, pp. 10ff; Komozin and Meshcherkin, 1986). Yet, Gorbachev evidently understood this, for by the end of his first year in office he was ready to push more radical proposals onto the agenda. At the 27th Party Congress

---

40. Background on the law can be found in Slider (1985) and Teague (1986b). Originally billed as a major increase in workers' control, the law has been described as almost totally inconsequential by Western and Soviet scholars alike. Gorbachev signalled his own displeasure in his December 1984 speech to the ideologists (1985a, pp. 29–30). In June 1985, the Central Committee formally criticized implementation of the law and ordered a special commission to draw up a "Commentary" on its use, in the hope of thereby raising its effectiveness (*Pravda*, June 28, 1985, pp. 1–2; interview with a commission member). The commission was instructed to report back within six months, although a subsequent editorial in *Pravda* (December 26, 1985) indicated that the work was going slowly. It is likely, however, that this effort has since been dropped, or at least de-emphasized, and that the pro-democracy forces are now devoting most of their energy to the new Enterprise Statute (see below).

41. "We will be able to really elevate the people's initiative and creativity," he told the January plenum (1987, p. 2), "if our democratic institutions actively and genuinely influence the state of affairs in every work collective, whether it be the planning and organization of work, the distribution of material and other benefits, [or] the selection and promotion to leadership posts of the most authoritative and competent people. One can say with confidence that the sooner each person feels these changes in his own experience, the more active will be his position as citizen, his participation in all public and state matters." Workplace reforms must, Gorbachev said using the standard phrase, make it so that each worker feels him- or herself to be "the genuine proprieter (*khozyain*) of the enterprise."

(1986a, p. 7), he endorsed the idea of enterprise councils, in principle an institutional alternative to the unions for representing workers' interests within the enterprise. In addition, Gorbachev proposed the election of certain categories of management personnel, and soon thereafter began to allude to the need for a new enterprise statute. Although it took another year to win their acceptance, both enterprise councils and managerial elections (including enterprise directors) were endorsed by the January 1987 Central Committee Plenum. These were subsequently incorporated into the draft of a new enterprise statute published a few days later (*Pravda*, February 8, 1987, pp. 1–3).

To be sure, this is hardly the end of the story, and in some respects the really important battles have just begun. For example, the draft of the Law on the State Enterprise specifies open voting for members of the enterprise council and *either* secret or open voting for the post of manager. Not surprisingly, many critics of the draft law fear that open voting, if preserved, will give "the formalists and bureaucrats" a means with which "to bury" the new institutions (Nikitin in *Pravda*, April 2, 1987, p. 2). Equally important, the draft law gives no serious attention to the issue of relations between the new councils and existing public organs like the trade unions. At the recent 18th Trade Union Congress, union head Stepan Shalayev argued that the fears of "some comrades," who believe that enterprise councils will narrow the role of union organs, are "completely wrong." He also suggested that the unions should themselves assume responsibility "for the creation of the councils" and for "generalizing and disseminating" the lessons to be learned therefrom (*Trud*, February 25, 1987, p. 5).[42] In short, it is too early to tell whether the new councils and managerial elections will become effective participatory institutions, or whether they will be captured by the authorities. On the other hand, the policy debate has shifted decisively, and the first obstacle to workplace democratization is now being confronted in serious fashion.

The same is true of the second obstacle—the enterprise's weakness vis-à-vis other organs. Yet here, uncertainty about the future is greater still. Although the stated intention of the new enterprise statute is to significantly strengthen enterprise autonomy, the public discussion has revealed numerous problems with the existing draft law. Most deficient, perhaps, is the "declaratory" character of the injunctions to higher level bodies not to interfere in enterprise affairs. Critics have argued forcefully, and probably correctly, that juridical guarantees of enterprise independence need to be provided, and clear judicial responsibility and penalties for unfounded interference established as well (e.g., Zagaynov in *Pravda*, March 28, 1987, p. 2; Nikitin and Parfenov, *Pravda*, April 8, 1987, pp. 1–2). On the other hand, even if this and similar issues are resolved fully in favor of the reformers,

42. The "anti-union" thrust of the councils and the unions' anxieties seem obvious. There was very little discussion of the prospective councils in the published record of the recent Trade Union Congress, and the councils merited only one, quite general reference in the Congress Resolution (*Trud*, March 1, 1987, p. 4). However, one speaker who did raise the issue directly (a brigadier from Perm') clearly was not satisfied with Shalayev's assurances: "Won't there be some confusion, an erosion (*razmyvaniye*) of the functions of both [the new councils and union organs]?" she asked. Are not the council and the union organs supposed to represent the same constituencies? "So far," she declared, "I have not heard a convincing explanation" (Trapeznikova in *Trud*, February 27, 1987, p. 4).

it is clear that the ultimate extent of enterprise autonomy (and workplace democratization) will depend on continued political support from above and, of equal importance, on the right external conditions, i.e., price reform, wholesale trade, an improved banking and credit system, and so forth—in other words, "radical" reform in other parts of the economy.

This interdependence between democratization and radical economic reform may well mean, as some suspect, that democratization is doomed. Or one might reverse the argument and suppose that as democratizing measures are instituted, the pressures in favor of radical reform will intensify. The latter has seemed increasingly to be Gorbachev's view. In his Krasnodar speech (1986b, p. 2), he asked rhetorically: for whom has restructuring been the most difficult so far? Not for the slackers, he replied, but for "the innovators, active people, the irrepressible, the restless." Such people, he continued, "are destroying some leaders' existing stereotypes of work, they are forcing them to get moving (*shevelit'sya zastavlyayut*)." It is the active people, he declared, who can and must be brought into the process of restructuring through democratization. At the January Plenum four months later, Gorbachev (1987) defined democratization as necessary for making reform "irreversible." Although short on specifics, Gorbachev now seems to imagine democratization more and more as a means of augmenting the voice of those individuals and groups scattered throughout society who support reform or stand to gain from it. If, as seems to be Gorbachev's assumption (and, arguably, he is right), democratization is likely *de facto* to broaden disproportionately the participatory chances and influence of the "winners" of reform, then the political changes now on the agenda can be seen first and foremost as required if the policy changes accompanying restructuring, included those in social policy, are to be institutionalized.

At the Center, the problems of institutionalization have mainly to do with prevailing norms of policymaking. The most important issue, from the standpoint of the reformers, is how to neutralize or win over those central bodies which in the past helped to protect the old social contract from attack in the course of normal, day-to-day decision making. Numerous organizations fall into this category; e.g., the State Planning Commission, the Ministry of Finance, and the State Committee on Prices, among others.[43] There are two agencies, however, which have been more intimately involved than the others in designing and implementing the specifics of social policy: the State Committee on Labor and Social Problems (Goskomtrud) and the All-Union Central Council of Trade Unions (VTsSPS). Redirecting the energies of these two bureaucracies is proving to be difficult in practice.

The problem in Goskomtrud's case is overcoming not so much its longstanding defense of traditional social policies, as its narrow preoccupation with wage policy to the virtual exclusion of anything else. Goskomtrud acquired

---

43. Numerous interviews with Soviet specialists have emphasized the role that the Ministry of Finance in particular has heretofore played a role in obstructing efforts to decentralize wage formation and to give managers more freedom over hiring.

this orientation under the long and effective leadership of Alesksandr Volkov, an important political ally of Khrushchev. Although the committee's influence continued to increase as a result of the Brezhnev administration's habit of deferring on many policy questions to the major institutions involved, Brezhnev himself grew increasingly dissatisfied with Goskomtrud's performance, and in 1974 Volkov was fired. For over two years no replacement was named. Then, when a successor to Volkov finally was announced in August 1976, the committee was simultaneously reorganized in an effort to allow and encourage the committee to pay more attention to other dimensions of the labor market besides wage regulation.[44] However, the committee's new head, Vladimir Lomonosov, turned out to be an undistinguished administrator (like many other late Brezhnev-era appointees), and there was little change in the committee's behavior. Soon after Brezhnev died, a renewed assault was launched against Goskomtrud in the central press, and on the same day the draft of the new Law on Laboring Collectives was published, Lomonosov was dismissed (*Pravda*, April 12, 1983, pp. 1–2), as if to drive home the point that the committee really ought to be spending less time on the details of wage regulation (and involving itself in the affairs of enterprises). Chairmanship of the committee now went to Yuriy Batalin, a construction executive who had made a name for himself building pipelines in Siberia, and who has turned out to be one of the Gorbachev administration's "high fliers." Batalin quickly moved to sweep out the rest of the committee's leadership, much of which had been holdovers from the Khrushchev days. Then, in January 1986, Batalin himself moved on and up; his replacement was Ivan Gladkiy, a VTsSPS Secretary.[45]

In principle, Goskomtrud should be ready to play a substantially different role from that which it performed in the 1960s and 1970s. In fact, there have been significant changes. The committee has clearly broadened its focus.[46] And it has changed its tune on wage policy, now conceding the need for larger rate differentials and a major cutback in the central regulations limiting enterprise discretion in questions of pay. Yet on several key issues the committee has continued to take a markedly conservative position. Most important, it has remained unwilling to support a departure from the central regulation of wages to anywhere near the degree that radical, or even moderate, reformers would like.[47] Perhaps equally troubling is the fact that there is almost no one in

44. The committee's mission now includes responsibility for the job placement service, the development and operation of an effective vocational counseling service, the organization of programs to facilitate workforce displacement, and a heightened role in planning and labor market analysis.

45. Interviews published before his appointment leave the impression that Gladkiy supports workplace democratization (*Trud*, August 18, 1985, p. 2; and *Literaturnaya gazeta*, October 2, 1985, p. 10).

46. It also broadened the focus of its chief research arm, the Scientific Research Institute of Labor, with the appointment (though apparently before Batalin's appointment) of Yevgeniy Antosenkov, an outstanding economist and one of the country's leading experts on labor turnover, as institute director.

47. For example, in an article published just when his tenure at Goskomtrud was ending, Batalin expressed generalized support for the Novosibirsk experiment, while urging modifications which would probably reduce the impact of enlarged brigades and almost certainly leave the labor committee's role in wage formation largely untouched. Of particular importance, Batalin would continue to plan (and allocate) separately the wage funds of blue collar workers and ITR, in part so as to allow "unnecessary psychological frictions to be avoided" (Batalin, 1986, p. 13).

government or the academic community who has thought much about what might be done concretely to turn the labor committee into a more supportive (or less obstructive) force with respect to reform.[48]

The situation in the trade unions is, by comparison, much bleaker. Although Western scholars disagree on this point, interview evidence in particular suggests that the VTsSPS has been a "player" of considerable influence in the making of social policy.[49] Like Goskomtrud, the VTsSPS owes its position to powerful and effective leadership in the past (under Viktor Grishin and Aleksandr Shelepin) and to Brezhnev's deferential policymaking style. Also like Goskomtrud, the VTsSPS became a target of the politicians' displeasure in the mid-1970s and for a long time was left without a chairman. Then, under the new head, Aleksey Shibayev, who turned out to be even less effective (and a good deal more corrupt) than his counterpart at the labor committee, the unions languished. In the early 1980s, the Polish crisis helped to bring labor policy and the unions' performance back onto the leadership's agenda. And, just prior to the opening of the 17th Trade Union Congress in early 1982, Shibayev was replaced by Stepan Shalayev, a union man for most of his career (Ruble, 1983).

The effect seems to have been minimal. For one thing, union leaders have been nearly invisible in the vigorous policy debates that have erupted since Brezhnev's death. When they have spoken up, it has been to register cautious but unmistakable skepticism of some of the more radical options under consideration.[50] Indeed, according to printed sources and interviews at the VTsSPS and elsewhere in Moscow, the national union leadership has taken a quite conservative stance on most of the social policy issues discussed earlier.[51] Meanwhile, Gorbachev has himself criticized the unions on several occasions (e.g., 1986b, p. 2, when he described the unions as "toothless"). In addition, a few anti-union exposés have appeared in the press (e.g., Palamarchuk in *Pravda*, April 16, 1985, p. 3). Still, it is the lack of attention that is most striking. While most other institutions appear to be debating, if not always

48. Based on interviews with a large number of labor specialists in April 1981 and September–October 1985. An otherwise unremarkable exception is Inga Maslova (1985, pp. 132–141), a senior economist at the Institute of Economics.

49. Based on my own interviews. But see Hough (1979) and Ruble (1981).

50. For example, in an important article published the summer before the 27th Party Congress, Shalayev (1985) voiced support for brigades and brigade contracting in principle, while worrying about leveling tendencies within brigades and emphasizing the importance of finding ways to preserve incentives for rate-busters (*peredoviki*) who might otherwise be discouraged by having to share their rewards with less energetic comrades. In his speech at the Congress, Shalayev concentrated on the housing problem. Yet his analysis included only a tiny and unspecific reference to the issue of improved distribution and stressed instead the need for more building (*Pravda*, March 3, 1986, p. 5). Although Shalayev had very little to say about the Laboring Collectives Law (in either of these statements), on the day the Congress opened, another VTsSPS Secretary, Leonid Kazakov, publicly blamed the lag in implementing the Law primarily on worker passivity (*Trud*, February 25, 1986, p. 2).

51. Among other things, the VTsSPS is apparently: (1) opposed to letting brigade members' income depend entirely on collective performance, arguing that the tariff should be considered a minimum wage for workers who show up, fulfill their norms, and otherwise perform conscientiously, regardless of the collective result; (2) lukewarm in its support of contracts and divided over the Novosibirsk experiment; (3) not enthusiastic about relaxing current restrictions on legal moonlighting (*sovmestitel'stvo*); (4) skeptical of the need for a big increase in the blue collar-white collar earnings gap; and (5) very resistant to consumer price reform or any serious expansion of the private sector and individual employment.

enthusiastically, the goals and tactics of "restructuring," there is little evidence of anything comparable going on within (or about) the unions. One has the impression that the union bureaucracy is opposed to large-scale restructuring and that the party leadership does not know what to do in response.[52]

Perhaps there is nothing the leadership can do. An attempt to democratize the workplace *through* the unions probably is not a realistic option, given the unions' present monopoly position and the material interests of most incumbent union organizers.[53] On the other hand, allowing the rise of an independent competitor (the Solidarity option) is probably no more feasible a solution. The remaining alternative is simply to avoid the question of union reform, i.e., to ignore the VTsSPS, even if tolerating its publicly voiced skepticism of change, and to proceed with efforts to undermine the unions and to strengthen worker self-management at the enterprise level by setting up the equivalent of company unions (enterprise councils). This is the direction the leadership seems to be moving in anyway. In view of all the ideological baggage that would inevitably become unpacked in the course of a full debate on union reform, Gorbachev may well think it preferable to let the issue lie.

Finally, there is an issue distinct from the need to cope with the particular interests and attitudes of various central bureaucracies: the legacy of Brezhnev's policymaking style. Brezhnev's deference to established institutional interests had its obvious political value as a means of consolidating support among the elite. But it also had its costs, perhaps most serious in its balkanizing effect on policymaking. Exerting political control over large, specialized bureaucracies is, of course, a problem that all modern governments face, and there are no easy or fully effective solutions. A harsher, more partisan personnel policy promises some returns in heightened agency discipline and accountability; but the effects are often short-lived and the long-term costs can be high. An alternative is to develop institutional mechanisms for compelling the aggregation and synthesis of competing bureaucratic interests before they get to the top, which is never a good place to make and enforce the necessary trade-offs.

Gorbachev has shown an interest in this kind of solution in other policy areas: e.g., the consolidation of agricultural agencies into Gosagroprom and the cautious move toward "superministerial" coordination in machine-building, energy, and construction. Now, the same is evidently to be tried in social policy, as suggested by the recent creation of a Council of Ministers' Bureau for Social Development (*Pravda*, October 17, 1986, p. 1). If implemented and

---

52. My initial reading of the published record of the just-concluded 18th Trade Union Congress has strengthened this judgment.

53. Just after the January 1987 Plenum, the Politburo endorsed a VTsSPS proposal that a draft of a new trade union charter be submitted for broad public discussion. The proposed changes were reportedly aimed at intra-union democratization (*Pravda*, January 30, 1987, p. 1). Gorbachev, meanwhile, had alluded to the need for electoral reform within the unions in his speech to the January plenum, another suggestion which the Central Committee chose to ignore in its resolution. Nevertheless, with all the public attention being given to competitive elections, it is surely indicative of the VTsSPS' position that the possibility of competitive elections for union officials was ignored at the Trade Union Congress (in general, the issue of intra-union democratization received very little attention), and that even Gorbachev chose not to raise the issue directly in his own address to the gathering (*Trud*, February 26, 1987).

utilized effectively, this mechanism may have several beneficial results. For one thing, it may reduce the government's effective dependence on Goskomtrud and the VTsSPS for expert advice and recommendations, by ensuring scrutiny and criticism of these agencies' submissions by other interested bodies. Furthermore, to the extent the new Bureau forces the labor organs' and unions' own interests and preferences out into the open, it may make it easier for the government to prevent covert opposition from undermining its policies at the state of implementation.

CONCLUSIONS

The Soviet Union is experiencing far-reaching internal change. Whether the outcome will be radical economic reform is not yet clear. What is clear is that the basic bargain between the regime and society—the "formula for rule" conceived by Khrushchev and largely preserved under Brezhnev—has reached, or is reaching, the end of its natural life. The first post-Stalin social contract has come unstuck; it no longer works well, and it has become an important cause of economic decline. Whoever the Soviet leader is, whatever the regime's economic strategy becomes, a new social contract will have to be crafted and installed in place of the old; otherwise, we are likely to see the continuation of poor economic performance and increasing social turmoil. Different leaders may speed up or slow down the process of transformation, smoothing it or complicating it, raising or lowering the price to be paid. But the process itself almost certainly cannot be stopped.

It also is clear that Gorbachev is not trying to stop or even delay this transformation; on the contrary, he is actively promoting it. Gorbachev appears to understand the important role which the old social contract played in containing social conflicts and in maintaining public consensus and order. He also seems to understand that the old social contract has become unraveled and that it must be replaced, not merely refurbished. Finally, one might reasonably infer from the record that he understands, at least instinctively, the different levels on which a new social contract must be constructed. To be sure, it is far from clear that Gorbachev's social program will be implemented successfully, let alone become the core of an enduring new social contract. Nor can one say with any confidence that a new social contract will be capable of sustaining radical economic reform, if that is what Gorbachev wants.

But surely the probability of radical reform has risen on account of what has been done since Gorbachev took power. Almost all observers agree, for example, that radical reform will lead to increased inequality and reduced economic security—if not to anything approaching the extremes of poverty and joblessness that obtain in many capitalist countries, then at least to a markedly less egalitarian, less secure society than exists presently. If anything, Gorbachev's program seems designed to make those results more palatable to the Soviet public. Most observers also agree that reform would elevate the status and influence of college-educated professionals and weaken the position of the traditional working class. In practice if not by intent, Gorbachev's program appears to be aimed precisely at mobilizing support for his leadership among the former, while exploiting the growing fragmentation and increasing marginality of the latter. Lastly, it is apparent that at some point the institutionalization of Gorbachev's social policies and radical economic reform are likely to become mutually interdependent. Yet, one might go further. Most citizens, whether workers or professionals, must for now be largely indifferent to such things as directive planning and administered pricing, for their incomes and individual security are generally assured, whatever central decision makers do. However, if democratization proceeds, if the wage system is decentralized, if enterprise collectives acquire more control over hiring and firing, and if they are held more accountable for their work—then public sensitivity to the consequences of directive planning and administered pricing is likely to intensify, and there may suddenly develop a great deal more popular support for radical reform than exists now. In this sense, Gorbachev's proposed social contract is not only compatible with radical economic reform, it may come to require it.

Ultimately, Gorbachev's fate and that of his program will depend very much on his skill, both as politician and as strategist. In many respects, Gorbachev's overall strategy seems remarkably similar to Khrushchev's. For one thing, it is "populist," in the sense of promising only pressure and no new favors for the political-administrative elite, and in its attempt to mobilize a broad coalition of support among the mass public. Of course, Gorbachev's coalition is different from the one Khrushchev tried to assemble. Gorbachev's appeals are aimed at groups which Khrushchev, and later Brezhnev, tended to discount or ignore, but which have become in the years since larger, more important economically, and more profoundly dissatisfied. Second, like Khrushchev (but very much unlike Brezhnev), Gorbachev's approach is neither to downplay or obscure social divisions and competing group interests, nor to suppress the inevitable conflicts associated with them. His approach is, rather, to exploit and accentuate conflict, and even to find new cleavages which previously lay dormant. Squeezing the traditional working class is an obvious recipe for heightened social conflict, not peace. Yet, if Gorbachev is serious about radical reform, then intensified conflict is inevitable. Radical reform by definition means major reallocations of resources and power, which are always going to involve a major struggle. Part of the solution, as Zaslavskaya has noted (1985, p. 22), is to demobilize, deflect, or weaken one's opponents. To some extent, this is an institutional problem, insofar as it consists in developing means of denying established constituencies their usual opportunities for voice. Gorbachev seems not unaware of this approach, although his attention to the problem probably has to increase if his program is to survive. At the same time, a larger pie would obviously help, which is perhaps why such emphasis has been placed on accelerating economic growth (and the growth of consumption) right from the start.

On the other hand, as alike as Gorbachev and Khrushchev may seem in their basic strategies, they are different in one, very crucial respect, which augurs well for (but hardly assures) Gorbachev's future. He may not have the "iron teeth" supposedly attributed to him by Andrey Gromyko in the latter's nominating speech at the March 1985 Central Committee plenum, but he surely has the "nice smile." Gorbachev, by all the evidence, is a smooth, charismatic politician, an intelligent, tactful, and personable man who appears to elicit respect and admiration wherever he goes. Khrushchev was never able to boast such personal qualities, and in the end it may be this which allows Gorbachev to escape his predecessor's fate.

Finally, a caveat. In the Western literature on the Soviet Union, there is an unfortunate tendency, expressed in this article as well, to oversimplify the struggle for reform and to trivialize or ignore altogether the moral-ethical aspects of the issues at stake. We too quickly and unthinkingly divide the Soviet world into "good guys" and "bad guys," routinely cheering on the reformers, while heaping scorn on their opponents. Reality is not so simple. In reading the public debates, and especially in interviews, one is struck by the deep sincerity of many of the antagonists on both sides of the issues and, more importantly, by the difficult and fundamentally ambiguous nature of the choices to be made. The arguments against reform, often arising out of a fear of its likely corrosive effects on social solidarity, deserve to be taken seriously. That reform is liable to make victims of "the old and the weak," in one Soviet journalist's phrase (Maksimova, 1985), ought to be cause for worry in any context and under any political-economic system. Officials like Batalin, who caution against making the incomes of ITR dependent on the votes of workers, are not merely defending the interests of the former. Nor is anxiety over the possibility of a large increase in inequality and its impact on the social fabric to be scoffed at. It is hardly intellectual obtuseness, as one of my colleagues unwittingly suggested, that leads ardent reform advocates like Zaslavskaya (1986b, pp. 21–22) and Shatalin (Shatalin and Gayder, 1986) to urge an uncompromising fight against speculators, the archetypal recipients of nonlabor incomes, or to warn about the risks of ignoring "the existence of objective social limits to the differentiation of incomes."

The point is that the debate over restructuring, in the Soviet Union as elsewhere, is animated by wrenching conflicts over ideals and principles, and not just by the competition among "interests" (political and material). It is important that we take this into account. One reason is that by ignoring the normative dimension of the debate, we risk misunderstanding what happens. An accurate explanation of the outcome may require a smaller role for self-interest and a larger stress on widely shared conceptions of "the public good" than we are accustomed to conceding. A second reason is that we risk mis-judging the impact of reform (or no reform) on people. Too often, we have simply assumed that a radically reformed Soviet political economy will make life better for the Soviet public, and perhaps for us as well. For some, that is sure to be true; but not for all—and almost surely not for many of the middle-aged, poorly educated manual workers who will find their enterprise-specific and previously highly paid skills no longer in demand. If we were more appreciative of the complex social consequences of restructuring, we might display more humility and even sympathy in our evaluations of the Soviet predicament. That might reduce the polemical component in our own scholarly debates and, in some small way, contribute to the easing of international tensions from which we all should benefit.

REFERENCES

Afanas'yev, Ye., and O. Medvedeva, "Organizatsionno-pravovyye, voprosy pereraspredeleniya vysvobozhdayemykh rabotnikov (Organizational-Legal Questions in Reallocating Displaced Workers)," *Sotsialisticheskiy trud*, 1:67–73, 1987.

Batalin, Yu.P., "Kollektivnyy podryad—deystvennoye sredstvo uskoreniya sotsial'noekonomicheskogo razvitiya (Collective Contract—An Effective Means of Accelerating Socio-Economic Development)," *Sotsialisticheskiy trud*, 1:6–20, 1986.

Beissinger, Mark R., "In Search of Generations in Soviet Politics," *World Politics*, 38, 2:288–314, 1986.

Bialer, Seweryn, *Stalin's Successors*. Cambridge: Cambridge University Press, 1980.

Breslauer, George W., "On the Adaptability of Soviet Welfare-State Authoritarianism," in Karl W. Ryavec, ed., *Soviet Society and the Communist Party*. Amherst, Mass: University of Massachusetts Press, 1978, 3–25.

Bushnell, John, "The 'New Soviet Man' Turns Pessimist," *Survey*, 24, 2:1–18, 1979.

Connor, Walter D., "Generations and Politics," *Problems of Communism*, 24, 5:20–31, 1975.

———,"Social Policy under Gorbachev," *Problems of Communism*, 35, 4:31–46,1986.

"Distsiplina truda v dinamike (Labor Discipline in a Dynamic Perspective)," *Ekonomika i organizatsiya promyshlennogo proizvodstva*, 9:17–45, 1981.

"Doklad o neobkhodimosti uglublennogo izucheniya v SSSR sotsial'nogo mekhanizma razvitiya ekonomiki (Report on the Need for More Profound Study of the Social Mechanism of Economic Development in the USSR)," *Materialy Samizdata*, 35/83, Radio Liberty August 26, 1983.

Dzhafarli, T. M., Sh. L. Kistauri, B. P. Kurashvili, and V. P. Rassokhin, "Nekotoryye aspekty uskoreniya naucho-tekhnicheskogo progressa (Certain Aspects of the Acceleration of Scientific-Technological Progress)," *Sotsiologicheskiye issledovaniya*, 2:58–63, 1983.

Feshbach, Murray, "Issues in Soviet Health Problems," in U.S. Congress Joint Economic Committee, *Soviet Economy in the 1980's: Problems and Prospects*, Part 2. Washington, D.C.: U.S. Government Printing Office, 1983, 203–227.

Gidwitz, Betsy, "Labor Unrest in the Soviet Union," *Problems of Communism*, 31, 6:25–42, 1982.

Gorbachev, M. S., *Zhivoye tvorchestvo naroda (The People's Vital Creativity)*, Report to the All-Union Scientific-Practical Conference on "The Perfection of Developed Socialism and the Party's Ideological Work in Light of the Decisions of the June (1983) Plenum of the Central Committee of the CPSU," December 10, 1984. Moscow: Politizdat, 1985a.

————, *Korennoy vopros ekonomicheskoy politiki partii (The Basic Question of the Party's Economic Policy)*, Report to the Central Committee of the CPSU Conference on "Questions of Acceleration and Scientific-Technological Progress," June 11, 1985. Moscow: Politizdat, 1985b.

————, "Politicheskiy doklad tsentral'nogo komiteta KPSS XXVII s'yezdu kommunisticheskoy partii Sovetskogo soyuza (Political Report of the Central Committee of the CPSU to the 27th Congress of the Communist Party of the Soviet Union)," *Pravda*, February 26, 1986a, 2–10.

————, "Rech' General'nogo sekretarya TsK KPSS M. S. Gorbacheva navstreche s partiynym aktivom Krasnodarskogo kraya (Speech of CPSU General Secretary M. S. Gorbachev at a meeting with the Party aktiv of Krasnodar Territory)," *Pravda*, September 20, 1986b, 1–2.

————, "O perestroyke i kadrovoy politike partii (On Restructuring and the Party's Cadres Policy)," Report to the January 1987 Plenum of the CPSU Central Committee, *Pravda*, January 28, 1987, 1–5.

Granick, David, *Job Rights in the Soviet Union: Their Consequences.* Cambridge: Cambridge University Press, 1987.

Grossman, Gregory, "A Note on Soviet Inflation," in U.S. Congress Joint Economic Committee, *Soviet Economy in the 1980's: Problems and Prospects*, Part 1. Washington, D.C.: U.S. Government Printing Office, 1983, 267–186.

Hauslohner, Peter Austin, "Managing the Soviet Labor Market: Politics and Policymaking under Brezhnev," Ph.D. Dissertation, University of Michigan, 1984.

————, "Reforming Social Policy: A Comment," in U.S. Congress Joint Economic Committee, *Gorbachev's Economic Plans, Vol. 2.* Washington, D.C.: U.S. Government Printing Office, 1987, pp. 344–352.

Heinemeier, Meredith M., "The Brigade System of Labor Organization and Incentives in Soviet Industry and Construction," in U.S. Congress Joint Economic Committee, *Gorbachev's Economic Plans, Vol. 2.* Washington, D.C.: U.S. Government Printing Office, 1987, pp. 272–281.

Hough, Jerry F., "Policy-Making and the Worker," in Arcadius Kahan and Blair Ruble, eds., *Industrial Labor in the U.S.S.R.* New York: Pergamon, 1979, 367–396.

Kapustin, Ye. I., and A. V. Vikhlyayev, eds., *Sovershenstvovaniye otnosheniy raspredeleniya: etap razvitogo sotsializma (Perfecting Distributive Relations: The Stage of Developed Socialism).* Moscow: Nauka, 1985.

Kazakevich, D. M., "K sovershenstvovaniyu potrebitel'skikh tsen (On the Perfection of Consumer Prices)," *Ekonomika i organizatsiya promyshlennogo proizvodstva*, 1:33–43, 1986.

Komozin, A. N., and A. K. Meshcherkin, "Kollektivnyye formy truda v usloviyakh ekonomicheskogo eksperimenta (Collective Forms of Labor in Conditions of the Economic Experiment)," *Sotsiologicheskiye issledovaniya*, 1:20–27, 1986.

Kostakov, V., "Odin kak semero (One as Seven)," *Sovetskaya kul'tura*, January 4, 1986a.

————, "Chelovek i progress (Man and Progress)," *Sovetskaya kul'tura*, February 1, 1986b.

————, "Zanyatost': defitsit ili izbytok? (Employment: Shortage or Surplus?)," *Kommunist*, 2:78–79, 1987.

Kutyryev, B. P., "Kak primenyat' kollektivnyy podryad v deyatel'nosti ITR (How to

Apply the Collective Contract in the Activity of ITR)," *Sotsiologicheskiye issledovaniya*, 3:42–48, 1985.

———, "Soyedinit' individual'nyye i obshchestvennyye interesy (To Unify Individual and Public Interests)," *Ekonomika i organizatsiya promyshlennogo proizvodstva*, 1:92–106, 1986.

Lapidus, Gail Warshofsky, "Social Trends," in Robert F. Byrnes, ed., *After Brezhnev*. Bloomington: Indiana University Press, 1983, 186–249.

Latsis, O., "Individual'nyyi trud v sovremennoy sotsialisticheskoy ekonomike (Individual Labor in the Contemporary Socialist Economy)," *Kommunist*, 1:74–82, 1987.

Livshits, R., and V. Nikitinskiy, "Sovetskoye trudovoye pravo: nauka i praktika (Soviet Labor Law: Science and Practice)," *Sotsialisticheskiy trud*, 5:101–108, 1985.

Maksimova, N. K., "Brigady na pereput'ye (Brigades at the Crossroads)," *Ekonomika i organizatsiya promyshlennogo proizvodstva*, 8:152–199, 1985.

Maslova, I. S., *Mekhanizm pereraspredeleniya rabochey sily pri sotsializme (The Mechanism of Labor Force Reallocation under Socialism)*. Moscow: Ekonomika, 1985.

Materialy plenuma Tsentral'nogo komiteta KPSS, 23 aprelya 1985 goda (Materials of the Plenum of the Central Commitee of the CPSU 23 April 1985). Moscow: Politizdat, 1985.

Narodnoye khozyaystvo SSSR v 1984 godu (National Economy of the USSR in 1984). Moscow: Finansy i statistika, 1985.

Nikitinskiy, V. I., and B. G. Rozovskiy, "Povysheniye effektivnosti distsiplinarnoy otvetstvennosti v poryadke podchinyennosti (Raising the Effectiveness of Disciplinary Accountability in the Regime of Administrative Subordination)," *Problemy sovershenstvovaniya Sovetskogo zakonodatel'stva*, 8:91–103, 1977.

Popov, G., "Tvoye rabochyeye mesto (Your Job)," *Pravda*, December 27, 1980, p. 2.

———, "Perestroyka v ekonomike (Restructuring in the Economy)," Part 2, *Pravda*, January 21, 1987, p. 2.

Pravda, Alex, "Spontaneous Workers' Activities in the Soviet Union," in Arcadius Kahan and Blair Ruble, eds., *Industrial Labor in the U.S.S.R.* New York: Pergamon, 1979, 333–366.

———, "East-West Interdependence and the Social Compact in Eastern Europe," in Morris Bornstein, Zvi Gitelman, and William Zimmerman, eds., *East-West Relations and the Future of Eastern Europe*. London: Allen and Unwin, 1981, 162–187.

———, "Is There a Soviet Working Class?" *Problems of Communism*, 31, 6:1–24, 1982.

Profsoyuzy i trudovoye pravo: sbornik nauchnykh trudov (The Trade Unions and Labor Law: A Collection of Scientific Works). Moscow: Profizdat, 1979.

Pryor, Frederic, L., "Growth and Fluctuations of Production in O.E.C.D. and East European Countries," *World Politics*, 37, 2:204–237, 1985.

Rimashevskaya, N., "O putyakh effektivnogo resheniya sotsial'nykh problem (On the Means of Effectively Resolving Social Problems)," *Kommunist*, 2:59–68, 1986a.

———, "Raspredeleniye i spravedlivost' (Distribution and Justice)," *Ekonomicheskaya gazeta*, 40:6–7, 1986b.

Rogovin, V. Z., *Sotsial'naya spravedlivost' i puti yeye realizatsii v sotsial'noy politike (Social Justice and Ways of Realizing it in Social Policy)*, 2 vols. Moscow: Institut Sotsiologii Akademii Nank SSSR, 1982.

Ruble, Blair A., *Soviet Trade Unions: Their Development in the 1970s.* Cambridge: Cambridge University Press, 1981.

———,"Soviet Trade Unions and Labor Relations After 'Solidarity'," U.S. Congress Joint Economic Committee, *Soviet Economic Prospects in the 1980's: Problems and Prospects*, Part 2. Washington, D.C.: U.S. Government Printing Office, 1983, 349–366.

Shalayev, S., "Sovetskiye profsoyuzy v sisteme sotsialisticheskogo samoupravleniya (Soviet Trade Unions in the System of Socialist Self-Management)," *Kommunist*, 10:34–44, 1985.

Shatalin, S., and Ye. Gayder, "Uzlovyye problemy reformy (The Crucial Problems of Reform)," *Ekonomicheskaya gazeta*, 29:6–7, 1986.

Slider, Darrell, "Reforming the Workplace: The 1983 Soviet Law on Labour Collectives," *Soviet Studies*, 37, 2:173–183, 1985.

———, "Worker Participation in a Socialist System: The Soviet Case," *Comparative Politics*, 18, 4:401–418, 1986.

"Sokrashcheniye shtata (Reduction in Force)," *Izvestiya*, June 6, 1985, p. 3.

Teague, Elizabeth, "Labor Discipline and Legislation in the USSR: 1979–1985," *Radio Liberty Research Bulletin*, Supplement, RL 2/85, October 16, 1985.

———, "A Greater Role for the Cooperative Sector," *Radio Liberty Research Bulletin*, RL 319/86, August 22, 1986a.

———, "The USSR Law on the Work Collectives: Workers' Control or Workers Controlled?" in David Lane, ed., *Labour and Employment in the USSR.* New York: New York University Press, 1986b, 239–255.

———, "Gorbachev's 'Human Factor' Policies," in U.S. Congress Joint Economic Committee, *Gorbachev's Economic Plans, Vol. 2.* Washington, D.C.: U.S. Government Printing Office, 1987, pp. 224–239.

Trehub, Aaron, " 'Social Justice' and Economic Progress," *Radio Liberty Research Bulletin*, RL 382/86, October 7, 1986.

Treml, Vladimir G., *Alcohol in the USSR: A Statistical Study.* Durham, N.C.: Duke University Press, 1982.

———, "Subsidies in Soviet Agriculture," in U.S. Congress Joint Economic Committee, *Soviet Economy in the 1980's: Problems and Prospects*, Part 2. Washington, D.C.: U.S. Government Printing Office, 1983, 171–186.

———, "Soviet Foreign Trade in Foodstuffs," *Soviet Economy*, 2, 1:19–50, January–March 1986.

"Trud—individual'nyy, pol'za—obshchaya (Labor—Individual; Its Use—General)," roundtable discussion, *Kommunist*, 18:24–29, 1986.

Tsepin, A. I., "Trudovoy kollektiv kak sub'yekt trudovogo prava (The Labor Collective as the Subject of Labor Law)," *Sovetskoye gosudarstvo i pravo*, 8:46–54, 1981.

Vaganov, S., and M. Shcherbachenko, "Na povorote (At the Turning Point)," *Trud*, August 3 and 5, 1986, p. 2.

"Vo imya sotsialisticheskoy spravedlivosti (In the Name of Socialist Justice)," views on the struggle with non-labor incomes by three leading officials in Voronezh province, *Kommunist*, 15:85–96, 1986.

"Vybor strategii (Choice of Strategy)," *Izvestiya*, June 1, 1985, p. 3.

White, Stephen, "Economic Performance and Communist Legtimacy," *World Politics*, 38, 3:462–482, 1986.

"Zakon o trudovykh kollektivakh v deystvii (The Law on Laboring Collectives in Action)," *Sovetskoye gosudarstvo i pravo*, 6:5–12, 1985.

Zaslavskaya, T. I., "Ekonomicheskoye povedeniye i ekonomicheskoye razvitiye (Economic Behavior and Economic Development)," *Ekonomika i organizatsiya promyshlennogo proizvodstva*, 3:15–33, 1980.

――――, "Ekonomika skovz' prizmu sotsiologii (Economics Through the Prism of Sociology)," *Ekonomika i organizatsiya promyshlennogo proizvodstva*, 7:3–22, 1985.

――――, "Chelovecheskiy faktor i sotsial'naya spravedlivost' (The Human Factor and Social Justice)," *Sovetskaya kul'tura*, January 23, 1986a.

――――, "Tvorchekaya aktivnost' mass: sotsial'nyye rezervy razvitiya (The Creative Activeness of the Masses: Social Reserves of Development)," *Ekonomika i organizatsiya promyshlennogo proizvodstva*, 3:3–25, 1986b.

――――, "Chelovecheskiy faktor razvitiya ekonomiki i sotsial'naya spravedlivost' (The Human Factor in the Development of the Economy and Social Justice)," *Kommunist*, 13:61–73, 1986c.

Zaslavskaya, T. I., and R. V. Ryvkina, "O predmete ekonomicheskoy sotsiologii (On the Subject of Economic Sociology)," *Izvestiya Sibirskogo otdeleniya Akademii Nauk SSSR: seriya ekonomiki i prikladnoy sotsiologii*, 1, 1:9–20, 1984.

CHAPTER 4

The Politics of Systemic Economic Reform

Timothy J. Colton

EVEN IF Mikhail S. Gorbachev had never uttered a word about reforming the Soviet economic system, the changes in economic personnel and policy since his advent as leader would grab our attention.

THE GORBACHEV RECORD

From his first days in office, Gorbachev proclaimed the acceleration (*uskoreniye*) of Soviet progress, on the basis of revived economic growth, to be a matter of life and death for the country. A means to this end, and to increase his personal control, was to make a sweep through the ranks of senior economic management. Here the numbers speak for themselves. Of those fourteen (of fifteen) March 1985 members of the Presidium of the Council of Ministers concentrating on economic questions, ten (71 percent) had been retired or replaced by July 1, 1987.[1] Among rank-and-file heads of economic agencies in the Council of Ministers, attrition has been less, yet it has still affected a majority of the pre-Gorbachev office-holders (thirty-eight of seventy-one, or 54 percent), and the press is reporting the exodus of lower-ranking economic bureaucrats in droves.[2] In the Secretariat of the party's Central Committee, ten of the fourteen economic specialists among the secretaries and department heads (71 percent) have been demoted or retired, only one of the rest going on to greater things.[3]

First published in *Soviet Economy*, 1987, 3, 2, pp. 145–170. [Eds.]
1. This does not include Nikolay V. Talyzin, who was promoted from a deputy chairman to a first deputy chairman in 1985.
2. The thirty-eight ministers and heads of state committees counted here include thirty-six demoted and two dead in office. This figure does not include the three ministers promoted to the Presidium of the Council of Ministers, the three transferred to other ministries, or the one who retained minister's rank after being moved into the new State Agro-Industrial Committee. Of the thirty-one officials left untouched so far under Gorbachev, twelve are relatively recent appointees, having been given their positions under party leaders Andropov and Chernenko.
3. This one is Nikolay I. Ryzhkov, appointed Chairman of the Council of Ministers in September 1985.

In all major economic institutions, the new faces are anywhere from one or two to thirty-five years younger than the old.[4] The result has been a moderate rejuvenation of an economic elite that for years had grown old and fatigued. In a little over two years, the mean age of economic administrators has fallen from sixty-nine to fifty-nine in the Presidium of the Council of Ministers, from sixty-four to fifty-eight among subordinate economic ministers, and from sixty-seven to fifty-six in the Central Committee apparatus.[5] The post-Stalin generation, born in the late 1920s and 1930s and come of age after Joseph Stalin's death, is finally gaining control of the economy.

Policy changes have started with the application of the principle of *glasnost'* or openness to the mass media, specialized periodicals, and even the party's theoretical organ *Kommunist*. In all these outlets, the Gorbachev thaw has allowed fuller, more probing, and more opinionated coverage of economic and socioeconomic issues. The trend of the late Brezhnev era toward withholding unflattering economic statistics has been reversed. Some of the new material is sensational by any measure and exceeds many Western accounts in the unsparingness of its indictment.

The new leadership has been equally quick to launch a series of programs aimed at specific economic and economic-related problems. In Gorbachev's first year, these were mainly punitive, notably the extensions of Yuriy V. Andropov's drives against corruption, alcohol, and malingering. Since then, the emphasis has shifted to affirmative policies. The Politburo has stepped up investment, given priority to technological modernization in the civilian sector, and started to supply the economy and school system with microcomputers. Planners and managers are being pressured to work harder to get goods and services to the consumer. A unified system of industrial quality control, put in place in January 1987, covers 1,500 large manufacturing enterprises. New procurement rules allow farms to sell all above-plan grain, and more of their other produce, at market prices.

Freshest in conception have been policy changes in respect to private and cooperative enterprise, foreign economic ties, income distribution, and enterprise autonomy. As of May 1987, economic activity by individuals and family firms has been legalized for twenty-nine types of consumer goods and services. There are new regulations to facilitate the establishment of cooperative businesses. Decrees of September 1986 and January 1987[6] authorize a number of industrial entities to trade directly with foreign partners and create legal scaffolding for joint commercial ventures on Soviet soil. The first moves were made in a September 1986 edict to force steep differentials in wages and benefits

4. The thirty-five-year gap occurred in the Ministry of Medium Machine Building, the nuclear weapons-manufacturing agency, where in November 1986 a minister born in 1898, Ye. P. Slavskiy, was replaced by L. D. Ryabev, born in 1933.

5. Ages are not known for two of the new heads of Central Committee departments. In a third case (the economic department), the position is apparently vacant.

6. Provisions of these decrees are described in detail by the Deputy Chairman of the State Commission on Foreign Economic Relations, USSR Council of Ministers, in Ivanov, 1987. [Eds.]

corresponding to productivity. And a June 1987 "Law on the State Enterprise" begins to give factory-level managers protection against detailed interference by head offices (Zakon, 1987).

Most intriguing about Gorbachev as an economic decision maker, however, is not his hiring and firing of officials or his specific policy remedies, but his dramatic championing of comprehensive economic reform. At the Twenty-Seventh Party Congress in February 1986 he called for a "radical reform" (*radikal'naya reforma*) of the economy, as the cornerstone of the national reconstruction (*perestroyka*) he holds to be mandatory (Gorbachev, 1986). In his June 1987 address to the party Central Committee he provided his fullest statement to date of what that radical reform might entail (*Pravda*, June 26, 1987). He now insists that the USSR cannot afford to repeat the halfhearted reforms of the past, most recently the September 1965 decentralization sponsored by Aleksey N. Kosygin, but must make changes as massive in their impact as those that produced the mature Soviet command economy two generations ago.

WHAT IS THERE TO EXPLAIN?

If the yardstick is the 1970s and early 1980s, what is now derided as "the period of stagnation," it is hard not to be impressed by Gorbachev's energy and inventiveness. If, however, the criterion is the far more exacting one that Gorbachev himself has held up, that of radical reform, then his early achievements are less impressive. While it is premature to be reaching final conclusions, Western analysts have had little difficulty demonstrating the snail's pace of structural economic change to date.[7] Gorbachev does not disagree. He declared to the June 1987 Central Committee plenum that, if valuable experiments and adjustments had been carried out, only "the first steps at assimilating new management methods" had been made and "the shifts achieved here have not been fundamental" (*Pravda*, June 26, 1987, p. 3).

This raises the question of how much progress we should be looking for (and how quickly), on which point we are on shaky conceptual ground. Neither the language of social science nor that of daily life draws a clear line beyond which changes are manifestly fundamental. Among historians and political scientists, the discrimination of systemic from non-systemic change is to no small degree a matter of subjective judgment and intellectual tradition. Was the New Deal in the United States a systemic reform? Did it result in something qualitatively different from what preceded? Liberal, neo-conservative, and Marxist historians would give differing answers. British scholars would be no more unanimous about the achievements of the post–World II Labour government.

---

7. A number of critical Western assessments have been published in *Soviet Economy*. A useful review is the roundtable discussion, "Gorbachev's Economic Reform" (1987, pp. 40–53), in the January–March 1987 issue, in which Herbert Levine of the University of Pennsylvania is quoted (p. 52) as predicting on the basis of Gorbachev's first two years that "really serious economic reforms won't come until after the year 2000."

If by systemic reform of the Soviet economy is meant its transformation into something diametrically opposed—a textbook capitalist economy with private ownership and unfettered markets—then this alchemy has not yet happened under Gorbachev and there is no chance that it will. But this is not what we should be puzzling over, any more than we should ponder why Ronald Reagan has not nationalized heavy industry and instituted a Gosplan of the United States. To speak of systemic reform, in the Soviet Union or elsewhere, is to speak of something that is more profound than tinkering or superficial reform but, by the same token, is less all-encompassing than revolution. A definition that does not leave room for the persistence of certain basics of the unreformed system is a misconstruction.

More interesting questions emerge if Gorbachev's economics are evaluated by three standards. One, as mentioned above, is the largely ineffectual record of Leonid I. Brezhnev, against which Gorbachev already stands up reasonably well. A second test is against the reform experiences of those other communist countries, like Hungary under Janos Kadar and China under Deng Xiaoping, which have embarked on what are generally conceded to be seriously conceived economic reforms. The third and most immediate touchstone is Gorbachev's floridly reformist rhetoric.

The present chapter is directed mostly at the second and third tests, by which Gorbachev's regime continues to stack up poorly. Some problems have been brushed aside. Many of the most critical ideas have not been converted into public policy. Some of the legislation that has made its way onto the books (the 1986 law on private firms, say, or the 1987 enterprise charter) is forbiddingly verbose and surrounds the changes with a thicket of restrictions. Generation of proposals for macroeconomic restructuring has been consigned to a body with the Kafkaesque title of Commission of the Council of Ministers for Improving Management, Planning, and the Economic Mechanism. And the press brims with reports of sabotage of the initiatives taken.

LEVELS OF ANALYSIS

Why has the road to economic reform been so rocky? And what do the political dynamics observed imply for the future prospects of major economic reform in the USSR? Some perspective comes from examining the problem in terms of five successive levels of explanation apt for a Soviet-type society: the top leader, the collective political leadership, the administrative machinery of party and state, nonbureaucratic sources of information and advice, and the population. On each plane, political forces may work either to aid or to impede fundamental reform.

Economic reform prospects are most favored by the presence of a strongly and intelligently pro-reform party head, of a collective leadership rallied around the reform banner, of a bureaucracy receptive to reform and willing to try to execute it, of economists and other advisers contributing workable reform suggestions, and of support and compliance among the population. This best case is depicted schematically in the lefthand column of Table 1. The second and third columns display political conditions that are progressively less congenial to major economic reforms. The outlook for reform darkens if the individual leader is ambivalent or confused about it, if the political leadership is split, or if reforms are only grudgingly accepted by the bureaucracy, policy analysts, and public, or are actively fought by subgroups within them. In the least favorable case, leadership, bureaucracy, advisers, and population are equally intransigent and economic reform joins the legion of lost causes.

These categories can be used to sketch in a very impressionistic way the state of play of the economic reform issue in the USSR. The evidence is often slippery, sometimes ephemeral. The odds of reform success cannot be gauged with precision. It is possible, nonetheless, to make some inferences and to sharpen questions for further study.

LEVEL I: THE TOP LEADER

It is best to begin with the man at the top. Leery perhaps of perceptions that he is promoting a "personality cult," he stated in an interview with the Italian communist newspaper *L'Unità* in May 1987 that "if there had been no Gorbachev, there would have been someone else" to spearhead reforms (*Pravda*, May 20, 1987, p. 1). Yet there is no denying that Mikhail Gorbachev more than anyone else has legitimized the economic reform cause and has made it impossible for others in the Soviet system to ignore it. At the same time, the murkiness of his reform vision, which has only lately gained coherence, has helped delay realization of reform.

What little we know suggests that Gorbachev's conversion to economic reformism has been gradual and recent. The unofficial transcript of his June 19, 1986, audience with Soviet writers, which gives revealing glimpses of his thoughts, contains a surprisingly fond allusion to the early Brezhnev years, which he spent as a regional party official in Stavropol': "We had a problem in Stavropol' in 1969—where to put all the meat and milk."[8] He did confide to *L'Unità* that he and "many comrades who worked in those years on the periphery" were becoming dissatisfied with the state of affairs. But he does not say just when disillusionment set in and is able to summarize his views then only negatively, stating that he was starting to feel "that it was impossible to continue doing things the same way" (*Pravda*, May 20, 1987, p. 1). There is no glimmer here of a positive program.

When transferred to Moscow as the party Secretariat's main agricultural specialist in November 1978, Gorbachev, regardless of his private opinions, could hardly have been perceived as a disruptive or even restless force. Given

8. All quotations from Gorbachev's comments to the writers are from the unofficial Russian-language version, in *Arkhiv samizdata* (Beseda, 1986), prepared by Radio Liberty, Munich. The best English language translation is provided by the Foreign Broadcast Information Service (FBIS, 1986).

Table 1. *Political Factors Promoting and Inhibiting Economic Reform in a Soviet-Type Society*

Level of analysis	Prospects for Implementation of Reform		
	Good	*Fair*	*Poor*
Top leader	Clearly and consistently pro-reform	Pro-reform, but ambivalent or inconsistent	Anti-reform
Collective leadership	Uniformly or preponderantly pro-reform	Divided; no stable pro-reform coalition	Anti-reform (uniform or coalition)
Bureaucracy	Consistent support and compliance	Grudging compliance; resistance by bureaucratic leaders or interest groups	Consistently anti-reform —resistance by bureaucracy as a class
Knowledge specialists	Support and supply of useful reform	Support uneven or not translated into concrete proposals	Consistently anti-reform —resistance by economists as a group or by intellectuals as a class
Population	Consistent support and compliance	Grudging compliance; resistance by societal interest groups	Consistently anti-reform —resistance by society as a whole

Brezhnev's growing conservatism and his demonstrated suspicion of high fliers, Gorbachev most likely was seen as a vigorous but politically safe technician from the boondocks, someone who could be counted on to bring in the crops and not ask too many questions.

It presumably was the ensuing setbacks and disappointments that ripened Gorbachev's discontent. His term as party secretary coincided with a string of miserable harvests and with the economic brushfire fighting of the early 1980s. According to Abel G. Aganbegyan, now his main economic adviser, Gorbachev, upon assuming full Politburo membership in 1980, began to meet informally with him and other critically inclined economists and to develop "a congruence of ideas" with them. The meetings became more frequent after Brezhnev's death, when Gorbachev became General Secretary Andropov's lieutenant and expanded his economic portfolio.[9] Gorbachev's alliance with Andropov must have included some shared understanding of reform imperatives, which Andropov was starting to broach in public, though it is curious how little credit Gorbachev has since given his patron for influencing him or the course of events.

It is no slur on Gorbachev to say that when he took over the party he was what Janos Kornai (1986) calls a "naive economic reformer," bandying concepts about without working through implications. Whatever his rapport with the reformist economists, his brave words about restructuring and radical reform rang hollow when set against deeds that stressed traditional remedies like purges, investment shifts, new boxes on the organization chart, and political pressure on unproductive factories and farms.

Damaging inconsistencies on discrete points were also evident in Gorbachev's early economic decisions. Appealing in one breath for higher production quality, he demanded in the next rapid quantitative increase in growth rates, as if oblivious to the tension between the two objectives. Only months after affirming Andropov's five-ministry experiment in streamlined industrial management, he was endorsing different and complicated arrangements for "full cost accounting" (*khozraschet*) and "self-financing" of enterprises. Simply mismanaged was the May 1986 party and government resolution on "unearned income," conceived of as a blow against corruption and illicit use of state property but interpreted by many enforcement officials as a license to crack down on forms of legitimate private activity that Gorbachev had already been lauding. Confusion was so rampant that Moscow had to send out a confidential message warning against improper restrictions (Hamman, 1986). Only that autumn did the new statute on individual economic activity furnish some small firms with the legal safeguards that Gorbachev had apparently intended to provide all along.

So substantial was the gulf between oratory and attainment in the first year or year-and-one-half of the Gorbachev administration that it raised the possi-

9. Philip Taubman's interview with Aganbegyan in the *New York Times*, July 10, 1987, pp. 25, 27.

bility that his espousal of economic reform was a masquerade. Yet this hardly squared with the fervor with which he advanced the need for reform. If he did not intend to do something about economic reform, why inflate elite and popular expectations, only to dash them later? Why not mimic Brezhnev, who did not want systemic reform but made no pretense of it, or Andropov and Konstantin U. Chernenko, who spoke blandly of "improving" and "perfecting" the economic system? And why express such irritation about roadblocks being put in the way of reform, as Gorbachev increasingly did after the party congress?

The question of Gorbachev's motivation has become less perplexing. There is abundant evidence that learning through experience in office, coupled with his gut conviction of the gravity of Soviet problems, has forced him toward more painful and far-reaching choices than he could have stomached at the outset. *Perestroyka,* he said generally of his program in January 1987, "has turned out to be more difficult, and the causes of the problems embedded in our society more profound, than we had imagined earlier." The further the party pushes reconstruction, "the clearer become its scale and importance, the more there move into view new, unresolved problems, left behind as a legacy from the past" (*Pravda,* January 28, 1987, p. 1). So it has been with economic reform, above all.

The most vivid index of the distance Gorbachev has travelled is his praise of a polemic against Soviet economic hypercentralization, and the underlying philosophy of "equal poverty for all," published by the economist Nikolay Shmelev in June 1987 (Shmelev, 1987, pp. 142–158). The portrait, Gorbachev told journalists, was "close to the actual state of things." To be sure, he disputed some of Shmelev's recommendations, chiefly that unemployment be tolerated in the USSR. Around this same time, Gorbachev cautioned at a Kremlin conference on economic problems against the forwarding of "anti-socialist alternatives" to the status quo. But the gist of his remarks was that debate should be encouraged and "diverse experience and diverse points of view" be brought to bear.[10]

Strong evidence of maturation and radicalization comes through in Gorbachev's landmark June 25, 1987, report to the Central Committee, "On the Party's Tasks Concerning the Essential Restructuring of Economic Administration."[11] The report accepts that progress on the "theoretical front" is a prerequisite of reform, and also that new theories cannot disregard the legitimate "interests of various groups among the population, of collectives, agencies, and organizations." It grants that economic reform might produce a temporary diminution of growth rates. It pays the greatest attention yet to reform in agriculture, dwelling at length on decentralization through "family contracting," and to cooperatives, which seem a genuine Gorbachev enthusiasm. It

10. Gorbachev's comments about Shmelev are in *Pravda,* June 22, 1987, p. 1, and about the economic debate, in *Pravda,* June 13, 1987, p. 3.

11. Quotations here are from *Pravda,* June 27, 1987, pp. 1, 3; emphasis added by the author.

calls for an end to most price subsidies and, in extreme cases, for the bankruptcy of insolvent enterprises.

Three features stand out in the June 1987 speech. First, it provides an actual timetable for introducing a reform package, with most legislation to be in place by the end of 1987, most measures effective by the end of 1989, and a debugged system functioning by January 1, 1991. Second, where his early statements traced Soviet economic difficulties back only to poor tactics starting around 1970, he now acknowledges that they are rooted in the Stalinist economic formula of mobilization and command from above. Accordingly, he pays tribute to past stirrings of reform, quoting from a 1964 article by the economist Vladimir S. Nemchinov. Third, and most remarkable, is that Gorbachev goes beyond administrative decentralization to make his first forthright admission, and the first by any General Secretary, of the need to incorporate market relations into the core operations of the planned economy. The Soviets, he said, have to achieve "the *systematic mastery and management of the market, with due regard for its laws,* and the strengthening and increase in the authority of the ruble," something which would be incalculably "more difficult than issuing commands and directives."

There can be little doubt that Gorbachev remains passionately attached to a few irreducibles of socialism, prime among them predominant state ownership and planning of some sort. But it cannot be said that these commitments are more rigid than the wedding of successful communist reformers elsewhere to the same core values or, for that matter, of Franklin Roosevelt to the ABCs of private enterprise. Nor is Gorbachev's design, at this early juncture, demonstrably more muddled than that of many other statesmen whom history records as great reformers. Roosevelt's road to the New Deal, to refer again to that case, was incredibly circuitous, marked by intermittent remappings and detours.[12]

To be sure, this is far from saying that Gorbachev's image of reform is a model of clarity. His embrace of the market and its "laws" remains partial and grudging; he would seem to find it as distasteful a tonic as it is necessary. Although his June 1987 speech and the new enterprise law provide a broad framework for reform, many of the components remain hazy. Far from certain are the real roles Gorbachev foresees for major institutions like Gosplan, the economic ministries, the new coordinating bureaus of the Council of Ministers, the municipalities, and the banks (their number is to expand to six). Fuzzy, too, are certain other key traits of the reform—the relative importance of what will be the three different kinds of prices (centrally fixed, negotiated, and market), the volume of economic activity to be covered by the state orders (*zakazy*) that will replace physical plans, the place of the "control figures"

12. The same, in fact, could be said of the revolutionaries who built the Soviet state between 1917 and the early 1930s. Few if any foresaw what the end product would be, and most were personally destroyed by the very institutions they helped create.

referred to in the documents (which some suspect will be physical targets smuggled in the back door), and the means of inducing competition between producers, to mention only a few. And it remains to be seen whether Gorbachev accepts fully the logic of some of the tradeoffs built into his proposals—between quality and quantity, security and dynamism, and individual and collective rights, for example.

In sum, some of the inconclusive outcome of reform to date can be imputed to gaps in the economic education and proposals of the very leader, Mikhail Gorbachev, who has done most to raise the profile of the reform issue. But this is only a partial explanation, and it probably will be of less moment in the future if his outlook continues to jell. Analysis on other levels is needed.

LEVEL II: THE POLITICAL LEADERSHIP

Like all heads of the party since the tyrannical rule of Stalin, Gorbachev must maintain general support among the collective leadership, meaning to all intents and purposes the party Politburo (especially its voting members) and Secretariat, and must secure this tiny group's assent in specific policy initiatives. Can it be, then, that economic reform is being thwarted at this level? Although the evidence is threadbare, a few things can be established.

We can surmise in retrospect that the Politburo majority that made Gorbachev General Secretary in March 1985 was razor-thin. Of the nine voting members other than himself, four have since been pensioned off (Grigoriy V. Romanov, Nikolay A. Tikhonov, Viktor V. Grishin, and Dinmukhammed A. Kunayev), only Tikhonov with dignity. A fifth (Andrey A. Gromyko) has been kicked upstairs to ceremonial head of state, remaining in the Politburo, but greatly lowered in influence. Had these five mainstays of the Brezhnev leadership, all of them more conservative in orientation than Gorbachev, voted as a bloc, the Politburo would have been deadlocked. Had Defense Minister Dmitriy F. Ustinov lived to side with them rather than dying in December 1984, or had they been joined by any one of the others (Vladimir V. Shcherbitskiy, for instance, a younger member of Brezhnev's "Dnepropetrovsk mafia"), then Gorbachev would be at his dacha today and Grishin or Romanov would be heading the country down a different path.

There is much water under the bridge since the accession, but all that we know about Kremlin politics indicates that Gorbachev is not yet in a position to dictate policy. In staffing decisions, politically the most sensitive, he has had to proceed with care and to accept compromises probably not much to his liking. He has promoted few clients of decades' standing (the equivalents of Brezhnev's Chernenko and Tikhonov) whom he can trust implicitly. Even where illegalities are attributed to his foes, as is the case with Kunayev's clients in Kazakhstan, change "goes slowly and meets with sophisticated opposition on the part of those who have compromised themselves but with the help of old connections are keeping themselves afloat'' (*Pravda,* January 7, 1987, p. 2).[13]

Within the crucial Politburo, Gorbachev's influence surely grew with the addition of three members in June 1987. For the first time, a majority of the voting members (eight of fourteen, not counting Gorbachev) have reached full membership during Gorbachev's tenure as General Secretary. But only four of the eight (Viktor P. Nikonov, Nikolay N. Slyun'kov, Aleksandr N. Yakovlev, and Lev N. Zaykov) were without at least candidate Politburo or Secretariat status before March 1985. They are still outnumbered by the politicians who scrambled most of the way up the political ladder without a hand from Gorbachev and can be assumed to think and act with some fair degree of independence.[14] While most are probably willing to defer to the General Secretary on routine issues, on matters of great consequence (and radical economic reform is one) their views are going to make themselves felt. Gorbachev-era promotees are a good deal more dominant among the Politburo candidates and nonranking secretaries (four of six and five of five, respectively). Gorbachev will thus have a freer hand than today once he has completed the renovation of the full membership of the Politburo and moved in officials from the rungs below, in large part younger and more dependent on him.

For the time being, then, and for some time to come, Gorbachev is best thought of as the head of a political coalition in which weight must be given to the opinions and interests of his partners. If this is reasonably apparent, however, the impact of coalition behavior on economic reform is not.

There can be little question that there are differences of emphasis and priority on economics among the members of the present party leadership. It is possible, though not provable, that such differences lie behind some of the lurches in Kremlin behavior, such as that displayed in the misapplication of the May 1986 decree on unearned incomes. This measure could conceivably have been pushed prematurely by Politburo conservatives who would not hold up their crusade against corruption until the bill on private firms was ready. Gorbachev, in this interpretation, would not have rallied his forces to push through the private enterprise law until the first edict misfired.

Gorbachev touched on the collective leadership at his meeting with the writers in June 1986 (Beseda, 1986). "Clashes (*stolknovleniya*) and arguments (*spory*) do occur" in the Politburo, he said at one point, using the present

---

13. The slowness to remove Kunayev from the Politburo (he was first attacked in the press a year before his January 1987 ouster) underlines the point. So does the survival in lesser posts of Brezhnev stalwarts whose policies have been repudiated, like the ex-party secretary for personnel matters, I. V. Kapitonov (moved in March 1986 to chairman of the party's auditing commission), or the ex-Minister of Culture, P. N. Demichev (retained as a Politburo candidate member in June 1986 and made First Deputy Head of State). Only several who served with Gorbachev in Stavropol' have made it to high Moscow office. Most prominent would be V. S. Murakhovskiy (First Deputy Premier for Agriculture), S. I. Manyakin (head of the People's Control Committee), and A. D. Budyka (Minister of Grain Products).

14. Two (not counting Gorbachev) were promoted under Brezhnev, three under Andropov, and four under Gorbachev.

tense. "Things were shelved for two or three years," he then said (using the past tense), but "now we want to act." The two or three years would seem to be those following Brezhnev's death. He offered no particulars about the Politburo consensus, emphasizing its resolve "not to evade the need to tackle pressing problems." "When we make decisions we may sometimes make mistakes. But we want to act, not to remain idle and allow things to pass us by." He was describing, seemingly, a consensus more about the urgency of doing something about Soviet problems than about any specific strategy.

Gorbachev made an unusual reference to leadership deliberations at the Kremlin meeting on economic reform on the eve of the June 1987 Central Committee plenum. The Politburo, he stated, had "studied practically every direction for improving the central organs of economic management" (*Pravda*, June 13, 1987, p. 1). "It has to be said," he continued, "that this business is not simple, that big discussions are under way at all levels," in which he evidently meant to include the Politburo. The Politburo, according to Gorbachev, had discussed drafts of a dozen pieces of economic legislation in addition to the enterprise law, "but we did not make decisions, we did not finally approve" the drafts, sending them back to staff for further work (*Pravda*, June 13, 1987, p. 1). Does this point to principled divisions at the top? Perhaps, but it is equally plausible that Gorbachev had the votes to ram through the decisions, but the group was unable to resolve doubts that all or most members, Gorbachev among them, shared about the feasibility of some of the proposed legislation. Only two weeks later, Gorbachev was capable of adding three full members to the Politburo, a convincing display of political muscle, and to get Central Committee concurrence in his framework for economic reform.

When one looks at the public statements and behavior of individual members of the leadership, the main impression is that they are taking Gorbachev's lead, though with varying degrees of enthusiasm. They also tend to be occupied with the reform problem in bits and pieces, a division of labor that probably both fragments potential opposition to Gorbachev and further smudges Moscow's grand strategy in reform.

Premier Ryzhkov, head of a Central Committee working group on economic management during his three years as party secretary, now appears largely to have been swallowed up by routine economic decision making. The one area where he sounds as if he is pressing on his own for reform action is foreign trade. His June 1987 speech to the Supreme Soviet, elaborating on the Central Committee resolution and introducing the enterprise law, indicates that he is very much in step with Gorbachev on economic change, if not actually showing the way.[15]

15. For example, Ryzhkov seemed to tout eventual marketization of the supply of raw materials and equipment to industry, a central point in any realistic radical reform: "It is important that there be real wholesale trade, without [centrally controlled] funds and orders, with wide application of negotiated prices, socialist competitiveness for customers, and the possibility of choosing a business partner. In the end this will create a socialist market in the means of production, which will put an end to the dictate and monopoly of the producer" (*Pravda*, June 30, 1987, p. 4).

Much has been made in the West of the dour attitude toward reform in general of the party's now second-ranking secretary, Yegor K. Ligachev, but the evidence for his conservatism is checkered and he, at any rate, is facing increasing competition for influence from more recent arrivals in the leadership. Aleksandr Yakovlev, who is more Gorbachevian than Ligachev (and maybe even than Gorbachev), now shares Politburo-level responsibility with Ligachev for ideological matters, and it would not be surprising to see Ligachev's star fade quickly in the next year or two. For the moment, he has been assigned some oversight role in agriculture, where his views do seem well shy of radical.[16]

Three other Politburo-ranking party secretaries have economic responsibilities. Two of them, Zaykov and Nikonov, remain ciphers, oddly unanimated in their public comments but apparently disposed to parrot the Gorbachev line. The Leningrader Zaykov, whose economic duties have now been whittled down to defense industry and machine building, has had a higher profile than Nikonov, who supervises agriculture with Ligachev.[17] That he has relinquished control of general economic coordination hints at some disappointment with him on Gorbachev's part.[18]

Nikolay Slyun'kov, brought into the Secretariat only in January 1987 and made a full Politburo member in June, has taken over control of economic planning from Zaykov and seems now to be the overall party orchestrator of economic reform. Although most of his career has been as an industrial and party executive in Belorussia, he was a deputy chairman of Gosplan from 1974 to early 1983, his path intersecting there with Ryzhkov, who was a first deputy chairman of Gosplan from 1979 to late 1982. Slyun'kov's only major statement on reform, shortly before the June 1987 plenum, echoed many of Gorbachev's main themes (*Pravda,* June 13, 1987, p. 1).

The other member of the party leadership directly involved in handling the reforms is Nikolay V. Talyzin, the head of Gosplan since October 1985 and a candidate member of the Politburo. Talyzin is also chairman of the Council of Ministers' commission on economic restructuring. But he has had so little to say in public about reform, and carries so crushing an administrative burden in the unreformed system, that one suspects his role in the commission to be minimal. He was criticized by Gorbachev in June 1987 for poor management and, like Zaykov, now seems rather overshadowed by Slyun'kov.

To summarize, the fragmentary evidence suggests that Gorbachev, even

16. Ligachev has insisted, like Gorbachev, that the process of social and economic renewal "has a revolutionary character, both in scope and in content" (*Pravda,* November 7, 1986, p. 2). Although he has on a number of occasions sounded less enthusiastic about cultural liberalization than Yakovlev, the fact is that cultural and ideological change have proceeded under his supervision at least as rapidly as economic reform. For his thoughts on agriculture, see especially Ye. Ligachev (1987, pp. 28–42).

17. For a noncommittal statement by Nikonov on agriculture, see Nikonov (1987).

18. Zaykov, the first Politburo member to have been promoted from outside the leadership, has been unusually fulsome in his personal praise of Gorbachev. For example, at a meeting on the new quality control system in industry, he lauded Gorbachev's modest speech for its "exceptionally capacious and profound analysis" (*Ekon. gaz.,* 1986b, p. 4).

with the addition of outsiders like Yakovlev and Slyun'kov, must for the present take the views of his leadership peers into account in arriving at economic decisions. Leadership accord appears more solid on the need to do something about the economy than on what that something should be, but there is no evidence of active opposition to Gorbachev's reforms. Kremlin conflict over the economy will perhaps be exacerbated if the reform process is marred by egregious blunders and failures. Barring these, Gorbachev will with time be better able to pack the leadership with individuals who share his orientation.

LEVEL III: THE BUREAUCRACY

We have it on no less than Gorbachev's authority that the most obdurate opponents of economic restructuring have been public administrators below the leadership level. This thread runs through all his speeches, and occasioned his most acerbic remarks in the closed session with the writers:

> Between the people who want and dream of changes and the leadership that encourages them, there is the administrative stratum (*upravlencheskiy sloy*), the apparatus of the ministries and of the party. They do not want changes because they do not want to part with certain rights connected with privileges (Beseda, 1986).

Whereas Gorbachev chose here to portray the bureaucracy as a homogeneous stratum or class, acting as one to uphold its privileges, caution must be used in interpreting his words. While Soviet administrators do have certain interests in common, some of which would be affected by systemic economic reform, we should not oversimplify. Gorbachev, playing to the corporate self-esteem of the writers, had good reason to dramatize the situation. He has since that time stated publicly that not all officials opposed to his reforms are scoundrels. The skeptics, he has now said, include "people who are honorable and unselfish but remain the prisoners of old concepts" (*Pravda*, February 26, 1987, p. 1).

Even in his comments to the writers, several of Gorbachev's comments underline the need for an appreciation of nuances in the interpretation of bureaucratic resistance. A moment after condemning bureaucratic privilege, he lashed out at economic managers who decline opportunities to increase their authority: "Many directors write to us to say, 'We need no rights or autonomy, let us leave everything as it was before.' " The problem with these individuals was that they wanted too few rights, not too many.

Further on, Gorbachev looks at the problem from a different angle by saying this of Gosplan, the State Planning Committee:

> As far as Gosplan is concerned, there are no authorities, no General Secretary, no Central Committee. Its officials do whatever they want. The

main situation that suits them is for people to come to their individual offices to request a million rubles, twenty or forty thousand tractors, or whatever. They like people to come and beg from them (Beseda, 1986).

It can hardly be literally true that Gosplan does whatever it pleases, especially when its chief, Talyzin, had been installed only eight months before and was himself a non-voting member of the Politburo. Moreover, the "people" who in Gorbachev's account come as supplicants to Gosplan are, in the normal course of things, fellow bureaucrats, seeking the scarce resources needed for their units. Soviet administrators, it follows from this example, do not have identical interests or inclinations.

Consider further the meaning of some of the anecdotes of bureaucratic resistance to economic change offered recently in the Soviet press. It should be stressed that they pertain to agencies that by and large are under new management, and they concern innovations that are mild compared to the proposals now winning party blessing.

• Factory directors now have more leeway to peg compensation to performance, but are having to fend off hindrances at every turn. "There have long since been no opponents of this very important principle of socialism [wages that reflect productivity], yet it is necessary to fight for it every step of the way." Latvian executives who voluntarily paid members of an independent construction brigade (*shabashniki*) above-norm rates have been investigated by the republic's people's control committee (*Lit. gaz.*, 1986a, p. 10).

• The industrial ministries are grumbling to the State Committee of Standards and their superiors in the Council of Ministers that the new system of quality inspections (*gospriemka*) threatens to get in the way of plan fulfillment. "As is well known," says one report, "to every pressure there arises counterpressure. And these forces [opposing the new system] are powerful. They would not mind going over to the offensive" (*Lit. gaz.*, 1986b, p. 10).

• A plant director in the Ministry of the Automobile Industry, in which planning and accountability were supposed to be simplified in 1986, expresses frustration that he is still "bombarded by an avalanche of planning indicators, the number of which has hardly been reduced." In the first nine months of the year he had received 18,000 circulars from various agencies (*Izvestiya*, October 20, 1986, p. 2). In other ministries, managers are finding that head offices juggle the new planning "normatives" to balance their own ledgers and continue to ratchet upward the targets of successful enterprises. One has called this ministerial "black magic" (*Sotsialisticheskaya industriya*, June 7, 1987, p. 1).

• The Ministry of Heavy and Transport Machine Building, which was in the original Andropov experiment, has been singled out by Gorbachev for formalistic compliance with the directive that it loosen the reins on its plant directors. But the chief of the ministry's planning section explains that other organizations, including Gosplan, Gossnab, the Ministry of Finance, the Council of Ministers' Bureau for Machine Building, the State Prices Committee, and the State Committee on Science and Technology, are handcuffing it from doing so. "It is impossible to raise the question of expanding the rights of the enterprises without resolving the problem of expanding the rights of the headquarters of the branch" (*Izvestiya*, December 17, 1986, p. 2).

● Kazan's officials have forced a local sovkhoz to cut the prices of produce it offers for sale in local markets, despite the farm's legal right to sell up to 30 percent of its planned non-grain production freely. Local farm administrators were also forbidden to release vehicles for marketing runs at harvest time, although demand and prices were unusually high. "The baggage of antiquated economic thinking keeps . . . these leaders from catering to the market. They live by only one concern, that there be a victorious report" on the prescribed form (*Pravda*, September 17, 1986, p. 2).

● The associations (*tovarishchestva*) that manage small suburban garden plots for city dwellers, which the Politburo has repeatedly endorsed, are still beset by petty confinements and get minimal cooperation concerning roads, drainage, and electricity. And the new cooperatives for reworking industrial scrap have been hurt by the claim of local executives that credit can be advanced for equipment and supplies only, not for needed renovations to the buildings housing them (*Ogonëk*, 1987; *Ekon. gaz.*, 1987).

One lesson of all this is to underline the need for greater clarity of purpose and design at the top, as the party leadership now seems to be acknowledging. Hiring and firing, homilies from the General Secretary, general injunctions to shape up, and patchwork reform schemes will not suffice to produce economic efficiency. Another implication is that bureaucratic resistance, while it may at a certain level of abstraction have the character of uniform, class-type behavior, often breaks down on closer inspection into a multitude of localized, uncoordinated actions. On reform issues, as in routine economic management and in resource conflicts, the highly complex structure of the Soviet bureaucracy generates an intricate politics of bargaining, posturing, and subterfuge.

Contrary to the claim in the vignette about quality control cited above, there is little to show bureaucratic foes of reform to be "going on the offensive" against it. Their maneuvers are essentially defensive, and even here the anti-reform army absorbs rather than repels blows, wearing the adversary down by invoking, day in and day out, standard operating procedures developed over a half-century. Its strength is less in its generals, be they in Gosplan or elsewhere, than in its inconspicuous and innumerable lieutenants. And they are motivated, not just by simple prejudice and defense of crass privilege, but by a conviction that they are doing their duty and, more often than not, by a sincere befuddlement about what they are expected to do.[19]

What tactics can Gorbachev use against uncooperative bureaucrats? Com-

---

19. For an especially convincing case of bureaucratic confusion, see the story about the Belorussian Ministry of Trade (*Pravda*, May 15, 1987, p. 2).

ments on his search for non-bureaucratic support will be offered below. Equally important must be the recruitment of allies within the bureaucracy itself. Offering material incentives to low-level officials (kolkhoz chairmen and brigade leaders, for instance) who persevere against obstruction from above is one tack to take. Another is to make a positive example of more senior officials who make specific reforms work, holding out to others who emulate them the prospect of career advancement. This has been tried in China, where the career of Zhao Ziyang soared after he successfully implemented Deng Xiaoping's market-oriented agricultural reforms in Sichuan province. New Soviet regional bosses like Boris N. Yel'tsin of Moscow and Gennadiy V. Kolbin of Kazakhstan have already been put forward as role models, though their reforms have mostly been first-stage ones such as stamping out corruption and defending *glasnost'*.

A daunting problem is how to involve the apparatus of the party, especially at the local and regional level, on the side of economic reform, something at which Gorbachev seems to have had limited success thus far. He has several times depicted party officials as "commissars of restructuring," nobly fighting for the new ways. Drawn from the civil war era, the figure of the commissar is a poor guide to action today.

In Moscow, one of Andropov's first changes was to retitle the "planning and financial organs department" of the CPSU Secretariat the "economic department," place the fifty-three-year-old Ryzhkov in charge, and assign it to study economic restructuring. In 1984, under Chernenko, a Politburo commission on improving the economic mechanism was formed, but its membership was kept secret, it never reported publicly, and it presumably was dissolved after Gorbachev's accession. Inexplicably, when Ryzhkov moved to the Council of Ministers in September 1985, no permanent replacement as head of the economic department was named and there is none to this day.[20]

The territorial party organs, because of their unique ability to cut through red tape and impose decisions across departmental barriers, are vital to the normal functioning of the segmented economic bureaucracy. But so far there is little sign that the local party secretaries are taking any kind of lead in economic change. Where, in an era of reform, the machine needs engineers who will redesign and modernize it, the local party bosses have long since been cast in the role of mechanics who keep it creaking and wheezing along without rebuilding.

Inertia, habit, and self-interest are the main reasons the local party organs are having trouble breaking the mold, in which respect they are not much different from the ministries and the factory managers. Decentralization of

20. B. I. Gostev, who had been head of the department (under its old title) before Ryzhkov, was briefly returned as head, but departed to become Minister of Finance in December 1985. A first deputy head and several deputies have since been identified, but no head. Slyun'kov is now supervising the department's work, and may even be its head, without being identified as such.

economic administration should, in theory, reduce the need for party intervention, but it may not always work out that way in practice. Many party officials, as one regional first secretary has observed, are so used to being "in the presence of authority" (*pri vlasti*), because of their indispensability as fixers and umpires, that they may unconsciously oppose any diminution in these roles, even in the name of economic rationality. When managers flounder, moreover, party prefects "rush to take their responsibilities onto their own shoulders," fearing, among other things, punishment from Moscow if local plans are not met.[21] Another problem is their ongoing responsibility for welfare functions, which centrally controlled enterprises have often in the past served only when compelled to by local party nursemaids. Even as the Politburo orders the party to get off the managers' backs as part of the reform process, it emphasizes the increased importance of social programs, something that gives the party secretaries greater incentive to stay involved.

A recent survey of local party secretaries in the Orenburg region discovered that 80 percent of them agreed that direct party interference in management was the fault of the malfunctioning of the economic bureaucracy. While all were aware of summonses to carry out "political leadership" of the economy, and to refrain from old-style administrative pressure, 79 percent of the secretaries "imprecisely understood the distinction" between the two styles of work. "It would be a shame," the story on the survey concluded, "if new economic initiatives clash with ossified, willful methods of party leadership" (*Pravda*, June 17, 1987, p. 2). Gorbachev surely agrees, but so far has been unable to come up with new methods.

LEVEL IV: THE KNOWLEDGE SPECIALISTS

Economists and other knowledge specialists have had less real influence over economic reform than any other group considered here, but they are now being activated and some of them may take a greater part in future.

It is no mystery why a party leader bent on radical reform would draw little direct inspiration from the Soviet Union's generally conservative economics profession. Nevertheless, Gorbachev's post-1980 tutorials with Abel Aganbegyan, the latter's claim that a "congruence of ideas" emerged at them, and the prominent role of Aganbegyan and others in the drafting and marketing of concrete proposals demonstrate that certain economists have played a role. Even if it is inconceivable that Aganbegyan sold Gorbachev on a finished reform plan, economic research has helped him explore and flesh out the possibilities.

Especially after the gutting of the 1965 Kosygin reform, most Soviet economists under Brezhnev stuck to safe themes and cautious recommendations. The most innovative work, and that now of most interest to Gorbachev, seems

21. V. A. Kuptsov in *Pravda*, September 1, 1986, p. 2.

to have been done in three places: the Central Economic Mathematical Institute in Moscow, created under Nikita S. Khrushchev to test new econometric methods and models; the Institute of the Economics of the World Socialist System, also in Moscow, which examines mostly the East European economies; and the Institute of the Economics and Organization of Industrial Production in Novosibirsk, directed by Aganbegyan and oriented toward socioeconomic questions. In all three cases, relatively unorthodox research was somewhat sheltered from political interference in the 1970s and early 1980s by technical abstruseness in the first instance, by "socialist" subject matter in the second, and by geography in the last.

One of the more interesting products of the Gorbachev thaw has been a spate of attacks on the moribund state of mainstream economic science. These accelerated sharply after the January 1987 plenum of the Central Committee, at which Gorbachev bluntly assailed conservative dogma in ideology and the social sciences. Some of the most devastating comments have come from inside the discipline, largely but not exclusively from younger scholars.[22]

Aleksandr I. Anchishkin (before his premature death at the age of fifty-four) was the youngest of the major institute directors (and a former colleague of Ryzhkov and Slyun'kov in Gosplan); he accused the majority of economists of having since the 1960s followed "the path of time-serving, shallow descriptiveness, and often primitive apologetics" (Ekonomicheskaya teoriya, 1987a). Pavel G. Bunich, a department head at a Moscow management institute, has faulted them for servility to state-dictated stereotypes, but has also blamed the conformist climate of the Brezhnev years: "It is not that there were no attempts at constructive analysis or at putting forward new ideas. But these did not receive support. Worse than that, the firm holders of the most radical views often fell 'into disfavor' " (Ekonomicheskaya teoriya, 1987b).

By giving key appointments of Aganbegyan (research director of the Talyzin commission and secretary of the economics branch of the Academy of Sciences) Gorbachev has signalled that he wants "new ideas" previously on the fringe of the profession to be taken seriously both within it and in wider circles. Leonid I. Abalkin, the new director of the Institute of Economics, and Oleg T. Bogomolov, head of the Institute of the Economics of the World Socialist System, are both said by Soviet informants to be counselling Gorbachev personally along with Aganbegyan. Bogomolov is the more reformist of the two, having recently spoken up against "Stalinist interpretations" of development, urged an end to the taboo against candid discussion of the socialist market, and proposed deep reforms in agriculture.[23]

It is difficult to predict the participation of economists as the reform effort unfolds. Some, like one of Bogomolov's deputies and Nikolay Shmelev of the U.S.A. and Canada Institute, have been emboldened to criticize current reform

22. Light is shed on the enlivened debate by Hanson (1987).
23. See especially Bogomolov's interview in *Izvestiya*, May 14, 1987, p. 2; and his remarks at the Central Committee conference on the economy, in *Pravda*, June 13, 1987, p. 2.

proposals as inadequate and to demand a transition by the mid-1990s to full-blown market socialism, with profit-maximizing firms and a convertible currency.[24] It is possible that these are the kinds of notions that Gorbachev considers "antisocialist." At the other extreme, there are those who agree with the economist from the Moscow Cooperative Institute who said in a roundtable that specialists should exercise a "healthy conservatism," advising the party against "rash decisions" (Protivorechiya, 1987, p. 31). Economists' future role will depend equally on whether, like many in the political leadership, their nagging doubts about the status quo will have led them toward critical but not "antisocialist" views—terms that will have to be defined in practice—and on whether Gorbachev and his associates are willing and able to find constructive ways to involve them in decisions.

In the final analysis, Gorbachev and his coalition partners are far less interested in the small band of economists than in the Soviet intelligentsia as a whole, which he has openly wooed as an ally against bureaucratic and other anti-reformers. This was Gorbachev's main message to the writers at the Kremlin colloquy of June 1986: "The Central Committee needs support. You cannot even imagine how much we need support from a group such as the writers" (Beseda, 1986). Here as much as anything is the fuel for the remarkable cultural liberalization that we have seen gain momentum since then. Gorbachev's hope is that a partially emancipated intelligentsia[25] will step up the social pressure on his opponents to hew to his program. It will help through its work to make the case for greater individual originality, entrepreneurship, and ethical responsibility, without which the Soviet economy cannot be modernized.

The risks of this strategy are immense, for it threatens to alienate the same political establishment that brought Nikita Khrushchev down after an earlier thaw. Gorbachev's task will not be made easier by the fact that his new allies in the intelligentsia are not going to be easy to bridle. Many cultural figures will defend personal rights and creativity, but not all will be devotees of technology and economic modernization. In fact, as the bitter debates over northern river diversion and historical conservation in Russian cities show, many of the best of them will be not only indifferent to economics but positively hostile to subordinating social and spiritual values to efficiency.

Special opportunities and hazards are posed by the historical revisionism that has been sanctioned by the cultural thaw in spite of some initial reluctance on Gorbachev's part. At first, little of the new anti-Stalin material was about economics—reflecting, in part, the endemic weakness of the field of economic history in Soviet institutes and universities—but this is beginning to change. Most provocatively, several authors have taken up what they describe as the willful falsification of economic statistics under Stalin, saying that this built a

---

24. V. Krivosheyev, as quoted in *Lit. gaz.* (1987, p. 10); and Shmelev (1987, pp. 148–158).

25. The word being used, *raskreposhcheniye*, is the same employed for the emancipation of the serfs in 1861.

lasting dishonesty into Soviet national accounts.[26] Shmelev goes as far as any Soviet author has in painting Stalin as an economic illiterate obsessed with personal and state power.[27] Since Stalin presided over the building of the economic edifice that Gorbachev now says needs renovation, it may be to his advantage to have his economic misdeeds exposed. The trick will be to allow this without inviting questioning of the legitimacy of the Soviet economic order as a whole.

LEVEL V: THE POPULATION

The final level at which the politics of economic innovation is being fought is the broadest of all, that of the population. Barring radical changes in the Soviet political system, the people will not any time soon have the option of affirming or rejecting reform, or any particular brand of it, in a multi-party election. But their influence over the outcome will be vast. If, as Lenin put it, Russia's trench-weary soldiers voted against World War I with their feet, ordinary Soviet citizens today can vote for or against economic renewal with their hands. Unless they in the end produce more and better goods and services, faster and more cheaply, economic restructuring is doomed.

Is the populace for or against systemic reform? Gorbachev in his dialogue with the writers (Beseda, 1986) at one point asserted that it was entirely for reform, remarking (in the passage quoted above) that only the bureaucracy stands between a pro-reform leadership and "the people who want and dream of changes." Later in his talk, however, Gorbachev muddied the picture. For example, on drunkenness:

People want the "dry law." At the same time people in [vodka] lineups come up with all sorts of epithets like "Mineral Secretary," "We will drink as we did before," "Let us dig up Brezhnev." [Despite all this], we will save the people, especially the Slavic people, . . . [from] the scourge of drunkenness.

The "save the people" theme, foretelling salvation imposed from above, is itself contradicted a paragraph later in a general comment on transformation: "Unless we involve the people, nothing will come out of it. We are depending on influencing the people."

As with the bureaucracy, there is much to be said for shunning generalizations about "the people" and considering the orientations of specific subsets of the population. This idea has been most consistently pursued by Academician Tat'yana I. Zaslavskaya, the Novosibirsk sociologist and advocate of economic reform. In a September 1986 article in *Kommunist* (Zaslavskaya, 1986, pp.

26. See especially Selyunin and Khanin (1987) and also Nikolay Bykov (1987). Bykov's article is about V. V. Obolenskiy, a victim of Stalin's purges and the USSR's chief statistician in 1926–1929 and 1931–1935.

27. Shmelev (1987, p. 144) goes so far as to speak of "extraordinary and inhuman circumstances" prevailing in the economy and more generally in Soviet life under Stalin.

63, 67), Zaslavskaya argued, as she has before in scholarly publications, that "the only management system that will be effective today is one that rests on a precise knowledge and skillful utilization of the interests of working people." These interests, she emphasized, "are many-sided, depend on a multitude of causes, and change under the influence of circumstances." Intergroup differences in attitude toward reform are clouded by the interdependence among groups and the internal differentiations within them. Writing of workers and managerial personnel, the key to economic development, Zaslavskaya reported that there are "both active supporters of the new, people who are full of initiative and enterprising, and the more passive and conservative-minded." It is necessary, she said, "to stimulate and support the former in every way, to give scope to their creative urges, and to prove to the latter the superiority of new relations" (Zaslavskaya, 1986).

A reading between the lines of Soviet discussions, reinforced by East European experience, suggests strongly that many Soviet blue-collar workers would, at least at the outset, be numbered among the "passive and conservative-minded" on systemic economic reform. Deep reforms, especially if they entailed marketization, would, among other effects, add greatly to the insecurity of working-class life. Zaslavskaya and others are now writing with enthusiasm of scarcity pricing for other consumer goods, housing, and daily services. This, we know from many sources, would be deeply resented by the majority of Soviet workers.

Widely shared Soviet attitudes toward change in general also figure in the political dynamics of economic reform. One is the pervasive skepticism, born of years of discounting bombastic sloganeering, that anything important is going to change, whatever the General Secretary and the Politburo say to the contrary. Another is the fear that, were change actually to occur, it might be for the worse rather than for the better. Stephen Cohen rightly refers to this as the Soviets' "abiding anxiety that another disaster forever looms" (Cohen, 1985, p. 148).

Fragmentary public opinion data back up these points and suggest, again, the lack of clarity in the regime's vision of reform. A large-scale poll by the Institute of Sociological Research, apparently done in early 1987, found that 90 percent of those asked were generally in favor of economic restructuring (*perestroyka*). But the majority of respondents believed that, for all the rhetoric, few significant changes had yet occurred, at least on the benefits side. But costs there were: "The majority feel restructuring today only in the greater pressure at work" (*Izvestiya,* May 5, 1987, p. 2).

The social value most antithetical to systemic economic reform is probably the egalitarianism, compounded of Marxism, envy, and habit, that mirrors the traditional, flattened rewards structure of the official economy. Nervousness about giving offense in this area crops up again and again in the published discussions of wages and earnings, small enterprise, and many other economic issues. Thus the director of the Elektrosignal electrical equipment plant in Voronezh:

> I know that the leaders of several subunits of our Elektrosignal think it is a sin to deprive a do-nothing of his bonus. Why offend people? And if only this were confined to us! . . . They "share" [premiums] among the workers, they "share" them among the engineering and technical personnel. They even share and reallocate work itself, all so that they can "with clean conscience" pay everyone as nearly as possible the same. The person who works better and more productively is often sent "to bring in the potatoes," or on an expedition: he has already met his norm, and when he is gone other people can get their pay up to the *peredovik* level. . . . We are afraid of paying, we are afraid of punishing, we do not face up to telling the idler that he is an idler. And that is today. What will we do with this psychology tomorrow, when we will have to implement the new system of labor compensation, which gives us incomparably greater rights? (*Ekon. gaz.*, 1986, p. 8).

The *Izvestiya* correspondent Aleksandr Vasinskiy has written eloquently about the philosophy of prohibitions (*filosofiya zapretov*), the regime or rule of prohibitions (*zapretitel'stvo*), and the naysaying busybodies (*nel'zyatchiki*) that influence all sides of the Soviet condition. Under this philosophy, Soviet citizens were once told how wide to cut their trousers and how long to wear their hair. In culture and science, the power to forbid was used "to interdict architectural styles, literary genres, musical directions, and even . . . laws of nature" (the last an allusion to Lysenkoism). As Vasinskiy demonstrates, the same approach continues to be felt in economics, and it is manifested by ordinary citizens as well as by officials. He cites a letter received from a Rostov resident demanding that there be size restrictions on sheds built on suburban garden plots, and they limit height as well as ground coverage lest avaricious gardeners put up high buildings, rent out the rooms, and thereby come into "unearned income." "I read this letter," Vasinskiy says, "and have to pinch myself: The devil take me, the next thing you know the owners of garden plots will be wanting to build income-generating skyscrapers" (*Izvestiya*, December 27, 1986, p. 3).

It is in this context that the broadening of Gorbachev's reform strategy into the cultural and political realms makes sense. Events in their own right are the extraordinary easing of restrictions on the press and the arts, the apparent shift in policy toward dissent, the quickening debate on legal rights, Gorbachev's proposals for political "democratization" and multi-candidate elections. But they also bear a direct relation to the process of economic change. Gorbachev clearly has concluded that economic reform is impossible without a measure of cultural and political reform. Particularly in culture, quick victories are possible for reformers in ways that they are not in economics. Intellectual liberalization, if all goes well, will enable searching study and discussion of the USSR's economic malaise. Political liberalization will involve white- and blue-collar workers in decisions inside the factory gates (through the election of managers mandated by the June 1987 Law on the State Enterprise) and outside (in decisions in the soviets and the party), and thereby reduce their alienation and elicit better work.

If the audacity of Gorbachev's assumption is plain, their workability has yet to be demonstrated. One problem may be that the benefits of different parts of his overall program will tend to be out of phase with one another. So far as the economy is concerned, political decompression, for all the good it will do eventually, may in the short run alienate both conservatives and reformists. Surveys show that many Soviet workers—24 percent in one sample in Kazakhstan—dislike economic *glasnost'*, considering "that a broad illumination of shortcomings and difficulties does more harm than good" (*Izvestiya*, May 5, 1987, p. 2). But for employees who are sympathetic to criticism, it may work to delegitimize the existing system before new structures are ready to replace it. Gorbachev's authority-building economic reforms, therefore, may be in a race with his early non-economic reforms, whose immediate effects are authority-dissolving.

LOOKING FORWARD

If events since March 1985 tell us anything, it is that the struggle for economic reform in the Soviet Union will be protracted, many-sided, and unpredictable. Reform, though as yet falling well short of Hungarian and Chinese precedents and of the rhetoric of Gorbachev himself, has moved forward as a cause. But pro-reform forces have made only initial inroads in a powerfully entrenched system embodied in the inertia of attitudes and institutions.

Several litmus tests will help us in the crucial months ahead to gauge the political chances of systemic economic reform gathering momentum:

• Will Mikhail Gorbachev be clearer than he has been in the past about the main principles of "radical reform" and, in particular, the role of market relations? Will he move forward when reformist decisions suffer setbacks? Brezhnev, whose heart was never really in the limited industrial reform of 1965, went the other way.

• Will Gorbachev manage to retain the support of the party leadership as reform proceeds? Will he bring into the leadership more politicians who are as committed as he is, or more so, to structural innovation in the economy?

• Will the authors of reform proposals devise ways of neutralizing opponents and rewarding supporters in the bureaucracy? Will they find some formula for bringing the party apparatus into the reform process?

• Will Soviet economists and social scientists generate detailed reform blueprints? Will other intellectuals go along with economic reform and reconcile it with their other values?

● Will the reformers find the right mix of carrots and sticks to sell reform to a work force that is disgruntled with the status quo but will find fault with almost every concrete proposal for improvement?

REFERENCES

"Beseda chlenov SP SSSR s M. S. Gorbachevym (Conversation of Members of the Writer's Union with M. S. Gorbachev)," *Arkhiv samizdat*, Radio Liberty Report No. 5785, Munich, 1986.

Bykov, Nikolay, "Po pravu pamyati (By Right of Memory)," *Ogonek*, 24:6–7, June 1987.

Cohen, Stephen F., *Rethinking the Soviet Experience: Politics and History since 1917.* New York: Oxford University Press, 1985.

Ekonomicheskaya gazeta, 43:8, October 1986a.

———, 48:4, November 1986b.

———, 24:16, June 1987.

"Ekonomicheskaya teoriya i praktika perestroyki (Economic Theory and the Practice of Restructuring)," *Kommunist*, 5:36, March 1987a.

———, *Kommunist*, 6:15, April 1987b.

FBIS. Foreign Broadcast Information Service, *Daily Report*, series III, October 9, 1986, pp. R1–R3.

Gorbachev, Mikhail S., "Politicheskiy doklad tsentral'nogo komiteta KPSS XXVII s''yezdu Kommunisticheskoy partii Sovetskogo Soyuza. Doklad General'nogo sekretariya TsK KPSS tovarishcha M. S. Gorbacheva. 25 Fevralia 1986 goda (Political Report of the Central Committee of the CPSU to the XXVII Congress of the Communist Party of the Soviet Union. Report of the General Secretary of the CC of the CPSU, Comrade M. S. Gorbachev)," in *Materialy XXVIIs''yezda Kommunisticheskoy Partii Sovetskogo Soyuza*. Moscow: Politizdat, 1986, pp. 3–97.

"Gorbachev's Economic Reform: A Soviet Economy Roundtable," *Soviet Economy*, 3, 1:40–53, January–March 1987.

Hamman, Henry, "Interview with Fedor Burlatsky," *Radio Liberty Research Report*, RL396/86, October 10, 1986, p. 7.

Hanson, Philip, "The Reform Debate: What Are the Limits?" *Radio Liberty Research Report*, RL 237/87, June 23, 1987.

Ivanov, Ivan, D., "Restructuring the Mechanism of Foreign Economic Relations in the USSR," *Soviet Economy*, 3, 3:192–218, July–September, 1987.

Kornai, Janos, "The Hungarian Reform Process: Visions, Hopes, and Reality," *Journal of Economic Literature*, 24, 1724–1726, December 1986.

Ligachev, Ye., "Chelovecheskiy faktor, khozraschet, i perestroyka v agropromyshlennom komplekse (The Human Factor, Economic Accountability, and Restructuring in the Agroindustrial Complex)," *Kommunist*, 4:28–42, March 1987.

Literaturnaya gazeta, 50:10, December 10, 1986a.

———, 51:10, December 17, 1986b.

———, 23:10, June 8, 1987.

Nikonov, V., "Polneye zadeystvovat' potentsial agropromyshlennogo kompleksa (To

More Fully Activate the Potential of the Agro-Industrial Complex)," *Kommunist*, 5:15–29, March 1987.

Ogonëk, 19:10–11, May 1987.

"Protivorechiya sotsialisticheskoy ekonomiki na sovremennom etape (Contradictions of the Socialist Economy at the Current Phase)," *Voprosy ekonomiki*, 5:31, May 1987.

Selyunin, Vasiliy, and Grigoriy Khanin, "Lukavaya tsifra (A Sly Figure)," *Novyy mir*, 2:181–201, February 1987.

Shmelev, Nikolay, "Avansy i dolgi (Advances and Debts)," *Novyy mir*, 6:142–158, June 1987.

"Zakon Soyuza Sovetskikh Sotsialisticheskikh Respublik o gosudarstvennom predpriyatii (ob'yedinenii) (Law of the Union of Soviet Socialist Republics on the State Enterprise [Association])," *Pravda*, July 1, 1987, pp. 1–4.

Zaslavskaya, T., "Chelovecheskiy faktor razvitiya ekonomiki i sotsial'naya spravedlivost' (The Human Factor in the Development of the Economy and Social Justice)," *Kommunist*, 13:63, 67, September 1986.

CHAPTER 5

The Social Dimensions of *Perestroyka*

Blair A. Ruble

TIMOTHY COLTON suggests that we may gain some insights and assess the prospects of the Soviet Union's major economic reform by considering the problem from five successive levels of explanation: the top leader, the collective political leadership, the administrative organs of party and state, the intelligentsia, and the population at large (Colton, 1987). This chapter will extend this analysis by exploring one level of explanation, the population, in greater depth. Such a "bottom-up" perspective on *perestroyka* greatly facilitates better understanding of the prospects for economic reform for, as Colton correctly notes, Soviet citizens must work harder if Gorbachev's economic restructuring is to result in improved economic performance. The Soviet population, then, is in a position to "vote" for or against economic reform "with their hands."

A basic argument advanced in this paper is that Soviet society has experienced substantial change over the past quarter century. As Tat'yana Zaslavskaya and other Soviet sociologists have indicated on several occasions, the process of change has added a number of new groups to the fabric of Soviet society (Zaslavskaya, 1985, 1986a, 1986b; Klopov, 1980, 1985). The members of many of these groups display attitudes toward labor and rewards that are quite distinct from those held by earlier groups and generations. Gorbachev's reform rhetoric and actions appeal to several of these new groups, suggesting political and economic change has not kept pace with a sweeping social transformation that is already well under way.

This state of affairs contrasts rather strongly with the social environment of Gorbachev's predecessors, the prevailing social context clearly differentiating the Gorbachev reform effort from that of Nikita Khrushchev, for example, who

First published in *Soviet Economy*, 1987, 3, 2, pp. 171–183. More than is usually the case, the author proceeded to structure this paper around numerous, and at times extended, communications and discussions with informed colleagues. In this connection, his reliance on helpful comments and suggestions received from Nancy Condee, Murray Feshbach, Peter Hauslohner, Ed Hewett, Gail Lapidus, Marion J. Levy, Jr., Vladimir Padunov, Richard Rockwell, Vladimir Shlyapentokh, S. Frederick Starr, and Andrew Walden is gratefully acknowledged. [Eds.]

91

Table 1. *Percentage of Total American, Italian, and Soviet Populations in Urban Areas, 1940–1981*[a]

Year	US	Italy	USSR
1940	56	. . .	33
1960/61	70	60	50
1970/71	74	65	56
1980/81	74	67	63

Sources: *Historical,* Part 1, 1975, p. 11; *Statistical,* 1986, p. 15; *Italy,* 1984, p. 106; *Narkhoz,* 1981, p. 7.

a. The urban population of Italy has been chosen for comparison with American and Soviet populations because Italy's level of per capita GNP is similar to that of the USSR.

confronted significantly different social problems as he sought political and economic change. This chapter contends, therefore, that in order to understand the array of support for and opposition to *perestroyka,* we must come to terms with the Soviet population, much as Mikhail Gorbachev will have to if he is to succeed in bringing about meaningful economic and political renewal.

SOCIAL TRANSFORMATION

An Urban Society

On an average day during the twenty years between the 1959 and 1979 Soviet censuses, roughly 5,000 to 7,000 Soviet citizens left their country homes and moved to town. This simple fact evidences a fundamentally important process of social change: during the post-Stalin period, the USSR has become an urban society. The USSR of the 1980s is overwhelmingly urban and has been so for nearly a generation (Table 1).[1]

The urban character of Soviet society is further highlighted by the rather dramatic recent growth of the number of cities having more than 100,000 residents (Table 2). This increase indicates that two related yet fairly distinct demographic processes have been at work in the USSR. First, existing cities are growing; second, new cities are being created. Both trends testify to the heightened urban character of Soviet life as well as to emerging similarities between patterns of urbanization in the USSR and the industrialized world in general.

A Better Educated Society

The urbanization process in the USSR, as elsewhere, has been accompanied by a marked improvement in the educational achievement of both the general

1. This pattern is amplified in the European USSR in general, and in the RSFSR in particular, where 73 percent of the 1986 population lived in urban areas (*Narkhoz,* 1986, p. 8). However, it has slowed in recent years as various programs intended to increase agricultural production have included incentives for farm workers to remain in the countryside and even for city dwellers to return to the country. One might also note that the rural population of Tadzhikistan increased during the 1980s.

Table 2. *Size Category of Large American and Soviet Cities,*
1939/40–1979/80

Year	Number of residents		
	100,000–499,999	*500,000–999,999*	*1,000,000 +*
1939/40			
US	78	9	5
USSR	78	9	2
1959/60			
US	109	16	5
USSR	123	22	3
1970			
US	127	20[a]	6[a]
USSR	188	23	10
1979/80			
US	147	16[a]	6[a]
USSR	224	26	21

Sources: *Historical*, Part 1, 1975, p. 11; *Statistical*, 1986, p. 15; *Itogi*, 1972, pp. 22–61; Morton and Stuart, 1984, pp. 3–4.
a. Taking into account metropolitan population data as reflected in the U.S. Census Bureau's Standard Metropolitan Statistical Areas, the U.S. figure for cities with 500,000–999,999 residents in 1970 was 26 while in 1979/80 it was 32; the figure for cities with more than 1,000,000 residents was 32 in 1970 and 35 in 1979/80.

Table 3. *Educational Level of the Soviet Population, 1939–1986*[a]

Educational level	1939[b]	1959	1979	1986
Primary or less	89.2	63.9	36.2	29.9
Secondary				
Incomplete		21.8	24.1	19.2
General		6.1	20.7	27.6
Special		4.8	10.7	13.1
Higher				
Incomplete		1.1	1.5	1.5
Complete	.8	2.3	6.8	8.7

Sources: *Narkhoz*, p. 27; *Narkhoz*, 1986, p. 27.
a. Percentage of population ten years of age or older.
b. People with an education ranging from secondary incomplete to higher incomplete accounted for 10.0 percent.

and elite populations. On the eve of the Second World War, nearly every Soviet citizen over ten years of age had scarcely more than a primary education (Table 3). Twenty years later, this situation had certainly improved, although nearly two-thirds of the Soviet population over ten years of age had completed no more than primary school. After another twenty years the educational achievement of the Soviet population had noticeably improved, with nearly two-thirds of Soviet citizens ten years of age or older having received at least some training at the secondary level.[2] Although it is possible to question the quality of particular Soviet educational institutions, especially rural schools, any examination of the aggregate quantitative data leaves little doubt that the Soviet population as a whole now receives more education than previous generations.

2. This figure is roughly comparable to the level of educational achievement of American citizens over the age of 25 in 1950 and Italians over the age of six in 1961 (*Statistical*, 1986, p. 133; *Italy*, 1986, p. 149).

Table 4. *Educational Level of Urban and Rural Populations of the Soviet Union, 1939–1986*[a]

Year	Some higher		Some secondary		Some primary	
	Urban	Rural	Urban	Rural	Urban	Rural
1939	1.9	.2	19.9	5.0	78.2	94.8
1959	4.0	.7	42.9	24.9	53.1	74.4
1970	6.2	1.4	53.0	31.8	40.8	66.8
1979	9.3	2.5	63.0	46.7	27.7	50.8
1986	11.9	2.6	65.3	53.6	22.8	43.8

Sources: *Narkhoz*, 1981, p. 28; *Narkhoz*, 1986, p. 28.
a. Percentage of population ten years of age or older.

Advances in educational achievement have for the most part been concurrent with urbanization, which indicates that a greater proportion of the Soviet school population is now enrolled in higher-quality urban schools. Thus, as elsewhere in the world, urbanization and widespread educational advancement appear to have gone hand-in-hand in the USSR, a pattern that is confirmed by the data contained in Table 4. Less uniform data on educational attainment also are available for the elite. They present a similar picture: broad segments of the Soviet population currently holding critical political, managerial, cultural, and scientific positions are better educated than the elites of any other period in Soviet (and, arguably, Russian) history (Hough, 1980).

Changes in the Workplace and Economy

The emergence of a reasonably well educated general population has very significant implications for a multitude of social, political, military, and economic interactions. Highly educated people certainly join patronage networks as readily as others, and frequently rely upon patronage for career advancement as well. However, higher levels of education are accompanied by skills which are readily transferable to a variety of institutional environments. In general, then, the more highly educated the person, the more independence he or she has from the traditional relationships of a patronage network. Consequently, the authority based on personal relationships typical of traditional societies becomes more fluid and open-ended as employees become less dependent upon employers.

Societies experiencing the kind of broad social change reflected in increasing levels of education and urbanization frequently undergo a similarly dramatic reorientation of economic effort. The destruction of a traditional peasant society accompanies (and frequently may be a consequence of) the dismantling of an agriculture-based (and the creation of an industry-based) national economic system. There is further evidence that as this revolutionary process continues industry eventually begins to lose its pride of place within the national economy to various service activities. Both trends are apparent in data on the struc-

Table 5. *Employment Structure of the Soviet Economy by Sector, 1940–1985*[a]

Economic sector	1940	1960	1970	1980	1985
Industry and construction	23	32	38	39	38
Agriculture and forestry[b]	54	39	25	20	20
Transport and communication	5	7	8	9	9
Services[c]	18	22	29	32	33

a. Percentage of total workforce.
b. Excluding private agricultural activities.
c. Trade, dining and supply, health, physical and social welfare, education, culture, arts, science and scientific services, government agencies, cooperative and social organizations, credit and insurance agencies, housing, municipal, and non-productive forms of consumer service.

ture of employment in the Soviet economy during the period 1940 to 1980 (Table 5).

Throughout the four decades between 1940 and 1980, the proportion of the Soviet workforce employed in agriculture dropped steadily from roughly one-in-two employees to one-in-five, a workforce ratio between agricultural and non-agricultural sectors roughly equivalent to that found in Italy in 1971.[3] Concomitantly, the Soviet Union's non-agricultural workforce grew, with the industrial and construction sectors dominating employment by the early 1960s.[4] Since 1965, however, the process of redistribution of the non-agricultural labor force among economic sectors has slackened, although service sector employment did surpass agricultural employment by 1970. The Soviet Union has come to resemble other advanced industrial societies in the degree of urbanization and, to only a slightly lesser degree, in the level of educational achievement. It has, however, only begun to make the transformation to a service-oriented economy.

NEW SOCIAL GROUPS

The far-reaching transformations outlined above are capable of spawning new social groups, which is clearly the case in the Soviet Union. Over the past generation or so, at least four distinctive social substrata—the working middle class, the young professionals, professional and paraprofessional women, and committed national elites—have emerged within the Soviet social hierarchy. Each group is discussed in turn below.

The Working Middle Class

The Brezhnev years represented the first period in Soviet history during which the industrial labor force had stabilized (Kahan, 1979; Pravda, 1982). Previously, a century of social disruption prevented the development of social and cultural (let alone political) continuity between the old and the new gen-

3. By the mid-1980s the Italian ratio had approached one-in-ten (*Italy*, 1986, p. 153).
4. This is about the same time that a majority of the Soviet population had come to live in cities.

eration of industrial workers. In addition, many members of the Soviet industrial workforce traditionally sought social mobility upward across a blue collar/white collar divide, rather than within the working class itself. The emergence of a multi-generational industrial work force with few opportunities for mobility out of the working class dramatically alters the relationship of the individual worker to his or her job. At the very least, the lack of opportunities for social advancement had led Soviet workers to seek incremental improvements in their present work environment and general quality of life instead of sweeping changes in their social status.

If social mobility is restricted across the major boundaries separating different strata within Soviet society, what of mobility within a given stratum? Overall, there is clear evidence of growing differentiation among workers.

During the 1950s, the Soviet working class was remarkably homogeneous. Fresh from the countryside, or one-generation removed at most, Soviet workers remained undereducated and underskilled. Reexamination of the educational data in Tables 3 and 4 indicates that at the close of the decade only a small minority of Soviet citizens (4.4 percent) had more than a secondary education, while nearly two-thirds of the total and just over one-half of the urban populations had no more than a primary education. It can be assumed, then, that industrial workers with very few exceptions had little more than a primary education.

As one proceeds toward the 1980s, not only does the quantity and quality of education rise for the population as a whole, but levels of education within the workforce become more differentiated or heterogeneous (Klopov, 1980, 1985). Many workers entering the industrial labor force during the 1950s with only a primary education are still a part of that workforce, whereas a new generation of workers comes from an environment in which a vast majority of the general and urban populations have at least some secondary education, workers included. The divergence of educational achievement within the working class has increased over the decades since the 1950s—from an educational profile encompassing almost solely primary education to one encompassing incomplete primary school through some form of post-secondary training.

This enhanced differentiation in educational levels shows up clearly upon examination of the changing pattern of skills levels among Soviet workers. Alex Pravda reports that between 1962 and 1979 the percentage of blue collar workers who were considered to be low or unskilled declined rather markedly,[5] while the percentage of high-skilled industrial manual workers similarly increased[6] (Pravda, 1982). This trend, which broadly follows heightened levels of educational achievement, produces new sub-groupings within the Soviet working class. For example, to borrow further from Pravda, we

5. From 38 percent to 26 percent.
6. From 13 percent to 23 percent.

may find a substantial cluster of "worker-technicians" whose skills and job duties overlap with the lower echelons of semi-professional engineering technical personnel (*inzhenerno-tekhnicheskiy rabotniki,* or *ITR*). We can thus identify an increasing divergence of qualifications within the Soviet working class ranging from unskilled laborers to skilled and sophisticated technicians. Recent growth in the percentage of workers in high-skill categories accentuates the pyramid shape of the industrial employment structure, in addition to whatever other changes are taking place in the relationship between workers and other employment groups in Soviet society. Such differences, of course, have a pronounced generational dimension; older workers tend to be concentrated in lower and semi-skilled professions, while younger workers tend to dominate higher skill ranks.

Alex Pravda goes on to argue that income, consumption levels, education, and prestige are similarly distributed among workers, with craftsmen, highly skilled manual workers, and worker-technicians forming a special substratum within the working class. When skill levels, economic sectors, and geography are taken into consideration, some groups of workers in this category receive greater compensation than do white collar employees. The blue collar/white collar divide once so pronounced in the Soviet social structure is increasingly blurred by the emergence of industrial substrata which provide opportunities for upward mobility within the working class to a new "working middle class."

The Young Professionals

The ongoing diversification in the Soviet white collar world is every bit as complex as that occurring within the industrial workforce. Over the past two decades a group of young, well-educated professionals has emerged within the country's metropolitan areas. Relatively small though this social group may be, its presence is evident in various aggregate social data. Between 1970 and 1980, for example, the percentage of the Soviet workforce engaged in material production declined modestly (*Narkhoz,* 1981, p. 356).[7] The most significant growth within the remaining workforce, employed in non-productive sectors, occurred in precisely those sectors which employ large numbers of well-educated professionals, namely health care, the arts, science, and education (*Narkhoz,* 1981, pp. 357–358).

Sub-national data for the same 1970 to 1980 period confirm the essentially urban nature of these developments. Statistics on employment patterns in such principal cities as Moscow and Leningrad reveal that both metropolitan regions have experienced significant growth in the number of white collar professionals, especially in science, culture, health, and the financial community (*Moskva,* 1985, p. 105; *Narkhoz Leningrada,* 1981, p. 68). These "Yuppies," as Peter

7. The decline was from 77.1 percent to 72.9 percent. The period from 1970 to 1980 has been chosen to illustrate this point because of the availability of comparable national and regional/local data. These trends are even more pronounced over a more extended period of time.

Hauslohner has labeled them, offer additional evidence of the consolidation of a mature industrial social structure with relatively stable, multigenerational subgroups (Hauslohner, 1986).

Professional and Paraprofessional Women

Urbanization, the broadening of educational achievement, and economic restructuring significantly disrupt the family patterns of traditional societies (Levy, 1986). Previously, most people lived out their lives in close proximity to other family members. Family proximity, however, breaks down as the establishment of new economic and social relationships proceeds.

David Lane has reported trends in Soviet sexual relations that are universal among industrial societies (Lane, 1986). Drawing upon the work of sociologist Igor Kon, Lane states that the sexual maturation of Soviet adolescents has been accelerating, the age of initial sexual experience has been declining, the differences in sexual behavior of men and women have been disappearing, sexual morality has been experiencing a period of liberalization, and so on. Overall, Lane concludes, the marital union has come to be viewed increasingly as a frequently temporary arrangement.

The very evident improvement in the level of female educational and professional achievement in the USSR promotes radical change in the patterns of family behavior, which show up in turn in changing Soviet employment patterns over the past half-century.

Economic contingencies forced large numbers of Soviet women into the labor force, at least as early as Stalin's initial five-year plans. By the Brezhnev period, significant numbers of urbanized and educated women had moved upward to white collar positions (*Narkhoz*, 1986, p. 65). Soviet women who a generation or more ago would have ended up driving a tractor on a collective farm are now finding their way into jobs as physicians, laboratory assistants, and librarians.

As is the case with the working middle class and the young professional elite (two groups, it should be noted, in which there are many women), the female labor force has become an articulate and aggrieved substratum of the Soviet population with some rather special needs. Tensions produced by the "dual burden" of work and family responsibilities have plagued Soviet women ever since they began to enter the work force in large numbers. The need to balance professional and familial responsibilities takes on added economic and political meaning at present as a consequence of demographic trends which have constrained the availability of manpower.

Numerous proposals designed to facilitate female participation in the workforce could become part of the Soviet political agenda. Women in the Soviet Union earn somewhere between 60 percent and 70 percent of the salaries earned by Soviet men (e.g., McAuley, 1981). Pressure is beginning to mount for the implementation of more flexible work schedules that would permit women to manage their "dual burden" more efficiently. At the same time, the need for women to balance professional and domestic demands on their time creates pressures for improved household goods and services. The long-standing and large-scale participation of women in the Soviet labor force, combined with higher levels of educational and professional achievement among Soviet women, confront Soviet policymakers and economic planners with far more complicated policy decisions relating to women workers than has previously been the case.

Committed National Elites

Intellectual, professional, and cultural elites in societies undergoing rapid social change may return to tradition for a sense of coherence and stability in an otherwise volatile environment. This search for normative continuity intensifies the appeal of traditional forms of cultural expression, leading at times to efforts to establish and demonstrate the uniqueness and individuality of those groups. Efforts directed toward a renewal of group identity over time usually generate an agenda for political action as well. Significantly, Soviet elites among many of the country's most important national and ethnic groups (including the Russians) now appear to be conforming to this cycle of heightened ethnic consciousness as reassurance increasingly is sought in traditional cultural forms.

In approaching nationality issues in today's Soviet Union, we must be mindful that personal and nationality policies throughout much of the 1960s and 1970s integrated local elites into a national political hierarchy, granting them unprecedented autonomy (Goble, 1987). This expanded autonomy for republic elites, when combined with urbanization and higher levels of educational achievement, served to differentiate younger cohorts of national political, economic, social, cultural, and intellectual leaders from their elders in many regions of the USSR (including predominantly Russian areas). Many younger Soviets of various nationalities are aware of their ethnic identity and are sufficiently articulate and well-placed within the political system to manipulate that system to their benefit. The very concept of nationality, then, has become imbedded in the institutional core of the Soviet political economy in ways which are unique to the present.

Looking to the future, recent student riots in Alma-Ata demonstrate the volatility of educated and culturally conscious urban-based elites among the various nationalities of the Soviet Union. The very existence of such groups demands that central policies become ever more sensitive to national aspirations.

SHIFTING AUTHORITY RELATIONS

The formation of each of these new strata and substrata within society fundamentally alters the nature of authority relationships throughout the Soviet political economy. To begin with, they constitute significant social groups that are likely to become strategically placed within the Soviet political economy over time. Given their levels of skill and the economy's continuing labor shortages, members of each of these social clusters promise to gain control over the commanding heights of the Soviet labor market.

In the past, Soviet citizens remained highly dependent upon their employers not only for wages but also for a wide array of goods and services. The mobility of these new social groups increases pressure to reduce employment-based access to goods and services throughout Soviet society. Expanding private markets (both legal and illegal) for housing and consumer goods respond to these new demands while enhancing the freedom of employees to maneuver in the labor market, and in society more generally. Soviet citizens from a variety of backgrounds command skills and gain access to goods and services outside of the workplace. Such accessibility affords many employees a greater degree of independence from their employers than the norm over the history of Soviet and Russian labor relations.

Under the "social contract" developed during the Khrushchev-Brezhnev era, a range of benefits intended to support less productive elements of society have gone into effect (Hauslohner, 1987). The expanding groups discussed above, on the other hand, in time may come to resent the linkage of social welfare benefits to the workplace. As Andrew Walder rightly argues, such distribution mechanisms accentuate the dependency of citizens upon system throughout the Communist world (Walder, 1986). Within this broader context, significant shifts in authority relations at the workplace assume larger significance for a range of relationships throughout the entire political economy.

The formation of new social/occupational groups—urban-based, professional, paraprofessional, and highly skilled—promises to qualitatively transform the nature of authority relations beyond the workplace, i.e., throughout the Soviet political economy. Until recently, however, there has been little relaxation of the network of paternalistic authority relationships within Soviet economic and political institutions. Throughout most of the Soviet period and even the preceding years, basic labor and political relations have been structured around displays of deference combined with a freedom from responsibility. These traditional attitudes toward authority on the part of superiors and subordinates alike appear, at least at first glance, to represent relics of the past.

Whatever the root causes, such dependency relations inflame tensions between increasingly independent yet highly productive workers and arbitrary policies administered in the economic, political, and ideological spheres. Soviet economic planners and managers must draw upon the energies and creativity of the aforementioned social groups in order to sustain dynamic growth over the next several decades. These groups tend to be motivated primarily by material incentives, expectations of being more fully informed, and a sense of increased participation in decision-making processes (Yanowitch, 1979). Gorbachev's wage policies, *glasnost'* campaign, and support of experimental worker participation mechanisms respond to these emerging demands. At least three of the four social groups mentioned here (the committed national elites being a possible exception) are likely to provide support for attempts to reform fundamental economic and political relationships.

POLICY CONSEQUENCES: CAN GORBACHEV CATCH UP?

The challenge confronting Mikhail Gorbachev and the entire Communist Party leadership at present is how to manage social conflicts effectively without destroying basic economic and political alignments. Policies that favor previous socio-political arrangements alienate important emergent social groups, while those that meet their increasingly articulate demands violate long-standing and frequently unstated compromises. These ''violations'' consist of the following:

- Rewards for increased productivity within the working middle class contradict previous notions of social equity;

- Increased availability of consumer goods and services demanded by working women redirects resources away from previously favored heavy industrial interests;

- Access to the information required by technologically advanced economic systems undermines the authority and control of entrenched bureaucratic elites; and

- Governance of union republics on the basis of competence alone erodes the position of those committed national elites whose claim to power has been ethnically derived.

Mikhail Gorbachev and his colleagues thus must make decisions that benefit some social groups at the expense of others. The political task faced by the new leadership is to manage these varied and complex competing interests in a manner that permits the Soviet political and economic system to adjust to a new social reality. The success of the economic components of *perestroyka* will depend to a considerable degree upon the capacity of the Soviet economic and political leaders to control and coordinate these unprecedented patterns of social interaction.

REFERENCES

Colton, Timothy J., ''Approaches to the Politics of Systemic Economic Reform in the Soviet Union,'' *Soviet Economy*, 3, 2:145–170, April–June 1987.

Goble, Paul, ''Running Against the Republics: Gorbachev and the Soviet Nationality Problem.'' Unpublished manuscript, 1987.

Hauslohner, Peter, "Gorbachev's Social Contract," *Soviet Economy*, 3, 1:54–89, January–March 1987.

———, "The Gorbachev Regime as a 'Yuppie' Administration." Unpublished paper presented at the conference, "Gorbachev's First Year," University of California, Berkeley, March 21–23, 1986.

Historical Statistics of the United States from Colonial Times to 1970. Washington, D.C.: U.S. Government Printing Office, 1975.

Hough, Jerry, *Soviet Leadership in Transition*. Washington, D.C.: The Brookings Institution, 1980.

Italy Today: Social Picture and Trends, 1985. Rome: Centro studi investmenti sociali, 1986.

Itogi Vsesoyuznoy perepisi naseleniya 1970 goda (Results of the All-Union Census of Population in 1970). Moscow: Statistika, 1972.

Kahan, Arcadius, "Some Problems of the Soviet Worker," in Arcadius Kahan and Blair A. Ruble, eds., *Industrial Labor in the USSR*. Elmsford, N.Y.: Pergamon Press, Inc., 1979, pp. 283–312.

Klopov, Ye. V., Sotsial'naya dinamika rabochego klassa SSSR (The Social Dynamics of the Working Class of the USSR). Moscow: Znaniye, 1980.

———, *Rabochiy klass SSSR (The Working Class of the USSR)*. Moscow: Mysl', 1985.

Lane, David, *Soviet Economy and Society*. New York: New York University Press, 1986.

Levy, Marion J., Jr., "Modernization Exhumed," *Journal of Developing Societies*, 2:1–11, 1986.

McAuley, Alastair, *Women's Work and Wages in the Soviet Union*. London: George Allen & Unwin, 1981.

Morton, Henry W., and Robert Stuart, eds., *The Contemporary Soviet City*. Armonk, NY: M. E. Sharpe, Inc., 1984.

Moskva v tsifrakh, 1985 (Moscow in Figures, 1985). Moscow: Finansy i statistika, 1985.

Narodnoye khozyaystvo Leningrada i Leningradskoy oblasti v 10 pyatiletke (National Economy of Leningrad and Leningrad Oblast in the Tenth Five-Year Plan). Leningrad: Lenizdat, 1981.

Narodnoye khozyaystvo SSSR v 1980 g. (National Economy of the USSR in 1980). Moscow: Finansy i statistika, 1981.

Narodnoye khozyaystvo SSSR v 1985 g. (National Economy of the USSR in 1985). Moscow: Finansy i statistika, 1986.

Pravda, Alex, "Is There a Soviet Working Class?" *Problems of Communism*, 31, 6:1–24, 1982.

Statistical Abstract of the United States, 1986. Washington, D.C.: U.S. Government Printing Office, 1985.

Walder, Andrew, *Communist Neo-Traditionalism. Work and Authority in Chinese Industry*. Berkeley: University of California Press, 1986.

Yanowitch, Murray, ed., *Soviet Work Attitudes*. White Plains, N.Y.: M. E. Sharpe, Inc., 1979.

Zaslavskaya, T. I., "Ekonomika skvoz' prizmu sotsiologii (Economics Through the Prism of Sociology)," *Ekonomika i organizatsiya promyshlennogo proizvodstva*, 7:3–22, 1985.

———, "Chelovecheskiy faktor razvitiya ekonomiki i sotsial'naya spravedlivost' (The

Human Factor in the Development of the Economy and Social Justice)," *Kommunist,* 13:61–73, 1986a.

————, "Tvorcheskaya aktivnost' mass: sotsial'nyye reservy razvitiya (The Creative Activeness of the Masses: Social Reserves of Development)," *Ekonomika i organizatsiya promyshlennogo proizvodstva,* 3:3–25, 1986b.

Part II

The Politics and Adversities of Change

The Politics and Adversities of Change: An Introduction

Timothy J. Colton

AN OFT-REPEATED native pun about Gorbachev's reforms is that his *perestroyka*, or high-minded "restructuring," opened with *perebranka*, Russian for "wrangling," and ended in *perestrelka*, or "crossfire." The play on words draws attention to three key characteristics of Soviet affairs since March 1985: the extent to which political activity, long practiced on the sly, has become an exuberantly public exercise in the USSR; the vigor and even violence with which politics has erupted into conflict; and the tendency for Mikhail Gorbachev to find himself in the middle of the exchange, facing fire from all quarters. The struggle in which he has been caught up has been about the essence of *perestroyka* itself and, through that, about no less than the future of state socialism and of the Soviet Union.

The 19th Conference of the Communist Party, convened in Moscow in June of 1988, was one of the first occasions on which the full scope and magnitude of the disagreements began to come into view. It is the subject of the first pair of the five chapters that follow in this section of *Milestones in Glasnost' and Perestroyka*.

Just the October preceding the conference, Boris Yel'tsin, then the head of the Moscow CPSU organization and a candidate member of the Politburo, had taken Gorbachev to task at a plenary session of the party Central Committee about what he submitted was the slow pace and compromising content of *perestroyka*. At the time, only a tendentious official account of the incident and of Yel'tsin's subsequent dismissal and humiliation was released. The 19th Conference, by contrast, was high political burlesque. Here was Gorbachev moving a brace of constitutional revisions, Yel'tsin crossing swords with Yegor Ligachev, other delegates demanding the dismissal of Andrey Gromyko and other high officials tainted by Leonid Brezhnev's "era of stagnation"—and all of it piped into tens of millions of Soviet living rooms by state television.

Chapter 6, excerpted from a *Soviet Economy* roundtable, discusses delegate selection and other preparations for the 19th Conference, General Secretary Gorbachev's objectives, the agenda of the conference and the ensuing debate, and the resolutions adopted as well as other results and consequences of the meeting.

Thane Gustafson of Georgetown University and Ed A. Hewett and Victor H. Winston, the editors of this volume, agreed on the candor and relative sophistication suffusing most of the conference's proceedings.[1] They concurred also on the difficulty of interpreting the event's impact in an unambiguous way. Gustafson, in particular, noted the disorganization of the procedures for choosing delegates, Gorbachev's apparent inability to win consent for a purge of the CPSU Central Committee, and the seeming contradiction between Gorbachev's support for competitive elections and his reassertion of the vanguard role of the party.

Chapter 7 reproduces an article on the politics of the 19th Conference and its aftermath by Jerry F. Hough of Duke University and The Brookings Institution, whose views on the Soviet scene were liberally cited at the roundtable. Hough contended that the most important outcome of the conference was the continued consolidation of Gorbachev's power. Conceding some awkwardness in explaining the lack of expulsion of "lame ducks" (retired officials) from the Central Committee, he wrote that this was at least balanced by news of the retirement of CPSU functionaries tied to Ligachev, Gorbachev's rather more conservative deputy, in the weeks after the conference.

Jerry Hough's use of Kremlinological evidence is a useful corrective to any tendency to place exclusive weight on what Soviet leaders say, as distinct from what they do. He closed his essay with the speculation that Gorbachev "has a scenario in mind" for removing aggrieved retirees from the Central Committee— precisely what happened the following April, when Gorbachev prevailed on more than 100 pensioners to submit their resignations. Hough's companion "guess" that Gorbachev's main concern at the conference and at other times was with economic reform, and that political change was used to divert others' attention "onto safe battlegrounds" while economic choices were being sorted out, will perhaps ring less true for many readers today. Nor will all necessarily be persuaded by Hough's judgment that the power struggle in the 1980s was being played by essentially the same rules as in previous decades. Georgiy Razumovskiy, whom Hough portrays as Gorbachev's "most trusted lieutenant" and as having been elevated to *de facto* second secretary of the CPSU in 1988, was to be retired, together with Ligachev, at the 28th CPSU Congress in July 1990. Nonetheless, Hough's chapter remains a fascinating contribution to the debate.

Questions about Gorbachev's intentions and power, and about the larger process unfolding around him, were the substance of a *Soviet Economy* roundtable held in Moscow in November 1988. Chapter 8 of this volume presents insights proffered at the roundtable by Andrey D. Sakharov, Yelena Bonner, Stephen F. Cohen of Princeton University, as well as by Ed A. Hewett and Victor H. Winston.[2]

---

1. Other valuable contributions to the 19th Conference roundtable not reproduced in either volume of *Milestones in Glasnost' and Perestroyka* included those of Gur Ofer of Hebrew University, Steven Shabad of Newsweek, Inc., and Jan Vanous of Planecon, Inc. (see The 19th Conference, 1988; The Aftermath, 1988).

2. The companion volume of *Milestones in Glasnost' and Perestroyka* carries comments made at the roundtable by three other Soviet participants. Not reproduced in this book are contributions by Vitaliy Korotich, Aleksandr Avelichev, Leonid Batkin, Aleksandr Gel'man, Vladimir Glotov, Igor Klyamkin, Gregory Massell, Peter Reddaway, Steven Shabad, and David K. Shipler (see Supporters, 1988).

Academician Sakharov's remarks, made thirteen months before his untimely death, find the greatest resonance in 1991. It was Sakharov's view that the defining issue in Soviet politics is not whether there should be a *perestroyka* but what form it should take. He boiled the possibilities down to a triad, which he termed "Stalinism," "enlightened monarchy," and "democracy, coming from below." Sakharov's reading of the draft constitutional amendments released since the 19th Conference inclined him to the view that the monarchic outcome was a strong possibility. This held the supreme danger, Sakharov said, that Soviet progress and "the fate of our country" would depend absolutely on one person, Gorbachev, and that all could be lost if that benign monarch lost power or changed direction.

A major theme in the roundtable was the interplay in *perestroyka* between internal and foreign policy issues. Stephen Cohen observed that one of Gorbachev's self-assumed tasks was reducing the drag of the East-West cold war on the domestic economy and society. He also argued that *perestroyka* had its friends and foes within the United States and that a comprehensive easing of tensions would entail "new thinking" and bold leadership on the American side as well as the Soviet. Yelena Bonner took exception to several of Cohen's points and made the observation that American "leftists" sometimes insist on looking at Gorbachev's Soviet Union "with their eyes closed." Stephen Cohen, evidently one of the leftists Bonner had in mind, objected. Readers can judge for themselves who got the better of the exchange, and can see through it the extent to which Soviet and American appraisals of changing realities in the USSR were starting to overlap and intermingle.

In hindsight, it is of interest that neither of the roundtables conducted in 1988 was greatly concerned with issues flowing from the Soviet Union's extraordinary ethnic diversity. Mikhail Gorbachev has since said that he underestimated the nationality issue and took insufficient account of it until it had already become inflamed. The same might be said of the Western Sovietological community.

The riot of December 1986 in Alma-Ata, Kazakhstan, was the first major outbreak of the ethnic disorder since Gorbachev's accession. The Azerbaijan-Armenian dispute over Nagorno-Karabakh, an Armenian enclave within Azerbaijan, heated up with a vengeance in the spring of 1988. Shortly before the 19th Party Conference, Baltic nationalism also began to stir, and before 1988 was out, mass-based "popular fronts" had taken shape in all three Baltic republics. This revival of nationalist feelings was weakly represented at the CPSU's conference and, naturally enough, not discussed in detail at the *Soviet Economy* roundtable following it.[3]

At the Moscow roundtable in November 1988, as can be seen in the excerpt

---

3. See the exchange at the roundtable (The Aftermath, pp. 218–220) between Ed Hewett and Jan Vanous. Responding to a question about possible destabilization resulting from Gorbachev's plan to give more decision-making authority to the republics, Vanous was confident that the problem could be contained. Even the most radical Estonians, he said by way of example, accepted the Soviet framework and the need to transfer some resources into the central budget: "They are not arguing against paying anything. Nor are Armenians or Georgians calling for a free Armenia or a free Georgia. They know that none of these little republics could survive."

in Chapter 7, Andrey Sakharov raised the issue of "separatist tendencies" within the USSR. His response was non-alarmist and liberal: better, he said, "to lose part of our country" than to hold on to non-Russian republics by force and nip decentralization and democracy in the bud.

Chapter 9, by Yitzhak M. Brudny, now of Yale University, was published in *Soviet Economy* in 1989. It examines the specific nationalism—that of the Russians, who still constitute slightly more than 50 percent of the USSR's population—that had least intruded on early treatments of the problem. Brudny's work is based on a close reading of the monthly "thick journals" which have given prominence to Russian nationalist ideas, above all *Nash sovremennik* (Our Contemporary) and *Molodaya gvardiya* (Young Guard). He distinguishes among "conservative nationalists," "radical Slavophiles," and "liberal nationalists," but stresses the prominence among Russian nationalist intellectuals of attitudes hostile to the pluralism of thought and expression that *glasnost'* was bringing into being.

A nagging question about self-identified Russian nationalists is about the breadth of their support among the population. As Brudny shows, Russophile candidates did miserably in the competitive elections to the USSR Congress of People's Deputies in the spring of 1989. In the wake of this defeat, however, nationalist intellectuals were working to build a coalition with established organizations (the trade unions among them) and were cooperating in the establishment of new associations (such as the United Front of Russian Workers, *Ob'yedinennyy front trudyashchikhsya Rossii*, set up in Leningrad in June 1989).

In Chapter 10 of this volume, completed in early 1990, Gail W. Lapidus of the University of California at Berkeley offers a comprehensive assessment of the rising tide of self-assertion by ethnic groups. It is a phenomenon which, she says, "now constitutes a fundamental challenge to the integrity of the Soviet state and the values and institutions that have sustained it."

Lapidus distinguishes among six different types of national problems, based on different patterns of socioeconomic and cultural cleavages: cohesive national movements for political and economic autonomy and independence; conflicts between national groups based on historical grievances; spillovers of economic tension into the ethnic arena; demands for upgrading of ethnic homelands into full union republic status; campaigns for the righting of wrongs committed against national groups in the Stalin era; and Russian nationalism. As Lapidus shows, all of these matters have been discussed and fought over in public since 1987–1988. The ever more unveiled nature of interethnic disagreement has contributed to an erosion of central authority, and this in turn has heartened ethnic spokesmen to press their cases with greater vigor, often in mass movements whose mere existence would have been unthinkable before 1985.

In the year after Lapidus's paper went to press, events in Moscow and the republics have offered backing for her assertion that the nationality question has become "the key dilemma of Soviet politics." Between the spring and autumn of 1990, multi-candidate elections, organized in many instances on a *de facto* party basis, brought independence-minded nationalist groups to power in five of the republics (Armenia, Estonia, Georgia, Latvia, and Lithuania) and had a less clearcut result in several other non-Russian areas. It also gave control of the government of the Russian republic, albeit narrowly, to Democratic Russia, a Westernizing movement whose objectives include extension of RSFSR control over national resources, economic decision making, and social policy on Russian territory. Boris Yel'tsin, chosen chairman of the RSFSR Supreme Soviet in May 1990, has broached bilateral negotiations with the Ukraine and several other receptive republics.

President Gorbachev, in turn, has proposed conversion of the USSR into what he says would be a genuine federation through a new "Union Treaty" between all the republics, and he has used a show of administrative and military force to try to bring nationalists to heel. Concern over the possible disintegrative effects on the constitutional structure seems to have been prime among the considerations that moved him to reject the "Shatalin Plan" for rapid marketization and privatization of the economy in September–October 1990. So it is that the nationality crisis, the uninvited guest at the table for the original makers of *perestroyka*, both feeds on and gives sustenance to the country's other mountainous problems.

REFERENCES

"Supporters and Opponents of Perestroyka: The Second Joint *Soviet Economy* Roundtable," *Soviet Economy*, 4, 4:275–318, October–December 1988.

"The Aftermath of the 19th Conference of the CPSU: A Soviet Economy Roundtable," *Soviet Economy*, 4, 3:181–222, July–September 1988.

"The 19th Conference of the CPSU: A *Soviet Economy* Roundtable," *Soviet Economy*, 4, 2:103–136, April–June 1988.

CHAPTER 6

The 19th Party Conference

Ed A. Hewett
with Thane Gustafson and Victor H. Winston

HEWETT: The 19th Party Conference was a watershed event in Mikhail Gorbachev's *perestroyka*—an exciting event, but one that needs to be viewed with caution. The delegate selection process seemed to be far less democratic than Gorbachev had hoped for; and the resulting composition of the various delegations was far more conservative than he had bargained on. The political reforms introduced at the meeting contain significant contradictions, leaving important questions unanswered; the Central Committee membership remains unchanged, contrary to what most believe to be Gorbachev's intentions. All told however, the conference was a historical event. It may not have been history in the way that we expected, because I thought there would be more substance. But it was clearly the sort of watershed that we will probably look back at and say, it gave the reform process new momentum.

This colloquium will ponder, collectively, the significance of the 19th Party Conference for Gorbachev's reform efforts. The discussion will be organized around general themes embracing the elections, the compromises on the agenda, and Gorbachev's opposition.

THE ELECTIONS

Gorbachev's Objectives

GUSTAFSON: Focusing on Gorbachev's objectives, the idea of the Conference was first broached in his Central Committee plenum speech in January 1987 (*Pravda*, January 28, 1987). He did not discuss in detail what he expected

Excerpts from a transcript of a roundtable on the 19th Conference of the CPSU and its aftermath held on August 11, 1988, at the Brookings Institution in Washington, D.C., under the auspices of the Joint Committee on Soviet Studies of the American Council of Learned Societies and the Social Science Research Council, which provided financial support. Substantially all the material in this chapter was first published in *Soviet Economy*, 1988, 4, 2, pp. 103–136 and 3, pp. 181–222. [Eds.]

from such a conference until June 1987 (*Pravda*, June 26, 1987). At that point he elaborated quite a bit on what purpose party conferences had served in the past. In so doing, Gorbachev told us, in his own words, what he expected the Conference to achieve and why he was summoning it.

He was frustrated over the resistance to *perestroyka* and he wanted the Party Conference to give him a fresh mandate for economic reform. Gorbachev also expected the Conference to give him a mandate for political reforms that he had hinted at in the January 1987 plenum.

The most eye-catching of his initial pronouncements was the point that party conferences in the past had been used for replacement of personnel. I believe he used the word *popolneniye* (replenishment). After the June 1987 plenum, various spokesmen for Gorbachev elaborated on that theme.

There was a good deal of head-scratching over what a party conference was allowed to do, so articles appeared with learned interpretations of what the party rules had said in various earlier versions going back to 1941 and before. The problem was that for most of the Khrushchev years and early Brezhnev years, the party rules made no provision for conferences at all. It seemed to have been a fossil that had been dropped. Then, later in the Brezhnev period, the party rules once again made a provision for a CPSU conference, but they did not describe what a party conference could do, so there was much debate about that.

Most commentaries cited rules that were in effect during the 1941 Party Conference, which allowed it to replace up to 20 percent of the voting members of the Central Committee with candidate, or nonvoting, members. People like Fyodor Burlatskiy,[1] who supposedly were insiders, were telling foreigners to watch for 20, 25 percent, and if it turned out to be less, then it would be a defeat for Gorbachev.

So it is fairly clear that until the spring of 1988 Gorbachev intended to use the Party Conference to reinforce his power in personnel. He also wanted it to get rid of the so-called dead souls—that is, the people who have lost jobs corresponding to Central Committee membership but have not been officially removed from the Central Committee. By a strange coincidence, the dead souls make up about 20 percent of the Central Committee.

In the spring of 1988, the insiders suddenly began telling us *not* to look for personnel changes. There did not seem to be any single event that prompted this turnabout; it was quite mysterious.

As the Conference approached, there were other indications that Gorbachev's game plan was falling apart. The elections of delegates were postponed by about six weeks amid signs of continuing debate at the top about what a conference would do and how the delegates would be elected. On the eve of the beginning of voting for delegates around the beginning of May, a group of intellectuals headed by Andrey Sakharov sent a petition to Gorbachev urging

---

1. Fedor Burlatskiy, a former aide to Nikita Khrushchev, was at the time a political commentator for *Literaturnaya gazeta*. [Eds.]

him to postpone the Party Conference because it was going to be loaded with conservatives. But the elections went forward, and they seem to have been a glorious mess.

The Election Procedure

GUSTAFSON: The procedures appear to have been somewhat chaotic. Every party committee conducted elections in its own way. Moscow often supplied each *obkom* (*oblastnoy komitet partii*, or oblast party committee) with its own list of notables. Some *obkoms* evidently elected delegates from lists of candidates that were drawn up at *obkom* headquarters. In those cases the elections could fairly be called rigged. But the procedures varied. If there was a common zone of procedure, it was that local bodies—the primary party organizations (PPOs)—voted to elect not delegates but candidates to be delegates, and those lists were forwarded to the next higher level. As a rule, the deciding level was the *obkom*, which actually approved or rejected candidates. Sometimes there was a secret ballot, sometimes there was not.

As a result of this very disorganized procedure throughout the country, 5,000 delegates were elected who, on the whole, had a fairly conservative appearance. A couple of details show that Gorbachev wanted to make sure that certain people were elected and to move against the *obkom* first secretaries who had committed the most egregious, obvious rigging. At the Moscow *gorkom* (*gorodskoy komitet partii*, or city party committee), a group of prominent reformers was not elected in the early rounds; so Gorbachev himself and a group of Politburo members went next door to the *gorkom* on Staraya Ploshchad'[2] and made sure that, at a meeting of the *gorkom*, a number of these people were included.

Those who never did make it included Gorbachev's adviser Academician Tat'yana Zaslavskaya, the venerable authority on Russian culture Academician Dmitriy Likhachev, economist Gavriil Popov, poet Yevgeniy Yevtushenko, dramatist Mikhail Shatrov, and economist Nikolay Shmelev (*Pravda*, June 30, 1988, p. 1).

As with Supreme Soviet elections, delegates were parceled out to various districts they had never been to in their lives, but the people I mentioned who were not elected were at the Conference as "representatives" of the public. Likhachev was repeatedly interviewed.[3] Shmelev and Zaslavskaya were also mentioned (*Pravda*, June 30, 1988, p. 1) as *predstaviteli obshchestvennosti* (representatives of the public). But the list of delegates has not been published yet.

---

2. Staraya Ploshchad' (Old Square) is the site of Central Committee headquarters and Gorbachev's office. [Eds.]

3. At the press conference, he severely criticized the anti-semitically oriented historic-patriotic society Pamyat'. [Eds.]

Voting Irregularities

GUSTAFSON: In other areas, when the delegate selection obviously went awry, it would appear that Central Committee staff—under the supervision of Razumovskiy[4]—moved to set things right. Let me cite some specific instances. There were four places where the rigging seems to have been so outrageous that public protests took place. Whether those protests were inspired from Moscow is an interesting question.

In one case, the long-term first secretary of the Yaroslavl' *obkom*, Fedor Loshchenkov, who is an old crony of Ligachev's, was elected as a delegate under these procedures. This caused such a hue and cry that the *obkom* was summoned, and Loshchenkov was "unelected." This reversal was doubly fascinating because he had been given a cushy job in the Council of Ministers' State Committee for Material Reserves. Yet his election was reversed. So much for Ligachev's clout.

In three other provinces, the abuses were so considerable that the *obkom* first secretaries were dismissed: Sakhalin, Kuybyshev, and Astrakhan'. In all three cases, the first secretary was a holdover from the Brezhnev era, and in all three cases they were replaced by people associated either with Gorbachev and Stavropol' connections or with Razumovskiy and Krasnodar connections. In all these instances, there were popular demonstrations, including a street rally in Kuybyshev and a meeting in the stadium in Sakhalin. I believe the delegation to the Conference was also changed in Sakhalin, but I don't know about the others. Presumably rigging occurred in many other places and Moscow may have tried to take action, but these are the four cases we know of.

Grassroots power was in evidence and pressure was exerted from below; the press reported on this pretty substantially. There was a great deal of marching and waving of banners and shouting at meetings, and in many cases that kind of pressure seems to have worked. I know of secret balloting, multiple candidates and so forth, but my impression is that, by and large, the *obkoms* managed to hold the lines through the procedures I described.

And yes, there was some rigging in places where the "liberals"—whatever that means—dominated. For example, in the elections held in the USSR Writers Union, Moscow section, the liberals were substantially in control, and they prevented the election of conservatives. In a number of *obkoms*, there are now first secretaries who are recent Gorbachev appointees. Interestingly, the proportion of elected scientists was relatively substantial.

WINSTON: And they were visible. There were at least seven speakers at the Conference who may have represented the scientific community. The President of the Academy of Sciences of the USSR, Academician Guriy I. Marchuk, spoke of the internationalization of scientific knowledge, clearly in favor of

---

4. Georgiy Razumovskiy, secretary in charge of organizational party work for the Central Committee and a candidate member of the Politburo, was chairman of the Credentials Commission at the Party Conference. [Eds.]

strengthening ties with his counterparts in the West. Interestingly, while comparing the scientific potential of the Soviet Union with that of the United States, he noted the relatively low productivity of Soviet scientists, estimating his country's potential in this area as being five times lower than America's (*Pravda*, July 1, 1988, pp. 2–3). Then there were the speeches of Georgiy A. Arbatov and Yevgeniy M. Primakov.[5] Roal'd Z. Sagdeyev, who heads the Academy's Institute of Space Research, participated officially only in the discussion and did not deliver a speech. Also among the elected delegates identified with science who later spoke at the Conference were Anatoliy A. Logunov, rector of Moscow State University; Gennadiy A. Yagodin, director of the State Committee on Public Education; Svyatoslav V. Federov (a surgeon); and, of course, Academician Leonid I. Abalkin, who received what some consider an unambiguous reprimand from Gorbachev.

The Role of *Obkoms*

GUSTAFSON: The elections were disorganized. My impression is that the *obkoms* were the overall winners. In terms of Gorbachev's objectives, he did not achieve what he wanted on personnel turnover, and he largely lost control of the delegate selection. The 4,991 delegates who appeared at the Palace of Congresses were, on the whole, a conservative bunch, and that showed in the patterns of applause, in the types of speeches, in the exchanges that took place. This may have been due to a political misjudgment, because Gorbachev did not pay enough attention to the process, or he may have been outmaneuvered and forced to compromise.

HEWETT: I think it is more likely he was outmaneuvered. How could he not pay attention to it? It was written up in the newspaper every day.

GUSTAFSON: Because the process had already gotten under way. For example, one early question was whether delegates would be selected by *obkom* plenums or *obkom* conferences. An *obkom* plenum would consist of official members who were previously elected; an *obkom* conference would be a kind of *ad hoc* gathering consisting of delegates elected separately, and it presumably would be less conservative. As early as the summer of 1987, commentaries suggested that the decision had been made to have the selection done by *obkom* plenums (Malyayev and Popov, 1987). So the prospect was raised already at that time that the process would be difficult to control.

One of Gorbachev's main objectives was to reach over the heads of the party apparatus to the party rank and file—and even outside the ranks of party members and play both ends against the middle. One way to accomplish that might have been to leave the *obkoms* out of the process altogether and let

5. Respectively, the feuding directors of the Institute for the Study of the USA and Canada and of the Institute of the World Economy and International Relations of the USSR Academy of Sciences. [Eds.]

delegates be elected at meetings of primary party organizations that nonparty members would be allowed to attend.

When a PPO holds a public meeting, incidentally, nonparty members are invited and given the right to vote. In fact, in a number of places that is exactly what happened. But instead of having the PPOs nominate candidates whose names would be forwarded to the *obkom*, the delegates could have been elected directly at the local level. For some reason I am not aware of, that was not done.

COMPROMISES ON THE AGENDA

GUSTAFSON: Compromises on the agenda are a fascinating subject, because, as far as I can tell, Gorbachev got exactly the agenda he wanted, without any essential changes. There were some reports, however, of dissenting votes. For example, there was a good deal of debate about the resolution on combining posts at the local level. As you recall, the provision is that in these newly beefed-up soviets, the chairman will be the *obkom* first secretary of the area or the corresponding party first secretary of the locality. According to some reports, as many as 200 delegates voted against that resolution, voting, in effect, against Gorbachev. They were liberals in particular, I think, at least that was the implication in an interview with Olzhas Suleymenov, the head of the Kazakh Writers Union, but he did not go into detail (*Literaturnaya gazeta*, July 13, 1988, p. 3).

In terms of the current political situation in the USSR, I think there was a compromise and a half. The one full compromise was on personnel turnover. I believe that the resolutions now make it official policy that future party conferences at all levels have the right to renew as much as 20 percent of the membership of the corresponding *gorkom*, *obkom* or, for that matter, the Central Committee.

This outcome suggests that, rather than losing on the issue, Gorbachev simply temporized. We know that the Central Committee adopted its theses, or proposals, before the Party Conference without this 20-percent provision. But we don't know if Gorbachev ducked the issue at that meeting, or tried to get the Central Committee to include it and failed. Presumably it had been thrashed out in the Politburo, and Gorbachev knew where it stood.

The *Ustav*, as currently written, contains no provision for automatic renewal of 20 percent of the membership (*Pravda*, March 7, 1986). But such a provision did exist in the 1939 version of the *Ustav*, which has been changed repeatedly. In fact, one could construct an entire *Ustav* genealogy. The last party conference, in 1941, still had the power to renew 20 percent (Khlevnyuk, 1988; Mann, 1988). But sometime in the 1950s the party conference was eliminated from the *Ustav* altogether (Malyayev and Popov, 1987). There was no reference to it at all for over a decade. Then, I believe in 1966, a new version of the *Ustav* restored the reference to a party conference, but did not spell out what its purpose was. Finally, the current version of the *Ustav* says only that the powers of a party conference will be defined by the Central Committee.

One can infer from all this that these matters were debated at the Central Committee plenum held a month before the Party Conference. A Politburo announcement in the beginning of April said the structure of the Party Conference had been debated within the Politburo. Then the Politburo presumably submitted to the Central Committee a resolution that contained the compromises it had struck.

Incidentally, in the weeks leading up to the Party Conference there were no reports of Politburo meetings. They just vanished from their usual weekly place in the press.

HEWETT: They did, but that was also during the period of the Reagan-Gorbachev summit, when the Politburo tends not to meet.

GUSTAFSON: True; now regarding the half-compromise, it is a difficult one to interpret because of the storm of criticism over *glasnost'* that came from all the voices at the Conference itself. The most extreme was Ligachev, who got up and called, in effect, for the dismissal of Vitaliy Korotich and Yegor Yakovlev[6] (*Pravda*, July 2, 1988, p. 11). Gorbachev responded to this with compromise language, saying, "Yes, we must not offend people; Yes, the criticism must be balanced and factual." Since then, he seems to have backed away from any compromise language, and in his plenum speech (*Pravda*, July 30, 1988, pp. 1–3),[7] in fact, he takes a few swipes at Yuriy Bondarev, the Russian nationalist writer who blasted the liberal press at the Party Conference (*Pravda*, July 1, 1988, pp. 3–4). And there is no sign that Korotich and Yakovlev are in danger of losing their jobs.

OPPONENTS OF *PERESTROYKA*

GUSTAFSON: How should we understand these compromises? Jerry Hough has made two arguments about Gorbachev's power and the course of reform from the beginning (Hough, 1988). One of them is that Western scholars as a group underestimate the institutional power of the General Secretary. He says we simply underestimate his power to control the agenda, to control the action, and even to control personnel. Therefore we should not be surprised that, even in dealing with such a seemingly conservative crowd as this one, Gorbachev carried everything that he wanted through the Politburo, through the Central Committee, and through the Party Conference and is now charging ahead with his agenda for change.

Hough's second point is that we in the West have consistently misjudged the nature of the opposition to Gorbachev. His argument is startling at first, but I have been pondering it recently, and I think it makes a lot of sense. His point is that Gorbachev's worst opponents are the intellectuals and his best

6. Respectively, the editors of *Ogonyok* and of *Moskovskiye novosti*. [Eds.]
7. The plenum convened on July 29, 1988. [Eds.]

friends are the bureaucrats. One's initial reaction is: What's all this? But his argument applies to the long term; he says that in the long run there is no satisfying intellectuals.

Ten years from now, according to Hough, the intellectuals will have realized that Gorbachev—reformer though he may be—is nevertheless an Establishment man, and they will oppose him. Wherever Gorbachev draws the line, the intellectuals will want to keep going.

The Bureaucrats

GUSTAFSON: But my point now has to do with the bureaucrats. Jerry Hough has insisted for some time that the bureaucrats are basically, first of all, Western oriented and much more modern than we give them credit for; second, they have a reformist half to them; third, they know there's no going back. In other words, they buy the essence of the Gorbachev argument.

They are uncomfortable over *glasnost'* and the excesses of *perestroyka*. Yet they are basically behind Gorbachev's reformist program—as is Ligachev. So Jerry would argue that it is no surprise that, given the power of the General Secretary and the basically hospitable attitude of the bureaucrats, even this stacked group of delegates would go along and give Gorbachev essentially what he wanted.

Now let me present the view of Michel Tatu, who is writing the lead article on the Party Conference in the September issue of *Problems of Communism*. I predict that he will say that the Party Conference proves him right, that his basic description in his book on Gorbachev last winter is still valid (Tatu, 1987). His argument is that Gorbachev faces such strong resistance from the bureaucrats and from within his own Politburo and Central Committee that he is, in effect, paralyzed.

The reason Gorbachev got the agenda he wanted, according to Tatu, is that the bureaucrats know, just as they knew under Khrushchev, that the old men can redraw the organization chart, but it does not make an ounce's worth of difference. Let him eat politics; let him eat reform. Meanwhile we bureaucrats, who have the real power, will make sure that this reorganization does not get out of hand.

The two-hats arrangement between the party committees and the soviets is the clearest sign of compromise in this case. It ensures that, no matter what games Gorbachev wishes to play with the soviets, the *obkom* first secretary will be there to make sure that essentially nothing changes. For Tatu, the key speech of the Conference would be Ligachev's, in which he dismissed the entire reorganization agenda with two comments. First, we must proceed "*osmotritel'no*" (circumspectly); the second derisive comment was that politics is "not like slurping down cabbage soup." It was, in other words, not even a *pro forma* endorsement of the reorganization plan. It was about as cold a comment as one could make.

That is the Tatu version. I must say, I am more and more impressed with Jerry Hough's argument. Tatu's analysis is very sound. But Hough's analysis is very insightful and stimulating, and I agree with it.

HEWETT: I understand that you can never satisfy the intellectuals; Jerry alerted us all to that. But I don't see the other half of the proposition—that the bureaucrats, in the long run, are Westernizers and they really have an interest in reform.

Just because you cannot satisfy the intellectuals, does not mean you will ever be able to satisfy the bureaucrats. The Soviet bureaucrats I know tend to be a distressingly conservative lot. They may admire Western consumer goods, but I see little inclination that—as a group—they support the tough reforms needed to radically alter the system and their role in it. Are you saying that you also agree with that part of the Hough thesis?

GUSTAFSON: I am impressed by it, up to a point. I think we have also underestimated the extent of the economic mess at the time of the Gorbachev succession. Everything we have been reading in the Soviet press since then suggests that a bureaucrat with eyes to see would agree that you cannot go back. You have to go forward. Therefore one has to have *perestroyka* of some kind. I think this is also essentially Peter Reddaway's argument in his recent *New York Review of Books* article (Reddaway, 1988). He says there is no conservative opposition in the Soviet Union today.

What we are dealing with are variations on *perestroyka*: a conservative-reform party group, or shall we say, a restrained-reform party group. Tatu, by the way, does not disagree with that. He does not think there are conservatives in the Politburo, either. His shorthand description of the Politburo is that it contains Andropovians and a small handful of Gorbachevians.

On balance, I am impressed with Jerry's argument that the party apparatus is not necessarily opposed to reform. I am more uncertain about his argument that the bureaucrats as a group are not necessarily the enemies of reform. But I am struck by something Jerry Hough has been writing for almost twenty years now: that we make the mistake of thinking of the party as more monolithic than it is. We overlook the cleavages within it. We overlook the possible reason why the party might support a change in the distribution of functions at the local level.

I am struck by the fact that Gorbachev and other speakers, such as Ligachev, seemed very concerned about delivering the message to the party that the leadership is not going to tolerate any challenge to its privileges. If anything, it is inclined to try to raise wages for party workers. It is concerned about stressing the party's vanguard role, no matter how the reforms go in the future; about safeguarding the real importance of the party apparatus at the local level; and about increasing the powers of the rank and file.

This runs through all of Gorbachev's recent speeches, and I think this may be the best way to put it: one should not necessarily think of the party apparatus and party officialdom as the enemy.

HEWETT: In essence, *perestroyka* has become a meaningless word because it is about everything, and therefore everyone can support *perestroyka*. Ligachev can genuinely say he supports the goals of *perestroyka*, as can Yakovlev. The disagreement is over the methods to be used in moving toward those goals. A major point I make about bureaucrats in my book (Hewett, 1988) is that the system they are working in naturally leads them to do many things in apparent opposition to the goals of *perestroyka*, and Gorbachev's own decrees have reinforced that tendency.

At the Party Conference Gorbachev said he held the Machine-Building Bureau and the ministries under it directly responsible for the slow pace of modernization. This is the man who is talking about the need for ministries to stay out of the affairs of enterprises, yet he says they are personally responsible for failures in the modernization program.

Now, if I am a bureaucrat in that system, even a well-meaning one, I am going to act in a certain way. What I would do, based on my experience, what I know, and what I think will work, all run counter to the decentralizing aspects of *perestroyka*.

The Common Enemy

WINSTON: I recently encountered in Moscow a very interesting neologism—*tormozitel'*[8] of *perestroyka*. It is a portmanteau combining *tormozheniye* with *vreditel'* (evildoer)—the word consistently used to whip up passions during Stalin's hate campaigns. But while the *vreditel'* of yesteryear was a certifiable adversary and also a moving target—the counterrevolutionary in the 1920s, the saboteur in the 1930s, etc.—the *tormozitel'* of the late 1980s is an amorphous hybrid, neither too clearly identified with any of the loosely defined groups, nor with any of the well defined groups. As a conceptual term, it seems to fill the bill for the bureaucrat who worries about his tenure, for the corrupt bureaucrat, and for the member of the Soviet mafia.

Since the party apparatchiks who stage-managed the Conference for TV and other audiences had to be sure that a live enemy was in reserve for everybody to pounce on (not unlike our party apparatchiks who had to orchestrate bursts of wall-to-wall solidarity at the Democratic Convention in Atlanta), a suitable whipping boy had to be in place. With the shopworn "American imperialism" mercifully gone—at least for the present—it might have been very difficult to establish a credible villain. But a powerful common enemy had surfaced in time thanks to the relentless, anti-corruption campaign spearheaded by the media. He was, of course, duly noted and condemned, directly or indirectly,

---

8. This Russian neologism, as yet not in the dictionary, is derived from *tormozheniye* (literally, applying brakes), which can be logically perceived as an antonym of *uskoreniye* (*uskoreniye's* more literal antonym is *zamedleniye*—deceleration). It may be joining the increasing array of lingustic hallmarks of the Gorbachev era. [Eds.]

by Gorbachev and Ligachev, by Korotich and Bondarev, and by most of the other delegates and participants.

Hard evidence of massive corruption has only recently been declassified and moved into the public domain. It is by no means a new item on the agendas of Soviet party meetings, but now it is on display in most newspapers, weekly magazines and particularly in *Ogonyok*, to be read and talked about almost every day of the week. In fact *Ogonyok's* editor, Vitaliy Korotich, prepared for the Conference agenda a virtual bombshell in the form of documents disclosing the names of four participating delegates about to be indicted on charges of bribe taking (FBIS, 1988, p. 39).

Most recently, *Literaturnaya gazeta* and particularly *Trud* have opened their pages to a vigorous and consistent flow of reportage featuring remarkable disclosures, statistics, and case studies of pervasive corruption in Soviet bureaucratic fiefdoms; such fiefdoms are said to breed and harbor Communists with a taste for flawless diamond rings and even lust for such eccentricities as safety deposit boxes in Western banks. The flow of information is so heavy that, for example, during the first week of this month *Trud* alone published three stories detailing estimates of tax evasion by illegal traders allegedly depriving the country of 3 to 5 percent of its national income (Osipenko, 1988); confessions of two formerly bemedaled party and state leaders in Uzbekistan— behind bars for payoffs and graft (Dmitriyev and Mayorov, 1988); and exposés of grand larceny and fraud in cooperative enterprises (Kislinskaya and Snegirev, 1988).[9]

In Gorbachev's strong hands, corruption is not only a useful scapegoat to unify (even if only temporarily) the bureaucrats and the intellectuals, but also an enemy of long standing to be strangled and then somehow resuscitated and co-opted into the new cooperative sector of the economy—away from the *tenevaya ekonomika*[10] mentioned in his opening speech (*Pravda*, June 29, 1988, p. 2). Gorbachev's experience in dealing with the issue can be traced to the anti-corruption campaign of Yuriy Andropov, whose full confidence he apparently earned and deserved (e.g., Medvedev, 1986, pp. 121, 126–127, 135). Legal training also may have added to his qualifications and ability to fumigate their Tammany Halls. But is Gorbachev prepared to focus on the common enemy's most lethal representative—the minions of organized crime in the USSR?

In the days when crime in the USSR was only rarely reported (and then mostly as occurrences traced to some "unsavory influences" from the West), it was not possible to visualize that criminal gangs were organized and that a great deal of professionalism similar to that of our *cosa nostra*, was very much

9. Within a day after the discussion at the roundtable meeting (i.e., on August 12, 1988), *Trud* published an estimate by a Gosplan economist to the effect that the country's shadow economy accounts for an annual turnover in excess of 70 billion rubles (Mostovshchikov, 1988). [Eds.]

10. Literally, the shadow economy which encompasses the shadow and the second economies—both first differentiated and clearly defined in the literature by Gregory Grossman (e.g., Grossman, 1977; 1979). [Eds.]

in evidence. And so, hand in hand with the corrupt bureaucrat, comes the new breed identified with the criminal mafias—a common enemy with guns to kill. At the Conference, the word "mafia" was mentioned in no fewer than three speeches—by Boris Yel'tsin (*Pradva*, July 2, 1988, p. 2), Vitaliy Korotich (FBIS, 1988, p. 39), and Viktor Postnikov, an agricultural executive from Stavropol'—from Gorbachev's former domain (*Pravda*, July 1, 1988, p. 5).

This past July, a random sprinkling of statistical detail in *Literaturnaya gazeta* (Shchekochikhin and Gurov, 1988) gave us a glimpse of mafia connections with the economy's new enterprise forms such as the reconstituted cooperatives.[11] One of the authors, a middle-ranking officer of the militia and graduate student at Moscow State University, has just defended his Ph.D. dissertation devoted to organized crime. He interviewed 109 detectives assigned to squads that handle organized crime, seeking their views about mafia activities that may be attributed to the development of producer cooperatives. Eighty-one percent of the respondents singled out extortion as the major growth area (they call it *reket*); 52 percent highlighted protection of cooperatives from extortion; while 22 percent—that's the most interesting part—focused on laundering (*otmyvaniye*) of illicit profits by investing in cooperatives. The clear implication from this fascinating opinion survey is that organized crime is as firmly entrenched in the USSR as it is in America.

Truly amazing comparisons shed some light on criminal lifestyles and profits. In 1958–1959, presumably official RSFSR sources reported the average annual losses from what was called "economic crime" within a range of 1.5 million to 2 million rubles. But at present, these amounts are about equal to "what a successful burglar makes in one year." Judging by such examples as 500,000-ruble stakes in card games, or a traced 300,000-ruble bribe offered to a militia detective, the authors suggest revenues in the billions of rubles. And they talk not only about crime in Moscow and Leningrad, but mention Kiev and Odessa, less prominent urban centers like L'vov, Donetsk, and Dnepropetrovsk, and even such typical Russian Peorias as Tambov, Penza, Yaroslavl', and Perm'. "The south is our Klondike," one of the authors says, and "Uzbekistan is not the only area."

HEWETT: A very interesting article. It confirms Gregory Grossman's thesis that organized crime was extremely important. So you believe that the mafia is one of the common enemies?

WINSTON: I do, though it could be a relatively marginal component of the enemy camp. And even though honest bureaucrats who need not fear Lubyanka[12] should be on the other side of the fence, I think that some, particularly the pencil pushers—in their late 50s and early 60s—the least productive ones whose job security is in jeopardy—have much in common with the "common

---

11. Reinvigorated by the draft law on cooperatives (Ryzhkov, 1988), more or less similar cooperatives also existed for a time prior to 1961 when they were abolished. [Eds.]

12. A prison complex. [Eds.]

enemy." They yearn for the relative stability of the Brezhnev era, and the public views them as *tormoziteli* of *perestroyka*—the unrelenting opponents of *glasnost'* and proponents of *status quo ante*.

BASIC THEMES OF THE CONFERENCE

HEWETT: That is undoubtedly interesting material. Let us now talk about some of the less sensational but no less significant subjects addressed by the Conference. We know that five commissions were created to handle six topics at the Conference (*Pravda*, July 2, 1988, pp. 1, 12). The first, which was chaired by Gorbachev, was looking at both the resolution on implementation of the decisions of the 27th Party Congress and the resolution on democratization of Soviet society and reform of the political system. Then there were commissions concerned with the battle with the bureaucracy, chaired by Yegor Ligachev; international relations, chaired by Prime Minister Nikolay Ryzhkov; *glasnost'*, chaired by Aleksandr Yakovlev; and legal reform, chaired by Andrey Gromyko. Economic reform, to the extent that it was discussed, was in that first omnibus commission.

There were 150 speakers at these commissions, more than twice the number as at the Party Conference itself. They apparently met contemporaneously with the Party Conference itself over those four days, and we know people were sometimes gone from the podium to attend some of these commission meetings. Gorbachev himself was gone sometimes, and someone else was chairing. The only results we have seen from these commissions are the final resolutions (*Pravda*, July 5, 1988).

The Conference "Theses"

GUSTAFSON: Those resolutions were foreshadowed by a list of ten "theses," or proposals, that were published before the Conference. Let me try to group them by the most significant themes.

The first is the attempt to change the functions of the party and to strengthen correspondingly the soviets at all levels. This is the most radical proposal of all, with important implications for economic policy. What is being proposed is an end to the economic functions of the party at the local level, at least as they are exercised through branch departments in the local party committees.

There are two questions about this proposal. First, can these functions be dispensed with? That strikes me as the crucial question about this whole package.

Second, if those functions can indeed be dispensed with, what does that do to the power of the party? I have believed for a long time that the power of the party grows out of those local functions. To the extent that the CPSU apparatus keeps the command economy on a somewhat even keel through its local functions, its power is born every day. If those functions are eliminated, one of two things will happen. Either the party will begin to lose power at the local level—and that is actually happening to some extent in Yugoslavia, where those functions have been considerably weakened. Or those functions will be reborn: the branch departments will rise again by another name, but within the CPSU apparatus, and things will go on essentially as before.

If I am wrong—if the power of the party in some sense originates from habit or comes from the top down—then perhaps those functions can be eliminated without any change in the essential balance of power. In that case perhaps the CPSU apparatus at the local level will not resist the changes. So the first theme in the proposals is the transfer of those economic functions to the local soviets.

Number two, and even more sweeping in its long-term implications, is the notion that one can put the Soviet government on a full legal footing. This is the theme of the *pravovoye gosudarstvo*, which I suppose would be "government of law" in English. But people in the West seem to be using the German term, *rechtsstaat*.

There is a fundamental contradiction here, because in the same breath Gorbachev reasserts the vanguard role of the party. He cannot have it both ways. If he is talking about a state of laws based ultimately on popular sovereignty, backed up in some cases with plebiscites, in other cases with voting, he cannot at the same time talk about the vanguard role of the party. We have here the political equivalent to what Janos Kornai says about the economy: you either look up to the bureaucrat or you look down to the consumer (Kornai, 1986). In politics, you either look up to the party or you look down to the voter.

Yet Gorbachev charges ahead, so this second group of themes clustered around the creation of a *rechtsstaat* is, in the long run, extraordinarily important for the shape of the Soviet state.

Democratization of the Party

GUSTAFSON: The third, and last, broad theme is the democratization of the party itself. The key notion here is that the CPSU member will be given a greater role in his dealings with the committees that he supposedly elects. So the *vybornyye organy*, or elective bodies, are to be the great gainers, top to bottom, throughout the system. This applies to the Central Committee in its relations with the Politburo, as well as the PPOs in their relations with their own party committees at the local level.

Secret ballot, multiple candidates, powers of recall and, as a new feature, limited terms of office—the debate over these issues at the Conference was most revealing of Gorbachev's interpretations and intentions.

The theses proposed two terms as a maximum tenure for the General Secretaryship, with the possibility of a third term by a two-thirds majority. There was a lot of sentiment against this at the Conference. Gorbachev was finally obliged to intervene and say, "We are not talking about personalities here."

In the end, the final resolution adopted two terms, with no extension. These proposals taken together, if applied literally, would break the power of the *obkom* first secretary and, conceivably, of the General Secretary himself.

HEWETT: Who precisely would be up for election? That is, how far up the party hierarchy? And who would elect them? Presumably, we are talking about primary party organizations for sure—the bottom links located at factories and other organizations.

GUSTAFSON: Yes, but whether that extends all the way up to the Politburo is not stated explicitly. I suppose it would. We may see the first test in the upcoming "accounting-and-elections" campaign within the CPSU apparatus, which starts in September and runs through December. A cynic would say it is "business as usual." The party puts itself regularly through this campaign, and it goes like a wave at a baseball stadium. It starts at the PPOs, and it goes all the way to the top.

The elected officials get up and give an account of themselves, an *otchet*. This is followed by an election, at which they are either confirmed or removed. In the past, the *otchet* and election were *pro forma*; now it is all supposed to be real.

There are reasons to believe that Gorbachev will proceed with a purge of CPSU members during the campaign in September. However, he says a lot of different things at once. In May, at a Central Committee *soveshchaniye* (conference) he said, "Look, we've had two-thirds turnover at almost all levels of the party since 1985 and we have got to stop, because *perestroyka* is not a waltz of personnel." He said essentially the same thing at the Party Conference and rejected the words of speakers who called for a purge. The "purging" process will not involve turning in party membership cards. There was a call in the theses for a so-called *attestatsiya*, or certification of members, which would have involved turning in party cards, but many speakers got up at the Party Conference and opposed it, and in the resolutions all reference to *attestatsiya* was dropped.

The New Role of the Soviets

HEWETT: We should spend a little time on the proposed shift of power at the local level from the CPSU to the soviets.

GUSTAFSON: Here we have another classic example of a contradiction in the program. Gorbachev presented the "two hats" scheme, under which the chairman of the local soviet would be "elected," but it would be the *obkom* first secretary. He justified this on the grounds that the soviet should be further reinforced with the authority of the party.

Several speakers at the Conference raised the point that a nonmember of the party could be head of the soviet. They said that the "two hats" idea is good in principle, but they wondered what that implies about the elective nature of the chairmanship of the soviet, and wouldn't it be desirable not to rule out in advance that even a nonparty member could become chairman of the local soviet. In the end, I think the resolutions adopted the "two hats" proposal.

HEWETT: The proposal is only a recommendation in the resolution because it has to be considered by the Supreme Soviet. It would mean a change in the law.

WINSTON: It's ironic if you flash back to 1917. The Bolsheviks in Petrograd and Moscow were saying, "All power to the soviets!" More than seventy years have gone by, and that slogan never really came true. Now at the Party Conference in Moscow, with people watching TV in Leningrad, again it is "Power to the soviets!"

HEWETT: The idea that there is another source of power and legitimacy represents a gamble in which even the most important parameters are unknown.

Let me give you an example. The *obkom* first secretaries now have awesome powers, and they are judged by Moscow on the basis of the economic performance of their region. So over a long period they have had a tremendous vested interest in the performance of their region. Now, stripping away all the verbiage, what is being added to that is some formal accountability to the people in the region by these *obkom* first secretaries. Another addition—and here it gets very fuzzy—is somewhat more authority for the local soviets, run by the *obkom* first secretary or local first secretary, over the enterprises in the area. Here it is very unclear what is happening.

The whole new stew may create very powerful bodies—local soviets married to the party—with one primary interest: the welfare of the region. The first consequence of that will be signals from every *obkom* first secretary, who will say, "We support the reform, but not one worker will be fired from one enterprise in our region. Not one enterprise will be closed in our region, because if it is closed I am going to be voted out of office."

So what will be created is an institutionalized opposition to the core of the economic reform. Economic reform is a polite word for closing some enterprises, and for firing people and moving them around.

Another potential consequence will be regional protectionism, such as now exists in China. The difference is that in the Soviet Union it will involve smaller regions, where enterprises will not allow products to come into their area if they are making those products. So, in an economy already highly protected from international competition, with a system in which the ministries also protect themselves, there will now be a third line of protectionism—regional protectionism. That, in turn, suggests an increase in existing tensions between the ministries and the localities that is left totally unresolved in the discussions at the Party Conference.

I think all the talk in the Soviet Union about the "crisis" and why they are not getting anywhere has gotten out of hand. If there is a crisis in the Soviet Union, it is a crisis in theory. These guys haven't thought things through. And the result is enormous chaos.

If you want a model that is probably most helpful in thinking about the

Soviet Union, I think of it as a very big U.S. Department of Defense. And they are setting up what are in effect congressmen out there in the provinces, who are beholden to the population of their areas. Now just think about how our congressmen act when you start talking about cutting defense expenditures. "We support cutting defense expenditures, except in our area!"

CONCLUDING COMMENTS

GUSTAFSON: It is conceivable in principle that we are going to witness a transfer of the *obkom's* power to the regional soviet. The regional soviet will get a budget, full-time functionaries, and all the resources that Gorbachev talked about in his speech. You put the *obkom* first secretary at the top, and you have, in effect, the party apparatus inside the soviet. They could, in fact, continue to rely on *podmena*[13] and micromanage from inside the soviet headquarters.

HEWETT: I don't quite see why this process does not end up destroying the CPSU as we know it and producing a true state, in which factional politics is built around the government.

If I were in the party now, I would wonder if Gorbachev was trying for what one might call the coup of the century, which is to shift the entire power base and recreate a whole new structure centered in the government. Why has he chosen that strategy?

GUSTAFSON: Let me try to sketch for you the range of views among the major political scientists, from one extreme to the other. Tatu is perhaps the firmest in saying that Gorbachev's political strategy has been flawed from the beginning. In fact, Tatu uses the word "naive." In particular, he says Gorbachev's emphasis on *glasnost'* and his reliance on the intelligentsia is a sign of essential weakness and also of political naïveté. In Tatu's view, the man just doesn't know what he is doing (Tatu, 1987).

At the other extreme is Jerry Hough, who is not very far from saying that everything Gorbachev has done fits into a very clear logic that he has thought out in advance. Hough believes it is a brilliant political strategy (Hough, 1988).

It seems to me that one should be able to go back to the speeches of December 1984, April and June 1985, and June 1986, and simply compare them, theme by theme, to see how they have evolved and to what extent *perestroyka* was already present in those early speeches.

I think the right analogy is to compare Gorbachev to a jazz pianist, who is improvising, to be sure, but within a definite key and a definite musical structure. That structure has, by and large, been present since December 1984 or even earlier; it was definitely present in outline in April 1985, and it has remained remarkably intact in his approach ever since.

WINSTON: But historically, at least, Gorbachev's reliance on the intelligentsia makes some sense. Russian intellectuals have played more than a mar-

---

13. *Podmena,* or substitution, is Soviet parlance for displacement of government powers by the party apparatus at the local level (Hough, 1969). [Eds.]

ginal role. The historian Natan Edel'man makes an interesting point: Every time intellectuals have sided with the people in power the revolutions inspired or supported by those in power succeeded. He cites the examples of Peter the Great, Catherine the Great, Alexander I, and Lenin. He argues that Gorbachev is supported by all those whom Aleksandr Griboyedov called *lishniye lyudi* (superfluous people).[14] These are people who are now coming into their own. Interestingly, Edel'man defines Gorbachev's political strategy as another case of a Russian revolution from above.[15]

GUSTAFSON: But Tatu would not agree. Michel Tatu's argument from the beginning has been that Gorbachev has lost his constituency by failing to get the economic benefits flowing, by appealing to an intelligentsia that has little political influence, and by alienating large segments of the population. However, Jerry Hough would argue that, to some extent, a politician should appeal to every Soviet citizen, because they all potentially belong to his constituency if he can appeal to them in the right way (Hough, 1988).

At this point, I would like to bring in a word from Max Weber. What is so entertaining is that Gorbachev's proposed reforms fit right in with a scheme that Weber developed. As one looks at world history, there are really only three basic types of domination: one that he called the traditional mode, basically hereditary kingship. The second is charismatic—basically Mohammed or Lenin. Then there is a third, the legal-rational mode, which was what Weber hoped for in Germany and which was developing there and in other Western countries (Weber, 1968).

The reason I mention this is that there has been some very interesting writing on the evolution of communist systems, such as the piece by Ken Jowitt (1983). Barrington Moore and his followers, he points out, always felt that eventually Soviet totalitarianism would move in the direction of legal-rational authority (Moore, 1954). This is the Westernization thesis, which is also Jerry Hough's argument. Jowitt argues that under Brezhnev we were seeing a kind of perverted return to origins, a sort of neotraditionalism—the clientelism, the corruption, and all the rest of it—a kind of reconstituted Ottoman Empire.

Lately there has been a marvelous book by Andrew Walder (1986) who takes basically the same approach as Jowitt; in fact, they are both Weberians. But Walder says that neotraditionalism is not a corrupt form of Leninism, that Jowitt is wrong. On the contrary, he contends that communist neotraditionalism always has been at the core of the Leninist system. The collective distribution of favors and the cultivation of personal loyalties at a factory level is what makes it work. That is how the communists have always managed their enterprises.

14. Griboyedov, an 18th-century satirist, introduced the term in the play *Gore ot uma* (Woe from Wit). [Eds.]

15. Based on extensive interviews in Moscow later published in abbreviated form by Vladimir Glotov (1988) of *Ogonyok*. Edel'man, who died in 1990 at the age of 60, was the author of more than 15 books and roughly 200 articles, including sophisticated biographies and insightful commentaries on Herzen, Pushkin, Peter the Great, Karamzin, and the Decembrists. [Eds.]

Gorbachev is trying to break away from this trend toward neotraditionalism and put the Soviet system back on the rails, as he might say, toward a legal-rational mode of authority. In doing so, he is using the charismatic mode of authority as his instrument—trying to revive the charisma of the party and using his own charisma to move toward a Westernized principle of authority.

If Jowitt is right and neotraditionalism is a corrupt form of Leninism, then what Gorbachev is doing is quite reasonable and may even work. If Walder is right—that neotraditionalism is the essence of Leninism and the key to its success—then Gorbachev is bursting wide open the entire working basis of the communist authority system. Not only is he going to fail; he is going to blow the whole country wide open.

REFERENCES

Dmitriyev, Yu., and Yu. Mayorov, "Rasplata: dva monologa s predisloviyem i poslesloviyem (The Settlement: Two Monologues With a Preface and Epilogue)," *Trud*, August 4, 1988, p. 4.

FBIS (Foreign Broadcast Information Service), *Soviet Union Supplement, 19th CPSU Conference*, July 5, 1988, p. 39.

Glotov, Vladimir V., "Optimizm istoricheskogo znaniya (The Optimism of Historical Knowledge)," *Ogonyok*, 44:2–4, 28–29, October 25–November 5, 1988.

Grossman, Gregory, "The Second Economy of the USSR," *Problems of Communism*, 26, 5:25–40, September–October 1977.

———, "Notes on the Illegal Private Economy and Corruption," in U.S. Congress, Joint Economic Committee, *The Soviet Economy in a Time of Change*. Washington, D.C.: U.S. Government Printing Office, 1979, pp. 834–855.

Hewett, Ed A., *Reforming the Soviet Economy: Equality versus Efficiency*. Washington, D.C.: The Brookings Institution, 1988.

Hough, Jerry F., *Russia and the West: Gorbachev and the Politics of Reform*. New York: Simon and Schuster, 1988.

Jowitt, Ken, "Soviet Neotraditionalism: The Political Corruption of a Leninist Regime," *Soviet Studies*, 35, 3:275–297, 1983.

Khlevnyuk, Oleg, "XVIII partkonferentsiya: Vremya, problemy, resheniya (The 18th Party Conference: Time, Problems, Resolutions)," *Kommunist*, 1:27–35, 1988.

Kislinskaya, L., and S. Snegirev, "Kooperativ spishet vse? (Will the Cooperative Write Off Everything?)," *Trud*, August 6, 1988, p. 6.

Kornai, Janos, "The Hungarian Reform Process: Visions, Hope and Reality," *Journal of Economic Literature*, 24, 4:1687–1737, December 1986.

Malyayev, V., and T. Popov, "Vsesoyuznaya partkonferentsiya (The All-Union Party Conference)," *Partiynaya zhizn'*, 14:30–32, July 1987.

Mann, Dawn, "Events of Party Conference in 1941 Recalled," *Radio Liberty Weekly Research Bulletin*, No. 93, February 10, 1988.

Medvedev, Zhores, *Gorbachev*. Oxford: Basil Blackwell, 1986.

Moore, Barrington, *Terror and Progress U.S.S.R.* Cambridge, Mass.: Harvard University Press, 1954.

Mostovshchikov, S., "Tenevaya ekonomika (Shadow Economy)," *Trud*, August 12, 1988, p. 4.

Osipenko, O., ''Chto razresheno 'individualu'? (What Is the 'Individual' Allowed to Do?),'' *Trud*, August 2, 1988, p. 2.

Reddaway, Peter, ''Resisting Gorbachev,'' *New York Review of Books*, August 18, 1988, pp. 36–41.

Ryzhkov, N. I., *O roli kooperatsii v razvitii ekonomiki strany i proyekte zakona o kooperatsii v SSSR (Role of Cooperatives in the Development of the Country's Economy and the Draft Law on Cooperatives in the USSR)*. Moscow: Politizdat, 1988.

Shchekochikhin, Yu., and A. Gurov, ''Lev prygnul (The Lion Jumped),'' *Literaturnaya gazeta*, July 20, 1988, p. 13.

Tatu, Michel, *Gorbatchev: L'URSS va-t-elle changer?* Paris: Le Centurion, 1987.

Walder, Andrew, *Communist Neotraditionalism*. Berkeley: University of California Press, 1986.

Weber, Max, *Economy and Society*, Vol. 1. New York: Bedminster Press, 1968.

CHAPTER 7

The Politics of the 19th Party Conference

Jerry F. Hough

THE 19TH Party Conference contained elements of high drama because so much of it was shown on television and because so many speeches had high drama: the unprecedented exchange between Boris Yel'tsin and Yegor Ligachev, the call by the First Secretary of the Komi ASSR[1] party committee for the removal of such high officials as Andrey Gromyko and Georgiy Arbatov, the suggestion by Leonid Abalkin that a multi-party system might be necessary, the denunciation of bureaucrats by several workers and directors. All of this seemed the perfect symbol of the new openness that Gorbachev is introducing in the Soviet Union.

IDENTIFYING WHAT IS IMPORTANT

Nevertheless, in a broader sense, we should not focus too much attention on the phenomena that were so visible on television. They were, indeed, the perfect symbol of the new openness, but with a few exceptions they were not that different from articles that have been appearing in the Soviet media during 1988. They were a visual reflection of an ongoing process, more than a breakthrough in and of themselves. By the same token, we probably should not give too much attention to the actual decisions that emerged from the Conference. First, much remains unclear. There will be a reorganization of the party apparatus: apparently a cadres department is to be created that will dominate the others, many or most of the specialized economic departments are to be abolished, and some major reorganization will occur within the legislative system. However, the details of these reorganizations and the way they will work in

First published in *Soviet Economy*, 1988, 4, 2, pp. 137–143. Professor Hough, originally scheduled to participate in the roundtable excerpted here in chapter 6, was unable to attend because of an unexpected delay in his return from foreign travel. References to his views on Gorbachev's power and the course of reform, however, were made at the roundtable (The 19th Conference, 1988), where his recent book was cited (Hough, 1988). [Eds.]

1. Autonomous Soviet Socialist Republic. [Eds.]

practice remain very hazy—and perhaps not only to us. Soviet intellectuals with very good access had no idea that the proposal to combine party and soviet leader, especially at the local level, was even under serious consideration, and with the decisions so tightly held in a few hands, details were not debated out. Inconsistencies may reflect the different agendas of the small number of insiders, and we will have to see how they are resolved.

Second, we should not overemphasize Gorbachev's dedication to democratization in the sense we and the radical reformers would understand the term. Much was said by intellectuals that Gorbachev was defeated because his supporters were not elected as delegates to the Conference and the party apparatus played the dominant role. In my opinion, the party apparatus is largely Gorbachev's political machine—and is becoming more so every month—and he wanted it to select the delegates. If nothing else, he understood that the free election of delegates would have to include the non-Russian republics, and he had no desire for freely elected delegates from Armenia, Azerbaijan, Estonia, and so forth.

Similarly, some of the inconsistencies—e.g., talk about separating party and state functions at the same time the party secretary is to become leader of the soviet—reflect Gorbachev's central concern with the consolidation of power. The acquisition of the top soviet job increases his authority and gets rid of Gromyko; the talk of separation of party and state means a restructuring of the Central Committee apparatus that makes his most trusted lieutenant, Georgiy Razumovskiy, the head of the all-powerful cadres department, and the new Second Secretary. If such arguments are valid, there is no reason to try to reconcile the language philosophically because it is not meant to be taken seriously as political theory. It is likely that some of the architects of the details—Lukyanov and Shakhnazarov—are including elements that they hope will lead toward democratization a quarter of a century from now (and may well), but that is difficult to discuss until the full details are evident.

In general, I continue to see economic reform as central to what is going on, and I continue to believe that "democratization" and debates about Stalin are largely intended to divert the battles between reformers and conservatives onto safe battlegrounds while the difficult decisions are implemented. The joint venture law was published on the day the January 1987 plenum on democratization was held, and was published without prior or concurrent debate. My guess is that the summer of 1988 will go down as the time of radical agricultural reform and the first important steps toward a loosening of the supply system, but with the public's attention diverted to less important questions of political structure.

WHAT WAS ACCOMPLISHED

Besides providing a Greek chorus demanding economic reform and drawing debate away from its hard choices to denunciations of bureaucrats, the most important thing about the Conference is the extent to which it facilitated Gorbachev's consolidation of power.

On this level the impression created is a strange one. The setting of the stage for the removal of Gromyko and the replacement of Ligachev by Razumovskiy as Second Secretary is enormously important, and the Conference as an event was totally dominated by Gorbachev. He was the only Politburo member to speak besides Ligachev, and Ligachev was defending the General Secretary from a frontal attack by Yel'tsin (who is trying to set himself up as the leader of the informal competing party or party faction in the system). Gorbachev intervened freely in the discussion, often using the familiar Russian "ty."

Yet, on the surface at least, the Conference did not accomplish one major aim. Decisions on constitutional change, on economic reform, and on reorganization of the party apparatus are fully within the competence of the Central Committee, and a party conference was not needed to deal with them. Indeed, the power of the Central Committee in the policy sphere was driven home by the decision to hold a Central Committee session four weeks after the Conference to pass decisions on economic reform and reorganization of the party apparatus.

It is also the Central Committee—and only the Central Committee—that has the power to elect and remove the General Secretary, other Central Committee secretaries, and members of the Politburo. The only powers that the Central Committee does not have are to co-opt new members (other than candidate) and to change the party rules.

Hence the obvious reason for the decision to hold the first party conference in 47 years was to change the party rules and to change some 15–20 percent of the voting members of the Central Committee. The Central Committee elected in March 1986 contained 307 voting members, approximately 275 of whom were high officials who were elected almost as representatives of the posts they occupied. As these people are retired, or seriously demoted, however, they normally remain members of the Central Committee until the next party congress (the congresses are held every five years, as a rule).[2] For example, the Minister of Defense and the Head of Air Defense who were fired when a small plane landed in Red Square are still members of the Central Committee, as are the First Secretaries of Armenia and Azerbaijan, removed after the riots. By June 1988, 17 percent of voting members were retirees or persons who had been seriously demoted. This in itself is not a dangerous figure for Gorbachev, but it will continue to rise (by September 1 it was at 18 percent) and by the scheduled party congress in 1991 it could be very worrisome—all the more so

---

2. The Central Committee does have the right to remove a member by a two-thirds vote, as well as to promote candidate members to voting membership. In the past, however, members were removed only for major political opposition (e.g., the so-called anti-party group of 1957) or for major corruption (in recent years the Krasnodar First Secretary Medunov, the Minister of Internal Affairs Shchelokov, and the Kazakh First Secretary Kunayev). Candidates have been promoted only to fill vacancies left by death. However, nothing prevents more substantial turnover via this route.

since Gorbachev has so many changes in government and party structure in mind.

By all indications, the Party Conference was going to deal with these questions that the Central Committee could not. Prior to the Conference, theses on changes in the party rules were formally presented, and they were widely discussed. In addition, throughout 1986 and early 1987 a number of well-placed figures told Westerners that retired members would be removed at the Conference and new members elected.[3] The changes in party rules proposed before the Conference actually called for a partial change of Central Committee members between congresses, and the Conference itself passed a resolution that conferences should be held regularly between congresses and should have the right to change 20 percent of the Central Committee membership.

Nevertheless, no members of the Central Committee were changed at the 19th Party Conference. Moreover, the decisions that were passed on changes in party rules were not to be implemented until the next party congress. In many ways this latter decision was more remarkable than the decision not to change Central Committee membership. A congress is more powerful and authoritative than a conference. Why in heaven's name should a conference be passing a resolution on the party rules to be implemented nearly three years later by a congress that obviously is not bound by the conference's decision?

INTERPRETING THE RESULTS

What happened? We don't really know. The first and most obvious hypothetical answer is that Gorbachev suffered a major defeat and wasn't able to continue the consolidation of power that is under way. The second hypothetical answer is that Gorbachev has in mind another solution to the problem of the lame ducks on the Central Committee—and there are, in fact, a number of ways to skin that cat. The third hypothetical answer is that there is no Central Committee problem—perhaps that the Politburo is so solidly behind Gorbachev that there is no leader who would appeal to the Central Committee, perhaps that power is in the Politburo, or perhaps that the army is so solidly behind Gorbachev and reform that Gorbachev is confident of military intervention against any civilian attempt to overthrow him.

Certainly the third hypothetical answer should not be dismissed out of hand. Ligachev did go out of his way to say that the Central Committee had been the body to elect Gorbachev in 1985 and that the Politburo would not have done so.[4] And surely a Politburo majority has no more ability today than before to defend Gorbachev against a Central Committee majority. Nevertheless, without an alternative leader in the Politburo who can command a majority in the

---

3. For example, 33 of 90 regions and republics represented by a voting member on the Central Committee elected in 1986 are now without representation because of a change in first secretary.

4. Ligachev did this by saying that Gorbachev would not have been elected without the support of people like Chebrikov, Solomentsev, and himself. Since these men were not Politburo members but Central Committee members, Ligachev was clearly saying that the possibility of an appeal to the Central Committee was decisive.

Central Committee, the latter will never remove the General Secretary, and the defeat of Yel'tsin removes the most dangerous opponent.[5] And since Deng Xiaoping is running China out of the military committee and has even given up his Politburo membership, one should not dismiss out of hand the supposition that the Soviet military is so worried about Chinese modernization and SDI that it will put down any conservative attack on Gorbachev.

The real problem with the third hypothetical answer is that Gorbachev seems to want to observe the legalities if he can, and therefore he must want to retain the solid base he had in the Central Committee in 1985 and 1986. If he had total confidence in his strength in the Politburo and/or the army, he had the strength to get the Party Conference to change the party rules and the Central Committee membership. While those steps were not specifically authorized by the party rules, they were not prohibited by it and would have been widely accepted.

The first hypothetical explanation for the Conference events—that Gorbachev suffered at least a partial defeat—is the one that is most plausible on the surface, and it has wide support in the community of analysts of Soviet affairs. It is often said that he conceded on the issue of Central Committee membership in order to get support for measures such as the joining of party and state offices (and his replacement of Gromyko as chief of state), acceleration of agricultural reform, etc.

The first problem with the explanation of a partial defeat is that the compromises posited really represent a near-total defeat. Every Soviet leader since Lenin has eventually combined the position of party leader with that of Chairman of the Council of Ministers or Chairman of the Presidium of the Supreme Soviet. The latter post could have been Gorbachev's for the asking. Moreover, if he, as Brezhnev's specialist on agriculture, hasn't had the authority to conduct any agricultural reform he wanted, he has been in deep trouble indeed. Finally, if he really was defeated in his attempt to change the Central Committee, it is an extremely serious defeat. If the old retired and demoted Central Committee members (and they are relatively old on the average) are strong enough to protect their position, they are strong enough to cause Gorbachev enormous trouble on other issues, especially if they are joined by other Central Committee members who develop a personal grievance against Gorbachev as he replaces them in the future.

The difficulty with the thesis of a Gorbachev defeat is that he has actually been showing enormous strength at the kind of detailed political level that usually is most revealing. In the month after the July plenum of the Central Committee, three of the most important *obkom* first secretaries—those of Kuybyshev, Novosibirsk, and Perm'—were retired, and they seemed to be key members of the old Kirilenko-Andropov machine with which Gorbachev had

---

5. Others believe Ligachev is potentially such a leader. but I disagree.

made an alliance, but never seemed to have long-term personal ties. The Novosibirsk First Secretary had ties with Ligachev—another member of the machine—that went back to the late 1950s. In the three months before the Conference, three more first secretaries of a similar type—those of Gorkiy, Irkutsk, and Sverdlovsk—were removed and sent into more ceremonial jobs (although ones that warrant continued Central Committee membership).

There is a strip of oblasts from the Urals to Siberia that always have seemed to have a closer connection with Ligachev: from west to east,[6] Perm', Sverdlovsk, Tyumen', Omsk, Novosibirsk, Kemerovo, Krasnoyarsk, Irkutsk, and Chita. With the exception of Tyumen' Oblast, all have had their first secretaries replaced since the 1986 Party Congress, all of them were demoted or retired except for two with apparent ties to Gorbachev. There are another twelve regions just to the west and southwest of this tier: the Bashkir ASSR, Chelyabinsk, Gorkiy, and Kirov oblasts, the Komi ASSR, Kuybyshev and Kurgan oblasts, the Mari ASSR, Orenburg Oblast, the Tatar ASSR, Ul'yanovsk Oblast, and the Udmurt ASSR. First secretaries have been changed in seven of them since the Congress, and in four of the other five they are agricultural specialists with likely long-time ties with Gorbachev.

Political ties almost always are matters of conjecture to a lesser or greater degree, and one can always explain personnel changes in various ways. Nevertheless, the pattern is striking, and if Ligachev has a connection with any area, it is this one. At a minimum, however, some very important oblast and autonomous republic secretaries—all voting members of the Central Committee—have been replaced in recent months, and none had an apparent connection with Gorbachev (not even an agricultural background) that would suggest an attack on the General Secretary. The Kuybyshev Secretary, in fact, was replaced by a man from Stavropol'. The question is: if Gorbachev is behind these changes as he seems to be, is he not strong enough to have changed the Central Committee? And if he is not strong enough to change the Central Committee, is it not wildly reckless to be increasing the number of discontents among its members?

As a consequence, there is a strong temptation to conclude that Gorbachev did not really suffer a defeat at the Conference and to assume that Gorbachev has a scenario in mind that will remove the ever-growing number of aggrieved retirees from the Central Committee. The most elegant solution would be to hold a party congress in 1989, for that would solve a number of problems ranging from the synchronization of party and state elections, election of congress delegates, introduction of new party rules, and election of a new Central Committee. But there are other possible solutions. The Central Committee does have the power to remove its own members on grounds other than corruption, and it can promote candidates (but not elect totally new members). Finally,

6. Tomsk Oblast, another such area, sits astride the northern border of Novosibirsk and Kemerovo Oblasts.

the trial of Brezhnev's son-in-law must remind a number of people of their vulnerability, and perhaps many retired members can be persuaded to resign, as happened in China.

Nevertheless, the kind of analysis presented here did lead to the conclusion in 1963 and 1964 that Khrushchev surely could not be acting as recklessly as he was with his political base unless he was absolutely confident of it. Gorbachev does seem a much more cautious and intelligent politician than Khrushchev, and in the past he has been more careful than one would have thought necessary (e.g., not annoying Gromyko with any foreign policy personnel changes until the eve of the Congress). Unless we want to posit a military base of power for Gorbachev, however, we should take the formal structure of power—and the crucial role of the Central Committee—with the utmost seriousness. We should keep thinking about the lame duck problem on the Central Committee and keep watching how Gorbachev does or does not handle it.

REFERENCES

Hough, Jerry F., *Russia and the West: Gorbachev and the Politics of Reform*. New York: Simon & Schuster, 1988.
"The 19th Conference of the CPSU: A *Soviet Economy* Roundtable," *Soviet Economy*, 4, 2:103–135, April–June 1988.

CHAPTER 8

Interpretations and Perceptions of *Perestroyka*

Andrey Sakharov
with *Yelena Bonner, Stephen F. Cohen, Ed A. Hewett, and Victor H. Winston*

SAKHAROV: It is gratifying to be among friends. Last month, Yelena Grigor'yevna and I attended a similar gathering in Georgia involving Soviet as well as American scholars.[1] I expect this meeting to be stimulating and productive.

HEWETT: Bilateral Soviet-American meetings to discuss world affairs with scientists, politicians, prominent businessmen—people in the news—seem to proliferate these days. But this joint *Soviet Economy* roundtable is very special and its proceedings may structure a chronicle of more than casual historical significance.

To begin with, there are Soviet participants in this room whose names will be oft repeated by students and historians for generations to come. Collectively, you are known to us (and at last to your Soviet compatriots as well) as the pioneers and fighters for the emerging democracy and human rights in the Soviet Union and, yes, you are the architects and builders of *glasnost'*, with all the limitations this word has yet to overcome.

At our end, it is not a coincidence that my American colleagues at this table are Sovietologists whose fluency in the Russian language is well above the

Excerpts from a transcript of a joint *Soviet Economy* roundtable devoted to discussions about supporters and opponents of *perestroyka*. The panel convened at the publishing house *Progress* on the eve of Academician Andrey Sakharov's historic trip to the U.S. in November 1988. Hosted by *Ogonyok*, it was transcribed in Russian and published in one of its December issues in the form of a condensed reportage (Vyzhutovich and Glotov, 1988). Substantially all material in this chapter was first published in *Soviet Economy*, 1988, 4, 4, pp. 275–318.

Other participants included Yuriy Afanas'yev of the Moscow State Institute of Historical Archives, Aleksandr Avelichev of Progress Publishers, Leonid Batkin of the Academy of Sciences of the USSR, Pavel G. Bunich of the Academy of the National Economy, Aleksandr Gel'man (noted Moscow intellectual), Vladimir Glotov of *Ogonyok*, Igor Klyamkin of the Academy of Sciences of the USSR, Vitaliy A. Korotich of *Ogonyok*, Gregory Massell of Hunter College and the Harriman Institute of Columbia University, Peter Reddaway of George Washington University and the Kennan Institute, Steven Shabad of Newsweek, Inc., David K. Shipler of the Carnegie Endowment for International Peace, and Nikolay P. Shmelev of the Institute of the USA and Canada of the Academy of Sciences of the USSR. The discussion with Yuriy Afanas'yev, Pavel Bunich, and Nikolay Shmelev comprises Chapter 16 of the *Milestones in Glasnost' and Perestroyka: The Economy*. [Eds.]

1. Apparently a reference to the Pugwash Conference. [Eds.]

average. Just about all of us come to Moscow regularly, and there are many evenings to remember in the privacy of your apartments when discussions such as this one about to begin took place—one of us the guest and one or two of you the gracious hosts. So we do not convene as relative strangers and the object of our discussion will not be persuasion (every participant here looks forward to *perestroyka*'s success), but rather a probing inquest to assess *perestroyka's* chances to survive. There are tape recorders on the table and no censors to stifle the proceedings. I think the prospective candor might set a precedent and the substance of this roundtable yield useful insights for our respective governments to digest. Shall we proceed?

THE POLITICAL ALTERNATIVES AND CONCEPTIONS

SAKHAROV: I would like to say a few words about the political alternatives that the country has. The first is Stalinism; the second, enlightened monarchy, if you will; and the third is democracy, coming from below. I think the only real way of carrying out *perestroyka* is the third method. The second path, which is very popular among the Soviet intelligentsia and our friends in the West, boils down to the slogan, "Don't Interfere with Gorbachev." I think that this is in fact a dangerous slogan—and dangerous for Gorbachev as well.

COHEN: I read many Soviet newspapers and journals on a regular basis, and as I read them I find that there is not one conception of *perestroyka* in the official Soviet press but at least three different conceptions. The first and still dominant conception is that of Mikhail Gorbachev and his most committed supporters, including the Soviet participants in this roundtable. It is the idea of *perestroyka* as "radical reform" or even as "revolution"—far-reaching, fundamental, progressive (even democratic), and one that changes the Soviet political and economic system.[2] At the other end of this spectrum is what I call the neo-Stalinist conception of *perestroyka*, which advocates "restructuring" and repairing the Soviet system by making the state, rather than society, more powerful. Calling upon Stalinist and tsarist traditions, which its proponents hardly bother or care to distinguish, it is a statist conception of *perestroyka* that finds solutions to Soviet problems in, as Pushkin put it, "the charms of the whip" rather than in democratization. And third, in the center, is a self-professed moderate conception of *perestroyka* whose advocates deplore and recoil from the "excesses" and "extremes" of the other two. Such people seem to believe that the Soviet Union's problems can be solved by limited, rationalizing economic reforms that do not require any kind of real political changes.

If my foundation of at least three different conceptions of *perestroyka* is generally correct, the question of who supports and who opposes *perestroyka* is doubly, or triply, complex. On the one hand, it means that everyone supports

---

2. This conception of *perestroyka* is reflected in the collection of essays (Afanas'yev, 1988) which includes contributions from three participants (Afanas'yev, Batkin, and Sakharov). [Eds.]

"perestroyka," as indeed almost every Soviet citizen professes to do. But on the other hand, it does not tell us which *perestroyka,* what kind of *perestroyka,* they support. A vivid illustration of how different these conceptions can be appeared in *Moskovskaya pravda* (September 2, 1987, p. 2), which featured the views of two factory party members on the country's economic problems. One exclaimed, "The Whip Is Needed" *(Nuzhen knut)*; the other replied, "No Return to the Past" *(Vozvrata net).* In short, two profoundly conflicting conceptions of *perestroyka,* and another chapter in the long struggle between neo-Stalinism and anti-Stalinism, which has been a central aspect of Soviet politics ever since 1953, as I have argued elsewhere (Cohen, 1985, chs. 4 and 5).

I should like to comment on Gorbachev's frequent statement, "There is no alternative to *perestroyka.*" I understand the political and moral imperatives behind this statement, but as a scholar I also know that in history and politics there are always alternatives. In this case, there are, for example, the alternatives represented by the two other conceptions of *perestroyka* that are to be found in the Soviet press and thus presumably in Soviet political circles. Personally, I do not think that a moderate or conservative version of *perestroyka* would stand much of a chance, for two reasons. The Soviet Union's problems are too large and deep-rooted to be solved by small-scale or partial reforms. And second, as a result of more than three years of *glasnost',* the nature and dimensions of those problems have become widely known throughout the country; the Brezhnev era cover-up is over. Indeed, national awareness of the problems seems to have "polarized" opinion, as is often reported in the Soviet press, which suggests that the center has collapsed, and with it any durable basis for policies that eschew all "extremes." Therefore, it seems unlikely that a limited, muddle-through *perestroyka* program would be able to cope politically or economically, at least in the long run.

As for the other alternative, what I call a neo-Stalinist or despotic *perestroyka,* it may not be a viable contender today. But for some near or remote tomorrow, the potency of its statist proposals and ideology, of tenacious traditions upon which it calls, and of its popular appeal cannot be excluded. Those of us at this table would no doubt agree that Gorbachev's *perestroyka* calls upon many of the best traditions in Russian and Soviet history, and the neo-Stalinist *perestroyka* upon the worst. But none of us really knows which will prove stronger and prevail at this turning point in the history of the Soviet Union.

THE RADICAL *PERESTROYKA*

COHEN: What does the kind of *perestroyka* proposed by Gorbachev and the Soviet intellectuals around this table mean? As I read Gorbachev's speeches and your writings, I understand it to include four general categories of radical reform. One is decentralization of control over the state economy, or in other words, transferring Moscow's economic powers and functions to the enterprises themselves. A second category of economic reform involves substantial privatization and marketization, that is, creating a sizable non-state economic sector composed of cooperatives and individual enterprises. The third category is the political reform that you call *glasnost'*, which I understand to mean a substantial reduction of state imposed bans and other forms of censorship in cultural and intellectual pursuits and in the mass media, along with considerably greater official toleration of a "pluralism" of views more generally. And fourth, there is what you call, still more generally, "democratization," about which there is still considerable confusion and controversy but which certainly includes plans to reduce the party-state's powers of appointment from above (the *nomenklatura*) by permitting multicandidate elections from below—at the workplace, to soviets, and even inside the Communist Party itself.

If I am right about these components of Gorbachev's *perestroyka*, we are close to an understanding of its essential meaning. All of these categories of radical reform go in one direction: Toward substantially reducing the monopolistic party-state controls imposed on society by the Stalinist regime more than 50 years ago, in the 1930s. Or to use an expression I recall reading somewhere in your press, Gorbachev's *perestroyka*, if actually implemented, promises to "liberate society" from the Stalinist system of administrative-bureaucratic controls, taboos, prohibitions, etc. You will recall that Klyuchevsky characterized early 18th-century Russian history as a time when "the state swelled up and the people grew lean." Might we say that Gorbachev's *perestroyka* would give the people a chance to swell up by making the state much leaner? But perhaps it is better to locate our understanding of *perestroyka* in the context of Soviet history. As Otto Latsis (1988) and other Soviet writers have rightly argued, the Stalinist model of Soviet socialism, and Stalin's enduring legacy, are thoroughly "statist." In this sense, we can say that radical *perestroyka* means a process of de-statization of the Soviet system, which also means, as Viktor Kiselev has written, "a process of decisive de-Stalinization" (Kiselev, 1988).

Again, if my formulation of the issue is correct, or even roughly so, a number of other questions arise. I will touch on them only briefly. Given the long, almost unbroken tradition of state power over society in Russian and Soviet history, we cannot avoid asking if Soviet society is now ready for such a process of de-statization and "liberation." This question involves what political scientists call political culture, and it interests me that a discussion of it has developed in your publications in recent years, though elliptically and inconclusively.

That raises another large question: What kind of new relationship between state and society do you radical *perestroyshchiki*, as many of our Soviet participants would call themselves, want to create? What is your ideal, what is your model, what are its institutions and mechanisms? I find no satisfactory discussion of this question in the Soviet press or at this table. Discussions about cutting the power of state ministries, about increasing the powers of soviets, about elections and legal reforms—all these touch on the question but do not address it directly. For example, you speak a great deal about the need for economic markets in the Soviet Union, but do you also see the political role of markets as a buffer or negotiating mechanism in a new state-society relationship?

Nor should we think that such a radical *perestroyka* will require only a few years, one or two five-year plans, as the Soviet press sometimes implies. In a country as large, diverse, and—forgive me—conservative as the Soviet Union, such a far-reaching reformation will certainly take decades, even if all goes well, which is unlikely. Robert C. Tucker, my colleague at Princeton University, has referred to the New Deal, begun under President Roosevelt in the early 1930s, as a kind of American *perestroyka*. Though the analogy may be imperfect, let us remember that the New Deal is generally thought to have more or less reached its fulfillment in the mid-1960s, under President Johnson, three decades later. I think that any serious analysis of a radical Soviet *perestroyka* must be framed in a comparably long period of time. This means that few, if any, of us in this room will live to see the end of the process.

It also means that even if the Gorbachev leadership is able to set the process fully in motion, radical *perestroyka* will almost certainly suffer serious setbacks in the years and decades ahead. That has been the case with great reforms in other countries, even successful ones. It is not hard to imagine, for example, that in time a Soviet leadership may emerge, based on changing sentiment in the political elite and among the populace at large, that will seek to slow or even halt the process of *perestroyka,* or to "consolidate" it, as such a government might argue. Nor is it hard to imagine a subsequent Soviet leadership that will seek to reradicalize or renew the process. Again, that would be the natural ebb and flow of such a historic and historical reformation. Indeed, we should remember that truly radical reforms, by their very nature, almost always generate new forms and waves of resistance and opposition because their success constantly threatens new realms of vested interests and conservatism.

THE POLITICS OF CONSTITUTIONAL CHANGE

SAKHAROV: The changes in the Constitution and the electoral law will define our political life for a very long time.[3] It will be difficult to change anything within this framework. So they must be thought out very carefully, and the one month that has been allotted for this process is clearly not enough. A thorough debate should take at least three months. During this period various groups of experts could compose alternative procedures, and the debate could proceed in journals and not only in newspapers, which discuss only particular details and cannot get into a very deep discussion. The only course that may

3. The reforms were adopted at a session of the Supreme Soviet on December 1, 1988. The changes in the Constitution were adopted on December 1, 1988, in the Council of Nationalities by a vote of 657 to 3, with 26 abstentions, and in the Council of the Union by 687 to 2, with 1 abstention. A new electoral law also was adopted (*Pravda,* December 2, 1988, p. 2). [Eds.]

yield a safe solution for our country's political development is a referendum on the key controversial issues, which must still be formulated.

As for the draft that has been presented, in my view it already contains time bombs of enormous danger—the danger of an orientation toward that second alternative, the alternative of *perestroyka* only from above. *Perestroyka* began as a result of the historic initiatives of Mikhail Sergeyevich Gorbachev, but it can develop only on a popular level, on a consistently democratic basis— otherwise it will be a succession of dead ends.

We see in the published draft a multiphase system: delegates are elected to the Congress of People's Deputies, then they must elect, within a short period, 400 people from their number. There is no democratic mechanism based on knowledge of these people's positions, which would make it possible to elect them rationally. In other words, it will be a choice based on slates and on what the government apparatus will suggest to them either directly or indirectly.

Then there is the head of state, who will also be the head of the party, i.e., a person endowed with absolute powers. He will even have legislative power in the period between sessions of the Supreme Soviet, and he may issue directives. Today it will be Gorbachev; tomorrow it could be anyone. We have absolutely no guarantees against such a mess, and, frankly, we have no guarantees against the possibility that various kinds of pressures might compel Gorbachev to change his own position. Everything continues to depend on one person. This is extremely dangerous—dangerous for *perestroyka* as a whole and dangerous for Gorbachev himself. This must be stated openly, because the fate of our country may depend on this question.

In addition, this entire system of elections to the Congress also contains a multitude of submerged rocks. The principal one is that the system is still designed for a one-party system. The terms for nominating candidates are formulated in such a way that even the popular fronts that are now appearing in the republics cannot nominate deputies, because they do not have a centrally located body, and they are essentially regional organizations. They reflect the interests of their respective regions, but they are not the kind of political force that can mitigate the covert threat posed by a one-party system.

The shortcomings of a one-party system become especially pronounced when the head of state has unlimited powers. In the United States, the President also has great powers and capabilities, but they are offset by the fact that it is a multiparty system. Here the powers are much greater, so to have a head of state with such powers as the draft law envisages, without a multiparty system, is simply madness.

The nature of the Supreme Soviet, which must ratify decrees, became clear when it voted those antidemocratic, anticonstitutional decrees on the freedom of assembly, of demonstrations, and especially on the emergency powers of internal troops. We already are seeing the results in the country, and after all, we know more about what is happening in Moscow. In the provinces everything has a different emphasis—one that is focused much more on the anti-*perestroyka* forces. We know that on the basis of these decrees a man was arrested in L'vov for calling for the creation of a memorial to the victims of Stalin's repressions. We know that on October 30 people who were simply going to a cemetery encountered internal troops, and an utterly brutal massacre followed.[4] Again the organizer of the Memorial Society was detained. That is how things are developing, and one must simply understand that *perestroyka* is now experiencing a very difficult, pivotal period, when a choice must be made between the second and third alternatives.

THE SURVIVAL OF *PERESTROYKA*

BONNER: Some issues relating to *perestroyka's* ability to survive have not been framed correctly. Rather than focusing on supporters or opponents of *perestroyka*, we should address the issue whether people have or don't have faith in *perestroyka*. I always was a believer, although there was a period when my faith was shaken. But today my faith in *perestroyka* is waning, and I often think of Vasiliy Grossman's novel *Forever Flowing* (Grossman, 1972), where he speaks of the theater: people say one thing and do something else. Isn't that what we are seeing now?

What will affect *perestroyka's* survival is the issue of our nationalities. What is needed is legislation under which large nationalities would stop holding on to small ones. Then small ones may even seek to live together with large ones. This requires that the small ethnic groups be given the freedom to decide their own fate. And the only way to avert a national catastrophe is to establish the principle of equality, regardless of whether it is 100 million Russians or 170,000 Karabakhites.

SAKHAROV: It has been suggested that we should be afraid of separatist tendencies. In fact we should fear not the separatist tendencies themselves but their causes, which are economic and purely ethnic, inspired by national culture. It is better to lose part of our country than hold on to every republic by force, which would only exacerbate the problems and increase tensions within the country. With proper democratic procedures, I don't think anything will be lost.

I would like to underscore what Yelena Grigor'yevna said. It is extremely dangerous for the central authority of a state, out of pragmatic considerations or even political, mafialike considerations, to apply different yardsticks to large and small national organizations. The disgraceful events in the Karabakh crisis could happen elsewhere. The only solution here is a general solution of the nationalities problem on the basis of a horizontal structure instead of a hierarchical, ramified system, under which large nationalities can suppress small ones, and small groups, as in the case of Karabakh, can suppress a smaller group in an enclave.

---

4. For a comprehensive discussion of that event, see *Literaturnaya gazeta.* December 28. 1988. p. 10. [Eds.]

The nationalities problem *per se* is a completely legitimate one, and there is no need to fear that the nationalities will present some claims. It is all totally natural, and the central leadership must show great tolerance and tact. What is dangerous is not the external symptom of the disease, but its deep-rooted causes.

HEWETT: Implicit in our discussion today, and implicit in many formulations here and in the West, is the notion that political and economic reforms must go hand in hand. Thus both the pace and extent of reform must involve not only economic but also political decentralization. I share the general excitement over political reforms now emerging in the USSR, and the frustration over their limits. But I do have some misgivings about the particular relationship emerging now between political and economic reform.

The economic reforms are beginning to place greater and greater emphasis on the decentralization of the state's economic management functions to lower levels, and to governmental levels—the republics and even the *oblasti*. The theory is that regions will become self-financing, that the regional governmental bodies, full of elected officials, will be closer to the wishes of the people and more responsible to them. Indeed that will surely be the case. And the people are likely to speak with one voice to local politicians that their task is to protect local factories from closing, and local jobs from being lost.

And therein lies the potential conflict with economic reforms. Reforms in the economy are a polite phrase for layoffs, factory closings, the major turmoil in the system necessary to squeeze out years of deeply ingrained inefficiencies. Local officials, close to their constituents, and flush with new powers in managing their regional economies, will be pressured to protect particularly the most inefficient factories, those which should be closed.

I see no easy solution to this potential contradiction. I simply note that the putative link between political and economic reforms is not as simple as some would have us believe.

COHEN: Ed Hewett worries that the decentralizing political reforms of *perestroyka* may jeopardize the economic reforms that are so essential. I understand his point, but I want to emphasize a crucial aspect of Gorbachev's "democratization" program that is rarely if ever discussed.

Most of us would agree, I think, that *perestroyka* faces a major problem: A radical leadership at the top of the Soviet system, headed by Gorbachev, wants to introduce far-reaching reforms, but it may be thwarted, particularly now that it has reached the stage of actual implementation, by a multi-echelon party-state bureaucracy composed of millions of people (though not all of them, of course) who actively oppose or passively resist the reforms. The power of the bureaucracy, including its ranking appointed officials (the *nomenklatura*) to ignore or even sabotage reform legislation is amply documented in modern Soviet history. I think of many reforms enacted under Nikita Khrushchev, the 1965 economic reform, and so forth. And so the question is, How can the radical reform leadership in Moscow implement its program throughout the country? My reading of the Soviet press and my discussions with many *perestroyshchiki* suggest that the leadership is counting on the support of millions of reform-minded people at the grass roots levels of the Soviet system—at workplaces, in local soviets, in schools, and in the Party. Evidently, the Gorbachev leadership believes that there are millions of radical reformers, or would-be radical reformers, at these lower levels, and that they are its best hope for implementing *perestroyka*.

But how can the leadership in Moscow establish an effective alliance with such people, even assuming they exist in large numbers, who have lacked any real power or authority in the past, and from whom the leadership is still separated by "the bureaucracy"? Until 1988, the Gorbachev leadership seemed to have relied mainly on what we loosely call *glasnost'*. That is, it used the Soviet media to inform and arouse the rank-and-file about the nation's problems, to attack "the bureaucracy" for inefficiency, corruption, and worse, and to embolden ordinary citizens to act. But the media alone cannot create or serve as an institutional alliance between Moscow reformers and would-be legions of reformers from below. Such an alliance requires real mechanisms of power. And that, I think, is to be the role, in the eyes of the Gorbachev leadership, of the "democratization" legislation enacted in 1988. On paper, at least, the legislation, particularly as it relates to elections, puts power within the grasp of previously disenfranchised citizens at the bottom (and perhaps the middle) of the Soviet system. Will they, can they, reach out and take power, or some power, from state, party, factory, and kolkhoz bureaucrats? I don't know. That great and fateful drama has yet to unfold. But if I am right about the importance of "democratization" for the implementation of economic *perestroyka*, Ed Hewett's concern may be misplaced.

SAKHAROV: I think there is more reason to fear the failure of *perestroyka* than its success. Our country always has enough soldiers, enough equipment, and enough research institutes for military expansion. But a failure for *perestroyka* would make expansion by our country politically inevitable; the Soviet Union would become extraordinarily dangerous for the strategic equilibrium. On the other hand, the fear that the Soviet Union could become economically competitive on the level of Japan if *perestroyka* succeeds is simply not plausible. It is enough to sketch the graphs of productivity growth to see that the curves for Japan and the Soviet Union would intersect beyond politically realistic limits, somewhere near infinity.

I think Gorbachev is quite right in saying that increased interdependence is a stabilizing factor. Not only does it deter expansionism and confrontation, it should also be a factor affecting the domestic political process. We are now living through a very dangerous period in *perestroyka*, and the West should be aware of this and, to some extent, keep its hand on the faucet. It should act in a clear-eyed fashion, so that not only Gorbachev but the entire decision-making level of our society understands that everything that happens here is under close scrutiny.

AMERICAN PERCEPTIONS OF PERESTROYKA

WINSTON: American perceptions of *perestroyka* represent a spectrum of views ranging from extreme optimism to unwavering skepticism and disbelief. An early view which has withstood the test of time is the cautious approbation of William Hyland (1985). Gorbachev is seen by Hyland as the first Soviet leader born after the Bolshevik Revolution—untested, largely unknown, and possibly a short-term leader. But America "must be prepared for a period in which the Soviet Union does attempt to throw off some of the dead weight of the past." Much less cautious and rather more optimistic about *perestroyka* nowadays are our American media. Thus, many politicians can be expected to give some thought to the consequences of jumping on the bandwagon. Most if not all of us wish General Secretary Gorbachev well. However, we are not participants but concerned observers who ought not to be called upon to declare themselves as either supporters or opponents of *perestroyka*. Accordingly, it may be more appropriate to refer to some of us as absentee cheerleaders, while *perestroyka's* American detractors may as well become known as boders of ill will from a distance.

The substantive issue, I think, is national defense. Optimists hope that Gorbachev will manage to reduce Soviet defense spending so that we, in turn, curtail our defense expenditures to materially reduce the budget deficit. The state of your economy appears to supply more food for pessimism in America than cheer. Many of our analysts simply point out that the strategies of de-centralization and encouragement of private initiative introduced by Gorbachev are incompatible with the basic principles of Marxism-Leninism. Also, these strategies will fail, they say, because the analogy with NEP is not in order. In the 1920s, Lenin could draw on the surviving merchant class, only one decade removed from active participation in Russian capitalism. But more than 70 years thereafter, the experience of competing for business or taking business risks is no longer here to be mobilized. So more than a few American skeptics are reluctant to participate in your joint ventures and inclined to view the opportunities with suspicion.

COHEN: Many of our analysts suggest that cold-war thinking about the Soviet Union has virtually come to an end in the United States. As a longtime opponent of the cold war, I wish this was so, but to think it is so would be euphoric and dangerous. A new, more positive stereotype is emerging in America, but it could be quickly displaced as a result of any one of many imaginable future conflicts in U.S.-Soviet relations.

More generally, I want to add that the legacy of 70 years of ideological cold war, and more than 40 years of militarized cold war, could not possibly be swept away by 3 years of *perestroyka*, summits, and media atmospherics. Powerful cold-war institutions, elites, and popular attitudes remain on both sides. To go beyond this mountainous cold-war legacy to some valley of enduring better U.S.-Soviet relations will require much more effort and bolder leadership on both sides. We may have begun that long march, but we have only begun. Nor should you imagine that America has become, or will easily become, a bastion of pro-*perestroyka* sentiment. We, too, have our friends and foes of *perestroyka*—those who want to meet Gorbachev's "new thinking" in foreign policy fully half way, and those who do not. And in this respect, we, too, are engaged in a long and uncertain struggle. A great many Americans have always insisted on the right to tell the Soviet Union how it should conduct its internal affairs. I, on the other hand, have always felt uncomfortable with this long American practice of preaching to the Soviet Union. We have the right, of course, to study Soviet affairs, to think critically about them, and to reach our own political and moral opinions. But I doubt that we Americans have the wisdom or the right to instruct the Soviet Union about its domestic affairs or its national destiny. That responsibility rightfully belongs to Soviet citizens, including those at this table. Whatever political wisdom and effort we Americans can muster should be directed toward our own problems at home. If America really wants to influence the affairs of other countries, the best and probably only real way to do so is by putting our own democratic and economic house in order. In other words, as we Americans discuss with you the current changes in your country, we do so not as preachers but as scholars.

BONNER: When our American colleagues say that there are people in their country who are opponents of *perestroyka* (like Jeane Kirkpatrick), I disagree. These people want to preserve peace no less than Stephen Cohen does. Stephen says that Americans insist on talking to us from a position of strength. I would like him to name just one Soviet leader who would talk from a position of weakness. We are not asking you to help our *perestroyka;* we are simply asking you to portray it accurately for Americans—and not according to the concepts that you develop while you sit in your office and pick out only those facts that suit your purpose. Stephen keeps saying that *perestroyka* is working, while we here say that it is not working. Stephen hears us and yet does not hear us. When I was abroad, I met with the most extreme rightists and the most extreme leftists. And very often the leftists, who are most effusive in declaring their love for our country, insist on looking at it with their eyes closed. Everyone must keep their eyes open.

COHEN: I must object to Yelena Bonner's charge that I sit in Princeton, blinded to Soviet realities by some left-wing ideology, seeing only what I want to see. Because her comments about me were so general, I cannot even guess exactly what it was I said that so offended her. Perhaps it was not even something I said here today. Nor do I consider myself to be a person of "the left" or of "the right." For me, those are geographic locations whose whereabouts are unknown. It may well be that I do not see or understand Soviet realities accurately or fully. If so, it means that my intellectual vision and power are lacking, not that I have an ideological axe to grind. I don't. Some evidence of that may be that people of very different ideological outlooks often object to what I write and say, both here and in the United States.

I will take this opportunity, however, to raise one question that interests me both as a scholar and as an American citizen. Sharing as I do Andrey Sakharov's conviction that we must end the cold war and the arms race, I am puzzled why the non-democratic Soviet system has produced a remarkably anti-cold-war, anti-arms-race leader, in the person of Mikhail Gorbachev, and democratic America has not yet quite done so. As a scholar, the question intrigues me. As an American, it troubles me. Incidentally, any intellectual history of what Gorbachev now calls the "new thinking" about international affairs would need to devote a major chapter to Sakharov's famous 1968 memorandum, published in the United States as *Progress, Coexistence, and Intellectual Freedom* (Sakharov, 1970). Certainly, in that pamphlet, he was one of the forefathers of the "new thinking."

WINSTON: Earlier, Stephen Cohen commented on our presidential candidates' emphasis on negotiating from strength. What else should one expect? Among other things, would Gorbachev respect an American president who is not wary of the enduring presence of Brezhnevites, neo-Stalinists, and other embittered advocates of the past in the Central Committee? Nor am I too comfortable with Stephen's perception of cold-war thinking in America. Manifestations of reasonably justified caution need not be viewed as evidence of bad faith. In this context, William Hyland's guardedly optimistic assessment of Gorbachev in the spring of 1985 (Hyland, 1985) seems to reflect a view that one should be able to endorse in the fall of 1988.

But caution tends to dissipate in time. Perhaps some of the concerns that have emerged in this roundtable may be answered by the lessons taught by historical determinists.

CONCLUDING COMMENTS

SAKHAROV: Now, a few concluding words about this slogan, "Don't Interfere with Gorbachev." It exists both in our country and abroad. Outside the country it signifies the support that the West can give to the USSR. I believe that *perestroyka* deserves a great deal of support from the West, and the West has a vital interest in it. But the support should be cautious. When such thorny and pivotal situations occur as we have now, however, that slogan may already prove harmful to the country—and, as I mentioned, to Gorbachev.

COHEN: Had such a roundtable discussion been held only a few years ago, the Soviet participants probably would have spoken in more or less one voice. And so might have the Americans. That is what happens when people feel themselves to be on opposite sides of a barricade. So I am impressed. It is further evidence of the very significant changes brought about by *glasnost'*. As I listened to our Soviet colleagues talk, I was reminded of Russia's 19th-century intelligentsia, with whom they have so much in common. Indeed, I suppose our Soviet colleagues here today are members of its present-day counterpart, again debating those eternal Russian questions: Whither Russia, and what is to be done? Perhaps the fact that they have no precise or full answers is a good thing. Unlike American commentators who sometimes write about the Gorbachev leadership and *perestroyka* as though they emerged accidentally or inexplicably in 1985, the Soviet participants in this roundtable know that the events of 1985 had a long prehistory, which is their own autobiography. As a person who believes that contemporary politics cannot be studied or understood apart from its history, I hope that if there is to be another Soviet-American roundtable on the fate of *perestroyka,* it will begin at the beginning.

WINSTON: We may as well turn to history and try to rely on what John Joyce (1984) defined as the "old Russian legacy." Encouraging is the ability of Russian people to take it as it comes, to muddle through, make do, and ride out adversities with their courage intact. Understandable is their reluctance to take too many risks in rapid succession. Theodore Shabad was an early believer when we first met in 1947—the cold war still in its infancy at the time. It greatly saddens me and his many friends in the profession that Ted didn't live to see this exciting period. When we last met in 1987 shortly before his death, he was cheerfully confident that a grim march backward into the pre-Gorbachev era will not materialize.

HEWETT: On behalf of the American participants, I should like to thank Messrs. Korotich, Avelichev, and Glotov for the exceptionally stimulating opportunity to partake of the views of our distinguished Soviet colleagues. I am particularly grateful to Yelena Bonner and Academician Andrey Sakharov for the their participation and creative contributions. History books will recount their courage and we are honored by such presence.

Perestroyka is our concern as well as yours, for what transpires here will affect the entire planet. We are thus eager to probe and learn, sharpen our approach, and understand your anxieties, expectations, and pride. We join you in hoping that your country is on the threshold of a new era—a new, exciting beginning.

REFERENCES

Afanas'yev, Yuriy, ed., *Inogo ne dano: perestroyka—glasnost', demokratiya, sotsializm (There Is No Alternative: Restructuring—Openness, Democracy, Socialism).* Moscow: Progress, 1988.

Cohen, Stephen F., *Rethinking the Soviet Experience: Politics and History Since 1917.* New York: Oxford University Press, 1985.

Grossman, Vasiliy, *Forever Flowing.* New York: Harper and Row, 1972.

Hyland, William G., "The Gorbachev Succession," *Foreign Affairs,* 63, 4:800–809, Spring 1985.

Joyce, John M., "The Old Russian Legacy," *Foreign Policy,* 55:132–153, Summer 1984.

Kiselev, Viktor, "Razvitiye teorii sotsializma v SSSR (The Development of the Theory of Socialismn in the USSR)," *Leninskoye znamya,* January 12 and 14, 1988.

Latsis, Otto, "Skazki nashego vremeni (Fairy Tales of Our Time)," *Izvestiya,* April 16, 1988, p. 3.

Sakharov, Andrey, *Progress, Coexistence and Intellectual Freedom.* New York: W. W. Norton, 1970.

Vyzhutovich, Valeriy, and Vladimir V. Glotov, *"Perestroyka:* kto protiv? (*Perestroyka:* Who Is Opposed?)," *Ogonyok,* 50:10–14, December 10–17, 1988.

CHAPTER 9

The Heralds of Opposition to *Perestroyka*

Yitzhak M. Brudny

IN MARCH 1985, at the time Mikhail Gorbachev became General Secretary, there were five Soviet literary monthlies, or "thick journals," as they are known in the USSR, which had a clearly defined Russian nationalist orientation. These journals were: *Molodaya gvardiya, Nash sovremennik, Moskva, Sever,* and *Don.* Their combined circulation was well over one million copies per year. Most important among them were the Moscow journals *Nash sovremennik* (circulation 220,000 copies) and *Molodaya gvardiya* (circulation 640,000). In four full years of Gorbachev's leadership these two journals became the leading organs of various Russian nationalist groups which oppose *perestroyka* and *glasnost'*.

This paper analyzes the fiction and non-fiction published in these two journals between March 1985 and May 1989, as well as the size of their circulation and subscription. This analysis provides a fairly clear picture of the nature, strategy, arguments, and popularity (at least among the Russian reading public) of the Russian nationalist opposition to ongoing reforms. The paper is divided into four basic sections: the first briefly describes the tradition of the Russian "thick" journal from pre-revolutionary times to the end of the Khrushchev era; the second analyzes manifestations of Russian nationalism on the pages of the journals *Novyy mir* and *Molodaya gvardiya* from the mid-1950s to the late 1960s; the third discusses the politics of *Nash sovremennik* in the Brezhnev era; and the final section portrays the politics of these two journals and measures the degree of popularity and power of this nationalist message from the time Gorbachev took office to May 1989.

THE TRADITION OF THE "THICK JOURNAL"

The pre-revolutionary Russian and post-revolutionary Soviet state did not allow (with the exception of the short period between 1905 and 1922) and still

First published in *Soviet Economy*, 1989, 5, 2, pp. 162–200.

does not allow the formation of Western-style political parties. The function of parties as institutions which aggregate and promote the socio-political concerns of social and intellectual elites is performed, because of the highly politicized nature of Russian literature, by the so-called thick journals (*tolstyye zhurnaly*). These are monthly publications, several hundred pages long, with sections of prose, poetry, literary and social criticism, economics, and politics.

To be more precise, in Russia and the Soviet Union the "thick journals" were and are: (a) a well-recognized means of shaping public opinion, (b) accepted arenas of permitted socio-political debate, and (c) important institutional bases of informal groups of politically like-minded members of the intellectual elite, usually headed by its leading representative. In 19th-century Russia, such publications as *Sovremennik, Sovremennyye zapiski, Moskvityanin*, and *Vremya* created and perpetuated this tradition. In the Soviet Russia of the 1920s, the journal *Krasnaya nov'*, edited by the old Bolshevik intellectual Aleksandr Voronskiy, continued to a large degree the pre-revolutionary tradition of the "thick journal" (Maguire, 1968).

In Stalin's Russia, open and even semi-open political debate disappeared. Literary journals were closely monitored by the party ideological apparatus in order to prevent any deviation from the party line and the enshrined principle of "social realism." In the post-war years, Politburo member Andrey Zhdanov was entrusted with the supervision of Soviet cultural life. Under Zhdanov, Stalinist intolerance toward the slightest deviation from the prescribed norm reached its apogee.

Thick journals were the primary victims of Zhdanov's cultural policies. On August 14, 1946, the Central Committee issued a decree entitled "Resolution on the Journals *Zvezda* and *Leningrad*" which fully revealed the Stalinist approach to the thick journals. The decree proclaimed that:

> Our journals are a mighty instrument of the Soviet state in the cause of the education of the Soviet people, and Soviet youth in particular. They must therefore be controlled by the vital foundation of the Soviet order— its politics. The Soviet order cannot tolerate the education of the young in the spirit of indifference to Soviet politics, in the spirit of a devil-may-care attitude and ideological neutrality. . . . Consequently any preaching of ideological neutrality, of political neutrality, of "art for art's sake" is alien to Soviet literature and harmful to the interests of the Soviet state. Such preaching has no place in our journals (Swayze, 1959, p. 37).

The resolution was prompted by the publication in the above-mentioned journals of works of Mikhail Zoshchenko and Anna Akhmatova. In the aftermath of the decree the journal *Leningrad* was shut down permanently, while *Zvezda*'s editorial board was purged.

During the first post-Stalin decade the number of "thick journals" drastically increased. According to a Soviet source, from 1955 to 1957 alone twenty-seven new "thick journals" appeared (Bocharov, 1988, p. 99). More important,

in this period the journals again became institutions of aggregation and artic-
ulation of ideas prevailing in the intellectual elite and, thus, major forums of
socio-political debate.

There were two main reasons why in the post-Stalin era Soviet leaders
tolerated the publication in "thick journals" of ideas which implicitly or explicitly challenged, both from the nationalist "right" and liberal "left" perspective, official policies. First Khrushchev and later Brezhnev and Suslov (the
party chief overseer of cultural life) might have reached the conclusion that it
is impossible to suppress such ideas effectively, if they prevail in large segments
of the society, without a revival of terror. The post-Stalin consensus in the
political leadership was, however, to prevent a recurrence of the terror. Second,
in the post-Stalin era the scope of views prevailing among members of the
political elite was very similar if not identical to that which prevailed among
members of the intellectual elite (Cohen, 1985, p. 133). Competing political
leaders could, therefore, perceive the socio-political debate among members
of the intellectual elite as an important extension of their own debates.

In the late Khrushchev-early Brezhnev era, the leading "thick journal" of
the anti-reformist and orthodox Stalinist end of the political spectrum was
Oktyabr', headed, from 1961 to 1973, by Vsevolod Kochetov. At the other,
reformist and anti-Stalinist end of the spectrum stood the journal *Novyy mir*.
Konstantin Simonov, chief editor from 1954–1958, and especially Aleksandr
Tvardovskiy, chief editor from 1950–1954 and again from 1958–1970, turned
Novyy mir into a major participant in the socio-political debate by publishing
some of the most important anti-Stalinist fictional and non-fictional works of
the period (Spechler, 1982).

RUSSIAN NATIONALISM IN *NOVYY MIR* AND *MOLODAYA GVARDIYA*, 1956–1970

In order to understand the present politics of *Molodaya gvardiya* and *Nash
sovremennik*, one should go back to the literary politics of the years 1956–1970.
The two main "thick journals" which published works of Russian nationalist
writers and critics in the years 1956–1970 were *Novyy mir* and *Molodaya gvardiya*.
Novyy mir was not simply an anti-Stalinist journal which called for socio-political
reform. It was the very first institutional basis of an emerging Russian nationalism
in the post-Stalin era. Between 1953 and 1970, the journal published a series of
fictional and non-fictional works whose common denominator was a sharp criticism
of various aspects of Stalin's legacy in the countryside, be it the methods of party
management of agriculture, the harsh living conditions of the peasantry, or even
collectivization itself. Because of its subject matter, this genre became known as
"village prose" (*derevenskaya proza*).[1]

---

1. On the "village prose" of the 1960s–1970s, see Hosking (1980, Ch. 3), Brown (1978, Ch. 12), Lowe
(1987, pp. 81–95), Zekulin (1971), and Lewis (1976).

Although all 'village prose'' writers who contributed to *Novyy mir* were extremely critical of party policies in the countryside, in retrospect one can discern very meaningful differences of opinion among them. By the mid- to late-1960s there were two "faces" to the "village prose" appearing in *Novyy mir,* which in fact represented two distinct types of Russian nationalism. The first type of "village prose" might be called "liberal-nationalist." It developed from the Valentin Ovechkin school of agrarian journalism of the early post-Stalin era.[2] Its leading exponents were such writers as Fyodor Abramov, Efim Dorosh, Boris Mozhayev, and Sergey Zalygin. Their prose was essentially an effort to write the true history of party policies in the countryside under Stalin and Khrushchev and their effect on the lives of Russian peasants.[3]

The second type of *Novyy mir* "village prose," which emerged in the early 1960s, could be called "conservative nationalist." Its leading exponents were such writers as Vasiliy Belov, Viktor Likhonosov, Aleksandr Solzhenitsyn, and Aleksandr Yashin. These writers equated Russian national identity with traditional peasant identity. They gave a highly idealized description of the traditional peasant way of life and morality, and presented its rapid disappearance as a national tragedy. Often this prose contained strong anti-urban and even anti-intellectual sentiments.[4]

From 1966 to 1970, another major Russian nationalist "thick journal" was *Molodaya gvardiya,* the organ of the Komsomol Central Committee.[5] *Molodaya gvardiya* was the first journal with an exclusively Russian nationalist orientation in the post-Stalin era. The Russian nationalism of *Molodaya gvardiya* also had two "faces," although these were very different from the "faces" of *Novyy mir.* The common denominator of the two types of nationalism found in *Molodaya gvardiya* was a rejection of the reformist politics of *Novyy mir,* an ecological orientation, and a concern for the preservation of the architectural remnants of pre-revolutionary Russia, in particular, ancient Russian churches.

One type might be called a "neo-Stalinist nationalism." Ecological orientation and preservationist concerns distinguished the neo-Stalinist nationalists of *Molodaya gvardiya* from the orthodox Stalinists of *Oktyabr'.* Neo-Stalinist contributors to *Molodaya gvardiya* did not limit themselves to praising Stalin's revival of the military and state-building traditions of the Russian tsars, but especially praised Stalin's retreat from the Bolshevik idealism of the revolutionary era. Moreover, they presented the Russian Revolution as a Russian national revolution. The second type of Russian nationalism appearing in *Mo-*

2. The September 1952 issue of *Novyy mir* contained a semi-fictional essay by Valentin Ovechkin (1904–1968) entitled "District Weekdays" (*Rayonnye budni*). Through the portrayal of a confrontation between District Party Secretary Borzhov, the local Stalinist bully, and reform-minded Second Secretary Martynov, Ovechkin blasted Stalinist methods of agricultural management. This essay became a landmark in Soviet social criticism since it gave birth to a school of agrarian journalists known at the time as "essayists" (*ocherkisty*). On Ovechkin and the "essayist school," see also Garden (1976) and Vilchek (1988).
3. See Abramov (1968), Dorosh (1958–1970), Mozhayev (1966) and Zalygin (1964).
4. See Belov (1968), Likhonosov (1963, 1967), Solzhenitsyn (1963), and Yashin (1962).
5. For an analysis of several major essays published in *Molodaya gvardiya* in the late 1960s, see Yanov (1987, Ch. 10).

lodaya gvardiya might be called "radical Slavophilism." The representatives of this type sharply attacked *Novyy mir* not for its anti-Stalinist stance but for what they perceived to be its pro-Western liberalism. In their essays, they combined strong anti-urban and anti-intellectual rhetoric with a highly idealized view of the Russian Orthodox Church and traditional Russian peasantry as it was portrayed in the "village prose."[6]

NASH SOVREMENNIK, 1970–1985

In 1970, Aleksandr Tvardovskiy and Anatoliy Nikonov, the editors of *Novyy mir* and *Molodaya gvardiya,* were replaced and the editorial boards of the journals purged as a part of a crackdown on both the liberal and nationalist intelligentsia. In 1972, the orthodox Stalinist writer Anatoliy Ivanov (b. 1928) was appointed editor of *Molodaya gvardiya,* a position he still holds as of this writing (May 1989). Although neo-Stalinist nationalists and radical Slavophiles continued to publish in the journal, it ceased to be their primary publication. In addition, after Tvardovskiy's departure, liberal and conservative "village prose" writers largely stopped contributing to *Novyy mir.* In the 1970s, the journal which emerged as the major Russian nationalist publication was *Nash sovremennik.*

The transformation of *Nash sovremennik* began in August 1968 with the appointment of the poet Sergey Vikulov (b. 1922), until then deputy chief editor of *Molodaya gvardiya,* as chief editor of the journal. Vikulov purged the editorial board of the journal, dropping ten of the twelve members of the old board and bringing in thirteen new writers and critics. From the very beginning, Vikulov brought to *Nash sovremennik* both the "village prose" writers of *Novyy mir* and the Russian nationalist historians and literary critics of *Molodaya gvardiya.*[7] This proved to be the key to the journal's success. It acquired the status of the most important Russian nationalist journal publishing views of all segments of the Russian nationalist movement, from the liberal nationalists to the neo-Stalinists. In short, *Nash sovremennik* became the leading institution of the Russian nationalist intelligentsia.

By the early 1980s, *Nash sovremennik* had become very popular among the Russian reading public. Its steadily growing circulation was a good indication of the popularity of the ideas identified with the journal. The circulation of *Nash sovremennik* rose from 60,000 copies in October 1968 (the last issue of the pre-Vikulov era) to 336,000 copies in February 1981.[8]

6. For examples of neo-Stalinist nationalism, see Sakharov (1970), Semanov (1970); for examples of radical Slavophilism, see Glinkin (1967), Lobanov (1968), Chalmayev (1968), and Zhukov (1969).

7. See Abramov (1972), Zalygin (1975), and Rasputin (1976) [liberal nationalist and conservative nationalist "village prose"]; Mikhaylov (1969), Paliyevskiy (1973), and Chivilikhin (1978–1984) [radical Slavophile and neo-Stalinist prose and literary criticism].

8. The interim statistics of *Nash sovremennik*'s circulation are: 70,000 copies in Janaury 1969; 100,000 copies throughout 1973; in the period between the January 1975 issue and the November 1979 issue the circulation grew from 119,000 copies to 205,800 copies; throughout 1980 the circulation was 300,000 copies; in January 1981 it was increased to 333,000 copies.

Such significant growth in the circulation of *Nash sovremennik* was combined with an official recognition of the journal's contributors as being among
the most important Soviet writers. This recognition came in the form of the
very prestigious RSFSR State, USSR State, and Lenin prizes, which were
awarded to the Russian nationalist writers closely associated with the journal,
and the reprinting of their works in millions of copies.[9] The growth in circulation
and official recognition bestowed upon its authors reflected the important role
Nash sovremennik and its contributors were to play in Brezhnev's and Suslov's
efforts to co-opt into the system those Russian nationalist intellectuals previously excluded from it.[10] This inclusionary strategy pursued two aims: (1) to
gain popular support for Brezhnev's policies of heavy investment in agriculture;
and (2) to regain the ability to mobilize the ethnic Russian population through
appeals to its nationalist sentiments since official Marxist-Leninist ideology
could no longer perform this function.[11]

I call Brezhnev's politics of inclusion a "political contract," to distinguish
it from Brezhnev's labor and social policies, conceptualized by Hauslohner
and others as a "social contract" (Hauslohner, 1987). Like the policies associated with the "social contract," the "political contract" failed because by
the end of the 1970s Russian nationalists refused to be a partner. This was due
to two factors: a rising level of expectations among the Russian nationalists,
fueled by the "political contract," in such areas as protection of the environment
and historical monuments, and a revitalization of the countryside—expectations
which the Brezhnev government could not or did not want to fulfill; and
secondly, the continuation of negative social trends including an overwhelming
increase in the incidence of alcoholism, a continuous depopulation of the countryside, and the Russian demographic decline—all processes which Brezhnev's
efforts could not reverse.

Using the 600th anniversary of the Kulikovo Field Battle (1980) and 160th
anniversary of Dostoyevsky's birth (1981) as a pretext, *Nash sovremennik* began
to publish a series of essays very critical of the social and political realities of
the Brezhnev era. The repercussions quickly followed. On February 1, 1982,
Pravda sharply attacked an essay of the radical Slavophile literary critic Vadim
Kozhinov, published in the December 1981 issue of *Nash sovremennik*, as a
part of its Dostoyevsky anniversary celebrations. This attack was followed

9. Vladimir Soloukhin (1979) and Georgiy Semenov (1981) were awarded the RSFSR State Prize. Fyodor
Abramov (1975), Gavriil Troyepolskiy (1975), Valentin Rasputin (1977), Viktor Astaf'yev (1978), Pyotr Proskurin (1979), and Vasiliy Belov (1981), all received the USSR State Prize for literature. Yuriy Bondarev (1972)
and Vasiliy Shukshin (1976) were awarded the Lenin Prize. Between 1967 and 1977 Astaf'yev's books were
printed in 3,608,400 copies; Bondarev's in 3,419,700 copies; Soloukhin's in 2,850,200 copies; Shukshin's in
2,744,000 copies; Abramov's in 2,629,000 copies; Belov's in 2,598,210 copies; Proskurin's in 2,441,000 copies;
Rasputin's in 1,427,000. These statistics do not include reprints of works of these writers in the popular *Roman-
gazeta* series. Each work in this series is printed in 2.5 million copies and sits virtually in every Russian peasant's
and worker's living room. Works of Bondarev, Soloukhin, Shukshin, Abramov, Belov, Proskurin, and Rasputin
were reprinted in these series (see Mehnert, 1983, pp. 36, 239, 268).

10. Jowitt interpreted the process of inclusion of members of social elites (he calls them "articulated
audiences") into Communist regimes as "the attempt to control society 'from within,' as opposed to commanding
it from an insulated position" (see Jowitt, 1975, p. 86).

11. On agriculture as Brezhnev's highest investment priority, see Gustafson (1981, Ch. 2).

shortly by lengthy attacks on Kozhinov and *Nash sovremennik* in other thick journals (Kozhinov, 1981; Kuleshov, 1982; Surovtsev, 1982). This signaled the end of the "political contract." Apparently Andropov was the man who stood behind this decision since he replaced Suslov as the party's chief ideologue at this time. In late July 1982, the Central Committee, for the first time in more than ten years, issued a resolution which contained an explicit condemnation of Russian nationalism. In January 1983, the circulation of *Nash sovremennik* was cut from 335,000 to 220,000 copies, a fact which points to Andropov's determination to crack down on Russian nationalism. These policies continued, although in a less harsh form, under Chernenko.[12]

The policies of the "political contract," nevertheless, transformed the Russian nationalists from being one among many groups within the Russian intellectual elite at the beginning of the Brezhnev era to being the most influential group (at least by perception) at its close. Environmentalism and the preservation of historical monuments, two issues with which Russian nationalism was very closely identified, had gained enormous popularity within Soviet society by 1985. Andropov and Chernenko recognized this reality and, unlike Brezhnev in 1970, did not try to eliminate the main institutional basis of Russian nationalism. The question of how to deal with Russian nationalist intellectuals and their institutional bases was left to Mikhail Gorbachev.

NASH SOVREMENNIK AND *MOLODAYA GVARDIYA* UNDER GORBACHEV

In the period under review (March 1985–May 1989), one can distinguish three stages in the development of Russian nationalism as it appears in the journals under review. At every stage the publication policies of *Nash sovremennik* and *Molodaya gvardiya* dutifully presented the positions of the different types of Russian nationalism toward Gorbachev's policies in general and his cultural policies in particular.[13]

The First Stage: March 1985–March 1987

Perhaps because Russian nationalists were allowed to be the most active political group throughout most of the Brezhnev era, they appeared to be better prepared for political action than the non-nationalist members of the Russian intelligentsia. They demonstrated this in the first year and a half of Gorbachev's leadership. While *Molodaya gvardiya* remained politically ineffective in this

---

12. The relationship between Russian nationalism and the Soviet state in the years 1981–1984 is fairly well described in Dunlop (1985, Chs. 1–3).

13. On Russian nationalism under Gorbachev, see also "Russian Nationalism Today," *Radio Liberty Research Bulletin*, December 19, 1988 (special edition of *RL Bulletin* which contains essays of John B. Dunlop, Darrell P. Hammer, Andrei Sinyavsky, Ronald Grigor Suny, and Alexander Yanov).

period, different groupings of the Russian nationalist movement successfully used *Nash sovremennik* to shape the terms of the socio-political debate.

Soon after Gorbachev took power, *Nash sovremennik* turned ecology, and especially the project to divert Siberian rivers to Central Asia, into one of the main issues on the political agenda.[14] In fact, the journal led the nationalist campaign against the project. In its July 1985 issue, *Nash sovremennik* published a "Round Table," in which twelve highly respected Soviet scientists warned that the river diversion would not bring the promised economic benefits, but could lead to ecological disaster (*Zemlya i khleb,* 1985). This was the beginning of a long campaign which ended on August 15, 1986, when the Politburo announced the halt of all field work on the project in order to reevaluate its economic and ecological consequences. This was in effect the cancellation of the project. Moreover, the opposition to the project was rewarded: one of the project's major opponents and an important contributor to *Nash sovremennik* in the 1970s, the liberal nationalist writer Sergey Zalygin, was appointed the chief editor of *Novyy mir* a week before the cancellation was announced.

In addition to the environmental issues, *Nash sovremennik* soon brought the subject of moral corruption in Russian society to the center of the political debate. *Nash sovremennik*'s success in raising the issue of moral corruption was a result of the publication in the journal of the works of such conservative nationalist "village prose" writers as Valentin Rasputin, Viktor Astaf'yev, Vasiliy Belov, and Aleksandr Astrakhantsev. Rasputin, in the novel *Fire* (Rasputin, 1985), Astaf'yev, in the collection of short stories *Place of Action* (Astaf'yev, 1986), Belov, in the novel *Everything Lies Ahead* (Belov, 1986), and Astrakhantsev, in the novel *Parting of the Ways* (Astrakhantsev, 1986), all portrayed Russian society as morally corrupt and argued that without a revival of traditional moral values, Gorbachev's reforms were doomed to fail. They searched for the agents of the moral corruption of Russian and found them in the Communist Party, the urban intelligentsia, urban emancipated women, rock music, and the national minorities, especially Jews and Georgians.[15]

During this period, *Nash sovremennik* did not limit itself to the publication of conservative nationalist critiques of Russia's moral corruption. Rather, *Nash sovremennik* was the very first journal in the Gorbachev era to publish neo-Stalinist and anti-Semitic attacks on the new, liberalizing trends in Soviet cultural life. In the June 1985 issue of the journal, the theater critic Mark Lyubomudrov lashed out at those theater directors who staged plays which

14. On the river diversion project in general and the Russian nationalist campaign against it in particular, see Petro (1987), Darst (1988), and Micklin and Bond (1988).

15. For his novel *Fire (Pozhar)*, Rasputin received the State Prize in 1987. Astafiyev's collection of short stories was preceded by the publication in the *Oktyabr*'s January 1986 issue of his novel *The Sad Detective Story [Pechal'nyy detektiv]* which dealt with the same issues. At the May 1987 discussion of journal publication in the RSFSR Writers Union Secretariat, *Nash sovremennik* was praised for being in the forefront of the ecological campaign and the struggle against moral corruption. See "Obsuzhdeniye raboty zhurnala 'Nash sovremennik'," *Literaturnaya Rossiya,* May 15, 1987.

gave a more realistic account of Soviet reality (Lyubomudrov, 1985). These plays, Lyubomudrov claimed, rather than giving Russia a clear national ideal to strive for, were exclusively preoccupied with the darker side of Soviet life. In many ways this article set the standard for all subsequent neo-Stalinist critiques of Gorbachev's *glasnost'* policies.

The radical Slavophiles in this period also used *Nash sovremennik* to revive the debate about the Slavophile legacy and its crucial importance in the present. They did so in order to suggest that Gorbachev would lose his mandate to rule if the essence of his reforms were the simple adoption of Western social, political, and cultural models. The historian Apollon Kuzmin stated that by borrowing Western values and culture, the post-Petrine autocracy and the aristocratic elite separated themselves from the rest of the Russian nation and became, in fact, "rootless cosmopolitans." Progressive forces in Russian society, such as the Decembrists, turned against the autocracy because it was a cosmopolitan institution bent on weakening and betraying the Russian state (Kuzmin, 1985, p. 189; Kuzmin, 1986, pp. 189–190).

By using the concept "cosmopolitans"—the euphemistic slogan of Stalin's anti-Semitic campaign—Kuzmin implied that those elites who wanted to introduce Western or Western-like models to the Soviet Union were alien social elements, as Jews are, and should be treated the way Jews were treated in the late 1940s–early 1950s. Kuzmin's argument was supported and elaborated by another radical Slavophile historian, Vadim Pigalev (Pigalev, 1986). In an essay on the Slavophile legacy, he asserted that the Russian nation is anti-bourgeois and anti-capitalist in its nature. The only way to undermine its strength is to turn the Russian people into "consumerist-philistine cattle." Thus Gorbachev was warned of the danger of turning Russia into a Western-style consumer society.

The Rise of Aleksandr Yakovlev

The ability of *Nash sovremennik* to set the agenda for socio-political debate, however, progressively diminished after the autumn of 1986. This was due to the fast rise in the Kremlin hierarchy of Aleksandr Yakovlev, a committed reformer and a long-time foe of Russian nationalism.[16] In March 1986, at the end of the 27th Party Congress, he was promoted to the position of Secretary of the Central Committee in charge of cultural life and in January 1987, he became a candidate member of the Politburo, rising to full membership six months later.

Yakovlev knew that control of the cultural realm was crucial for creating wide popular support for *perestroyka*. In order to achieve this he made several key appointments over the course of 1986. Vasiliy Shauro, Russian nationalist sympathizer, and a leading supporter of the policies of the "political contract"

---

16. See his two-page essay "Protiv antiistorizma," *Literaturnaya gazeta*, November 15, 1972.

in the party apparat, was replaced by Yuriy Voronov in the position of head of the Cultural Department of the Central Committee, and Vasiliy Zakharov replaced another Brezhnev appointee, Pyotr Demichev, in the post of Minister of Culture.

More important, Yakovlev handed control of several Moscow newspapers, popular magazines, and literary journals to the reform-minded intellectuals. Vitaliy Korotich replaced an old Stalinist, Anatoliy Sofronov, as chief editor of the popular, mass-circulation weekly *Ogonyok,* while Albert Belyayev and Yegor Yakovlev became chief editors of the newspapers *Sovetskaya kul'tura* and *Moskovskiye novosti.* Yakovlev seized the opportunity of the vacant positions of chief editor at the journals *Znamya* and *Novyy mir* to appoint Grigoriy Baklanov as the chief editor of *Znamya* and Sergey Zalygin as the chief editor of *Novyy mir.* Finally, Yakovlev used his influence to support the election of Elem Klimov as the first secretary of the Filmmakers' Union (May 1986) and of Kiril Lavrov as the first secretary of the newly created Union of Theater Workers (December 1986), thus helping supporters of cultural liberalization to gain control of these two important artistic unions.

These nominations signified the beginning of the Gorbachev "political contract." The beneficiaries of Gorbachev's "contract" were liberal and liberal-nationalist members of the intellectual elite. Not only did they control important newspapers and journals, but the circulation of these pro-reform publications was allowed to skyrocket while the circulation of *Nash sovremennik* essentially remained frozen at its 1983 level.[17]

At the beginning of the period, the leading conservative nationalists and members of *Nash sovremennik*'s editorial board, Rasputin, Belov, and Astaf'yev, adopted a position of political "fence sitting." They supported some aspects of *perestroyka,* such as the anti-Stalinist campaign, reform in the countryside, tough anti-alcohol policies, and publication of previously forbidden works of literature, and opposed others, such as the opening up of Soviet society to Western cultural influences, in general, and the legitimation of rock music, in particular. Later on, however, they joined another prominent conservative nationalist member of the *Nash sovremennik* editorial board, Yuriy Bondarev, who by March 1987 had become the unchallenged leader of the united Russian nationalist opposition to Gorbachev's cultural policies.

Progressively losing the ability to shape the agenda of the socio-political debate and increasingly repulsed by events in Soviet cultural life, the conservative nationalists, radical Slavophiles, and neo-Stalinist nationalists launched a frontal attack on the liberalization of cultural life and, by implication, on *perestroyka* in general. This assault began in March 1987 at a meeting of the Secretariat of the Russian Republic Writers' Union. On this occasion, Bon-

17. The circulation of *Ogonyok* rose from 1,500,000 copies in 1985 to 3,350,000 copies in 1989; the circulation of *Znamya* went up from 175,000 copies in 1985 to 980,000 in 1989; the circulation of *Novyy mir* increased from 425,000 copies in 1985 to 1,573,000 copies in 1989. In comparison, during the same period of time, the circulation of *Nash sovremennik* grew only from 220,000 to 250,000 copies.

darev, one of the secretaries of the Union, spoke of the "pseudo-democrats of literature, who have lit over an abyss the light of *glasnost'* which they stole from justice and truth." He equated the situation of Russian national culture today to that of Russia in July 1941, when it was on the brink of defeat by Nazi Germany. He called upon the nationalist opponents of reform to rally for a "cultural Stalingrad" (*Literaturnaya Rossiya,* March 27, 1987).

In the months following the meeting of the RSFSR Writers Union, there was a "revival" of *Molodaya gvardiya.* It not only joined *Nash sovremennik* as a very important forum of Russian nationalist reaction to the cultural liberalization but, in fact, it became the most important publication of the neo-Stalinist nationalists who opposed Gorbachev's reform projects. The publication of hitherto forbidden works of literature, avant-garde art, the liberalization of Soviet television, the acceptance of rock music, the liberal reformist intelligentsia, and newspapers and journals which supported the reforms were all assailed with increasing intensity (Pisarev, 1987; Andreyev, 1987; Baygushev, 1987a). The leading voice in this campaign was Vyacheslav Gorbachev, the deputy editor of *Molodaya gvardiya.* In a series of essays, he defended Stalin, extolled traditional family values, criticized the publication of Nabokov's works and the exhibition of Chagall's paintings, attacked Jews, freemasons, rock music, the liberal reformist intelligentsia, and its newspapers and magazines such as *Ogonyok, Moskovskiye novosti, Sovetskaya kul'tura,* and *Nedelya* (Gorbachev, 1987a; Gorbachev, 1987b; Gorbachev, 1987c).

After *Ogonyok* sharply responded to Vyacheslav Gorbachev's vicious attack in the July 1987 issue of *Molodaya gvardiya,* the party apparatus, fearing that the situation was getting out of hand, intervened to stop the infighting between the journals. A high party official, in an article in *Pravda* which he signed under the pseudonym "Vladimir Petrov," called upon both *Molodaya gvardiya* and *Ogonyok* to restrain themselves. The neo-Stalinists of *Molodaya gvardiya,* however, insisted on having the last word in this confrontation. In the September 1987 issue of the journal, twenty-two nationalist historians, writers, and literary critics elaborated in sixty-eight pages Vyacheslav Gorbachev's arguments against Mikhail Gorbachev's cultural policies. This was the strongest attack (until March 1988) on Mikhail Gorbachev's reform program since his rise to power.[18]

In essay after essay, the contributors assailed the Soviet press for its reports on drug addiction and prostitution, criticized rock music, the publication of forbidden works of literature (especially those of Nabokov), and the exhibition of avant-garde art (especially that of Marc Chagall), demanded the cessation of attacks on Stalin, and argued against the rehabilitation of Bukharin and Trotsky. Mikhail Gorbachev's idea that the radical restructuring of Soviet society requires the encouragement of diverse social and political views was proclaimed to contradict the Russian historical experience and its national traditions. As one of the contributors bluntly stated: "cultural 'pluralism,' the

18. *Ogonyok,* No. 30, 1987, pp. 26–27; Vladimir Petrov, "Kul'tura diskussii," *Pravda,* August 3, 1987; "V otvete za vremya," 1987.

uninterrupted 'free competition' of different, [and] at the same time, entirely contradictory points of view, tastes and predilections, implies the rejection of the main idea which unifies the Soviet people, of traditional spiritual values, and of deviation from the main road of our history'' (Fomenko, 1987, p. 280).

The principle of democratization was assailed as leading to social anarchy, and the liberal-reformist intelligentsia, which pressed for the democratization of Soviet politics, was accused of undermining the strength of the Russian state. What Russia really needed was, as another contributor asserted, ''a strong and responsible state power, which knows the troubles and the needs of the nation'' (Karpets, 1987, p. 243). In the next six issues of *Molodaya gvardiya* (October 1987–March 1988), the attacks continued on various aspects of *perestroyka* and *glasnost'*, be it the publication of Pasternak's *Doctor Zhivago*, works of fiction and literary criticism of liberal reformers, rock music, and the content of Soviet television programs, or Nikolay Shmelev's proposals for radical economic reform (Markova, 1987; Lisenkov and Sergeyev, 1987; Khatyushin, 1987; Doronin, 1987; Baygushev, 1987b; Bushin, 1988a; Antonov, 1988; Trukhin, 1988).

Nash sovremennik tried to keep up with *Molodaya gvardiya* in its attacks on *perestroyka* and *glasnost'*. The two journals, however, opposed Gorbachev's reforms from different Russian nationalist viewpoints. As mentioned earlier, the *Molodaya gvardiya* perspective was definitely that of the neo-Stalinist nationalist. Despite the fact that *Nash sovremennik* also published neo-Stalinist attacks on *perestroyka* (Shevtsov, 1986; Lyubomudrov, 1987; Baygushev, 1988), it served primarily as a forum for the radical Slavophiles. This line of the editorial board of *Nash sovremennik* meant the end of the journal as a forum for all branches of the Russian nationalist movement. From late 1986 on, such prominent liberal nationalists as Dmitriy Likhachev, Sergey Zalygin, Boris Yekimov, and Boris Mozhayev no longer contributed to *Nash sovremennik*. In fact, the column on agrarian journalism was the only section of the journal which continued to publish liberal nationalist journalists. It was *Novyy mir* which became, from the time of Zalygin's appointment as its chief editor, the main liberal nationalist journal.[19]

The contributors to *Nash sovremennik* in particular saw a grave danger to Russian national existence in the pluralism of cultural forms which Gorbachev encouraged. They pointed to the policy of removing all obstacles from the performance of rock music as an example of how *perestroyka* contributes to the spread of harmful Western political and cultural values among the Russian youth. And as in the case of *Molodaya gvardiya*, the attack on rock music as a symbol of Gorbachev's cultural policies went on in *Nash sovremennik* simultaneously with vicious attacks on the reformist intelligentsia (Dunayev, 1988; Kazintsev, 1986, 1988a; Bushin, 1987). Another device used by contributors to *Nash sovremennik* to attack *perestroyka* was to discredit the recently

19. On Zalygin and his editorial policies at *Novyy mir*, see Brudny (1988).

rehabilitated Bukharin and his legacy. They portrayed Bukharin as a Trotskyite in disguise, a man who hated Russia, who organized the persecution of leading representatives of Russian national culture, and even as an enemy of NEP and the Russian peasantry (Dubrovina, 1987, pp. 181–183; Kozhinov, 1987, pp. 164–165; Kuzmin, 1987, p. 176).

During this period, however, *Nash sovremennik* tried to do more than simply criticize Soviet reformers. As in the preceding stage, the journal attempted to concentrate on one policy area around which most Russian nationalists, as well as wide sections of the general public, could unify in order to create strong pressure in favor of a major policy change. If in 1985–1986, *Nash sovremennik* was campaigning for the cancellation of the river-diversion projects, in 1987–1988, the journal lobbied for the imposition of a "dry law" on Soviet society.

On May 17, 1985, the Politburo announced a policy severely restricting production and sales of alcoholic beverages. These restrictions were accompanied by the creation of a voluntary Sobriety Society, known after its Russian acronym of VDOBT (*Vsesoyuznoye dobrovolnoye obshchestvo borby za trezvost'*), the aim of which was to spread the idea of sobriety among the masses. By mid-1987, it was clear that the policy was not only failing to achieve its goals but also causing serious damage to the Soviet economy. In many places local authorities quietly increased sales of alcoholic beverages. Moreover, instead of becoming an aggressive Russian nationalist organization, the VDOBT turned out to be a very ineffective institution staffed with ex-party and government bureaucrats.

All these developments prompted *Nash sovremennik* to start a campaign for the imposition of a total ban on the production and sale of alcohol and for the revitalization of the VDOBT. The campaign began with the publication in the July 1987 issue of the journal of an essay by Dr. Fyodor Uglov, a member of the Soviet Academy of Medical Sciences and the chief Russian nationalist spokesman on problems of alcoholism. In the essay, Uglov notes that alcoholism threatens the very existence of the Russian nation (Uglov, 1987). He insists that the income the state generates from alcohol sales cannot outweigh the damage alcohol abuse inflicts on the economy and national defense.

Uglov brings up two main causes of the evident failure of the May 1985 policies. First, these policies were at best only half-measures. Second, there is a conspiracy between bureaucrats who see in alcohol sales the easiest way to generate revenues, and ethnic non-Russians in the mass media who oppose the idea of a sober Russian nation.[20] The only way to save the Russian nation from physical extinction is, in his view, to reimpose the complete ban on the production and sale of alcohol which existed in Russia in the years 1914–1925, and to transform the VDOBT into a grassroots movement led by prominent Russian nationalist advocates of "dry law" policies.

20. In his 1986 book (Uglov, 1986), Uglov openly blames pre-revolutionary alcoholism in Russia on Jews.

Uglov's ideas were elaborated and defended by Lapchenko and Kovalenin in the March 1988 issue of *Nash sovremennik*. In his essay, Boris Lapchenko argues that the policy of restricting production and sale of alcohol is bound to remain ineffective while an acute shortage of consumer goods exists (Lapchenko, 1988). Lapchenko calls for a complete ban on alcohol production and sale, combined with a saturation of the market with consumer goods. The essay by A. Kovalenin, a member of the Novosibirsk chapter of the VDOBT, contains a detailed program to fight alcoholism (Kovalenin, 1988). At its center stands a proposal to elect Uglov and other well-known Russian nationalists to head the VDOBT, to have new elections in all regional chapters of the society, and to impose a total ban on the production and sale of alcohol by December 19, 1989, the 70th anniversary of the Bolsheviks' decision to continue pre-revolutionary "dry law" policies.

Finally, the period between March 1987 and March 1988 witnessed the emergence in the Soviet political arena of a new form of Russian nationalist opposition to *perestroyka*. Exploiting Gorbachev's policy of permitting the formation and activities of non-official societies with a political agenda, the nationalist and rabidly anti-Semitic Moscow organization *Pamyat'* was able to transform itself from a small cultural club into a very visible, if not significant, factor in Soviet politics. Although the leaders of *Pamyat'* presented themselves as ardent supporters of *perestroyka,* through their arguments about a pervasive Judeo-Masonic conspiracy against Russia, they in fact challenged *perestroyka* from radical Slavophile positions taken to the very extreme.[21]

It was natural that *Nash sovremennik* would be the first journal to defend *Pamyat'* from its liberal critics. The first to address the subject of *Pamyat'* on the pages of the journal was the leading radical Slavophile theorist, Vadim Kozhinov. He rejects many of *Pamyat'*s arguments because they contain, in his words, too much "ignorance" and "infantilism" which finds its expression "in all kinds of emblems, myths, [and] fantastic images." Kozhinov refused, however, to condemn *Pamyat'*, claiming that its extremism is an unavoidable by-product of the ongoing transformation of Russian nationalism into a mass movement. Finally, this refusal to denounce the organization went hand-in-hand with a long and harsh attack on *Pamyat'*s critics (Kozhinov, 1987, pp. 167–172).[22]

This defense was seconded by that of the conservative nationalist Valentin Rasputin in the January 1988 issue (Rasputin, 1988, p. 171). Rasputin spoke about "the left-leaning (*davshaya levyy kren*) press" which violates the principles of *glasnost'* by attaching to *Pamyat'* the label of the "Black Hundreds," and by denying *Pamyat'* the right to defend itself in print. *Pamyat'* ought to be defended, Rasputin argues, because behind attempts to discredit and crush

---

21. For a useful recent summary of Soviet and Western writings on *Pamyat'*, see Laqueur (1989, pp. 135–145).

22. For a similar attack on *Pamyat'* critics, see Kuzmin (1988, pp. 154–156).

the organization stands a desire to discredit and crush the entire Russian nationalist movement.

The Third Stage: March 1988–May 1989

It was not surprising that *Nash sovremennik* defended *Pamyat'* regularly, beginning in late 1987. This was a period of growing confrontation between the supporters of *perestroyka* and its opponents. One of the most important arenas for this confrontation was a meeting of the governing board of the USSR Writers Union, which took place on March 1–2, 1988. Russian nationalist opponents of *perestroyka* used the forum to attack the reforms. As in March 1987, the assault was led by Yuriy Bondarev, who portrayed *glasnost'* as "unruliness of all-negating emotions," and accused reformers of depicting all Russian and Soviet history exclusively in black colors. He openly labeled the historian Yuriy Afanas'yev, one of the main spokesmen of reformers, as the "apostle of sensation and slander." Other nationalist writers and critics defended *Pamyat'*, criticized the rehabilitation of Bukharin, and blamed the reforms for weakening the state and thus setting the stage for the Nagorno-Karabakh affair.[23]

This confrontation at the meeting of the Writers Union's governing board was an ominous prelude to the publication of an essay by a college teacher, Nina Andreyeva, entitled "I Cannot Give Up Principles" (*Ne mogu postupitsya s printsipami*). Spread over a full page in the March 13, 1988, issue of the daily *Sovetskaya Rossiya*, it was a frontal attack on *perestroyka* made from the neo-Stalinist nationalist point of view. Andreyeva defended Stalin as the leader who turned Russia into a superpower, criticized *glasnost'* policies, and accused reformist writers Shatrov and Rybakov of falsifying Soviet history in their recently published works. The essay was rabidly anti-Semitic: it emphasized the Jewishness of Trotsky and even argued that Jews are a counterrevolutionary nation. The unprecedented length of the essay and the fact that it was reprinted in regional newspapers throughout the Soviet Union and in Eastern Europe clearly pointed to Yegor Ligachev, the second-ranking Politburo member at the time, as its main sponsor.[24]

Despite official condemnation of Andreyeva's article in *Pravda* (April 5, 1988), its publication encouraged the editors of *Molodaya gvardiya*, who, sensing the support for their ideas within the Politburo, proceeded to intensify their assault on *perestroyka*. In its April 1988 issue, the journal published an essay by Mikhail Malakhov, the deputy head of Gosplan under Khrushchev. It was the first serious effort to forge an alliance between Russian nationalist

23. *Literaturnaya gazeta*, March 9, 1988. In addition to Bondarev's speech, see also the speeches of Prokhanov, Kunyayev, and Prokushev.

24. According to a prominent reformist intellectual, Vasiliy Selyunin, Ligachev himself praised the essay in two meetings with Soviet press editors and pressed them to reprint it. See *Christian Science Monitor*, April 27, 1988, pp. 1, 10.

intellectuals and the anti-reformist forces in the Soviet political elite (Malakhov, 1988).

The content of the essay is very similar to that of Andreyeva's. It is an outright apology of Stalinism. It praises collectivization and industrialization and the principles of Stalinist industrial management. In the same breath, Malakhov sharply criticizes the de-Stalinization reforms of Khrushchev. Finally, Malakhov warns that Gorbachev's re-opening of the Stalin question would inevitably lead to anarchy and the undermining of socialism.

Alongside Malakhov's essay, *Molodaya gvardiya* resorted to a strategy of selectively publishing readers' letters in order to renew its attacks on such manifestations of *perestroyka* and *glasnost'* as the rehabilitation of Bukharin, private businesses, rock music, and the publication of formerly forbidden anti-Stalinist works of fiction. As before, the reformist intelligentsia bore the main brunt of the attack. They were accused of undermining national morale by filling literary journals with works which ''attempt to prove that the last seventy years were the most dirty and disgusting in the history of our nation.'' They also were found guilty of weakening the Russian state by using the existing freedom of expression to preach ideological rapprochement with the bourgeois West (Khochu, 1988; Nesti, 1988; Podmena, 1988; Kak nashe, 1988).

Like *Molodaya gvardiya, Nash sovremennik* made an effort to establish a tie with the anti-reformist forces in the Soviet political elite. *Nash sovremennik* tried to present Ligachev and his appointees as leaders whose records show a deep understanding of Russian nationalist concerns. The May 1988 issue of the journal contained Yevgeniy Chernykh's essay about the anti-alcohol policies of the Tomsk regional party secretaries, Ligachev, and his successor (and presumably appointee) Zorkal'tsev. Chernykh claims that already in the 1970s, Ligachev, on his own initiative, severely restricted the number of alcohol sales outlets and their working hours. As a result of this policy, the consumption of vodka in the region fell by one-third in the period 1974–1984. After the introduction of the anti-alcohol policies in May 1985, Zorkal'tsev closed several main alcohol producing facilities in the region, left open only a few liquor stores and restaurants which serve liquor, and banned deliveries of alcoholic beverages from outside the region (Chernykh, 1988, pp. 156, 158–159). The message of the article is clear: Ligachev and his people deserve Russian nationalists' strongest support.

Alongside the promotion of Ligachev, *Nash sovremennik*'s publication policies between April and June 1988 were aimed at strengthening the unity of the Russian nationalist opposition to *perestroyka* on the eve of the 19th Party Conference. As a symbolic act of solidarity with the editorial line of *Molodaya gvardiya, Nash sovremennik* carried in its May 1988 issue a long interview with Anatoliy Ivanov, the chief editor of *Molodaya gvardiya*, which contained a straightforward apology for Stalinism and a harsh attack on *perestroyka*. Ivanov tries to shift the blame for the violence which accompanied collectivization, and for the destruction of several Moscow churches in the 1930s, from Stalin to his Jewish lieutenants, Yakovlev and Kaganovich, and justifies the terror of the 1930s as a defensive act against internal enemies. The terror, he declares, saved the Soviet Union from a counterrevolution of the kind East Germany experienced in 1953, Hungary in 1956, and Czechoslovakia in 1968. Finally, like the rest of the neo-Stalinists, he repeats the warning that the reforms are leading Russia to anarchy, as they did in Eastern Europe (A. Ivanov, 1988).

Ivanov's neo-Stalinist and anti-Semitic assertions were seconded by the radical Slavophile stance of Vadim Kozhinov. The April 1988 issue of the journal contains his programmatic essay in which he blames the Jews for terrorizing the Russian peasantry during collectivization and for blowing up Moscow's churches in the 1930s. Contrary to Ivanov, Kozhinov is not apologetic toward Stalin. He presents Stalin as a good Leninist and as a man who merely perfected the machine of terror which Lenin built during the Civil War. Moreover, he states that both Lenin and Stalin were only executioners of the will of the world Communist movement which was under Jewish domination (Kozhinov, 1988).

Publication of the articles of Ivanov and Kozhinov reflected the strategy of *Nash sovremennik*'s editors. Anti-Semitism was to serve as the "glue" of the nationalist opposition to the reforms. Indeed, in the months preceding the 19th Party Conference, anti-Semitic attacks on *perestroyka* in *Nash sovremennik* reached an unprecedented level. *Nash sovremennik* now openly endorsed a theory of Judeo-Masonic conspiracy by publishing Viktor Ivanov's novel *The Day of Judgment* (V. Ivanov, 1988). The novel, of a kind which had not appeared in print in the Soviet Union since Ivan Shevtsov's rabidly anti-Semitic novels of the 1960s, portrayed the subversive activities of a Judeo-Masonic espionage network in the Soviet Union of the Khrushchev era. *Nash sovremennik* also rallied in defense of Vladimir Begun, the leading anti-Semitic theorist in the Soviet Union, from attacks by reformers who accused him of plagiarizing from Hitler's *Mein Kampf*. The *Nash sovremennik* editors not only published a letter in defense of Begun but also endorsed it (Protiv, 1988).

The anti-Semitic line of *Nash sovremennik* was quickly picked up by *Molodaya gvardiya*. The July 1988 issue of the journal, which appeared during the Party Conference, carried a dialogue between Ivan Shevtsov himself and Air Force Marshal Ivan Pstygo. They assail "Zionism" and present it as "the agency of world imperialism" and as the most vicious enemy of the Soviet state. Moreover, the authors openly praise *Pamyat'* for its efforts to make the public aware of the "Zionist" threat. Shevtsov and Pstygo, indeed, go on to present *Pamyat'* as a patriotic society which deserves the open and unqualified support of the party and the military (Shevtsov and Pstygo, 1988, pp. 226–228).

The 19th Party Conference proved that Russian nationalist opposition to *perestroyka* has substantial support inside the party. Such prominent opponents of *perestroyka* as Yuriy Bondarev and Anatoliy Ivanov were elected to the

Conference as delegates. In his speech before the Conference, Bondarev defended the publication policies of *Molodaya gvardiya* and *Nash sovremennik* and viciously attacked *glasnost'*. He accused the reformist newspapers and journals of propagating national nihilism and immorality, Western ideas and values, and warned that *glasnost'* was destabilizing the Soviet state. Bondarev's ideas found support among many delegates who interrupted his speech with applause, and who booed Baklanov, the editor of *Znamya*, who sharply criticized Bondarev's speech (*Pravda,* July 2, 1988).

While broad support of Russian nationalist opposition to *perestroyka* was evident among the delegates, this was not reflected in the Conference resolutions. In fact, one resolution contained an implicit condemnation of Russian nationalist opposition; the policies of *glasnost'* were upheld while the "activities aimed at ... stirring up national and racial hatred" were condemned (*Pravda,* July 2, 1988). Moreover, in early fall 1988, the Russian nationalists suffered a major defeat: Gorbachev disregarded the renewed pressure of *Nash sovremennik* to impose a total ban on alcohol production (Khukhry et al., 1988; Dusha, 1988) and cancelled the 1985 anti-alcohol policies.

Despite the defeat of the anti-alcohol campaign, Russian nationalists were extremely encouraged by the hostility of the Conference delegates toward reformist Moscow intellectuals. To them, this was the best indicator of the views prevailing among the party elite. Moreover, Ligachev openly expressed his support of their views by endorsing Bondarev's Conference speech at a meeting with local journalists in Gorkiy in August 1988.[25]

At the September 1988 meeting of the Secretariat of the RSFSR Writers Union in Ryazan', the leaders of the coalition of Russian nationalist opponents to *perestroyka,* encouraged by this endorsement, began a new assault on Gorbachev's cultural and economic policies. It is worth pointing out that the intensity of the assault did not diminish after Ligachev lost his position as the second-ranking Politburo member in the September 30, 1988, Politburo reshuffle.

Rasputin, in the meeting's keynote address, spoke about the destructive impact on Russia and its culture of such Western imports as rock music, beauty contests, sex education, and the defense of homosexuality. The radical Slavophile economist Mikhail Antonov attacked the legalization of joint ventures and the move toward integration into the world economy as leading to the transformation of Russia into a "colony of multi-national corporations." Another leading radical Slavophile, the literary critic Anatoliy Lanshchikov, added to Antonov's argument a warning that Gorbachev's policies would cause Russia to fall victim to "Western 'peaceful' technological aggression and the equally

25. Answering a reporter who praised Bondarev's speech at the Party Conference and complaining that *Ogonyok* is engaging in sensationalism and destructive criticism of Soviet achievements, Ligachev argued that the Party Conference rejected reformers' attempts to portray Soviet history exclusively in negative terms. He went on to emphasize that during the Stalin and post-Stalin periods, the Soviet Union transformed itself from a backward country into a world superpower (see Povyshat', 1988, p. 5).

'peaceful' Eastern demographic aggression.'' He, as well as other participants, also complained about the anti-Russian nature of *Ogonyok* and other leading reformist publications.[26]

Elaboration of Rasputin's argument that *perestroyka* undermines the moral health of the Russian nation by exposing it to Western cultural aggression fit perfectly into the aim of the editorial boards of *Nash sovremennik* and *Molodaya gvardiya* to redefine the nature of the socio-political debate. Already the October 1988 issue of *Nash sovremennik* featured a special section dedicated to the dangers of rock music to Russian youth. The contributors present rock music as the Western "Trojan Horse" which destroys from within the most basic unit of Soviet society, the family, and call for enactment of legislation limiting the activities of rock bands (Chistyakov and Sanachev, 1988; Chirkin, 1988; Gunko, 1988). Both *Nash sovremennik* and *Molodaya gvardiya* followed Rasputin in attacking "pornography" in Soviet cinema, theater, and arts, the defense of homosexuality, and sexual education as leading to the corruption of youth (Andreyev-Rayevskiy, 1988; Lyubomudrov, 1989, pp. 177–179; Lugovoy, 1989; Matveyets, 1989; Shiropayev, 1989, pp. 183–184; Zelenevskiy, 1988).

Of equal if not higher importance to the campaign against rock music and sexuality in arts were the journals' efforts to discredit the radical reformers and their publications both in the eyes of the party elite and the general public. Between October 1988 and May 1989, almost every issue of both journals printed polemical essays and readers' letters which violently attacked *Ogonyok* and *Znamya,* their leading contributors, and their editors. Korotich and Baklanov. The strategy was to blend character assassination with political accusations. So, Korotich's reformist credentials were challenged on the ground that in the past the *Ogonyok* editor had praised Brezhnev's literary genius. *Ogonyok* itself was denounced as "an omnipotent ideological narcotic" which demoralizes Russian people by denying their past achievements and undermining their belief in the idea of socialism. Baklanov, the editor of *Znamya,* in turn, was accused of distorting the history of World War II, especially Stalin's war record, and spreading malicious allegations against *Pamyat'* (Bushin, 1988b; Bushin, 1989a; Bushin, 1989b; Ekologiya, 1988, pp. 245–250; Fed, 1989a, pp. 13–16, 1989b, pp. 175–179; Gorbachev, 1989, pp. 250–257; 1989, pp. 277–281; Kozhinov, 1989, pp. 143, 173–175; Lapin, 1989; Litsom, 1989, pp. 217–226, 228–232).

The same basic strategy was applied against the liberal Moscow intelligentsia and cultural avant-garde associated with it. *Molodaya gvardiya* published letters from readers in which the Moscow intelligentsia was labeled "intellectual bourgeoisie" and was accused of attempting to take from the party its control over the nature of the reform process (Litsom, 1989, pp. 228, 233). In addition to these political accusations, *Molodaya gvardiya* portrayed the avant-garde

26. An abridged stenographic report of the Ryazan' meeting of the RSFSR Writers Union Secretariat was published in the October 28, 1988, issue of *Literaturnaya Rossiya.*

poetry and prose of younger members of the Moscow intelligentsia as elitist and detached from the concerns of the people (Bulin, 1989; Khatyushin, 1988; Salutskiy, 1989).

Anti-intellectualism also constituted an important dimension in *Nash sovremennik*'s and *Molodaya gvardiya*'s evaluation of Stalinism, its roots, and the political and economic alternatives to it. It is clear that the two journals would like to avoid extensive treatment of Stalinism, since it meant both the acceptance of the agenda of the socio-political debate set by radical reformers and the danger of a potential breakdown of the Russian nationalist alliance over this issue. Stalinism and its political, social, and economic legacy, indeed, was not discussed at the Ryazan' meeting.

Russian nationalists, however, were dragged into this very debate because of the extremely wide publicity which accompanied publication of such anti-Stalinist works of fiction as Grossman's novel *Life and Fate* or Voynovich's *Life and Adventures of Ivan Chonkin;* the foundation by leading members of Moscow reformist intelligentsia of the *Memorial* society dedicated to commemorating the victims of Stalinism in the fall of 1988; and an intensification, due to the progressively worsening food supply situation and the sharply diminishing availability of consumer goods, of the debate about the potential of a command economy and the future direction of economic reform.

Although the strategy of *Molodaya gvardiya* and *Nash sovremennik* in dealing with the issue of Stalinism and the Stalinist legacy differed significantly, both journals heavily emphasized anti-intellectual and anti-Semitic elements in order to keep the nationalist alliance together. *Molodaya gvardiya*'s policy primarily was to publish essays and letters of orthodox Stalinists, be it simple workers, intellectuals, or former high party officials (Benediktov, 1989; Konotop, 1988; Matveyets, 1988; Mostafin, 1989; Zhitnukhin, 1988).[27]

The orthodox Stalinists aggressively justify all aspects of Stalinism, including collectivization and the terror, as the necessary price Russia had to pay to become a superpower. They follow the editor of *Molodaya gvardiya*, Ivanov, in transferring the responsibility for the excesses of the terror from Stalin to his Jewish subordinates, Mekhlis and Yakovlev, and to Jewish officers in the security police. Finally, this defense of Stalinism includes a justification of the command economy, created by Stalin, and criticism of Khrushchev's reforms and their apologists among the liberal Moscow intelligentsia. These reforms, they argue, only undercut the vitality of the command economy by weakening discipline in the party and in the society as a whole. The solution to the Soviet Union's economic problems is not its marketization but rather a strengthening of the work ethic and the selection of proper party cadres to supervise the

---

27. Among these neo-Stalinist essays, that of the late (d. 1983) Ivan Benediktov (Benediktov, 1989), Commissar and Minister of Agriculture in the years 1938–1958 and later Soviet ambassador to India and Yugoslavia, clearly stands out. The essay is based on a series of interviews with Benediktov conducted in 1980–1981 but published only in April 1989. This is the most elaborate defense of Stalinism published in the USSR in the post-Stalin era. Recently it was claimed that the Benediktov essay was a fabrication (see Gennadiy Vychub, "Maket krasiv, A dal'she?" *Sovetskaya kul'tura*, December 9, 1989, p. 3).

economic sphere (Benediktov, 1989, pp. 19–21, 62–64; Konotop, 1988, pp. 237–243).

In the period between fall 1988 and late spring 1989, *Nash sovremennik's* approach to dealing with Stalinism and its legacy was far more sophisticated than that of *Molodaya gvardiya*. The orthodox Stalinist defense of collectivization, the terror, and the command economy was entirely absent from the *Nash sovremennik* pages. What the journal published instead were essays by conservative nationalists and radical Slavophiles which attempted to discredit the reformers' view of Stalinism and its origins, the nature of the command economy, and the desired direction of economic reform. All the essays effectively deny Stalin's responsibility for collectivization and the terror by tracing the foundations of the Stalinist system back to the politics and ideas of the 1920s, or even to the revolution itself.

The conservative nationalist Soloukhin and the radical Slavophile Lanshchikov thus follow up Solzhenitsyn and reject the reformers' attempt to attach the label "Stalinist" to such events as collectivization, industrialization, and the terror. Reformist intellectuals from *Ogonyok* and the *Memorial* society employ the term "Stalinist" in order to whitewash the record of their spiritual and biological fathers, the party intellectuals who perished in the purges of the 1930s. This party intelligentsia, however, was responsible for the murder of the tsar and his family, and for millions of victims during the Civil War and collectivization.

While Soloukhin does not mention Lenin explicitly, Lanshchikov does. It was Lenin, according to Lanshchikov, who came up with the idea of the rapid collectivization of the Russian peasantry. During the NEP, this idea was ignored by the party until Stalin reintroduced it. The idea of a breakneck pace for industrialization was not Stalin's invention either, but was borrowed from Trotsky. There was no such thing as the Stalinist terror, they argue, only a Communist terror, which eventually justly victimized its initiators. The attempt of the reformers to distinguish Stalinism from other forms of socialism, Lanshchikov and Soloukhin imply, is merely a strategy to legitimize Western-oriented socialism which combines political and cultural pluralism with market economics (Lanshchikov, 1988; Soloukhin, 1988).

The radical Slavophiles Kunyayev and Kozhinov elaborate this argument while Kozhinov, together with two other radical Slavophiles, Antonov and Kazintsev, link it to the ongoing debate about the direction of economic reform. In his poetry and criticism, Stanislav Kunyayev aggressively put forth the idea that the terror of the 1930s was fair retribution for the crimes against Russia, which were committed by communist intellectuals of predominantly Jewish origin from the time of the revolution to collectivization. Moreover, the reformist intelligentsia today, the so-called children of the Arbat, must bear the responsibility for the crimes of their fathers.[28]

---

28. In August 1989 Sergey Vikulov resigned as chief editor of *Nash sovremennik* and recommended Stanislav

Trotsky, Bukharin, and other Jewish Communists are Kunyayev's main targets. It was not Stalin but Trotsky, whom he calls Leib Bronshtein to emphasize his Jewishness, who invented the concentration camp system in the early 1920s. Kunyayev carefully singles out all senior NKVD officers in the early 1930s with Jewish-sounding names to assert that Jews played a key role in the emerging GULAG system. Bukharin, the only non-Jewish Communist attacked by Kunyayev, is found guilty of initiating the terror against Russian national culture in the 1920s (Kunyayev, 1988a, 1988b).

Jewish intellectuals, Bukharin, and the NEP era also appear on Kozhinov's list of villains. In the 1920s and the 1930s, he states, Jewish intellectuals eagerly destroyed Russian national culture by branding it as anti-Semitic. Moreover, according to Kozhinov, Jewish intellectuals were the beneficiaries of Stalinism, not its victims. Even in 1950 and 1951, during the anti-cosmopolitan campaign, a third of the Stalin Prizes for Russian-language literature was awarded to Jews (Kozhinov, 1989, p. 170).

Bukharin, however, is a far more important target of Kozhinov's attack than the Jewish intelligentsia. Bukharin, he argues, provided the ideological justification for a drive to transform radically Russian society and destroy its centuries-old national traditions as well as the intellectuals defending these traditions. There were no principal disagreements between Stalin and Bukharin about the collectivization of the peasantry, only disagreements about tactics. Bukharin was concerned not with the fate of millions of Russian peasants as such, but with the impact of collectivization upon the tempo of economic development and the stability of Soviet power (Kozhinov, 1989, pp. 151–153, 155, 157).

Kozhinov's attack on Bukharin and the NEP era is not simply an academic effort to present the Russian nationalist views of Soviet history. It is an integral part of his debate with the liberals about the desired course of Gorbachev's economic reforms. While in the 1920s Bukharin sought the destruction of Russian national traditions, Bukharin's modern day followers attempt to use his ideas in order to justify the introduction of Western-type economic models and American-style family farm agriculture, both of which are alien to Russian national traditions. The Russian economy, concludes Kozhinov, ought to rely on centuries-old Russian national traditions (Kozhinov, 1989, pp. 167, 173–174).

This linkage between Bukharin's ideas and the current debate over the direction of the economic reforms is the central subject of Mikhail Antonov's essay. Although Antonov's interpretation of Bukharin's ideas completely contradicts that of Kozhinov's, their conclusions are identical. According to Antonov, the main spokesman for Bukharin on economic questions was the famous economist Kondrat'yev. Bukharin and Kondrat'yev came up with an interpretation of the economic principles of NEP which fundamentally differed from

Kunyayev to be appointed as his successor. Vikulov's recommendation was approved by the Secretariat of the RSFSR Writers Union. Kunyayev unveiled his plans for the 1990 *Nash sovremennik* in an interview in *Literaturnaya gazeta* (see *Literaturnaya gazeta*, August 16, 1989).

that of Lenin. While Lenin's conception of NEP never envisioned the unrestricted development of market relations, Bukharin's and Kondrat'yev's did.
If their ideas were accepted by the party, Antonov asserts, Russia soon would
have fallen prey to Western economic imperialism (Antonov, 1989, pp. 136–
138).

In rejecting Bukharin's idea of market socialism, Antonov does not accept
the Stalinist model of the command economy. The latter, in addition to being
an economic failure, is responsible for the systematic destruction of the environment and ought to be dismantled (Antonov, 1989a, pp. 126–133).[29] The
Stalinist command economy, however, should not be replaced by the contemporary versions of Bukharin's and Kondrat'yev's ideas. Shmelev, Abalkin,
Aganbegyan, Bogomolov, and other champions of Soviet integration into the
world economy are wrong, Antonov argues, because their program does not
go beyond the narrow framework of Western economic theory.

The primary purpose of the economic reform must not be the attainment of
capitalist-level efficiency and productivity, but the "real improvement of the
physical and spiritual health of our compatriots and an increase in their well-
being." Relying on this definition, Antonov argues that the true indicators of
the country's socioeconomic development should be demographic growth, levels of fertility and mortality, average life span, health and real income of the
population, changes in land yield, the ecological balance, and the crime rate.
In order to achieve positive results on all of these indicators, the Russian national
economic model should not rely on command-administrative methods, nor on
the market mechanism, but on "socio-political means based on spiritual and
moral values which include both economic and administrative means" (Antonov, 1989a, p. 147).

Antonov, however, does not go beyond this extremely vague statement, or
the equally ambiguous assertion that Russian economics should be based on
millennium-old Russian national traditions. Neither here, nor in any of his other
numerous essays, does he explain how economics based on traditions ought to
function or how it would differ from the existing system. However, he spares
no effort in criticizing market economics as socially unjust, and works to
discredit Soviet supporters of a market system. Since market economics and
plutocratic and individualistic Western democracy are inseparable, the hidden
agenda of the reformist economists is to turn Russia into a province of the
West (Antonov, 1989a, pp. 143, 146, 149–150).[30]

While Antonov's argument against the ideas of Bukharin and Abalkin stops
short of providing a clear answer to how Russian nationalist economics should
function, Kazinstsev's attack on the anti-Stalinist writings and liberal dissidents

29. Mikhail F. Antonov, the head of a section at the Institute of World Economics and International Relations
(IMEMO), is the main Russian nationalist speaker on economic reform. His August 1987 essay is the most
elaborate Russian nationalist analysis of the failures of the command economy. (Antonov, 1987).

30. In his speech at the Ryazan' plenum and in other essays, he passionately argues against the policy of
foreign investments and joint ventures as leading to the effective transformation of the Soviet Union into a
Western colony (Antonov, 1989b).

does at least provide a partial answer. In many ways he carries the ideas of Kozhinov, Antonov, and other radical Slavophiles to their logical conclusion. Kazintsev's specific targets are several anti-Stalinist works of fiction, especially those of Grossman and Voynovich. Under the guise of portraying the evils of Stalinism, these writings slander the Russian people and Russia's millennium-old history. Publication of such "Russophobic" works, Kazintsev asserts, is an integral component of the reformers' drive to discredit Russian national traditions and its defenders (past and present) in order to justify imposition of Western-type pluralism. The next stage of this drive is already on its way with the publication of the writings on contemporary Russian nationalism of the emigre scholar Alexander Yanov (Kazintsev, 1988b; 1989).

The marketization of the Soviet economy and the growth of private business are as dangerous to the Russian people and their traditions as the reformers' literary politics. This situation requires the unity of all forces opposing the reforms. Russian nationalists, therefore, must make the painful choice between the bureaucratic command economy and the socially unjust market system. Kazintsev sees both as evil, but the bureaucratic command economy is definitely the lesser of the two. Nationalists will manage a compromise with the bureaucrat, who is now scared of the reformers, but not with the emerging Soviet entrepreneur. Thus, Kozhinov's and Antonov's Russian national economics, as interpreted by Kazintsev, is merely a modification of the existing command economy (Kazintsev, 1989, pp. 167–168).

Kazintsev's justification for the alliance between Russian nationalists and anti-reformist forces in the political elite, and his readiness to accept the essentials of the Stalinist economic structure had yet another important reason: the fast growth of the anti-Russian nationalist movements in the Caucasus and, especially, in the Baltic republics. Kazintsev implicitly accuses reformers of a willingness to accept the secession of the Baltic republics from the Soviet state (Kazintsev, 1989, p. 161). Indeed, as nationalist movements in the Baltics became stronger and more aggressive, *Molodaya gvardiya* and *Nash sovremennik* increasingly challenged these claims and called for strengthening the alliance with the anti-reformist wing of the party.

In January 1988, *Molodaya gvardiya* argued that the demographic decline of ethnic Russians is the only Soviet nationality problem. But by November 1988, it already admitted that a lack of knowledge of the Estonian language by local Russians constituted a legitimate basis for the natives' discontent. This admission, however, was made under the assumption that language is the only aspect of the nationality problem which Russians are willing to recognize and discuss. Those members of the Estonian nationalist movement who call for secession from the Union are labeled "anti-Soviet" and "anti-communist" (Troitskiy, 1988; Teterin, 1988a, 1988b).

In January 1989, *Nash sovremennik* proclaimed that "Russophobia" and "anti-Soviet activity" are one and the same and accused the Baltic nationalist movements of both. The author also identified the reformers in Moscow as supporters of local nationalist movements (Kuzmin, 1989). The journal asserted that the preservation of the integrity of the Union is of major interest to the Russian nationalist movement and the anti-reformist forces in the party.

Finally, in April 1989, *Molodaya gvardiya* published a long essay on the situation in Lithuania which harshly attacked the policies of the local Communist Party and the Lithuanian National Front (*Sajudis*). The author, a Russified Dagestani who lives in Lithuania, accused the local party of imposing discriminatory language requirements on the Russian-speaking population. He argued that *Sajudis,* in its essence, is both an anti-Russian and anti-Soviet secessionist movement. The implicit agenda of this essay is clear: it is a call to the party in Moscow to suppress nationalist movements in the Baltics and restore to the Russian-speaking population in these areas the rights it enjoyed prior to *perestroyka* (Kaziyev, 1989).

The Russian nationalist positions on Gorbachev's cultural, economic, and nationality policies were aired at the Congress of People's Deputies. Vasiliy Belov and Valentin Rasputin, both members of the *Nash sovremennik* editorial board, argued that policies of cultural pluralism are forcing upon Russia a dangerous "pluralism of morals." They complained about the "spread of Russophobia" in the Baltics and the Caucasus, criticized the cooperative movement, and openly expressed their support for Ligachev and the anti-reformist wing of the party (*Izvestiya,* June 3, 1989; June 7, 1989).

In sum, between March 1985 and May 1989, the Russian nationalist movement split between the reform-supporting minority and the reform-opposing majority. This majority consisted of three groups with very different opinions, but the differences were outweighed by strong opposition to Gorbachev's cultural, economic, and nationality policies. *Molodaya gvardiya* and *Nash sovremennik* played crucial roles in Russian nationalist politics during the period. Their editorial policies were aimed at: maintaining the unity of Russian nationalist opposition to radical reforms; forging an alliance between this opposition and opponents of radical reforms in the political elite; discrediting leading reformist intellectuals, their journals, and their causes; and convincing the party to limit, if not reverse, Gorbachev's policies of cultural pluralism, economic reform, and greater autonomy to the non-Russian republics.

POPULARITY OF RUSSIAN NATIONALIST APPEAL

No adequate procedure for measuring the popularity of Russian nationalist (or reformist) appeal yet exists. Poor showing of Russian nationalist candidates at the elections to the Congress of People's Deputies is a misleading indicator, since most Russian nationalists showed a Slavophile-like disdain for the election process, and because most of their outspoken opponents were elected in Moscow, which is hardly representative of the RSFSR as a whole.[31] Russian na-

31. This disdain for parliamentary politics was expressed even by Russian nationalist delegates to the

tionalists who were elected, however, turned out to be popular among the Congress deputies: Vasiliy Belov, the only Russian nationalist candidate to the Supreme Soviet, was elected to the Council of Nationalities with a vast majority of 1,984 to 165 votes, while Boris Yel'tsin and most of the reformist Moscow candidates failed to win seats (*Izvestiya, May 28, 1989*). Incidentally, Belov was elected to the Congress from the party list. Both facts suggest that Russian nationalist ideas are popular among the party elite.

As for the ability of Russian nationalists to influence the policy process, the results are inconclusive, at least for now. Russian nationalists were in the forefront of the successful campaign against the river diversion projects, but these were always controversial. They failed to reverse Gorbachev's cultural policies and they were defeated in their attempt to force the party to impose a total ban on the production of alcohol. Yet, on June 6, 1989, the Supreme Soviet of the RSFSR went along with Russian nationalist demands and imposed high taxes on the gross income of cooperatives. The cooperatives, however, are unpopular among both the Russian general public and the RSFSR bureaucracy. The decision to tax them highly may have to do as much with these factors as with the Russian nationalist campaign against cooperatives.

Finally, data on the circulation and subscription to *Molodaya gvardiya* and *Nash sovremennik* could provide useful insights into the popularity of Russian nationalism among Russians. This is especially true because both journals refuse, as a matter of principle, to publish previously forbidden or unpublished works of fiction and non-fiction—one of the main causes of the meteoric increase in circulation of such reformist journals as *Znamya, Druzhba narodov,* and *Novyy mir,* as well as the Russian nationalist journal *Moskva.*

Analysis of circulation and subscription to *Molodaya gvardiya* suggests that orthodox Stalinist and neo-Stalinist nationalist ideas which dominate the journal are not very popular among the Russian reading public, especially Muscovites. The journal's circulation fell from 870,000 copies in 1981 to 655,000 in 1989.[32] Moreover, most of its still large circulation consists of institutional subscribers: it is a periodical to which all military and Komsomol libraries must subscribe.

In the beginning of 1987, *Molodaya gvardiya* had only 5,900 personal subscribers and 1,900 general library subscriptions in Moscow—the lowest of the Moscow "thick journals." The journal's total distribution in Moscow (including sales at newsstands), was 7,941 copies, i.e., only 1.2 percent of its total circulation. From rather fragmentary data we also know that in 1988 the distribution of the journal in Moscow was still below 2 percent of its total circulation. In comparison, 23 percent of the circulation of *Novyy mir* was distributed in the capital in 1988.

At the same time, an analysis of the subscriptions and circulation of *Nash*

Congress. *Izvestiya* (June 7, 1989) quotes Rasputin as calling its activities "legislative chicanery" (*zakonodatel'noye kryuchkotvorstvo*).

32. All the data in this section are based on Bocharov, 1988; Gudkov and Dubin, 1988; Gudkov, 1988; *Sotsiologicheskiye issledovaniya,* 6:60–62, 1988; and *Izvestiya TsK KPSS,* 1:138–139, 1989.

sovremennik suggests that the popularity of the conservative nationalist and radical Slavophile ideas associated with the journal is meaningful and growing, even in Moscow. Although in 1989 the journal did not reach its 1982 level of 335,000 copies, its circulation stood at 250,000 copies, including 243,000 (mostly personal) subscriptions. Moreover, in 1986 and 1987 *Nash sovremennik* was the second most popular journal in Moscow after *Novyy mir,* with 13,000 personal subscribers in 1986 and 16,000 in 1987.[33]

A circulation of 250,000 copies is rather small compared to the reformers' journals. However, the journal's circulation is still tightly regulated. Its editors complained that while all other "thick journals" were permitted unrestricted subscriptions in 1989, *Nash sovremennik* was allowed only a 20 percent increase *(Nash sovremennik,* 1:192, 1989). This suggests that reformers in the party leadership are trying to limit the spread of ideas associated with the journal.

Today *Nash sovremennik* is clearly the most important journal of the Russian nationalist opposition to the reforms. Its future positions will provide a clear indication of the direction of Russian nationalist politics. Changes in its editorial board and its circulation figures may also serve as a measure of the popularity of the Russian nationalist appeal and the support it enjoys in the political elite.

Afterword

After this article was accepted for publication, I was invited to add an afterword detailing the results of my four-week stay in the Soviet Union, through October 14, 1989. While in Moscow, I interviewed a dozen of the leading Russian nationalist contributors to *Molodaya gvardiya* and *Nash sovremennik,* visited the editorial offices of *Nash sovremennik* twice, and had lengthy talks with its new editor, Stanislav Kunyayev, and his deputy, Aleksandr Kazintsev.

The contributors and editors to *Nash sovremennik* said that competition for the hearts and minds of ethnic Russians is intense. It is heightened by the deepening economic crisis and efforts of nationalist movements in the Baltics and the Caucasus to secede. The situation, they said, calls for the transformation of Russian nationalist-controlled newspapers and journals into considerably more effective media capable of shaping the political views of ethnic Russians. *Nash sovremennik* plays a very important role in this new strategy.

To broaden support among the members of their traditional constituency (the middle classes and the intelligentsia of provincial Russian cities), and to reach constituencies with no significant Russian nationalist following (the Russian working class and Russian-speaking population of the Baltic republics), the RSFSR Writers Union replaced Vikulov, the editor of *Nash sovremennik,* in August 1989. City-born, Moscow University–educated, and younger than Vikulov by ten years, Kunyayev calculates that he can broaden the journal's

---

33. In comparison, *Znamya* had 10,000 subscribers in 1986 and 13,500 in 1985; *Druzhba narodov,* 4,800 and 8,100; and *Oktyabr',* 6,600 and 9,700, respectively (Bocharov, 1988, p. 99).

appeal by publishing in 1990 Solzhenitsyn's *October 1916* and new novels of Bondarev and Pikul', two writers especially popular among members of the Russian working and middle classes. These publications and the conspicuous absence of works by the well-known "village prose" writers, the mainstay of the journal's prose section in the Vikulov era, clearly point to *Nash sovremennik*'s shift from a rural to an urban focus.

The editors told me that they commissioned non-fictional works on economics and politics to emphasize the ideas most popular with the urban Russian-speaking population, such as: the integrity of the Russian-dominated Soviet state; support of the authoritarian one-party system; defense of the military from attacks by reformers; social justice as the guiding principle of economic reforms; and a high priority for ecological concerns. The content of the August and September issues already illustrates this shift.[34]

Another part of the new strategy is a sharp increase in the number of speaking engagements by *Nash sovremennik* editors and contributors, and a diversification of audiences. In the summer and early fall of 1989, they appeared before employees of science institutes, KGB and MVD officers, factory workers, and high school and university students, to name a few.[35] This strategy seems to be successful. Subscriptions to the journal jumped by 97 percent above the 1989 level reaching 480,000 copies—the biggest increase among Moscow and Leningrad "thick journals" (*Literaturnaya gazeta*, January 10, 1990).[36]

In recent months *Nash sovremennik* as an institution and its leading contributors as individuals are attempting not only to shape public opinion favorable to Russian nationalist ideas but also to create a powerful coalition capable of making a serious impact on the direction of political and economic reforms. This coalition includes, in addition to Russian nationalist institutions and societies, workers, trade unions, conservative party officials, intellectuals, economists and their publications, and members of the Supreme Soviet.

This coalition uses the umbrella of the United Front of Russian Workers (*Ob''yedinennyy front trudyashchikhsya Rossii*, or OFT), a working-class organization founded in Leningrad in June 1989 with the support of the local party organization. In September 1989, OFT convened its First All-Russian Congress in Sverdlovsk at which Anatoliy Salutskiy, a leading writer of *Nash sovremennik* on economic reform, took an active part (see Salutskiy, 1989). Soon after the Congress, the Sixth Plenum of trade unions decided to give OFT full financial and organizational support (see *Trud*, September 9, 1989).

Headed by Venyamin Yarin, a rolling mill operator from Nizhniy Tagil and

34. See Solzhenitsyn's essays (1989), Antonov's programmatic article on the subject of economic reform (1989c), and readers' letters dealing with such questions as the construction of nuclear power stations, activities of cooperatives, and even price formation of heavy industrial goods (Iz nashey, 1989).

35. According to People's Deputy Yuriy Shchekochikhin, the MVD held regular meetings with *Nash sovremennik* editors between June 1989 and January 1990. See *Radio Liberty Daily Report*, No. 20 (January 29, 1990).

36. The aggressive nationalism of *Molodaya gvardiva* also seems to gain popularity; its 1990 subscriptions rose by 11 percent over 1989, reaching 697,000 copies (*Literaturnaya gazeta*, January 10, 1990). Since institutions are no longer requesting new subscriptions, this increase reflects a growth in individual subscriptions.

a Supreme Soviet deputy, OFT demands an increase in the percentage of workers in the Supreme Soviet. The OFT platform calls for the election of two-thirds of deputies to local and republican Soviets from workplaces and only one-third from territorial districts. It also demands a restriction in the activities of cooperatives and proclaims that the cost of economic reform will not fall on the shoulders of Soviet workers. With the support of Moscow trade unions, on October 3, 1989 OFT staged a mass rally with 10,000 to 20,000 participants, in which its principal demands were aired.[37]

Salutskiy claims to have been instrumental in introducing the OFT leadership to such conservative Communist intellectuals as the former *Kommunist* editor, Richard Kosolapov and the economists Aleksey Sergeyev and Vladmir Yakushev. As a result of Salutskiy's mediation, Kosolapov became the movement's chief ideologue, while Sergeyev and Yakushev took charge of developing the alternative model of economic reform presented at the OFT conference in Leningrad on October 21, 1989 (*Sovetskaya Rossiya,* October 22, 1989). Their main economic publications will be *Ekonomicheskiye nauki* and *Planovoye khozyaystvo* (Sergeyev, 1989; Salutskiy, 1989). *Trud* and *Sovetskaya Rossiya* appear to be the newspapers poised to publish material supportive of OFT positions (see *Trud,* September 10, 1989, October 15, 1989; *Sovetskaya Rossiya,* October 22, 1989, November 24, 1989, December 30, 1989).

Concluding Note

In October 1989, the coalition between the Russian nationalist intellectuals writing for *Nash sovremennik,* the OFT, and conservative members of the Supreme Soviet from the Russian Republic acquired an organizational form. On October 20–21, a group of 51 People's Deputies from the RSFSR met in the city of Tyumen' (for an account of the meeting, see Pavel Emelin, "Russkiy vopros," *Literaturnaya Rossiya,* November 17, 1989). At the end of the meeting 28 deputies signed a declaration, published in the December issue of *Nash sovremennik.* The content of the declaration was remarkably similar to the ideas Russian nationalist intellectuals have articulated in their thick journals.

The declaration: a) protests the discrimination of Russians in the Baltic republics and Georgia and claims that they are lacking legal protection and representation; b) charges that the financial resources of the RSFSR are being pumped into the other republics; c) expresses concern over the reformers' efforts to discredit the military, denounces Gorbachev's policies of unilateral disarmament, and calls for education of Soviet youth in the idea of territorial integrity and strength of the Soviet state; d) demands the creation of a RSFSR Academy of Sciences, RSFSR radio and television agency, and new RSFSR newspapers and publishing houses; and e) appeals for the adoption of new educational and cadre policies based on the principle of proportional representation of each

37. See *Trud,* October 5, 1989, and *Moskovskiy komsomolets,* October 6, 1989.

nationality in the Soviet population. Citing the lack of action on these issues by the RSFSR Council of Ministers, the declaration calls for the formation of a club of RSFSR People's Deputies which would defend the national interest of ethnic Russians (*Nash sovremennik*, 12:3–6, 1989).

On October 24, 1989, the founding meeting of the Deputies Club "Rossiya" took place in Moscow. The "Rossiya" Club was sponsored by OFT, *Sovetskaya Rossiya*, and such Russian nationalist institutions as the Russian Republic Writers Union, *Nash sovremennik*, the *Unity* ["Yedinstvo"] society, and the "Committee for Rescuing the Volga River" (*Sovetskaya Rossiya*, October 25, 1989). Yarin was elected chairman of the club, Salutskiy one of the co-chairmen, and Kunyayev of *Nash sovremennik*, a member of the club's executive council. "Russia" was clearly designed to be both the alternative to the Inter-Regional Group of radical deputies and the coordinating forum for participants in the conservative alliance on the eve of the March 4, 1990, elections to the local and RSFSR Supreme Soviet.

On December 29, 1989, this alliance, which began to call itself the Bloc of Social-Patriotic Movements of Russia (*blok obshchestvenno-patriotiche-skikh dvizheniy Rossii*), published its electoral platform, which is an elaboration of the Tyumen' declaration. Challenges to the policies and ideas of radical economic reform occupy major parts of the platform. It claims that the economic crisis deepened because of the senseless effort to destroy the existing economic structure and to replace it with an unregulated market mechanism. It opposes the policies of free-economic zones, concessions, and "semi-colonial-type joint ventures" which would turn Russia into a supplier of raw materials and a dumpster for the nuclear and chemical waste of capitalist countries.

The document declares the Bloc's opposition to the legalization of private property (even though it does support private agriculture) and demands that the issue be subject to a national referendum. Hand-in-hand with its declared opposition to private property comes a proposal for currency reform officially aimed at killing the "shadow economy." This reform would consist of exchanging old rubles for new ones of the same value up to the level of 10,000 to 15,000. A declaration on the sources of income would be required for those wishing to exchange amounts above this ceiling. The introduction of a progressive inheritance tax is proposed as a supplement to the monetary reform.

In the sphere of political reform, the platform demands the creation of the RSFSR Communist Party, RSFSR Academy of Sciences and research institutes similar to those of the USSR Academy. Like the Tyumen' document, the platform calls for the creation of an RSFSR radio and television agency. Since they propagate values of "immorality and individualism, pornography and violence," the All-Union radio and television would stop broadcasting all but the news in the Russian republic. RSFSR radio and television would operate in accordance with a new RSFSR "law on morality" which would protect Russians from propagation of immorality.

In the realm of inter-republican relations, the platform concedes the possibility of secession from the Union, but calls for reconsideration of the republics' borders since they were arbitrarily established in the 1920s and later. The program reiterates the Tyumen' declaration demand to halt the subsidization of republican economies and the standard of living of citizens of other republics beginning in 1991, and adds to this a call for all All-Union organizations, ministries, and legislative organs located in the RSFSR to pay rent for their facilities. Finally, the platform proposes designating Moscow as the sole capital of the RSFSR and moving the All-Union capital elsewhere ("Za politiky narodnogo soglasiya i rossiyskogo vozrozhdeniya," *Literaturnaya Rossiya*, December 29, 1989; for further analysis of this document, see Paul Goble, "A Program for Russia: The Appeal of the Bloc of Russia's Social-Political Groups," *Radio Liberty Report*, January 3, 1990).

The impact of these developments on the pace of the economic reforms is hard to judge at this point. However, it does not appear out of line to argue that this emerging conservative alliance does present a very serious challenge to the successful execution of radical economic reform.

REFERENCES

Abramov, Fyodor, "Pelageya (Pelageya)," *Novyy mir*, 6:31–70, 1969.

———, "Al'ka (Al'ka)," *Nash sovremennik*, 1:2–36, 1972.

Andreyev, Aleksey, "Vospitaniye krasotoy i agressivnost' bezobraznogo (Education by Beauty and Aggressiveness of the Ugly)," *Molodaya gvardiya*, 7:264–271, 1987.

Andreyev-Rayevskiy, Aleksey, "S kogo zhe delat' zhizn'? (On Whom to Model Life?)," *Molodaya gvardiya*, 11:247–257, 1988.

Antonov, Mikhail, "Tak chto zhe s nami proiskhodit? (So What's Happening to Us?)," *Oktyabr'*, 8:3–66, 1987.

———, "Idti svoim putyom (To Follow One's Own Path)," *Molodaya gvardiya*, 1:195–200, 1988.

———, "Nesushchestvuyushchiye lyudi (Nonexistent People)," *Nash sovremennik*, 2:125–150, 1989a.

———, "Speshim—kuda i zachem? ([We] Are Rushing—Where and Why?)," *Literaturnaya Rossiya*, March 31, 1989b.

———, "Vykhod yest'! (There Is a Solution!)," *Nash sovremennik*, 8:71–110, 9:138–158, 1989c.

Astaf'yev, Viktor, "Mesto deystviya (The Place of Action)," *Nash sovremennik*, 5:100–140, 1986.

Astrakhantsev, Aleksandr, "Razvilka (A Parting of the Ways)," *Nash sovremennik*, 12:53–82, 1986.

Baygushev, Aleksandr, "Preodoleniye (Overcoming)," *Molodaya gvardiya*, 4:227–253, 6:232–254, 1987a; 12:229–251, 1987b.

———, "Letopis' pokoleniya (The Chronicle of a Generation)," *Nash sovremennik*, 1:185–191, 1988.

Belov, Vasiliy, "Plotnitskiye rasskazy (A Carpenter's Stories)," *Novyy mir*, 7:7–56, 1968.

————, "Vse vperedi (Everything Lies Ahead)," *Nash sovremennik*, 7:29–106, 8:59–110, 1986.

Benediktov, Ivan, "O Staline i Khrushcheve (On Stalin and Khrushchev)," *Molodaya gvardiya*, 4:12–67, 1989.

Bocharov, A., "Zhurnaly v fokuse mneniy (Journals in the Focus of Opinions)," *Literaturnoye obozreniye*, 1:98–100, 1988.

Brown, Deming, *Soviet Literature Since Stalin*. Cambridge: Cambridge University Press, 1978.

Brudny, Yitzhak M., "Between Liberalism and Nationalism: The Case of Sergei Zalygin," *Studies in Comparative Communism*, 21, 3/4:331–340, 1988.

Bulin, Yevgeniy, "Otkroyte knigi molodykh! (Open the Books of the Young!)," *Molodaya gvardiya*, 3:237–248, 1989.

Bushin, Vladimir, "S vysoty svoyego kurgana (From the Heights of One's Hill)," *Nash sovremennik*, 8:182–185, 1987.

————, "Yesli znat' i pomnit' (If One Knows and Remembers)," *Molodaya gvardiya*, 2:269–279, 1988a.

————, "S vysoty nasypnogo Olimpa (From the Heights of an Artificial Olympus)," *Molodaya gvardiya*, 10:262–280, 1988b.

————, "Kak Arkadi Mikhailovich uzh bol'no shibko Grigoriya Yakovlevicha nas-troshchal, a tot yego za eto na poltora goda upek (How Arkadi Mikhaylovich Scared Grigoriy Yakovlevich to Death and the Latter Sent Him off for a Year and a Half to Jail for This)," *Nash sovremennik*, 1:190–191, 1989a.

————, "Deyeniya svyatogo otkazchika (Acts of a Holy Renouncer)," *Molodaya gvardiya*, 2:254–262, 1989b.

Chalmayev, Viktor, "Neizbezhnost' (Inevitability)," *Molodaya gvardiya*, 9:259–289, 1968.

Chernykh, Yevgeniy, "Nastupleniye prodolzhayetsya (The Offensive Continues)," *Nash sovremennik*, 5:150–160, 1988.

Chirkin, Albert, "Podrostok, semiya i rok-muzika (The Adolescent, Family, and Rock Music)," *Nash sovremennik*, 10:141–149, 1988.

Chistyakov, V., and I. Sanachev, "Troyanskiy kon' (The Trojan Horse)," *Nash sovremennik*, 10:126–141, 1988.

Chivilikhin, Vladimir, "Pamyat' (Memory)," *Nash sovremennik*, 1, 1978; 8–12, 1980; 5–6, 10–11, 1983; 3–4, 1984.

Cohen, Stephen F., *Rethinking the Soviet Experience*. New York: Oxford University Press, 1985.

Darst, Robert G., Jr., "Environmentalism in the USSR: The Opposition to the River Diversion Projects," *Soviet Economy*, 4, 3:223–252, July–September 1988.

Doronin, Anatoliy, "O roke—bez prikras (On Rock Music without Embellishment)," *Molodaya gvardiya*, 12:213–228, 1987.

Dorosh, Yefim, "Derevenskiy dnevnik (A Village Diary)," *Novyy mir*, 7, 1958; 7, 1961; 10, 1962; 6, 1964; 1, 1965; 1, 1969; 9, 1970.

Dubrovina, Elida, "Ne otgoryat ryabinovyye kisti (The Ashberry Bunches Shall Not Burn)," *Nash sovremennik*, 9:180–187, 1987.

Dunayev, Mikhail, "Rokovaya muzyka (Fatal Music)," *Nash sovremennik*, 1:157–168, 2:163–172, 1988.

Dunlop, John B., *The New Russian Nationalism*. New York: Praeger, 1985.

"Ekologiya pravdy (The Ecology of Truth)," *Molodaya gvardiya,* 12:238–257.

"Dusha dorozhe kovsha (The Soup Is More Valuable Than the Ladle)," *Nash sovremennik,* 9:142–172, 1988.

Fed, Nikolay, "Poslaniye drugu, ili pis'ma o literature (Message to a Friend, or Letters about Literature)," *Nash sovremennik,* 4:3–20, 1989a; 5:169–185, 1989b.

Fomenko, Aleksandr, "O samom glavnom (Of the Greatest Importance)," *Molodaya gvardiya,* 9:278–281, 1987.

Garden, Patricia, "Reassessing Ovechkin," in Richard Feeborn, R. R. Millner-Gulland, and Charles A. Ward, eds., *Russian and Slavic Literature.* Columbus: Slavica, 1976, 405–424.

Glinkin, Pavel, "Zemlya i asfal't (Earth and Asphalt)," *Molodaya gvardiya,* 9:240–255, 1967.

Goble, Paul, "A Program for Russia: The Appeal of the Bloc of Russia's Social-Political Groups, *Radio Liberty Report on the USSR,* 2, 1, January 3, 1990.

Gorbachev, Vyacheslav, "Chto vperedi? (What's Ahead?)," *Molodaya gvardiya,* 3:250–277, 1987a.

———, "Perestroyka i nadstroyka (Restructuring and Superstructure)," *Molodaya gvardiya,* 7:220–247, 1987b.

———, "Prinyat' k deystviyu (To Take Action)," *Molodaya gvardiya,* 8:228–245, 1987c.

———, "Arendatory glasnosti? (The Renters of Glasnost'?)," *Molodaya gvardiya,* 1:229–267, 1989.

"Granitsy prilichiya (Limits of Decency)," *Molodaya gvardiya,* 4:260–288, 1989.

Gudkov, Lev, "O chem skazali tirazhi (What Circulations Said)," *Sovetskaya kul'tura,* September 22, 1988.

Gudkov, Lev, and Boris Dubin, "Chto my chitayem? (What Are We Reading?)," *Literaturnoye obozreniye,* 1:93–97, 1988.

Gunko, Boris, "Dve estetiki (Two Aesthetics)," *Nash sovremennik,* 10:121–125, 1988.

Gustafson, Thane, *Reform in Soviet Politics.* New York: Cambridge University Press, 1981.

Hauslohner, Peter, "Gorbachev's Social Contract," *Soviet Economy,* 3, 1:54–89, January–March 1987.

Hosking, Geoffrey, *Beyond Socialist Realism.* New York: Holmes & Meier, 1980.

Ivanov, Anatoliy, "Chernyy khleb isskustva (The Black Bread of Art)," *Nash sovremennik,* 5:171–179, 1988.

Ivanov, Viktor, "Sudnyy den'" (Day of Judgment), *Nash sovremennik,* 4–6, 1988.

"Iz nashey pochty (From Our Mailbox)," *Nash sovremennik,* 9:180–192.

Jowitt, Kenneth, "Inclusion and Mobilization in European Leninist Regimes," *World Politics,* 28, 1:69–96, 1975.

"Kak nashe slovo otzovetsya (How Our Word Will Be Received)," *Molodaya gvardiya,* 6:265–278, 1988.

Karpets, Vladimir, "Povorot k nravstvennosti (A Turn to Morality)," *Molodaya gvardiya,* 9:241–245, 1987.

Kazintsev, Aleksandr, "Litsom k istorii: Prodolzhateli ili potrebiteli (With the Face to History: Continuers or Consumers)," *Nash sovremennik,* 11:166–175, 1986.

————, "Ochishcheniye ili zlosloviye? (Purification or Vilification?)," *Nash sovremennik*, 2:186–189, 1988a.

————, "Istoriya—ob''yedinyayushchaya ili razobshchayushchaya (History—Unifying or Setting Apart)," *Nash sovremennik*, 11:163–184, 1988b.

————, "Novaya mifologiya (The New Mythology)," *Nash sovremennik*, 5:144–168, 1989.

Kaziyev, Bagautdin, "Tolcheya na puti k pravde (A Crowd on the Way to the Truth)," *Molodaya gvardiya*, 4:235–250, 1989.

Khatyushin, Valeriy, "O novykh veyaniyakh v kritike (On the New Trends in Criticism)," *Molodaya gvardiya*, 10:243–255, 1987.

————, "O mnimom i podlinom v poezii (On the Imaginary and the Real in Poetry)," *Molodaya gvardiya*, 9:260–275, 1988.

"Khochu vyskazat' svoye mneniye (I Want to Express My Own Opinion)," *Molodaya gvardiya*, 4:276–278, 1988.

Khukhry, A., A. Tarakanov, and I. Ivanov, "Tuman nad alkogol'noy propost'yu (Fog over the Alcoholic Abyss)," *Nash sovremennik*, 8:92–97, 1988.

Konotop, Vasiliy, "V chiikh interesakh traktuyutsya nashi idealy i interesy? (In Whose Interests Are Our Ideals and Interests Interpreted?)," *Molodaya gvardiya*, 10:230–244, 1988.

Kovalenin, A. V., "Trezvost'—oruzhiye perestroyki" (Sobriety—the Weapon of *Perestroyka*)," *Nash sovremennik*, 3:143–145, 1988.

Kozhinov, Vadim, "I nazovet menya vsyak sushchii v ney yazyk ... (And Each of Its People Shall Speak My Name ...)," *Nash sovremennik*, 11:153–176, 1981.

————, "My menyayemsya? (Are We Changing?)," *Nash sovremennik*, 10:160–174, 1987.

————, "Pravda i istina (Truth and Rightness)," *Nash sovremennik*, 4:160–175, 1988.

————, "Samaya bolshaya opasnost' ... (The Greatest Danger ...)," *Nash sovremennik*, 1:141–175, 1989.

Kuleshov, V., "Tochnost' kriteriyev (Accuracy of Criteria)," *Pravda*, February 1, 1982.

Kunyayev, Stanislav, "Razmyshleniya na Starom Arbate (Reflections on the Old Arbat)," *Nash sovremennik*, 7:26–27, 1988a.

————, "Vse nachinalos' s yarlykov (It All Started with Labels)," *Nash sovremennik*, 9:180–189, 1988b.

Kuzmin, Apollon, "V prodolzheniye vazhnogo razgovora (The Continuation of an Important Conversation)," *Nash sovremennik*, 3:182–190, 1985.

————, Otvety, porozhdayushchiye voprosy (Answers Which Beg Questions)," *Nash sovremennik*, 5:189–190, 1986.

————, "Meli v eksterritorial'nom potoke (Shoals in the Exterritorial Torrent)," *Nash sovremennik*, 9:173–179, 1987.

————, "K kakomy khramy ishchem my dorogy? (To Which Temple Are We Searching a Path?)," *Nash sovremennik*, 3:154–164, 1988.

————, "Kto vinovat i komy eto nuzhno? (Who Is Guilty and for Whom Is It Necessary?)," *Nash sovremennik*, 1:191–192, 1989.

Lanshchikov, Anatoliy, "My vse glyadim k Napoleony ... (We Are All Looking to Become Napoleons ...)," *Nash sovremennik*, 7:106–142, 1988.

Lapchenko, Boris, "Ne oboronyat'sya—nastupat'! (Not to Be on the Defensive—to Advance!)," *Nash sovremennik,* 3:130–143, 1988.

Lapin, V., Pust' ne drognet pistolet progressa (The Pistol of Progress Should Not Shake)," *Molodaya gvardiya,* 3:268–270, 1989.

Laqueur, Walter, *The Road to Freedom: Russia and Glasnost.* New York: Scribners, 1989.

Lewis, Philippa, "Peasant Nostalgia in Contemporary Soviet Literature," *Soviet Studies,* **3,** 4:548–569, 1976.

Likhonosov, Viktor, "Bryanskiye (Bryansk Folk)," *Novyy mir,* 11:142–145, 1963.

———, "Rodnyye (Relatives)," *Novyy mir,* 2:145–159, 1967.

Lisenkov, Anatoliy, and Yuriy Sergeyev, "Kolovert bespamyatsva (The Whirling [Forces of] Delirium)," *Molodaya gvardiya,* 10:256–270, 1987.

"Litsom k pravde (With a Face Turned to the Truth)," *Molodaya gvardiya,* 3:212–236, 1989.

Lobanov, Mikhail, "Prosveshchennoye meshchanstvo (Educated Philistines)," *Molodaya gvardiya,* 4:294–306, 1968.

Lowe, David, *Russian Writing Since 1953.* New York: Ungar, 1987.

Lugovoy, E., "Bilet na poshost' (The Ticket to Vulgarity)," *Molodaya gvardiya,* 4:287–288, 1989.

Lyubomudrov, Mark, "Teatr nachinayetsya s Rodiny (Theater Starts with the Motherland)," *Nash sovremennik,* 6:163–178, 1985.

———, "Kak nashe slovo otzovetsya (How Our World Will Resound)," *Nash sovremennik,* 7:167–175, 1987.

———, "Izvlechem li uroki? (Will We Learn the Lessons?)," *Nash sovremennik,* 2:170–183, 1989.

Maguire, Robert A., *Red Virgin Soil: Soviet Literature in the 1920s.* Princeton: Princeton University Press, 1968.

Malakhov, Mikhail, "Smysl nashey zhizni (The Meaning of Our Life)," *Molodaya gvardiya,* 4:257–275, 1988.

Markova, Yekaterina, "Otbleski golubogo ekrana (Reflections of the Blue Screen)," *Molodaya gvardiya,* 10:228–242, 1987.

Matveyets, G., "Ne v nem odnom delo (He Was Not the Only One)," *Molodaya gvardiya,* 12:240–244, 1988.

———., "Dorogoye udovol'stviye za 30 kopeyek (A Costly Pleasure for 30 Kopecks)," *Nash sovremennik,* 4:192, 1989.

Mehnert, Klaus, *The Russians and Their Favorite Books.* Stanford: Hoover Institution Press, 1983.

Micklin, Philip P., and Andrew R. Bond, "Reflections on Environmentalism and the River Diversion Projects," *Soviet Economy,* 4, 3:253–274, July–September 1988.

Mikhaylov, Oleg, "V chas muzhestva (In the Hour of Courage)," *Nash sovremennik,* 4:106–114, 1969.

Mozhayev, Boris, "Iz zhizni Ivana Kuzkina (From the Life of Ivan Kuzkin)," *Novyy mir,* 7:42–118, 1966.

Mustafin, Dmitriy, "Narod pomnit vse (People Remember Everything)," *Molodaya gvardiya,* 3:234–236, 1989.

"Nesti lyudyam slovo dobroye, svetloye (To Bring People the Good and Bright Word),'' *Molodaya gvardiya*, 5:265–279, 1988.

Paliyevskiy, Pyotr, "Mirovoye znacheniye M. Sholokhova (The World Significance of M. Sholokhov),'' *Nash sovremennik*, 12: 167–173, 1973.

Petro, Nikolai N., "The Project of the Century: A Case Study of Russian Nationalist Dissent,'' *Studies in Comparative Communism*, 20, 3/4:235–252, 1987.

Pigalev, Vadim, "Chto oni ishchut u slavyanofilov? (What Are They Looking for in the Slavophiles?),'' *Nash sovremennik*, 10:156–162, 1986.

Pisarev, Yuriy, "Nuzhna li nam rokovaya muzika? (Do We Need Rock Music?),'' *Molodaya gvardiya*, 7:273–278, 1987.

"Podmena (Substitution),'' *Molodaya gvardiya*, 6:250–264, 1988.

"Povyshat' sozidatel'nuyu rol' pressy (Promoting a Constructive Role for the Press),'' *Zhurnalist*, 9:1–9, 1988.

"Protiv podmen (Against Substitutions),'' *Nash sovremennik*, 5:189–190, 1988.

Rasputin, Valentin, "Proschaniye s Matyoroy (Farewell to Matyora),'' *Nash sovremennik*, 10:3–71, 11:17–64, 1976.

―――, "Pozhar (Fire),'' *Nash sovremennik*, 7:3–38, 1985.

―――, "Zhertvovat' soboyu dlya pravdy (To Sacrifice Oneself for the Sake of Truth),'' *Nash sovremennik*, 1:169–176, 1988.

Sakharov, A. N., "Istoriya istinnaya i mnimaya (True and Imaginary History),'' *Molodaya gvardiya*, 3:297–320, 1970.

Salutskiy, Anatoliy, "Poiski istiny i 'pop-nauka' (Searches of Truth and 'Pop-Science'),'' *Ekonomicheskiye nauki*, 10:78–85, 1989.

Semanov, Sergey, "O tsennostyakh otnositel'nykh i vechnykh (On Relative and Eternal Values),'' *Molodaya gvardiya*, 8:308–320, 1970.

Sergeyev, Aleksey, "Iz segodnya v zavtra ili pozavchera? (From Today into Tomorrow or into Yesterday?),'' *Ekonomicheskiye nauki*, 9:121–131, 1989.

Shevtsov, Ivan, "Spolokhi (Lightening),'' *Nash sovremennik*, 12:174–187, 1986.

Shevtsov, Ivan, and Ivan Pstygo, "Vospitat' patriota (To Educate a Patriot),'' *Molodaya gvardiya*, 7:221–230, 1988.

Shiropayev, Aleksey, "Kozlinnyy dukh, ili na dvore 'dvadtsatyye gody'? (The Goat Spirit, or Are the 'Twenties' Back?),'' *Nash sovremennik*, 1:180–185, 1989.

Slavetskiy, Vladimir, "Ishchu stikhi! (Searching for Poems!),'' *Molodaya gvardiya*, 1:279–282, 1989.

Soloukhin, Vladimir, "Pochemu ya ne podpisalsya pod tem pismom (Why I Did Not Sign That Letter),'' *Nash sovremennik*, 12:186–189, 1988.

Solzhenitsyn, Aleksandr, "Matryonin dvor (Matryona's Home),'' *Novyy mir*, 1:42–63, 1963.

―――, "Pomenal'noye slovo o tvardovskom (Eulogy for Tvardovskiy)'' and "Zhit' ne po Izhi (Live Not a Lie),'' *Nash sovremennik*, 9:159–162, 1989.

Spechler, Dina R., *Permitted Dissent in the USSR*. New York: Praeger, 1982.

Surovtsev, Yuriy, "V stile ekstaza (In the Style of Ecstasy),'' *Znamya*, 3:202–224, 1982.

Swayze, Harold, *Political Control of Literature in USSR, 1946–1959*. Cambridge, Mass.: Harvard University Press, 1959.

Teterin, Igor, "Realisty protiv ekstremistov (The Realists Against the Extremists)," *Molodaya gvardiya,* 11:196–209, 1988a; 12:218–237, 1988b.

Troitskiy, E., "Russkaya sotsialisticheskaya natsiya segodnya (Russian Socialist Nation Today)," *Molodaya gvardiya,* 1:277–287, 1988.

Trukhin, Aleksandr, "Sem' raz otmer' (Measure Seven Times)," *Molodaya gvardiya,* 1:217–225, 1988.

Uglov, Fyodor, "Glyadya pravde v glaza (Staring Truth in the Eye)," *Nash sovremennik,* 7:150–157, 1987.

———, Iz plena illyuzii (From the Captivity of Illusions). Leningrad: Lenizdat, 1986.

Vilchek, L. Sh., *Peyzazh posle zhatvy (The Landscape After the Harvest).* Moscow: Sovetskiy pisatel', 1988.

"V otvete za vremya (Responsibility for the Times)," *Molodaya gvardiya,* 9:219–287, 1987.

Voznesensky, Andrei, "A Poet's View of Glasnost'," *Nation,* June 13, 1987.

Yanov, Alexander, *The Russian Challenge and the Year 2000.* Oxford: Blackwell, 1987.

Yashin, Aleksandr, "Vologodskaya svad'ba (The Vologda Wedding)," *Novyy mir,* 12:3–26, 1962.

Zalygin, Sergey, "Na Irtyshe (On the Irtysh)," *Novyy mir,* 2:3–80, 1964.

———, "Komissiya (Commission)," *Nash sovremennik,* 9–11, 1975.

Zekulin, Gleb, "The Contemporary Countryside in Soviet Literature: A Search for New Values," in James R. Millar, ed., *The Soviet Rural Community.* Urbana, Ill.: University of Illinois Press, 1971, 376–404.

Zelenevskiy, V., "A vy izuchaite nas! . . . (Study Us! . . .)," *Molodaya gvardiya,* 12:273–282, 1988.

Zhitnukhin, Anatoliy, "Sokhranyaya preyemstvennost' (Keeping the Continuity)," *Molodaya gvardiya,* 10:23–33, 1988.

Zhukov, Dmitriy, "Svyaz' vremen (The Link of Times)," *Molodaya gvardiya,* 6:300–304, 1969.

CHAPTER 10

Gorbachev and the "National Question"

Gail W. Lapidus

THE CENTRAL Committee's recent endorsement of the principle of a multi-party system marked a watershed in Soviet history. Having earlier renounced the Communist Party's monopoly on truth to endorse a "socialist pluralism" of ideas,[1] the Soviet leadership has now renounced the other main tenet of Leninism: its claim to a monopoly of power. The key issue of Soviet politics today is no longer the fate of *perestroyka;* it is the outcome of the more fundamental transformation of the Soviet system that is clearly under way.

The process of liberalization and democratization in the USSR, however, confronts more profound and far-reaching obstacles than similar processes occurring in Eastern Europe. Not only does the mounting economic crisis add to the already formidable constraints on economic marketization; the very definition of the Soviet political community is itself being called into question. By helping erode the core values and institutions which traditionally held together the Soviet multinational system, *glasnost'* and democratization have unleashed powerful centrifugal forces which Moscow can no longer readily contain. As Aleksandr Prokhanov vividly asserted, "Today we are a galaxy that has exploded and is flying off in all directions, with a black emptiness at its center" (Prokhanov, 1990).[2]

The rising tide of national self-assertion now constitutes a fundamental challenge to the integrity of the Soviet state and the values and institutions that have sustained it. Central to these have been the myth of internationalism, the

First published in *Soviet Economy,* 1989, 5, 3, pp. 201–250. The author would like to thank Philip Goldman and Sergei Drobizhev for research assistance, and Tony Reese for editorial help. She would also like to express her appreciation to the Carnegie Corporation for its support of the larger research project on which this article is based.

1. Indeed, in the latest of a protracted series of efforts to define a new model of socialism, a recent *Pravda* editorial entitled "Our Ideal—A Humane, Democratic Socialism" contains no reference to either Marx or Lenin (*Pravda*, Feb. 1, 1990).

2. Prokhanov goes on to argue that the assault on centralism is responsible for destroying the integrity of the Soviet multinational state and carries with it the danger of an apocalyptic civil war. Similar concerns are expressed by Eduard Volodin (1990).

federal political structure, the centralized command economy, the Russification of cultural life, and the use of the military and the KGB as instruments of central power. After examining current challenges to each of these traditional mechanisms for managing the Soviet multinational system, this paper will analyze the leadership's response to current challenges and assess the scope and adequacy of its efforts thus far to contain these pressures by restructuring the federal system.

SIX VARIETIES OF NATIONAL SELF-ASSERTION

From Alma-Ata to Abkhazia, from Tallinn to Tbilisi, virtually no region of the Soviet Union has proven immune to the rising tide of national unrest. Whether in the form of anti-Russian demonstrations, or in the emergence of national political movements demanding greater economic and political autonomy, if not outright independence, or in more volatile outbursts of communal violence that result in a tragic loss of lives and many thousands of refugees, as in Armenia, Azerbaijan, and Uzbekistan—all pose a growing threat to central authority and to the prospects for a relatively benign transition from authoritarianism to a more liberal and democratic system.[3]

The "national question" in the Soviet Union today embraces not one but six different types of national problems, structurally distinct from each other and deriving from different configurations of socioeconomic and cultural cleavages. First and foremost are the growing demands by powerful and cohesive national movements for political and economic autonomy, and increasingly for outright independence, centered in—but not limited to—the Baltic republics. No longer content with resisting or reversing pressures toward integration, they have moved to challenge the very legitimacy of Soviet rule over their territories. These efforts have in turn provoked the counter-mobilization of national minorities—whether Russians in Estonia, Latvia, and Moldavia, Poles in Lithuania, or Abkhazians and South Ossetians in Georgia—demanding protection of their own national rights, proclaiming their own right to autonomy or secession, making desperate appeals to Moscow for support.

A second group of problems derives from conflicts between national groups, stemming from long-simmering territorial, religious, and political rivalries. The protracted and increasingly bitter struggle between Armenia and Azerbaijan over Nagorno-Karabakh, which defies Moscow's efforts at resolution, has not only escalated into armed struggle but has increasingly discredited the authority of the center, which is perceived as unwilling or powerless to come to the defense of either side.

The dramatic eruptions of inter-ethnic violence in Central Asia—in the

---

3. Both regional and nationalist movements share a common impulse toward self-determination and seek to curb the center's domination of economic and political life in the periphery. However, in the case of national movements ethnic grievances are superimposed on center-periphery tensions, and common nationality and shared historical grievances are proving to be the most powerful of all potential bonds.

Fergana Valley, in Novyy Uzen, and in Tadzhikistan—are a manifestation of yet a third category of problems: the spillover of economic grievances into communal violence. An amorphous but intense and potentially explosive sense of resentment, particularly strong among unskilled workers and underemployed or unemployed youth in Central Asia and the Transcaucasus, exacerbates inter-ethnic tensions as economic grievances are displaced onto ethnic hostility directed against "outsiders." Moreover, these are not random or isolated outbreaks; the growing explosiveness of inter-ethnic relations in the region reflects a broader socioeconomic and demographic crisis in Central Asia, the legacy of a distorted pattern of economic and political development which is now being openly challenged.[4]

A fourth set of problems stems from demands to extend the principles of Soviet federalism to national groups lacking the status and protection afforded by territorial homelands with full union republic status. The increasingly outspoken and insistent demands of a number of national minorities—from Tatars and Bashkirs to Abkhazians—for upgrading the status of their national homelands are supported by many Soviet reformers who favor elimination of the hierarchical state structure of the present Soviet federation.

A fifth category of demands are those voiced by the "punished peoples" of the Stalin era—among them, the Crimean Tatars, Chechen Ingush, and Volga Germans—calling for full historical rehabilitation and the restoration of their national homelands, demands which would also require redrawing borders throughout the USSR. In trying to respond to these demands the Soviet leadership confronts a difficult tradeoff between correcting what it explicitly acknowledges were grave historical injustices and opening up a Pandora's box in which redress of the grievances of one national group can be achieved only at the expense of another.

A final dilemma is posed by the rise of Russian nationalism. The growing intensity of ethnonationalism among the non-Russian nationalities of the USSR, and increasingly overt expressions of anti-Russian and anti-Soviet sentiments, have in turn provoked an increasingly resentful and hostile reaction among Russians and contributed to the recent growth of Russian national consciousness. While it has prompted reform-minded intellectuals and scholars to openly re-examine the viability of the empire, to reject the fusion of Russian nationalism and Soviet imperialism, and to defend the principle of national self-determination up to and including the right of secession, it has also stimulated chauvinistic, xenophobic, and anti-Semitic forms of Russian nationalism in-

---

4. The extremely high rates of unemployment among young males in Azerbaijan and Central Asia has been a particular Soviet concern in recent years. A recent issue of the Central Committee's journal *Izvestiya TsK KPSS* (1989, p. 79) confirmed that Azerbaijan and Uzbekistan, both scenes of major ethnic violence, also have the highest rates of young adults not employed in socialized production—23 percent and 27 percent, respectively, compared to a figure of 8 percent in the Russian republic. See also the important roundtable discussion in *Kommunist* (1989), as well as recent articles by Kozlov (1988), Mukomel' (1989), and an earlier survey by Rumer (1989).

sistent on preserving the integrity of the Soviet state and demanding that central authorities take drastic measures to curb centrifugal forces.[5]

This tide of ethnonational mobilization has ramified across every domain of Soviet life: rising ethnic tensions have reverberations in enterprises and offices, in classrooms and military units, in theatrical troupes and artistic collectives, in primary party organizations as well as in the Supreme Soviet, complicating interpersonal relations as well as policy making at every level of the Soviet system. The strains are particularly acute within the Communist Party itself, as growing frictions and cleavages along ethnic lines further erode the Party's capacity to preserve a vestige of internal unity in conditions of societal fragmentation and growing political pluralism.

EMERGING POLICY DEBATES

The growing intensity of ethnonationalism among Russians and non-Russians alike has not only provoked growing alarm among Soviet citizens and leaders; it has also precipitated an unprecedented controversy over Soviet nationality policy and over the nature and future of the Soviet federal system itself. During the past two years a gamut of sensitive issues previously closed to public discussion have become the subject of heated debate: the extent to which the national republics which comprise the Soviet federation should enjoy real sovereignty, the legal status of territories like the Baltic republics annexed as a consequence of the Molotov-Ribbentrop pact, the criteria for resource allocation among the regions of the USSR and the degree to which more developed areas should subsidize the less developed, the representation of different nationalities in leadership positions, the language and cultural rights of different national groups, as well as the role of Russian as a *lingua franca*, and above all, the question of where the right to make such decisions should reside.

Conventional assumptions and approaches have been directly challenged in public discussions unprecedented in their scope and frankness. If the existence of policy debates among Soviet political actors once had to be teased out of the esoteric and Aesopian language of scholarly publications or state and party documents, these differences have now been displayed in full public view in the mass media. Indeed, scholars, intellectuals, and local leaders, many newly transformed into national political actors, if not media stars, have now been able to directly translate their views into legislative proposals for discussion and possible adoption by the new Congress of People's Deputies and the Supreme Soviet.

Two conflicting visions of the Soviet system have contended with each other. The first, which gives greater political recognition to national diversity, views the USSR as a confederation of sovereign national republics which should

5. For recent contributions to the debate, see Volodin (1990), Menshikov (1989), Prokhanov (1990), and Anisimov (1989). Two excellent overviews by Western scholars are Szporluk (1989) and Brudny (1989).

enjoy substantial economic and political autonomy in shaping the destiny of their historical homelands (Koroteyeva et al., 1988). The second, which assigns highest priority to economic and political integration, argues—by analogy with the American model—that the individual rather than the group should be the subject of political rights. It views the Soviet Union as "our common home" and insists there should be no corner of the territory of the USSR where any Soviet citizen could not feel at home (Tishkov, 1989a, 1989b; Bromley, 1989). While the Soviet leadership has sought to straddle the issue, it has become clear that difficult policy choices must be made.

To critics of Gorbachev's increasingly far-reaching agenda of economic and political change, including members of the top party leadership itself, the growing tensions and dangers resulting from rising national self-assertion constitute additional evidence that *glasnost'* and democratization have gone too far. Soviet achievements, they charge, are regularly maligned in the media; unofficial political groups challenge the leadership and the very legitimacy of the party; and national movements are taking advantage of an excessively tolerant political environment to marshal forces which would ultimately challenge Soviet rule. In the view of these critics, current developments are exacerbating interethnic relations in general, posing a growing threat to the Russian settler communities dispersed throughout the non-Russian regions of the country, and ultimately threatening the cohesion and very stability of the Soviet system (Ye. Ligachev, in *Pravda,* July 22, 1989).

In the view of Soviet reformers, by contrast, *glasnost'* and democratization—compounded by sharply deteriorating economic conditions—have simply brought to the surface long-simmering resentments and grievances and provided legitimate outlets for their expression. The eruption of national tensions in the past few years is for them dramatic evidence that traditional ways of managing the multinational Soviet system has reached a dead end, demonstrating the urgency of a fundamental *perestroyka* of nationality policy as well as the restructuring of the Soviet federal system. Echoing Gorbachev's own words, they insist that turmoil is inseparable from revitalization, and that some degree of instability is a necessary condition of any far-reaching change. Not only would the resort to political repression provoke explosions of increasing scale and ferocity, and strengthen separatist tendencies; it would entail the demise of the reform process itself, further economic decline, and a return to a more authoritarian system of political rule. The critical challenge, in their view, is to draw a clear line between legitimate economic and political protest, and impermissible discrimination and violence against other ethnic groups.

The leadership's difficulty in coping with these problems is compounded by two additional factors. First is the absence of well-developed mechanisms in the Soviet system for dealing with social and ethnic conflict in non-repressive ways. While Gorbachev's reforms were clearly intended to create new political and legal institutions capable of conflict-management at the all-Union, republic, and local levels, and to shift major responsibilities to the network of legislative bodies, these new institutions and mechanisms are only beginning to take shape. At the same time, a broader breakdown of authority which accompanied the reform process—most visibly manifested by Moscow's inability to control escalating communal violence in the Transcaucasus and Central Asia—emboldened local activists to acts of further defiance.

In late 1988, Gorbachev had announced that 1989 would usher in a new phase of *perestroyka* devoted to the harmonization of inter-ethnic relations. A restructuring of the federal system, including a substantial decentralization of political and economic power, was placed on the reformist agenda (*Izvestiya*, November 30, 1988). A special Central Committee plenum would serve as the capstone of this process, elaborating a party platform on inter-ethnic relations that would lay out the framework for future policy and strike a suitable balance between the need for political and economic integration and the demands for greater political, economic, and cultural autonomy.

The decision to convene a special plenum of the Party's Central Committee to formulate new directions for Soviet nationality policy was both a response to growing tensions and demands and a catalyst in stimulating public debate over alternative proposals. It revealed a recognition by the Soviet leadership that previous Soviet policies were exhausted, and that rapidly moving developments required more than just a stream of tactical adaptations. Merely tinkering with existing arrangements was no longer adequate; fundamentally new thinking about nationality theory, and fundamental changes in Soviet institutions and policies, were now required. How far-reaching these departures should be, and what direction they should take, became the subject of heated debate.

The preparations for the Central Committee plenum precipitated an unprecedented public debate over nationality policy. In keeping with its espousal of *glasnost'* and political participation, the party leadership solicited broad public input into the process. During the eighteen months that elapsed between the initial proposal to hold the plenum and the actual meeting which finally convened, after four postponements, on September 19–20, 1989, a massive nationwide discussion of the whole gamut of issues connected with inter-ethnic relations took place. Roundtable discussions and interviews with a wide range of experts filled the pages of scholarly journals and the mass media. Special television programs were devoted to the topic. A questionnaire soliciting the views of hundreds of officials and experts on controversial issues was prepared by researchers at the Institute of Ethnography, and an entire volume setting out the views of dozens of specialists—plaintively entitled *What Is to Be Done?*—included excerpts from their responses (*Chto delat'*, 1989). The party Central Committee alone received over 60,000 letters on the subject, and since many of these had groups of signatories, the total number of individuals who sought to register their views on the subject was larger still (*Kommunist*, No. 15, October 1989, p. 46).

The inputs into the preparation of the party's platform came from four major sources. The scholarly community, and particularly the social science institutes of the Academy of Sciences, constituted a first and most visible source of inputs, providing both criticism of existing arrangements and proposals for change. Legal scholars set forward recommendations for changes in state structure and drafts of revisions to the constitution; economists grappled with the technical aspects of regional and republic self-financing and its relationship to broader economic reforms; historians reexamined the evolution of Soviet nationality policy and debated the legacies of Lenin and Stalin; ethnographers proposed measures to address the language and cultural rights of national minorities; while the party's Institute of Marxism-Leninism struggled to develop a new theoretical framework for nationality policy that would correct the distortions of the Stalin and post-Stalin era and provide a genuinely Leninist approach to contemporary problems.

Party and state officials in the central bureaucracies in Moscow constituted a second major source of input into the platform. The preparation of the platform was coordinated within the Central Committee apparatus, under the overall direction of the Legal Affairs Commission headed by Secretary Viktor Chebrikov. Other Politburo members shared responsibility for its preparation, including Nikolay Ryzhkov as head of the Politburo Commission on Questions of Inter-ethnic Relations and Vadim Medvedev as head of the Central Committee Commission on Ideology.[6]

Republic and local party and state officials also played an important role in the preparation of the platform, not only submitting proposals to the Central Committee for consideration but also participating in high-level meetings with Politburo members and with Gorbachev himself. Indeed, their views on a number of issues under discussion can be inferred from the speeches at the plenum itself, which frequently expressed dissatisfaction with one or another aspect of the final platform.

Finally, there were broad opportunities for ordinary Soviet citizens, including activists in a variety of social and political movements, to add their own input to the broader public discussion. The receptivity of the media to different points of view varied considerably from one republic to another, but there were few issues—and few points of view—that did not find some expression in the course of this nationwide discussion. Moreover, the input of social movements also took more dramatic forms, as public rallies, demonstrations and even political strikes were and continue to be utilized by activists to focus attention on their demands and bring direct pressure to bear on local and central authorities.

---

6. Chebrikov chaired the two-day Central Committee conference in May 1989 which discussed draft materials for the plenum, and it was he who was interviewed by *Pravda* concerning the draft program following its publication on August 17, 1989. Ironically, Chebrikov's removal from the Politburo was announced at the conclusion of the September plenum which adopted the new program (*Pravda*, August 18, 1989).

"NEW POLITICAL THINKING" ON NATIONAL RELATIONS

Perhaps the most striking feature of this entire discussion was the degree to which conventional treatments of "the national question" were being supplanted by new and quite unprecedented formulations of the issues. The public debates revealed the emergence of what could appropriately be considered "new political thinking" about nationality problems, and a shift in the center of gravity of the entire discussion toward new approaches.

"New thinking" about national relations was already beginning to develop in the Brezhnev era, as ethnographers and sociologists conducting empirical research on ethnic processes began to challenge traditional assumptions and to reformulate the issues in fresh ways. But the obligatory tone of self-congratulation that permeated scholarly writings in that "era of stagnation" reduced the utility of these studies in preparing either the political leadership or the public for the problems ahead.

In the new political environment of the Gorbachev reforms, which had delegitimized earlier norms and policies in this as in other spheres, and in the face of mounting ethnic problems, the search for new approaches sanctioned the expression of previously heretical views. The emerging "new thinking" can best be captured in the changing treatment of three issues which formed the heart of the Soviet approach to national development.

The first novel point of departure in these discussions of national relations was the explicit abandonment of the myth that the "national question" could be once and for all time "solved." For several decades, Soviet policy was based on the expectation that modernization and socialism would automatically erode national identities and loyalties and that a new multinational community, based on the equality, prosperity, harmony, and increasing uniformity of all its members, would be the outcome. The fact that such illusions have largely vanished was reflected in a change in Soviet rhetoric: the focus on "solving" [*resheniye*] the national question has been replaced with a concern over "managing" [*upravleniye*] it.

Yet a second concept that once occupied a central place in Soviet discussions, but that has now virtually vanished from the pages of official documents as well as current publications is the view that *sliyaniye*—convergence or fusion of nations and nationalities—is a possible and indeed desirable object of policy. While Soviet scholars and officials have acknowledged for a number of years that national identities are less malleable and more enduring than classical socialist theory posited, what is novel in current Soviet discussions is the considerable value now attached to national distinctiveness and diversity, and the notion that its disappearance would constitute an irreparable human loss.

This new approach is captured in the words of a distinguished Soviet ethnographer, Sergey Arutyunov. Taking issue with the traditional view that ethnic assimilation is not only a natural but a progressive phenomenon, he argued:

Any disappearance of an ethnos is a tragic phenomenon. . . . The concept of ethnic pluralism should have its Communist variant. . . . Soviet society has an interest in preserving the specific cultural heritage of all ethnoses, since de-ethnicization leads to a divorce from historical roots with the inevitable ensuing growth of soullessness, the coarsening of behavioral norms, and the loss of the most important moral-ethical (*Natsional'nyye*, . 1987, p. 94).

Perhaps the most eloquent statement of this newly legitimate view was made by the First Secretary of the Estonian Communist Party, Vaino Valijas. In his address to the Central Committee Plenum, Valijas affirmed:

The nation is the basic form of human existence, with roots that reach back into the distant past and ahead into the foreseeable future; its national culture, which takes shape over centuries by absorbing the experience of generations, is the foundation of universal human values. It is nations and peoples, not a formless mass of people, that are the makers of history. Destroying their integrity leads inevitably to moral decline, the deformation of culture, neglect of the everyday environment, ecological anomalies and, finally, stagnation (*Pravda,* September 21, 1989).

This growing interest in rediscovering, reviving, and protecting national groups and their cultural heritage in effect repudiates earlier assimilationist goals. It argues that the newly discovered espousal of pluralism should be extended to ethnicity. If diversity is to be cultivated both at home and abroad, rather than eradicated, as many scholars and officials now argue, the fundamental challenge is to reduce the potential for conflict and to create mechanisms for managing it non-repressively.

This recognition has in turn forced a rethinking of the whole meaning of the term "internationalism," long associated with the struggle against national traditions, identities, and values. For the countless party officials and scholars who have devoted a lifetime to this struggle, the "new thinking" requires a wrenching shift in mental outlook.[7] Nonetheless, the main thrust of the "new thinking" is to reframe the concept of internationalism to make it compatible with national values.

A third element in the emerging "new thinking" about national relations involved a repudiation of the striving for uniformity. The recognition that a country as vast and diverse as the USSR cannot be treated as a monolithic whole called for the development of differentiated policies suited to the dis-

7. See, for example, the novel assertion by a leading party theorist of national relations that, "as V. I. Lenin believed, the satisfaction of national demands is the most important way to strengthen internationalism" (Bagramov, 1989).

tinctive problems and needs of different regions of the country.[8] Increasingly varied patterns of economic, political, and cultural life, and different kinds of ties between center and periphery, would inevitably be the outcome. How such variation could be accommodated within the framework of a single political, economic, and legal universe now has emerged as a major subject of discussion.

OUR COMMON HOME: RESTRUCTURING THE FEDERAL SYSTEM

The Soviet leadership's belated recognition that restructuring the federal system was an essential element of democratization was a vivid illustration of a learning process which has characterized much of Soviet policy under Gorbachev. During Gorbachev's first months as General Secretary, he gave no indication that nationality policy was part of the reform agenda, or that it was itself in need of reassessment. As he would later confess, the leadership initially underestimated the urgency of the entire issue:

> It must be admitted that at the beginning of restructuring we by no means fully appreciated the need for updating nationalities policy. Probably we were too slow in resolving a number or urgent questions. Meanwhile, natural dissatisfaction with the economic and social problems that had accumulated began to be perceived as an infringement on national interests . . . (*Pravda,* May 31, 1989, p. 7).

The demonstrations in Alma-Ata in December 1986 were the first in a series of jolts that would transform the leadership's view of national relations from complacency to alarm. By 1988 Gorbachev identified nationality policy as "the most fundamental, vital issue of our society" and in July 1988, in a speech to the Central Committee plenum, he called for a comprehensive restructuring of nationality policy, including a transformation of the federal system itself.[9]

Throughout Soviet history both the functions performed by the republics and, indeed, the very sanctity of the original federal arrangement have been the subject of continuing controversy. During Stalin's lifetime, Soviet federalism largely served to provide a fig-leaf of legitimation for Moscow's control over the periphery, while facilitating the recruitment of local cadres to administer central policies. Moreover, Lenin's endorsement of a federal system was treated by Stalin as highly conditional, motivated by tactical expediency, and

8. One of the earliest scholars to make this argument publicly was Yu. V. Arutyunyan (1969). It was bolstered with detailed socioeconomic data in Gintner and Titma (1987). The argument was extended to the political sphere by a Soviet legal scholar, I. Muksinov, who argued for diverse types of federal relations between the center and different republics (1989).

9. A more comprehensive treatment of the evolution of Gorbachev's approach to the national question is presented in a forthcoming study by the author, *Eroding Empire: Ethnonationalism and the Soviet Future.*

premised on the view that it was a "transitional form" on the path to a unitary state.[10]

Despite the fact that the union republics were formally endowed with many attributes of sovereignty, it was ultimately the center that defined the scope and limits of their jurisdiction. The ministerial structure of economic organization excluded large areas of economic life from their direct control. Moreover, under Stalin, several republics and autonomous areas were arbitrarily abolished; in most cases—as in the Crimean Tatar, Kalmyk, Volga German, and Chechen-Ingush republics—their populations were forcibly removed. Although these abuses were exposed and denounced by Khrushchev, they were not fully rectified; and it was during Khrushchev's rule that the Karelo-Finnish Republic lost its status as a union republic.

At the same time, the very existence of a federal system gave some substance to the claims of republic elites that they represented more than mere administrative subunits. Unlike a territorial *oblast,* union republics were formally endowed with constitutions, "sovereignty," the right of secession, the right to engage in diplomatic relations with foreign states, and until 1938, the right to their own military units—however much these rights were circumscribed in practice. The political relaxation which followed Stalin's death, and the process of de-Stalinization initiated by Khrushchev, brought the latent controversy over federalism once more to the fore.

The publication of several of Lenin's long-suppressed late writings, including his letter of December 1922 "On the question of nationalities or 'autonomization,' " challenged Stalin's interpretation of Lenin's views on federalism and revealed important differences between Lenin's and Stalin's approaches to nationality policy. The reignited controversy over federalism continued in the Soviet press and scholarly journals throughout the Khrushchev period.[11]

During the Brezhnev era, a prolonged controversy over the status and powers of the Union republics again erupted and indeed delayed the adoption of the 1977 Constitution. Although the debate appeared to revolve around the question whether Lenin viewed the creation of the federal structure as a temporary and tactical expedient or as an expression of a durable political principle, more sensitive policy problems lurked beneath the surface.[12] Moreover, while the new constitution preserved the existing structure—although with some diminution of the republics' autonomy—Brezhnev's report on the discussions which preceded its adoption did not challenge the principle of a unitary system but

10. Stalin's account of Lenin's views was distilled in one frequently quoted passage: "In Lenin's book *The State and Revolution* (August 1917), the Party, in the person of Lenin, made the first serious step towards recognition of the permissibility of federation as a transitional form to a centralized republic; this recognition, however, being accompanied by a number of substantial reservations" (Stalin, 1952, v. 3, p. 31).

11. For a discussion of these earlier controversies, see Hodnett (1967).

12. Among the proposals under discussion, according to a later account, were measures to liquidate union and autonomous republics or sharply restrict their sovereignty, to introduce a statute that identified all Soviet citizens as members of a single, *Soviet,* nationality, and to abolish the Council of Nationalities and establish a unicameral Supreme Soviet (Paskara, 1982).

indicated only that major changes were inexpedient at the time (*Izvestiya*, October 5, 1977; see also Shtromas, 1980).

The debate was not ended by the adoption of the new constitution; it continued in muted form into the 1980s,[13] and was given new impetus in the late Brezhnev era by controversies over economic, political, and demographic trends. Advocates of reducing the role of the republics further, or of eliminating the federal republics altogether, urged their case on grounds of economic rationality (holding that existing boundaries were an obstacle to optimal economic planning); as a matter of political control (arguing that retention of the federal structure impeded political integration); and as a response to demographic trends (which reduced their titular nationality to a minority in several union and autonomous republics). Defenders of existing federal arrangements cited Lenin on their behalf and asserted that the federal system had by no means exhausted its utility and that its retention was a precondition for further rapprochement among nationalities. Their insistence on the need for an exceptionally careful and sensitive approach was coupled with the scarcely veiled warning that ill-considered measures to restrict the powers and independence of national republics would inflame national prejudices.

These seemingly esoteric discussions of the durability of the federal republics, and of the conditions under which they might become superfluous in the future, represented a crypto-dialogue with considerable economic and political stakes. They reflected an ongoing struggle by local elites in a highly centralized political and economic system to enhance the power and resources available to them, and to reshape policy across a broad range of highly sensitive issues. Expanded access to central decision-making organs, and particularly to Gosplan, would increase their leverage over key resource allocation and personnel decisions. Increased economic and political autonomy would give republic authorities greater control over industrial enterprises within their boundaries as well as of resource flows across those borders; over migration policies which affected the ethnic balance of the population within each republic; or over language policy, with all its implications for the status and job opportunities of different nationalities in every sphere of economic, political, and cultural activity. By adding an affective dimension to center-periphery conflicts, the federal structure of the Soviet system, with its reinforcement of national boundaries by political-administrative ones, complicated Soviet efforts to combine a high degree of centralization of power with responsiveness to local interests and demands.

This entire debate over the nature of the federation burst into the open, and took a radically new direction, in the context of Gorbachev's reforms. The attacks on the Soviet command-administrative system unleashed by *glasnost'* opened the door to a serious discussion of the Soviet state structure. What was

---

13. A sketch of these controversies is presented in Karakeyev et al. (1982).

once an esoteric scholarly debate was now transformed into an open political struggle. Moreover, under the impact of democratization, republic political elites and mass movements now became major political actors in a campaign for far-reaching structural reform. Advocates of fundamental changes in the Soviet federal system challenged the status quo as a distortion of genuine federalism. The Soviet state, they argued, represented a centralized, unitary system cloaked in the legal form of a federation; restructuring was needed to give federalism real content.

In calling for major changes that would strengthen the status and role of the union republics, the advocates of reform also rejected the idea that the federal structure was a transitional one. The republics, they argued, represented an enduring expression of nationhood.

In their campaign for changes in the federal structure, the reformers sought their ultimate legitimation in Lenin himself, and particularly in Lenin's late writings. Arguing that Stalin had distorted both Lenin's conception of the federal system and its implementation, they drew on a newly developing body of historical studies reassessing the early history of the Soviet federation to support their views.[14] Even the Central Committee's Institute of Marxism-Leninism acknowledged that its previous understanding of these early developments was incomplete and distorted and promised a new and comprehensive study of Soviet nationality theory and practice.[15]

The alleged differences between Lenin's and Stalin's views of the nature of federation turned on a number of broad issues. First was the definition of self-determination itself. Lenin, it was argued, took a broad view of self-determination, treating it as a process rather than a single political act. Self-determination included not only political choice but opportunities for national-cultural development. Stalin, by contrast, reduced the notion of self-determination to a single political act—that of secession—which in turn provided the rationale for restricting union republic status to territories which had an external border.[16]

A second difference between Lenin and Stalin, it was now suggested, lay in their understanding of national autonomy. For Lenin, national autonomy included the right to form independent political units and was inseparable from federalism itself. Stalin, by contrast, emphasized territorial rather than national autonomy, in effect blurring the distinction between purely territorial *oblasts* and national territories. This difference in turn shaped their conceptions of the federation. Lenin, it was argued, conceived it as a union of equal republics, while Stalin, in calling for "autonomization" within the RSFSR, in effect proposed to subordinate other nations to Russia.

Finally, Lenin, it was emphasized, conducted a life-long struggle against great-power, Russian chauvinism and was prepared to bend over backward to

14. For examples of a burgeoning literature, see Khallik (1988), Nenarokov (1989), and Zotov (1989).
15. Interviews by the author, May and August 1989.
16. Advocates of enhancing the status and powers of autonomous republics and regions, or of upgrading them to union republic status, had an important stake in this argument.

respond to the sensitivities and concerns of national minorities. Stalin, by contrast, pursued a policy of Russification and reinforced the metaphor of Russians as "elder brothers." Indeed, the very decision not to create separate political institutions for the Russian republic effectively conflated Russia with the USSR and undermined the very principle of genuine federation.

By endorsing the need for structural changes in the Soviet federal system, and calling for discussion and recommendations by legal specialists across the country, the 19th Party Conference of June 1988 invited a major debate over the future of Soviet federalism.[17] The central focus of the controversy was the proposal by advocates of radical constitutional reform that a new federal system be established on the principle of genuine republic sovereignty.

Both reformers and moderates agreed on the need for changes in the constitution and related legal documents that would clearly define the respective competence of central and republic authorities; it was widely recognized that the existing provisions were inadequate and full of internal contradictions.[18] Major differences erupted, however, over the balance to be struck between the two, and indeed over the fundamental character of the federation itself.

The radical reformers proceeded from the principle that the USSR was a federation of sovereign, equal republics which enjoyed extensive rights of self-determination up to and including the right of secession. The republics, in their view, retained all rights not explicitly transferred to all-Union institutions, and they took a relatively restrictive view of all-Union functions.[19]

This approach was contested by others who acknowledged the need for greater decentralization, and supported an expansion of the rights and status of the republics, but who viewed this as a transfer of rights and responsi-

17. The Institute of State and Law of the Academy of Sciences in Moscow created a special department to study problems of federalism and organized an important roundtable discussion of the subject which brought together specialists from around the country. A summary of the proceedings was published in *Sovetskoye gosudarstvo i pravo* (1987a and 1987b); see also Maslov (1989).

18. Internal contradictions in the Soviet 1977 Constitution, for example, were brought into sharp focus during the dispute between Armenia and Azerbaijan over the status of Nagorno-Karabakh. Both sides could find justification in the constitution for their conflicting claims.

19. A speech by A. V. Gorbunov, chairman of the Presidium of the Latvian Republic Supreme Soviet, to the USSR Congress of People's Deputies (*Izvestiya*, June 1, 1989), pointed out fundamental contradictions in the definition of republic rights. He noted that Article 76 of the present constitution, which proclaims that a union republic is a sovereign socialist state, is at variance with other articles of the constitution, including Article 73 which presents such a vague interpretation of the jurisdiction of the USSR that virtually all powers could be assigned to the center. It is equally contradicted by Article 74, according to which any USSR law, even if it deals with questions that are within the exclusive jurisdiction of the union republics, has higher legal force than the laws of the union republic. Gorbunov also noted that Article 174, which sets out the procedure for changing the USSR Constitution by a decision of the Congress of People's Deputies is worded in such a way that, even if all of a republic's deputies to the Congress voted against such changes, and they were rejected by the republic's supreme lawmaking body, a law changing the USSR constitution would still go into force on the territories of all the union republics. In effect, the terms on which sovereign Soviet socialist states have united can be changed not only without their consent, but also against their will. He proposed to reword Article 70 of the USSR constitution as follows: "The Union of Soviet Socialist Republics is a federal, multinational state, formed in conditions of a federal compact as a result of the voluntary association of equal Soviet socialist republics. This association is based on the principle of the free self-determination of nations. "The new legislation would proceed from the premise that the union republics are primary while the federation derives from them. Only the republics can transfer to the union or restore to themselves various powers, not the other way around, because the republics created the union. Finally, "a republic cannot be considered sovereign if it cannot be independently in charge of its own territory and resources."

bilities from the center.[20] Assigning high priority to political and economic integration, they defended the view that all-Union organs could take into their purview any question which they considered to have all-Union significance. Both sides in the debate acknowledged that questions of basic foreign and security policy fell largely within the purview of the center; the disagreements focused primarily on jurisdiction over economic life. But at a more fundamental level, the debate brought into the open a fundamental cleavage between advocates of a strong center, exercising substantial control over political and economic life, and those who viewed the republics as the basic constituent units of the USSR and sought to reduce the functions and powers of the center to a minimum.

The discussions on restructuring the federal system also addressed the need for new mechanisms to resolve potential conflicts between republic and all-Union legislation. The issue was raised in the Congress of People's Deputies in response to a law adopted in Lithuania specifying that all-Union legislation could not take effect within the republic until it had been explicitly ratified by the Lithuanian Supreme Soviet. Moreover, several republics insisted on their right to protest all-Union legislation or to challenge decrees that, in their view, violated republican constitutions. This issue was further complicated by the insistence of the Baltic republics that, since they were not party to the original federal arrangements of 1923, a new treaty of federation was now required to resolve their anomalous position. By the time the Soviet leadership explicitly acknowledged the need for a new treaty of federation, events had already outrun its evolving policy. The growing strength of separatist sentiments in the Baltic republics, reflected in the victory of pro-independence candidates in the 1990 elections, culminated in a decision by the newly elected Lithuanian Supreme Soviet on March 11, 1990, to denounce as illegal the republic's annexation in 1940 and to demand negotiations with Moscow aimed at restoring its independence. Gorbachev's insistence that the republic's action was illegal, and that it would be required to observe procedures for secession that were being developed by the Supreme Soviet, provoked a very serious political confrontation which at the time of this writing has not been resolved.

The status of the Russian republic itself raised an additional set of policy dilemmas. Amid a rising tide of complaints from Russian cultural and political figures about the absence of distinct state and party organizations for the republic, a number of reformers themselves now argued that the creation of a more genuine federation of equal and sovereign republics required the establishment of separate institutions for the Russian republic which heretofore had not existed. Under growing pressures from the Russian nationalist movement, the Gorbachev leadership offered some support to these demands. However, it sought to resist pressures for the creation of a separate Russian party orga-

---

20. See, for example, the report of the Maslyukov commission (Obshchiye, 1989) and the debate that followed its publication in *Pravda* during the summer of 1989.

nization, conceding only the reestablishment of a Russian *byuro*, within the Central Committee, headed by Gorbachev himself.[21]

The debates over the federation brought other unresolved issues of state structure into the political arena, prompting proposals for the rationalization of the existing federal structure or the redress of past grievances. The existing state structure of the USSR—comprising 15 union republics, 20 autonomous republics, 8 autonomous provinces, and 10 autonomous regions—came in for widespread criticism on several grounds. The higher any given entity stands in this hierarchy, the greater the advantages it tends to enjoy. But the rationale for these arrangements was highly arbitrary and no longer seemed persuasive.[22] Officials and activists in a number of autonomous republics and regions— Tataria and Bashkiria, among others—demanded an upgrading of their status, insisting that they deserved to be made union republics. A number of major national groups that lacked their own state structure now sought the creation of one, arguing that nations rather than state structures ought to be the subject of the Soviet federation. Other groups, such as the "punished peoples" (e.g., the Crimean Tatars, among others), demanded the restoration of state structures that were abolished under Stalin. Disputed territories, like the autonomous region of Nagorno-Karabakh, presented an additional set of problems. Even the long-neglected "small peoples of the north" now pressed for greater protection of their interests.

The trend toward increased autonomy for union republics triggered violent protests among minorities within these republics who feared that their own rights might be curtailed. Russians in Estonia and Moldavia used demonstrations and strikes to protest new laws infringing their traditional prerogatives; protests in Abkhazia touched off the demonstrations in Tbilisi which led to military actions and a tragic loss of lives in April 1989. However, elevating the status of autonomous republics and regions, or creating state structures for national groups that do not presently have them, would infringe on the rights of the present republics and challenge their status and powers.

A final set of issues involves the need for new political institutions to assure all nationalities adequate political representation, whatever federal structures or new arrangements are adopted. One proposal widely supported by minority groups would mandate the creation of bicameral legislatures in all union republics; the second chamber, a chamber of nationalities, would address issues

21. At the first meeting of the Russian *byuro* on April 3, 1990, a number of local and regional Party officials continued to press for the creation of a full-fledged Russian Party organization. They succeeded in keeping the issue alive by convening a Russian Party Conference to be held just prior to the CPSU Congress planned for June 1990.

22. The absence of clear criteria concerning national state structures has led to a number of anomalies. Estonia, for example, with a population of just over 1 1/2 million, has the status of a union republic, while 7 million Tatars have only an autonomous republic. The autonomous region of Adzharia has virtually no Adzhars in it, while the Jewish autonomous republic contains less than one percent of the Jewish population of the Soviet Union. For several perceptive discussions of anomalies in the existing state structure and proposals for reform see *Vek XX i mir* (1988), and the roundtable discussion in *Sovetskoye gosudarstvo i pravo* (1989).

involving rights or conflicts among the nationalities within any given republic. The reorganization of the executive branch provides for the representation of the heads of all union republics in a new Council of the Federation.[23] Finally, Gorbachev has proposed a restructuring of the Communist Party which would eliminate the present Politburo and create in its place an expanded Presidium that would include representatives of republic party organizations. Proposals are also under consideration to provide for the representation of all union republics in a new Council of the Presidency, as well as in a restructured Communist Party Politburo.

THE ECONOMICS OF FEDERALISM: REPUBLIC ECONOMIC SOVEREIGNTY

The calls for restructuring the Soviet federal system were not confined to issues of political-state structure; they embraced a fundamental reorganization of the economic system as well. Increasing dissatisfaction with the performance of the Stalinist planned economy had generated growing pressures for reforms that would reduce the reliance on highly centralized decision making and give increasing scope to the play of market forces. But if most reformers viewed enterprise autonomy and marketization on an all-Union basis as the answer to current problems, pressures were building in support of an alternative approach based on republic economic sovereignty.[24]

Virtually all advocates of economic reform took as their point of departure the view that the existing "command-administrative system" with its extreme concentration of power in the hands of central economic ministries, was incapable of carrying out policies that would effectively address regional economic and social needs and stimulate local initiative. This understanding extended to the highest level of the Soviet leadership; Aleksandr Yakovlev, in a speech to Latvian party activists in August 1988, explicitly included in his catalog of problems inherited from the past "conflicts between the interests of comprehensive territorial development and the economic activities of central departments" (*Pravda*, August 11, 1988). Support was building among economic reformers and government officials alike for some degree of economic decentralization that would expand the role of republic and regional authorities in economic decision making and management, and increase the financial resources available to them. Some steps in this direction had already been taken in 1986 and 1987, and further measures along these lines were envisioned by

23. The first session of this council, on March 30, 1990, was largely devoted to the Lithuanian crisis; the council was essentially used to endorse harsh measures against the Lithuanian leadership.

24. The term most widely used in the discussions, republic *khozraschet* (literally, self-financing or accountability), was a rather fuzzy concept which encompassed a whole range of possible meanings. Since self-financing could also be applied to cities or regions, "republic economic sovereignty," with its connotation of self-management, better conveys the broader political implications of the demand.

a high-level government commission headed by Yuri Maslyukov, then chairman of the State Planning Committee. The commission proposed draft legislation which would have devolved further economic responsibilities to the republics, altered Union-republic budgetary relations, and expanded the role of republic authorities in economic planning and coordination.[25] A number of specialists criticized these proposals for their failure to provide local officials with adequate resources to cope with these new responsibilities. But others considered the entire approach a totally inadequate response to critical problems, and demanded not merely the expansion of republic responsibilities but a more radical restructuring of center-periphery economic relations. Their proposals were intended to sharply curtail the prerogatives of central authorities and give republics broad powers over economic activity within their borders.

The argument for republic economic sovereignty joined considerations of economic productivity, political democratization, and national self-determination. From an economic perspective, its advocates contended, the existing system was structurally incapable of making rational economic decisions. The ministries' pursuit of their own narrow departmental interests inevitably resulted in a neglect of regional and local needs and interests, and produced outcomes which were economically unproductive, socially destabilizing, and environmentally disastrous.

Industrial ministries, as these critics charged, were responsible for extreme distortions in the economic and demographic life of the republics, promoting industrial expansion in developed urban areas in order to exploit the existing social and cultural infrastructure, and overburdening local communities while forcing them to bear the additional costs. Heavy reliance on workers from outside the republic—involving substantial immigration by Russians and Ukrainians—placed additional strains on already-tight housing suppplies, and brought changes in demographic balances that in republics such as Estonia and Latvia threatened to make the titular nationality a minority in its own republic. Between 1979 and 1989, according to the latest census data, in-migration accounted for over half the total population increase in Estonia and Latvia, reducing Latvians to half the population of the republic and Estonians to 61 percent.[26] Local economists estimated that every worker brought into these republics imposed a significant burden on local communities. Consequently, the Latvian and Estonian governments not only sought to restrict new enterprises relying on labor from outside the republic, and to limit residence permits, but required enterprises to pay that cost to local soviets.[27] Adding to the resentment of local

25. See Obshchiye (1988). See also Maslyukov's defense of this approach in "Sil'nyy tsentr; sil'nyye respubliki," *Pravda*, March 23, 1989. The proposal was endorsed by the USSR Council of Ministers and the CPSU Politburo, but was subsequently rejected as inadequate by the Supreme Soviet and sent back for redrafting. For a discussion of the draft legislation see John Tedstrom (1988). The Supreme Soviet discussion is reported in *Izvestiya*, October 18 and November 20, 1989.

26. *Atgimimas*, no. 37/50 (October 20–27, 1989), as cited in RL Report, vol. 1, no. 45 (November 10, 1989).

27. Conversation with Estonian economists, Tallinn, April 1989. In Riga, for example, the city's Chief Architect, G. K. Asaris, used the visit of Central Committee secretary Vadim Medvedev in November 1988 to

residents was the fact that many of these projects—from nuclear power plants to the mining of phosphorites—involved dangerous or environmentally destructive activities, and that regulations on environmental protection were flagrantly and routinely violated.

Central ministries were accused of playing an equally destructive role in agricultural development, imposing irrational crop priorities, misusing land and water, and encouraging destructive use of chemical fertilizers and pesticides harmful to the health of local populations. Appalling economic, social, and health problems in Central Asia were a direct result of their behavior. Only by transferring economic decision making to those with a direct and immediate stake in the welfare of the local populations would economic productivity and social welfare by enhanced.

In political terms, republic economic sovereignty constituted, in the view of its advocates, a logical extension of the process of democratization, ensuring both expanded participation in decision making by those most affected by it, and greater accountability for outcomes. Indeed, in the view of its supporters, it constituted the economic foundation of political *perestroyka,* fulfilling Lenin's call for vesting all power in the system of soviets.[28]

Finally, such a shift in the locus of decision making from Moscow to the republics was arguably a mechanism for reducing ethnic tensions. Moscow would no longer be the target of blame for economic and environmental mismanagement, or for migration processes that threatened national survival; republic and local leaders would now bear the primary responsibility for the welfare of their populations.

Inspired in part by the short-lived experiment with regional economic councils [*sovnarkhozy*] under Khrushchev, and in part by the economic reforms introduced in China and Hungary, the first proposals for republic self-management in the USSR were drawn up by a group of Estonian social scientists in October 1987 (Kallas et al., 1987) in response to the June 1987 Central Committee plenum's call for innovative approaches to economic problems. The authors' ideas were developed further by a group of Estonian economists and social scientists, and culminated in the publication of IME, a plan for republic self-management in Estonia.[29]

The Estonian proposal, and others that would subsequently draw on it as a model, had three key elements. First, it sought to establish the republic's control over all economic activity within its borders, arguing that with the exception of foreign and military policies which were properly the competence of all-Union authorities, the inhabitants of Estonia themselves should be masters of

---

point out that, despite a resolution of the USSR Council of Ministers limiting new industrial development in the largest cities, central ministries continued to expand industry in the city, resulting in a growth of population by 41% more than had been planned. Housing grew only 16%, leaving some 75,000 families on the waiting list for apartments (*Sovetskaya Latviya,* November 15, 1988, pp. 1–3; cited in Bahry (1989)).

28. Interview with M. L. Bronshetyn, *Kommunist Estonii,* No. 11 (July 1988), p. 23.

29. Problemnyy sovet IME, 1989; the term "IME" is a play on words and signifies "miracle" in Estonian.

their territory. Its most radical feature was the assertion of republic ownership over all enterprises and natural resources within its territory.

Second, it provided for extensive republic autonomy in the management of both internal and external economic affairs. Self-financing and self-management based on the introduction of market relationships and price reforms would replace the existing system of centralized state planning and allocation, and trade with other regions of the USSR, as well as with foreign partners, would be based on direct ties between producer and customer. The development of foreign economic ties, as well as intra-Soviet trade, would be furthered by the establishment of currency convertibility and the creation of either a separate Estonian currency or its functional equivalent to mediate the relationship between the Estonian and all-Union economies. The republic would have the power to regulate labor migration into its territory, as well as flows of capital from foreign investors and potential partners.

Finally, the plan would involve a transformation of the existing system of taxation, in which revenues flowed directly from enterprises to the center, to one in which the republic would receive all revenues from enterprises within its jurisdiction. The size of the republic's contribution to the all-Union budget would be negotiated with central authorities and formally established by the Supreme Soviet. Under these arrangements a substantially greater share of revenues than in the past would be retained within the republic and would be devoted to scientific-technical development, raising living standards, expanding social services, improving the social and cultural infrastructure of the republic, and environmental protection. Moreover, the resources available to the republic would rise in direct proportion to its successes in improving productivity.

The Estonian project was not explicitly intended as a model for other republics. Indeed, a fundamental assumption of its authors was the view that the USSR was too complex and differentiated, and its republics too diverse in their needs, to be managed through a uniform, monolithic approach. IME's authors sought to portray their approach as a limited, localized experiment which, if successful, might yield lessons from which other regions of the country might benefit. Nonetheless, the idea of regaining local control over economic ministries, had widespread appeal throughout the Soviet Union. Although only a few republics—Latvia and Lithuania in particular—were prepared to adopt the Estonian program in its entirety, republican and regional *khozraschet* became, in effect, an umbrella covering a great variety of economic demands and proposals.[30] Although economic independence would be most feasible in more highly developed republics, and to the disadvantage of those dependent on substantial economic subsidies from the center, the demand for substantial republic economic autonomy was even taken up by some officials and scholars in the Central Asian republics, although primarily as an expression of resent-

---

30. On May 19, 1989, the Supreme Soviets of the Estonian and Lithuanian republics adopted laws which laid the foundations for economic independence; the Supreme Soviet of Latvia followed suit on July 27.

ment directed at the center for what was perceived as exploitation of their economies.

The Baltic proposals, however, were highly controversial for symbolic as well as practical reasons, and elicited a barrage of criticism on several grounds.[31] Some of the concerns were economic and technical, and shared by conservatives and reformers alike. They stemmed from the fear that conceding substantial economic powers to the Baltic republics would threaten the integration of the all-Union economy by disrupting the ties which bound the republics into a single all-Union economic complex. Central ministries and planning agencies feared it would increase the barriers to central investment in, and management of, projects of all-Union importance. Growing regional protectionism had already complicated a whole range of economic activities, from siting new industrial enterprises to exporting food and consumer products from one republic to another. Not only in the Baltic but increasingly in Moscow and other cities of the Russian republic, restrictions were being imposed on purchases of scarce goods by non-residents. These developments already held out the danger of increasing fragmentation of the Soviet economy along national-territorial lines. Greater republic autonomy, critics feared, would only exacerbate the problem.

Economic reformers in Moscow were themselves divided, and at best ambivalent, about the Baltic proposals. On the one hand, they sympathized with the argument that traditional economic institutions and priorities had had devastating consequences in many republics. Academician Leonid Abalkin, the distinguished economist and Vice Premier of the USSR, affirmed the importance of treating national republics as something more than territorial subdivisions:

> It is necessary to recognize a union republic's sovereign right to solve any problems associated with the construction of new enterprises, regardless of whether they are detrimental to nature or not. After all, when we talk about a territory we mean more than just a shaded area on a geographical map. It means a people's habitat, a social and cultural sphere within which a people's history evolved. And these very sensitive factors, which are impossible to translate into the language of economic calculations, must without fail be taken into account when solving problems of republic self-management (*Ekonomicheskaya gazeta*, April 15, 1989, pp. 4–5).

At the same time reformers feared these changes could merely result in the substitution of republic *diktat* for that of Moscow. Only the shift of decision making to the enterprise itself, and reliance on the market to integrate economic decisions across the entire country, offered, in their view, a promising approach to economic reform (*Ekonomicheskiye*, 1989).

31. See the roundtable discussions organized by the journal *Voprosy ekonomiki*, "Respublikanskiy khozrashet: problemy i perspektivy" (1989). Also illuminating was a roundtable discussion with Baltic economists and public figures organized by *Kommunist*: "Slushat' drug druga," 1989. See also "Federativnyy soyuz," *Pravda*, July 12, 1989, for a key segment of a debate carried in *Pravda* throughout the summer of 1989.

Critics also attacked proposals for republic economic sovereignty as a step backward, an anachronistic movement toward autarchy at a historical moment when other nations—particularly in Western Europe—were moving toward ever-closer economic integration.[32] Confederations, they argued, were inherently unstable political formations, and historical experience showed that they resulted either in disintegration, or in movement in the direction of greater unification. While there were ample grounds for concern about the disruptive consequences of localism—from Yugoslavia to China—another set of concerns, less openly addressed, lay beneath the surface: the fear that developing economic integration across the Baltic republics, including plans for a Baltic common market, and expanding economic ties to Scandinavia and Western Europe, was laying the economic foundations for ultimate secession.

A further set of objections stemmed from ideological-political considerations, and centered on the whole question of property. The assertion that the republics rather than the union "owned" the enterprises and resources on their territory, and should control their disposition, was a highly contentious proposition. It directly challenged the power and prerogatives of central economic ministries, and not surprisingly they mounted a major campaign against it.[33] Moreover, in view of the announced intention of the Baltic republics to legalize private property on their territories, the controversy also turned on whether the regulation of forms of property should be a function of all-Union authorities, uniform throughout the USSR.[34]

A final objection stemmed from concern that republic economic sovereignty would sharply increase regional inequalities. In view of the enormous variations in levels of economic development, resource endowments, and demographic trends across the territory of the USSR, critics argued, resource redistribution by the center was essential to promoting some equalization of economic and social conditions among republics. Indeed, they noted that at the 19th Party Conference proposals for republic economic sovereignty were supported only by delegates from economically advantaged regions, while those from less developed regions of the country—especially Central Asia—had expressed serious reservations. Such subsidies were particularly important to the Central Asian republics, where high rates of population increase and a deteriorating economic and ecological situation demanded resources beyond the capacity of

32. See, for example, "Vpered v ... proshloye?" (*Pravda*, May 22, 1989, p. 2): "Federativnyy soyuz" (*Pravda*, July 12, 1989). In a speech to the Congress of Deputies, an Estonian Deputy, Klara Khallik, retorted that the real obstacle to greater integration of the USSR with the international community was bureaucratic centralism, and affirmed that the Baltic republics sought increasing interaction with Scandinavia and Western Europe.

33. The campaign relied on three basic arguments: first, that ownership of republic resources had been surrendered to the Union by the act of federation itself; second, that republics had no claim on enterprises created by the contribution of resources from Moscow; and third, that republic ownership contradicted the principle of public ownership over the means of production. As the more sophisticated Soviet economists pointed out, much of this debate reflected simplistic and outdated conceptions of property.

34. Legislation presented to the Supreme Soviet in the fall of 1989 provided for four types of state property: all-Union, union-republic, republic, and communal (reported by N. I. Ryzhkov, *Pravda*, October 3, 1989, pp. 2–4).

the republics themselves to provide. While the Baltic delegates and their allies conceded that regional disparities might well increase, in their view the costs would be more than offset by the stimulus to local initiative and productivity (Shkaratan, 1989).

Notwithstanding the intense controversy which the entire issue generated, the Supreme Soviet during its fall session formally approved a law giving the Baltic republics broad latitude for experimenting with economic independence.[35] While the implementation of this legislation will involve a protracted struggle between republic and central authorities, it is clear that a considerable number of officials and delegates—as well as many Soviet citizens—view these arrangements as a thinly disguised step toward secession. Although critics acknowledge that enhanced local autonomy could conceivably yield economic benefits, they fear that it would contribute to strengthening already mounting centrifugal forces and to reinforcing national cleavages with socioeconomic ones.

LANGUAGE POLICY

While debates over restructuring the Soviet federation were largely the province of legal and economic specialists, controversies over language policy exploded into major public demonstrations involving hundreds of thousands of participants. Throughout 1988 and 1989, in republic after republic, beginning with the Baltics and sweeping southward to Central Asia, demands to make the language of the titular nationality the state language of the republic became the focal point of efforts by national activists to mobilize mass support.[36]

These campaigns to enhance the status of the republic language at the expense of Russian, as a guarantee of linguistic survival and a first step toward recovery, were typically led by a coalition of political elites, intellectuals, and professionals whose status and career opportunities would be enhanced by the shift, and by workers resentful of competition from Slavic immigrants into their republics. Proposed legislation would mandate the use of the national language in the workplace, in economic life, in party and state agencies, and in cultural life, including the media. It would become the language of instruction at higher and secondary educational institutions, as well as a mandatory subject in all general-education schools conducted in Russian. The massive campaigns in republic after republic in support of such legislation represented a protest against Russification, a challenge to the prerogatives of the Russian-speaking settler communities, and a struggle to redefine community identity. It was bitterly opposed by a substantial part of the Russian-speaking settler communities, by

35. Zakon o ekonomicheskoy samostoyatel'nosti Litovskoy SSR, Latviyskoy SSR i Estonskoy SSR," *Pravda,* December 2, 1989, p. 1.

36. The Transcaucasian republics were largely immune to these developments because their national languages had long had the status of state languages. Protests in Azerbaijan focused on the failure to implement these provisions in practice.

Russified party and state officials, and even by local elites closely identified with the instruments of central power for whom the revival of national self-assertion posed severe dilemmas.

A letter to *Izvestiya* from a Russian worker at the Ignalina Atomic Power Station in Lithuania eloquently captured the bitterness of these struggles, as well as the intimate connection of economic and linguistic policies, of issues of power and identity. As a skilled worker, the author recounts, he had responded to the call to help create "Lithuania's atomic sun," and was now among the 35,000 residents of the plant's largely Russian settlement. "We used to be virtual heroes," he reports. "We built the power station. But now we're becoming anti-heroes for the same reason. . . . Since the onset of the psychological attack against 'occupiers' and 'foreigners'—and that covers practically all the personnel of the atomic power station—the mood in our settlement has been one of wanting to pack up and leave. . . ." The new language laws would require the plant either to hire Lithuanian specialists, who don't yet exist, or to arrange the translation of all documents; "to learn a language so well within two years that it is possible to keep a fiery nuclear steed in rein is hardly possible for the majority of specialists." And without legal guarantees concerning the use of Russian, "who will we be in 15–20 years? Who will our children grow up to be?" (*Izvestiya,* March 10, 1989, p. 3).

Sentiments like these underlay the mobilization of Russian-speaking communities in opposition to the proposed new laws. Rallies, demonstrations and strikes, accompanied by inflammatory and abusive accusations and counter-accusations, brought to the surface latent ethnic hostilities and intensified them further. The height of bitterness was reached in Moldavia in August 1989 when crowds estimated at 300,000 to 500,000 people assembled in Kishinev to demand official status for the Moldavian language in the republic. The demonstrators were harshly denounced by *Pravda,* which published an article attacking the Popular Front of Moldavia as a "nationalist, separatist and anti-Russian [organization] seeking to ride to power on the turbid scum of chauvinism" and warned deputies preparing to attend the Moldavian Supreme Soviet meeting to vote on the language law that a vote in favor of the "discriminatory drafts" would be a vote for "national discord, the isolation of Moldavia, and the violation of its ties with the other fraternal republics" (*Pravda,* August 28, 1989). A counter-demonstration by 30,000 Russian-speaking workers in Tiraspol, on strike to put pressure on the legislature, voted to eliminate from the city's libraries and bookstores two newly published books of classical Moldavian literature printed—for the first time since World War II—in the Latin script.

Attitudes within the Russian communities were not altogether monolithic. Although the dominant sentiment was hostile, examples abounded of individuals or groups speaking out in support of the language laws and asking their fellow-Russians to show empathy. A Russian philologist in Moldavia, for example, noted that while all Moldavian students in the groups she/he taught were Russian-speaking, the Russian students were, as a rule, not bilingual, a situation she/he considered unfortunate. While endorsing the idea that the USSR was a "common home," it was decidedly not a communal apartment.[37]

These disputes over language policy threatened to loom large in the preparations for the Central Committee plenum. However, the repeated postponement of the plenum, and the rapid pace of events in the national republics, brought the issue to a head before the plenum even convened. The adoption of new language laws by the Supreme Soviets of a number of republics substantially preempted the issue before Moscow had a real opportunity to come to grips with it.

As republic after republic moved to adopt new language laws, the controversy focused on the status and future role to be accorded to Russian. A first approach, which offered the most minimal guarantee to the Russian-speaking population (and which it opposed most violently), was to designate the language of the titular nationality both the official language of the republic and the language of inter-nationality communication, while simply guaranteeing "the free use" of Russian and of other national languages. This approach, which was embodied in the draft legislation proposed by the Moldavian Supreme Soviet, was amended by the republic's Party secretary after a direct conversation with Gorbachev. The final decision made both Moldavian and Russian the languages of interethnic communication.

A second approach, adopted in a majority of cases, identified Russian as the "language of communication among nationalities," leaving open precisely what this would mean in practice. A third approach, strongly defended by the Russian-speaking communities but violently opposed by most of the national movements, would have guaranteed Russian equal status with the indigenous language within the republic.

Whether the adoption of these new republican language laws will help to defuse more radical demands for political autonomy or secession, as was the case in Canada, Spain, Belgium, and India, remains to be seen. Moreover, while the adoption of the language laws offered important symbolic satisfaction to the indigenous national movements, and may contribute to a degree of ethnic demobilization, conflicts over implementation are likely to keep these issues alive in specific local settings in years to come. In the absence of any real experience training Russians in national languages, carrying out the intent of these new measures will demand major investments in language training, preparing language teachers with the necessary expertise, developing curricula

---

37. "When we take up residence (permanently or temporarily) in another republic, and especially when we go there as guests or tourists, as a rule we do not know the language of our hosts, and we are totally confident that everyone should want to speak with us in Russian. We are offended when we do not encounter this desire, and we give no thought to the fact that this confidence of ours, our lack of consideration for the language of our hosts, our unwillingness to learn a few polite phrases ('Hello,' 'Good-bye,' 'Please,' 'Thank you,' 'Excuse me'), sometimes combined with not very high standards of behavior, are offensive and irritating. When this sort of irritation builds up over the years, it can reach a critical point" (*Pravda*, March 6, 1989).

and textbooks, and managing the delicate problems of a transition period. The burden will now fall on local elites to manage the balance between demands for rapid expansion of the use of the national language and the protection of the linguistic rights of Russian and minority communities.

These trends create particularly sharp dilemmas for non-Russian national-cultural minorities, whose treatment varies considerably from one setting to another. In some instances republic authorities have demonstrated unusual consideration for their needs. Whether out of a genuine commitment to support cultural pluralism or out of a desire to divide and thereby weaken potential coalitions of Russian speakers, the creation of new cultural associations, educational programs, and even religious facilities for national minorities has been encouraged in a number of republics.[38] In other cases, however, where national minorities are perceived to threaten the political or cultural hegemony of the titular nationality, less hospitable and more coercive measures have been applied.

From the perspective of Moscow, these decisions will carry a significant cost. To the extent that they increase the cultural and linguistic distinctiveness of the national republics, they create potentially important new obstacles to interregional mobility. The center's ability to deploy cadres across the entire territory of the USSR—whether to staff major industrial enterprises or to fill key positions in a republic party organization—will be very substantially diminished.

These decisions are also likely to accelerate current trends toward increasing ethnic homogeneity of the union republics. The out-migration of "outsiders" from increasingly unfriendly environments, and the return of individuals to the more protected environment of their "own" republics, is likely to be accelerated by these developments. Indeed, recent census data indicate that such a process is already under way. Increasing ethnic homogeneity, which is likely to reinforce political and economic cleavages with linguistic and cultural ones, would constitute a dramatic reversal of the trend toward greater dispersion characteristic of the USSR for most of its history, as well as of other industrial societies, and add to the difficulties of maintaining integration in the face of growing centrifugal pressures.

Indeed, the growing alarm over this prospect prompted numerous proposals to the Central Committee plenum that special measures be taken to protect the status of the Russian language, including provisions to formally establish it as the state language of the USSR. Such a decision—clearly contravening Lenin's explicit views on the subject—would be widely perceived as an effort to undo the decisions of republic legislative bodies and would undoubtedly reignite intense passions across the country. The central leadership has therefore resisted

---

38. Jewish associations and cultural-religious institutions have been established in the Baltic republics and in Moscow; the Ukrainian Popular Front "Rukh" has asked the government to restore closed synagogues; the creation of a Nationalities Forum in Tallinn and of a Polish Association in Vilnius are but a few examples of these trends.

such an approach, while searching for less confrontational ways of achieving the same goals.[39]

NATIONALITY AND THE SOVIET ARMED FORCES

Rising tensions among ethnic groups, and growing challenges to traditional Soviet policies across a whole range of dimensions, have inevitably extended to the Soviet military as well. Relying as they traditionally have on universal male conscription, the Soviet armed forces have long been assigned a major role in integrating diverse nationalities, socializing them into common norms of behavior, and imbuing them with patriotic consciousness. These integrative functions are now facing a serious challenge.

How successfully the Soviet military has performed these functions in comparison with other multinational armies has long been a subject of controversy among Western specialists (Wimbush and Alexiev, 1982; Jones, 1982; Jones and Grupp, 1982; Wimbush, 1985). Official Soviet claims of success are given indirect support by the testimony of some dissidents, who describe Soviet military service as a "de-nationalizing" experience that tears young conscripts from their roots (Dzyuba, 1968). At the same time, there was ample evidence even before the advent of *glasnost'* of ethnic tensions and frictions within the armed forces, and explicit calls in Soviet military publications for more decisive efforts to curb discriminatory attitudes and practices. The need for more widespread and effective "internationalist" and "patriotic" education in the armed forces, and for more emphasis on the achievements of Soviet nationality policy in creating harmonious relations among peoples, were obsessive themes in Soviet writings of the Brezhnev era.

Further complicating the tasks of the military has been inadequate knowledge of Russian language—the language of command and control—by non-Russian conscripts, particularly from Central Asia, and their poorer educational and technical qualifications. Demographic trends compounded these problems by rapidly increasing the proportion of Central Asians in the conscript pool. Between 1959 and 1979, for example, the Moslem population of the USSR increased some 45 percent, compared to 13 percent for the Great Russians; by 1989 the share of Russians in the Soviet population had declined to 50.8 percent, while the share of Central Asians had risen to 12 percent (*Rahva Haal*, September 19, 1989). As a consequence of these trends, conscripts from Central Asia and the Transcaucasus constituted 37 percent of the total of new recruits in 1988 (Deryugin, *Argumenty i fakty*, 35, 1988, pp. 1–2). Throughout the 1970s and early 1980s, the leadership's concern about the impact of these trends on military effectiveness was clearly reflected in Politburo reports, in the stepped-up campaign of the early 1980s to

---

39. At this writing, a draft law under discussion by the Supreme Soviet would declare Russian to be the language of all-state (*obshchegosudarstvennyy*) and interethnic communication of the USSR as a whole. Critics of this approach fear it would undermine the position of the national languages in the republics, and have proposed instead that Russian be declared the "official" language and the "language of federal communication," which would limit its mandatory use to areas of all-Union competence.

expand and intensify Russian language instruction in Central Asia, and in statements and resolutions that explicitly linked this effort to military as well as broader economic and social objectives.[40]

Wide disparities in the linguistic and educational preparation of different nationalities were also largely responsible for the *de facto* patterns of ethnic stratification within the Soviet military. Even if there were no discriminatory intent, uniform policies of recruitment and assignment would necessarily have a differential impact, given variations in education and skills among recruits. Consequently, Central Asian conscripts tended to be disproportionately concentrated in noncombat units, such as construction battalions, and largely absent from branches that place a premium on sophisticated technical skills. Moreover, because the officer corps remained largely the preserve of Slavic elites, the prevalence of units in which non-Slavic troops were commanded by Slavic officers was a built-in source of tension.

During the Brezhnev era, efforts were launched to step up the recruitment and training of officers of non-Russian nationalities as well as to combat attitudes prejudicial to their promotion. As one of many such articles in Soviet military journals affirmed, "the party constantly points to the necessity to be concerned that all nationalities of the country are adequately represented in military training institutions and in the Soviet officer corps" (Nikitin, 1982).

The Gorbachev era brought two additional sources of strain to an already difficult situation. On the one hand, democratization contributed to a process of "de-militarization" of Soviet society, involving challenges to the traditional priority of defense in Soviet values as well as budgets, and to the inculcation of military ideals in Soviet institutions. The process of de-ideologization in Soviet domestic and foreign policy, and the diminished perception of external threat, have called into question the predominance of military claims on a strained economy, while the withdrawal from Afghanistan, and the use of military forces against civilians in Tbilisi, fed a major public debate over military policies. Millions of Soviet viewers were exposed to sharp criticism of Soviet military policies in the course of the televised sessions of the Supreme Soviet.[41] At the same time, rising ethnonationalism in Soviet society more broadly has inevitably carried over into the armed forces, complicating the management of ethnic tensions within the military and provoking growing challenges to the existing military system from a variety of national movements.

These challenges stem from several sources. Under the impact of *glasnost'*, the armed forces and their role in Soviet society have been subjected to unprecedented scrutiny. Some of this attention has focused on the brutal mistreatment of younger soldiers by those who have completed part of their service [*dedovshchina*], often with the tacit collusion of officers. These practices have

---

40. In his speech to the Central Committee plenum on nationality issues in September 1988 Defense Minister Yazov complained that 125,000 draftees lacked a real knowledge of Russian, a figure twelve times higher than it had been 20 years earlier (*Radio Liberty Report on the USSR*, September 27, 1988).

41. For a more extended discussion, see Holloway (1990).

been exacerbated by ethnic tensions, arousing public indignation and charges by Baltic leaders that conscripts from their republics have been singled out for especially harsh treatment.[42]

An even more serious set of challenges comes from rising pressures for changes in military structure and practices that would bring the armed forces under greater control by republic authorities. Amid spreading anti-military protest and draft resistance, and student boycotts of military education programs at universities and other educational institutions around the country, demands have been voiced for the creation of national military units, and for the right of non-Russian conscripts to carry out their military service in their own republics.[43] These demands have been endorsed by high-level officials in several republics. In April 1989, for example, after mounting pressures from republic activists and public organizations, including the Estonian Women's Congress, the Estonian leadership submitted a series of proposals on military service to the authorities in Moscow, incuding demands that Estonian conscripts serve in the Baltic Military District, that republic militia units and border troops be heavily staffed by residents, that alternative service be permitted for conscientious objectors, that military training in schools be reduced or abolished, and that decisions on troop deployments be made in consultation with republic authorities (*Homeland*, 1989).[44] "The Army is no longer under the control of civilian authorities," the Chairman of the Estonian Council of Ministers, Indrek Toome, complained, "and this can no longer be tolerated" (Vosem', 1989). Similar demands have been voted by the Lithuanian and Latvian Supreme Soviets, and in Azerbaijan even the head of military conscription has called for the establishment of national units (Foye, 1989). An even more radical position has been taken by activists in the Baltic republics and Georgia who argue, citing the Geneva Convention, that the conscription of non-Russians for service in what is essentially an occupying army constitutes a violation of international law. In March 1990, the newly elected president of the Lithuanian republic explicitly endorsed this position, provoking a confrontation with the Soviet military authorities over Lithuanian deserters from the armed forces.

Negotiations between republic authorities and senior military officials in Moscow appear to have elicited some concessions to republic demands. Toome announced that 25 percent of Estonian conscripts would now serve in the Baltic Military District, compared to 2 percent previously.[45] A number of republics

42. One particular case involving a young Lithuanian private who shot and killed eight fellow soldiers when they tried to rape him after months of beating him up attracted wide attention. A television documentary about the episode elicited a wave of sympathy and a campaign calling for his acquittal of charges of murder; Holloway (1990) discusses this episode at greater length.

43. More than 200 Latvians reportedly refused to serve in the armed forces, and a senior Soviet general claimed that 1,500 Georgian youths had failed to report for induction. Demonstrations and hunger strikes outside conscription centers have been reported in a number of republics (Foye, 1989).

44. Interview with Indrek Toome, then Chairman of the Estonian Council of Ministers (*Sovetskaya Estoniya*, April 21, 1989, p. 3).

45. The Chairman of the Lithuanian Council of Ministers, Vitautas Sakalauskas, indicated that 9% more Lithuanian draftees were serving in the Baltic military district in 1989 than in 1988 (*RL Daily Report*, November 10, 1989).

are also introducing provisions for alternative service themselves. Moreover, if major cutbacks in the size of the Soviet armed forces are carried out in the next few years, the pressures to shift from a conscript to a professional military are likely to grow. Meanwhile, the reluctance of local authorities to take action against draft evaders of their own nationality has contributed to a de facto toleration of draft violations and made it more difficult for the military to enforce its priorities. Forced onto the defensive, the military leadership has stepped up its attacks on informal groups and national movements for seeking to discredit the Soviet armed forces, inspire draft evasion, and heighten ethnic tensions within the military.[46] These tensions are likely to grow, however, as increasingly assertive republic officials attempt to increase their control over military installations and activities within their borders.

NATIONAL MINORITIES: THE REVENGE OF OTTO BAUER

The upsurge in national consciousness and political self-assertion across the USSR, accompanied by efforts to enhance the power and status of union republics and of their titular nationalities, has had powerful reverberations among the non-titular nationalities of the union republics and galvanized them to organize on behalf of their own interests. While smaller nations and nationalities already possessing their own state structures within the union republics (for instance, the Abkhazians, the Yakuts, and the Bashkirs) began to demand that their status be upgraded, the position of national minorities without such structures (such as the Gagauz in Moldavia or the Poles in Lithuania) or living outside their republics (in particular, the Russians dispersed throughout the non-Russian republics) began to appear increasingly problematic (see Table 1).

According to recent Soviet data, more than 55 million Soviet citizens live outside the borders of their "own" republics or lack any state structure of their own. Because Soviet nationality policy rests on the close association of nationality, territory, and cultural rights, national minorities lacking state structures enjoy relatively little protection of their rights to national-cultural development.

The 1918 Constitution had included explicit affirmations of the equal rights of all citizens irrespective of nationality, and forbade encroachments on the rights of national minorities. These provisions were dropped from the 1924, 1936, and 1977 constitutions. In the Stalin era, the brutal treatment of minority groups was simply one more manifestation of the general lawlessness and repression, as well as of the assimilationist thrust of Soviet policy. In the more benign environment of the Khrushchev era some measures were taken to address the needs of a variety of national groups, but they were largely halted under

---

46. For example, in a November 12, 1989 interview with TASS, Defense Minister Dimitriy Yazov condemned "nationalist, extremist, and separatist forces" which were "seeking to seize power" in the country.

Table 1. *National Composition of Soviet Union Republics, 1979 and 1989*

	Population (millions)		Native (%)		Russian (%)		Other (%)	
Republic	1979	1989	1979	1989	1979	1989	1979	1989
Russian	137.4	147.0	83	82	83	82	17	18
Ukrainian	49.6	51.4	74	73	21	22	5	5
Uzbek	15.3	19.8	69	71	11	9	20	20
Kazakh	14.7	16.4	36	40	41	38	23	22
Belorussian	9.6	10.1	80	79	12	13	9	9
Azerbaijan	6.0	7.0	78	82	8	6	14	12
Georgian	5.0	5.4	69	70	7	6	24	24
Moldavian	3.9	4.3	64	64	13	13	23	23
Tajik	3.8	5.1	59	62	10	8	31	30
Kirghiz	3.5	4.3	48	52	26	22	26	26
Lithuanian	3.4	3.7	80	80	9	9	11	11
Armenian	3.0	3.3	90	93	2	2	8	5
Turkmen	2.8	3.5	68	72	13	9	19	19
Latvian	2.5	2.7	57	52	30	34	13	14
Estonian	1.5	1.6	65	62	28	30	7	8

Sources: Compiled from data in Kozlov (1982) and *Natsional'nyy* (1989).

Brezhnev. The Gorbachev reforms, with their emphasis on democratization and the new commitment to universal values and human rights, generated a new sensitivity to the treatment of national minorities.

This heightened awareness and moral concern were most directly expressed in regard to the so-called small peoples of the north. Ancient inhabitants of the Siberian north and the Russian Far East, distantly related to Aleuts and Eskimos resident in the Western Hemisphere, they were coming to be perceived as victims of the mindless exploitation of the region for its valuable natural resources both during and after the Stalin years. The ruthless encroachment on their traditional habitat, which threatened the destruction both of their economic livelihood and of their cultural survival, elicited from the conscience-stricken Russian intelligentsia proposals for their relief and assistance. Politically this was a comparatively cost-free crusade: its major target was the central ministerial apparatus of the "command-administrative system"; it joined environmental protection to the defense of national culture; and it did not require the displacement of other national groups.

Also evoking sympathy but raising more difficult problems was the fate of national groups exiled from their homelands before and during World War II and now pressing for the restoration of their rights: Koreans and other Asians deported in 1937; Germans from the Volga region deported in 1941–1942; and the "punished peoples" (including Crimean Tatars, Chechens, Ingush, Kalmyks, and Meskhetian Turks) whose national homelands were liquidated. Although the accusations against them had been declared baseless, their demands to return to their original places of settlement—long since incorporated into other republics and occupied by new inhabitants—created painful and difficult dilemmas. Despite widespread sympathy for the view, expressed by one Kalmyk activist, that "the forcible resettlement of nations and their destruction were the greatest of Stalin's crimes," and that "it is from there that the tangled ball of nationality problems has rolled into the present day," it was equally clear that "now it is not so simple to unravel it" (Kugul'tinov, 1988).

The case of the Volga Germans, whose demands for the reestablishment of an autonomous German republic were pressed by the increasingly vocal representatives of this community, exemplified the larger policy dilemma.[47] Speaking on behalf of the Soviet German community before the Central Committee plenum, Natalya Gellert warned the Soviet leadership that without the reestablishment of an autonomous area, the continuing erosion of German cultural life would fuel a rise in emigration to West Germany (*Pravda*, September 20, 1989). While professing sympathy for the Crimean Tatars, Volga Germans, and Meskhetian Turks (and special commissions under the Supreme Soviet were looking into their causes), the Soviet authorities were reluctant to redraw boundaries, fearing to provoke the hostility of those populations who had meanwhile settled in their former territories.

An equally challenging problem was posed by the growing demands of a number of subnational groups for autonomous structures of their own. Galvanized by the political mobilization of the titular nationalities of their republics, and in some cases by increasing hostility toward them, activists from among the Gagauz in Moldavia and Poles in Lithuania, among others, found increasing support for efforts to organize their own movements. As in the case of subnational groups possessing their own autonomous regions or provinces, they also found sympathy and support in Moscow, which had long utilized interethnic hostilities to gain leverage vis-à-vis union republic elites. Once again the opportunity to use representatives of subnational groups as real or potential allies in containing the aspirations of republic elites was no doubt welcome to centralists in Moscow.

But the most promising opportunity of all was presented by the growing anxiety of Russian settler communities who saw their own status threatened by the upsurge of national self-assertion in the non-Russian republics. The struggle over language laws, and over the efforts of the Baltic republics to establish residence requirements for voters and candidates for public office, precipitated the organization of countermovements like Interfront and Unity which appealed to Moscow for support. These appeals were bolstered by actual political strikes by Russian workers in Estonia and Moldavia in the fall of 1989 designed to bring additional pressure to bear against local leaders. While Mos-

47. The Volga German Autonomous SSR was created in 1924. Abolished on September 24, 1941, its territory was divided between the Saratov and Stalingrad [now Volgograd] oblasts of the RSFSR. In 1964, a decree was published clearing the Germans of the charges for which they were deported in 1941. In 1979, prompted by pressures from the community and a rising tide of emigration to the German Federal Republic, the Soviet leadership attempted to restore an autonomous territory, but in Tselinograd, Kazakhstan rather than on the Volga. This effort failed because of resistance from the Kazakh population.

cow reproached them for using strikes as a political weapon, it endorsed their view that these measures introduced in the republics were discriminatory and deprived them of their equal rights as Soviet citizens, and pressed the republics to modify or rescind these measures.

Moscow's support encouraged some local groups to contemplate even more radical actions. In those republics where occupational stratification had created compact regions almost exclusively inhabited by Russian settlers, local activists were attempting to form autonomous political units capable of challenging the republics' jurisdiction over their affairs. Whether as an effort to gain leverage in political bargaining or as a veiled effort at intimidation of republic authorities, these activities appeared to have clear backing in Moscow. Similarly, when republic Communist parties declared their independence from Moscow, the Soviet leadership lent political and financial support to the factions which remained loyal to the center. In the confrontation with Lithuania in the spring of 1990, Moscow openly intervened against the republic authorities and sought to use the local Russian population in its efforts at intimidation.

All these conflicts brought to the fore an underlying dilemma of Soviet nationality policy: what balance to strike between the rights of nations and the rights of individuals or groups constituting minorities within a given republic. Treating the union republics as the national homelands of their titular nationalities and guaranteeing the right of national self-determination necessarily circumscribes to some degree the rights of other national groups residing on these territories and carries with it the dangers of a "dictatorship of the majority" (Guboglo, 1989). What rights should be guaranteed to all citizens of the USSR and what mechanisms should be established to protect them became the subject of a major debate.

A number of scholars and public figures have concluded that the present structure of the Soviet federal system makes this an intractable problem, necessarily pitting the interests of national groups against each other and compelling central authorities to choose among them. They conclude that only a drastic alteration of the entire federal structure is capable of resolving the issue. While some scholars and political activists, including the late Andrey Sakharov and Galina Staravoyteva have proposed to equalize the status of all nationalities and nations by endowing them with their own political structures, others have argued for, in effect, abolishing the republics altogether, and thereby severing the linkage of nationality and territory. Advocates of this view argue, by analogy with the American case,[48] that individual citizens rather than nations should be the subjects of the Soviet polity, and that national identity should be treated as irrelevant to citizens'

48. See, for example, Tishkov (1989a, 1989b). The relevance of the American model to the Soviet scene, however, is questionable. The population of the United States is largely composed of dispersed immigrants rather than peoples inhabiting historical homelands, and American state borders are purely political-administrative and do not correspond to ethnic boundaries.

rights.[49] Here the advocacy of human rights serves, in political terms, as a vehicle for the promotion of an integrationist policy.

A more promising approach takes the existing state structures as its point of departure, but calls for the expansion of voluntary associations devoted to the national-cultural development of national minorities or people living outside their republics. While this strategy would not address all the sources of political grievances and inter-ethnic conflicts, the creation of a rich network of cultural associations, clubs, and educational programs could help nourish national identity and satisfaction of needs in culturally alien environments. Moreover, the republics themselves would be drawn into this effort by providing cultural facilities for their co-nationals under the sponsorship, where appropriate, of their Permanent Representations—institutions that its advocates would expand from their current role in Moscow to the capitals of other union republics. There has also been increasing advocacy of re-creating national soviets—local political institutions for national minorities living in compact settlements—which performed useful functions in the 1920s but were abolished under Stalin (Bromley, 1989).

Ironically, the thrust of this entire discussion of how to provide for the national-cultural needs of a multinational society evokes the turn-of-the-century debates within the socialist movement. Indeed, many of the proposals of contemporary Soviet reformers are strikingly reminiscent of the ideas of the 19th century Austro-Marxists Karl Renner and Otto Bauer, whose advocacy of national-cultural autonomy was bitterly attacked by Lenin and Stalin, and whose views about the future of nations under socialism remained anathema for many decades.

THE PROBLEM OF PARTY FRAGMENTATION

The process of reform had dramatic consequences for the role of the Communist Party itself as an instrument of national integration. The 1989 elections to a newly constituted Congress of Deputies exposed the party to unprecedented political competition from a variety of new political forces, and brought key local party officials to humiliating defeats by local voters. A Central Committee meeting to assess the results of the elections was marked by bitter recriminations; regional party secretaries accused the center of placing them in an untenable position, while they in turn were accused of failing to adapt to changing conditions. The profound disorientation and demoralization of the party leadership was reflected in the remarks of Nikolay Ryzhkov, Chairman of the Council of Ministers:

> The Party, practically speaking, is losing authority in the eyes of the people. . . . Consciously or unconsciously, the appearance is continuing to

---

49. As a first step in implementing this approach, many urged that designations of individuals' nationality should be removed from Soviet passports (Kozlov, 1989).

be preserved that nothing special has occurred, that the basic levers remain
in our hands as before and that with their help, with the same old methods,
we can still control the complicated processes that are developing in our
country, but this is being done at a time when influence, power, and the
possibility of influencing everything that is occurring in society is being lost
(*Pravda,* July 21, 1989, p. 3).

At the same time, growing national self-assertion was adding additional
sources of cleavage to an increasingly divided organization. The dilemma of
maintaining central control over local party officials while encouraging them
to be responsive to local constituencies was exemplified during the dispute
over Nagorno-Karabakh: in June 1988 virtually the entire leadership of the
Armenian republic supported the transfer of Nagorno-Karabakh to Armenia,
while the Azerbaijani leadership voted to retain the territory. This division
marked a watershed in Soviet political life. For the first time in its history, the
Communist Party itself had fragmented along national lines.

Not only were the party organizations of different republics at odds with
each other; growing national tensions within the party organizations of a number
of republics were making it increasingly difficult to maintain party unity and
discipline in the face of conflicting pulls. The problem was particularly acute
in the Baltic republics and Moldavia, where Russians in the party membership
expressed growing outrage at what they considered the leadership's deviation
from party principles.

By mid-1989, while the newly elected Congress of People's Deputies was
debating the virtues of a multi-party system, many Soviet citizens were claiming
that, *de facto,* one already existed. In virtually every republic, embryonic
political organizations had emerged, embracing a broad spectrum of political
positions, from explicitly separatist parties in several of the non-Russian republics, to extreme Russian chauvinist organizations like *Pamyat',* to the progressive Popular Fronts, to Christian, Social-Democratic, Green, and other
movements. Faced with the erosion of their position in this broadening political
spectrum and the prospect of a bruising round of local elections in 1990, the
Communist Party organizations of the non-Russian republics were increasingly
pushed to identify with national interests and to distance themselves from
Moscow.

Public opinion surveys carried out by newly created research centers in
Lithuania and Estonia indicated just how precarious the party's position had
become in these republics. In Lithuania, a survey asking respondents which of
a number of political organizations they would vote for in elections found that
the Communist Party would receive only 20 percent of the vote, with 48 percent
going to Sajudis, 8 percent to the Christian-Democratic Party, and 7 percent
to the Greens (Girnius, 1989). Russian and Polish respondents tended to have
a more positive view of the party than Lithuanians, who gave much stronger
support to Sajudis. Asked to express their views about the future status of the

Communist Party, 77 percent of the Lithuanians but only 36 percent of non-Lithuanians favored the establishment of an independent Communist Party, while 8 percent of Lithuanians and 30 percent of non-Lithuanians wanted the party to seek greater autonomy within the CPSU.

Opinion surveys in Estonia were even less heartening to the Communist Party, with little more than 5 percent of Estonian respondents prepared to vote for them in an election in June 1989.[50]

In response to the poor performance of leading party officials in the 1989 elections, and in line with his plans to introduce reforms of the party organization itself, Gorbachev had promised significant changes in the party's statutes at the Party Congress scheduled for 1990. But even these measures seemed too little too late to republic party organizations facing the imminent prospect of marginalization in the forthcoming local elections. Increasingly under pressure from more radical political forces, even the most reform-minded parties moved to increase their autonomy and to distance themselves from Moscow.

The most dramatic challenge came from Lithuania, whose Communist Party—further emboldened by developments in Eastern Europe—declared its independence from Moscow. A new draft program discussed at the Party Congress in December 1989 affirmed that the Lithuanian Party would no longer consider itself a constituent segment of the Communist Party of the Soviet Union, and that its ultimate goal was the establishment of a Soviet Lithuanian state. Summoned to Moscow for urgent consultations to head off the move, the party's First Secretary, Algirdas Brazaukas, sought to reassure Moscow of the party's desire to avoid an open split, and insisted that independence need not signify a rupture of close ties with Moscow.[51]

The Soviet leadership's position was unambiguously hostile; all members of the Politburo reportedly signed a resolution criticizing the Lithuanian Party and its First Secretary for allowing "hesitations, inconsistencies, and deviations" from the principles of the CPSU, and calling on it to resolutely reject the federalization of the party. But the prospects of serious party fragmentation

---

50. *Noorte Haal* of July 12, 1989, reported the following party preferences in response to two 1989 surveys which attempted to allocate seats in a non-existing independent Estonian parliament:

	Estonians		Non-Estonians	
Selected political party	April	June	April	June
Popular Front	50.3%	56.1%	8.9%	10.7%
Estonian National Party	9.6%	6.3%	0.9%	2.2%
Estonian Communist Party	7.2%	5.5%	32.2%	19.2%
Interfront	0.0%	0.2%	10.9%	11.6%
Joint Council of Workers	0.3%	0.0%	17.8%	11.6%

A similar survey conducted in December, 1988 and reported in *Noorte Haal* of May 6, 1989 yielded comparable results. In actual elections to the Estonian Supreme Soviet on March 18, 1990, the Communist Party won 29 seats—significantly less than the Popular Bloc progressives with 49 seats, but slightly ahead of conservative non-Estonians opposed to independence who won 27 seats (Kionka, 1990).

51. The Estonian party followed suit in the spring of 1990. In Latvia, the loyalists won a narrow vote on April 6, but the departure of the pro-independence wing left the party severely damaged.

Table 2. *Political Attitudes in Lithuania, March 1990*
"On March 11, 1990, the Supreme Council of the Republic of Lithuania declared an act restoring the independence of the Lithuanian state. What is your attitude to this act?"

Response to declaration of independence	Lithuanians (%)	Non-Lithuanians (%)	Overall (%)
Approve	69	22	60
Approve but consider too early	28	45	31
Disapprove	3	33	9

Source: Center for the Study of Public Opinion, Lithuanian Academy of Sciences (*Baltimore Sun*, April 4, 1990, p. 4A).

also became entwined, in the summer and fall of 1989, with growing pressures for ending the Communist Party's monopoly of political power and for the introduction of a multi-party system. The rapid pace of political change in Eastern Europe, where one party after another was compelled to renounce its political monopoly and to acquiesce in sharing power, merely served to accelerate the pressures already building across the Soviet Union.

The Soviet leadership's response made clear to what extent the defense of the role of the party had itself become entwined with the "national question." In the face of growing centrifugal pressures and inter-ethnic strife, the leadership insisted that the party was the single institution capable of performing the essential functions of national integration. As Yegor Ligachev put it:

> Recently calls for a multi-party system have been heard. In the conditions of a federative government such as the Soviet Union, this is simply fatal. A multi-party system would mean the disintegration of the Soviet system.... The Communist Party is the only real political force which unites all the peoples of the country into a single union of republics. There is no other (*Pravda*, July 21, 1989, p. 3).

Lukyanov put it more starkly still: "without Party leadership, the federation would fall apart."[52]

In February of 1990 the Party Central Committee acquiesced in the inevitable, effectively renouncing its monopoly of power and paving the way for multi-party electoral competition. But the republican and local elections held in the spring of 1990 made it clear that the struggle to maintain party unity in the face of fragmentation would become increasingly difficult. The victory of national movements in a number of republics placed increasing strains on existing Communist parties and increased the pressures toward fragmentation. The public reactions to the Lithuanian declaration of March 11, 1990, restoring the independence of the Lithuanian Republic, dramatized these pressures (see Table 2).

52. Interview on Moscow Radio, as reported in *FBIS*, August 23, 1989.

POWER AND POLITICS

All the policy debates and dilemmas addressed above involved challenges to the key mechanisms through which the Soviet multinational system had long been integrated. The struggles over ideology, federalism, republic economic sovereignty, language and cultural policy, and social redistribution involved challenges to the highly centralized pattern of political and economic decision making characteristic of the Soviet system, and the myths which had helped to sustain and legitimize it, just as the efforts to assert greater local control over economic and cultural life, and over military arrangements, similarly challenged long-standing patterns of central control. The *de facto* fragmentation of the party under the impact of conflicting political orientations as well as national demands was now compounded by pressures to sanction the process by permitting the explicit federalization of the party, the quintessential integrating mechanism of a Leninist system.

Of course, all these issues above were not debated in the antiseptic vacuum of an ivory tower; rather, they were hotly contested both in the traditional and in the newly nascent political arenas across the USSR. Not only did they engage intense emotions on the local level, but they also fed—and became the objects of—larger political struggles at the center. Alignments over nationality issues intersected with and complicated battles among groups and institutions over reform and, ultimately, over the distribution of power in the Soviet system more broadly.

By the spring of 1990, the spectrum of diverse orientations toward the Soviet federal system had crystallized around four positions. At one end of the spectrum were those individuals and groups committed to one degree or another to separatism. Primarily but not exclusively concentrated in the Baltic republics and Georgia, and composed almost exclusively of members of the titular nationalities, these were supporters of the Gorbachev reforms only insofar as they saw them as an avenue toward independence for their own nations.

A second orientation, increasingly difficult to distinguish from the first, was represented by the advocates of republic sovereignty who, while accepting the framework of the Soviet federal system, sought to transform it into a *de facto* confederation. The national fronts and their equivalents in the various republics had initially been the most prominent exponents of this view, but over time several of them had moved toward advocating outright independence. This orientation also drew on significant support from among progressive Russian intellectuals and political figures, and particularly the Interregional Group of Deputies elected to the new Supreme Soviet—either as a matter of conviction or as a facet of parliamentary coalition-building.

A third orientation was prepared to contemplate a limited devolution of economic and political functions to republics and regions but sought to preserve a substantial concentration of political power at the center. This position, widely held in the party and governmental establishment in Moscow and in the ministries and enterprises in the republics tied to the center (particularly those of the military-industrial complex), was exemplified by the recommendations of the Maslyukov Commission.

A fourth and final orientation was represented by the integrationists, of both liberal and conservative stripe. The liberals—Russian and non-Russian alike— sought, in the name of universal human rights, to make the individual citizen, regardless of nationality, the basic unit of the Soviet system, and to treat the republics as administrative rather than national units. The conservatives shared their hostility to centrifugal nationalist tendencies, but their insistence on maintaining law and order was typically colored by neo-Stalinist or Great Russian values.

These four categories necessarily represent something of an oversimplification. Moreover, no institutions—whether the Popular Fronts or the party apparatus—were monolithic, and the boundaries of individual commitments were both fuzzy and fluid. In addition, the considerable variations in the character and aspirations of national movements from one region of the country to another inevitably elicited differentiated approaches to them.

Nor is it easy to attach a specific political weight to each of these positions. The universe of articulated views did not—and could not—give adequate expression to the instincts of a vast and silent bureaucracy, suspicious and fearful of the reforms but socialized into disciplined conformity.

For the Gorbachev leadership in particular these were bitterly divisive issues. Yegor Ligachev and Viktor Chebrikov had openly and repeatedly expressed their concern about the "excesses" of *glasnost'*, their hostility to the burgeoning informal groups and national fronts, and their fears that the weakening role of the party jeopardized its survival at a time of serious crisis. The use of force to put down demonstrations in Tbilisi in April 1989 was not out of keeping with their approach to law and order, but appears to have prompted bitter differences within the Soviet elite. On other issues, however, there was probably a greater degree of consensus. The entire leadership evidently shared a sense of alarm at the explosions of interethnic violence in the Caucasus and Central Asia, and at the mounting separatist tendencies in the Baltic and elsewhere, though it was divided over the best means of handling it.

As for Gorbachev's own position, his approach to the key issues of nationality policy was entwined with his efforts to manage the process of reform more broadly. By mid-1989, beset by mounting and simultaneous political and economic challenges, his commitment to change was balanced by the need to maintain a modicum of stability at a time of intense social strain. Maintenance of the momentum of the reforms to which he remained fully committed and preservation of the political coalition which sustained them required support for a significant restructuring of the Soviet federal system pressed by his more radical allies among republic elites. At the same time, he considered it essential to keep the support of moderate conservatives (as well as of the military and security establishments) to avoid an open split of the party leadership over these issues. The political struggles behind the scenes reflected Gorbachev's effort to strike a compromise between the two middle positions, while isolating the protagonists at both extremes of the spectrum. This effort was put to the test by the Lithuanian decision to reaffirm its independence on March 11, 1990.

THE CENTRAL COMMITTEE PLENUM

In announcing the decision to hold a Central Committee plenum on inter-ethnic relations, the Soviet leadership had hoped to use the occasion to provide an authoritative framework for nationality policy. This framework was intended to provide a way to rectify the major "deformations" of the past and respond to grievances and demands for change, while preserving the political and economic integrity of the Soviet system.

By the time the plenum actually convened on September 19, 1989, events had overtaken part of its original purpose. So rapid was the pace of change in Soviet political life that the plenum proved to be less a mechanism for shaping new policies than a forum reacting to initiatives already undertaken by local officials and organizations. Its key purpose was as much political as theoretical: to define a strategy around which a new political coalition could be constructed. This strategy required finding a politically acceptable balance between advocates of a radical transformation of the existing federal system and political forces which at most sought merely to "perfect" it.

The most repeated postponements of the plenum offered testimony to the enormous difficulty of the undertaking. Moreover, the intense tug and pull of political forces was reflected even in the differences between the draft platform published for discussion on August 17 and the final document approved by the plenum one month later.[53] Without departing from the commitment to an integrated political and economic system, the draft went considerably further toward accommodating the pressures for radical change than the document finally adopted by the plenum.

The very discussion in the preamble of the document of why a radical renewal of the federal system was necessary itself reflected the new political mentality. It acknowledged that reforms were dictated by the defects of past policies, as well as by the new requirements of contemporary Soviet and international development, which could not be accommodated within the framework of "ossified" structures.

In dealing with the legacy of the past, the document singled out five features of Soviet development which had had a particularly disastrous effect on national relations: the policies of mass repression and deportations of entire peoples pursued under Stalin and the failure to adequately address their consequences

53. The draft platform, "Natsional'naya politika partii v sovremennykh usloviyakh," was published in *Pravda* on August 17, 1989, pp. 1–2, followed by an important interview with Chebrikov about the document on August 19, pp. 1–2. The final version adopted by the Central Committee plenum on September 20 appeared in *Pravda* on September 24, pp. 1–2; Gorbachev's concluding speech on September 20 and a summary of the discussions appeared on September 22, pp. 1–7.

after they were denounced by the 20th Party Congress; patterns of economic development and management which ignored their social, ecological, and cultural consequences and led to distorted forms of growth; the pursuit of rigid and uniform policies by an overcentralized and monolithic political/economic system which failed to take account of regional differences and which extinguished the independent powers of the republics; the pursuit of *sblizheniye*, which belittled national and spiritual diversity and impeded recognition of national needs; and indifference to demographic and social processes that became a major source of interethnic tension. Contributing to the accumulation of problems was the failure to properly analyze or take account of worldwide trends in national development which had their parallels in the USSR as well: the tension between trends toward integration and the striving for increased national independence.

In addressing the central policy dilemma facing the Soviet leadership—how far to go in altering center-periphery relations—the program typically sought to occupy a middle ground. Referring to the debates of 1922 as the precedent for rejecting both unitary and confederational tendencies, it called for a genuine federation as Lenin himself allegedly envisioned, composed of a "strong center and strong republics," a voluntary association of "sovereign socialist states" in a single Union within which each republic retained its independence [*samostoyatel'nost'*].[54] It evaded the demand of the Baltic republics for a new treaty regulating their status by arguing that the Soviet Constitution was itself a "treaty document."

The actual delineation of the competence of central and republic authorities envisioned in the platform would retain key powers in the hands of the center. In addition to substantive responsibilities for foreign and security policy, and for coordinating and deciding common tasks in economic, scientific and cultural life, the center reserved the right to define the principles of the political system as well as the principles governing the utilization of property rights assigned to the republics. The draft platform acquiesced to substantial republic control over natural resources and economic activities on its territory, but the final text retreated some distance from this stance. While republics would have the right to challenge all-Union legislation, republic legislation which went beyond the republics' authority would be subject to revocation. A provision for a new institution—a Constitutional Oversight Committee—to resolve conflicts was one of the more novel but controversial elements in the program.

No less important, the document affirmed the republics' right to participate in the adoption of common decisions. While this provision might have been little more than ritual deference to the Union republics, there is reason to think that it reflected a more serious strategy. Both the document and accompanying speeches by Gorbachev and other leaders suggested that this new emphasis on

54. Western discussions of this issue are confused by the use of the single term, "independence," to translate two somewhat different Russian words, *samostoyatel'nost'* and *nezavisimost'*. The first connotes autonomy but not necessarily secession.

the republics' role in domestic and foreign policy decision making—presumably to be reflected in new institutional arrangements—represented a deliberate effort to channel the aspirations and ambitions of some republic elites from republic-based to all-Union influence, so as to give them a greater personal stake in the federal system.

Possibly the most significant feature was the alteration in the bases of legitimation of the federal union. By contrast with earlier Soviet affirmations that the federation represented the nucleus of a world socialist system, the new arguments shifted from an ideological to a pragmatic rationale. Seeking to avoid contentious arguments about the formation of the union, the leadership stressed that it should be regarded as a *fait accompli;* regardless of how it was formed, the fact of its existence should now be taken as the point of departure. Gorbachev's speech to the plenum, as well as his subsequent remarks on the issue, stressed both the economic benefits of cooperation and the mutual economic dependence of the republics. A similar pragmatism pervaded the discussion of border changes between or within republics: without claiming that existing boundaries were justified, the leadership took the position—just as it had with respect to borders in Europe—that efforts to alter them would be destabilizing.

Breaking with decades of Soviet constitutional practice, the platform called for the creation of separate state institutions for the Russian republic—much the largest unit of the Soviet Union and until now lacking the full range of economic, political, scientific, and cultural organs of its own. It also envisaged the creation of a Russian Bureau within the Central Committee of the party to coordinate the activities of RSFSR party organizations. These decisions were politically important for at least three reasons. First, they sought to place the Russian republic on the same level as the other members of the federation by ending the fusion (and confusion) of Russian republic and all-Union institutions. Second, they would have the further benefit of dissociating the Russian people from the "command-administrative system," treating them—along with the non-Russians—as its victims. Finally, they served an important tactical purpose in both providing a constructive outlet for rising Russian national sentiment and for mobilizing the support of Russian party and state officials behind the new platform.

If some of the provisions of the platform expanded the rights and resources of the union republics, these were balanced by explicit guarantees of the rights of all Soviet citizens, regardless of nationality or place of residence. Not only did this limit the scope of republics' powers and portray the center as the guarantor of minority rights, it did so in the name of progressive values and human rights.

In his closing speech at the plenum, Gorbachev affirmed once more the importance of resisting the fragmentation of the party: "everyone came out unanimously for the unity of the CPSU—in full conjunction with the ideas of Lenin, who was for a federation of peoples, for a Union government, but who categorically rejected federalism in the construction and functioning of the Party.'' Precisely because the Soviet Union was moving toward increased decentralization, it was all the more essential that the party play a consolidating role (*Pravda,* September 22, 1989, p. 1).

The party platform—the first systematically to deal with policy concerning the nationalities—amounted, strictly speaking, to recommendations by the Communist Party to the organs of state, and their implementation would require action by the newly created legislative organs. In any event, it left unsatisfied both the advocates of radical republic autonomy and the stalwarts of centralism. It also failed to address many of the demands made by representatives of smaller nations and peoples. Nonetheless, from the point of view of the Gorbachev leadership it accomplished several objectives. It gave the party's endorsement to some of the changes in the federal system long advocated by reformers, thereby depriving some entrenched defenders of the status quo of party legitimation. Partly thanks to the vagueness of the language, it helped to hold together a political coalition across the center of the spectrum by appealing to a variety of orientations.

Ironically, even so elaborately prepared a meeting and widely debated a document no longer carried the weight they might once have commanded. It was a measure of the diminishing authority and power of the party and of the growing autonomy and radicalization of political life that struggles and conflicts continued as if unaffected by these events. In the fluidity of the Soviet political scene, the platform and plenum were soon overtaken by new rounds of dramatic events, from Nagorno-Karabakh to Lithuania, and by the political actions of newly assertive legislative bodies in the republics as well as in Moscow.

CONCLUDING REMARKS

In embarking on an ambitious program of reform, Mikhail Sergeyevich Gorbachev could not have anticipated that the nationality problem, which was then barely on the periphery of his vision, would come to pose a formidable challenge to his leadership and indeed to the integrity of the Soviet system. And yet, there was a logic in the political and social upheavals unleashed by the process of reform. The combination of *glasnost'*, democratization, and the diminished scope of repression altered the costs and benefits of authentic political initiative and contributed to the political mobilization of previously quiescent groups. In ethnically homogeneous societies such as Poland, Hungary, and the GDR, these newly awakened political forces would be translated into a variety of political and ideological orientations. In a multinational and federal system such as the Soviet Union, by contrast, the new political activism was bound to be channeled, at least in part, into national movements, especially under conditions in which the central government was suffering from a severe loss of authority. Themselves heterogeneous, the national movements were fed both by surviving—and reviving—older national currents and by the search for new identities in the context of widespread alienation from the existing order. Moreover, in conditions of economic stringency, national enmity, hatred, scapegoating, and bigotry become all too easily responses to deprivation or envy.

Nor could Gorbachev have anticipated how the "national question" would become entwined with the larger struggles over reform. A realignment of political coalitions was clearly taking place in which advocacy of radical political and economic reform was increasingly joined to advocacy of restructuring the federal system, while supporters of preserving more centralized political and economic institutions were seeking allies both within those segments of the working class fearful of the consequences of marketization and among the burgeoning Russian national movements, both in the RSFSR and in the non-Russian republics.[55] The growing prominence of conservative Russian nationalism, and Gorbachev's concern to both respond to and co-opt it, was symbolized by his inclusion of Rasputin and Yarin in the new Presidential Council.

The evolution of Gorbachev's approach to the "national question" captures in microcosm the interplay between development, learning, and politics which characterized his political program more broadly. The Soviet pattern of state-sponsored socioeconomic development, and the distinctive patterns of ethnic stratification it generated, were being transformed, in the Brezhnev era, from a successful mechanism of integration into a growing source of strain. Compounded by the effects of ideological erosion, political ossification, and economic stringency, they created a context for a potential exacerbation of inter-ethnic tensions which was not properly understood at the time.

The accession to power of a reform-minded leadership provided the catalyst for a reassessment of policies and a reconfiguration of political coalitions. Gorbachev's growing appreciation of the scope and depth of the problems the new leadership confronted, as well as an increasingly critical assessment of past approaches, resulted in a progressive radicalization of the reform program. The search for new ideas and approaches was given urgency, in the area of nationality policy, by the emergence of new political forces as well as by growing unrest and outbreaks of communal violence, which by generating a growing sense of crisis gave the issue high salience within the elite. The emergence of new political thinking on the nationality issue involved a reevaluation of goals, and not merely of political strategies. However, this process of learning remained highly differentiated within the political elite as different members of the leadership drew different lessons from unfolding events.

In seeking to sustain a viable political coalition while maintaining some momentum for controlled within-system change, Gorbachev's freedom of maneuver was limited at both poles. His commitment to reform precluded a return

---

55. In late 1989 this coalition between conservatives, Russian nationalists, and the United Front of Russian Workers took on more organized form with the creation of the Bloc of Social-Patriotic Movements of Russia, the adoption of a joint electoral program, and the formation of the Deputies Club "Rossiya." For a more detailed account, see Brudny (1989) and Goble (1990).

to a more tightly centralized economic and political system; his political survival precluded his presiding over the dismemberment of the Soviet Union. At the same time, the ability of the center to control, let alone shape, events across the country was increasingly being eroded. Whether the national movements that the process of reform had unleashed would ultimately jeopardize the entire undertaking, or whether his considerable political skills would enable Gorbachev (or his successors) successfully to manage an increasingly turbulent Soviet scene, is by no means clear.

In the course of five years of *perestroyka*, the "nationality problem" emerged as the key dilemma of Soviet politics. It was entwined with, and indeed has become a metaphor for, all the major issues of reform: the dilemmas of decentralization, the scope and limits of de-Stalinization, the interdependence of domestic and foreign policy, and the tension between democratization and control. Its fate is as problematic as the future of the Soviet system as a whole.

REFERENCES

Anisimov, Ye., "Splinters of the Empire," *Moscow News,* 51, December 24–31, 1989, p. 10.

Arutyunyan, Yu. V., "Konkretno-sotsiologicheskoye issledovaniye natsional'nykh otnosheniy (Concrete Sociological Research on National Relations)," *Voprosy filosofii,* 12:129–139, 1969.

Bagramov, E. A., "Obzor vystupleniy (Survey of Presentations)," *Sovetskaya etnografiya,* 1:19, January–February 1989.

Bahry, Donna, "Perestroika and the Debate over Territorial Economic Decentralization," *The Harriman Institute Forum,* 2, 5:1–8, May 1989.

Bromley, Yu. V., "O razrabotke natsional'noy problematiki v svete resheniy XIX partkonferentsii (On Working Out the National Problem in Light of the Decisions of the 19th Party Conference)," *Sovetskaya etnografiya,* 1:4–18, January–February 1989.

Brudny, Yitzhak, "The Heralds of Opposition to *Perestroyka,*" *Soviet Economy,* 5, 2:162–200, April–June 1989.

Chto delat' *(What Is To Be Done).* Moscow: Akademiya Nauk SSSR, 1989.

"Demokratiya yest' konflikt (Democracy Is Conflict)," *Vek XX i mir,* 12:8–17, 1988.

Dzyuba, Ivan, *Internationalism or Russification?: A Study in the Soviet Nationalities Problem* (translated from the Ukrainian). London: Weidenfeld & Nicolson, 1968.

"Ekonomicheskiye problemy mezhnatsional'nykh otnosheniy v SSSR na sovremennom etape (The Modern Stage of Economic Problems of Interethnic relations in the USSR)," *Voprosy ekonomiki,* 5:8–29, 1989.

Foye, Stephen, "Growing Anti-Military Sentiment in the Republics," *Radio Liberty Report on the USSR,* 1, 50:1–4, December 15, 1989.

Gintner, Yu. O., and M. Kh. Titma, "Stravnitel'nyy analiz sotsial'nogo razvitiya soyuznykh respublik (A Comparative Analysis of the Social Development of the Union Republics)," *Sotsiologicheskiye issledovaniya,* 6:3–10, 1987.

Girnius, Saulius, Sociological Surveys in Lithuania," *Radio Liberty Report on the USSR,* 1, 45:24–26, November 10, 1989.

Goble, Paul, "A Program for Russia: The Appeal of the Bloc of Russia's Social-Political Groups," RLR 17/90, January 3, 1990, also appears as "Platform of the Russian Patriotic Bloc," *Radio Liberty Report on the USSR,* 2, 2:11–12, January 12, 1990.

Guboglo M., "Natsional'nyye gruppy v SSSR (National Groups in the USSR)," *Kommunist,* 10:53–58, 1989.

Hodnett, Grey, "The Debate Over Soviet Federalism," *Soviet Studies,* 18, 4:458–481, April 1967.

Holloway, David, "State, Society and the Military under Gorbachev," *International Security,* 14, 3:5–24, Winter 1989–1990.

Homeland (supplement to the Estonian *Koduma* weekly), April 19, 1989, p. 1.

"Ideologicheskiye problemy mezhnatsional'nykh otnosheniy (Ideological Problems of Interethnic Relations)," *Izvestiya TsK KPSS,* 6:78–89, 1989.

Jones, Ellen, "Minorities in the Soviet Armed Forces," *Comparative Strategy,* 7, 4:285–318, 1982.

————, "Manning the Soviet Military," *International Security,* 7, 1:105–131, Summer 1982.

Jones, Ellen, and Fred Grupp, "Political Socialization in the Soviet Military," *Armed Forces and Society,* 8, 3:355–387, Spring 1982.

Kallas, Siim, Tiit Made, Edgar Savisaar, and Miik Titma, "A Proposal for Self-Management for the Entire USSR," *Edasi,* September 26, 1987 (Tartu).

Karakeyev, K. K., I. Ya. Kopylov, and R. A. Salikov, *Problemy upravleniya stroitel'stvom sovetskogo mnogonatsional'nogo gosudarstva* (Problems of Administration in Building a Soviet Multinational State). Moscow: Nauka, 1982.

Khallik, K., *Natsional'nyye otnosheniya v SSSR i problemy perestroyki* (National Relations in the USSR and Problems of Perestroyka). Tallinn: Dom politprosveshcheniya universiteta Marksizma-Leninizma TsKKP Estonii, 1988.

Kionka, Riina, "Elections to Estonian Supreme Soviet," *Radio Liberty Report on the USSR,* 2, 14:22–24, April 6, 1990.

Koroteyeva, V., L. Perepelkin, and O. I. Shkaratan, "Ot byurokraticheskogo tsentralizma k ekonomicheskoy integratsii suverennykh respublik (From Bureaucratic Centralism to the Economic Integration of Sovereign Republics)," *Kommunist,* 15:22–33, October 1988.

Kozlov, V., *Natsional'nosti SSR (Nationalities of the USSR).* Moscow, 1982.

————, "Osobennosti etnodemograficheskikh problem v sredney Azii i puti ikh resheniya (Features of the Ethnodemographic Problem in Central Asia and Routes to Their Solution)," *Istoriya SSSR,* 1:41–51, January–February 1988.

————, "Natsional'nyy vopros i puti yego resheniya (The National Question and the Road to Its Solution)," *Sovetskaya etnografiya,* 1:59–73, 1989.

Kugul'tinov, David, "Ot pravdy ya ne otrekalsya (I Didn't Renounce the Truth)," *Ogonyok,* 35:24–25, 1988.

Maslov, A., "O pravovykh osnovakh ekonomicheskogo suvereniteta (On the Legal Bases of Economic Sovereignty)," *Kommunist,* 7:37–60, May 1989.

Menshikova, T., "Guest Nation Syndrome," *Moscow News,* June 11–18, 1989.

Mukomel', V., "Vremya otvetstvennykh resheniy (Time for Responsible Decisions)," *Sotsiologicheskiye issledovaniya,* 1:9–15, 1989.

"Natsional'nyye protsessy v SSSR: itogi, tendentsii, problemy; beseda za "kruglym stolom' (National Processes in the USSR: Results, Tendencies, Problems; A Roundtable Discussion)," *Istoriya SSSR,* 6:50–120, 1987.

Natsional'nyy sostav naseleniya (Nationality Composition of the Population). Moscow: Goskomstat, 1989.

Nenarokov, A. P., "Za svobodnyy soyuz svobodnykh narodov (For a Free Union of Free Nations)," *Istoriya i politika KPSS*, 3:3–64, 1989.

Nikitin, Ye., *Agitator armii i flota*, 23:10–14, 1982.

"Obshchiye printsipy perestroyki rukovodstva ekonomikoy i sotsial'noy sferoy v so-yuznykh respublikakh na osnove rasshireniya ikh suverennykh prav, samoupravleniya i samofinansirovaniya (General Principles on the Restructuring of the Economic and Social Leadership in the Union Republics on the Basis of Widening Their Sovereignty Rights, Their Self-management, and Self-financing)," *Ekonomicheskaya gazeta*, 12:10–13, 1989.

Paskara, P., "Sovetskiy narod—novaya sotsial'naya i internatsional'naya obshchnost' lyudey (The Soviet Nation–A New Social and International Community of People)," *Kommunist Moldavii*, 12:80–86, December 1982.

Problemnyy sovet IME, *Kontseptsiya IME: Proyekt (Concept of the IME: Draft)*. Manuscript, Tallinn, 1989.

Prokhanov, A., "Tragediya tsentralizma (The Tragedy of Centralism)," *Literaturnaya Rossiya*, January 5, 1990, pp. 4–5.

"Respublikanskiy khozraschet: problemy i perspektivy (Republican *khozraschet:* Problems and Prospects)," *Voprosy ekonomiki*, 4:33–39, 1989.

Rumer, Boris, *Soviet Central Asia: A Tragic Experiment*. Boston: Unwin Hyman, 1989.

Shkaratan, O. I., "Obzor vystupleniy (Survey of Presentations)," *Sovetskaya etnografiya*, 1:18–19, January–February 1989.

Shtromas, A., "The Legal Position of Soviet Nationalities and Their Territorial Units According to the 1977 Constitution of the USSR," *Russian Review*, 3:265–272, July 1980.

"Slushat' drug druga (To Listen to Each Other)," *Kommunist*, 6:62–80, 1989.

"Srednyaya Aziya i Kazakhstan: prioritety i al'ternativy razvitiya (Central Asia and Kazakhstan: Priorities and Development Alternatives)," *Kommunist*, 14:23–43, September 1989.

Stalin, J. *Works* (English language edition). Moscow: Foreign Languages Publishing House, 1952.

Szporluk, Roman, "Dilemmas of Russian Nationalism," *Problems of Communism*, 38, 4:15–35, July–August 1989.

Tedstrom, John, "USSR Draft Program on Republican Economic Self-Management," *Radio Liberty Report on the USSR*, 1, 16, April 21, 1989.

Tishkov, V. A., "O kontseptsii perestroyki mezhnatsional'nykh otnosheniy v SSSR (On the Concept of a Restructuring of Interethnic Relations in the USSR)," *Sovetskaya etnografiya*, 1:73–88, January–February 1989.

———, "Narody i gosudarstva (Peoples and States)," *Kommunist*, 1:49–59, 1989.

Volodin, E., "Novaya Rossiya v menyayushchemsya mire: realisticheskiy prognoz (New Russia in a Shrinking World: A Realistic Prognosis)," *Literaturnaya Rossiya*, January 26, 1990, pp. 3–4.

"Vosem' predlozheniy po delam voyennym (Eight Proposals on Military Affairs)," *Estoniya*, April 14, 1989, pp. 1, 3.

Wimbush, S. E., "Nationalities in the Soviet Armed Forces," in S. Enders Wimbush, ed., *Soviet Nationalities in Strategic Perspective*. New York: St. Martin's, 1985.

Wimbush, S. E., and Alexander Alexiev, *The Ethnic Factor in the Soviet Armed Forces: Historical Experience, Current Practices, and Implications for the Future— An Executive Summary.* Santa Monica, Calif.: The Rand Corporation, 1983.

Zotov, V., "Natsional'nyy vopros: deformatsii proshlogo (The National Question: The Deformations of the Past)," *Kommunist,* 3:79–89, 1989.

Part III

The Stirrings of
Democratization

The Stirrings of Democratization: An Introduction

George W. Breslauer

THE LIBERALIZATION of Soviet political life began in late 1986, with the first stirrings of *glasnost'*, while the democratization of Soviet political institutions commenced in January 1987, with Gorbachev's presentation of a program for *demokratizatsiya* at a plenary session of the CPSU Central Committee. Political struggles ensued throughout 1987 and 1988, both within society and within the establishment, over the scope and limits of *glasnost'* and democratization. Conservatives sought to limit the challenge to the party-state's monopoly over ideology, politics, economics, and socio-political organization. Democratizers sought to destroy that monopoly, and to construct a more competitive system. A public competition of ideas (a "marketplace of ideas") was the promise of radical *glasnost'*. Multiple candidate elections, based on an open nomination process and secret balloting, was the hallmark of *demokratizatsiya*. The proliferation of voluntary associations and political self-organization (the *neformal'nye*) was the hallmark of the effort to revitalize public life, stimulate authentic public initiative, mobilize new social forces into politics, and break the party-state's monopoly over socio-political organization.[1]

The establishment of a Congress of People's Deputies, a new Supreme Soviet, and a new position of "President," along with the liberation and revitalization of *soviets* (legislative councils) at all levels, created new arenas of power to compete with the Communist Party apparatus for both organizational resources and popular legitimacy. During 1990, Article 6 of the Soviet Constitution was formally abrogated, thus ending the party's juridical claim to being the only legal political party on the Soviet scene. At the 28th Party Congress in July 1990, changes in personnel, structure, and rules drastically diminished the extent of the party's "leading role" within the newly competitive political order. The once-ruling Politburo was reduced to a rubber-stamp body that would meet irregularly and would include only officials of the party itself. The Central Committee's powers were curtailed, as were the powers of party officials at all levels to appoint and discipline officials of other institutions.

The consequences of these manifold changes in politics and policy took many

---

1. For a good overview of these trends, see White, 1990, chapters 2–3.

forms, not all of which boded well for the institutionalization of a democratic order within the territorial boundaries of what is now the USSR. During 1989–1990, intercommunal violence spread within the southern republics of the USSR. An inter-republic war between Armenia and Azerbaijan erupted and dragged on. About 800,000 refugees from this and other violence, mostly Russians and Armenians, crowded into the major cities. The legislatures of the Baltic, Georgian, Moldavian, and Armenian republics declared their independence of the USSR. In response to both the violence and the legislative defiance, Moscow on several occasions sent troops to intimidate and cow the local populations, to crush insurrection, or to separate and disarm the local combatants. In most cases, military intervention only served to further radicalize the ethnic populations, or amounted to a holding operation that did not prevent perpetuation of a state of siege.

Other consequences of political reform took less violent, but equally momentous, forms. The proliferation of informal organizations in 1989 and 1990 reached a total of more than 60,000, encompassing the majority of urban citizens between 20 and 50 years of age. In relatively free elections in spring 1989 and spring 1990, the immunity of prominent party and state leaders from public accountability was broken, even though the majority of party officials who ran for office nationwide secured election (by one means or another).[2] Most significantly, radical majorities were elected to the city councils of Moscow, Leningrad, Kiev, the major cities of the Western Ukraine, and several large cities in the Urals, Siberia, and the Far East, while radical separatists came to control the republican legislatures, and most city councils, of the Baltic states, Georgia, Armenia, and Moldavia. In the Russian Republic, the Supreme Soviet defied Gorbachev and elected Boris Yel'tsin as President in June 1990, since which time the two leaders have struggled continuously over the relative powers of the all-Union versus RSFSR authorities.

In response to these trends, the conservative and reactionary forces within the system have counter-mobilized, capturing the newly created Communist Party of the Russian Republic, organizing a substantial faction within the Congress of People's Deputies, forcing leading radicals out of Gorbachev's cabinet, sharply restricting the scope of *glasnost'* on television and in selected newspapers, and demanding a more resolute crackdown on public "disorder" and separatism. As this conservative backlash is a focus in Part IV of this volume, I will not review it further here.

Not all the stirrings of democratization amounted to either ethnic violence and separatism, on the one hand, or polarized politics within elected assemblages and voluntary associations, on the other. During 1989, large-scale strikes of coal miners broke out in Siberia (the Kuzbas), Ukraine (the Donbas), and

---

2. "Out of 191 republican and regional level first secretaries nominated, 38 lost, including *all 32 who faced competition*" (Hahn, 1990, p. 169; emphasis added), in addition to incumbents who ran uncontested, yet had their names crossed off the ballot by more than fifty percent of the voters. See also Urban (1990, p. 112). These data on the correlation between political competition and the defeat of incumbents cast a different light on Jerry Hough's observation, in his chapter in this section of the reader, that "eighty percent of the republic and *obkom* secretaries who were on the ballot did win."

Arctic Russia (Vorkuta). These resumed sporadically in 1990, and broke out again in sustained fashion in March 1991. Of course, there had been labor strikes before Gorbachev came to power, just as there had been incidents of interethnic violence. But those tended to be sporadic, short-lived, and easily contained by the authorities. In contrast, the labor unrest of 1989–1991 was sustained, widespread, and incapable of being controlled by Moscow. Most significantly, it resulted in the emergence of a fairly widespread anti-*system* consciousness among the strikers, and the development of strike committees into Regional Workers Councils that would compete with the party-state for the right to represent the interests of workers. The articles in Part III of this volume examine these stirrings of democratization from several vantage points. Jerry F. Hough takes a "top-down" view, exploring Gorbachev's ability to manipulate the democratization process in ways that would simultaneously increase his own powers and encourage, as well as contain, the instability in society. Timothy Colton and Peter Rutland offer "bottom-up" views. Colton zeroes in on the Moscow City Council races of March 1990, attempting to specify who won and why. Rutland presents an in-depth account of the miners' strikes of 1989–1990, exploring their causes and their possible consequences for democratization of the system.

Hough claims that "the very 'democratization' that went on during 1988 and 1989 was an important technique in [Gorbachev's] consolidation of dictatorial power." First, Gorbachev manipulated the nomination processes so as to ensure that few officials associated with him faced real electoral competition, while those he sought to replace or intimidate were typically placed in competitively disadvantageous positions. Having thereby "packed" the Congress of People's Deputies, "the results of the Congress were essentially what Gorbachev wanted. The radicals were defeated on all contested ballots, and Gorbachev and all his key appointments were easily approved."

Second, Gorbachev used the democratization process to conduct a strategy of "directed chaos." This involved encouraging popular unrest and challenge of varied sorts, so as to create a perception of crisis that would intimidate elites into conferring on him emergency powers and deferring to his eventual program of radical economic reform. Televising the proceedings of the Congress of People's Deputies was a way of simultaneously raising popular consciousness, stimulating popular defiance, and intimidating rival politicians. Intentionally allowing shortages to beset the consumer markets was designed to raise popular fury against officials resistant to major corrective action. Thus, according to Hough, by manipulating the electoral process, and by stoking an atmosphere of crisis, Gorbachev has crafted a situation in which "the political base for reform has been created."

Hough argues, however, that Gorbachev is not a democrat. He will not tolerate a toppling of Communist Party hegemony or a break-up of the Union. He must therefore anticipate, and guard against, "the possibility that things will get out of hand." On this score, the articles by Colton and Rutland suggest forms of radicalization that Gorbachev may not have anticipated, or that may yet defy the limits of his orchestration.

For as Colton points out, "few aspects of political flux in the contemporary Soviet Union hold the revolutionary potential of the advent of competitive elections for governmental office." Colton's article examines one such election: that held in Moscow in March 1990 to choose a new city council. Colton shows how radical forces associated with "Democratic Russia" swept majority control of the *Mossovet* (Moscow Municipal Soviet). He attributes their victory to more than their intrinsic electoral appeal as democratic alternatives to a discredited establishment. He also finds that the electoral rules favored the insurgents, while lack of "elan and [tactical] ingenuity" among the old guard candidates allowed insurgents to seize the initiative against them. The result was a Moscow city council dominated by forces increasingly critical of Gorbachev's unwillingness to break the back of Communist Party rule. Indeed, the Mayor and Vice-Mayor, Gavriil Popov and Sergey Stankevich, joined Boris Yel'stin and Leningrad Mayor Anatoliy Sobchak, in turning in their party cards after the 28th Party Congress (July 1990).

The coal miners' strikes were another form of turmoil that Gorbachev perhaps did not anticipate or desire (though he did use it as justification for purging opponents and radicalizing reform proposals). The initial strikes in the three major coalfields "were restrained and highly disciplined affairs," and were defused only through assurances by Moscow that the miners' economic and social grievances would be met in full. Gradually, however, the miners realized during 1989–1990 that the government was unwilling or unable to deliver on its promises. This resulted in further strikes and a major escalation of political demands to include the resignation of Gorbachev himself.

Among the miners, among the radical democrats in major cities, and among separatist forces in many republics, Gorbachev has been outflanked to the left. Yet all three articles in Part III reach conclusions that suggest caution about the prospects for consolidating a democratic alternative in the USSR. Hough believes that "on the question of real democracy, of a multiparty system, the Russians—including many well-educated and liberal ones—remain quite conservative," fearing a break-up of the country more than they yearn for "complete political freedom." Colton notes that many things could undermine the future prospects of Democratic Russia: changes in electoral rules (such as the choice of proportional representation); increased tactical sophistication by centrist and independent candidates; infighting within the Democratic Russia forces now in power; growing popular disenchantment with economic conditions; and disenchantment with the inability of radical democrats to improve them. Rutland, in turn, notes the "extreme fragmentation of the [miners'] movement—both over the tactics to be followed and over the general goals to be pursued." He skillfully identifies the conflicting perspectives and interests of miners in the three coalfields, and bemoans their failure to share a united vision of "what kind of political and economic system" they want. Perhaps such a unified version will emerge from the strikes of 1991, but Rutland's article demonstrates how much organizational and agitational work remains to be done.

These limitations notwithstanding, the social base for democratization will remain strong and widespread, as Blair Ruble's study of the social dimensions of *perestroyka* has demonstrated.[3] As Rutland discovered, well-educated miners, of whom there were many among the strikers, were heavily involved as strike leaders and "became a major factor in the radicalization of the workforce." As Colton found, a democratic alternative to the party-state establishment was able to win a large majority in Moscow. And, perhaps most significant, party officials must worry greatly about a pattern displayed in both the 1989 and 1990 elections: radical victories in major urban centers and many minority republics (outside Central Asia), accompanied by old guard victories in rural Russia and Central Asia. This post-Leninist re-creation of an urban-rural split, but this time with the "Bolshevik" support concentrated in the most backward areas, cannot but affect the morale and unity of party officials.

Despite these trends, the USSR could slip back into an authoritarianism of the left or the right, or could for some time be marked by chronic instability and recurrent political crises. The tasks are so difficult, and the economic conditions so austere, that people with democratizing inclinations could nonetheless support authoritarian solutions. No responsible observer should attempt to predict with confidence the precise outcome of the current turmoil in the USSR. Yet before we assume that turmoil will henceforth favor only an authoritarian backlash by the old guard, we should bear in mind Jerry Hough's warning: "Regimes often fall when too many members of an old elite finally decide that it is not worth fighting and give up. The Soviet Union is more vulnerable on this point than is generally appreciated."

REFERENCES

Hahn, Jeffrey W., "Boss Gorbachev Confronts His New Congress," *ORBIS* 34, 2:163–178, Spring 1990.

Ruble, Blair A., "The Soviet Union's Quiet Revolution," in George W. Breslauer, ed., *Can Gorbachev's Reforms Succeed?* Berkeley: University of California, Center for Slavic and East European Studies, 1990.

Urban, Michael E., *More Power to the Soviets*. London: Edward Elgar, 1990.

White, Stephen, *Gorbachev in Power*. Cambridge: Cambridge University Press, 1990.

---

3. See Chapter 4 of this volume.

CHAPTER 11

The Politics of Successful Economic Reform

Jerry F. Hough

1989 HAS BEEN an extraordinary year in Soviet history. The first competitive elections in 65 years, a transformation of the legislature into a body in which deputies made unprecedented statements on live television, the first long strike since the 1920s, the demand of sovereignty not only by Baltic extremists but by party officials—these events followed each other in breathtaking succession.

When the year began, Soviet intellectuals and many American observers were talking about conservative workers and bureaucrats as major obstacles to reform in the Soviet Union. The autumn began with many talking about a Soviet population, specifically including the workers, so radical that Mikhail Gorbachev's power was threatened in the streets and about the imminence of anarchy—or, maybe, a democratic success such as seemed to be occurring in Poland.

And, yet, despite all the political excitement, one political fact transcended all the others in the short run in the spring of 1989: Mikhail Gorbachev's position within the existing political structure was greatly strengthened. By all the traditional indicators, he completed one of the most rapid consolidations of power in history. A conservative coup d'état seems impossible now, except through assassination, and the very "democratization" that went on during 1988 and 1989 was an important technique in this consolidation of dictatorial power.

The assumptions about a Gorbachev consolidation of power within the Communist Party and an imminence of anarchy in the street are not necessarily incompatible. It is at least conceivable that Gorbachev could have unleashed forces in his consolidation of power that then got—or will get—out of hand. At a minimum, however, the fact that Soviet and American anxiety about the fate of Gorbachev and *perestroyka* persisted while the underlying analysis underwent a 180-degree change should give us pause. We should ask ourselves

First published in *Soviet Economy*, 5, 1, pp. 3–46.

whether the problem is within us, i.e., whether we simply cannot face up to a fundamental rethinking of the assumptions of the postwar era, and whether as skilled a politician as he is has really made the horrendous mistakes we attribute to him.

In my view, the Soviet Union is far from anarchy or a failure of *perestroyka*. Instead, Gorbachev has understood that economic reform cannot be conducted in some clinical manner. "Surely," he said in July, "it is not necessary to panic when revolutionary processes become a reality. It was *we* who produced them with our policy. Didn't we understand this when we discussed all this?" (*Pravda*, July 21, 1989, p. 1). He has the sense that progress can be made only with a policy of controlled chaos, that only an exaggerated and even artificial economic crisis is necessary to push things forward. If we understand the centripetal as well as the centrifugal forces in Soviet society, we can see why he has such well-placed confidence that the chaos is under strict control. Stalin had a similar policy from 1927 to 1931, and Russia today is less out of control than it was then.

HOW GORBACHEV CONSOLIDATED POWER

Reshaping the Central Committee

I would argue that Gorbachev has essentially been "tsar" for the last several years and has had the political strength of Stalin in 1928–1929. Boris Yel'tsin has been confirming this interpretation in his recent interviews, saying that Gorbachev never faced any organized opposition in the Politburo. Despite all the talk of Yegor Ligachev's opposition to Gorbachev (which supposedly even drove out Gorbachev's closest ally, Yel'tsin), the recently published steno-graphic report of the "Yel'tsin" plenum of the Central Committee makes it clear that Yel'tsin always perceived Gorbachev and Ligachev as working to-gether and that he was indirectly attacking Gorbachev with his criticism of Ligachev (*Izvestiya TsK KPSS*, No. 2, 1989, pp. 209–287).[1] At this plenum, Gorbachev himself referred to Ligachev as a part of his "team" (*komanda*) (*Izvestiya TsK KPSS*, No. 2, 1989, p. 243).

By the spring of 1989, however, Gorbachev completed several key steps to forestall any weakening of his position in the future. One of these received no public notice at all, while another has been largely forgotten in the excitement of the elections and the Congress of People's Deputies. The first was the endorsement by the 19th Party Conference in June 1988 of the principle that

---

1. Actually when Philip Taubman of *The New York Times* first broke the story in 1987, he had its main points essentially correct (*The New York Times*, October 30, 1987, p. 1, November 1, 1987, p. 22, and November 2, 1987, p. 1), and his version was confirmed by the type of esoteric communication in the Soviet press that is almost always correct. However, Aleksandr Yakovlev and his supporters inaccurately told reporters that stories of a Yel'tsin attack on Gorbachev and on the speed of *perestroyka* were (in Yakovlev's words at a press conference) "a fantasy," and this information was widely accepted. See, for example, *The Washington Post*, October 31, 1987, p. 1, and November 4, 1987, p. 33 (for the Yakovlev quotation).

subsequent party conferences (to be held midway in the period between party congresses) could replace up to 20 percent of the Central Committee.[2] The second was the "resignation" of 74 of the voting members of the Central Committee (24 percent of the total) at the April 1989 plenum of the Central Committee and promotion of 24 candidate members as a partial replacement for them (*Pravda*, April 26, 1989, p. 1).[3]

These developments were of the utmost importance, for the General Secretary is officially elected by, and removable by, the Central Committee. While many Westerners have assumed that this subordination is a formality and that the Politburo is really the dominant institution, this is not the case. For example, if the Politburo really had the power to select a General Secretary, the Politburo members of March 1985—seven of nine of whom have been removed, with the other two on the way out—clearly would not have elected Gorbachev.[4] A year before that the Politburo had included Konstantin Chernenko as General Secretary and Dmitriy Ustinov as Defense Minister, and the majority suspicious of Gorbachev was even stronger. If the Chernenko Politburo had had the power to clip Gorbachev's wings or at least build up a challenger to him, it surely would have.

Hence even the surface evidence of 1985 indicated that the Politburo must have been forced to defer to the desires of the Central Committee majority concerning the successor to Chernenko. If there was any doubt on the question, however, Ligachev resolved it at the 19th Party Conference when he stated flatly that Gorbachev would not have been selected if he had not had the active support of many men who were not voting members of the Politburo, including KGB chief Viktor Chebrikov and "a number of *obkom* first secretaries" (*Pravda*, July 2, 1988, p. 11).[5] Such men would have had an influence only if the Central Committee had the ultimate power.

Obviously the dependence of a General Secretary on the Central Committee normally makes him very sensitive to the political necessities of gaining and maintaining support there—sensitivities that have certainly been heightened by memories of Nikita Khrushchev's fate in October 1964. Gorbachev, in fact, acted very cautiously in his first year of office while he was still dealing with the Central Committee elected in 1981 under Brezhnev. Instead he concentrated on changing personnel so that as many as possible of the officials elected to the Central Committee in 1986 would be beholden to him. In practice, he

2. The Theses published prior to the conference simply referred to the "partial" renewal of the Central Committee at the party conference (*Pravda*, May 27, 1988, p. 2). The resolution adopted at the conference modified this to say "partially, up to 20 percent" (*Pravda*, July 5, 1988, p. 2).

3. The biographies of living Central Committee members (including candidates who had been promoted to full membership since the congress) were published in *Izvestiya TsK KPSS*, No. 2 (February), 1989, pp. 44–114. No doubt, the purpose of the publication was to show the current occupation—or nonoccupation—of members and thus to prepare the way for the "resignation" of the retirees. In addition, several other members were retired between February and April.

4. The members, besides Gorbachev, were Geydar Aliyev, Viktor Grishin, Andrey Gromyko, Dinmukhamed Kunayev, Grigoriy Romanov, Vladimir Shcherbitskiy, Mikhail Solomentsev, Nikolay Tikhonov, and Vitaliy Vorotnikov.

5. *Obkom* is short for *oblastnoy komitet partii*, or oblast party committee.

succeeded in obtaining a Central Committee from the 27th Party Congress which had nearly 40 percent of its voting members newly elected.[6]

Nevertheless, an activist General Secretary who wants to restructure and rejuvenate the political-administrative elite still has a problem with the Central Committee. Most members of the Central Committee have been elected to that body because they occupy a post deemed worthy of Central Committee membership, and they normally are removed from the Central Committee when they are demoted to a lesser job or retire. Unfortunately from a General Secretary's point of view, this occurs only at the next party congress except in extraordinary circumstances (corruption or membership in an "anti-party" group). Thus when a General Secretary demotes or retires high officials, he is at the same time demoting or retiring members of the Central Committee who have the power to retire him, and the retired members have a vote in a crisis that is equal to any other member, including one who sits on the Politburo.

These "lame ducks" on the Central Committee—or "dead souls," as the Russians call them—posed little problem for Stalin in the 1920s, since party congresses were held very frequently (and less problem later because of police terror). Now, however, the congresses are normally held only every five years, and that provides time for a large number of lame ducks to accumulate. Brezhnev solved the problem by changing very few officials, and 90 percent of the living Central Committee members were re-elected at the last two party congresses of the Brezhnev period (Hough, 1982, pp. 46–47). Gorbachev had a much more severe problem because of his frequent changes in personnel: 28 percent of the voting members of the new Central Committee elected in March 1986 had already been retired or demoted by April 1989, and this figure rose to some 38 percent by the end of July.[7] It clearly threatened to approach or exceed 50 percent by the time of the 28th Party Congress, which was expected to be held in early 1991 (but now late 1990).[8] If anti-Gorbachev forces attempted a coup in the Central Committee, many of these lame ducks would surely support the effort for personal reasons as well as policy ones.

Many sophisticated Soviet observers predicted that the 19th Party Conference of June 1988 would remove the roughly 50 lame ducks who were on the Central Committee at the time, and this prediction seemed to be borne out when the draft of the Party Rules proposed before the conference sanctioned partial replacement of Central Committee members at party conferences. But only party congresses are legally empowered to change the Party Rules, and it was

6. For further discussion see Hough (1988a, pp. 145–175).

7. As this is written, the personnel changes are still under way, and it is unclear which persons who have lost jobs have been retired and which may receive other high jobs. It is also unclear which posts will warrant Central Committee membership in the future. For example, the first secretary of the Chechen-Ingush *obkom*, a voting member of the Central Committee, resigned to become chairman of the Supreme Soviet Committee on Glasnost' and Rights and Appeals of Citizens. We (and, fortunately for Gorbachev, probably the chairmen of the new committees) don't know whether this category of official will be elected to the Central Committee at the next Congress (*Izvestiya*, July 13, 1989, p. 2).

8. Gorbachev has now proposed a fall 1990 congress (*Pravda*, July 17, 1989, p. 3). See also the speech of V. A. Medvedev in *Moskovskaya pravda*, June 23, 1989, p. 7.

decided that the 19th Party Conference would only recommend rule changes (including the 20-percent replacement rule) and that it not attempt to remove any Central Committee members.

Gorbachev in no way remained defenseless. For example, he could force an early convening of the 28th Congress, or he could try to persuade the lame ducks to resign "voluntarily," as had been done in China.[9] The latter path was the one chosen, and the delay from June 1988 to April 1989 permitted 74 voting members to be removed instead of 50. The result of the April plenum was a Central Committee that looked quite different on May 1 than it had on April 1. The average age of the voting members had dropped from 62 to 59. The proportion of members who were lame ducks fell from 28 percent to 4 percent. The figure rose back to 16 percent by late summer, but it would have been some 38 percent without the April plenum.

The balance of occupations among Central Committee members also changed with the April plenum. Twenty-four military officers and former industrial or construction ministers were among the voting members who resigned. Although there were 22 such officials among the candidate members, only two of them were promoted to full membership. At the same time every worker and peasant among the candidates was promoted, and the proportion of them among voting members rose from 8 to 13 percent.[10]

Lenin had had the idea of stacking the Central Committee with workers in order to increase his independence from the other party leaders, and Gorbachev acts as if he has learned from Lenin on this point. The editor of the Central Committee journal, *Kommunist*, has even proposed selecting academics and workers for the party Politburo instead of high officials (*Christian Science Monitor*, Aug. 7, 1989, p. 2), and Gorbachev may even begin doing this in the future.

Gorbachev was not, however, concerned only with the removal of Central Committee members who had been retired. Historically the power of the General Secretary had rested on his ability to control the selection of regional first secretaries and on their ability to control the selection of delegates to party congresses, which had the power to select the Central Committee. This "circular flow of power," as Robert Daniels called it, was the mechanism by which the General Secretary had traditionally built his political machine,[11] and Gorbachev gave every sign of understanding this.

At the January 1987 plenum of the Central Committee, Gorbachev said that "some comrades" favored the competitive election of regional first secretaries, and Soviet intellectuals (as well as many Western observers) assumed that, contrary to the circular-flow-of-power theory, the regional first secretaries were Gorbachev's greatest enemies. According to this view, contested elections of

9. See the discussion of options in Hough, 1988b, p. 143. One analyst speculates that the conservatives called the April plenum to limit Gorbachev, but that he managed to turn the tables on them (Teague, 1989). This interpretation seems very unlikely.

10. This figure includes a handful of collective farm chairmen.

11. For such an interpretation, see Hough and Fainsod (1979, pp. 144–145, 260–261, 454–455).

party officials and the free elections of delegates to the 19th Party Conference were indispensable to Gorbachev. Although party control of delegate selection had formerly been interpreted as a sign of a General Secretary's power, this time such controlled elections were interpreted as a defeat for Gorbachev.

Controlling Party Appointments

Gorbachev himself, however, has behaved as if the theory of the circular flow of power was absolutely correct. Even though he has deplored the lack of democracy in the latest party elections, he has shown little inclination to loosen Central Committee control over the appointment of the key first secretaries of *obkoms* and republics.[12] The posts of all *obkom* and republic secretaries, not just those of the first secretaries, are still in the *nomenklatura*[13] of the Central Committee. This fact was dramatized in 1989 by the monthly publication of the names of the confirmed secretaries in the new journal, *Izvestiya TsK KPSS*.[14]

The Yel'tsin Affair. In practice, Gorbachev has not indicated any doubt about the nature of "confirmation" in the case of important first secretaries. So far as can be judged, this was one of the key issues that lay at the base of the Gorbachev-Yel'tsin conflict. Yel'tsin had already begun to break with Gorbachev almost a year earlier with a memorandum whose contents have not been revealed, and then he delivered a speech at the June 1987 plenum of the Central Committee that was so radical that no other Central Committee member supported it. Yel'tsin had agreed to step down after the celebration of the 70th anniversary of the revolution in November 1987, and the October plenum was called simply to approve Gorbachev's speech for the celebration. Yel'tsin, however, completely disrupted the plenum by rising at the conclusion of Gorbachev's speech and attacking the speed of *perestroyka*.[15]

Yel'tsin's central strategy was clear enough: he was provoking an open break with Gorbachev in one of the most scandalous manners possible in order to stake out a position as the radical alternative to the General Secretary. There was, however, a subtle—and crucial—aspect to Yel'tsin's behavior and Gorbachev's response. Yel'tsin was essentially demanding that the democratic forms of the Party Rules be followed. If he had stepped down quietly after the November celebration, the decisions would have been made within the Politburo

12. In the party elections, only half of the secretaries of primary party organizations were elected in competitive elections, and a much smaller number of *gorkom* and *raykom* secretaries and only a handful of *obkom* and republic secretaries faced opposition. (*Gorkom* is short for *gorodskoy komitet partii*, or city party committee; *raykom* stands for *rayonnyy komitet partii*, or *rayon* party committee.)

13. In this narrow sense, *nomenklatura* denotes a list of posts for which a certain party committee has the right of approval. In the broader sense, it refers to the entire system of such appointments.

14. The list is published under the heading "Vybory i utverzhdeniye partiynykh rabotnikov" (Elections and Confirmation of Party Functionaries). It began with the No. 2 issue (pp. 154–157) and has continued every month thereafter.

15. For Yel'tsin's speech, see *Izvestiya TsK KPSS*, No. 2, 1989, pp. 239–241. Gorbachev's summary of the Yel'tsin position on p. 241 clarifies some of the issues.

framework. But the Party Rules say that Politburo members are chosen by the plenum of the Central Committee, and Yel'tsin decided to make his case at the plenum and offer his resignation as a candidate member of the Politburo. At the same time, the first secretary of the Moscow *gorkom* is, of course, formally elected by the Moscow *gorkom*, and Yel'tsin told the Central Committee members that the question of his tenure as Moscow leader would be decided by the *gorkom*.

Gorbachev generally handled the Yel'tsin challenge at the plenum calmly, but he reacted with cold fury at the Yel'tsin statement about the Moscow *gorkom*. Gorbachev made it absolutely clear that the Central Committee, rather than the Moscow party committee, would decide who would be Moscow first secretary—and it would not do so in plenary session. The issues that Yel'tsin raised in his late 1986 memorandum and his June 1987 plenum speech, which led to the break, have not been revealed. But the internal evidence of the plenum discussions strongly suggests that Yel'tsin called for much looser control by the Central Committee Secretariat over regional party organizations—probably including meaningful elections of regional party secretaries from below rather than their "recommendation" from above. His criticism of Ligachev was more a criticism of the role Ligachev was playing as Central Committee secretary than of Ligachev's performance as such, and it is quite possible that Gorbachev's reference in January 1987 to "some comrades" who were calling for the competitive election of regional secretaries was a reference to Yel'tsin's memorandum.

Although Gorbachev called for more competitive party elections, in July 1989, he also traveled to Leningrad to attend the plenum of the Leningrad *obkom* that replaced the first secretary, Yuriy Solov'yev. The communique on the plenum reported that "M. S. Gorbachev offered a motion to elect Boris Veniaminovich Gidaspov first secretary of the Leningrad *obkom*." Gidaspov himself stated that he had not been consulted about his candidacy and did not think he was qualified.[16] (He was a scientist who had never held a party or governmental position.) When other candidates were nominated, Gorbachev gave no indication that this was desirable, and these candidates withdrew their names. One delegate described the situation with unusual frankness when he expressed gratitude that Moscow had selected a local person rather than imposing a "Varangian" (*varyag*) from the outside. At the end of the plenum, Gidaspov himself said that he wanted to express his "sincere gratitude to Mikhail Sergeyevich Gorbachev" (*Leningradskaya pravda*, July 14, 1989, pp. 1–3).

Moscow's role in the selection of first secretaries in the republics has sometimes been equally ostentatious. When trouble erupted in the Nagorno-Karabakh

16. This statement was made on Soviet television on July 12 (FBIS, *Daily Report—Soviet Union*, July 13, 1989, p. 43), and it should be treated with some skepticism. Gidaspov was named chairman of the Credentials Committee of the Congress of People's Deputies—normally a post reserved for a politically important person, and he spoke for the Leningrad organization on questions of nominations. Clearly he had been either anointed or well on his way to anointment by this time.

Autonomous Oblast, the first secretaries of Armenia and Azerbaijan—both in their fifties—resigned "for reasons of health" on the same day, each time at a plenum which two Central Committee secretaries attended, one liberal and one conservative.[17] Republic first secretaries were replaced in 12 of 14 republics between November 1985 and July 1989 (in fact twice each in the republics of Kazakhstan, Lithuania, and Uzbekistan). Normally the presence of Georgiy Razumovskiy, Gorbachev's personnel secretary, at the plenum tipped Moscow's hand. In Estonia, the visiting Politburo member, Nikolay Slyun'kov, "informed [the plenum] that the Politburo of the Central Committee recommended V. I. Vialis as first secretary of the Central Committee of Estonia." Two other candidates were nominated from the floor, but withdrew (*Sovetskaya Estoniya*, June 17, 1988, p. 1).

Moscow has also continued the practice of keeping a second secretary in each republic who is a Russian. Gorbachev has, however, apparently decided to respond to local sensitivities by abandoning the practice of sending an outside Russian who does not even know the language. The three second secretaries who have been elected since June (in Georgia, Kirghizia, and Uzbekistan) have all come from within the republic.[18]

Gorbachev not only retained the right to approve personnel changes in the key posts of republic and *obkom* first secretary, but he exercises it frequently. He was personnel secretary of the Central Committee under Yuriy Andropov and Chernenko and has been General Secretary since March 1985. In the nearly three-and-a-half years before the 27th Party Congress that he occupied these posts, the first secretary was replaced in 83 of the 146 republics and oblasts that elected delegates to the Party Congress, and 62 percent of the delegates came from these areas.

Changes among first secretaries in the last three-and-a-half years since the Party Congress have continued at exactly the same pace. Between March 1986 and early September 1989, the first secretary was replaced in 83 of the 142 current units. In addition, the first secretary was changed in three of the four large republics in which delegates are elected at the oblast level, and a change in the fourth (the Ukraine) is clearly imminent. More personnel changes can be expected on the eve of the upcoming local elections and next fall's Party Congress, but the Central Committee has even issued a decree demanding that the local party committees convene quickly to "decide urgent personnel questions" (*Pravda*, Aug. 3, 1989, p. 1). The turnover may be quite substantial.

Some analysts suggest that Gorbachev may really democratize the Communist Party, perhaps even to the point of abandoning his control over the

---

17. Ligachev and Georgiy Razumovskiy attended one plenum, and Yakovlev and Vladimir Dolgikh the other (*Pravda*, May 22, 1988, p. 2).

18. The biography of the new Georgian second secretary, A. Yu. Pavshentsev, is found in *Zarya Vostoka*, June 18, 1989, p. 1. However, the new Kirghizian second secretary (N. M. Chepelev, the chairman of the Osh *obispolkom*, or oblast executive committee) and the new Uzbek second secretary (A. S. Yefimov, the chairman of the Uzbek Committee on People's Control) did not have their biographies published at the time of their election (*Sovetskaya Kirgiziya*, July 29, 1989, p. 1, and *Pravda Vostoka*, July 30, 1989, p. 1).

party apparatus—which has been the traditional source of power for a General Secretary—and relying on his control of the Supreme Soviet as the source of his power.

Such speculation is little more than the dreams of radical Soviet intellectuals. As will be discussed in the next section, Gorbachev undoubtedly has been building up the Congress of People's Deputies and Supreme Soviet in order to lessen his dependence on the Politburo. But he does not seem interested in becoming any more dependent on the Supreme Soviet than on the party apparatus. All the evidence suggests that he wants to be able to play one off against the other, while retaining the party structure as the dominant one in the country.

From this perspective, Gorbachev must exercise caution in approaching competitive elections to the key party positions. If—as in the Baltic states—he is relying basically on the threat of military force as the main instrument of control, he has an interest in having first secretaries who have popular appeal and can act as a "good cop," an intermediary between the center and the local population. But in the RSFSR and the Ukraine, where the application of military force is more dangerous, he must be leery about first secretaries who fear only the local populace and not the General Secretary.

There are cases where competitive elections are not threatening. For example, Aleksandr Khomyakov, a long-time associate of Razumovskiy in the Krasnodar party apparatus, was made first secretary of the Saratov *obkom* in 1985 and now has been appointed chairman of the RSFSR Gosplan. Presumably he selected top lieutenants whom he trusted, and three of them (an *obkom* secretary, the first secretary of the Saratov *gorkom*, and the first deputy chairman of the executive committee of the oblast soviet) competed in the election at the obkom plenum to succeed him.[19] Gorbachev presumably had nothing to fear, regardless of who won, but it is crucial that the participants know he has the ability to play a deciding role, as he did in Leningrad. If his highest goal were to democratize the party, he would not have intervened in the way he did in Leningrad.

A Shift Toward Political Skills

Nevertheless, a significant change appears to be taking place in the party apparatus, both in the type of official chosen and perhaps even in the structure of the party. However, this entails a change not in the relationship between the central party leader and the regional party leaders, but in the role that the latter are supposed to play.

In recent decades Moscow has given the regional party officials two main tasks: the maintenance of political stability and the fulfillment of the economic

---

19. The *obkom* secretary won (*Pravda*, August 11, 1989, p. 2). A similar election was held in Rovno where the competitors were the second secretary of the *obkom*, the chairman of the *oblispolkom*, and a lesser *obkom* secretary. The *oblispolkom* chairman won (*Pravda*, August 30, 1989, p. 2).

plan. For non-Slavic areas, the central leaders have acted as though they attached priority to the first task, and they normally selected republic first secretaries with political backgrounds and skills, but relatively little experience in economic management (Freeman, 1990). (Eduard Shevardnadze is a good example.) However, since political stability was taken for granted in the RSFSR and the Ukraine, the leadership usually selected as first secretaries men with great experience in economic management, who seemed best qualified to help achieve plan fulfillment. Lev Zaykov in Moscow is a former factory manager, and Solov'yev in Leningrad a former high construction official. Whatever their merits may be, factory managers and construction officials do not, on the whole, make the most natural electoral politicians in the United States, and there is no reason to suppose that they are well suited for this role in the Soviet Union.[20]

Zaykov himself cited precisely this factor in explaining the electoral disaster of the party in Moscow. He complained that party officials were still being chosen for their skills in economic management, and they still had a "technocratic approach [rather than] an ability to interact with people to convince and lead them, to deeply understand social processes" (*Moskovskaya pravda*, June 22, 1989, p. 2). He and others called for the selection of party officials with political skills, and the term now has a different meaning than it did in the past. When Gidaspov was elected first secretary in Leningrad, it was not accidental that he was praised as a man who is able to communicate (*kommunikabelen*) and "adapts very well to a new situation" (*Leningradskaya pravda*, July 14, 1989, p. 2).

Similar change is necessary at the national level. As both rank-and-file Communists and Premier Nikolay Ryzhkov complained, one of the most remarkable features of the sessions of the Congress of People's Deputies was that Politburo members (other than Gorbachev and Ryzhkov as rapporteurs) never spoke to defend party policy. Politburo members are very skilled at closed-committee politics, but they are clearly not comfortable in the give-and-take of parliamentary debate. The leadership needs people who are skilled debaters and public speakers and can serve as party leaders in parliamentary forums.

Finally, the structure of the party may have to be changed to reflect the new situation. When Lenin formed the Communist Party, he based it on party cells in factories, and the principle has continued to this day. The lowest structural unit of the party is not the precinct, but the primary party organization at the place of work. (The exception is the pensioner who is enrolled in a primary party organization where he or she lives.) The key lower-level party official is not the precinct captain, but the secretary of the primary party organization at work.

---

20. When Solov'yev was removed as first secretary in Leningrad, he was often praised, even by people who did not seem to be conservative party officials. He was a former subway-construction official, and it is quite possible that he was good at organizing plan fulfillment, but out of his element when he had to offer other qualities to a demanding electorate.

The building of the Communist Party on the base of the primary party organization at the place of work was one of the most dramatic facets of the party's production orientation; it was also a major instrument for preserving it. Since party leaders usually began their careers at the factory, the construction site, the collective farm and so forth, they tended to be engineers and agronomists who proved their mettle at least partially by their ability to secure plan fulfillment. Naturally they often retained this orientation as they rose through the hierarchy.

Zaykov noted, however, that "many" Communists question the efficacy of the old party structure and suggest that the basic party unit be transferred to the place of residence. It is a good idea. The powerful political machines in America were built around precinct captains who had a real feel for people's moods, who could help them out in their daily lives and who received political support in return. A party structure with low-level political work concentrated in the election precinct seems far better suited to produce leaders who are sensitive to their constituents' needs.

A major change in party structure and in the career path of party leaders may be wrenching for young party officials who are already on a different career course, but people like Gorbachev have nothing to fear. Indeed, as the market takes over an increasing share of supplies procurement and microeconomic coordination, local party organs will lose one of their traditional roles (Hough, 1969, chs. 10 and 11), and the continued appointment of party secretaries with a managerial background will become counterproductive. The problem is not so much that such officials will actively resist economic reform; but they will naturally tend to interfere in economic decision making when short-term problems arise. The advent of competitive elections will lay the groundwork more smoothly for a new type of politician in the role of party secretary than if it were a matter of economic exigency alone. The young production-oriented party officials, like their counterparts in China, can move into the private sector and prosper economically. Everyone will benefit.

THE ELECTIONS TO THE CONGRESS OF PEOPLE'S DEPUTIES

Of all the events of 1989 that created the impression of a party out of control, none was more important than the elections to the Congress of People's Deputies in March—as well as the runoffs in April and May. The coal strikes in July also had a major impact on our perceptions, but to a large extent they themselves were signaled by the election defeat of party leaders in the coal districts and stimulated in part by the fiery oratory of the electoral campaign. (The *obkom* first secretary lost in all of the mining and heavy-industrial centers of the Urals and Western Siberia—Chelyabinsk, Kemerovo, Orenburg, Perm', Sverdlovsk, Tomsk, and Tyumen'.)

Outsiders are not the only ones who have described events in alarmist terms. On June 20, the second secretary of the Moscow city party committee said in an interview that "if we speak completely frankly, it is impossible not to see that we are engaged in a struggle for power" (*Vechernyaya Moskva*, June 20, 1989, p. 2). The next day, at the plenum of the Moscow *gorkom*, a plant director, A. S. Samsonov, said that "we Communists are losing" (*Moskovskaya pravda*, June 23, 1989, p. 4). Lev Zaykov, the *gorkom* first secretary and Politburo member, endorsed the view that joining the party might be risky today, not something to do for careerist reasons (*ibid.*, June 22, 1989, p. 2). The premier, Nikolay Ryzhkov, said that "the party, practically speaking, is losing authority in the eyes of the people," while the first secretary of the Chita *obkom* in Siberia (one of the losers in the March elections) asserted: "The events in Kuzbas [coal fields] have thrown me into shock to a certain degree. I think that if Siberia has not stood firm, if people have been reeling even here, then we are almost on the brink" (*Pravda*, July 21, 1989, pp. 3 and 4).

The Party's Anxiety

On the surface, the reason for such alarm is not that clear. The Congress of People's Deputies has an even larger percentage of party members among its deputies (87 percent) than the old Supreme Soviet (71.5 percent) (*Deputaty*, 1984, p. 3).[21] A total of 191 secretaries (not just first secretaries) of republic central committees, *kraykoms* and *obkoms*, were on the ballot, and 153 of them won. Of the 126 who were single candidates in a district, 120 won, while 33 of 65 won in contested elections.[22] As will be discussed, the actual parliament, the Supreme Soviet, was chosen at the Congress of People's Deputies rather than through direct elections and seems even more moderate than the Congress.

In fact, the reasons for the anxiety are actually several-fold. First, if one follows the election results closely and reads the Soviet commentaries closely, it is quite clear that the more alarmist statements are coming from people who lost their elections (or from speakers like Ryzhkov who lost in the Supreme Soviet). Without question, these people have something to worry about on the personal level, and they have a natural tendency to speak of a setback to the party rather than to themselves.

Second, the election results were clearly a surprise to the intelligentsia, and perhaps some party officials were caught unawares as well. The intelligentsia had long contended that the masses were conservative and xenophobic, and in

21. This source also provides the biographies of the deputies as well as statistical information about them. For the 1989 deputies, see *Izvestiya*, May 26, 1989, p. 2.

22. *Argumenty i fakty*, No. 21 (May 27/June 2), 1989, p. 8. It is said that the data take account of the second round of voting, and perhaps some officials who lost the first time are counted as winners if they won in the second round.

the period before the elections it deplored the restrictions on full democratization. One-third of the 2,250 deputies' seats of the supreme legislative body—the Congress of People's Deputies—were allocated to the official "public organizations." The Communist Party and the trade unions were guaranteed 100 seats each; the Women's Committee, the Young Communist League, and the Veterans' Committee were each given 75; the remaining 325 public-organization deputies were distributed among a wide range of organizations, from the various cultural unions (with 10 representatives each) down to the Temperance Society with one deputy.[23]

In addition, candidates for the 1,500 territorial districts (750 in a Council of the Union and 750 in a Council of Nationalities) were not nominated in any primary system, but through a two-stage process that gave local party leaders many opportunities to shape the outcome. In practice, this process ensured that 399 of the districts had the familiar one-candidate elections and that 85.3 percent of the candidates were members or candidate members of the Communist Party (*Izvestiya*, March 11, 1989, p. 1).[24] People knew that the Party Rules still explicitly obligate party members in any elected body to carry out the decisions of the appropriate party body—in the case of deputies to the Congress of People's Deputies and Supreme Soviet, the decisions of the Central Committee and the Politburo. Many observers expected that party officials would be protected in one-candidate elections and that competitive elections would be limited in the way that they have been in Eastern Europe in the past.

In fact, many party secretaries were protected by one-candidate elections, and some of the elections did appear to be controlled. Thus, the voters in Gorbachev's home Stavropol' Kray were organized into 13 electoral districts—1 large Council of Nationalities district, 7 for the Council of the Union, and 5 additional for the nationality-based subdistrict within the kray, Karachayev-Cherkess Autonomous Oblast. There was a single candidate in seven of the districts. In the others, a factory manager ran against a factory manager; a collective farm chairman against a state farm director; an airplane pilot against a locomotive engineer; one factory worker against another factory worker; a shepherd against a tractor driver; the head of a dermatology division of a sanatorium against a rank-and-file doctor. The kraykom first secretary won 209,288 to 21,903, the chairman of the executive committee of the kray soviet 48,174 to 3,582, and the first secretary of the autonomous *obkom* 52,851 to 2,827—but all ran unopposed. No candidate received a majority of the vote in three contested elections, and in the second round, a factory worker ran unopposed in one of the districts, a collective-farm mechanic opposed the leader of a welders' brigade in a second, and a worker ran against a state-farm brigade leader in the third. In none of the original elections or the reruns did a man

---

23. A list of the number of seats for each public organization, together with the number of candidates nominated for each, is found in Mann (1989).

24. At that time only 384 of the districts were said to have single candidates; 953 with two candidates, and 163 with more than two. By election day the number of one-candidate districts had risen to 399, while 952 had two candidates (*Izvestiya*, March 11, 1989, p. 1 and April 5, 1989, p. 1).

oppose a woman; hence the gender balance of the delegation (12 men and 4 women) was determined from the first.[25]

The elections in neighboring Krasnodar—the home of Gorbachev's personnel secretary, Grigoriy Razumovskiy—were more competitive, but of a totally different character from the contests in Moscow. Here there were 20 districts— 1 for the Council of Nationalities, 14 for the Council of the Union, and 5 for the nationality-based subdistrict, the Adygey Autonomous Oblast. Only three districts had a single candidate, and the chairman of the executive committee of the kray soviet, the first secretary of the Adygey *obkom*, and a rural *raykom* secretary ran in competitive elections. The *obkom* first secretary won 31,493 to 10,303; the *raykom* secretary lost; and no one received a majority in the district in which the official of the kray soviet was a candidate. Nevertheless, two-thirds of the candidates were of the traditional worker, peasant, and collective-farm manager type, and none seemed radical. In the second round the chairman of the executive committee of the kray soviet was allowed to run unopposed in the same district where he had failed in a competitive election, and this time he won 185,303 to 30,622. (The first secretary of the party *kraykom* had run in the large Council of Nationalities district unopposed, and had won 2,682,604 to 541,096.)[26]

Electoral Surprises

The surprises were several-fold. First, a number of regions had elections with a very different look than Stavropol' and Krasnodar. A number of radicals were able to overcome the nominating barrier in Moscow, and Boris Yel'tsin was nominated in the most sensitive district of all—the Council of Nationalities district that embraced all of Moscow. His opponent held little appeal; he was the director of the huge Likhachev Auto Works. Several high military commanders (for example, the commanders of troops in East Germany, Leningrad, Moscow, and the Far East) ran against fairly attractive candidates. The first secretary of the Leningrad *gorkom* faced a young engineer at a research institute. The results of these elections were not surprising, but the fact that the officials faced any opposition was.

Second, the controls on the elections did not prove as effective as many had expected. Voters had to cross off the names of unwanted candidates from their ballot instead of putting an "X" beside the name of the candidate they wanted, and they could even cross off all the names on the ballot if they saw fit. Moreover, the rules specified that a candidate had to receive a majority of the votes cast in order to win. Thus, even if there was only one candidate on the ballot, he could be defeated if a majority of the voters crossed off his name.

25. The results of the original elections were published in *Stavropol'skaya pravda*, March 29, 1989, p. 1, and those of the second round in *ibid.*, May 16, 1989, p. 1. Here, as elsewhere, the occupations of the losers have to be found in the reports of candidate nomination and registration from late January to early March.
26. *Sovetskaya Kuban'*, March 29, 1989, p. 1, and May 14, 1989, p. 1.

This happened in a number of cases, including—most spectacularly—the candidacy of Yuriy Solov'yev, the first secretary of the Leningrad *obkom*, a candidate member of the Politburo.

The "controlled" elections of representatives of the public organizations also proved subject to outside influence. When the Academy of Sciences nominated just enough candidates to fill its allocated seats in the Congress and left Andrey Sakharov and other radicals off the list, a number of scientists conducted a campaign to cross out the names of all the candidates in order to force a new set of nominations. When 20 of the original 26 candidates were defeated in the Academy elections, the Academy leadership retreated and nominated Sakharov on the second round (*Izvestiya*, March 22, 1989, p. 1; March 24, 1989, p. 1; April 14, 1989, p. 2; April 21, 1989, p. 3).

The third surprise was the depth of popular dissatisfaction in a number of key areas. To repeat, we should not exaggerate: eighty percent of the republic and *obkom* secretaries who were on the ballot did win. Party officials fared especially well in the non-Russian areas. Some very important officials lost in the Ukraine, but in the republic as a whole only 4 *obkom* first secretaries of 25 went down to defeat. No *obkom* first secretary lost in Central Asia, including Kazakhstan, where riots took place in December 1986 because of the appointment of a Russian first secretary from outside the republic. In general, the Central Asian delegates were not seething with a spirit of revolt, but presented such a solid conservative phalanx against the radicals that the latter complained. With the exception of Karelia (which has a solid Russian majority), none of the first secretaries in the 16 autonomous republics of the RSFSR was defeated. The Baltics had a fervent political process, with candidates nominated by the Popular Front often winning; but even there the party apparatus seems to have won some legitimacy as a necessary intermediary between the local population and Moscow.

The first secretaries in the core oblasts and krays of the Russian republic did more poorly on the whole, with 21 of 55 going down to defeat. But the geographical distribution was far from balanced. Only 4 of 12 first secretaries lost in the central region around Moscow, and only 1 in 16 in the Volga, Chernozem, and Kuban' areas.[27] The *obkom* first secretary in Saratov won 189,300 to 22,665, the first secretary in Tambov 215,559 to 19,150, the first secretary in Penza 254,406 to 30,387, and the first secretary in Voronezh 196,382 to 14,317. (In Voronezh, a Politburo member, Vitaliy Vorotnikov, won 2,283,013 to 415,658.)[28]

Where the party leadership did poorly, however, it sometimes did so spec-

---

27. The names of all the *obkom* first secretaries who were defeated were printed in *Argumenty i fakty*, no. 21 (May 27/June 2) 1989, p. 8. I am using the groupings of RSFSR regions found in the Soviet statistical handbooks. Kaliningrad (where the first secretary won) is not grouped with other oblasti and is not included in the calculations.

28. All these elections featured a single candidate (*Kommunist* (Saratov), *Tambovskaya pravda*, *Penzenskaya pravda*, and *Kommuna* (Vorenezh)—all on March 28, 1989, p. 1). I am grateful to Darrell Slider for these references.

tacularly. Nowhere was this truer than in the country's three biggest and most visible cities—Moscow, Leningrad, and Kiev. In Kiev the first secretary of the *gorkom* and the chairman of the executive committee of the city soviet were defeated, despite being the only candidates on the ballot in their respective districts (FBIS, March 29, 1984, p. 34). In Moscow, the huge Council of Nationalities district gave 90 percent of its vote to Boris Yel'tsin, who had been removed as Moscow party leader in disgrace 17 months earlier. The voters of Moscow did not seem in a particularly ugly mood, but on balance they elected some fairly radical deputies. The chairman of the city soviet and second secretary of the *gorkom* went down to defeat in competitive elections.[29]

The mood of the Leningrad voters seemed much angrier, and they expressed their feelings about the party leadership across the board. With the exception of a scientist, Boris Gidaspov, who barely won an uncontested election with 56 percent of the vote, the members of the bureau of the Leningrad *obkom* (six of them) suffered heavy defeats. One party official said that it was enough for activists to write "member of the *obkom*" on the poster of one worker-candidate for her to be defeated.[30] Even the number of votes against Gidaspov is striking, for *Leningradskaya pravda* never published a profile of him or a statement of his views—only a critical article about the nominating meeting that resulted in his being the only candidate on the ballot. This made it clear that he was not a favored candidate and that he was in some way opposed to the Leningrad leadership he was destined to replace in June.[31]

As already mentioned, the party did well in the agricultural regions of the Russian republic, but four of six first secretaries lost in the northwest region dominated by Leningrad (the one losing autonomous republic, Karelia, was also located in this region). Twelve of 20 first secretaries lost in the Urals, Siberia, and the Far East—12 of 17 if we exclude the three grain-producing regions of Altay, Novosibirsk, and Omsk.

Assessing the Party's Overall Performance

Judged on their own, the March elections were not all that disastrous for the party. The party won a heavy majority, and the votes against party officials often were against unpopular candidates and policies, not against the system of one-party rule. Governors and mayors can wear out their

29. The second secretary finished a distant third in a three-way race, but the experience of the chairman of the soviet shows the peculiarity of the election law. He actually defeated a woman plasterer 84,701 to 49,526, but since 111,282 voters crossed his name out, he was not elected. (His opponent's name was crossed out by 146,457 people.)

30. For the report on the defeat of six members of the bureau, see the speech of I. A. Korsakov, *Leningradskaya pravda*, April 6, 1989, p. 2. For the report on the defeated candidate, see the speech of S. B. Petrov, *ibid.*, April 7, 1989, p. 3. Of course, the fact that a statement was made does not guarantee its accuracy. The woman worker was running against a male worker, and women did very poorly in the elections across the country. An examination of two-candidate contests in Moscow, Leningrad, the krays, and the autonomous republics uncovered 65 in which a man ran against a woman. The man received more votes in 54 of them.

31. For the Gidaspov nomination meeting, see *Leningradskaya pravda*, Feb. 4, 1989, p. 1.

welcome in the United States and be repudiated as individuals, and the same obviously happens in the Soviet Union. Certainly the Leningrad party establishment richly deserved to be defeated. It had long been dominated by engineers from the city's heavy and defense industries. It had long been culturally conservative in a city that prided itself on being the old "window on the West," and it had focused on industrial growth at the expense of nontechnical values (Ruble, 1989). Moreover, by building a dam on the Neva that was widely considered to be an ecological disaster in order to control periodic flooding of the city, the party leaders gave their critics a very powerful symbol of party insensitivity, even on issues not of central importance to it. Finally, the organ of the *obkom*, *Leningradskaya pravda*, was outrageously biased in the preferential treatment it gave favored candidates—a decision that backfired.

The defeats of some of the party leaders may also be attributable to tactical mistakes in the elections. The Leningrad first secretary ran in a central city district on the Neva River (it was, in fact, called the Neva district), while the first secretaries of Altay and Krasnodar ran unopposed in rural areas. The first secretary of the Komi *obkom* had gained local support by calling for the resignation of Andrey Gromyko and several other national leaders on television at the 19th Party Conference (and by denouncing Moscow for using Komi as a dumping ground for exiled convicts); he managed to run against a deputy chairman of the executive committee of the city soviet, and he won handily. By contrast, the first secretary of the Khabarovsk *kraykom*—a former head of the transportation department of the Central Committee—ran in a rural district against a 39-year-old state-farm director who sharply denounced the agricultural bureaucracy and called for more independence for the farms, but cagily said little about leasing.[32] The first secretary lost by a wide margin. Certainly many party officials in Moscow and Leningrad were lamenting their lack of experience in electoral politics. As they learn to choose safer districts for top party officials, as they learn to stack nominating meetings more carefully and to use the other techniques of successful machine politicians, they may have higher success rates.

Another factor leading to the defeat of party officials was the changing nature of the legislature itself. As long as the Supreme Soviet met for four or five days a year and voted unanimously on bills, it made sense to have symbolic representation: a certain quota of workers, peasants, factory managers, military officers, party secretaries, and so forth. The situation becomes very different as the legislature becomes a more meaningful body. Of course, policy views become relevant, but so do the characteristics of the deputies. A poorly educated peasant is not likely to be an effective representative for his district; a person with a college education and some verbal skills is likely to be superior. Anecdotal evidence indicates that people were, indeed, making such a calculation,

---

32. For the platform of this director (Yu. M. Chichik), see *Tikhookeanskaya zvezda*, March 12, 1989, p. 2.

Table 1. *Results of March 1989 Elections in the RSFSR, by Occupation*

Position of candidate	"Won"[a]	"Lost"[a]
High party, state, and military officials and top factory directors[b]	8	28
Middle-level party, state, and military officials and factory directors[b]	29	26
Chairmen of collective farms or directors of state farms	19	13
Persons in education, science, medicine, the law, or the media[c]	61	24
Officials and specialists at industrial enterprises[d]	33	22
Officials and specialists at farms	21	21
Brigade leaders and foremen in industry[d]	28	24
Industrial workers[d]	23	50
Peasants	10	22

Sources: These figures are based on all two-candidate elections, including the runoffs, in Moscow, Moscow Oblast, Leningrad Oblast, all six krays, and all 16 autonomous republics. The newspapers were read in the Newspaper Room of the Lenin Library, Moscow, and the figures do not include a few contests reported in missing newspapers.

a. "Won" means that the candidate received more votes than his or her opponent, even if both received less than the required 50 percent and hence both "lost."

b. "High" denotes first and second secretaries of party committees and chairmen of soviets at the levels of oblasts, autonomous republics, krays, and cities (but not rayons), commanders of military districts, and directors of plants that seemed among the largest in the city. "Middle-level" means the others.

c. This category includes many of the political radicals, but there was not much variation across the different occupations. For example, 15 of 19 medical doctors and hospital officials won, but they did not seem to be a radical group. Gender was more important. Only nine of 19 women running against men of other categories won, but 52 of 66 men running against candidates of other categories won.

d. "Industry" includes construction and transportation.

and Table 1 shows its impact upon the fate of those with relatively low socio-economic status.

Paradoxically, the same factors that hurt workers and peasants in the elections also operate against important officials. Such men have the education and the connections to be fine representatives, but they simply do not have the time. If the legislature is going to take an active role, then an important official like the director of Likhachev Auto Works (Yel'tsin's opponent) will not be an active legislator unless he announces beforehand (as Yel'tsin did) that he would resign to become a full-time legislator.[33]

The decision to have a Congress of People's Deputies and a smaller full-time Supreme Soviet was partly motivated by a desire to get around this problem, but it does not really solve it. If a district elects a high official who does not intend to give up his post, the district gives up the possibility of being represented in the more important Supreme Soviet. Consider the choice voters faced in the huge Far East District No. 11 for the Council of Nationalities. The commander of the Far East Military District ran against a local social scientist—herself a Nanai by nationality—who was concerned with problems

33. The bias against both high officials and the poorly educated were at work in Ivanovo, where a worker defeated a relatively new *obkom* first secretary. The worker's supporters said he was "more accessible" and that there was "no reason for an *obkom* first secretary to have a deputy's seat." The other side was expressed by the man who said, "I feel that USSR people's deputies should be educated in all respects, juridically, politically, and economically" (FBIS, April 17, 1989, p. 76).

of the peoples of the North. Whatever one's views about the party or the military, the commander would clearly have been too busy to do much of value in the Congress, and he could never be elected to the Supreme Soviet. The scholar (Ye. A. Gayer), on the other hand, could be elected to the Supreme Soviet and have an impact on a question that is poorly handled in the Soviet Union. A person totally loyal to the system should have voted for her unless she had shown anti-party views herself. She was, in fact, elected, and many Westerners wrongly concluded that the defeat of the Far East commander was a repudiation of the regime.[34]

Finally, as we assess the significance of the elections, we cannot ignore the striking fact that the uneven pattern of results happened to correspond very closely with Gorbachev's political interests in the Politburo. We have already seen the lack of popular challenge to the party in Stavropol' and Krasnodar, and, in general, there were very few defeats for party officials associated with Gorbachev. By contrast, four conservatives of the Politburo suffered crushing defeats—Ligachev, Zaykov, and Vladimir Shcherbitskiy among the voting members and Solov'yev among the candidate members. (As will be discussed in the next section, Ryzhkov was humiliated in the Congress of People's Deputies and the Supreme Soviet.)

Ligachev himself was among the 100 candidates nominated for the 100 seats guaranteed the Communist Party. His "electors" were the 417 members and candidate members of the Central Committee and the members of the Auditing Commission of the Central Committee, and 249 other regional and governmental officials who were "members of other elective party organs." He received the most votes against—78.[35] In addition, the *obkom* first secretary in his native Tomsk was defeated, as was his own second secretary in Tomsk, A. G. Mel'nikov, who had become first secretary of the Kemerovo *obkom*. In general, however, Ligachev's political base has been precisely the Urals-Siberian area where party leaders suffered such a defeat. Shcherbitskiy, the first secretary of the Ukraine, was himself elected, but a number of his key subordinates were defeated. The defeats of the leadership in Kiev, the heavy-industry secretary of the Central Committee, and the first secretary in L'vov (a former Central Committee secretary) were especially painful.

By the time of the March elections, Ligachev and Shcherbitskiy were the oldest members of the Politburo and clearly in political eclipse and moving toward retirement. With Ligachev's decline as a potential successor, Zaykov— the party secretary of Moscow and the Central Committee secretary for defense and the defense industry (the country's real defense minister)—became the

---

34. She actually was a candidate for deputy chairmanship of the Council of Nationalities and spoke out for the rights of peoples of the North (*Izvestiya*, June 10, 1989, p. 3, and June 12, 1989, pp. 3–4).

35. For the election, see *Pravda*, March 16, 1989, p. 1, and for the number of votes, see *Pravda*, March 19, 1989, pp. 1–2. The old lame ducks were still on the Central Committee at this time, and it is, therefore, surprising that the reformers did not fare worse. But surely the other 249 voters were mostly newly appointed (and members of republic and *obkom* bureaus) and were chosen to ensure that Gorbachev would not be too surprised by the results.

most reasonable conservative alternative to Gorbachev. It is not a coincidence that he was the Politburo member who lost the most in the March elections. The smashing victory of Boris Yel'tsin came in the face of Zaykov's obvious efforts to discredit him, and Zaykov, a former first secretary of the Leningrad *obkom*, also had played a key role in selecting many of the officials defeated there.

In addition, we should not forget Zaykov's part in supervising the military and his likely role in trying to defend its budgetary position in the Politburo. In general, high military officials were allowed to run unopposed in elections, and most of them won easy victories, even though they often proudly publicized their fulfillment of their "internationalist" duty in Afghanistan.[36] Yet, the military in the Far East, where Defense Minister Dmitriy Yazov and the chief of the General Staff, Gen. Mikhail Moiseyev, were based, were forced to run in competitive races and lost. The same was true of the commanders associated with Zaykov. The current commander of the Leningrad military district and the Moscow military district had to run against attractive, educated candidates, while the commander of the Leningrad military district at the time Zaykov was first secretary there[37] was given a district in Ivanovo Oblast and had to compete against a dissident lieutenant colonel. Some of the election results may have been a surprise to the leadership, but surely not those involving the various military commanders.

To some extent, the shock produced by the March elections stemmed from a lack of appreciation of some of these factors and reflected the novelty of party defeats in general. Still, fundamentally the alarm was based not so much on what happened in March, as on a sense of foreboding about the future. Revolutions tend to center in the capital and major cities of a country, and it would do the party little good if it controlled a strong majority of the inland provinces but could not keep Moscow and Leningrad from exploding. The alarm about the Kuzbas coal strikes was really about their larger implications: they crystallized the fear that a combination of revolutionary moods among Ural-Siberian workers and among the Moscow and Leningrad intelligentsia would be fatal to the regime, regardless of the sentiment in rural Russia and Central Asia.

In addition, people understood that local elections are imminent and that Gorbachev had talked about combining the posts of regional first secretary and

---

36. For example, the deputy minister of defense who heads the inspector-general service, M. I. Sorokin, played a very major role in Afghanistan from 1981 to 1987, and his biography was frank about his "internationalist duty" in Afghanistan (*Altayskaya pravda*, February 24, 1989, p. 1). L. V. Shustko, the commander of the North Caucasus military district, was reported to have "participated in the rendering of internationalist help to Afghanistan" (*Sotsialisticheskaya Osetiya*, February 18, 1989, p. 1). He won, 35,987 to 5,927. The deputy minister of defense for strategic missiles, Gen. Yuriy Maksimov, had been the commander of the Turkestan military district and won the Hero of the Soviet Union medal for fighting in Afghanistan. He publicly favored increased aid to Afghanistan (*Tuvinskaya pravda*, March 1, 1989, p. 3, and *Krasnoyarskiy rabochiy*, March 14, 1989, p. 1). He won, although I do not know by what margin. A deputy minister of defense and commander of the ground forces, Gen. Valentin Varennikov, who planned the Afghan war, won 14,792 to 1,254 (*Sovetskaya Kalmykiya*, March 29, 1989, p. 1).

37. Gen. Boris Snetkov, commander of Soviet troops in East Germany at election time.

chairman of the soviet. It was easy to imagine the radicals organizing themselves and fielding slates of candidates that would sweep the elections. When party secretaries were defeated in elections to the Congress of People's Deputies, it was an embarrassment, but it did not have profound practical consequences. American governors do not serve simultaneously in the U.S. Congress, and it is an anachronism that regional first secretaries seek such a role in the Soviet Union. But if party secretaries hold the job of chairman of the soviet and are defeated in local elections, then widespread defeats of party officials could turn into a disaster. These are issues to which we will return shortly.

THE CONGRESS OF PEOPLE'S DEPUTIES AND THE SUPREME SOVIET

In many ways the Congress of People's Deputies was more dramatic than the elections themselves. The proceedings were broadcast on live television (and, according to a high Soviet official, resulted in a 20 percent reduction in production because of the widespread public interest).[38] The tone of the Congress discussions went well beyond that which the American public would find normal or even "responsible," and in the Soviet Union it was a real shock.

Thus, with everyone watching—including Armenians and Azeris—Armenian and Azeri delegates denounced each other's positions on Nagorno-Karabakh intemperately and emotionally. The army commander in charge of troops that suppressed a demonstration in Tbilisi on April 9 blamed the local party leaders for the deaths, while the former Georgian first secretary blamed the army. A number of delegates treated the action as a deliberate provocation—presumably aimed at overturning Gorbachev's policy—while others poured scorn on the notion that Moscow was not involved in what happened. Economic and ecological conditions (including those in the coal industry) were described in the darkest terms, and the economist Nikolay Shmelev went so far as to say that "the degree of the exploitation of the labor force in our country is the highest of all the industrial countries" (*Izvestiya*, June 9, 1989, p. 9).

Nevertheless, we need to be extremely cautious about the idea that the Congress, in any significant sense, was out of control. Gorbachev certainly knew that the radicals would take the opportunity to make themselves heard, but he made no effort to limit their access to the microphone—except at the very end when he cut off Andrey Sakharov's microphone because Sakharov had grossly exceeded the time allocation. Sakharov spoke nine different times during the session, and the radicals of the so-called Moscow group so dominated the proceedings that other delegates often complained. Nothing would have been easier than to reduce their role in the name of fairness.

The day-to-day organizational planning of the Congress left much to be

38. FBIS, June 27, 1989, p. 3. Sometimes such statements should be taken skeptically. Soviet industrial production is very cyclical, with pre-deadline rush periods (*shturmovshchina*) followed by periods of time off and repair. The first ten days of June would normally be a slow period.

desired, but the results of the Congress were essentially what Gorbachev wanted. The radicals were defeated on all contested ballots, and Gorbachev and all his key appointments were easily approved.[39] The election of the Supreme Soviet went according to schedule, except for an emotional exchange regarding the two deputies for the Nagorno-Karabakh Autonomous Oblast. Indeed, other than several ill-starred experiments in Moscow and the RSFSR, the number of nominees was the same as the number of seats, and hence the elections were uncontested.[40]

The discussion at the Congress, in fact, made it clear that the Congress' elections to the Supreme Soviet should be noncompetitive, at least on the floor of the Congress. If the Congress were to elect deputies to the Supreme Soviet from a comprehensive list, some regions inevitably would be overrepresented and other regions underrepresented or not represented at all. Inevitably quotas of representatives had to be established for each region. A number of deputies, especially from Moscow, suggested that each area nominate more deputies than allowed by its quota, at least in the Council of the Union, and that the Congress of People's Deputies have a real electoral choice. However, such a system would mean that an area's representatives would be chosen by deputies from other areas, and deputies from the Baltic republics adamantly opposed any such arrangement. The Lithuanians even threatened a walkout on the issue. The debate on the subject was a sophisticated one that touched on the most fundamental questions in the theory of representation,[41] but the arguments of the Baltic deputies were the only realistic ones, especially in a multinational state.

Preventing the Ouster of the Leader

From Gorbachev's perspective, the most significant change was introduced almost without controversy, in part because it was made a question of party discipline. (See the speeches of V. B. Kryzhkov and B. N. Yel'tsin in *Izvestiya*, May 27, 1989, pp. 2 and 4.) Gorbachev had already been elected chairman of the Presidium of the Supreme Soviet in October 1988, but the new constitution changed the post to chairman of the Supreme Soviet. Gorbachev was duly elected the new chairman.

Superficially the change did not seem all that important. Some Soviet in-

39. Actually, the nominee for chairman of the Supreme Court was rejected in the meeting of the party group of the Congress before the Congress began. The nominee, the chairman of the Moscow city court, was rejected on the grounds of being too young and inexperienced (he subsequently became chairman of the RSFSR Supreme Court), but this was an appointment in which Gorbachev had no real stake (*Izvestiya*, June 9, 1989, p. 7).

40. In Moscow, 55 out of the 195 members of the delegation wanted to be elected to the Supreme Soviet, and the Muscovites, instead of making the choice within their own group, left the choice to the Congress. The result was that the Congress delegates, especially those from Central Asia, voted for the conservative candidates, to the great consternation of the radicals who had fought for the choice. In the election of the RSFSR delegation to the Council of Nationalities, Boris Yel'tsin insisted that there be a choice, and 12 persons were nominated for the 11 slots. As will be discussed, he was the one defeated (*Izvestiya*, May 31, 1989, p. 6).

41. These debates were carried in *Izvestiya* (May 27, 1989, pp. 4–5, and May 28, 1989, pp. 1–7).

tellectuals have referred to Gorbachev as "president" in his new role, but this is an attempt to legitimate the future popular election of the chief executive, which is the hallmark of a presidential system rather than an accurate description of the new post.[42] Under both constitutions the chairman was elected by the legislature, but now he is elected by the Congress of People's Deputies rather than the Supreme Soviet. If a majority of the Central Committee voted to remove Gorbachev as general secretary, it surely would also require the deputies to remove him as chairman of the Supreme Soviet, and the Party Rules require the Communist deputies to vote the Central Committee line.

The problem is that in a real political crisis the normal political rules of a country do not prevail. Formerly the chairman of the Presidium of the Supreme Soviet could be removed behind closed doors, but now it must be done in open session by the Congress. Gorbachev has talked about separating the functions of party and state, and he is perfectly capable of declaring that the Central Committee has been seized by antidemocratic (even antiparty) forces and that he has the duty of filling out his term as head of state. He is chairman of the Defense Council in his capacity as Chairman of the Supreme Soviet (*Pravda*, December 3, 1988, p. 2, Art. 121), and he can order the military to "defend the Constitution" against the majority in the Central Committee.

Conservatives in the Central Committee who might think of overthrowing Gorbachev—and it is extremely difficult to imagine a majority in the Central Committee that would want to overthrow Gorbachev in favor of a more radical alternative—must ask themselves two questions. First, would the Congress of People's Deputies, one-fifth to one-third of whose members seem more radical than Gorbachev, vote for a more conservative alternative when no such leader of any standing has emerged in the country?

Second, if the Congress assembled to vote on Gorbachev and began a debate, what would happen in the streets, especially if Gorbachev is calling upon the people to demonstrate for "democracy" and for him? As the military decided whether to support the Central Committee or the chairman of the Defense Council, it would have to ask itself whether it wanted to take on the task of controlling what could add up to millions of people in the streets. The military was painfully reminded in the elections about the lack of popular support for top commanders when they were forced to participate in competitive elections.

This central fact is absolutely crucial for an understanding of the political developments of this spring and summer. Most Americans found them quite unexpected, but we should be cautious about assuming that the leaders, and especially Gorbachev, were all that surprised. Many of the *obkom* secretaries opposed Gorbachev's proposal to combine the posts of regional party leader and chairman of the local soviet; they clearly had a keen sense that they would

---

42. See the speeches of Adamovich and F. M. Burlatskiy in *Izvestiya*, June 9, 1989, p. 6. Not surprisingly, Gorbachev objects to the word "president" (*Pravda*, August 20, 1989, p. 2).

face additional problems and even dangers. Paradoxically, radicals such as Andrey Sakharov and Roal'd Sagdeyev also opposed this change, but for the opposite reason. Not surprisingly, the regional secretaries understood the political system better.

If Gorbachev's major goal was to emancipate himself from Central Committee and Politburo control without making himself dependent on popular elections, he would have engineered precisely the results that occurred. The major conservatives on the Politburo had to be discredited, and a Congress of Deputies had to be produced that was to the left of Gorbachev, but without a thoroughly radical majority. The military had to be frightened out of any thought of staging a coup—or of supporting a conservative coup—with the specter of uncontrollable demonstrations in the streets or coal mines. Gorbachev might have miscalculated his own ability to control the streets or the next elections, but the results were too convenient to him in the short run to have been wholly accidental.

The Chief Conservative

While the election results and the subordination of the chairman of the Supreme Soviet to the Congress of People's Deputies instead of the Supreme Soviet essentially emancipated Gorbachev from the danger of a conservative coup d'état, the actual proceedings of the Congress and the Supreme Soviet discredited the one major Politburo leader who was not touched by the elections—Nikolay Ryzhkov.

When Ligachev and Zaykov were discredited in the election, the man who emerged as the potential conservative counterpoint to Gorbachev was Ryzhkov. In my judgment, Ryzhkov has long been the real leader of the conservative opposition in the Politburo rather than Ligachev, at least on questions of economic reform, and Soviet intellectuals report that his authority grew substantially in 1989 because of the way that he handled the Armenian earthquake crisis. Gorbachev has a history of undercutting any potential rival, and he needed to overcome Ryzhkov's opposition to economic reform.

Hence it hardly is surprising that by mid-July Ryzhkov had a quite different reputation than he had in mid-May. A physician-deputy referred to this fact directly when she returned to her home district in the Karelian Autonomous Republic. Ryzhkov's authority was "unquestioned" after the Armenian earthquake, she said, but it fell sharply under "the cross-fire of questions during the discussion of his candidacy" in the Congress of People's Deputies (*Leninskaya pravda* [Petrozavodsk], June 11, 1989, p. 2).

In large part, the sharp decline in Ryzhkov's position was the result of his own appalling performance in his confirmation hearings. He criticized the Law on the State Enterprise for granting too much independence to the enterprises, and he promised an end to the food problem in two or three years simply by investment in rural infrastructure (*Izvestiya*, June 9, 1989, pp. 2–3).[43] But Gorbachev, who praised Ryzhkov's dedication to *perestroyka* in nominating him, set the stage for sharp questioning by carefully dissociating himself from the government's performance and from the economic reform Ryzhkov was introducing. Gorbachev specifically said that the reform began with the law on the enterprise instead of reform at higher echelons "at the initiative of the Council of Ministers" (*Izvestiya*, June 9, 1989, p. 2). While he cited this as evidence of Ryzhkov's democratic character, informed observers knew that the reform's failure to be extended to the ministries and Gosplan was the reason that all Soviet economists were giving for its failure. In addition, Gorbachev followed his praise of Ryzhkov with the following chilling words:

> Having thus characterized Comrade Ryzhkov, I also want to say that, of course . . . serious errors were made . . . For all of us and for the government above all, this is an occasion for learning serious lessons . . . It seems that it is important now . . . to appoint him chairman of the Council of Ministers and thereby give him the opportunity to develop further the plans that he has, to rectify the omissions, to draw lessons from the past (*ibid.*).

Once Gorbachev had legitimized criticism of Ryzhkov, it was not long in coming. The very first speaker to question Ryzhkov asked, since it was being acknowledged that "the former Council of Ministers made very serious errors," what were they specifically? Some of the deputies were respectful, and others asked neutral questions, but on balance the session features a drumbeat of criticism: on Ryzhkov's attitude to the Baltic republics, on the amalgamation of ministries (which was called a second Gosagroprom,)[44] on "the deafness of the Council of Ministers to suggestions . . . about bureaucratic obstacles introduced into the laws" with respect to economic reform, and on the government's "half-measures" in the wake of the March 1989 Central Committee session on agriculture.[45]

When Ryzhkov proved so conservative on economic reform and so over-optimistic on the food situation, many must have felt what A. Chabanov, a factory director, stated openly: "I have to say that I am depressed by Nikolay Ivanovich's answers to today's questions" (*Izvestiya*, June 9, 1989, p. 4). The General Secretary, however, must have been purring to himself. If "the plans that he [Ryzhkov] has" do not work out, if the food problem

43. Ryzhkov did this, Ligachev later disclosed, while making major cutbacks in agricultural investments (*Pravda*, July 21, 1989, p. 3).
44. Gosagroprom, the State Agroindustrial Committee, was created in 1985 to replace six ministries. The agency, acknowledged as a bureaucratic fiasco, is now being dismantled.
45. The exchanges are published in *Izvestiya*, June 9, 1989, pp. 2–4. For agriculture, see A. K. Miloserdnyy (p. 3) and A. K. Mukametzianov (p. 4); for the similarities of reorganization to Gosagroprom ("which was the most successful action of the CIA against our country"), see Yu. T. Komarov (p. 3); for the Baltics, see K. D. P. Prunshene (p. 4) ("Many deputies from the Baltics are, mildly speaking, astonished by the repeated statements of Comrade Ryzhkov that provoke hostility to us from other republics").

isn't solved in two or three years, it is not difficult to imagine who one of the scapegoats will be. Indeed, the new deputy chairman of the Council of Ministers in charge of economic reform, Leonid Abalkin, suggested publicly that the government should resign in two or three years if the economy has not improved.[46]

A scheduled Gorbachev trip to West Germany had been the perfect guarantee that the radical demand for prolonging the sessions of the Congress of People's Deputies would not be met, and attention shifted to the Supreme Soviet. Ryzhkov's authority deteriorated further when he presented a cabinet to the Supreme Soviet that was treated very roughly.

The proceedings in the Supreme Soviet were less dramatic than in the Congress, but in a sense the Supreme Soviet seemed less controlled. The first order of business was the confirmation of the cabinet—a question on which party discipline is strong in any political system and on which the Communist Party had always been especially jealous of its prerogatives. The ministerial posts still remained within the *nomenklatura* of the Central Committee, and this time too the nominees went through the normal clearances. The Soviet media reported that "to begin with, the Council of Ministers submitted nominations to the Party's Central Committee, where they were examined" (FBIS, July 17, 1989, p. 47). Nevertheless, as Table 2 indicates, 11 of Ryzhkov's nominees to the 70 posts on the Council of Ministers were rejected either in committee or on the floor of the Supreme Soviet—although he subsequently was able to rescue two of them. Other nominees had sizable votes cast against them. (Since a nominee had to receive a majority of the votes cast—indeed, until the rules were changed, a majority of the total 542 deputies—an abstention had the same effect as a "no" vote.)

The performance of the Supreme Soviet in the confirmation process was not impressive. The defense-industry ministers were the group of administrators under Brezhnev most responsible for failing to introduce high-quality, high-technology goods into the civilian economy (their ministries produced the television sets, computers, electronics, and so forth), but they were confirmed without thought or opposition.[47] The mere seven votes against the minister of the coal industry symbolized the total indifference of the deputies to the needs of all workers, and this indignity may have been the last straw for the miners. The votes on the economic managers (particularly the rejection of the chairman of Gosbank and of the State Committee for Prices) were more informed, but elsewhere the pattern of votes shows a virtually exclusive interest in ecological issues, which now are the prime concern of the intelligentsia. (The rejection

46. Moscow Radio domestic service, June 27, 1989, translated in FBIS, June 28, 1989, p. 51. For a fuller presentation, see *Trud*, June 29, 1989, p. 2, translated in FBIS, June 30, 1989, p. 42.

47. Six of the deputy chairmen of the Council of Ministers had this background: I. S. Belousov, V. Kh. Doguzhiyev, Yu. D. Maslyukov, L. D. Ryabev, I. S. Silayev, and L. A. Voronin. The ministers are B. M. Belousov, I. V. Koksanov, V. G. Kolesnikov, V. F. Konovalov, Ye. K. Pervyshin, V. I. Shimko, O. N. Shishkin, and A. S. Systsov. It was said that the votes against Pervyshin were not against him personally, but against the decision to merge the Ministry of Communications with the Ministry of the Communications Media Industry.

Table 2. *The USSR Council of Ministers*

Post	Official	Votes against and abstentions
The Presidium of the Council of Ministers		
Chairman of the Council of Ministers	N. I. Ryzhkov	—
First dep. ch. of the C of M (for general issues)	L. A. Voronin	?
First dep. ch. of the C of M (and chairman of Gosplan [State Planning Committee])	Yu. D. Maslyukov	18
First dep. ch. of the C of M (and ch. of Commission for State Food Supplies & Procurements)[a]	V. V. Nikitin	?
Dep. ch. of the C of M (and ch. of Commission on Economic Reform)	L. I. Abalkin	21
Dep. ch. of the C of M (and ch. of Commission for Military-Industrial Affairs)	I. S. Belousov	14
Dep. ch. of the C of M (and ch. of Bureau for Social Development)	A. P. Biryukova	68 +
Dep. ch. of the C of M (and ch. of State Committee for Emergencies)	V. Kh. Doguzhiyev	4
Dep. ch. of the C of M (and ch. of Bureau for the Chemical-Timber Complex).	V. K. Gusev	35
Dep. ch. of the C of M (and ch. of State Committee for Science and Technology)	N. P.Laverov	9
Dep. ch. of the C of M (and ch. of State Committee for Material and Technical Supply	P. I. Mostovoy	94
Dep. ch. of the C of M (and ch. of Bureau for the Fuel and Energy Complex)	L. D. Ryabev	7
Dep. ch. of the C of M (and ch. of Bureau for the Machinery Industry)	I. S. Silayev	?
Dep. ch. of the C of M (and ch.of State Foreign Economic Relations Commission)[b]	?	
All-Union Ministries		
Automobile and Farm Machinery Industry	N. A. Pugin	9
Aviation Industry	A. S. Systsov	9
Chemical and Petroleum Refining Industry	N. V. Lemayev	54
Civil Aviation	A. N. Volkov	18
Coal Industry	M. I. Shchadov	7
Construction of Petroleum and Gas-Industry Enterprises	V. G. Chirskov	94
Defense	D. T. Yazov	143
Defense Industry[c]	B. M. Belousov	2
Electrical-Equipment Industry and Instrument Making	O. G. Anfimov	9
Electronics Industry	V. G. Kolesnikov	32
Fishing	N. I. Kotlyar	73
Foreign Economic Relations	K. F. Katushev	65
General Machinery Industry (Rockets)	O. N. Shishkin	5
Geology	G. A. Gabrielyants	11

continued

Table 2. *Continued*

Post	Official	Votes against and abstentions
Heavy-Machinery Industry	V. M. Velichko	5
Machine-Tool and Tool-Making Industry[d]	N. A. Panichev	21
Medical Industry	V. A. Bykov	47
Merchant Marine	Yu. M. Vol'mer	7
Metallurgy Industry	S. V. Kolpakov	30
Nuclear Power Generation and the Atomic Energy Industry	V. F. Konovalov	6
Petroleum and Gas Industry[e]	L. I. Filimonov	9
Radio Industry	V. I. Shimko	9
Railroads[f]	N. S. Konarev	133
Shipbuilding Industry	I. V. Koksanov	20
Transport Construction	V. A. Brezhnev	20
Water-Resources Construction[g]	?	

Union-Republic Ministries

Post	Official	Votes against and abstentions
Communications	E. K. Pervyshin	131
Culture[h]	?	
Finance	V. S. Pavlov	54
Foreign Affairs	E. A. Shevardnadze	0
Health	Ye. I. Chazov	39
Installation and Special Construction Work	A. I. Mikhal'chenko	18
Internal Affairs	V. V. Bakatin	35
Justice	V. F. Yakovlev	7
Power and Electrification	Yu. K. Semenov	23
Timber Industry[i]	V. I. Mel'nikov	3
Trade	K. Z. Terekh	21

All-Union State Committees

Post	Official	Votes against and abstentions
Computer Technology and Information Science	B. L. Tolstykh	14
Hydrometeorology	Yu. A. Izrael'	?
Quality Control and Standards	V. V. Sychev	10
Science and Technology[j]	N. P. Laverov	9

Union-Republic State Committees

Post	Official	Votes against and abstentions
Cinematography	A. I. Kamshalov	36
Construction	V. M. Serov	?
Environmental Protection[k]	N. N. Vorontsov	8
Forestry	A. S. Isayev	4
Labor and Social Problems	V. I. Shcherbakov	?
Material and Technical Supply[j]	P. I. Mostovoy	94
Physical Fitness and Sports[l]	N. I. Rusak	35
Planning[j]	Yu. D. Maslyukov	18
Prices[m]	V. K. Senchagov	?
Publishing	N. I. Yefimov	18
Public Education	G. A. Yagodin	102

continued

Table 2. *Continued*

Post	Official	Votes against and abstentions
Safety Supervision in Industry and the Atomic-Power Industry	V. M. Malyshev	6
State Security	V. A. Kryuchkov	32
Statistics	V. N. Kirichenko	?
Television and Radio Broadcasting	M. F. Nenashev	19
Other Officials		
Administrator of Affairs	M. S. Shkabardnya	3
Chairman, Gosbank (State Bank)[n]	V. V. Gerashchenko	7
Chairman, Committee for Light Industry, U.S.S.R. Gosplan	L. Ye. Davletova	31
First deputy chairman, U.S.S.R. Gosplan	V. A Durasov	7

Sources: The list of ministries and state committees was published in *Pravda*, July 6, 1989, p. 1. The information on nominees and votes came largely from FBIS, *Daily Report—Soviet Union* for the period of the confirmation process, but specific footnotes are provided in cases of special interest. The biographies of the members of the government are published in *Pravitel'stvennyy vestnik*, No. 14-15 (July), 1989, pp. 2-24, No. 16 (August) 1989, pp. 2-3, and No. 17 (August) 1989, pp. 2-5.

a. Ryzhkov's first nominee, V. I. Kalashnikov, was defeated at the committee stage (FBIS, June 28, 1989, p. 54).

b. Ryzhkov's nominee, V. M. Kamentsev, received a majority of the votes, but not of the total number of Supreme Soviet deputies, and hence was defeated by the rules then in force (FBIS, June 30, 1989, p. 39). Then, with the rules changed to require only a majority of the votes cast, even more voted against Kamentsev and he was defeated once more. (200 votes were in favor, 172 were opposed, and 47 abstained.) (FBIS, July 7, 1989, p. 68).

c. Originally it was announced that another man, S. P. Chevrov, would be nominated as Minister of the Defense Industry (*Trud*, June 14, 1989; in FBIS, June 21, 1989, p. 51). However, Belousov was the only man who was formally nominated.

d. Ryzhkov originally withdrew Panichev's nomination after unspecified questions arose about him in committee (FBIS, June 28, 1989, p. 40). But he resubmitted Panichev's name to the Supreme Soviet without explanation, and the latter was easily confirmed (FBIS, July 7, 1989, p. 55 and July 21, 1989, p. 86).

e. Ryzhkov's first nominee, G. P. Bogomyakov, was defeated in committee (FBIS, June 27, 1989, p. 37).

f. Ryzhkov's nomination of Konarev was first defeated in the Supreme Soviet with 130 votes in favor, 204 against, and 40 abstentions (FBIS, July 10, 1989, p. 72). Then, allegedly at the demand of the railroad workers and management (and with Yel'tsin's support), Ryzhkov resubmitted Konarev's name and won—although not comfortably (FBIS, August 7, 1989, pp. 49–52).

g. Ryzhkov's nomination of P. A. Polad-zade was rejected in the agricultural committee, with 25 of 30 votes against (FBIS, June 28, 1989, p. 54). Ryzhkov still submitted Polad-zade's name to the full Supreme Soviet, but he lost again with 125 votes in favor, 187 votes against, and 24 absentions (FBIS, July 21, 1989, p. 86).

h. Ryzhkov's nominee, V. G. Zakharov, was defeated at the committee stage, and the issue was (and is) in substantial part whether there should be a ministry (*Sovetskaya kul'tura*, June 24, 1989, and July 11, 1989, p. 3). (FBIS, June 3, 1989, p. 35.)

i. Ryzhkov's first nominee, M. I. Busygin, was defeated in the Supreme Soviet, with 85 votes in favor, 272 votes against, and 43 abstentions (FBIS, July 12, 1989, p. 71). The new nominee, V.I. Mel'nikov, was first secretary of the Komi *obkom*. He created a sensation at the 19th Party Conference by calling for the resignation of two Politburo members, Gromyko and Solomentsev, as well as the editor of *Pravda* and the director of the Institute of the USA and Canada.

j. The chairmen of these committees are also deputy chairmen of the Council of Ministers.

k. Originally Ryzhkov did not nominate a candidate, asserting on the television show, *Vremya*, that four people had turned him down—essentially for lack of courage (FBIS, June 29, 1989, p. 35). N. N. Vorontsev is a scientist who does not belong to the Communist Party—the only non-party member in the cabinet.

l. Ryzhkov's first nominee, M. G. Gramov, was rejected at the committee stage (FBIS, June 23, 1989, pp. 34–35).

m. Ryzhkov's first nominee, L. I. Rozenova, was rejected in committee, with only one vote in favor (FBIS, June 27, 1989, pp. 38–39).

n. Ryzhkov's first nominee, V. G. Gribov, was rejected in committee (FBIS, June 30, 1989, p. 48).

of the first deputy chairman of the Council of Ministers for agriculture resulted from his support for irrigation projects, a central concern of the environmentalists.)[48]

It is not quite clear what the confirmation process of the Supreme Soviet meant in political terms. Ryzhkov obviously was shaken by the experience,

48. For a denunciation of Kalashnikov's continued support for the river diversion projects, see Zalygin (1988, pp. 228–237).

and publicly, at least, he treated the events as a loss of power for the Politburo (*Pravda*, July 21, 1989, p. 3). In principle, this was a reasonable interpretation, for the Politburo had confirmed the nominees, but, in practice, Leonid Abalkin insisted that Ryzhkov was "absolutely free" in choosing his cabinet.[49] Ryzhkov's manifest shock at the "unanticipated surprises" in the Congress and the Supreme Soviet lend credence to Abalkin's assertion.

In the short run, the experience clearly left Ryzhkov both an angry and chastened man. He criticized his Politburo colleagues in an absolutely unprecedented way: "Is it permissible that two members of the Politburo [Ligachev and Nikonov] are concerned with agriculture? I think not." "The inertia of the departments and secretaries of the Central Committee in the most important [ideological] sphere of party activity [Yakovlev and Medvedev] leads—and it is necessary to say this directly—to the fact that a very great de-ideologization of society is occurring." Even Gorbachev should "give more attention to his party obligations. We have to free him from the detailed questions which overwhelm him" (*Pravda*, July 21, 1989, p. 3).

Unfortunately, the growing openness of Soviet society has not reached the point where one can be confident about the exact political meaning of these statements. Ligachev's strong direct attack on the level of military spending and the reduction of money invested in agriculture—almost surely a thrust at Ryzhkov and the men of the military-industrial complex whom Ryzhkov has made his first deputies—suggests that Ligachev is the agricultural secretary whom Ryzhkov considers unnecessary. But one could imagine that Ryzhkov simply wants Ligachev back in charge of ideology. Similarly, it is not clear whether Ryzhkov meant the details "overwhelming" Gorbachev flow from his actual chairing of Congress and Supreme Soviet sessions (surely a point that anyone can agree with) or from his interference in the work of Ryzhkov's Council of Ministers.

The same is true of Ryzhkov's most despairing statement: "Consciously or unconsciously the appearance is continuing to be preserved that nothing special has occurred, that the basic levers remain in our hands as before and that with their help, with the same old methods, we can still control the complicated processes that are developing in our country. But this is being done at a time when influence, power, and the possibility of influencing everything that is occurring in society is being lost." Clearly Ryzhkov thinks—indeed, he says directly—that the Politburo is losing control, but it was not always clear to what degree he meant the party's loss of control of society or the Politburo's loss of control over Gorbachev.

It seems to me that control of Gorbachev is what Ryzhkov primarily should be worrying about. Ironically, Ryzhkov—like Aleksey Kosygin and Nikolay Tikhonov before him—actually had the public persona of a chief of state above the fray, while Gorbachev had the public persona of a combative, deeply

49. Moscow Radio World Service in English, June 29, 1989, in FBIS, June 30, 1989, p. 43.

involved prime minister. But behind the scenes Ryzhkov had a powerful role in industrial reform. In a real sense, he—not Ligachev—was the leader of the opposition. Now he has a choice of concentrating on "chief of state" situations such as the Armenian earthquake, where he distinguished himself, or getting into the pits of the Supreme Soviet, where he did not and where he has to fight Gorbachev. With the appointment of Leonid Abalkin as the man in charge of economic reform, Ryzhkov has the choice of deferring to Abalkin or being savaged in the Supreme Soviet at Gorbachev's will.

After all the complaints, Ryzhkov spoke as if he understood the situation and was making the correct decision:

> Hearing all that was said about me, I caught myself thinking that in some cases I was insufficiently self-critical. . . . In this month and a half that I had to stand face to face with the people's deputies, I fully realized that this is a process of rectification. From all this I will draw fundamental conclusions about the essential improvement of the government's work and of my own work. It is difficult, of course, but in many respects I have to re-examine my views and approaches to what was done and what needs to be done. I agree that so long as we do not solve the basic economic problems, this will be reflected in the general political situation in the country. And I think that the new government which will be formed has to draw very, very serious conclusions.

A THREAT FROM THE LEFT?

But even if Gorbachev has made a conservative coup d'état virtually inconceivable in the foreseeable future, has he unwittingly unleashed forces on the left that will bring him down? Will several more years of predictable economic difficulties and political turmoil strengthen dissatisfaction to the point where it will do away with party control altogether, including that of Gorbachev?

The question cannot be answered with any certainty. Revolutionary situations have a peculiar character. Regimes often collapse very quickly in the face of dissatisfaction and pressure that seem no stronger than what has been successfully controlled for years. Yet other situations that seem just as "impossible" and "intolerable" can go on for decades. The difference between the two types of cases is frequently not very apparent to the outside observer. Crane Brinton (1938) correctly noted that a critical variable is the will of the elite to fight to preserve the old system. Regimes often fall when too many members of an old elite finally decide that it is not worth fighting and give up.

The Soviet Union is more vulnerable on this point than is generally appreciated. All the talk about the privileges of the bureaucracy and the apparatus has been fundamentally inaccurate. Soviet administrative salaries are very low in comparative terms, and living conditions are poor. The first secretary of the

Minsk *gorkom* lives in a two-bedroom apartment with his wife, married daughter, and her husband, while the top construction official in Leningrad lives in a one-bedroom apartment with his wife. Officials of such organizational-administrative ability would do much better in a Western European system, and they now know it. In the past, officials received moral and psychological compensation for their economic deprivation; but if they lose it under *glasnost'* and democratization and they are left with naked economic self-interest, the Soviet populist proponents of egalitarianism may be surprised by the support they gain and their impact on income distribution.

Despite this factor, it seems to me that Gorbachev's confidence is justified. Nine months ago the testimony of the Soviet intelligentsia about conservative obstacles to change was still widely accepted. This talk grossly underestimated the drive of a highly educated population (60 percent of Russian adults have a high-school diploma or better) for a more liberal and open society, but it was based on a correct perception of some aspects of reality. We should not suddenly swing to the other extreme in our analysis before exploring the character of those aspects.

For one thing, we must keep the results of the March elections, the manifestations of Estonian anger, and coal-miner strikes in perspective. They do not prove any sudden loss of faith in the party. There has always been considerable alienation among the Soviet population—even among people who ultimately supported the system. (The ambivalence that a George Wallace showed in flying the Confederate flag above the American flag above the Alabama State House, but asserting that those who burn the American flag should be run over, can be found in other countries as well, including the Soviet Union.) The fact that this alienation can now be expressed is not proof that it has increased.

Nor is it proof that it cannot be controlled. Some of the analysis of the Soviet Union in the U.S. media can arguably be described as hysterical and even irrational. Some commentators say that it is evidence of a failure of economic reform if things stay the same, if rationing is introduced, or if there is inflation. There are no other alternatives. Eastern Europe is said to be in crisis whether it is suppressed (and therefore seething) or whether Gorbachev calmly lets Poland go. And, of course, Gorbachev has lost control whether there are popular strikes and Supreme Soviet independence or whether he is forced to abandon his democratization program and use the army.

Assessing Gorbachev

A most remarkable thing has happened in the treatment of Gorbachev. In the past only left-wing fellow-travelers called Soviet dictators democrats, but now even American conservatives confuse Gorbachev with Lech Walesa and write about his "attempt to transfer power from an unredeemable Communist Party to a revamped hierarchy of popularly elected soviets" (Reddaway, 1989, p. B1). As this article has emphasized, we desperately need a more realistic view of Gorbachev. He is deeply committed to economic reform and integration into the West, and they are surely irreversible—indeed, they will accelerate—regardless of who is General Secretary. Gorbachev is also deeply committed to the types of political reform that accompany economic reform (greater freedom of information and travel). But we must not exaggerate his support for the types of political reform that are closest to the hearts of the radicals.

We should not think that Gorbachev is a weak or even a nice man. Whether or not Andrey Gromyko actually said that Gorbachev had "teeth of steel" while nominating him as General Secretary in March 1985, it is an accurate description.[50] When Chernenko died, Gorbachev had all Soviet newspapers carry the news of his own election as well as his own paragraph and biography on page one while the news of Chernenko's death and Chernenko's obituary were relegated to page two. Gorbachev has shown that kind of ruthlessness a number of times. The speed with which he crushed the Kazakh and Georgian demonstrations and the way in which he controlled the Stavropol' local elections leave little doubt about how he would act if he thought he was in danger in the future.

It has been very useful for Gorbachev to hold elections in which his opponents were humiliated and to hold legislative forums in which a sense of economic crisis is heated up. It has been very useful for him to rechannel the outrage of conservatives into rather meaningless discussions of Stalin, away from the far more important redefinition of property. But just as Stalin turned against the right when it no longer served his purpose, one should not assume that Gorbachev will not turn against the radical intelligentsia, the radical non-Russian nationalists, or against electoral mechanisms if they come to seem counterproductive to him. If this happens, of course, Gorbachev's propagandists will say that "poor" Gorbachev has been defeated by the conservatives, and those with a rosy view of the Soviet leader in the U.S. will, as before, echo that line. We should not be fooled. Anarchy comes from the inability to apply force successfully, not from its successful application.

One may, of course, assume along with Nikolay Ryzhkov that only the appearance of the old levers of control is being maintained and that Gorbachev only thinks that he still has teeth of steel. In the short and medium run at least, this is a doubtful proposition. When Nina Andreyeva's conservative letter was published in *Sovetskaya Rossiya* in 1988, the most striking fact was the terrorizing effect it had on the Soviet intelligentsia. The most startling aspect about the 1989 elections was how well the party leaders fared in Kazakhstan, which had presumably resented the appointment of a Russian first secretary.

---

50. Dusko Doder reported the use of this phrase, but it did not appear in the published version of Gromyko's nominating speech. In this case it is quite possible that the published version was edited (*Washington Post*, March 7, 1985, p. 1). Gromyko's speech is in *Kommunist* (no. 3 [March], 1985, pp. 6–7).

At a minimum, it is going to take some time before the population is convinced that the levers of power have disintegrated.

In addition, we should not forget the nearly universal assumption of the recent past that the Russian people were too conservative to accept reform. On one level this view represented a real misreading of Russian public opinion, but it was not made out of whole cloth. On the question of real democracy, of a multiparty system, the Russians—including many well-educated and liberal ones—remain quite conservative. They have long sensed what Ligachev put bluntly into words: "A multiparty system would mean the disintegration of the Soviet federation and . . . the Communist Party is the only real political force which unites and consolidates all the peoples of the country" (*Pravda*, July 21, 1989, p. 3). Consequently, they have been extremely suspicious of intellectuals like Andrey Sakharov who want real democracy. Indeed, they have been inclined to treat such people as traitors who have a program that would break up the country and who accept assistance and encouragement from Americans who have this conscious goal.[51] The tenacity of this attitude was clearly evident at the Congress of People's Deputies in the vociferous reaction to Sakharov's criticism of the Soviet Army's role in Afghanistan (*Izvestiya*, June 4, 1989, p. 5).

In short, the electoral behavior and strikes by the Russian people this year makes clear that on balance they are not conservative on the question of reform. But as the Soviet intellectuals have long sensed, the Russians remain quite conservative on the question of a revolution against the Communist Party—or even complete political freedom—that would permit separatism to function freely in the non-Russian parts of the country. Churchill once said that democracy is the worst system of government in the world except for all the rest. A similar sense about one-party rule in the Soviet Union has always been the central glue in the system. As a result of the decades of censorship, many Russians apparently were unaware of the depth of national feeling in the non-Russian areas; Gorbachev, in my view, has deliberately given extremists in small and safe Estonia their heads, has deliberately allowed the safe Armenian-Azerbaijani conflict to work itself out, and has permitted media coverage of these events (not to mention emotional debate in the Congress of People's Deputies about them) so that the Russians vividly understand the centrifugal forces in the country. It seems to me that Boris Yel'stin had the potential to be a real national force if he had moved to become leader of an elected trade-union movement. But now that he has associated himself with people such as Yuriy Afanas'yev, Gavriil Popov, and Sakharov in the Inter-Regional Group and has begun talking about a multiparty system and freedom for the Baltic states, he no longer poses a realistic challenge to Gorbachev.

51. For a discussion of this combination of social pressure for liberalization with the social unwillingness to accept the disintegrating consequences of full democracy, see Hough and Fainsod (1979, pp. 561–570).

GORBACHEV'S CALCULATIONS

We generally have the sense that Gorbachev is extremely skilled in shaping the international environment in ways that are favorable to him both at home and abroad. We marvel at how the General Secretary turns an apparently difficult domestic situation to his advantage. But we never give Gorbachev credit for creating a domestic situation favorable to himself, for creating the political opposition he takes advantage of, or even for putting a spin on a story in order to generate popular support or undercut opposition. If the purveyors of conventional wisdom in the United States are surprised by an event in the Soviet Union—as has usually been the case of late—they assume that Gorbachev is also surprised and, of course, that these unexpected events also jeopardize his position.

Not even a mediocre politician could be as politically naive as the Gorbachev of our imagination. It is even less likely that a politician of such naivete could have had the skills to have risen in Brezhnev's Politburo while planning radical reform and to have outmaneuvered his rivals in consolidating power. Unfortunately, the American conventional wisdom derives from the rumors and analysis circulating among the radical Moscow intelligentsia. Extreme radicals in the United States—people like Angela Davis—have very little sense of the tactical political considerations of U.S. Establishment politicians, and their counterparts in the Soviet Union are no more incisive. Indeed, the situation is even more muddled in the Soviet Union, since the intelligentsia is one of the groups whose views Gorbachev is most eager to manipulate.

The precise nature of Gorbachev's calculations is, of course, difficult to determine. At times, to be sure, Gorbachev has been surprised by events. At other times he has acted like any politician who tries to create a situation in which he can take advantage of any course of events that ensues. Still, Gorbachev could not have lacked a political strategy or an understanding of the forces he was unleashing and the nature of public opinion. Besides secret public-opinion polls, he has at his disposal the reports of the KGB, the flow of information and letters into the Central Committee, and the warnings of all the regional party secretaries and ministers.

Any political system has its own behavioral norms. An American President rarely fires a subordinate without preparing the groundwork through leaks, and even when the official departs, the president expresses his regret but seldom discusses his feelings honestly in public. A Soviet General Secretary does not have the legal authority of a U.S. president, and the norms of collective leadership demand a more careful "preparation" of a major policy or personnel change. Even Stalin behaved this way as he set the stage for the Great Purge of 1937–1938 and the Cold War.

Historically, it has taken each General Secretary four or five years before he is willing to make his great personal power fairly obvious—longer than it has actually taken him to get a hold on the real levers of power. Gorbachev has followed more or less the same pattern. He has been far more ruthless and dramatic in his recent personnel policy than before, but he has been more active in floating rumors—misinformation, really—about his opposition in the Central Committee and Politburo, and the result has been the same.

Gorbachev has been fortunate that the time required before a consolidation of power is acknowledged has been more or less the same needed to set the stage for a serious economic reform. Quite aside from any Politburo opposition, effective economic reform is technically very difficult, and no one knows for certain exactly what the most effective measures are. In addition, effective economic reform carried the risk of political demonstrations and strikes among the population as a whole.

The technical requirements of the various reforms are best served by one or two years of incomplete reform that basically can be used as an experiment. The political requirements of reform include a fundamental modification of ideology that cannot be introduced suddenly by fiat because it is not being aimed just at the ideologists, but at deep-seated popular attitudes as well. Especially if Leonid Abalkin has been correct that radical agricultural reform must coincide with radical industrial reform because industrial inputs are crucial to the improvement of agriculture, the pace of economic reform in the three years since it began with the 27th Party Congress has been close to ideal.

Let us assume in any case that Gorbachev believes the pace and staging of economic reform have been near optimal. Let us assume that the Politburo has maintained basic consensus on economic reform, with Gorbachev taking what he considers the necessary first steps in reform and letting more conservative members of the Politburo think that these first steps will not be pushed radically forward for some years. But let us also assume that Gorbachev felt that the fourth year of his consolidation of political power was also the time when he intended to push economic reform to a new stage. How should an intelligent General Secretary act, based on that set of assumptions? (Actually one could assume that Gorbachev thought the first steps of economic reform would prove adequate and then concluded in 1987–1988 that he was wrong. The problems he would have to face would be similar.)

Gorbachev's Political Needs

The first political need for a General Secretary who is determined to break the Politburo consensus of previous years would be to create a crisis—a profound crisis. Stalin faced this problem in 1927 and created an entirely artificial war scare to launch his class-enemy theme and brush the so-called opposition aside (Fitzpatrick, 1978). Gorbachev can't generate a war scare since he wants to reduce military spending and integrate the Soviet Union into the world economy. But he needs the perception that there is an economic crisis that must be solved in two or three years if the regime is not to collapse. A continuation of the status quo must be perceived as the most dangerous option of all.

The second political need for a radical General Secretary is an institutional change and an increased involvement by the public that makes the conservatives fear the consequences in the streets if they try to modify the status quo in a counterrevolutionary direction. But that involvement must be controlled so that it does not turn against him in a dangerous way, either. If the glue of the system among the Russians is the fear of the breakup of the country, the General Secretary needs to ensure that nationality policy stirs up the non-Russians enough to remind everyone (including the non-Russians) that excessive democratization could mean civil war—without stirring them up to a boiling point.

The third political need is to set up a situation that inexorably drives economic reform forward. The notion that some commission could set up a neat formula to solve the various price and wage reforms in a quiet manner is simply foolish. The cotton farmers think that cotton prices are too low, while outsiders think that the Central Asians receive too much. Nikolay Shmelev tells Soviet factory workers that they are the most exploited in the world, while the managerial class thinks that the manager-worker wage gap is much too narrow. Many think that the correct exchange rate is the black-market one, yet a realistic currency reform would raise the value of the ruble instead of cutting it. Any attempt to introduce change "rationally" would lead to enormous turmoil and resentment. The only way to do it is "irrationally": to set up "impossible" situations that compel corrective action in the desired direction as the only solution. Revolutions (even economic ones) *are* like omelets, and they require some eggs to be cracked.

If such a strategy is to be followed, the target date for genuinely significant change must be the summer of 1990 so that the 1991–1996 Five-Year Plan can incorporate it.[52] For good measure, the 28th Party Congress should be pushed forward from March 1991 to the fall of 1990 so that any resistance to change in the Central Committee and Politburo can be broken at the Congress— and, if necessary, by the election of a very different Central Committee there.

The fourth political need is to change the character of the lower party secretaries, not because they are resisting him directly, but because their entire managerial career will make it difficult for them not to interfere in economic decision making as things go wrong.

We should not regard Gorbachev as a man who has foreseen and even planned every event of the last six months and the next six months. Part of a policy of directed chaos is the confidence that any likely set of events can be played in a way to turn them to one's own advantage. Nevertheless, a leader with a policy of directed chaos thinks carefully about scenarios and strategy because of the possibility that things will get out of hand. And out of that planning can come some deliberately planned steps.

52. Leonid Abalkin was already emphasizing this point in private in 1988 and then expressed it in an article in the Central Committee journal, *Kommunist*, "Kakim byt' novomu pyatiletnemu planu?", No. 6 (April), 1989, pp. 10–19.

My view of the events of 1989 was well expressed by the Kirghiz party leader, Absamat Masaliyev, in July: "The impression is being created that someone is skillfully directing popular dissatisfaction with the party" (*Pravda*, July 21, 1989, p. 2). Masaliyev did not identify that "someone," but only the general secretary has the power to do so, directly or through others. Similarly, conservatives are very angry about the way in which the Central Committee dealt with Yel'tsin ("They created Yel'tsin"),[53] and Yel'tsin himself seems right when he said, "If Yel'tsin did not exist, Gorbachev would have to invent him."[54]

In particular, the deteriorating shortages and rationing of soap—what Ligachev correctly calls "the height of shame" for "our mighty state" (*Pravda*, July 21, 1989, p. 2)—is extraordinarily difficult to explain other than in deliberate terms. The problem—like the shortages of tea and coffee—originated in the decision to economize on foreign currency and reduce the importation of soap and especially some components in soap production. It is easy to imagine that a simple bureaucratic mistake occurred at first, probably a miscalculation about when new Soviet soap or soap-component factories would come on line. But the decision not to spend the trifling amount of foreign currency necessary to correct the problem when it arose, the decision to go ahead with rationing—in which the coupons were not always covered by supply—was a deliberate one. It must have been known that at the time of the first competitive elections this would be perceived as "the height of shame," the symbol of economic chaos in a period when retail turnover was actually rising quite sharply, even corrected for inflation.

In short, it seems to me that Gorbachev wanted to produce a huge volume of complaints at precisely the time the population was to be given an opportunity to act. One purpose was to create the situation about which the Kirghiz leader complained, "Communists and leaders of party committees are afraid of being conservatives." Another purpose was to force the selection of more nontechnocratic party leaders on the model of Eduard Shevardnadze and Gorbachev himself. Still another purpose was to foster an unduly negative public perception of economic performance when Gorbachev became chairman of the Supreme Soviet and the unquestioned leader so that the impending improvement in living conditions would be thought to be even better than it was and Gorbachev would get the credit.

One can, of course, assume that Gorbachev is dealing with an economy that cannot be improved and must conduct reform that is impossible. It is for an economist to judge the consequences of the current investment policies, but the statistics are showing a sharp rise in retail trade. An increase in the money supply, coupled with an inflationary psychology, is contributing to the problem of shortages, but that is a different matter than falling living standards. Individual savings are crucial for an economy that will need to rely more on private investment, and the proper investment opportunities may bring the money

53. Z. I. Khromilina in *Leningradskaya pravda*, April 6, 1989, p. 2.
54. *Corriere Della Sera*, June 16, 1989, cited in FBIS, June 19, 1989, p. 44.

situation very quickly under control—indeed, force an acceleration in the increase of the money supply.

One can also assume that it will take far too long to introduce reform. However, in reading Soviet materials of recent months, I have been struck by the way in which the political base for reform has been created. For example, at a time when economic reformers had given up on price reform as politically impossible, the combination of coal strikes and movement toward economic autonomy for the Baltics actually has Russian workers and the RSFSR leader, Vitaliy Vorotnikov, demanding price reform (*Pravda*, July 21, 1989, and FBIS, August 31, 1989, p. 48).

I have also been struck by conservative complaints about reform that suggest greater movement on reform than suggested by the radicals. The first secretary of the Tadzhikistan Central Committee, for example, stated, ''I think we should reexamine the system of material-technical supply and should return to a strictly centralized distribution of resources for certain sharply deficit goods'' (*Izvestiya*, June 2, 1989, p. 6). There have been a series of such complaints, including from coal miners who said that the strikes did not harm anything because customers were not taking the coal that was piling up and from a range of people talking about the barter system developing among regions and plants. Something seems to be happening with the decline in the proportion of state orders, even if we do not understand it.

Similarly, some of the complaints about the cooperatives have a very different character than the usual ones about prices:

> Huge production buildings and premises crammed with expensive equipment stand idle on account of the absence of workers. It is a pity that hundreds of workers are rushing to the cooperatives in pursuit of huge wages (FBIS, August 15, 1989, p. 64).

> Last year the cooperatives of Moscow took 311 million rubles from the banks of Moscow and deposited only 12. For the five months of this year they already took 976 million and deposited 38. If they don't control their appetite, they will take 4 billion a year in Moscow alone. . . . The monthly wages of all employees of Moscow is 1.1 billion rubles, and . . . the annual city budget is 4.2 billion (*Izvestiya*, June 4, 1989, p. 6).

Conditions are in place for a major breakthrough as the next five-year plan is prepared if Gorbachev is as decisive as he says.

Finally, of course, one can assume that Gorbachev is a political incompetent. One can assume that despite the great skill he showed in rising in the Brezhnev Politburo, that despite all the sources of information at his disposal, he has still totally misjudged public opinion and has unleashed forces that he will be unable to control. One can depict him riding the back of a tiger that is certain or nearly certain to devour him.

In my judgment, Gorbachev is a Cossack firmly mounted on his horse, wreaking havoc on the old boyars who have few defenses. His willingness to show strikes and nationalist demonstrations on television, to let the speakers at the Congress of People's Deputies run wild and to permit competitive elections is the strongest evidence that the Soviet people are nowhere near a revolutionary stage. Gorbachev has been far too cautious in the way he has handled his consolidation of power within the party to have allowed these things if there was the slightest chance that they would get out of control. The evidence from KGB reports, from public-opinion polls, and other information probably confirms what already seems so apparent: the non-Russians are too small and divided to challenge the regime, while the Russians are too committed to the preservation of the nation to carry democracy too far at this stage.

The American problem of understanding the Soviet Union is an enormous one. Our society—including our Sovietologists—has been shocked by events such as the release of Andrey Sakharov and the creation of a Solidarity government in Poland, not to mention coal strikes, that were completely predictable. We have had a strong instinctive tendency to focus on dangers and obstacles because they are quite obvious and require no research or knowledge to discuss. To consider Gorbachev's strategy, his consolidation of power, and the ways in which economic reform might work requires a knowledge of details that are not easy to acquire in the *glasnost'* era of information overload. The only way that we in Sovietology will begin to extricate ourselves from this period of deep *zastoy* (stagnation) is to launch a reorganization of our work. It must ensure that our own labor and that of our graduate students yield a sharp rise in productivity, a *perestrokya* that gives us ways of processing and learning the vast amount of information that is now at our disposal. Otherwise we will continue to serve our society as badly as we have for the last fifteen years.[55]

55. On September 20th, after this article was written, a plenary session of the Central Committee was held. It passed a program on the nationalities and union republics that will set the stage for a major struggle on the degree of economic reform implicit in regional economic autonomy—the extent of the reforms in planning, budgeting, and supplies procurement, as well as in wholesale prices in order to make inter-republican supplies deliveries equitable.

While the ultimate meaning of the decisions must remain unclear, the plenum also made major changes in the Politburo. Viktor M. Chebrikov (Central Committee secretary for security questions), Viktor P. Nikonov (Central Committee secretary for agriculture), and Vladimir V. Shcherbitskiy (Ukrainian first secretary) were removed as full members of the Politburo and Yuriy F. Solov'yev (former Leningrad first secretary) and Nikolay V. Talyzin (former deputy chairman of the council of Ministers) were removed as candidate members.

In their place Vladimir A. Kryuchkov (chairman of the KGB) and Yuriy D. Maslyukov (chairman of Gosplan) were elected full members of the Politburo and Yevgeniy M. Primakov (chairman of the Council of the Union) and Boris K. Pugo (chairman of the Party Control Committee) were elected candidate members. Andrey N. Giriyenko, Yuriy A. Manayenkov, Yegor S. Stroyev, and Gumer M. Usmanov were elected Central Committee secretaries (they had been *obkom* first secretaries in the Crimea, Lipetsk, Orel, and Tataria, respectively).

Those who thought that Gorbachev and even central control were threatened had reason to think the changes were major. For me, these were normal cabinet shifts by a man who before and after dominates his cabinet even more thoroughly than Margaret Thatcher dominates hers. With the plenum decisions promising much greater regional economic autonomy, the personnel changes signalled a determination not to let it get out of control. The chairmen of the KGB and Gosplan are clear signs, but, in addition, Chebrikov, Nikonov, and Shcherbitskiy were all men with extensive experience in non-Russian areas, and Shcherbitskiy is a Ukrainian. Kryuchkov and Maslyukov are Russians who have long worked in the central Moscow apparatus, while Primakov made an extraordinary de facto proposal for Russification in the republican administrative apparatus at the 19th Party Conference. The 11 voting members of the Politburo now include only two non-Russians (the Belorussian Nikolay Slyunkov and the Georgian Eduard Shevardnadze). Those who see anarchy coming from the non-Russians are engaged in wishful thinking about Gorbachev's intentions.

REFERENCES

Brinton, Clarence Crane, *The Anatomy of Revolution* (New York: W. W. Norton, 1938).

Deputaty Verkhovnogo Soveta SSSR, Odinnadtsatyy sozy (Deputies of the Supreme Soviet of the USSR, Eleventh Meeting). Moscow: Izdatel'stvo Izvestiya, 1989.

Fitzpatrick, Sheila, "The Foreign Threat During the First Five-Year Plan," *Soviet Union,* No. 1, 1978.

Freeman, Adair, "Changing Variations in Republican First Secretaries," *Journal of Soviet Nationalities,* No. 1, 1990.

Hough, Jerry F., *"The Soviet Prefects: The Local Party Organs in Industrial Decision-Making.* Cambridge, Mass.: Harvard University Press, 1969.

———, "Changes in Soviet Elite Composition," in Seweryn Bialer and Thane Gustafson, eds., *Russia at the Crossroads.* London: George Allen & Unwin, 1982.

———, *Russia and the West: Gorbachev and the Politics of Reform.* New York: Simon & Schuster, 1988a.

———, "The Politics of the 19th Party Conference," *Soviet Economy,* 4, 2:137–143, April–June 1988b.

Hough, Jerry F., and Fainsod, Merle, *How the Soviet Union Is Governed.* Cambridge, Mass.: Harvard University Press, 1979.

Mann, Dawn, *"Elections in the Congress of People's Deputies Nearly Over,"* Radio Liberty. Report on the USSR,* Vol. 1, No. 15 (April 14, 1989), p. 9.

Reddaway, Peter, "Is the Soviet Union on the Road to Anarchy?", *The Washington Post,* Outlook Section, Aug. 20, 1989.

Ruble, Blair A., *Leningrad: Shaping a Soviet City.* Berkeley: University of California Press, 1989.

Teague, Elizabeth, "Gorbachev Outfoxes the Opposition,"in Radio Liberty, *Report on the USSR,* 1, 9:1–13, May 12, 1989.

Zalygin, Sergey, "Nastupayem ili otstupayem" (Are We Advancing or Retreating?), in Yuriy N. Afanas'yev, *Inogo ne dano (There Is No Alternative).* Moscow: Progress, 1988.

CHAPTER 12

Labor Unrest and Movements in 1989 and 1990

Peter Rutland

THE YEAR 1990 has been a bewildering one for observers of the Soviet political and economic scene. Amid dramatic changes within the Soviet Union and Eastern Europe, attention has shifted away from a significant phenomenon of 1989—the appearance of mass worker unrest in the USSR. The purpose of this paper is to investigate what lasting changes may have resulted from that unrest. To what extent has an organized labor movement become a force to be reckoned with in Soviet politics? Will the workers' movement advance or delay moves toward a market economy and multiparty democracy?[1]

Most analysts familiar with the new workers' movements see them as one of the few positive developments in an otherwise bleak period for the Soviet system. The authority of many established political and economic agencies has been eroding rapidly, but the new groups and institutions which have emerged in their wake are weak and divided. The miners' movement seems to be one of the few anti-entropic forces to have emerged from the debris of the old, collapsing system. Sympathizers of that miners' movement argue that it has the potential to form the core of a new, pluralist, and market-oriented political system.

Time will tell whether optimism proves to have been warranted. The main argument of this paper, however, is that it would be premature to see the miners' movement as the harbinger of a new civil society in the USSR. The worker unrest of 1989–1990 has been a complex and contradictory phenomenon. It is being pulled in a number of directions, and is compatible with a wide range of possible Soviet futures. The replacement of Vadim V. Bakatin by Boris K. Pugo and Boris V. Gromov, followed by the resignation of Eduard Shevardnadze in December

First published in *Soviet Economy*, 1990, 6, 4, pp. 345–384. The author gratefully acknowledges the Sociology Exchange of the International Research and Exchanges Board (IREX) for supporting research in Moscow during June-August 1990 on which this paper is based. He is also grateful for the interviews granted him by many specialists and activists (some cited below), for the helpful comments on earlier drafts by George Breslauer, Bruce Cumings, Brendan Kiernan, and Jim McGuire, and for assistance in Moscow by Alison Mitchell and Irene Stevenson.
    1. A move much slowed down and possibly derailed by the events of December 1990.

287

1990, make it somewhat difficult to believe that a new society is emerging from the debris of the old regime. And some evidence reviewed by this author in the USSR earlier in the summer tends to indicate that the mobilization of the miners was merely yet another symptom of the collapse of the old economic system. As such, its ultimate character as a positive force remains unformed.

The worker unrest of 1989 had several distinctive features, which illustrate the extent to which it was a product of the old system. *First*, one is struck by the plethora of demands, ranging from constitutional changes to minor aspects of wage policy, which miners advanced within hours of going on strike. All the grievances and discontent which had been suppressed for decades rapidly surfaced. This added to the powerful, explosive impact of the strikes, but was not conducive to the emergence of a strong, institutionalized workers' movement.

A *second* noteworthy feature has been the extreme fragmentation of the movement—both over the tactics to be followed, and over the general goals to be pursued. The strikers found themselves in a contradictory position: one day calling for the removal of local and national leaders, the next day signing agreements with them. Perhaps any nascent workers' movement would be plagued by such confusion and compromises, but the contradictions faced by Soviet miners trying to define a role for themselves in the midst of a disintegrating economy and political system have been particularly acute in comparison with other countries.

This paper begins with an overview of Soviet industrial relations before 1985 and examines the analytical categories used by Western writers to explain Soviet worker behavior. It then provides case studies of the 1989 strikes in the three most politically significant coal basins—Vorkuta (Pechora Basin), the Kuzbas (Kuznetsk Basin), and the Donbas (Donets Basin). The differences in economic interests and political outlook between these three regions are considerable, suggesting a need for caution when generalizing about the workers' movement in the USSR.

The paper then explores national and regional efforts to institutionalize the miners' movement in the wake of the strikes, as well as efforts by the central authorities to contain the phenomenon by incorporating the nascent workers' movement. The paper subsequently offers several reflections on the way the miners' strikes relate to our understanding of the political and economic dynamics of the USSR. The conclusion presents four alternative scenarios for the future development of the workers' movement.

SOVIET INDUSTRIAL RELATIONS BEFORE *PERESTROYKA*

In the past, workers in the USSR had been effectively deprived of opportunities to make their presence felt as independent political actors. The CPSU, with its network of cells in every workplace, asserted a monopoly over the representation of workers' political interests, while the official trade unions (one for each industry) claimed to defend their social and economic interests.

In practice, the workers were indifferent to or alienated from these structures, seeing them as integral parts of the ruling party-state apparatus.

By and large, the trade unions (*profsoyuzy*) functioned as a branch of management, in that their primary duty was to help ensure plan fulfillment. They participated alongside management in deciding and implementing policy with regard to hiring, promotion, wages, work norms, and the like. They also served as a combined welfare agency and personnel department, supervising the allocation of social benefits such as housing, daycare, holidays, and pensions.[2] The *profsoyuzy* came closest to serving as a defender of worker interests in their role in enforcing legislation protecting workers from unfair dismissal. This was one of the few areas where Soviet legislation served to protect individuals against the state.

Soviet workers enjoyed impressive formal rights to participate in management, particularly through the elective work collective councils, introduced in 1983. In reality, such participatory channels were dominated by plant management. Since 1987, many workforces were permitted to elect their director in competitive elections, and this did lead to a shift in power within some plants. In June 1990, however, amendments to the Law on the State Enterprise curtailed this right, presumably because workers had started to exercise it, and were selecting compliant managers.

Independent protest actions by workers prior to 1985 were confined to occasional short stoppages at the workplace, about which little is known (Pravda, 1979). On some two dozen occasions in the past thirty years these stoppages lasted several days, sometimes engulfing entire towns. The authorities responded with a mixture of carrots and sticks, promptly dispatching scarce food supplies to the region and sending top leaders to conciliate strikers' demands, yet also often deploying the riot police and arresting ringleaders after the strike was over.[3] However, mass labor unrest of the kind which repeatedly surfaced in Poland was absent from the Soviet scene.

Western scholars differed in their assessment of this state of affairs. Some interpreted the workers' passivity as a sign that they accepted the legitimacy of the Soviet state in return for a guaranteed job and minimum living standard. Thus Lane (1978) writes of the Soviet worker as "incorporated," while Hauslohner (1987) argues that an implicit "social contract" was forged during the Brezhnev era.

Even among those who did not perceive the existence of a social contract between the workers and the Soviet state, there was a widespread view that the absence of a highly competitive labor market gave Soviet workers more control over the labor process than their Western counterparts enjoyed. The

2. A comprehensive treatment of the subject is provided in Ruble (1981).

3. The most turbulent strike was the one which occurred in Novocherkassk in June 1962. According to one of the most recently published accounts, 22 workers died when riot police were sent in (*Komsomol'skaya pravda*, June 2, 1989, p. 4). In a rare pronouncement, a KGB colonel referred to the past practice of the KGB being called in by party officials when unrest occurred in a factory "as a matter of putting the workers in their place" (*Tyumenskaya pravda*, March 2, 1990, p. 2).

unusually high rate of capital investment and the absence of a "hard budget constraint" meant that managers had no incentive to resist wage inflation and overstaffing. Thus the peculiarities of the Soviet planning system led to a high degree of collusion between workers and managers, geared toward mutual protection against the demands of the central planners (Andrle, 1976).

Alternatively, some scholars argued that Soviet workers were deeply alienated from the nation's political leadership and from local managers, and were in all respects in a worse position than their Western counterparts (Godson, 1981). According to this school, only fear of repression prevented them from expressing this discontent.

Given the limited data at our disposal, it is difficult to test these alternative hypotheses about workers' attitudes and about the relationship between attitudes and behavior. In any event, in 1987 the situation of worker passivity began to change. There were reports of brief work stoppages, mostly in response to pay cuts caused by changes in work rules. In January 1987, a new system of centrally managed quality control (*Gospriyomka*) was introduced, which led to a wave of unrest and, subsequently, the quiet abandonment of this reform. By and large, however, the workers remained passive observers of the *perestroyka* process between 1985 and 1988. A few halting efforts to create independent unions never involved more than several hundred persons.

A significant change took place in 1988, with the appearance of mass strikes as a weapon in ethnic disputes in the Caucasus and the Baltic republics. Depending on how one defines a strike, there were anywhere from 200 to 2,000 strikes in 1988–1989 (Redlikh, 1990). The bulk of the seven million work days lost through strikes in 1989 are traceable to these ethnic conflicts (Teague and Hanson, 1990, pp. 1–2). The summer of 1989 witnessed a wave of coal miners' strikes in Russia and Ukraine which were not related to ethnic disputes but to political mobilization of sections of the Soviet working class—for the first time since the 1920s.

The miners' strikes caught the Soviet leadership, and many Western observers, by surprise. They did not, however, come as a surprise to the workers and managers of the coal industry, who for months had felt the tremors of the impending earthquake.

If one explains earlier worker passivity as the product of satisfaction with a social contract, one would explain the strikes by arguing that workers took the deterioration in living standards since 1980 to mean that the regime had reneged on the "agreement." Or one could argue that workers perceived Gorbachev to be abandoning the contract by stating his intention to introduce a market economy, with its attendant specters of unemployment, inflation, and growing inequality.

Alternatively, analysts who treated earlier passivity as a product of fear could argue that the toleration of informal political groups after 1987 meant that workers no longer feared repression. Thus they felt free to voice the discontent which they had harbored for decades.

These rival approaches are formulated in such general terms that the behavioral evidence of the past two years is compatible with either interpretation, while the attitudinal evidence required to settle the issue is unavailable. Yet the situation has changed so radically with the advent of mass worker unrest that there is little to be gained from remaining within the confines of the old analytical categories. Instead, the workers' movements will be viewed in this paper as a new phenomenon, calling for a new framework of analysis. Not only is the situation novel, it is still very much in flux, and has not yet reached a stable outcome.

BACKGROUND OF THE COAL MINERS' STRIKES

The miners' strikes came as a surprise to the Soviet public and to the country's political leadership, since the coal industry had always been regarded as a favorite of the central planners. This privileged status originated in the coal industry's pivotal role in the creation of the socialist economy in the 1930s. Alexey Stakhanov, after all, was a miner. Hence it was widely assumed, by leaders and masses alike, that miners enjoyed high wages and privileged access to industrial supplies and consumer goods. The 1989 strikes shattered these illusions, and the preceding fifty years' manipulation of the miners as a symbol of proletarian purity backfired on the political leadership.

Some 2.2 million people work in the Soviet coal industry, providing 19.7 percent of the country's energy (*Narkhoz 1989*, 1990, p. 377). In order to trace the events of 1989, attention is focused on the three coal basins where labor activism was intense, and about which information is available: Vorkuta, Donbas, and Kuzbas. In terms of miners engaged directly in underground work, 150,000 are employed in Kuzbas, 300,000 in Donbas, and 23,000 in Vorkuta. In 1988, out of a USSR total of 772 million metric tons, Donbas produced 200, Kuzbas 159, and Vorkuta 32 million tons (*Soviet Geography*, 1990, No. 4, p. 298).

Miners the world over share certain common features, which often place them at the forefront of labor struggles. The harshness of their profession and the fact that they work in close proximity to each other tend to promote a strong sense of group solidarity. This is reinforced by the fact that miners usually live together in towns located over the coal deposits, often in isolation from other population centers. They also represent a strategic resource: disruption in supplies can rapidly pose hazards such as potential power shortages, damage to furnaces, and the like. Moreover, the spatial character of mining, concentrated at a few specific locations, makes it particularly vulnerable to problems of long-term economic decline, as pits become exhausted and unprofitable and miners come under pressure to move elsewhere. There are few other industrial sectors which share this combination of circumstances.

In addition to geographic features, Soviet mining has certain aspects which make it even more distinctive than its Western counterparts. Apart from the prominent political image mentioned above, it is unusual in comparison with other countries in attracting a high proportion of well-educated workers. The high wages available to miners have led many specialists with middle and even higher educations to abandon the profession for which they were trained and to work instead in the mines. These trained personnel ("ITRs," or "engineering technical workers" in Soviet parlance), account for about 15 percent of all Soviet miners. Many strike leaders were to emerge from the ranks of these proletarian engineers, who seem to have been a major factor in the radicalization of the workforce.[4]

Thus it is not too surprising that miners were the first working group in the USSR to challenge the state. The fact that miners took the lead may also help explain why these strikes were restrained and highly disciplined affairs, far from the urban jacqueries which many had feared would result when Russian workers took to the streets.

While the miners shared many common grievances, there were also certain unique features which shaped the course of the movement in the three regions under study. The links between the regions in the course of the strikes were rather tenuous. Unlike Poland's Solidarity in 1980, there was no network of truckers ferrying messages between the regional centers. What linked the Soviet strikers was an interregional demonstration effect—the knowledge that miners elsewhere had struck and were wringing concessions from the government.

Certain characteristics of the three regions also influenced the course of their strike movements. Thus brief sketches of the regions are presented before a description of the events of July 1989.

Kuzbas. The Kuznetsk Basin of West Siberia has rich, relatively accessible deposits (about one-quarter are mined open-cast). High productivity and the Siberian regional wage bonus of 25 percent yielded relatively high wages of 500–600 rubles per month, double the 1989 USSR average industrial wage of 240 rubles.

Even in Kuzbas, however, the economic situation in the mines had deteriorated in comparison with the preceding decade. Output per man fell by 40 percent during 1975–1985, because of poor management and chronic underinvestment. In the Soviet coal industry as a whole, output per man fell by almost 50 percent during that period (Federov, 1989, p. 80). Average labor productivity in Soviet pits is very low, U.S. and German pits being 700 percent more productive (*Krasnoye znamya,*[5] October 21, 1989, p. 1). The wage system is highly bureaucratized and still closely tied to plan targets. This means that a 10 percent shortfall in plan fulfillment causes forfeiture of bonuses and can

---

4. A point stressed by Leonid Gordon of the International Workers' Institute, USSR Academy of Sciences, Moscow (interview, August 6, 1990). This group, present in all regions, was particularly visible in Kuzbas.

5. Four regional (oblast) daily newspapers were consulted for this study: *Krasnoye znamya* (from the Komi ASSR, where Vorkuta is located); *Sotsialisticheskiy Donbass* (Donetsk); *Kuzbass* (Kemerovo); and *Tyumenskaya pravda* (Tyumen'). Unofficial newspapers consulted by the author include *Nasha gazeta* (published by the Kuzbas Council of Workers' Committees); *Kuzbasskiye vedomosti* (Novokuznetsk); and *Press-byulleten'* (Novosibirsk). Additional information was culled from the *Reuters* and *Tass* wires.

lead to a 50 percent drop in pay (*Trud*, June 14, 1989, p. 2). Thus, miners directly felt the impact of declining productivity.

Despite the relatively high wages, living conditions in Kuzbas are extremely primitive. One-quarter of the miners live in barracks. The strikers painted a sign at the entrance to Novokuznetsk reading "Welcome to the Stone Age." On a visit in the spring of 1989, Prime Minister Nikolay Ryzhkov is reported to have said that "he never saw a worse town" (Makashova, 1989, p. 65).

Siberia depends on food and consumer goods imported from other regions. In 1987, a decentralization of the supply system meant that regional authorities were suddenly responsible for persuading distant provinces to meet their delivery contracts. This led to a sharp deterioration in the availability of meat, vegetables, and consumer goods in Kuzbas. An additional shock was the national soap shortage, caused by production problems and consumer hoarding. The miners had already been straining under a 1923 norm which allocated individuals only 400 grams of soap per month. The disappearance of soap from the shops was, therefore, a catalyst for taking action. Thus the miners marched downtown, determined to show local party leaders their blackened faces.

Donbas. The Donets Basin is the old, traditional mining area of East Ukraine. Its plight was documented in a series of articles in 1988 in the national newspaper *Sotsialisticheskaya industriya*.[6]

Donbas mines are old and near exhaustion, marked by deep shafts (in excess of one kilometer), high temperatures, narrow seams (less than one meter, on average), high accident rates, and low pay (220–250 rubles per month). Accidents in Soviet mines are some twenty times more frequent than in the West. Ten thousand miners died in accidents during 1980–1988, and 670 in the first six months of 1989 (*Kuzbass*, July 13, 1989, p. 2). The death rate per 1,000 miners fell from 0.45 a year in 1980 to 0.27 in 1989, but this still represents one death for every 1.15 millions tons of coal mined (*Na gora*, April 1990, p. 7).

A report of the USSR Academy of Sciences in the late 1970s declared Donbas to be economically infeasible in the long run; as a result it has been starved of investment. Two-thirds of the mines have not undergone reconstruction for 20 years, and 50 percent of underground work is by hand. Decisions taken in 1988 further undermined living conditions and increased the insecurity of miners. For example, the USSR Coal Ministry's housing plan for Donbas was cut by 20 percent because of a brick shortage. Also, the new emphasis on cost accounting in the economy put additional pressure on uneconomical mines. A major reorganization in 1988 abolished the Ukrainian republic coal ministry and decentralized decision making to individual mines. This was widely perceived as laying the groundwork for mine closures, and a letter was sent by mine directors and local party leaders warning that the workers were disturbed by these developments. In the light of these trends and developments, an article

6. The series appeared from July 29 to August 3, 1988 under the title "Zhizn' shaktyora" (Life of a Miner); see also Marples (1990).

in a local newspaper on the eve of the strikes asked "Is It the End of Donbas?" (*Sotsialisticheskiy Donbass*, July 7, 1989, p. 3).

Vorkuta. The Vorkuta and Inta mines of the Pechora Basin are located north of the Arctic Circle in the Komi Autonomous Republic. Living conditions for some 23,000 miners are poor and the climate severe, with snow nine months of the year. Wages, however, are high: 800–1,000 rubles per month. Most workers apparently intend to stay for 10–15 years and then move south. In 1989 food supplies significantly deteriorated, with rationing introduced for tea and alcohol on July 1. Items such as meat and butter had been rationed for several years.

The combination of geographic isolation (there are simply no automobile roads into the area) and Vorkuta's past history as a gulag zone meant that local elites were used to ruling in an authoritarian manner, independent of Moscow. A survey of the strikers in November 1989 showed that 38 percent expected activists to be persecuted once the strike was over (Levinson, 1990). Few such fears were voiced in other regions during the July strikes.

Worker-manager relations seem to have been poor throughout the Soviet mining industry, but particularly tense in Vorkuta. In 1988 the coal trust director reneged on promises to award automobiles to workers in return for dangerous emergency repair work (*Krasnoye znamya*, February 10, 1990, p. 2). When another shipload of automobiles arrived in April 1989, the new trust director again reneged on the deal, claiming not to be bound by agreements signed by his predecessor. In March 1989, workers at the Severnaya mine had tried to set up a "Solidarity" organization and voted to dismiss the mine director. Thus, the signs of unrest were clearly visible in Vorkuta well before the strike wave began.

THE EVENTS OF JULY 1989

The Strike Wave's Beginnings in Kuzbas

The strike wave began with a refusal to work by 90 miners on July 10 in the Shevyakov pit in Mezhdurechensk, Kuzbas. Their initial 20 demands were modest and mostly internal to the enterprise: 800 grams of soap per month; a water machine; more salads in the canteen; three-year maternity leave for women; and a ban on party meetings during working hours. They also demanded a 60 percent regional Siberian wage bonus (*Kuzbass*, July 12, 1989, p. 1; Apenchenko, 1989; Makashova, 1990).

The strike was not a surprise to local officials. Even the head of the official miners union, Mikhail Srebnyy, conceded that "it was to be expected sooner or later" (*Kuzbass*, July 18, 1989, p. 2). There already had been a dozen work stoppages in mines in various parts of the country since January 1989. A report in a national paper on the most recent stoppage, in Krasnyy Lug, Ukraine, had apparently influenced the Mezhdurechensk workers to drop their tools (*Trud*, June 14, 1989, p. 2). This is a very direct example of the way *glasnost'* stimulated the emergence of the labor movement.

Since the spring of 1989, miners in Mezhdurechensk had been sending letters detailing grievances to numerous party and governmental organizations and had set a deadline of July 10 for a reply. On June 28, the central committee of the Coal Miners' Union received a letter informing it of the deadline, but forwarded the letter to the coal ministry. The Communist Party regional committee (*obkom*) responded by threatening to expel strikers from the CPSU, and on July 4 the works council told the radicals that their demands were "utopian" (*Trud*, August 3, 1989, p. 3). Even as late as July 16, the First Secretary of Kemerovo *obkom* was still threatening to punish CPSU members for participating in the strikes (*Kuzbass*, July 16, 1989, p. 2).

The strike spread rapidly to other pits in Kuzbas. Workers outside the coal industry offered to join, but the miners told them to keep working. For the most part, miners did not stop shipments of coal, and even let some mines continue working to feed local power stations and steel mills.[7] The miners elected strike committees in each pit, which in turn formed city and region-wide strike committees.

In each of the major mining cities in Kuzbas, miners occupied the main downtown square in round-the-clock meetings. The workers in Victory Square in Prokop'yevsk, which became the base for the Kuzbas regional strike committee during the strike, declared July 13 "Democracy Day." One of their placards bore the slogan "It's Impossible to Live Like This."

The strikers organized a militia to keep order and to close alcohol shops for the duration of the strike. They also set up commissions to take control of the distribution of local food supplies. In Prokop'yevsk, the chief of the regional police gave the strikers daily reports ("as you instructed") on the situation in the town, and referred to them as "lads" (*muzhiki*) rather than "comrades" (Makashova, 1990, p. 70).

The situation in these towns took on a carnival atmosphere. Social roles were turned upside down as the authority of officials evaporated. People were exhilarated, and felt they were behaving as they had never behaved before. For example, a delegation from the strike committee went to investigate how luxurious were the apartments of local party officials. They reported that the contents of their refrigerators were the same as everyone else's (*Kuzbass*, July 16, 1989, p. 2). To add to the general sense of unreality, Russia was experiencing a heat wave, with temperatures reaching 40°C.

What of the reactions of the local authorities? Local CPSU leaders seem to have been almost paralyzed by fear. The situation was clearly beyond their control, and elicited deeply rooted fears that there would be a violent mass uprising (*bunt*) of the kind which periodically shaped Russia's history. As it

---

7. According to official figures, the number of strikers peaked at 177,682, in 158 enterprises, on July 17 and fell to 33,690 on July 20 (*Argumenty i fakty*, 1989, No. 30, p. 6).

turned out, of course, the miners were peaceful and highly disciplined, and this exaggerated fear never materialized. In some areas, local party officials were active in trying to "calm" the workers, but mostly they simply maintained a very low profile. There were reports of miners throwing out party and management officials who tried to infiltrate their meetings (*Kuzbass*, July 18, 1989, p. 2). On the other hand, many individual CPSU members took part in the strike, accounting for 25 to 40 percent of the strike committees (*Pravda*, August 21, 1989, p. 2).

The official trade unions were completely bypassed by the striking miners. They occupied themselves with the maintenance and safety work, and provided hot meals for the strikers. There were some cases of coal industry managers cooperating with the strikers. For example, in Prokop'yevsk they helped to draw up their list of demands. However, this case seems to have been atypical. In many mines relations between managers and workers were hostile before and during the strikes.

The initial reaction of the local and central press was to ignore the strikes or to print blatant untruths.[8] The government quickly established an official "line," arguing that the grievances of the miners were just, *but* that the strike weapon was an "extreme" measure, and unnecessary now that the government was working on the problem.[9] Within the first week the argument was being made that the strikes represented "*perestroyka* from below," and therefore were a reaffirmation of Gorbachev's policies. This official line was pushed relentlessly by the press, which also expanded on the alleged economic losses caused by the strike—for example, the difficulties faced by steel mills dependent on a regular supply of coal. In fact, none of these dire consequences seem to have materialized.

Elements of the press continued to try to undermine the miners' position, by hinting at the unfairness of special treatment for the strikers. One report tried to discredit them by citing false reporting and "dead souls" at a Donetsk mine (*Komsomol'skaya pravda*, July 27, 1989, p. 4). Another frequent theme was to describe alleged attempts by "extremists" such as the Democratic Union to exploit the strike for their own purposes (*Trud*, July 16, 1989, p. 1). The miners grew angry with the initially negative press coverage (at some meetings, newspapers were ceremonially torn up), and this redoubled their determination to stay out on strike.

The Strikers' Demands

The initial open letter drafted by the Mezhdurechensk strikers included a wide range of demands, from emergency shipments of medical supplies to calls

8. For example, *Trud* reported on July 20, 1989 (p.1) that the Pavlodar miners had voted against joining the strike, when they had in fact done the opposite.

9. See, for example, *Sovetskaya Rossiya*, July 16, 1989, p. 1, or the interview with Stepan Shalayev, head of the official trade unions, in *Trud*, July 23, 1989, p. 1.

for a new Constitution by November 7. Placards at the public meetings ranged from "Clean Air" to "Meat for All." A distinctive feature of all the strikes was the range and number of demands that were raised. It was as if all the social, economic, political, ecological, and personal grievances which had accumulated over the years had suddenly surfaced. This "polyfunctionality" of the strikers' demands (Gordon, 1990) initially confused the authorities, but they subsequently learned to use it to their advantage, conceding on some issues while resisting others.

From the outset the demands of the Kuzbas strikers were a mixture of mundane economics and high politics, with economic issues predominating. There were no clear barriers separating economic from political issues, although it may tactically have been useful for miners in the beginning to pretend that their demands were "purely" economic.[10] The central demand of economic autonomy may be construed as either economic or political, since the quest for economic autonomy may or may not be achievable within the existing political system.

The strikers did not trust the "local powers," and insisted on negotiating directly with officials from Moscow. Coal Minister Mikhail Shchadov happened to be in Kuzbas on another task, and traveled immediately to Mezhdurechensk. He addressed the crowd in the square for three hours on July 11, spoke to Moscow by telephone, then continued speaking to the crowd until 5:00 a.m.

The authorities do not seem to have considered repression to be a serious option. Moscow's response was to quickly cave in to the strikers' demands, at least those that could be immediately assuaged. On July 13, they promised to grant the mines full economic independence. Additional supplies were immediately shipped into Mezhdurechensk, ranging from extra meat and sugar to a consignment of 25,000 disposable syringes (*Kuzbass*, July 16, 1989, p. 1). By July 14 the Mezhdurechensk miners were back at work; but by then the strike had spread to towns throughout Kuzbas.

On July 16, Gorbachev announced the formation of a commission under the then Politburo member Nikolay Slyun'kov to investigate the miners' grievances. Slyun'kov flew out the next day, joined by the head of the central trade union council, Stepan Shalayev and First Deputy Prime Minister Lev Voronin.

The initial 17-point agreement signed by Coal Minister Shchadov and the Kuzbas regional strike committee covered the following points (*Trud*, July 22, 1989, p. 1):

Demands for Structural Reform

(1) Full economic independence for the mines;
(2) The right to sell above-plan coal for dollars;
(3) A promise to study the feasibility of increasing the purchase price of coal;

10. For example, how is one to evaluate the statement of V. Dimidov, head of the Novokuznetsk strike committee (as reported in *Financial Times* of July 24, 1989) that the strike was not political but economic?

(4) Complete autonomy for each mine in deciding work hours and practices;

(5) A cut in the amount of paperwork required for mine operations, and a 20 percent cut in mine management staff.

Compensation Demands

(6) Forty percent night-shift and 20 percent evening-shift bonuses:

(7) Abolition of compulsory Sunday work (introduced five years earlier);

(8) Pay for travel time inside the mine (averaging two hours per day for each underground worker).

Demands Relating to Benefits and Conditions

(9) Improved death benefits;

(10) Longer holidays (e.g., 42 days for underground workers, 24 days for surface workers), and longer maternity leave;

(11) A safety review;

(12) A general review of pension eligibility;

(13) Increased pension levels, e.g., for underground workers 70 percent of the previous wage after 25 years' service;

(14) Improved invalid pay, and increased provisions of medical supplies and equipment, e.g., for dealing with spinal injuries;

(15) Improved pensions for surface transport workers;

(16) Guaranteed long-service bonuses;

(17) A review of the work of mine rescue teams (VGSCh).[11]

The Slyun'kov commission signed a 35-point protocol which fleshed out the Shchadov agreement with specific pledges of action by a host of government agencies to improve living conditions. These covered everything from the provision of ten extra buses for Kemerovo to a new pig farm (*Kuzbass*, July 19, 1989, p. 1). The Kuzbas regional bonus was raised to 30 percent. The Slyun'kov protocol also promised to pay miners back pay for the duration of the strike (at the level of the base wage), and guaranteed that no disciplinary sanctions would be applied to strikers.[12]

By the time negotiations came to an end there was considerable tension between the strike committee and the mass meeting still in progress on the central Prokop'yevsk square. The strike committee had a hard time persuading the meeting to accept the deal, but by July 20 Kuzbas was back at work.

The government concessions were of two basic types. First, there was a package of measures to improve local pay and living conditions, presumably

11. Workers in industries other than mining were approaching the strike committees with their grievances, but these do not seem to have surfaced in the signed agreements.

12. One of the miners' demands was for an end to work on the construction of a reservoir and hydroelectric power station at Krapivinsk, on the Tomsk River. Only after a two-hour warning strike on August 2 did the oblast soviet yield and suspend all work at the site (*Kuzbass*, August 3, 1990, p. 1).

to be paid for with money and supplies taken from elsewhere. On July 19 Gorbachev announced on television that 10 billion rubles in hard currency had been set aside for the purchase of consumer goods abroad—double the amount planned before the strike.[13]

Second, the concessions involved a promise to free the mines from detailed tutelage by central planners. The question of economic independence would turn out to be one of the thorniest problems in future months. Mining enterprises in Kuzbas, for example, had *already* been granted nominal autonomy ("regional cost accounting"), beginning January 1, 1989. It had proved to be nearly impossible, however, to find ways to turn this autonomy into a reality. For the time being, effective July 20 the internal price of coal was raised from 12 to 20 rubles per ton.[14]

The alacrity with which the government conceded the strikers' demands confused and disarmed the workers. Their situation was very different from that experienced by strikers facing a capitalist employer, or that of a non-socialist government facing a "hard budget constraint." In presenting their demands to the Soviet government the striking miners found themselves pushing at an open door, and beginning to worry about what they would find behind it.

The miners reacted to this uncertainty by insisting on guarantees. They demanded that top government officials pledge to honor the deal, and insisted on written guarantees with a specific timetable for the implementation of the items. Among the workers there eventually arose a feeling of disillusionment, and of having been betrayed by their strike committees. Some of the strike leaders suggested that they had once again succumbed to naive faith in the "good tsar" coming from Moscow, promising to put things right (Makashova, 1990).

The Strikes Spread to Other Regions

Having persuaded the Siberian miners to return to work, the government's problems were still far from over. Miners in other regions had begun to follow the Kuzbas example.

On July 15, the unrest spread to Makeyevka, in Donbas, the initial excuse for the refusal to work being the lack of wood props at the Yasinov mine. In fact, already on July 2 a shift had struck at the Rossiya mine because of a shortage of materials (*Sotsialisticheskiy Donbass*, July 2, 1989, p. 1; Friedgut and Siegelbaum, 1990). By July 20, 88 of the 121 mines in the region had followed the lead of Makeyevka, sharing their grievances, and not wanting to be left out of any concessions from the authorities.

A huge, round-the-clock meeting got under way in the central square of

13. Not all of the 10 billion rubles in hard currency would be earmarked for the miners.
14. As reported in *Financial Times* of July 28, 1989, the 20-ruble price excludes transport costs, which double the price of Kuzbas coal. But 20 rubles a ton is still far below the world price, which ranged from $25 to $49 a ton, or 500 to 980 rubles, at the rate dollars were trading in currency auctions in 1990.

Donetsk. This was the setting for one of the more curious events of the strike, the sight of the director of the Skonchinskogo mine leading a column of his striking miners into the town square. He later admitted that "until the last possible moment I tried to persuade my miners not to strike," but went along when they voted to strike (*Sotsialisticheskiy Donbass*, August 8, 1989, p. 1). It was also reported that local party officials summoned the police to stop the miners' columns marching into town, but that the police instead provided them with an escort to the center (*Reuters*, July 19, 1989).

Deputy Prime Minister Lev Ryabev was flown in to tackle the situation. Gorbachev and Ryzhkov sent a telegram, promising that the Kuzbas agreement would also apply to Donbas ["with allowance for regional conditions"] (*Sotsialisticheskiy Donbass*, July 21, 1989, p. 1).

In a meeting on July 21, agreement was reached by the Ryabev commission on a package of 47 demands which the Donbas regional strike committee had presented to him. The Donbas demands generally mirrored those of Kuzbas, but included their own local detail, such as demands for a back injury hospital, a brick factory, and the return of housing taken from the mines by the local soviet since 1987.

Like their Kuzbas colleagues, the Donetsk miners were suspicious of a sell-out by their strike leaders, and for two days resisted the regional strike committee's recommendation to return to work. Another Gorbachev-Ryzhkov telegram was sent on July 22, but an 18-hour-long meeting in the Donetsk central square failed to approve the deal. Tension was running high. The head of the strike committee passed out from heat exhaustion. Ryabev promised to resign if he had not managed to fulfill the agreement within six months. The local paper reported in a sinister fashion that outsiders were dressing up as miners and infiltrating the square (*Sotsialisticheskiy Donbass*, July 24, 1989, p. 1).

The turning point seems to have been Gorbachev's television interview on July 23, in which he eloquently linked the miners' strike to his own reform program. He recognized the legitimacy of the miners' grievances, and blamed local officials hostile to *perestroyka* for having allowed the situation to deteriorate. However, he avoided making any specific promises, and argued that the strike should end, as its continuation would threaten *perestroyka* (*Vremya*, July 23, 1990). Gorbachev's public intervention seemed to have the desired effect: by July 25 the Donetsk miners had returned to work.

Meanwhile, in the Far North the Vorkuta miners were joining the strike wave. Nine of the thirteen mines in Vorkuta stopped work on July 13. A meeting in Vortuka on July 21 drew up a list of 43 demands, ranging from the resignation of the USSR coal minister to the construction of a local brick factory. The government and Central Committee of the CPSU responded with a 17-point plan conceding all the main demands. In addition to the concessions offered in the Kuzbas agreement, the Vorkuta plan offered to raise the regional pay bonus to 60 percent, and to earmark 2,800 cars for sale in the region

(*Krasnoye znamya*, October 21, 1989, p. 1). Prime Minister Ryzhkov held a televised meeting with the Vorkuta strike representatives on July 25.

It was from Vorkuta that the first explicitly political demands surfaced during the July strikes. In a nationally televised speech before the USSR Supreme Soviet, a miner deputy elected from Vorkuta, Vladimir Lushnikov, spelled out the political demands of the miners: the removal of Article 6 from the Constitution (which stipulated the leading role of the CPSU); direct election of the chairmen of soviets at all levels, including Gorbachev himself; and an end to guaranteed seats in the soviets for social organizations [CPSU, unions, etc.] (*Krasnoye znamya*, July 25, 1989, p. 1).

The miners received strong support from deputies from their regions in the USSR Supreme Soviet: it was fortunate for them that the televised meetings of the opening session of the Supreme Soviet coincided with the strike wave. The deputies were quick to underline the political resentments and demands of the strikers. Thus, Deputy Yuriy Golik stated: "Our leaders kept telling us what a good working class we are. But when this class took to the streets, they did not recognize them" (*Trud*, July 25, 1989, p. 1). Deputy Aleksey Boyko, a professor from Donetsk, stated that "it was the lack of justice, and not the lack of soap, that drove people onto the streets" (*Trud*, July 25, 1989, p. 2). The miners themselves did not necessarily share these views: indeed, some seemed to resent moves by politicians (albeit radical ones) to utilize the strikes for their own political ambitions.

Events in the other mining regions mirrored those in the three main centers of unrest. On July 19, the miners in Pavlodar (Kazakhstan) struck and prepared a list of 50 regional demands, while on July 20 miners in neighboring Karaganda went out on strike. Separate commissions were sent to these regions, and they were promised treatment comparable to that of the Kuzbas.

THE AFTERMATH OF THE STRIKES

Four trends are noteworthy in the year following the July strikes:

(1) A gradual realization by the miners that the government could not or would not meet all the promises made in the signed agreements, particularly regarding economic autonomy;

(2) Maneuvering by local and national elites to contain and co-opt the workers' movement, showing that they believed themselves capable of riding out the storm. The workers' committees themselves cooperated in an uneasy partnership with central and local authorities;

(3) Increasing institutionalization and politicization of the workers' movement, with strike committees transforming themselves into permanent workers' committees—initially to monitor the implementation of the strike agreements. The institutionalization took different forms in different regions,

and remained at a low level of development. A different emphasis emerged in each of the three regions: political radicalism in Vorkuta, regional autonomy in Kuzbas, and industrial unionism in Donbas; and

(4) Attempts, at best partially successful, by workers in other sectors to flex their muscles and to share in some of the benefits won by the miners.

This section begins by examining national policy after the strikes, and then looks at the way institutionalization played out in the different regions.

The Government Reaction: Implementation of Resolution 608

The various measures promised by government plenipotentiaries in the July agreements were consolidated into Resolution 608, issued by the USSR Council of Ministers on August 3. Roughly one-fifth of the items involved changes in central regulations, while four-fifths enumerated special measures to be taken in the regions.

Deputy Prime Minister Ryabev claimed in November 1989 that 381 items under Resolution 608 had been implemented, at a cost of one billion rubles, over and above the annual six billion-ruble subsidy paid to the coal industry (*Sotsialisticheskaya industriya*, November 1, 1989, p. 1). Throughout 1990, reports continued to filter in on the details of the fulfillment of Resolution 608, but it is very difficult to tell exactly what has been achieved (*Krasnoye znamya*, February 11, 1990, p. 1; *Nasha gazeta*, January 23, 1990, p. 1). The implementation of Resolution 608 sank into a sea of bureaucratic confusion, from which it has not yet emerged. With the paralysis in national government which has resulted from the standoff between the Russian republic and Gorbachev in October 1990 and the uncertain outcome of the events of December 1990, it is increasingly dubious that any significance can be attached to the changes resulting from Resolution 608.

Consider, for example, the most important concession which the miners won: the pledge to grant economic independence to the mines. Since the strike, many mines have been granted formal autonomy. However, these mines are still subject to compulsory delivery plans, and failure to meet them will mean the freezing of capital funds (*Krasnoye znamya*, December 15, 1989, p. 1). In principle, mines can sell any above-plan output for hard currency on the world market (subject to a 20-percent tax), but even in February 1990 the ministry was still blocking such sales (*Krasnoye znamya*, February 24, 1990, p. 1). Above all, mine autonomy is fatally restricted by failings elsewhere in the Soviet economy. In the course of 1990, the centralized supply system (*Gossnab*), has slowly disintegrated, and enterprises have been left to fend for themselves through "direct contracts." In May 1990, for example, the Vorkuta miners began preparing a strike to protest the shortage of freight cars, which was limiting their ability to meet plan targets (*Krasnoye znamya*, May 29, 1990, p. 1).

Paradoxically, the miners found the value of their autonomy eroding as other sectors of the economy also achieved greater independence. In July 1990, Karaganda miners complained of being held to ransom by engineering suppliers, who were using *their* newly granted economic freedom to increase the price of mining equipment (*Sotsialisticheskaya industriya*, July 26, 1989, p. 2). *Perestroyka* also has reinvigorated local elected bodies, which has occasionally constrained the autonomy of mines. Thus mines found themselves under increasing pressure from local soviets to hand over the farms and apartment blocks that they had accumulated for their own use over the years (*Sotsialisticheskaya industriya*, July 16, 1989, p. 2).

Growing discontent in mining regions with the pace and effectiveness of the reforms led the government and official unions to create a special commission to monitor the implementation of Resolution 608. The commission consisted of seven representatives chosen by regional strike committees in the principal mining regions (Polozheniye, 1989). Also established was an "informal" commission of 60 miners' representatives, which met periodically to review implementation of Resolution 608.

Generally speaking, these commissions had little success when it came to using Resolution 608 as a vehicle for resuscitation of the mining industry. To some extent they seem to have lost interest in the specific demands contained in 608, as attention shifted to other, more dramatic political demands. The informal commission subsequently played a leading role in moves to create a new coal miners' union, and has reportedly become an effective lobbyist for worker interests in the corridors of the RSFSR and USSR Supreme Soviets. They reportedly had a strong influence in the drafting of the new pension law in September 1990.[15]

Central and local authorities continued to argue about who was responsible for the sluggish implementation of Resolution 608. Donetsk *obkom* First Secretary E. Mironov stated in May 1990 that "If some decisions cannot be implemented immediately, the government must have the courage to say so. It is unacceptable for local organs to be blamed for the mistakes and errors of the center—like before" (*Sotsialisticheskiy Donbass*, May 29, 1990, p. 2).

The official union structures struggled to respond in the wake of the 1989 strikes, which had completely discredited their already tattered claims to represent workers' interests. During the past year they have been fighting for their political and economic survival, with opinion polls showing a complete lack of faith in the unions by the general public.

In past decades, the unions' power and influence stemmed from their role in the bureaucracy, and not from public popularity. The rules of politics are changing, however, in that *glasnost'* and democratization are forcing organizations to improve their public image. The official unions are trying to develop popular appeal, portraying themselves as defenders of workers and

15. Personal communication from Ludmilla Thorne of Freedom House, September 27, 1990.

the poor, who are allegedly threatened by inflation and incipient market reform. It is too early to say whether this strategy will work: The public still seems deeply suspicious of the official unions. However, in the meantime the unions continue to be treated by the central authorities as if they are influential organizations.

The official coal miners' union, totally discredited by the July 1989 strikes, has tried to keep itself afloat and win back the loyalty of the miners. At its 15th congress on March 30, 1990, it adopted new statutes, elected a new leadership, and proclaimed itself to be an "independent" union.[16]

A year-long debate over the role of the entire official trade union movement culminated in the 19th trade union congress from October 22–27, 1990, which saw the abolition of the old All-Union Central Council of Trade Unions (VTsSPS) and its replacement by a "General Confederation of Trade Unions" under a new leader, Vladimir Shcherbakov (*Argumenty i fakty*, 1990, No. 44, p. 1). It is not yet clear whether the official unions will be able to break away from their centralized bureaucratic style of the past.

The official unions' efforts are not helped by the fact that neither the government nor the Supreme Soviet has shown much interest in passing new legislation regulating trade union activity. Presumably, such a law would also make it easier for the new independent unions to start organizing. One may speculate that Gorbachev is not eager to speed adoption of a new law on unions because it would help workers to consolidate their institutional representation. The unions (official and independent) would then be better placed to oppose Gorbachev's political maneuverings and reform programs.

Vorkuta: A Soviet "Solidarity" in the Making?

After the July strike wave had subsided, the Soviet government made a weak attempt to extinguish the workers' movement, by imposing strict legal limits on strike activity. The radicals in the Vorkuta mines spearheaded the campaign to halt this "counter-revolution." Some hoped that the strikes of 1989 could be turned into a mass revolutionary movement which would topple the Soviet system. In this they proved to be mistaken: the Soviet strikes failed to generate a broadly based working class movement along the lines of Poland's Solidarity.

In response to the events of July 1989, the government rushed to introduce legislation limiting strikes, hitherto not covered by Soviet law. Discussion of the legislation began very rapidly in the USSR Supreme Soviet Committee on Legislation, Law, and Order, on July 18 (*Tass*, July 18, 1989). A draft law was published in *Izvestiya* (August 16, 1989, p. 1). The pressure on the government was increased by a wave of unrest in August among railway and auto

16. Interview with one of the five secretaries of the official miners' union. Dinmukhamed Abdramanov, August 10, 1990, and from the new official coal union paper *Na gora* (opening issue, April 1990, p. 3).

plant workers, who were seeking to emulate the miners' success (*Izvestiya*, September 29, 1989, p. 2).[17]

However, radical deputies persuaded the Supreme Soviet to deny Gorbachev's request for an emergency 15-month ban on strikes. Instead, on October 3 the Supreme Soviet introduced a compromise measure, forbidding strikes in certain key industries such as defense and railways and imposing strict ballot and arbitration procedures on other strikes. The law was passed on October 9 and came into force on October 24 (Zakon, 1989).

These actions prompted another wave of militancy in the coalfields, with a two-hour warning strike by 20,000 workers in Mezhdurechensk on October 23. The battle with the new law was, however, to be led by the Vorkuta miners.

The radical miners of Vorkuta were confronted by a tough local apparatus which was more than willing to go along with the center's efforts to turn back the workers' movement. Thus, on September 10 the Komi government overrode the objections of workers and unions and raised local retail prices. Even in the key Vorgashorskaya mine, where 3,000 of the region's miners work, the unpopular director managed to ride out the July strikes. He was finally given a vote of no confidence by the work collective on October 13.

The Vorkuta miners held a strike ballot on October 19, and work stoppages began on October 23. The strike was to last 38 days—the longest in recent Soviet history. It represents the most serious confrontation thus far between the government and the workers' movement.[18] Their demands included the removal of Article 6 from the constitution and the resignation of the leaders of the city party organization, the city soviet, and the national coal union (*Krasnoye znamya*, October 24, 1989, p. 1). Apart from the issue of economic autonomy, the only specific items of Resolution 608 that they complained had not been fulfilled were fairly minor ones, such as a refusal to grant the regional bonus to youths entering their first job.

The Vorkuta miners were split over the wisdom of a political strike. At the meeting announcing the walkout, the existing regional trade union head managed to win re-election over the city strike committee leader, indicating the strength of conservative sentiment among some miners. On October 26 the city strike committee voted for only a 24-hour strike, but the Vorgashorskaya miners announced that they would stay out until their demands were met. A crucial factor pushing them toward militancy was the inability of their delegation to get an audience with Nikolay Ryzhkov in Moscow on October 24 (*Krasnoye znamya*, October 25, 1989).

On October 27, the Komi Republic court ruled the Vorkuta strike illegal, on the grounds that it did not go through arbitration and had not won a two-thirds majority in the pre-strike ballot. On October 28, in elections for a new

17. Also as reported in *Financial Times* of October 6, 1989.
18. In addition to the local paper *Krasnoye znamya*, information on Vorkuta comes from interviews with Igor Brummel, the representative of the Vorgashorskaya miners in Moscow and Ludmilla Thorne of Freedom House.

director at Vorgashorskaya, the former deputy director won by 2 to 1 over a challenge by strike leader I. Gudirov. By now the strikers were coming under strong pressure from the nearby Cherepovets steel combine, which complained that its furnaces would be damaged if coal supplies were not resumed (*Krasnoye znamya*, October 31, 1989, p. 1). The city-wide strike was held on November 1, but it ended up being reduced to just a two-hour stoppage. On November 5, miners in the nearby town of Inta voted not to join the strike.

The local political elite stepped up the pressure on the Vorgashorskaya miners, revoking recognition of the city strike committee, spreading rumors that the strikers had been promised extra meat rations, and even distributing material in schools condemning the strike. The miners felt that the central and local media were mounting a campaign of calumny against them.

On November 11, the Soviet government issued a decree suspending elections of managers in the Vorkuta coal trust, and on November 16 the Russian Republic Court confirmed the decision of the Komi court declaring the strike illegal. Even the weather turned against the strikers: on November 13 the temperature plunged to $-20°C$. This did not affect the miners' ability to hold open-air meetings in the town square, but it did mean that coal would start to freeze in the cars held up at the rail station. By this time only two of the region's 13 mines were still on strike: Vorgashorskaya and Promyshlennaya.

On November 17, representatives of the strikers finally got their meeting with Ryzhkov, who made a series of promises to them. The next day, however, the strike committee declared the meeting unsatisfactory, and voted to continue the strike "until the end." At this stage they were advancing the following demands: (1) new work rules in the mines; (2) punishment for officials who had failed to implement Resolution 608; (3) restoration of legal status for the strike committee; and (4) the regional bonus for new youth workers.

It was clear that the representatives feared that the authorities would prosecute the leaders of the "illegal" strike. This had not been a prominent issue in the other coalfields during the July strikes. On November 21 several Vorkuta miners went on hunger strike. A day thereafter, letters from Ryzhkov and the Komi court promised that there would be no punishment of strike leaders, provided the strike ended before November 24. The strikers declined to meet that deadline, since they were still waiting for the documentary record of the November 17 meeting with Ryzhkov.

The strike committee decided to try to hold out until December 12, when the second session of the USSR Supreme Soviet was due to begin, in the hope that public support from radical deputies might tip the balance in their favor. Leading radical deputies such as Vladimir Tikhonov had traveled to Vorkuta to address the miners. The strikers had also been in touch with Andrey Sakharov, who was canvassing support for the idea of a general two-hour strike to call for the removal of Article 6.

In fact, a compromise was reached. The strike ended on December 2, in return for a promise from Coal Minister Shchadov guaranteeing Vorgashorskaya complete economic independence.[19]

The Significance of Vorkuta. One should not underestimate the significance of the November strike. The Vorkuta miners were able to turn back an attempted "counter-revolution" by the Soviet state which could have destroyed the embryonic workers' movement. The Vorkuta episode also triggered a sharp radicalization of the miners' movement. The strike was significant in that it forced the government to back down from its plan to impose legal limits on strike activity. The new anti-strike law remains on the statute book,[20] but has been quietly ignored.[21]

How close did the Vorkuta miners come to igniting a mass political movement capable of bringing down the Soviet system, along the lines of the Polish Solidarity? Western media coverage of the Vorkuta strikes exaggerated the parallels with Poland. It was really only 3,000 miners at Vorgashorskaya who were espousing the most radical ideas. They gained only patchy support from the 20,000 other miners in Vorkuta, and still less from miners elsewhere in the country. The Mezhdurechensk miners did hold a two-hour sympathy strike in the middle of the dispute, but the Donetsk strike committee refused to endorse the Vorkuta demands (*Interfax*, November 14, 1989). In contrast, within days of the strike at the Lenin shipyard in Gdansk, Poland, in August 1980, a national network of workers' committees sprang into being and spread to cover more than half the workforce.

Also, the goals of the Vorkuta strikers may not have been as politically radical as initial reports suggested. A survey of 323 strikers in November 1989 found that 8 percent considered the strike "mainly political," 35 percent "mainly economic," and 50 percent a mixture of the two (Levinson, 1990). Thus their general discontent had not yet achieved a clear political focus. The dominant attitude seems to have been one of suspicion toward all forms of political organization. As reported by Levinson (*ibid.*), answers to the question "with whom should the strike committee establish close links?" indicated the following (in percent):

International labor		U.S. trade unions	10
organizations	27	Cooperators' Union	
Independent trade unions	11	(radicals)	8
Russian Popular Front		Democratic Union (extreme	
(democrats)	11	radicals)	5
United Workers Front		Pamyat' (extreme	
(nationalists)	10	nationalists)	3

19. The day after the strike ended, 120 Panasonic television sets arrived in the nearby town of Syktyvkar (to placate the miners, perhaps?). The queue turned into a riot, which the police dispersed with tear gas (*Krasnoye znamya*, December 3, 1989, p. 1).

20. Between November 1989 and August 1990, only two strikes were taken to court: one in a Moscow construction trust in June, and one in a Chelyabinsk engineering plant in July-August. Both were small, involving a few hundred workers, and concerned a wage dispute as well as an argument about an appointment of the director (interview with Valentin Lysenko, editor of "Infovzglyad," August 9, 1990).

21. The miners also succeeded in forcing the question of Article 6 of the Constitution to the top of the Soviet political agenda. In March 1990, the article was indeed dropped from the Constitution.

The Vorkuta miners even displayed an extreme lack of trust in their own elected strike committee leaders, particularly as many of those leaders moved into comfortable jobs in the local soviet and unions,[22] and even in mine management.[23] One year after the July strikes, the Vorkuta miners were on their fourth round of strike committee leaders.

In the first half of 1990, the miners of Vorkuta created a host of new politically oriented organizations whose distinguishing characteristic was their desire to avoid compromises with the existing political and economic institutions. Examples include *Demokraticheskiy Trud* (Democratic Labor) and *Professional' no-Obshchestvenyy Soyuz* (Professional and Social Union). Thus far, however, these organizations remain relatively small and disunited. If one wishes to draw an analogy with Poland, the 1989 strikes would parallel the unrest of 1970 or 1976 (not 1980), and these small radical groups, dominated by intellectuals, may (or may not) prove equivalent to the KOR network which sprang up after 1976 (Lipski, 1987).

Kuzbas: The Quest for Regional Self-Management

In contrast to Vorkuta, the strike movement in Siberia was powerful enough from the outset to overwhelm the "local powers." In Kuzbas a hierarchy of factory, city, and regional workers' committees quickly emerged, representing all industrial sectors. Despite the lack of any clear legal status they effectively enjoy a veto power over the decisions of the official soviet, party, and trade union bodies in the region. The situation is one of "dual power" (a reference to the period March–November 1917), with strike committees sharing power with local party and mine managers (*Sovetskaya Rossiya*, August 29, 1989, p. 1).

The strength and unity of the Kuzbas miners allowed the region to become the main source of leadership for the national workers' movement in 1990. Although the region also has more than its share of political radicals, the distinctive contribution of Kuzbas miners has been to push for *regional* self-management. They are confident that their mines are profitable, and feel exploited by the central planners (in the classic Marxist sense of getting less than the full value of their labor).[24] They have a strong sense of identity and pride as Siberians, and are confident that they can prosper on their own. This desire for autonomy cuts both ways, however: they are more interested in being left alone than in trying to change the power structure in Moscow.

22. For some reason, in Soviet parlance superfluous political appointees are called "snowdrops" (*podsnezhniki*).

23. For example, half of the leaders among a delegation sent to the United States in December 1989 were removed after their return, under (unfounded) accusations that they had appropriated gifts from U.S. miners for their personal use.

24. See for example the interview with the head of the regional strike committee, Teimuraz Avaliani, in *Trud* (July 26, 1989, p. 1). At the 28th Party Congress in July 1990, Avaliani ran against Gorbachev for the post of General Secretary.

The Kuzbas leaders were partly radicalized by witnessing the events in Vorkuta in October 1989. On November 18 a *Soyuz Trudyashchikhsya Kuzbassa* (Union of Kuzbas Workers) was formed by radicals within the workers' committees (*Kuzbasskiye vedomosti*, 1990, No. 2, pp. 1–5). While the workers' committees are elected directly at the place of work, the Union of Kuzbas Workers' (UKWs') 20,000 members are recruited on a voluntary basis. In Novokuznetsk, where it is strongest, it consists of a core of 500 activists who play a leading role in coordinating the activities of the workers' committees.

Since December 11, 1989, the regional council of workers' committees (RWC)[25] has published its own weekly newspaper, *Nasha gazeta* (*Our Paper*). This has managed to achieve a circulation of 110,000, despite lacking official recognition and having to be printed under the auspices of a variety of local industry newsletters. It finally received official permission to register in August 1990, and publishes an interesting mixture of articles on the coal industry, interviews with national democratic political leaders, and exposés on local corruption.[26]

As the months wore on and effective implementation of Resolution 608 failed to materialize, the workers' committees grew increasingly hostile toward the Ryzhkov government. A press conference of the Ryabev commission in early February announced that the price of coal would be raised to 22 rubles per ton (still below the 32 rubles the miners were asking for), but argued that plans for fuller economic autonomy were being obstructed by various Moscow ministries and state committees. M. Kislyuk, deputy head of the RWC, suggested the need for "*a diktat* of the workers against the *diktat* of the ministries," and approvingly quoted Margaret Thatcher on the logic of nuclear deterrence (*Nasha gazeta*, February 6, 1990, p. 2).

Between December 1989 and March 1990, most of the energy of Kuzbas activists flowed into the electoral campaign for republic and local soviets. They enjoyed partial success, endorsing 92 candidates for the Kemerovo oblast soviet, and wining 33 of the 250 seats. The RWC leaders refused to nominate someone to head the soviet, insisting on a direct popular vote instead of the existing system of indirect election by the soviet. In the absence of a miners' candidate, the apparatus nominee (a local railway director and former party *obkom* secretary) was elected as chairman of the oblast soviet (*Izvestiya*, June 18, 1990, p. 2).

Thus the regional soviet was deadlocked. Although the old "local powers" had a formal majority, they did not dare to defy the policy preferences of the RWC (*Kuzbass*, April 12–21, 1990, pp. 1–3). In cities within the region such as Kiselevsk and Novokuznetsk, however, the workers' movement was able

---

25. Known as *Sovet Rabochikh Komitetov Kuzbassa* (Council of Kuzbas Workers' Committees).

26. One scandal they exposed involved the misallocation of televisions in Mezhdurechensk. Six out of 25 sets given to the workers' committee for distribution in the town ended up in the homes of committee members (*Nasha gazeta*, February 6, 1990, p. 2)!

to achieve a clear majority in the soviets, and even captured leading positions in the local party apparatus. For example, former RWC head Teimuraz Avaliani became the First Secretary of the Kiselevsk *gorkom*.

The strike committees, consequently, found themselves in an ambiguous position, sharing responsibility for the allocation of supplies with regional managers and lining up alongside the "local powers" when lobbying Moscow for the fulfillment of Resolution 608. A puzzled local journalist asked the two RWC deputy chairmen "do you consider yourselves to be the opposition, ombudsmen, or the ruling group?" One answered "all three," while the other replied "none of those" (*Kuzbass*, April 7, 1990, p. 1). By June 1990 the chair of the RWC, V. Golikov, was declaring that they were "in opposition" to the regional soviet because it had rejected their program demands (*Nasha gazeta*, June 5, 1990, p. 2). As relations with the regional party deteriorated, the RWC started to pressure the regional soviet to seize all CPSU assets, and to ban party organizations from all enterprises (*Nasha gazeta*, July 24, 1990, p. 1).

The Confederation of Labor

By mid-1990, the Kuzbas leaders were recognizing the need for a more concerted effort to strengthen the workers' movement at the national level. From April 30 to May 2, 270 representatives of small independent unions from around the country gathered in Novokuznetsk to form the *Konfederatsiya Truda* (Confederation of Labor).[27] The sponsors of the conference included the Kuzbas RWC, the Kuznetsk Coal Trust, and, ironically, the official trade union association (VTsSPS). More than half the delegates came from coal mining districts (mainly the Kuzbas), with the remainder being individuals representing workers' clubs in various plants and regions of the country, such as the "Sotsprof" (Socialist Trade Unions) organization, led by Sergey Khramov.[28]

The organizers of the Confederation of Labor hoped that the conference would lead to the creation of a new, independent national trade union federation. No such organization has yet emerged: the Confederation of Labor cannot claim such a role. For example, a survey of delegates to the June 1990 miners' union conference in Donetsk revealed that 62 percent had not even heard of the Confederation of Labor.[29] Most of the workers' clubs at the conference from

27. The main sources of information on the conference are interviews with Professor Leonid Gordon of the USSR Institute of the International Workers' Movement, Ludmilla Thorne of Freedom House, Valentin Lysenko of "Infovzglyad," and documents provided by Yuriy Bobrovnikov of the Center for the Study of the Workers' Movement in Moscow. Press coverage included, for example, F. Yemchenko, "Na puti i . . . neizvestnosti (The Road to . . . Obscurity)," *Trud*, May 13, 1990, p. 2, and *Nasha gazeta*, May 15, 1990, p. 3).

28. For a rather hostile review of these groups, see I. Baganov, "Chego khotyat neformaly? (What Do the Informals Want?)," *Trud*, May 15, 1990, p. 2. For a brief description of the formation of the "*Spravedlivost*" (Justice) union in Leningrad, see the report on the talk by Ivan Dashkevich (1990).

29. Unpublished data from a survey conducted of 115 delegates at the Donetsk conference of June 11–16, 1990 by L. Gordon of the Institute of the International Workers' Movement in Moscow.

non-mining industries seem to have at most a few dozen members.[30] Thus it is not clear that one can yet talk of a "workers' movement" in the USSR beyond the ranks of the miners.

A secondary goal of the conference was to link the miners with the new radical political forces that had emerged from the March 1990 elections. Much of the conference was given over to speeches by representatives of Moscow-based political movements, such as Nikolay Travkin of the newly formed Democratic Party. Although the miners' sympathies clearly lie with the "Democratic Russia" bloc, no close, direct ties between the miners and political groups seem yet to have been forged. The UKW itself is divided over how to proceed, and a rift is appearing between the intelligentsia and rank-and-file members (Thorne, 1990).

Donbas: Cautious Steps Toward a New Union

The Donbas miners are divided and uncertain over the course of action they should follow. The miners appear to want to create powerful unions capable of defending their interests, along the lines of industrial unionism in the West. However, the following stands in their way: (1) the economic weakness of the Donbas mines; (2) the peculiar character of the socialist economic system, with its "soft budget" constraint; and (3) the fact that official unions already exist, and are trying to co-opt the function of defender of workers' interests.

The precarious economic situation of the Donbas mines (compared with those of the Kuzbas) made the region's miners more skeptical of the virtues of an approach stressing economic independence and regional self-management. Their industry could not survive without central subsidies or massive new investments, so the jobs of 300,000 miners hang in the balance. According to one survey, only 21 percent of Donbas strikers listed the lack of economic independence as a cause of the July 1989 strike: at the top of the list were food shortages (86 percent) and wages (79 percent) (Rubin, 1990).

As opposed to regional self-management, the Donbas miners have shown more interest in creating union structures capable of defending their threatened local economy. These sentiments could lead to the emergence of a form of industrial unionism not dissimilar to that in other countries. However, the situation is complicated by the fact that the miners are uncertain as to whether they should create a new miners' union or try to reform the old one from within. They are reluctant to break completely with the official union and create a new one because of the vast resources which continue to be at the disposal of the official unions: pension funds, housing, sanatoria, hotels, holiday complexes, etc. Hence, many of the miners' leaders advocate a strategy of trying to take over the official union from within.

---

30. Valentin Lysenko of "Infovzglyad" reported that his provincial stringers were unable to locate groups represented at the founding conference who described themselves as "United Workers of Belorussia" and "Volzhskiy Car Plant Workers' Club" (interview, August 9, 1990).

The union reform movement grew out of the structures created to monitor the implementation of Resolution 608. In September 1989, a coordinating committee of regional strike committees was formed in Moscow, under the auspices of the official national coal union. The strikers' representatives also were granted voting rights at the plenum of the official union, which met the next day.[31] Ironically, to set up this national network the strike committees demanded, and received, money from the official union.

In Donbas, opinions were divided over how the workers' movement should proceed. A radical minority sought to use the campaign for elections to republic and local soviets in February 1990 to radicalize the miners and link them with the national democratic movement. Donetsk was swept up in the wave of political mobilization which engulfed many parts of Russia and Ukraine in the course of the election campaign. A non-stop meeting was held on the Donetsk main square between February 7 and 14.[32] The meeting began after the spread of a rumor that a shipment of imported shoes had arrived, and citizens demanded to know its whereabouts.

The public meeting, coinciding with a wave of similar protests in Moscow, caused panic and a split in the ranks of the party *obkom*. The *obkom* first secretary resigned on February 9. However, repeated calls for a one-day strike to force the resignation of the entire *obkom* failed to gain the support of the Regional Workers' Committee (RWC), and a week-long hunger strike by 28 people, beginning on February 28, petered out without result. In the end, 100,000 Donbas and 20,000 Kuzbas miners joined a two-hour strike in March to call for abolition of Article 6 and direct election of the President, but that was the peak of the political radicalism. There was also an attempt, apparently abortive, to create a "Union of Donbas Workers"—in emulation of the Kuzbas organization.

The miners emerged with 49 of the 150 seats in the Donetsk oblast soviet, enough to exert powerful influence but not sufficient to take complete control. It is anyway unlikely that the Donetsk miners were united enough in their goals to be willing and able to take on such a task. In general, the Donbas workers' committees have been less assertive than those in the Kuzbas. For example, not until August 15, 1990, did they create their own newspaper, *Novosti i sobytiya* (registered under the auspices of the Donetsk Coal Trust workers' committee).

Political radicalism in Donbas has been restrained by the complicating factor of ethnicity. The region's miners are overwhelmingly Russian, and have looked askance at the remarkable renaissance of Ukrainian nationalism which has taken place in the western and central regions of the republic in 1990. And representatives of those regions have looked equally askance at the impact of strike

---

31. Interview with Professor Boris Rakitskiy of the Central Economics-Mathematical Institute (TsEMI), July 5, 1990.

32. Information in this paragraph comes from the local paper, *Sotsialisticheskiy Donbass*. A full account is also to be found in Friedgut and Siegelbaum (1990).

activity in Donbas. As the sovereignty movement gathers pace in Ukraine, the relationship with Donbas seems to be deteriorating.[33]

The New Coal Miners' Union

The electoral activity of January–February 1990 temporarily diverted energy and attention from the creation of new national workers' organizations outside the existing union structure. However, at a meeting of the official miners' union in March, the Donbas delegates broke away, declaring their intention to form a new, independent union for miners. The idea was to break entirely with the old party-dominated union bureaucracy. For example, its draft statutes excluded managerial personnel from membership in order to prevent the apparatus from infiltrating the new union.

A founding conference to create the new miners' union, which convened in Donetsk June 11–15, 1990, was unable to generate a consensus on the need to break completely with the old union. A survey of delegates at the June conference revealed wide differences over how to proceed.[34] Only 56 percent were in favor of forming a new independent union, while the large minority wanted to work within the old union structure, albeit with a radical decentralization of power. Sixty-four percent wanted independent workers' organizations in each enterprise, with the central union institutions restricted to a coordinating role.

At the June conference radicals pressed ahead with calls for a one-day political strike on July 11, 1990. The strike demands were to include: (1) resignation of the current USSR government; (2) dissolution of the existing USSR and republican soviets, and their re-election on a more democratic basis (e.g., with participation by several political parties); (3) nationalization of CPSU property; and (4) depoliticization of the army, KGB, and police.[35]

The Donetsk RWC was split over whether or not to recommend participation in the strike. In the end, it was left to individual collectives to decide. The strike proved to be an anticlimactic, largely token affair which failed to draw any support from outside the mining areas.

A follow-up conference of miners' delegates from around the country was held in Donetsk from October 21 to 26.[36] The congress demanded Ryzhkov's

33. This information comes from the comments of Ukranian participants in a conference on Economic Reform in Ukraine, held at the John F. Kennedy School, Harvard University, November 13, 1990. According to Volodomyr Pylypchuk, Chair of the Economic Reform Committee of the Ukrainian Parliament, subsidies for the Donetsk region will drain 13 billion rubles from the Ukrainian budget in 1990. Volodoymyr Chernyak of the Ukranian Academy of Sciences argues that since July 1989 the Donetsk miners have ignored the Kiev authorities, preferring to negotiate directly with Moscow for special treatment. For example, he alleges that special consignments of imported consumer goods have gone straight to Donbas, and have not been seen elsewhere in Ukraine. There also are reports that parliamentary deputies from the region met on November 12, 1990, to discuss the secession of Donetsk and other eastern oblasts from Ukraine.

34. Data provided in draft form by Leonid Gordon.

35. Soviet television news (*Vremya*, July 10, 1990).

36. As reported by Ludmilla Thorne of Freedom House, who attended the conference, and to whom I am very grateful for sharing her insights. See also *Radio Liberty Report on the USSR*, November 2, 1990, p. 39, for wire reports.

resignation, and called for direct election of the President of the USSR. However, one-third of the delegates were *apparatchiks* from the official *profsoyuz*, who managed to maintain control of the meeting, turning away calls to create a new independent union. In a dramatic reversal of fortune, on the final evening of the conference, a break-away group of Kuzbas delegates declared their intention to form such a new union. And during the course of a turbulent final session the following morning, the conference voted to approve its creation. The developments of December 1990 militate against predicting how successful the radicals will be in putting together this new organization, and whether they will be able to prevent the old officials from infiltrating it so as to use their organizational skills to pervert its mission.

Thus, in the year after the strikes, the miners' main achievement has been to consolidate strong regional organizations—an effort found to be much easier than the task of forming and sustaining a new national miners' union.[37]

The most visible political consequence of the July 1990 strike was to put the call for Ryzhkov's resignation at the forefront of national political debate. Prime Minister Ryzhkov became a symbol of the failures of the old regime because of his perceived role in the "betrayal" of Resolution 608. Just as Article 6 had been the focus of radical wrath in February, the ouster of Ryzhkov was to be the rallying cry of the mass demonstrations in support of radical economic reform in Moscow in September and October 1990. Though overshadowed by the drift away from democratization in December 1990, it still continues to be the symbolic bone of contention between the rival camps of Gorbachev and Yel'tsin. Evidently, the miners have played an important role in shaping at least the rhetorical political agenda of 1990, even though they have not had a decisive influence on national policy.

Strike Activity in Other Sectors

On several occasions in 1990 the government narrowly averted potentially crippling strikes in key sectors of the economy, as workers tried to emulate the miners' success. In some cases, however, the threat of worker unrest was artificially manipulated by managers maneuvering for favorable treatment for their industry in the face of mounting economic chaos.

In January 1990, as part of its program for the phased introduction of a market economy, the government raised fuel prices paid by Soviet firms. This cut into enterprise profits and immediately led to cuts in worker bonuses in industries which are heavy energy consumers, such as steel mills and pulp plants (*Sotsialisticheskiy Donbass*, January 12, 1990, p. 1). An energetic campaign of opposition by the official unions, combined with strike threats from many major plants, caused the government to retreat. Special compensation

---

37. The task proved to be extremely difficult because of such factors as the sheer size and diversity of the USSR and the practical difficulties of communicating between regions thousands of kilometers apart. Moreover, the miners have had to deal with skillful political maneuvering by the CPSU, government, and union officials.

payments were introduced for affected firms, which nullified the impact of the reform (*Tyumenskaya pravda*, March 4, 1990, p. 1).

On March 10, 1990, Tyumen' oil workers threatened a 15 percent cutback in oil production unless their demands were met. The list of demands included pay bonuses equal to those won by the miners during the summer of 1989 and guaranteed delivery of scarce consumer goods from other regions (*Tyumenskaya pravda*, March 10, 1990, p. 3). Like the miners, the oil workers noted the discrepancy between the world price of oil, at $100 to $150 per ton, and the internal price of 30 rubles.[38] Within a week of the strike threat, the region's *obkom* had a meeting with the CPSU Politburo, and on March 28 Prime Minister Ryzhkov promised to take specific steps to improve the flow of supplies from other provinces (*Tyumenskaya pravda*, March 15, 1990, p. 3; March 31, 1990, p. 2).

In 1990, strikes (or more precisely strike threats) became a standard way of gaining attention for a host of pressing demands. In April, for example, Kazakhstan miners threatened to call a general strike to protest the continued nuclear explosions at the Semipalatinsk underground test site (*Radio Liberty Report on the USSR*, April 27, 1990, p. 36). In Belorussia, 53 plants staged a strike on April 26 to protest the failure to deal with certain consequences of the Chernobyl' nuclear accident (*Sel'mashevets*, June 9, 1990, p. 2), while in Moscow day-care workers threatened to strike to protest their low pay. However, outside the mining areas such unrest has not yet generated a network of new organizations capable of articulating and defending workers' interests.

PRELIMINARY ASSESSMENT

What, then, is there to show for this wave of worker agitation? The miners' movements remain strong, but their strength has not yet achieved a stable national organizational form. Also, their success in creating new regional organizations has not yet been emulated by workers in other industries (except those in plants located within mining regions). Strictly speaking, it is premature to refer to a *workers'*, as opposed to *miners'*, movement in the USSR. Worker mobilization has only been under way for 12 to 18 months. While it is too early to suggest in December 1990 what shape it might finally take (and when), several preliminary observations can be made.

The Strikes as a "Historic" Phenomenon

The most distinctive feature of the workers' movement is that it is still perceived by participants and bystanders as a "unique" phenomenon. It is described in "historic" rather than "functional" terms.

In the West, political life usually proceeds without a perceived need to

---

38. Tyumen' Oblast's 700,000 oil workers produce about 60 percent of the country's oil (*Soviet Geography*, 1990, No. 4, p. 281), and oil accounts for half the nation's hard currency exports.

translate political events into a general theory of history. In contrast, Russian political culture is still inclined to interpret political life in Hegelian terms. There is a widespread belief that Russia alternates between long periods of stagnation and short bursts of "historic" activity, during which there is a breakthrough from one epoch to another. *Perestroyka* is just such a period of historic change, consisting of a succession of "unique" events: the first free elections in 70 years, the first direct criticism of Lenin, and now the first sustained wave of strikes.

The participants in these "historic" events feel both exhilarated and disoriented. They are privileged to have "changed history," but confused as to what happens the next day. The shift from history to normal daily life is invariably a disappointment, and it is accompanied by feelings ranging from pessimism and despair to betrayal and a search for scapegoats.

Accompanying this sense of participating in a historic sea-change have been widespread complaints that the society has reached a dead end (*tupik*). There are so many contradictions and problems that it seems impossible to imagine how political or economic reform could succeed. Instead, there is a feeling that one must somehow start again from the beginning.

These observations are directly relevant to the current status of the workers' movement. All those caught up in the movement—CPSU officials, liberal journalists, and the strikers themselves—describe the strikes as something extraordinary, an aberration, brought about by the critical situation facing the USSR. It was the very uniqueness of the strikes which explains their tremendous impact, and accounts for their carnival-like quality. However, as yet few people have gotten used to the idea of strikes as a regrettable but normal way of resolving conflicts of interest in industry. Of the delegates to the June 1990 miners' conference, 72 percent saw strikes as "an extreme measure," as opposed to "the only way to defend workers' interests," or "a normal way to solve problems." A clear separation is not being made between the interests of workers, managers, consumers, and society as a whole.

In the longer term, the workers' movement will not be able to continue capitalizing on the uniqueness of its protest, but will have to develop more stable institutional forms for voicing its interests, as distinct from the interests of other social groups. Workers will have to shift from a "historic" to a "functional" mode of reasoning. However, it will be difficult for them to carve out a functional position in society, when the political and economic institutions of Soviet society are in such a state of crisis and breakdown. The workers' movement itself is divided over what sort of political and economic forms to adopt.

The Workers' Movement and Political Reform

From the outset the strikes were seen as an intervention in the process of political reform, and not merely as an expression of economic discontent.

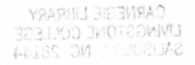

However, in 1990 the miners' movement has been overtaken in the national arena by events even more dramatic than the sight of striking workers.

During the past year, we have witnessed the collapse of communism in Eastern Europe; an accelerating spiral of nationalist violence in Central Asia and the Caucasus; radicals seizing control of the Moscow, Leningrad, Kiev, and Russian Republic soviets; declarations of sovereignty enacted in 14 of the 15 republics; mass resignations from the CPSU; a possible swing to dictatorship as enunciated in the memorable resignation speech of Shevardnadze; and a perilous deterioration in the standard of living. Against this background, the issues raised by the 1989 strikes seem to have slipped off the national political agenda.

The fact that the strikes have faded from view is clearly connected to the failure of the miners, to date, to develop a strong, coherent national organization. It is a common pattern in countries undergoing rapid political change for trade unions to play a vanguard role in the struggle for democracy (O'Donnell and Schmitter, 1986). Typically, they have the manpower, resources, and organizational structure lacked by other pro-democratic elements such as peasants, dissident groups, churches, or nascent political parties. This pattern is visible not only in Poland, but in countries as diverse as South Korea and South Africa. However, in the USSR this does not seem to be happening; or at least it is very slow to emerge.

At best, the process of political reform in the USSR is still at an early stage. Old institutions are losing their power, but new ones, capable of winning the trust of the public and becoming effective decision makers, are slow to emerge.[39] The main contribution of the July 1989 strikes was to discredit still further the central planning system and the local party-state apparatus. In the face of such political fragmentation, it is difficult for the nascent workers' movement to map out a viable political strategy. Should they rally behind Gorbachev's reform program—or abandon him? Can Yel'tsin be trusted, or is he another man in the Gorbachev mold? Will it pay to sink one's political energies into the newly elected republican and local soviets? Worker organizers have embraced no clear answers to such questions at the present time.

The Workers' Movement and the Economic System

While the workers seem broadly to favor a radical reform of the political system, their economic interests are more conservative, or at least divided.

---

39. For example, in an August 1989 survey reported by Zdravomyslov (1990, p. 14), the percentage of the public expressing "full trust" in public institutions was:

republic soviets	32	press	30
informal groups	27	CPSU	22
religious groups	22	local soviets	16
official trade unions	16	ministries	14
Komsomol	11	legal organs	10

The workers' movement has not yet produced a clear concept of what kind of economic system it wants, and what role workers' committees and trade unions should play within it. Arriving at such a conception has been made doubly difficult by the continuing deadlock in Moscow over economic reform (Åslund, 1990), and by the disintegration of the centralized system of planning and supplies.

This uncertain and fluid situation leaves the workers' movement in a quandary. The *de facto* decentralization of economic management which is now under way deepens the problem of *adresnost'*: who is responsible for economic decisions and to whom should one's appeals be directed? What guarantees are there that promised policies will be implemented?

As for the long term, the workers still have not decided whether they are for or against a market reform as a solution to the ills of the Soviet economy. The miners are for marketization if it means they can get a higher price for their coal. But they are against marketization if it means mine closures, free rein for speculators, increased food prices, or the selling of state industries to private citizens or foreigners. Ironically, the fact that the highly unpopular Ryzhkov government began to promote marketization in 1990 merely served to further discredit the idea of the market in the eyes of the workers, since it can be seen as just another government ploy to cut living standards.

There seems to be a strong syndicalist current among the miners, particularly among their intellectual advisers (for example, People's Deputy Oleg Rumyantsev), which favors handing over mines and factories to their workers. It is not clear how seriously one should take such ruminations. However, one may be troubled by the reluctance of these nascent syndicalists to take note of the failure of self-management in Yugoslavia.

The difficulties facing the workers' movement in formulating an economic strategy are not merely a product of temporary crisis conditions. They also reflect deep-seated cultural and economic conditions generated by the command economic system. Drawing upon classical Marxism, Soviet authorities have justified their economic system by drawing a sharp distinction between issues of "production" and "distribution" of the social product (Zaslavskaya, 1986). Production is rather mechanically depicted as depending on the availability and quality of factors of production and the level of technology; it is treated as a given. The main area where social choices have to be made is that of distribution (*raspredeleniye*).[40]

Distribution of the social product is treated as an entitlement, determined by one's place in the officially defined socioeconomic hierarchy. A vast bureaucratic system has emerged to administer this distribution function. It ranges from a State Committee on Labor, which produces multi-volume handbooks defining all job positions, to an elaborate nonmarket system for the distribution

---

40. The chair of the Kuzbas RWC, V. Golikov, wrote an article attacking the *raspredeleniye* philosophy, arguing that instead of helping the regional soviet "redistribute things that do not exist" the workers' movement should concentrate on self-sufficiency (*Nasha gazeta*, June 12, 1990, p. 2).

of consumer goods.[41] Factories too have elaborate networks to secure supplies for their workers. They build their own housing and operate their own farms. Special orders (*zakazy*) of deficit items are sold to employees at one's place of work, and these account for 15 to 40 percent of the food supply.[42]

This system of *raspredeleniye* cultivates a variety of attitudes not conducive to economically efficient behavior: (1) a feeling of dependency on the state in general and the employer in particular; (2) a failure to see the linkage between individual work effort and rewards; (3) a shift of energy from productive activity to efforts to secure advantage in the distribution sphere (shopping, queuing, contacts or "blat," etc.); and (4) an excessive concern with direct comparisons of living standards of adjacent social groups (vertical and horizontal).

This "distribution syndrome" was created by the network of economic institutions formed from above in the 1930s, but it seems to have become deeply implanted in popular culture. Public opinion surveys clearly show a preference for rationing and closed distribution systems over allocation through market forces (Zdravomyslov, 1990, p. 28).

Unfortunately, there is as yet no sign that the workers' movement itself has broken out of the "distribution syndrome." The survey of delegates to the June 1990 miners' conference cited above (see note 29) showed 60 percent to favor some sort of rationing system for the allocation of scarce consumer goods, while only 11 percent favored market pricing. On the other hand, 73 percent recognized unemployment as unavoidable in the near future.

As noted above, the miners' demands are mostly oriented toward a restructuring of the existing system, ironing out perceived breakdowns and inequalities within it. The system is increasingly less capable (in the short term) of absorbing their demands for more resources for their own sector, as it absorbed similar demands in the past from local managers and regional party officials. In the absence of a "hard budget constraint," managers and ministry officials can promise to improve pay, build housing, or cut hours. However, the central authorities become overloaded with conflicting commitments, and promised improvements fail to be realized. Neither industrial unionism of the kind found in many Western countries, nor economic self-management as promulgated in Kuzbas, is likely to take root in such an economic environment.

Only if there is a breakthrough to a market economy, in which horizontal, money-based transactions replace the bureaucratic allocation of resources, are autonomous unions likely to find a true role for themselves. As of the end of 1990, the Soviet economy is more of a planned than a market economy, albeit an increasingly badly planned economy. Whether the transition to a market will or will not occur remains an open question—as is the attitude of the workers themselves toward such a development.

41. For example, each local soviet runs its own rationing system, issuing tickets for everything from meat to alcohol, and maintains a network of special stores for pensioners and war and party veterans.

42. A thorough account of the *zakaz* system is to be found in the newspaper published by the electors' club in the Sevastopol' district of Moscow (*Slovo*, 1990, No. 2, p. 2).

FOUR SCENARIOS FOR THE FUTURE

If one examines Soviet and Western commentary on the miners' activities of the past 18 months, one can discern four alternative projections for their future development: (1) the Western trade union model; (2) *perestroyka* from below; (3) revolution; and (4) Peronism. Within several years it should be possible to ascertain which of the following hypothetical scenarios is being realized.

The Western Trade Union Model. This view maintains that the 1989 strikes indicate the awakening of workers as a social group able to articulate and defend their own interests. In the longer term one can expect them to form autonomous trade unions, which will take their place in the pluralist polity and civil society now emerging in the USSR.

These unions would function as defenders of the workers' economic interests in a manner akin to Western unions, albeit within a different (and as yet unknown) economic environment. If successful, these new workers' organizations may even go on to create political parties to defend their interests in parliament, along the lines of the social democratic parties of Western Europe.

Perestroyka **from Below.** By 1989, Gorbachev's attempt to reform the system from above was still being blocked by bureaucratic resistance. Gorbachev had to reach out and mobilize sympathetic sectors of society to accelerate his reforms (Breslauer, 1989, pp. 321–322).

In this light, many observers see the miners' strikes as popular mobilization in defense of *perestroyka*.[43] Before 1989, party conservatives seem to have believed that the "dark people" were on their side, and could if necessary be mobilized against Gorbachev's liberal reforms. The miners' strike of July 1989 proved just the opposite. Their demands for increased enterprise independence and an end to the CPSU's political monopoly were congruent with Gorbachev's plans for political pluralism and a regulated market economy. Attempts by conservatives to create a compliant workers' movement (through groups such as the United Workers' Front) failed to generate a mass following, and were ignored by the miners.[44]

Thus, according to this interpretation the intervention of the miners in the political arena frightened party conservatives, and cleared the way for Gorbachev to consolidate his personal power in 1990; abolishing Article 6 of the Constitution, creating the post of President, and emasculating the Politburo and Central Committee.

Skeptics might criticize the "*perestroyka* from below" position by arguing

---

43. An interpretation vigorously advanced by Leonid Gordon (1990) and by Friedgut and Siegelbaum (1990). This view is shared by many of the miners' leaders. For example, M. Kislyuk, deputy head of the Kuzbas Regional Workers' Committee, stated that "When a revolution is launched from above and from below, we may be able to change something in this unhappy country of ours" (*Kuzbass*, April 11, 1990, p. 2).

44. Information on the patriotic workers' organizations was provided by Anatoliy Salutskiy, a secretary of the RSFSR Writers' Union, in a series of interviews in July 1990. Mr. Salutskiy, an outspoken conservative, takes a more sanguine view of the role of these groups.

that workers are not likely to be ardent supporters of marketization. However, Leonid Gordon (1990, p. 29), argues that civil society is so poorly developed in the USSR that there are no social groups other than the workers capable of organizing themselves to press for liberalization. If the workers do not perform this task themselves, there is no bourgeoisie available to do it for them. Electoral campaigns run by the intelligentsia will not be sufficient by themselves to get the population involved in the resolution of the economic and political tasks facing the USSR. In sum, this scenario treats the workers not as Westernized democrats, but rather as allies of the reformist leadership in Moscow in seeking to destroy the party-state domination of the working class. Beyond that, this perspective is noncommittal as to the positive preferences of Soviet workers regarding the future economic and political structure of their society.

Revolution. Some argue that the workers' goals extend far beyond *perestroyka*, and amount to a social revolution based on direct democracy and social ownership.[45] According to this view, vigorously articulated by left-radical intellectuals, the miners' strikes represent the rebirth of the self-conscious workers' movement which created the soviets in 1917. The workers' movement will fuse with the radical forces in the soviets, overthrowing the CPSU's monopoly of political power. It will then institute a unique combination of political *and* economic democracy, neither statist nor capitalist.

Peronism. The three preceding models see the workers' movement as a sign that systemic change is under way in the Soviet Union. But the evidence tends to suggest that it is premature to see the workers' movement as necessarily capable of breaking out of the existing political and economic structures. The movement is arguably a child of the past rather than a harbinger of the future: it is a product and reflection of the fragmentation of the *existing* Soviet economic system.

The workers are trying to defend their interests within a highly unstable environment. Those focusing on Western solutions, *perestroyka* from below, or revolution, clearly overestimate the likelihood that a new, viable socioeconomic system will be created on the territory of the USSR in the foreseeable future. It is more probable that the workers' movement will have to function in a socioeconomic limbo, in a situation of deprivation and chaos. This means that unions cannot function along the lines of those in the developed capitalist countries (as predicted by the first model). Nor is it likely that a "third way" will be found, combining elements of planning and the market (as is necessary for models relating the outcome to *perestroyka* from below or revolution).

The new labor movements which develop in the USSR might conceivably resemble those of a country such as Argentina, where the weakness of political and economic institutions allowed unions to emerge as powerful actors, with a veto over many areas of social decision making. Despite this influential

45. An approach vigorously advocated by Professor Boris Rakitskiy of the Central Mathematical-Economics Institute of the Academy of Sciences of the USSR, one of the co-founders of the Moscow Center for the Study of the Workers' Movement (interview, July 5, 1990).

position in society, Argentinian unions failed to develop a political party under their own control. Instead, they were drawn into the populist movement assembled by Juan Peron, and came to rely on repeated strike threats and complex backroom maneuvering to defend their interests.

The lesson to be drawn from Argentinian experience is that labor unions may not be able to transcend the national political context within which they are located, and will not necessarily promote the emergence of multiparty democracy. There is a fundamental contradiction between the radicalism of organized labor's political demands, and the conservatism of its economic interests. According to the Peronist analogy, even if a coherent and powerful labor movement emerges from the unrest of 1989 (and that of 1990), it is unlikely to be capable of generating a national political party of its own. It is far more likely to come under the sway of bureaucratic (and/or pseudo-populist) leadership.

It is possible, but unlikely, that the Soviet system will produce a full-blown populist movement along Peronist lines. The workers remain highly skeptical of central authority, and no obvious Peronist figure is available to mobilize them. Short of that, the Argentianian analogy suggests that the emergence of strong labor unions may cause a further decline in the ability of the central authorities to govern the USSR, and could well accelerate the partial or total fragmentation of the Soviet state.

CONCLUDING COMMENTS

Soviet politics during the last two years can best be seen as a race between institution-building and institutional collapse. As the overt power of the CPSU and central ministries wanes, can new forces arise (other than the military, or KGB-MVD—i.e., soviets, new political parties, trade unions) to restore some measure of social order? The evidence in this paper suggests that models based on Western labor unions, *perestroyka* from below, or revolution are flawed by internal contradictions, and that there is no sign yet that the workers' movement will create stable institutions capable of performing as predicted by these models. That leaves us with a model suggesting a Soviet version of Peronism. The decisive factor in favor of this scenario is the extent to which the workers' movement has been and remains a prisoner of the old centrally planned economy.

Western Marxists have long argued that the central paradox of unions is that they arise to defend workers' interests as defined by the capitalist system. It has proven extraordinarily difficult to persuade workers to define their interests in terms other than those set by capitalism—that is, to adopt a revolutionary rather than a reformist strategy. The same paradox holds true for workers under socialism: their interests are defined by and within the structures of the old economic system. Unfortunately for Soviet workers, they are locked into an economic system which is sinking rapidly and leaves precious little room for maneuver.

In Poland, too, the workers found themselves in the midst of a collapsing economy and a discredited political regime. Yet they proceeded to create Solidarity, and brought down the whole system. Like the Russian workers' movement, Solidarity also lacked a clear vision of an alternative economic future. Indeed, the presidential elections in Poland in 1990 indicate that Solidarity's leaders are still divided over the extent to which state ownership of industry should be preserved. Thus, lack of a clear economic program is not an insurmountable barrier to system change.

However, in Poland the social consensus on an alternative *political* future— a future where decisions would be made in Warsaw, free of Soviet influence— was strong enough to submerge the differences over economic alternatives. In Russia, however, it is proving much harder (if at all possible) to build a political consensus on the need for system change.

To be sure, the non-Russian republics of the USSR are coming to resemble the Polish path toward "national liberation." In Russia itself, however, the communist system was home grown, and cannot simply be dismissed as an alien imposition. Russian workers do not have a clear vision of national independence to console them, or to provide them with the ideological unity necessary to effect a political revolution.

Russian nationalist groups have tried to provide such a vision of a new future for Russia, but their dismal showing in the March 1990 elections indicates that they have failed to ignite a mass following.[46] With a handful of exceptions, the nationalists have not addressed the question of what kind of political and economic institutions they would construct to lead Russia into the 21st century. They have withheld approval from such Western artifacts as parliamentary democracy and a market economy, but failed to specify what workers might have in their place.

Boris Yel'tsin's invocation of sovereignty for the Russian republic *may* yet prove capable of filling this political vacuum. However, there are still too many ambiguities in the relationship Yel'tsin envisions between the Russian republic and the central organs of Soviet power. Russia's workers will continue to look to Moscow to provide a system which can give them some semblance of sustenance and security. But the battle over precisely what kind of political and economic system will govern their lives remains undecided, and Russian workers have not yet come up with a clear answer of their own.

All told, however, the debate over what package of concessions will satisfy the miners may prove academic. President Gorbachev's apparent "shift to the right" in December 1990 suggests that he will not give the miners the economic decentralization which they have been demanding since the summer of 1989.

Gorbachev refused to accede to the radicals' demand to fire his Prime Minister, Nikolay Ryzhkov, who finally departed following a heart attack. Moreover, by nominating Gennadiy Yanayev as Vice-President, Gorbachev

---

46. Rather than a program for a new Russia, to date they have only managed to conjure up visions of Russia's glorious past.

sent a clear signal that he prefers to work through the old bureaucratic apparatus.[47] And should an authoritarian crackdown occur, it is likely to include a ban on strikes, and possibly a suspension of the activities of workers' committees.

REFERENCES

Andrle, Vladimir, *Managerial Power in the Soviet Union.* New York: Saxon House, 1976.

Apenchenko, Yuriy, "Kuzbass: zharkoye leto (Kuzbas: the Hot Summer)," *Znamya,* 10:163–186, 1989.

Åslund, Anders, "The Making of Economic Policy in 1989 and 1990," *Soviet Economy,* 6, 1:65–93, January–March 1990.

Breslauer, George W., "Evaluating Gorbachev as Leader," *Soviet Economy,* 5, 4:299–340, October–December 1989.

Dashkevich, Ivan, "Leningrad Democratic Activists," *At the Harriman Institute,* 3, 12:1–2, 1990.

Federov, V., "Tri retsepta uglepromu (Three Prescriptions for the Coal Industry)," *Ekonomika i organizatsiya promyshlennogo proizvodstva,* 11:80–96, 1989.

Federov, V., and N. Zhdankin, "Nagruzhat' Kuzbassa ili navodit' poryadok v ugleprome? (Burden Kuzbas, or Put the Coal Industry in Order?)," *Energiya,* No. 5, 1989.

Friedgut, Theodore, and Lewis Siegelbaum, "*Perestroyka* from Below: The Soviet Miners' Strike and Its Aftermath," *New Left Review,* Summer 1990, pp. 5–32.

Godson, Joseph, and Leonard Schapiro, eds., *The Soviet Workers.* London: Macmillan, 1981.

Gordon, Leonid, "Novoye v rabochem dvizhenii (New Trends in the Workers' Movement)." Unpublished manuscript, July 1990.

Gordon, Leonid, and E. Klopov, "Perestroyka i novoye rabocheye dvizheniye (*Perestroyka* and the New Workers' Movement)," in *Cherez Ternii (Through the Thicket).* Moscow: Progress, 1990, pp. 748–770.

Hauslohner, Peter, "Gorbachev's Social Contract," *Soviet Economy,* 3, 1:54–89, January–March 1987.

James, Daniel, *Resistance and Integration: Peronism and the Argentine Working Class, 1946–76.* New York: Cambridge University Press, 1988.

Lane, David, *The Soviet Industrial Worker.* London: Martin Robertson, 1978.

Levinson, Aleksey, "Zabastovka shakhterov Vorkuty (The Vorkuta Miners' Strike)." Moscow: VTsIOM, 1990 (pamphlet).

Lipski, Jan J., *KOR: A History of the Workers' Defense Committee in Poland, 1976–81.* Berkeley, Calif.: University of California Press, 1987.

Makashova, N., "Zabastovka (Strike)," *Ekonomika i organizatsiya promyshlennogo proizvodstva,* 11:65–79, 1989.

Marples, David, "Turmoil in the Donbass," *Radio Liberty Report on the USSR,* 2, 41:13–15, October 12, 1990.

47. Yanayev served as the head of the floundering official trade union movement between April and October 1990, and his appointment as Vice-President can only make it less likely that the miners' demands for reform will be answered.

McGuire, James M., ''Peronism without Peron: Unions in Argentine Politics,'' Ph.D. dissertation, University of California, Berkeley, Department of Political Science, 1989.

Narkhoz 1989, Narodnoye khozyaystvo SSSR v 1989 g. (National Economy of the USSR in 1989). Moscow: Finansy i statistika, 1990.

O'Donnell, Guillermo, and Philippe C. Schmitter, *Transitions from Authoritarian Rule*. Baltimore: Johns Hopkins, 1986.

Polozheniye, ''O gosudarstvenno-obshchestvennoy komissii po kontrol'yu za vypol-neniyem postanovleniya SM SSSR ot 3 Avgusta 1989 no. 608 (Decree on the State-Social Commission to Monitor Implementation of Resolution 608 of the USSR Council of Ministers of August 3, 1989).'' Moscow, November 24, 1989.

Pravda, Alex, ''Spontaneous Workers' Activities in the Soviet Union,'' in Blair Ruble and Arcadius Kahan, eds., *Industrial Labor in the USSR*. New York: Pergamon, 1979.

Redlikh, R., ''Rozhdeniye svobodnykh profsoyuzov v SSSR (The Birth of Free Unions in the USSR),'' *Poseyev*, 3:59–70, 1990.

Rubin, V., ''O prichinakh zabastovki (The Reasons for the Strike),'' *Na gora*, 2:1, April 1990.

Ruble, Blair, *Soviet Trade Unions: Their Development in the 1980s*. Cambridge: Cambridge University Press, 1981.

Teague, Elizabeth, and Philip Hanson, ''Most Soviet Strikes Politically Motivated,'' *Radio Liberty Report on the USSR*, **2**, 34:1–2, August 24, 1990.

Thorne, Ludmilla, ''Organizing for Free Enterprise,'' *Los Angeles Times*, October 18, 1990.

Zakon SSSR, ''O poryadke razresheniya kollektivnykh trudovykh sporov (Law of the USSR on the Procedure for Resolving Collective Labor Disputes).'' Moscow, October 9, 1989.

Zaslavskaya, Tat'yana, ''Chelovecheskiy faktor i sotsial'naya spravedlivost' (The Human Factor and Social Justice),'' *Kommunist*, 13:61–73, 1986.

Zdravomyslov, A. et al., *Politicheskoye soznaniye trudyashchikhsya i problemy yego konsolidatsii (The Political Consciousness of the Workers and Questions of Its Consolidation)*. Moscow: Akademiya Obshchestvennykh Nauk, 1990.

CHAPTER 13

The Moscow Election of 1990

Timothy J. Colton

FEW ASPECTS of political flux in the contemporary Soviet Union hold the revolutionary potential of the advent of competitive elections for governmental office. Uncontested elections were a clockwork-regular and compulsory ritual of the Communist dictatorship from its infant years onward.[1] Top-heavy with notables and model workers, the line-ups of candidates were sanitized and in great part preassembled by organs of the ruling party. For the Soviet citizen, as Merle Fainsod (1963, p. 382) wrote in *How Russia Is Ruled*, voting on cue was a drill in "manipulated unanimity . . . designed to create an illusion of representation and participation in public affairs."[2] Conversely, the right to choose from among several pretenders to leadership is emblematic of nearly every school of liberal democratic thought. With the ante so high, who would not be curious about how much Soviet practice has discarded the authoritarian percept of "one boss, one seat" for the Western "one person, one vote"?

In addition to their innate interest, multi-candidate elections are of instrumental value in flagging the trends emerging in opinion and behavior at both the mass and the elite level. Close empirical reading of their outcomes should uncover shifting moods at the grassroots. It would be enlightening in equal measure about the capacity of would-be leaders, outside yet also inside the

First published in *Soviet Economy*, 1990, 6, 4, pp. 285–344. The author is grateful to Professor Gary King of the Department of Government, Harvard University, for his advice on methodology. For generous assistance with the research and analysis, he wishes to thank Josephine Andrews, Joshua Blatt, Patricia J. Colton, Steven Solnick, and Margaret Trevor. [Eds.]

1. The only more or less unconstrained elections after the fall of the tsarist government were for municipal councils and the Constituent Assembly in the summer and autumn of 1917. The Bolsheviks circumscribed electoral competition soon after their victory and eliminated it entirely, along with the vestiges of opposition parties, in the early 1920s. In the city of Moscow, all local balloting beginning with the election of December 1922 involved single slates. A fair number of citizens abstained from voting until the early 1930s. Turnout in the local elections in Moscow was 84 percent in 1931, 97 percent in 1934, 99.8 percent in 1939, and over 99 percent from then until 1990.

2. Among the best studies of Soviet elections as exercises in mass propaganda and legitimation are Mote (1965) and Friedgut (1976, chapter 2). A later work accepts the view that elections before Gorbachev were "largely ceremonial" (Hahn, 1988, p. 28).

Communist Party of the Soviet Union (CPSU), to attract followers from below and to mobilize them into coalitions for governing.

Because multi-candidate balloting on a wide canvas goes back no further than the spring of 1989, when it was used to help select the USSR Congress of People's Deputies,[3] scholars are just now sizing up the challenge of studying it. This is easier said than done, if for no other reason than that most Sovietologists, having been confronted all their careers with pseudo-elections, have not had the chance or the incentive to acquire the research frameworks and skills mastered by students of *bona fide* electoral activity in other parts of the world. The elections breakthrough in the USSR hits us collectively off guard. Preliminary discussion has been by and large of two kinds: appraisal of the nature and intent of the liberalization of Soviet election procedures, and a thumbing through of some electoral results, as often as not with an eye to diagnosing the political health of Mikhail S. Gorbachev or prognosticating his program. Statistical treatment generally has been confined to elementary and potentially misleading cross-tabulations. The more commodious quantitative techniques that abound in scholarship on elections in Western and many Third World countries have scarcely been utilized.

The present chapter rests on the premise that, while scholars are in a position today to probe well beyond the objectives and hopes of Soviet electoral reform, and beyond the dispatches of journalists writing to deadline, generalization will best await the accumulation of first-hand description and analysis of specific instances of freer electioneering and voting. This chapter is about a single electoral clash, that over the Moscow Soviet of People's Deputies, the municipal council of the Soviet Union's largest metropolis. I was an eyewitness to this one election and was able to collect and examine in depth a good deal of data about it.[4] Given Moscow's population of nine million, its subdivision for the city election into almost 500 electoral units, and the entry of more than 3,000 candidates, certain of that data lends itself to statistical analysis predicated on a large number of observations.

The Moscow election belongs to the second wave of competitive elections, more disruptive than the all-Union balloting, held for parliamentary bodies in Soviet republics and localities starting in late 1989 and continuing through 1990. It ushered into Moscow government an arm of Democratic Russia (*De-mokraticheskaya Rossiya*, or DR), the movement that came to the fore in 1990 as the most potent political force to Gorbachev's left among the Russian population. Apart from the administration of the Russian Federation (RSFSR) itself, over which Democratic Russia narrowly gained leverage at the same juncture,

3. Two-thirds of the 2,250 seats in the Congress were filled in territorial elections, the first round held March 26, 1989. In 399 of those districts, there was only one name on the ballot, and there was an average of 3.4 candidates in the remaining 1,101 districts.

4. I was in Moscow in early January 1990 and again in the several weeks surrounding the first-round balloting of March 4. I also conducted interviews with participants during research visits to Moscow in the summer and autumn of 1990.

Moscow, the capital of the RSFSR as well as of the USSR, is the most prized trophy it yet has bagged.

No claim is made here of Moscow's perfect representativeness of the USSR or RSFSR in their entirety or even of all Soviet or Russian cities. But Moscow has been on the cutting edge of developments that, whether or not they are fully echoed in the provinces, are shaping events and mentalities. Its election is a porthole through which to peer at the transformations rippling through Soviet and Russian politics, the strengths and weaknesses of a spearhead of change, and the complexities of what must be recognized as the budding subfield of Soviet electoral studies.

FORMAL ORGANIZATION OF NOMINATIONS AND CAMPAIGNING

Legal scaffolding for the Moscow content was created in a prolix statute updating election procedures in the localities of the RSFSR adopted by the outgoing Supreme Soviet of the republic October 27, 1989 (*Zakon*, 1989).[5] By companion decree of the Presidium of the RSFSR Supreme Soviet the same day, the first round in the pioneering elections under the amended rules was called for Sunday, March 4, 1990, one week before the fifth anniversary of Gorbachev's accession to power. The local elections were to be synchronized with the first revamped elections to an RSFSR Congress of People's Deputies.

Preparations in the Moscow arena started with implementation of a reapportionment plan trimming the city soviet from 800 to 498 seats, in deference to the reform principle of making legislatures less cumbersome and more collegial. All seats were to be filled in single-member territorial districts (*okrugi*), numbered, oddly, 2 through 499 (district 1 being reserved for the mythic and long-deceased Lenin).[6] The electoral districts were all subareas of one of the city's 32 rayons (boroughs) or of the satellite town of Zelenograd, which functions as a thirty-third rayon (see Figure 1). The number of electoral districts per rayon was pegged to population and extended from five districts in Baumanskiy and Solntsevskiy rayons to 35 in Moscow's most populous rayon, Krasnogvardeyskiy. Although average size balanced out at the rayon level, individual electoral districts ranged from 6,385 to 20,654 voters; the mean district electorate was 13,481 voters (standard deviation 2,391). This oscillation in representation obeyed no overt principle and discomfited city officials for assigning some votes greater weight than others.[7]

5. The text of the law also was published in *Sovetskaya Rossiya*, November 3, 1989, pp. 1–3.

6. The RSFSR election statute did permit multi-member districts, but no such districts were created in Moscow except for several two-member districts in the rayon soviet of Zelenograd. RSFSR law also allowed experimentation with electing deputies on the "production principle," directly from places of work. In Moscow, this was done in 1990 for some seats on the soviets of two rayons (Perovskiy and Tushinskiy), but not for the city soviet.

7. See the interview with the chief of the Department for Work of the Soviets of the Executive Committee of the Moscow City Soviet (*Moskovskaya pravda*, January 4, 1990, p. 1). The official said, misleadingly, that the range was 11,000 to 19,000 voters.

Figure 1. *Moscow Rayons*

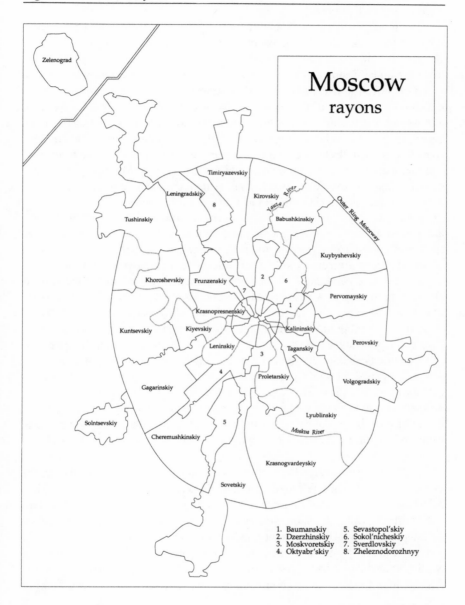

Each electoral district, large and small, was broken down into polling precincts (*izbiratel'nyye uchastki*), 3,048 in all. It was in these neighborhood-level divisions that ballots eventually were to be cast and tallied. Compendia of the postal addresses constituting the various precincts and districts, but not maps of either, were posted in public places in November. Lists of the 6,713,548 enfranchised voters, virtually all of Moscow's resident citizens aged 18 or over, were issued in February.[8]

The municipality's total expenditures on the election were to be 10.2 million rubles, five or six times its outlays on the last stage-managed election, in 1987. The costliest item was the 70 tons of paper for posters and ballot slips imported from Finland.[9] There was little tinkering with the modest election machinery relied on since the late 1930s. The Department for Work of the Soviets of the Executive Committee of the Moscow City Soviet was responsible for logistics and was outfitted with several microcomputers to speed paperwork. To act as returning officers, uphold propriety, and referee complaints, the holdover city council appointed electoral commissions (izbiratel'nyye komissii), five to twenty-one members strong, in all precincts and districts and for Moscow city. Under the part-time commissioners were small temporary staffs, mostly, I was told, with seasoning in the ceremonial elections of earlier times.

In the interests of legislative independence, Article 12 of the 1989 election law barred almost all senior municipal administrators (along with judges and state arbitrators) from election to local soviets in the RSFSR.[10] Any other qualified Moscow voter, as well as any nonresident employed in Moscow, was eligible to be a candidate. Nomination (vydvizheniye) of candidates was to proceed, according to Articles 10 and 34 of the statute, from a triad of sources. The first and second of these—factories and other places of work ("labor collectives") and public organizations (obshchestvennyye organizatsii)—were fixtures of prior legislation and practice, with workplaces, under the tight rein of CPSU units, habitually having made the lion's share of nominations. The new law opened the door a crack to nominations from a third origin, convocations of voters in residential areas, but equivocated by empowering local officials to veto the gathering and by stipulating that 150 residents had to attend, no small quotient in the dead of Russian winter. The bulk of the nominations were once again to come on the motion of assemblies of employees at places of work.

Trickling in from early December, nominations swelled to a steady stream as the January 2 deadline for filing protocols neared. For the Moscow Soviet, 3,793 names were placed in nomination, about 5 percent of them by more than one source.[11] Only 67 of the nominees (1.8 percent) had ever before served as a deputy. Two thousand, eight hundred and one (73.8 percent of the 3,793) were nominated by labor collectives, as compared to 885 (23.3 percent) by public organizations and a paltry 266 (7.0 percent) by residential assemblies. Almost four times as many nominations were offered for the lower-ranking

8. The lists of addresses and eligible voters were compiled by municipal clerks on the basis of information supplied by the passport and registration desks of the rayon departments of police. Maps were not prepared.

9. Author's interview, Department for Work of the Soviets, June 1990.

10. The officials excluded were members of executive committees of the given soviet (with the exception of the "mayor," the chairman of the soviet) and heads of administrative departments and directorates. Lower-ranking civic employees were eligible to run, and the exclusions applied only to the soviet in which the individual had executive responsibility.

11. There were 3,793 men and women nominated, but 3,952 acts of nomination.

local councils, 13,509 persons for the 33 rayon soviets (Zelenograd included) and 285 for the five hamlet and village soviets in the Moscow orbit. At 78.2 percent, the fraction of nominations to lower-echelon soviets originating in workplaces was higher than for the city soviet.[12]

To grant or withhold the formal registration (*registratsiya*) that would put nominees' names on the ballot was the business of the district electoral commissions. The RSFSR's local election law obliged them to render registration decisions by January 23, 40 days before election day. There was slippage from that timetable and no cap on appeals, which dragged on through February. Hefty inserts in *Moskovskaya pravda* of February 2, 6, and 8 printed the names and vital statistics of 3,329 registered candidates for the city soviet, expunging 464 of the original nominees (12.2 percent) who had either been denied registration or dropped out.[13] This was not the final repertory, as several dozen of the unregistered later were accorded recognition on appeal, one candidate had his registration nullified,[14] and still others withdrew. Come March 4, the total of certified candidates had settled at 3,262, 14.0 percent fewer than those first nominated.

Considering the historical legacy, the post-January 2 attrition pales before the survival of 6.6 candidates per electoral district—6.6 times as many as there would have been in years gone by. Table 1 shows the distribution of hopefuls by districts. As can be seen, no electoral district went begging for candidates. In only three districts was there a single candidate unopposed. In only 18 were two-way races held. In 70 districts the contestants numbered ten or more (2.1 percent of the districts, but 27.0 percent of the candidates), and in the limiting case there was a throng of twenty-three candidates.

As is plain from Figure 2, districts in the central area of Moscow, the thirteen rayons located (in part or wholly) inside the *Sadovoye kol'tso* (Garden Ring), tended to have the most candidates. The number of candidates averaged 10.6 per inner city district, as compared to only 5.5 in the outlying rayons.[15] The imbalance sprang from the city core's disproportionate grip on metropolitan employment. Crammed with government offices, older industry, science and higher education, and service outlets, the central rayons had 51.5 percent of Moscow's jobs in 1989, as opposed to 21.2 percent of the population. For some of the commuters into the city center, participation in the election was the outgrowth of an understandable interest in the social and political life of the local area in which they spent their working hours and, quite often, shopped for food and consumer products. Nonresidents comprised a goodly majority (61.2 percent) of candidates in the downtown rayons but only 34.2 percent in

12. Source: Moscow City Electoral Commission.
13. *Moskovskaya pravda* (February 4, 1990, p. 1) put the number of registered candidates at 3,361 or 32 more than the number of names on the lists.
14. This candidate was Pavel N. Sokolov in district 360, a Siberian exposed March 3 as having neither domicile nor job in Moscow.
15. Adjusting the number of candidates for population makes little difference, since there was no systematic variation in electoral district size between inner and outer city. The average district had 13,338 voters in the inner rayons and 13,587 in the outer rayons.

Table 1. *Distribution of Candidates for the Moscow Soviet across Electoral Districts*[a]

Number of candidates in district	Districts		Candidates	
	N	*Percent*	*N*	*Percent*
1	3	0.6	3	0.1
2	18	3.6	36	1.1
3	38	7.6	114	3.5
4	66	13.3	264	8.1
5	91	18.3	455	13.9
6	87	17.5	522	16.0
7	44	8.8	308	9.4
8	49	9.8	392	12.0
9	32	6.4	288	8.8
10	24	4.8	240	7.4
11	11	2.2	121	3.7
12	7	1.4	84	2.6
13	6	1.2	78	2.4
14	8	1.6	112	3.4
15	3	0.6	45	1.4
16	3	0.6	48	1.5
17	4	0.8	68	2.1
18	1	0.2	18	0.6
21	1	0.2	21	0.6
22	1	0.2	22	0.7
23	1	0.2	23	0.7
Total	498	100.0	3,262	100.0

a. On the first round ballot, March 4, 1990.

rayons closer to the city limits.[16] In-rayon candidates were fairly close to equal in the two zones—4.1 per district in the inner 13 rayons, 3.6 per district in the outer 20.

In no area of Moscow was registration of candidates a prelude to free-wheeling campaigning. Far from it, for the city bureaucracy and the electoral commissions did their utmost to keep stumping within preset channels. Following Article 13 of the RSFSR election law, candidates did not have their own warchests and could not solicit campaign donations; all expenses were to be covered from the election budget of the local government. No other forums but district all-candidates' meetings were approved for verbal discussion. The only acceptable posters were officially prepared composites, presenting for every candidate in the district a passport-style photograph (unsmiling and with one ear exposed, by injunction of the RSFSR electoral commission), a biographic cameo, and a mini-statement of "program," dry as dust and winnowed of "elements of agitation." These were not put on display until the week of February 17, the next to last of the campaign.

16. This information is readily derived from the published nomination data. The rayon in which a candidate worked was not made public, but the name of the enterprise usually was. In most verifiable cases, the enterprise was located in the same rayon in which the nonresident candidate stood for election.

Figure 2. *Average Number of Candidates per Electoral District*

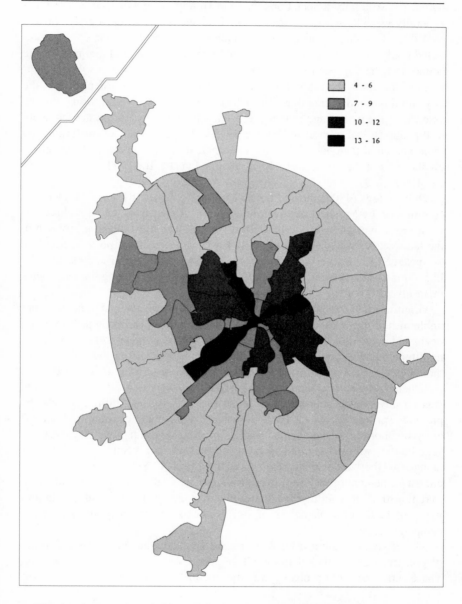

Nomination, registration, and campaigning all had their share of rancor. About 70 appeals against decisions of the district electoral commissions percolated to the city commission in January and the first half of February. The early disputes were preponderantly over nomination procedures, usually about the credentials of the entity that had forwarded the candidate's name. The

Department for Work of the Soviets impugned the voters' clubs (*kluby izbira-teley*), the voluntary associations that had sprung up in Moscow in 1989 and generally were left-wing in orientation. It maintained that most clubs did not qualify as "public organizations," a laurel always reserved for CPSU-pene-trated bodies such as the trade unions and the Komsomol, and that many were counterfeit, having been founded purely to nominate candidates. When nom-inees of the clubs and several legal experts took issue with the department, the city commission declared that "in each concrete case" it would "look into the essence of the matter and render a verdict," invoking as criteria the longevity of the club (it had to predate October 29, 1989) and its scale of operations (no more parochial than one of the city's rayons). It ruled in favor of the appellant on about 60 of the 70 (*Moskovskaya pravda*, January 10, 1990, p. 1; February 13, 1990, p. 3).

Only a few of the 30 additional cases adjudicated by the city electoral commission by March 4 involved registration. Rather more entailed disagree-ment arose over the wording of official posters. The most nagging problem in the latter stages was discord over dirty tricks: defacement of posters, heckling of speakers, telephone harassment of candidates and official agents, and the like. This nastiness pinned commissioners in a crossfire among the candidates themselves.[17]

Granting that the organization of nominations and campaigning was not unblemished, the local election of 1990 was, nevertheless, incomparably more open and more conflict-laden than any in Moscow since 1917. The sheer multitude of contestants—to say nothing for the moment of the substance of their views or the outcome of the election—betokened a giant stride away from precedent. As concerns the nominations that sculpted voters' alternatives, there was an advance in approach over even the selection of USSR deputies the previous spring. There was far less of an effort on this occasion to choke off entry of unorthodox candidates, probably because nominations chicanery the year before was widely seen to have aroused popular suspicions and boom-eranged to the benefit of radicals—notably Boris N. Yel'tsin, who harvested almost 90 percent of the votes in the Moscow-side balloting. The radicals were to remonstrate only mildly about nomination abuses in 1990,[18] and they in turn may not have been blameless of infringements of the election code at the campaign stage.[19]

The glaring deviation from Western standards continued to be the exclusion of political parties other than the CPSU from nominations and campaigning. The election of 1990 probably was the last to be fought in Moscow and the

---

17. Interview with Vladimir S. Afanas'yev, secretary of the commission.

18. The left's main grievance was that "against every democratic candidate there have been several outright or masked henchmen of the *nomenklatura*," not that the CPSU apparatus had kept left candidates off the ballot (quotation from *Pozitsiya*, No. 3 (February 1990, p. 1). The RSFSR election law did not provide for the district "pre-electoral assemblies" that were sometimes used to frustrate registration of radicals in the USSR election.

19. *Moskovskaya pravda* (March 6, 1990, p. 1) alleged that leaflets promoting left candidates were put in postal boxes in some districts the morning of March 4, flouting the ban on agitation on election day.

RSFSR under the restrictive old rules, for, prodded by a hitherto querulous Gorbachev, the Soviet leadership was at that very moment coming to the historic decision to rescind the CPSU's monopoly on party activity. The constitutional amendment enshrining the change was enacted too late—March 14, 1990— to affect the formalities of the Moscow balloting. But, as will be seen, enough had already transpired informally to make this a quasi-party election, a bridge between past and future on which the CPSU found itself in an awkward position.

VOTING AND WINNING

Before we turn to the pith of the election, a word is in order about the rules delimiting voter choice and the determination of winners. The most salient revision to come out of electoral reform had to do with confidentiality, an underpinning of electoral democracy vividly flouted in the Soviet past. Article 47 of the law of October 1989 was minutely explicit about the requisite physical layout: "Voting is to be carried out in places reserved for the purpose, where booths or rooms sufficient in quantity for secret voting are to be fitted out, places for distributing ballots are to be demarcated, and ballot boxes are to be emplaced. The ballot boxes are to be installed in such a way that as voters approach them they will necessarily pass through the booths or rooms for secret voting."

To judge from precinct 51/218 in Kievskiy rayon, not far from the Foreign Ministry building, where I spent several hours the morning of March 4, the spirit if not the exact letter of the revised law was respected. The polling station, an auditorium in a printing plant decorated in cut flowers, an austere bust of Lenin, and a wall decal proclaiming Lenin's enthusiasm for democracy and the soviets, was open from 7 a.m. to 8 p.m. The subsidized snack bar that had long graced such occasions opened at 8 a.m., but with a skimpier selection than usual. Upon presentation of identification papers, voters were handed *byulleteni* or ballot slips by members of the precinct electoral commission, who ticked off their names on lists. There was one color-coded ballot each for the city and rayon soviets and the two classes of RSFSR deputy, reciting the candidates in alphabetical order. Several elderly persons, of whom there are a great many in the precinct, quizzed the commissioners about the length and intricacy of the slips.

Perhaps two-thirds of those voting entered curtained cabins to bend over their ballots in privacy. But there were only four of the cubicles, too few to handle demand smoothly, so the remaining one-third made selections in the main hall, writing on their knees or on four open tables. There was occasional banter with neighbors and accompanying youngsters. These voters then were permitted to sidle around the closed booths and join the file of those exiting the booths, dropping their slips like the rest into the two plywood ballot boxes. When I had visited the precinct the day before, the deputy chairman of the electoral commission insisted that the four closed cabins—the same number as before reform—would suffice. On March 4 he shrugged off the problem with the comment that the crush of citizens forced adaptability.

The nonchalance of these arrangements was a flagrant violation of Article 47. My judgment is, all the same, that ballots were tendered without the intimidation and fear of surveillance that sullied past Soviet elections. Had it been otherwise, voters and candidates in Moscow, in the climate of high *glasnost'*, would if nothing else have demurred after the event; that they did not do so may safely be taken as evidence of a sea change. Voters interviewed at precinct 51/218 gave every appearance of having made an uncoerced choice. Heretofore they would have had but one option: either ratify the single, CPSU-backed candidate by inserting the ballot untouched into the box, or cross off that name, for which they had to duck into the polling booth.[20] The act of entering or shunning the booth told all. In 1990 the profusion of candidates forced all voters to address their ballots. Even when some circumvented the booths, there was no one signal that would have alerted a KGB informant, a neighborhood busybody, or a staff member to how individual voters had opted.

The secrecy safeguards aside, three other, interlocking features of the electoral system warrant comment. They are oddities in Anglo-American terms and can handily confuse the inexpert onlooker. The first is a turnout component. It dictates that no candidate may be elected at any phase in the voting progression unless a majority of the qualified voters in the district have cast valid ballots. A candidate could scoop up 100 percent of the votes in this district but still be denied a mandate if less than half of the electorate had showed up to vote.

The second trait, providing for negative voting, is a carryover from the unreformed Soviet system, in which the only way the voter could wield discretion was to pencil out the name of the single candidate on the ballot. Throughout the USSR, this strikeout clause has been retained, irrespective of the number of candidates. To vote (in single-member constituencies like Moscow's), the citizen scratches out the name (to be precise, the *familiya*, or family name) of every candidate he disfavors, leaving the name of his one preferred candidate intact. If, as almost never happened in Moscow in 1990, one candidate runs unopposed, acclamation is precluded; the voter in that district gets to choose, as in the old days, between rejecting the one name by drawing a line through it or confirming it by leaving it be. However many candidates he is faced with, the voter is entitled to express unhappiness with the lot of them by striking out all named on the ballot slip. An all-negatives ballot is considered valid for turnout purposes,[21] yet patently cannot count in any contender's positive vote ledger.

The third procedural anomaly consists of a baroque formula for runoff and repeat elections in the eventuality that the opening round of voting has not

20. This was the situation since nominally secret balloting was introduced in the Stalin Constitution of 1936. Prior to that time, Soviet citizens voted by public show of hands at meetings in workplaces.

21. Such a straight-no vote is not the same as a ballot intentionally or unintentionally rendered invalid (*nedeistvitel'nyy*), usually by leaving more than one candidate's name uncrossed-out. About 1 percent of ballots were spoiled in the Moscow election.

Table 2. *Outcomes for Candidates in First Round (March 4, 1990)*

Place in race	Elected	Advanced to runoff	Eliminated
Came in first			
With majority	35[a]		
Eligible for runoff		449	
Of 2 candidates, but without majority			13
Encountered low turnout			1
Came in second			
Eligible for runoff		449	
To winning candidate			32
Of 2 candidates			13
Encountered low turnout			1
Came in third or lower			2,269
Withdrew after March 4	—	(3)	
Total	35	895	2,329

a. Of these, 3 ran unopposed and 32 were opposed.

thrown up a legitimate winner. A victor may be declared outright in a first round, as in Moscow March 4, only in those districts in which (1) one candidate has gained an absolute majority of the valid votes cast and (2) turnout has been not less than 50 percent. If the second condition has been consummated, but not the first, in most cases the two top-drawing candidates collide within fourteen days in a runoff vote (*povtornoye golosovaniye*); in the runoff only a plurality of the valid votes, not a majority, is needed to win, but the turnout floor still applies.

Where the runoff is aborted by low turnout, a repeat election (*povtornyy vybor*) from scratch is scheduled within two months, starting with fresh nominations for which the first-round losers are ineligible. Districts glide straight from the first race to repeat elections in cases where in that race either (1) there were only one or two candidates, none procuring a majority, or (2) turnout undershot 50 percent. Repeat elections are scored like first-round elections and trigger runoffs if the majority and turnout criteria have not been satisfied. The cycle is to be reiterated until victors have been anointed in each district.

The outcomes on election day (March 4) are given in Table 2. Winners were determined in merely 35 electoral districts; in 449 districts, decision was deflected to the runoff, while 14 districts passed directly to follow-up elections. The main hurdle in the first race was not the proviso regarding turnout, which was 64.3 percent overall and was shy of 50 percent in only one district (where the two candidates were ousted). With candidates averaging almost seven per district, the far harder task was to attain the absolute majority of the valid votes needed for election. The mean number of candidates in districts that spawned winners in the first round was 4.0; these districts encompassed all three of the single-candidate constituencies and five of the eighteen with two candidates.

The Moscow runoff vote was held March 18 after two weeks of at times

Table 3. *Outcomes for Candidates in Runoff Vote (March 18, 1990)*

Place in race	Elected	Eliminated
Came in first		
With majority	277[a]	17[b]
With plurality	151	4[b]
Came in second		446
	—	
Total	428	467

a. Of these, 3 ran unopposed and 274 were opposed.
b. Eliminated due to low turnout.

desultory last-minute campaigning by the 895 finalists. The thinned-out field and the less stringent plurality condition paved the way for inaugurating many more winners, 428 (see Table 3). But turnout, which slid to 58.9 percent of what was now a smaller pool of eligible voters,[22] was more of a factor. In 21 districts, among them 17 in which one candidate got a clean majority of the votes cast, turnout dipped below 50 percent and prevented a decision from being reached. First-lap front-runners fared much better in the runoff than erstwhile runnerups, conquering 342 (79.9 percent) of the districts decided.

Supplementary elections in the 35 districts still undecided began April 24, 1990, and have limped on to the time of writing without final resolution.[23] They will not be scrutinized in the present article. Nor is there any necessity to do so. The selection of 463 legislators March 4 and 18 cast the die for the new council and provides plenty of grist for the analytical mill.

THE CANDIDATES

Whose were the faces in the crowd of candidates? Were some segments of the populace overrepresented among them and/or among the winners, and if so to what extent? Table 4 affords answers on the five personal attributes about which the authorities made information on all candidates available.[24]

The prototypical flesh-and-blood candidate who steps out of the cells of the table might be thought an unlikely revolutionary: a middle-aged man, a dues-paying member of the CPSU, a resident of the borough in which he was running, and the holder of a job with above-normal status and rewards. The average gladiator was 45 years old; the oldest had been born in 1907, the youngest in 1971, and almost two-thirds of the candidates were born between 1930 and 1949.

22. The number of eligible voters in the balloting for the city soviet dropped from 6,713,568 to 6,013,845 because there was no voting in 49 districts. Despite the briefness of the interval, in each of the 449 contested districts the list of eligible voters was fine-tuned from the March 4 list to correct for deaths and changes of residence. While most adjustments were microscopic, some were as high as several hundred.

23. In the repeat election and runoff held April 24 and May 15, only seven deputies were elected. The city then postponed further voting until November 25, when a repeat election in 26 of the 28 remaining districts, in which turnout was abysmally low, failed to settle on a single deputy or even to send one contest to a runoff. Yet another round of elections will have to be held in 1991.

24. The most serious lacuna in that information concerns ethnicity, which was not given in the press listings or on most official campaign posters. Posters for candidates for RSFSR deputy did identify the person's nationality.

Table 4. *Characteristics of Registered and Winning Candidates*

Characteristic	All candidates[a]		Winners[b]	
	N	Percent	N	Percent
Age[c]				
60 and over	233	7.1	16	3.5
40–59	2,140	65.6	274	59.2
39 and under	889	27.3	173	37.4
Gender				
Men	2,787	85.4	421	90.9
Women	475	14.6	42	9.1
CPSU affiliation				
Full member	2,374	72.8	266	57.5
Candidate member	36	1.1	7	1.5
Komsomol member	46	1.4	7	1.5
None	806	24.7	183	39.5
Area of residence				
Same rayon as electoral district	1,846	56.6	378	81.6
Adjacent rayon	406	12.5	21	4.5
Other rayon[d]	1,010	31.0	64	13.8
Occupational group				
Faculty members and researchers				
Higher education	287	8.8	62	13.4
Academy of Sciences	105	3.2	25	5.4
Other institutes	333	10.2	55	11.9
All	725	22.2	142	30.7
Figures in media and arts				
Writer	16	0.5	0	0.0
Artist[e]	21	0.6	7	1.5
Entertainer	18	0.6	0	0.0
Journalist, editor	74	2.3	16	3.5
All	129	4.0	23	5.0
Managers in production sector				
Manufacturing[f]	293	9.0	30	6.5
Construction	67	2.1	4	9
Transport, communications	80	2.5	1	0.2
All	440	13.5	35	7.6
Core public administrators				
USSR or RSFSR government	56	1.7	6	1.3
Local soviets	128	3.9	17	3.7
CPSU apparatus	161	4.9	16	3.5
People's Control	19	0.6	1	0.2
Trade unions	65	2.0	3	0.6
Komsomol	35	1.1	1	0.2
Military[g]	111	3.4	29	6.3
KGB[h]	12	0.4	5	1.1
MVD, local police	86	2.6	13	2.8
All	673	20.6	91	19.7

(continued)

Table 4 *(continued)*

Characteristic	All candidates[a]		Winners[b]	
	N	Percent	N	Percent
Engineers and technical specialists				
Production	123	3.8	18	3.9
Research and higher education	128	3.9	28	6.1
Applied science, design bureaus	147	4.5	28	6.1
Public administration and services	13	0.4	2	0.4
All	411	12.6	76	16.4
Managers and professionals in service sector				
Health	88	2.7	17	3.7
Education, daycare	118	3.6	13	2.8
Trade, consumer services, culture, recreation	151	4.6	6	1.3
Lawyer, procurator, judge	36	1.1	6	1.3
All	393	12.0	42	9.1
Personnel of semi-official organizations				
Artistic unions	11	0.3	0	0.0
Established voluntary associations[i]	45	1.4	4	0.9
Youth units[j]	36	1.1	8	1.7
Cooperatives	41	1.3	4	0.9
Informal political associations[k]	5	0.2	1	0.2
All	138	4.2	17	3.7
Other white-collar personnel	31	1.0	3	0.7
Blue-collar workers in production sector	177	5.4	15	3.2
Blue-collar workers in services	40	1.2	5	1.1
Miscellaneous				
Student, graduate student	16	0.5	7	1.5
Housewife	4	0.1	1	0.2
Retiree	70	2.2	2	0.4
Unemployed	10	0.3	1	0.2
Clergy	4	0.1	3	0.7
Invalid	1	0.0	0	0.0
All	105	3.2	14	3.0

a. All 3,262 candidates on the ballot March 4.

b. All 463 winners declared as of the runoff of March 18.

c. Strictly speaking, the nomination data gave year of birth, not age. Age is considered here to be the age the candidate will have reached by his or her 1990 birthday.

d. Includes 65 residents of Moscow Oblast, outside Moscow city limits.

e. Includes film and television directors, composers.

f. Includes power generation plants.

g. Includes political officers, faculty and students in military academies and institutes, and 1 military procurement agent in defense plant.

h. Includes 1 faculty member and 1 student at KGB Academy.

i. Examples are Red Cross, invalids' societies, veterans' councils.

j. Organizations for young adults not directly controlled by Komsomol.

k. Two candidates reporting positions in neighborhood self-government committees, 1 each from Rossiya Deputies' and Voters' Club, Reborn Russia Foundation, Concord (Sodruzhestvo) Foundation.

The maleness of the field is staggering, men outnumbering women nearly six to one. The gender gap runs through all age groups and subsets of candidates. One has to parse Table 4's occupational groups into smaller subgroups to identify two niches—rayon-level municipal officials and low-ranking health administrators—where females made up more than 50 percent of the candidates.

It is not happenstance that these are both spheres in which women loom large in the work force.[25] Overall, their participation was shockingly low, worse than in the pre-reform Soviet system, where quotas gave rise to rates of involvement double or more those recorded in the Moscow election. The determinants of this pattern, which cannot be plumbed here, must have to do equally with reticence among women and lack of succor from family and other institutions.

There is nothing untoward about the preeminence of CPSU members and affiliates (candidate members of the party and members of the Komsomol). It reflects the party's long-standing saturation of the middle- and higher-status, better-educated lines of work out of which the overwhelming majority of the 1990 Moscow candidates emerged (Hough, 1977). The crisis of morale within the CPSU and the exodus of thousands of intellectuals and others from it in recent months may foretell the end some time soon of the party's ideological and organizational hegemony, but in the winter of 1989–1990 Moscow's aspiring leaders still were drawn heavily from its ranks.

In terms of domicile, it was only to be anticipated that the greater number of elective politicians, especially amateurs and novices at the game, would want to be nominated and to compete in the areas in which they made their homes, where they and their families were clients of most local services, and where they had the greatest familiarity with issues and voters. This proved to be true for better than half of the Moscow candidates in 1990.

Central-city candidates were less likely to be running in their home rayons than candidates on the periphery, as was noted above. A nomination close to the place of residence was more common than the average among women and among candidates in their pension years, both groups whose routines bind them more to home life and less to work than others.[26] Among working-age candidates, members and associates of the CPSU (in downtown and peripheral districts alike) were less likely than others to stand for office in their home rayons, evidently because of their engrossment in some political issues in their job units through party cells there.[27] Since official bulletins recorded only the rayon of residence of the candidate, not the vest-pocket electoral district, it unfortunately cannot be ascertained how much of a homing instinct there was at the neighborhood level.

25. Women accounted for more than one-third but less than one-half of the Moscow candidates in seven other occupational subgroups: physician, teacher, school administrator, manager in a retailing or catering firm, blue-collar worker in a government department, local trade union official, and writer. Except for the last, these would normally be thought "women's work" in the Soviet Union.

26. Among women, 65.5 percent stood in their rayons of residence; among men, it was 55.1 percent. Of candidates born 1930 or earlier, 65.2 percent ran in their rayons of residence, as opposed to 55.9 percent among the younger candidates. Women were the more likely to run in their home rayons in both age groups: 71.4 percent among the candidates born 1930 or earlier and 65.2 percent among those born after 1930.

27. Among candidates born after 1930, 52.1 percent of CPSU members and affiliates ran in their rayons of residence as against 67.3 percent of the other candidates. The gap was 14.4 percent in electoral districts in the thirteen innermost rayons and 16.6 percent in the outer rayons. Among candidates born 1930 or earlier, Communists were slightly more likely (65.6 percent to 63.2 percent) to run in their home rayons.

Although we lack data on the education and incomes of the contenders, information on their vocations and empolyers was divulged during the nomination process. It reveals a strong bias toward the intermediate and upper rungs of the occupational ladder. A trivial 217 candidates (6.7 percent) were blue-collar workers in production or services. The largest grouping was the 725 faculty members and researchers in higher education and science, followed by the 673 in basic administrative pursuits, the 440 managers in industrial and other material production firms, and the 411 engineers and technical specialists. These four main white-collar groups, plus the smaller band of media and arts figures, accounted for 72.9 percent of all candidates. Managers and professionals in the under-funded human services, personnel in semi-official organizations, and miscellaneous categories roll the non-clerical white-collar ratio up over 90 percent.

These people may loosely be called members of Moscow's middle class. One may quibble over the label, for, carelessly applied, it glosses over differences between Soviet and Western social structure. We may also want to move some from one category to the next (police officers, for example, who are joined with core public administration, with CPSU, and with other officials with much fuller perquisites and decision powers). On the whole, however, there can be little doubt—particularly when it comes to the academics, bureaucrats, managers, engineers, communicators, and artists who made up almost three-quarters of the cast—that the candidates greatly exceeded Moscow and Soviet norms on any imaginable index of social position. With few exceptions, their work had a high intellectual component, was relatively clean and safe, had decent side benefits, and could be entered only with a post-secondary diploma.

Before being scandalized, the reader should be reminded that stratification by status and occupational group was not unknown within the bounds of traditional Soviet politics.[28] It is more accurate to think of it as having proliferated and changed valence in the USSR today than as having been invented from thin air. More to the point, comparative research tells us that electoral politics in a Western democracy is apt to be dominated by persons with generic attributes grossly akin to those of the Moscow candidates. From this standpoint, Soviet democratization is supplanting forms of political inequality based on the power of the Communist Party—not with egalitarian utopia, but with the differential rates of participation revolving around uneven possession of individual and group resources, that probably are one of the ineluctable prices of greater freedom. There is an apt analogy in the income disparities that are liable to accompany transition from central planning to market coordination in economics.

The third and fourth columns in Table 4 describe the 463 winners March 4 and 18. They add to the impression of white-collar bias and make for instructive comparisons with the longer list of eligible candidates. The scarcity of women,

28. This point was forcefully argued by Jerry Hough (see Hough and Fainsod, 1979, pp. 305–312).

for example, was accentuated by events after the nominations; persons aged under 40 show the obverse effect, being more prominent at the finish than at the starting line.

In social situations such as this, with many actors and data on many variables, not too many conclusions can be extracted from line-by-line comparisons in matrices like Table 4. The problem, among others, is that the table does not control for the possible interdependencies among the variables. If, say, women did worse than men while younger candidates outclassed older ones, the table would be of no use in disproving the hypothesis that women come out more poorly than men because they tend to be older. For sorting out this manner of evidence, the more powerful method of multivariate regression analysis will be employed later in the article.

THE PARTY THAT WASN'T

The narrative, artificially limited so far to individual candidates, has to be made more realistic here by bringing in the collective players. Yuriy A. Pro-kof'yev, the first secretary of the Moscow city committee (*gorkom*) of the CPSU and a member of the Politburo, was distorting only slightly when he said afterward that the Moscow election was "in essence carried out on a multi-party basis" (*Moskovskaya pravda*, November 30, 1990, p. 1). The role of near-parties, if not full-fledged parties, was the contest's most novel and most propitious feature. That role, ironically, was made possible by the refusal of the CPSU, the only accredited party, to perform like a normal political party. Previously unassailable, it was caught napping by opposition forces which, in a further irony, had one foot planted inside the CPSU.

Prokof'yev, acknowledging the spring balloting as a defeat (*porazheniye*) for the Moscow CPSU, has indicated that the Communists' "chief mistake" was the fact that they "did not manage to become aware in time" of the altered logic of the situation (*Moskovskaya pravda*, November 30, 1990, p. 1). This was in spite of the cold shower of the general election of the preceding March, when voters snubbed most nominees from the local establishment[29] and sent one of the most liberal contingents to the USSR Congress of People's Deputies. The city's CPSU boss during that trail-blazing election was Lev N. Zaykov, the Leningrader imposed by the Central Committee after it stripped Boris Yel'tsin of the Moscow first secretaryship in November 1987. Regardless of his burden at the national level, where he retained the post of CPSU secretary for defense production and national security,[30] Zaykov by all accounts planned to lead the Moscow CPSU into the local election and to be made chairman of the new city soviet under the policy of "combination of posts" (party and

---

29. One of them was Prokof'yev, then second secretary of the *gorkom*.

30. Besides supervising defense matters in the Central Committee Secretariat, Zaykov chaired a secret commission of the Politburo on "military-technical aspects of international policy," which dealt with arms control and the withdrawal from Afghanistan, and was a member of the USSR Defense Council. See his account in *Pravda*, July 4, 1990, p. 3.

legislative) enunciated by Gorbachev at the Nineteenth CPSU Conference in 1988. He was so cocky about success that he commissioned renovation of a city hall office, with private elevator, for his use as mayor.[31]

It presumably was pessimism about Zaykov's mettle as a vote getter that induced his replacement November 21, 1989, by Yuriy Prokof'yev. Sixteen years Zaykov's junior, a Moscow insider, less wooden in style, and not chained to the military-industrial complex, Prokof'yev was a sounder bet and acted as if he felt himself under marching orders to improve on the earlier outing. Unlike Zaykov, who was named to the USSR Congress by the Communist Party, he made a show of valor by contesting a territorial district (No. 388 of the Moscow Soviet, in the remote Butovo section of Sovetskiy rayon). On December 20, 1989, before nominations were over, Prokof'yev's *gorkom* adopted "Political Theses" looking ahead to the campaign and pledging a CPSU-controlled city soviet to "political stability" and "constructive dialogue" with other groups.

Stalwarts of the Moscow CPSU have since mounted blistering criticism of the party's battle-worthiness. Here is the assessment of one *raykom* (rayon party committee) first secretary:

> The Party *gorkom* has been less and less successful at shaping public opinion, directing it down a constructive channel, and harmonizing the activity of the rayon party organizations. . . . The absence of coordination by the *gorkom* was especially noticeable during the pre-election campaign. We entered into it disarmed, with no strategy or tactics for action, without objective appraisal of the situation or experience of a political struggle for power. The political leaders, theoreticians, and ideologists of the city Party organization came across as downright helpless. Their whole approach was disconnected and unprofessional. There was no single platform to unite everyone. A significant portion of the Party *aktiv* was passive. All this is what brought us to those reverses whose fruits we are now reaping.[32]

The point about the lack of experience of electoral combat does not deserve to be buried and does not bear on Moscow alone. Nothing in their biographies had groomed the apparatchiks for the rigors of open jousting for votes. The CPSU machine had been anchored in places of work since before 1917, and since Stalin's day it had busied itself primarily with economic management and plan fulfillment. Movement away from a production-branch toward a more "political" structure, part of Gorbachev's plan to modernize the party since the Nineteenth Conference, was halting. Apart from chapters in some apartment blocks, mostly for retirees, the CPSU still had a feeble presence in the residential realm in which voting and other acts of citizenship take place.

In terms of campaign message and delivery, the CPSU decidedly did not behave like a win-oriented political party in Moscow in 1990. There was no

---

31. On the office renovation, see the interview with Gavriil Popov in *Kuranty*, No. 1 (September 29, 1990), p. 4.

32. V. S. Afanas'yev of Pervomayskiy rayon (*Moskovskaya pravda*, December 1, 1990, p. 2).

one to take charge of its campaign, no headquarters having been formed to that end. Prokof'yev, preoccupied with his Butovo district, was a phantom in the rest of Moscow. The *gorkom*'s "Political Theses" were not modified after December 20, the restlessness of the electorate notwithstanding. The theses were mostly incantations of good wishes, with scant reference to the Moscow context, and of warmed-over promises about local amenities. They waffled on some divisive issues (property ownership, for one) while squandering precious space on belaboring dissidents for promoting a schism within the CPSU's own walls. The most heartfelt clauses in the document were peevishly conservative, climaxing in the allegation that persons and factions unnamed, "taking cover under the slogans of *perestroyka*," were conniving to "restore capitalist relations" in the USSR and to bind Moscow over to unsavory profiteers and money changers (*Moskovskaya pravda*, December 21, 1989, p. 1).[33]

As Prokof'yev confided, what concrete agitation CPSU units did mount in the electoral districts "was oriented as before to the personality factor" (*Moskovskaya pravda*, November 30, 1990, p. 1). The exemplary character of the candidate had been the one feasible sales pitch in the age of the one-name ballot. It did not square with new election realities in several respects.

For one thing, there was no easy way to limit a raft of candidates to personality issues or to get voters to heed personality differences only. Worse, there was now a plethora of *Communist* candidates—three out of every four nominees in Moscow, or almost five per district—and the party set up no clearing house or listing or ranking device to keep them out of one another's way or inform the electorate. One thousand, eight hundred and six Communists (and affiliates), or 73.6 percent of the Communists running, were to arrive at March 4 without the blessing of any of the several slates (see below) that sued for the voters' affections on the basis of more fine-grained programs. In motion, they brought to mind more a herd of elbow-swinging marathon athletes, their CPSU sponsorship stenciled to their jerseys in barely legible letters, than a team swaying to a common rhythm. It was predictable under the circumstances that party propaganda would be woolly and that the smartest candidates would fend for themselves, knowing that the CPSU vote, if there were such a thing, was going to be split among a handful of Communists in the given district. Even the sympathetic voter was left "to make his choice either intuitively or . . . by guesswork," in Prokof'yev's glum words (*Moskovskaya pravda*, February 15, 1990, p. 3).

To take blandness an extra notch, the *gorkom*'s "Theses," revisiting the apolitical lexicon of earlier times, counseled Muscovites to embrace salutary "Communists and non-Party members," therein diluting the very admonition to vote Communist. In the latter weeks of the campaign, as the realization dawned that the left slate, in particular, was hitting home with an audience, CPSU publicists hammered away at the nostrum of "consol-

---

33. Among the specific promises rehashed were those to provide every family with a separate flat by the year 2000, equip every microrayon with shops and consumer services, and restore architectural landmarks.

idation of healthy forces" which also had acquired primacy in Mikhail Gorbachev's rhetoric. Coverage in *Moskovskaya pravda* and *Vechernyaya Moskva*, the two daily papers under *gorkom* direction, for the most part took the shape of symposia and roundtables, where the utterances of the candidates were excerpted in disjunction from one another and the tone was one of a quest for technically competent but politically dispassionate custodians of a unitary public interest.

We will never know how the CPSU would have fared had it nominated single candidates by district and pulled out all the stops to get them elected, perhaps brandishing pork barrel promises as well as more philosophic positions. Some party officials have claimed, with a tinge of self-pity, that voters were so soured on the party by 1990 that no dike could have arrested the tide. It is true, as one account puts it, that "the backing of certain party committees would have guaranteed a candidate's complete downfall" in Moscow.[34] And yet, as this same observer points out, some Moscow party bosses did run unscathed. Prokof'yev was one of them. Quantitative analysis (see below) brings out no measurable tilt against CPSU officials as such, or against ordinary members of the party. All of this is to say that bad election generalship shares blame, together with the pervasive wilting of the party's authority, for the unsatisfactory election result.

THUNDER ON THE LEFT

If the organs of the Communist Party were unwilling or unable to submit a definite choice to the electorate, others were glad to step into the breach. A staple of the literature on party systems has been what Maurice Duverger a generation ago called "contagion from the left," the primacy in political innovation of new elites bent on upsetting the social and economic status quo (Duverger, 1964, p. xxvii). So it has been in Moscow and many places in the USSR.

The main gambit came from a small corps of activists who had first worked in unison in the capital *ad hoc* during the 1989 USSR election, when they decried Kremlin harassment of Yel'tsin and co-signed several declarations to the voters. Consultation after the balloting forged a consensus on the practicality of outflanking Gorbachev to his left in the upcoming RSFSR and local elections and on the exigency this time of an organizational springboard for cooperation. The sparkplugs of the effort were two academics elected USSR deputies in 1989 and still, at the time, members of the CPSU: Gavriil Kh. Popov, age 53, editor of the journal *Voprosy ekonomiki* and a former dean of economics at Moscow University, and the 35-year-old Sergey B. Stankevich, an Americanist at the Institute of World History of the Academy of Sciences. It was Popov who proposed formation of the Inter-Regional Group of deputies, the liberal caucus in the USSR parliament, in the summer of 1989. Stankevich, the drafter

---

34. V. Shutkin in *Moskovskaya pravda*, November 3, 1990, p. 2.

of the first pro-Yel'tsin letter, was more attuned to local affairs. He was a pivotal figure by the autumn in twin organizations with overlapping memberships and left-leaning programs, the Moscow Association of Voters (*Moskovskoye Ob''yedineniye izbirateley*, or MOI), the umbrella for the fledgling voters' clubs, and the older and more militant Moscow Popular Front (*Moskovskiy Narodnyy Front*, MNF).

During the Moscow and RSFSR nominations, Stankevich co-authored an MNF manual on the approach that a "democratic bloc" could ride to victory. He noted that voters were betraying "a certain fatigue with political globalism" and would look for "much more concretization and program" than in the USSR election. For candidates to the city soviet, he submitted the following war cry:

> Here what should prevail, obviously, is the theme of a Megapolis in which the problems of the whole country are incredibly concentrated. A winning moment in the program of a candidate to the local soviet should be [the need for] a Law on the Capital which will give special powers to the city authorities to curb agency [ministerial] dictates and in which removal of the seat of government from Moscow is not to be excluded. [We should speak about] granting Moscow special administrative status, about making Moscow comfortable for Muscovites, about declaring a three-to-five-year moratorium on industrial construction and simultaneously reorienting all building capacities to housing, of converting rayon road departments into contract units to rid the streets of rubbish, of making municipal property of all enterprises dealing with the recycling of scrap materials, the sanitary cleaning of the streets, and the manufacture of the goods that Muscovites need. Protection of green zones, and conferring on them the status of city and rayon parks, is another very important idea. An indispensable theme will be anything connected with the development of self-government (Stankevich and Shneyder, 1989, pp. 5, 7).

From matters of policy, the pamphlet went on to tactics, dispensing cool counsel on agitation, exploitation of positive and negative symbols, picketing and visual aids, and coping with "apparatus candidates." Nominees were urged to make participatory process as much of a drawing card as policy reform and so to turn omissions in the action program into an asset:

> When you are in contact with the voters, you must underline that your tasks as a deputy will not be to settle every problem in the district on your own— to say that would be deliberately misleading—but to open up as many opportunities as possible for citizens themselves to come together in associations for the defense of consumer rights, in ecological groups, in neighborhood patrols to guard playgrounds and transport stops, and so on. Every time a voter heaps doubt upon the practicality of resolving these or other problems—and there will be dozens of times—immediately suggest to him that he join the *aktiv* of the future deputy, that he become your plenipotentiary

for dealing with the issue that is sorest and most urgent to him. . . . It is especially important that the candidate react flexibly to the situation, carry out polemics in "enveloping (*obvolakivayushchem*) style," following up an attack with agreement and confession of the gravity of the problem, and then with a summons to reflection: "Yes, you are right, you have a basis for believing that way, but let us THINK TOGETHER about these other things that you have not yet brought out" (Stankevich and Shneyder, 1989, p. 12).

Preliminary publicity materials aired around the turn of the year referred to an "Alternative-90" slate trained solely on the Moscow and rayon soviets. But on January 20–21, 1990, attempts to expand the horizon of the drive culminated in the founding convention, held in Moscow's Youth Palace, of Democratic Russia, an "electoral bloc" of candidates for republic and local deputies' positions all over the RSFSR. Delegates from Moscow, Leningrad, and 20 oblast centers, setting aside differences on the nuances, adopted a generally worded coalition manifesto vowing to take Russia, "following the majority of the European countries," down "the difficult but peaceful and democratic path of parliamentary transformations, which in the final analysis will give bread and freedom to all." The only alternative, it said apocalyptically, was "bloody shocks" and social breakdown.[35]

Hailing the Inter-Regional Group and the political testament of Andrey D. Sakharov, the conference came out for conversion of the USSR into a genuine federation in which Russian rights would be recognized, for multi-party democracy, and for constitutional enthronement of civil liberties, including abolition of censorship, parliamentary sovereignty over the KGB, and full religious freedom. While more circumspect on economic change, and careful not to make the semantic rupture with "socialism,"[36] the manifesto saluted the market as "the basic regulator of the economy" and called for "legal equality of the various forms of property," all of this wedded to "mighty mechanisms for ecological security and social defense" (among them price controls and indexation of pensions during the transition to the market). Social-democratic icing was subsidiary to the body of the cake: espousal of the fundamental Westernization of Russian society.

It was beneath this ensign that the left slate fought and won the Moscow election. It did so, as I have postulated, as a near-party, an aggregation with some but not all of the hallmarks of a conventional political party. It had a party's crucial win orientation and agreement on the main planks of a serviceable platform, both so egregiously missing in the CPSU. Unlike a normal party,

---

35. Quotations from Sozdan, 1990, pp. 17–18.

36. The convention manifesto sidestepped the question this way: "The argument now heating up about economic policy . . . often acquires ideological coloration: socialism or capitalism? Moving the conversation onto this plane will not tell us what kind of economy we need. It is time to draw practical conclusions from what the experience of the entire world has proven."

however, it had no stylized decision-making structure, relying instead on adjustment of interests and on self-appointed spokesmen like Popov, Stankevich, and their fellow USSR deputy, Nikolay I. Travkin, a candidate in the RSFSR race. Nor did Moscow Democratic Russia enjoy legal shelter for its participation in the election. It did not come into being until three weeks after nominations ceased; not being an authorized "public organization," it could not have nominated candidates in any event. Election posters and ballot slips were silent about it or any other bloc. Democratic Russia had no entree to the official local media, not getting so much as a mention in *Moskovskaya pravda*, the morning daily, until March 2.

How then, one might ask, did the insurgents accomplish what they did? Although Stankevich and others coaxed some candidates into the ring, especially in districts that would otherwise have been vacant,[37] the locomotive power in the early stages was from individual nominees—veterans of the Moscow Association of Voters and Moscow Popular Front and neophytes— and from troupes of boosters, all with minimal central orchestration. The election law did not foreclose radicals coming forward through workplaces, and, as mentioned above, the city electoral commission let pass some of the proposals of the leftish voters' clubs. Two loopholes in the law—the lack of a ceiling on nominations emanating from any one proposer, and the acceptability of nominations from subunits (of at least 30 employees) in work units with more than 150 employees—allowed radicals to unleash volleys of nominations from strong points such as departments of institutes or faculties of Moscow University.

Rather more concertation was effected after the Democratic Russia conclave of January 20–21. Invitations to sign onto the left slate were tendered to nominees—though not in every instance, as I spoke to two candidates whose names cropped up on Democratic Russia lists without them having given prior consent.[38] The main billboard of Democratic Russia candidates, in a four-page newspaper called *Pozitsiya* (Position) in late February, was imprecise and amateurish in composition.[39] A different problem was the misplacement of effort stemming from flaccid coordination. Only 264 leftists (42.6 percent) of the 619 finally registered stood as the exclusive Democratic Russia candidate in their electoral districts; 128 districts had 2 Democratic Russia candidates each and 30 districts had an unruly 3 or more.[40] Had its troops been deployed

37. In an interview in May 1990, Stankevich could not say how many eventual Democratic Russia candidates had been induced into running, but stressed that it was a minority.

38. Both candidates got in touch with Democratic Russia organizers and let their names stand, and both won their seats.

39. *Pozitsiya*, identified as a publication of the Concord Foundation (*Obshshestvennyy fond "Sodruzhestvo"*), published a complete list of Democratic Russia candidates for the Moscow Soviet in its issue No. 3 (February 1990, pp. 2–3). Five of the individuals mentioned had withdrawn from contention by mid-February, seven seem never to have been duly registered as candidates, two were running in different districts than the one indicated, and one had his name misspelled (as Gorovitsyn rather than Korovitsyn).

40. There were 25 districts with three Democratic Russia candidates, two with four, two with five, and one district with six Democratic Russia candidates.

evenly, there would have been no district in Moscow without a Democratic Russia contender, and had their number been hedged there would have been none of the friction between Democratic Russia candidates found in some districts and no risk of fratricide on election day.

In any event, fratricide did not occur, partly because the other players were themselves too disorganized to capitalize on the left's indiscipline.[41] Most important, on March 4 there were Democratic Russia loyalists on the ballot in an impressive 422 (84.7 percent) of the electoral districts. Figure 3 shows their location across Moscow's rayons. In only one rayon (Volgogradskiy) did Democratic Russia average less than 0.50 candidates per electoral district, and in seven others less than one candidate.

Some characteristics of the left roster may be seen in Table 5. Its relative youthfulness would be predicted for advocates of change, but not its sub-average proportion of women. Slightly more than half of the Democratic Russia candidates were members or affiliates of the CPSU, testifying to the group's roots in the progressive wing of Gorbachev's party, while they ranked midway between the right and center slates, but far above the city mean, in terms of closeness of riding to residence.

Most striking about the left slate was its occupational profile. With 64.3 percent of its candidates coming out of higher education, science, the media and arts, or engineering pursuits, it was above all representative of Russia's humanistic and technical intelligentsia. It is instructive, nonetheless, that 10.3 percent of the left candidates were members of the inner administrative elite. Twenty-two military officers, two from the KGB, and seven from the local police carried the Democratic Russia banner, as did eight Komsomol leaders, two trade unionists, eight officials in civilian USSR and RSFSR departments, and seven local government officials. Senior among the latter was Nikolay N. Gonchar, chairman of the executive committee of Baumanskiy rayon. The left even had a smattering of friends within the salaried CPSU apparatus: five secretaries in primary party organizations, three officials of *raykoms*, and one first secretary of a rayon. The *raykom* boss, 42-year-old Aleksandr F. Kapustin of Krasnogvardeyskiy rayon, was one of two Democratic Russia candidates in district 161.

The left bloc was obliged by circumstances to be inventive about transmitting its appeal to the voters. It received a blaze of publicity at two street demonstrations in Moscow pushing the CPSU to speed up political reform: the massive meeting of February 4, which Gavriil Popov addressed and which may have attracted 200,000 participants; and the gathering of February 25, smaller and more obstructed by the police. Banished from the mainstream local press,

---

41. Democratic Russia either won the first round or advanced a candidate to the runoff in 90.9 percent of the districts with one Democratic Russia candidate, in 91.4 percent of the districts with two Democratic Russia candidates, and in 96.7 percent of those with three or more candidates. Among those, first-round Democratic Russia winners were declared in 6.1, 5.5, and 0 percent of the districts, respectively.

Figure 3. *Average Number of Left Candidates per Electoral District*

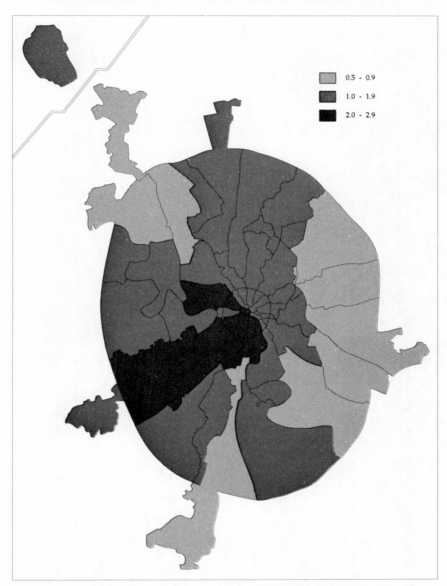

0.5 - 0.9
1.0 - 1.9
2.0 - 2.9

Democratic Russia got a hand from liberal tribunes in the national media, notably the weekly newsmagazine *Ogonyok*, which reported on its founding conference and carried a rambling essay by Popov on the eve of the first round of the election (Popov, 1990). It also eked out space in several of the 20-odd rayon newspapers, less subservient to the CPSU apparatus, which had mater-

Table 5. *Selected Characteristics of Candidates by Slate (percent)*

	Slate[a]			
Characteristic	Left (N = 619)	Right (N = 146)	Center (N = 265)	None (N = 2,232)
Age under 40[b]	35.2	15.8	24.5	26.1
Women	15.2	17.8	18.5	13.7
Member or affiliate of CPSU	50.7	54.8	97.0	80.9
Residence in same rayon as electoral district	73.3	85.6	57.0	50.0
Occupational group				
Faculty members and researchers	37.0	29.5	9.8	19.1
Figures in media and arts	6.1	13.0	0.4	3.2
Managers in production sector	2.9	4.8	21.1	16.1
Core public administrators	10.3	8.2	37.0	22.4
Engineers and technical specialists	21.2	19.2	5.7	10.6
Managers and professionals in service sector	7.4	6.2	14.0	13.5
Personnel of semi-official organziations	5.3	5.5	3.0	4.0
Other white-collar personnel	1.1	1.4	0.8	0.9
Blue-collar workers in production sector	3.1	5.5	5.7	6.0
Blue-collar workers in services	1.3	0.0	0.0	1.4
Miscellaneous	4.2	6.8	2.6	2.8
Running as exclusive candidate of slate in district	42.6	82.2	39.2	n.a.

n.a.—not applicable.

a. Twenty candidates were endorsed by two slates. Nineteen times, the second listing was by the center bloc, which did not reveal itself until the eve of the first round of the election. As a simplifying assumption, cross-endorsed candidates are reckoned here and throughout the article to belong to the slate that endorsed them first. Thus 13 candidates endorsed by both left and center are counted as left candidates, and 6 backed by center as well as right are considered right candidates. In 1 case, a left candidate was subsequently endorsed by the right bloc; he is counted as a leftist.

b. Average year of birth 1946 for left slate, 1945 for center, 1943 for right, 1944 for unendorsed candidates.

ialized in Moscow's boroughs during 1989.[42] Democratic Russia's all-Moscow listing in *Pozitsiya* (an unregistered newspaper priced at 50 kopeks) was complemented by what have to have been hundreds of thousands of handbills doled out free, mostly at the rayon and district levels, and by a myriad of posters slapped up during the stretch drive of the campaign at shops, subway stations, bus shelters, house vestibules, and the like. The authorities winked at this self-advertisement, which badly contravened the RSFSR election law.[43]

Spokesmen for the Communist Party in Moscow have after the fact gone so far as to pay grudging homage to the aggressive tactics of the opposition. One postmortem bears quoting at length:

> Mastery of agitation deserves special study, because here the Democratic Russia bloc in every respect outstripped the Party [CPSU] committees. Those "all-encompassing" official election posters, with their boring portraits of each candidate, faceless biographical texts, and indistinguishable programs, naturally could not captivate the voters.
>
> Everyone remembers the veritable "war of the pamphlets" that erupted on the eve of the election. It is difficult to say who came out on top in this . . . but Democratic Russia, while taking part in the pamphleteering, placed its bet on forms of agitation significantly more incisive and popular, and consequently more effective: pre-election rallies; people with megaphones in underground passageways and on the streets; posters that hit the target head on, showing not only the merits of the candidates supported by the bloc but criticizing their rivals, and sometimes discrediting them; support groups acting in the *mikrorayony*, in sections of apartment houses, at traditional places of congregation of city dwellers; and sound trucks. Let us be frank about it: all this made an impression.
>
> Meanwhile, the official structures—not only Party committees but also the trade unions and all the other public organizations—neglected to carry out this kind of operative and purposeful work (*Moskovskaya pravda*, November 3, 1990, p. 2).

On the sidewalks of their districts, left candidates were free to extemporize on the mutual Democratic Russia program. Many did so with alacrity, highlighting micro-issues or directing appeals, not infrequently emotion-laden ones, to defined groups of voters.

Thus Vladimir K. Abushayev, a Democratic Russia nominee in electoral district 3 (Leninskiy rayon), proposed a municipal payment to central Moscow's copious old-age pensioners and demanded an end to "the seizure by the CPSU Central Committee, the Council of Ministers, and other agencies of land [in

---

42. For example, the newspaper published by the CPSU and Komsomol committees and the soviet of Pervomayskiy rayon carried a message from the rayon voters' club endorsing 13 Democratic Russia candidates for the city soviet in that rayon (*Izmailovskiy vestnik*, 1990, No. 4, p. 3).

43. Some Democratic Russia posters were torn down or written over—without central direction, as far as I could tell—but the great majority remained intact until March 4.

the rayon] for their villas'' and to the issuance of police residency permits to "bankrupt" CPSU and government dignitaries.[44] Yuliy S. Gusman in nearby district 185 (Krasnopresnenskiy rayon) called for a state health insurance scheme, financed in part by profits piped off from Soviet "big sport," and for dedicated flats in rebuilt downtown housing for native Muscovites displaced by urban renewal. In district 337 (Proletarskiy rayon), Irina V. Bogantseva pushed for eviction from Moscow of all of the foundries of the gigantic Likhachev Auto Works, for diversion of the works' and other factories' investment budgets to housing, and for creation of a public park in the Nagatino Floodlands. Bogantseva, a researcher in the Academy of Pedagogical Sciences, also said she would speak up for a new school textbook on Moscow history.

Viktor M. Matveyev in district 189 (Krasnopresnenskiy rayon) was unusual in construing Democratic Russia's platform as a blueprint for "municipal socialism," such as, he said, had been "successfully implemented by left forces in the countries of Western Europe"; his poster said that grassroots groups over a threshold (unspecified) in size should have the right to space in local newspapers and time on TV and radio. One of the few incumbents in the race, Nellya N. Rogacheva in district 86 (Gagarinskiy rayon), campaigned on her record of helping to scuttle an apartment project reserved for high functionaries and to shut down a closed shop selling imported goods to Muscovites in hard currency. Aleksandr P. Braginskiy in district 117 (Kievskiy rayon) declaimed in favor of a "radical improvement" of street sweeping and trash collection, more auto service stations, and orders to defense plants to make spare parts for private cars and municipal buses. More flamboyantly, Lyudmila T. Shekhova in district 149 in north Moscow (Kirovskiy rayon) drew attention to her role in the mass crusade to derail construction of the Severnaya TETs (Northern Heat and Power Station)[45] and excoriated local and national officials for inflicting "ecological genocide" on the capital.[46]

THE SPOILER SLATES

There were two more groups of candidates, from very different bands on the political spectrum, in the swim in Moscow. Neither was large enough to have a mathematical chance of gaining control of the new city legislature. Had their candidates thrived, however, they would have laid bare veins of fervently

44. Abushayev's and other candidates' positions as described here are taken from posters seen by the author in Moscow.

45. Three hundred thousand residents of Moscow and neighboring Mytishchi had signed a petition against the power plant and its towering smokestacks.

46. Abushayev, Bogantseva, Braginskiy, and Shekhova, the sole Democratic Russia candidates in their districts, won their seats in the runoff of March 18. Rogacheva, one of three Democratic Russia candidates in her district, finished second to another Democratic Russia candidate March 4 but won the runoff. Gusman, one of six Democratic Russia nominees, and Matveyev, one of two Democratic Russia nominees in his district, both finished third March 4 and were eliminated.

and moderately conservative sentiment among the voters and might have torpedoed the left's bid at a majority.

The right-wing slate, dubbing itself the "Bloc of Public and Patriotic Movements of Russia," was the more diminutive but also the more viscerally motivated of the spoilers. Like Democratic Russia, it conducted concurrent RSFSR and Moscow campaigns. Its declaration, "In Favor of a Policy of Social Harmony and Russian Rebirth," was first published in December 1989 in *Literaturnaya Rossiya*, the organ of the reactionary and xenophobic RSFSR Union of Writers, and reprinted several times in the new year (Za politiku, 1989).

Signing these broadsides were a dozen extant societies and clubs: *Narodnoye Soglasiye* (Social Harmony, also known as the United Council of Russia), *Yedinstvo* (Unity, subtitled the Association of Lovers of Russian Literature and Art), the *Rossiya* (Russia) Deputies' and Voters' Club, the All-Russian Cultural Foundation, the All-Russian Society for the Preservation of Historical and Cultural Landmarks, the United Toilers' Front of Russia (*Ob''yedinennyy front trudyashchikhsya Rossii*, or OFT), the Public Committee to Save the Volga, the Association of Russian Artists, the Russian Branch of the International Foundation for Slavic Literatures and Cultures, the League for Spiritual Rebirth of the Fatherland, the Voluntary Society of Book Lovers of the RSFSR, and the Foundation for Rebuilding the Cathedral of Christ the Redeemer.

All of these organizations, not excluding the last (devoted to raising money to resurrect a Moscow basilica demolished on Stalin's edict in 1931), were RSFSR-wide rather than Moscow-specific in scope. Most, as is palpable from their titles, have principally taken up Russian cultural and spiritual issues. One important variant on this pattern is the Rossiya club, which originated in the USSR Congress of People's Deputies and Supreme Soviet as a counterweight to the liberals in the Inter-Regional Group. A second exception is the OFT, founded in 1989 with the aim of pulling ordinary workers into the political battle against what the Russian right laments as the excesses of *perestroyka*.

The Russophiles' platform was not without its subtleties. Its championing of Russian prerogatives against the homogenizing and top-heavy Soviet state commanded wide public sympathy in the RSFSR by 1989–1990 and was found in some guise in every faction's program. The right was hospitable to popular environmental causes, such as cleaning up the Volga, permanently interring the plan to divert Siberian rivers to Central Asia, and halting the construction of atomic power plants. It shrewdly phrased its reverence toward Russian Orthodoxy and critique of past mistreatment of the church so as to cast the issue, in part, as a civil libertarian one.

These, however, were secondary notes in the chorus on the right. The primary chord was recoil against the kernel of the Westernizing reforms launched since 1985 and spleen at groups branded as benefiting illicitly from *perestroyka* or wanting to hasten its pace. The right slate's nationality policy was stoutly

"Big Russian," that is, for prolongation of Russian dominion over the minority peoples of the USSR; slighted was the go-it-alone "Little Russia" sentiment which has been gaining currency among Russian nationalists.[47] Lauding the staunchness of the armed forces and police, the right bloc raged at proposals for a non-conscript army and at the "naive" doctrine of "prudent sufficiency" in Soviet defense. To offset the Gorbachev Politburo's "accommodationist" posture toward Russia's internal and external foes, it espoused creation of a hierarchical ("Leninist") Russian Communist Party as the stiff backbone of a redisciplined CPSU. Liberals within and without the CPSU it lumped together with anti-Russian nationalists in a "bloc of separatists and 'left radicals,' " whom it portrayed as itching "to dismember the USSR and sell out our national wealth to Western 'partners.' " Democratic Russia, by these lights, was guilty of little less than treason.

The only extended comments by the right on socioeconomic policy were a vituperative enumeration of the "Mafioso groupings," "machinator-cooperators," "racketeers," "swindlers," and "bribetaking bureaucrats," who lately had fattened themselves and, hand in glove with liberal politicians, were seeking the legalization of private property that would crown them "bosses of the country." The Bloc of Public and Patriotic Movements went out of its way to savage foreign investment, taking a leaf from Marxist movements in the Third World by denouncing "joint enterprises of the neocolonial type, which operate on the principle "They get the income and we get the scrap" (*U nikh dokhody, u nas otkhody*). On local Moscow issues, it had little to say other than the stock oath to protect and restore architectural landmarks (giving no cost estimates) and the more controversial idea of creating a new "administrative center for the USSR" (but not necessarily, it seems, a new parliamentary center) somewhere outside of Moscow, easing development pressure on the capital region. The bloc was mute about the housing and other welfare issues that figured prominently in Democratic Russia propaganda. Municipal voters would have perceived it as offering a pinch more urban conservation and a harsher line on corruption, but otherwise fidelity to socialist orthodoxy.

The Russophiles were slow to solidify organizationally. The list of approved candidates for the Moscow Soviet in the mid-February edition of the Rossiya club's newspaper, *Rossiya*, was only 34 names long. The pre-election *Literaturnaya Rossiya* thrust 150 names before the public, of whom 146 were actually on the ballot March 4; this is not counting Yevgeniy B. Balashov, the chameleon candidate in district 171 (Krasnogvardeyskiy rayon), who somehow was endorsed by both the left and the right slates.[48]

---

47. Within a renewed Soviet federation, however, the right bloc did call for greater political and economic autonomy for the RSFSR, creation of an RSFSR Academy of Sciences and television network, reduced RSFSR subsidies to the other republics, and proportional representation of delegates of the RSFSR in central Soviet institutions. The quotations in the text of this paragraph and the two that follow are from Za politiku (1989, pp. 2–3).

48. These lists are in *Rossiya*, No. 4 (February 1990, p. 1) and *Literaturnaya Rossiya*, No. 9 (March 2, 1990, p. 17). Balashov, a researcher in a Ministry of Defense institute, was easily elected in the runoff with

Backers put together some outdoor pep talks the weekend of the election, but otherwise mustered little presence on the streets, giving out almost no handbills or posters that I could see. Here and there, zealots who may or may not have been leagued with the bloc pasted up placards alluding to perfidious ties between Democratic Russia and the three planetary bogies of "international Zionism," the big banks, and the CIA. "If we do not stop them," one poster blared, "Russia may share the sad destiny of Poland, Panama, and Palestine. Keep in mind that every vote given to the yellow bloc falsely calling itself 'Democratic Russia' is a shot in Russia's back, a blow at the future of our children."[49] The anonymous authors smeared the left slate, but in fairness it should be said that they did not tout either the Bloc of Public and Patriotic Movements or any specific right-wing candidate.

Figure 4 shows the geographic reach of the right slate. It disputed only 133 electoral districts, 120 with lone candidates and 13 with pairs of candidates. Interestingly, these districts peppered all but three of Moscow's rayons. That and the infrequency of pairing both denote a resolve to avoid intra-bloc conflict and to fly the flag in all parts of the city.[50]

In Table 5 one can see that the right nominees were, as expected for the most conservative of the aspirants, the oldest of any slate's. They also were the most likely to run in their rayons of residence and more likely than Democratic Russia (but less than the center bloc) to be women. The fact that no more than 54.8 percent of the right candidates were CPSU members or affiliates, just 4.1 percent more than Democratic Russia, implies alienation from the Soviet mainstream in this quarter no less than on the left. Virtually as many right candidates (61.7 percent of the slate) were in higher education, research, the media and arts, and engineering occupations as on the Democratic Russia team, with about twice as many of them in the media/arts category as for Democratic Russia. Core public administrators seem to have been scared off by the right's vitriol. In all Moscow, the bloc convinced only three military commanders, four minor CPSU secretaries, three USSR civil servants, and two trade union bureaucrats to sport its colors; together these candidates comprised 8.2 percent of its list, less than on the left and about 40 percent of the city average. It garnered not a single municipal, Komsomol, or police official.

The last of the three organized slates in the Moscow election barely qualifies as such. Centrist in temperament, it was cobbled together at the eleventh hour by officials in the *gorkom* and several *raykoms* of the CPSU, acting with the

---

65.5 percent of the vote. I count him in the statistical analysis as a Democratic Russia candidate. Besides Balashov, the final right list included two individuals who had withdrawn from contention, one who seems never to have been registered, two who were placed in the wrong electoral districts, and three with their names misspelled.

49. Quotation from a poster seen March 3 in the Medvedkovo area of Babushkinskiy rayon. The same day, I saw Stars of David scrawled over several Democratic Russia posters in central Moscow, evidently a crude attempt to link the left slate with Zionists and Jews.

50. It is an odd and inexplicable fact that two of the three rayons in which there were no right candidates were the very two rayons in Moscow in which Russophile rayon-level newspapers were being published—*Golos Tushina* in Tushinskiy rayon and *Vybor* in Kievskiy rayon.

Figure 4. *Average Number of Right Candidates per Electoral District*

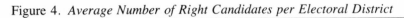

approval if not at the bidding of First Secretary Prokof'yev. According to
interviews, a prime instigator was Aleksey M. Bryachikhin, the workaholic
construction engineer and ex-municipal executive whom Yel'tsin installed as
first secretary of Sevastopol'skiy rayon in March 1987. The only borough
official on the bureau of the *gorkom*, Bryachikhin had been exhorting the
Moscow CPSU to take electoral imperatives more seriously and was one of

the few party bosses to have courted the politicized grassroots clubs and associations.

The March 3 *Moskovskaya pravda* and *Vechernyaya Moskva* splashed the following announcement, autographed by 284 candidates for the city soviet and several dozen for RSFSR deputy, over a half-page:

> Esteemed voters!
>
> We candidates for deputy in your districts are waging an honorable struggle for the votes and trust of the electors. We have diverse programs. Judge for yourselves which is better. But we have a common concern: the fate of *perestroyka* is in jeopardy!
>
> We see the exit from the crisis in political stability and civil accord, in assertion of democratic order and legality, in a just allocation of national property. We are convinced that this alone will make it possible to create the life that you and your families deserve, provide a better future for your children, and resolve the vital problems people have with housing, work, food, and consumer goods.
>
> We call upon you to make your choice March 4, 1990.

Certain of the signatories indubitably had propounded highly diverse programs, which they did not now forsake: 13 had previously been endorsed by the left slate and six by the right. The implication was that there was common sanctuary between the two poles and that all factions shared an interest in the tranquility that would allow *perestroyka* to unfold. Saying nothing tangible about how to rectify housing and other urban problems, the epistle left the impression that the mundane needs of citizens would be given short shrift if ideological passions were at the boil.

The soothing intonation was reminiscent of passages in the *gorkom*'s December "Theses" and of the technocratic roundtables that flooded the official press in the waning days of the campaign. The provenance of the center slate is further avouched by the identities of its candidates. Setting aside the 19 who were cross-endorsed,[51] almost all—97 percent—were associated with the CPSU (Table 5). The group had more women than the right or left blocs, but was intermediate in age and had many more outside-rayon candidates than either bloc. Most conspicuous was the stacking of the center list with senior administrative personnel; almost three nominees in four were either core public administrators or managers in production or service enterprises. The bloc was especially well armed with officials in central or local government (29) and the organs of the CPSU (36). Bryachikhin was joined by no less than eight other *raykom* first secretaries.

The group's last-minute debut left others no opportunity to object to the transgression of the RSFSR electoral law that the newspapers perpetrated by

51. As with the left and right slates, there were errors in the March 3 advertisement. One of the candidates listed had withdrawn, one was placed in the incorrect district, and two names were misspelled.

Figure 5. *Average Number of Center Candidates per Electoral District*

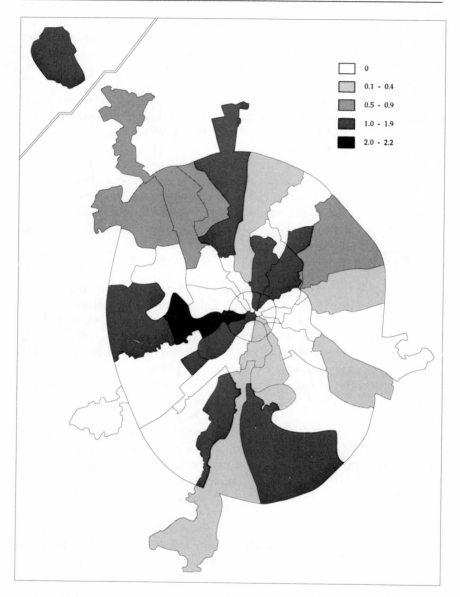

printing its manifesto. Helpful as this may have been, the fragment of time
given voters to digest the missive, and the impossibility of following up the
March 3 article with others, were assuredly unhelpful. The odds of the center
coalition acting as an efficacious spoiler were further reduced by its patchy
territorial organization (see Figure 5). Its 265 candidates were concen-

Table 6. *Selected Parameters of Election Returns*

Parameter	Slate			
	Left	*Right*	*Center*	*None*
First round				
District contested	422	133	178	487
Candidates	619	146	265	2,232
Deputies elected	22	0	3	10
Candidates in runoff	418[a]	32	65	383[b]
Runoff				
Districts contested	365	32	64	320
Candidates	416	32	65	382
Deputies elected	260	12	19	150

a. Includes two second-place finishers who withdrew before runoff.
b. Includes one first-place finisher who withdrew before runoff.

trated in just 178 electoral districts.[52] One hundred and forty-six (55.0 percent) were huddled in the nine rayons in which CPSU first secretaries were on the slate, and another 55 (20.8 percent) were in Krasnogvardeyskiy rayon. In 14 of 33 rayons, the center had no candidates whatsoever, as compared to three empty rayons for the tiny right bloc and none for Democratic Russia on the left.

THE VOTERS SPEAK

Once the votes had been laboriously tallied and verified, as they were without incident, and the returns published and deciphered,[53] it was clear that neither right, center, nor independents had spoiled the left bloc's parade. For a movement whose life span was reckoned in weeks, the election was a dazzling achievement. Tables 6 and 7 speak for themselves. The left returned the most legislators in the initial round. It commenced the second round with almost half the finalists and with the luxury of posting the only candidates in 53 of the districts.[54] On March 18 it increased it popular vote by 300,000 and stockpiled the most deputies' seats by far. Two-hundred and eighty-two of the seats filled as of the runoff, or 60.9 percent, were Democratic Russia's, dwarfing

52. There were single center candidates in 104 districts, two centrists in 62 districts, three in 11 districts, and four in 1 district.
53. Official results were printed in the local press March 6–7 and, for the runoff, March 20–27. From the researcher's point of view, they had numerous omissions, apart from the remediable lack of reference to candidates' slates. The first-round results gave raw votes earned for only the winning candidates; for those 35 districts, no other information was provided. For the districts from which candidates advanced to the runoff, the communique supplied the percentages earned (but not the raw votes and not the total votes cast) for the two top finishers. There was no information about the districts in which the balloting ensued in a repeat election. For the runoff, the press provided complete information for all the districts but one in which a winner was declared, but nothing about district 101 and only turnout figures for the others. I could not have written this article without the comprehensive district-by-district data I received from city hall's Department for Work of the Soviets. I am indebted to Andrey V. Shirokov of the Department for his assistance in this regard.
54. There were two runoff candidates from the left in 51 districts and two districts where a single left nominee ran unopposed.

Table 7. *Distribution of Votes by Slate*

| Slate | First round | | | Runoff | | |
| | | Percent | | | Percent | |
	Total (N)	Total	In contested districts	Total (N)	Total	In contested districts
Left	1,313,374	30.4	35.7	1,615,790	45.6	56.0
Right	138,414	3.2	12.0	104,340	2.9	41.9
Center	284,658	6.6	17.9	193,428	5.5	37.2
None	1,833,131	42.5	43.3	1,223,496	34.5	48.9
Negatives[a]	748,250	17.3	17.3	404,793	11.4	11.4
All	4,317,827	100.0	n.a.	3,541,847	100.0	n.a.

n.a.—not applicable.
a. Valid ballots cast by voters who rejected all candidates.

the contingents from the right (12 deputies) and center (19) and, less drastically, the 150 unendorsed entrants. Democratic Russia was assured of a majority in the next local legislature without having to await the repeat elections required in 35 districts.

Figures 6, 7, 8, and 9 show the drawing power of the three lists and of unendorsed candidates in the first round, summed by city rayon. Left votes are the only ones depicted for the runoff balloting, in Figure 10.

The left was the one slate posing a threat in all sections of Moscow. Its allotment of the votes cast March 4 was nowhere less than the 14.7 percent it received in Perovskiy rayon and rose to 49.9 percent in Zelenograd; it was between 25 and 35 percent in 20 of 33 rayons. In the runoff the range was 17.0 percent (Baumanskiy rayon) to 75.7 percent (Zelenograd).

The gaping holes in the other slates inescapably produced an erratic spatial array of votes. The right bloc got zero first-round votes in the three rayons where it had no candidates and an anemic 0.8 to 8.1 percent in the others. In the runoff the right was blanked in 16 rayons and polled between 2.3 and 12.0 percent in the rest. The center sat out 14 rayons in the first round and 16 in the runoff; in the rayons in which it was engaged, its vote share gyrated between 0.5 and 24.3 percent March 4 and between 2.0 and 20.9 percent March 18. Unaligned candidates, meanwhile, commanded slices of the vote pie ranging from 19.7 to 62.4 percent in the first race and from 12.0 to 60.2 percent in the second.

It is not possible to say how much the left's ascendancy owed to the Moscow campaign as such and how much it mirrored autonomous swings in public opinion, spurred by exogenous events such as countrywide economic woes and the upheavals in Eastern Europe. A poll done by the Institute of Sociology at the end of January detected "a radicalization of the views and aims of Muscovites" and concluded that a majority of the electors "intend to support those candidates in the elections who come out for immediate and decisive changes in our life," and not the disciples of either moderation or reaction (*Moskovskaya*

Figure 6. *Left Candidates' Share of Popular Vote in First Round*

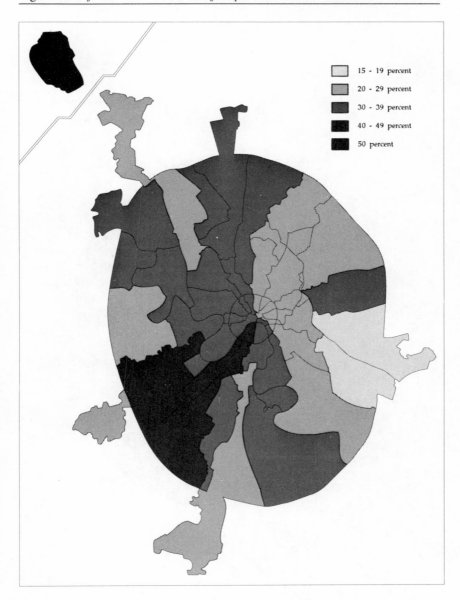

pravda, February 3, 1990, p. 2). The timing of this discovery—more than a month before March 4, and just as Democratic Russia was putting in its oar as a group—suggests that the drift of grassroots opinion was already firmly in the left's favor.

And yet, the facts are not evocative of an attitudinal riptide sufficiently

Figure 7. *Right Candidates' Share of Popular Vote in First Round*

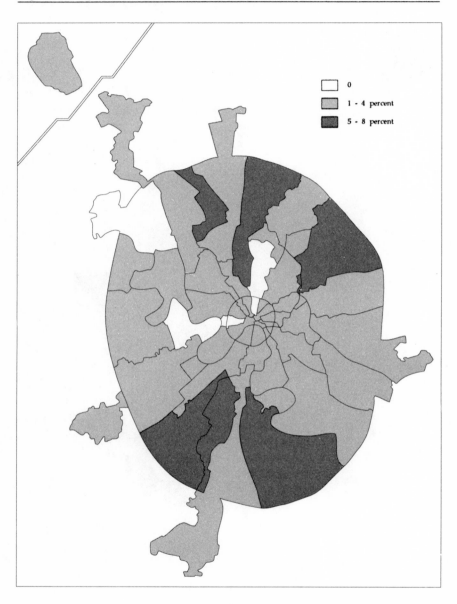

massive and unequivocal to have foreordained the election. Conceding a radicalizing tendency among the voters, the left still needed (1) to get enough
credible names on the ballot to have a shot at a majority of the deputies chosen,
and (2) to persuade prospective supporters that it and no one else would best
transact "immediate and decisive" reforms.

Figure 8. *Center Candidates' Share of Popular Vote in First Round*

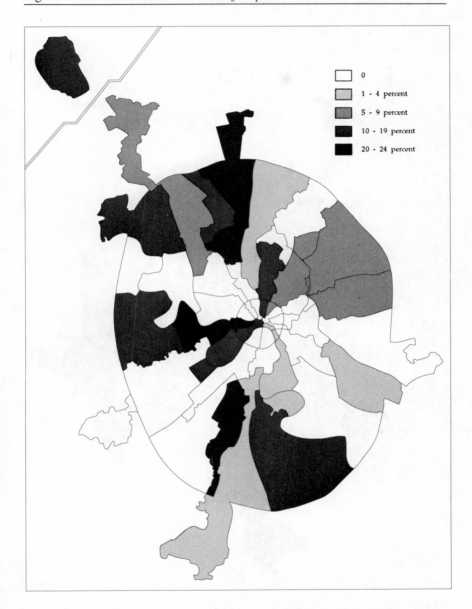

On the second score, the peaks and valleys in the outcome suggest that popular preferences were loosely articulated and asymmetrically distributed and that at a minimum those voters with latent left sympathies had to have them activated by efficient signaling. At one extremity, Sergey Stankevich of Democratic Russia could breeze through with 70.4 percent of the first-round votes

Figure 9. *Unendorsed Candidates' Share of Popular Vote in First Round*

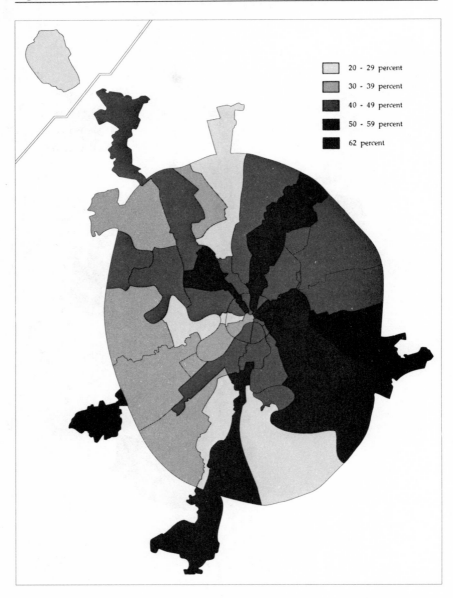

in district 478 (Cheremushkinskiy rayon);[55] at the other, Andrey N. Kovalev, a computer scientist sworn to the same program, could entice no more than

55. Stankevich received the highest vote share of any candidate (Democratic Russia or other) running in a contested district. One Democratic Russia nominee running unopposed, Vladimir E. Gefenider in district 183 (Krasnogvardeyskiy rayon), was the only candidate to receive a larger share (81.2 percent).

Figure 10. *Left Candidates' Share of Popular Vote in Runoff*

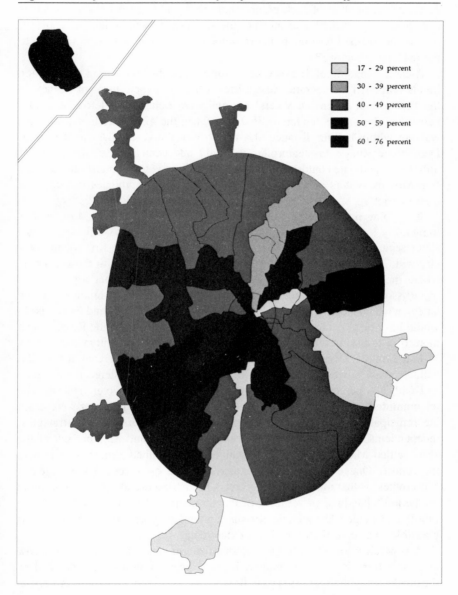

1.1 percent of the electors in district 286 (Moskvoretskiy rayon).

Aggregating left votes by electoral district lessens the variation without eliminating it. Left candidates' joint share in the first round was as lofty as 86.1 percent and as dismal as 8.8 percent, a ratio of almost ten to one. For rightists, first-race shares by district ranged from 0.9 to 38.2 percent, for centrists from 0.49 to 59.4 percent, and for independents from 0.2 to 69.2 percent. The number of each group's nominees and a series of other variables are statistically predictive of much of the variance (as will be laid out shortly), but an unexplained residual remains, some of which can wisely be imputed to the leadership factor.[56]

A careful reading of Tables 6 and 7 further qualifies the notion that opinion trends propelled Democratic Russia irresistibly to victory. In point of fact, in the first round, when the voters' options were richest, the left bloc's 30.4 percent of the ballots tendered (35.7 percent in the 422 districts it contested) was not within hailing distance of a majority of the votes. Easy as it was for Democratic Russia to steamroller the right and center slates, the horde of unlabeled candidates outdrew it by one-half million votes. Almost one in every five Moscow voters chose to vote against all of the candidates registered in their districts.

It is doing no disservice to the left to say that its burden in Moscow was immensely lightened by its antagonists' ineptitude. Whereas right and center slates secured a calamitously low 3.2 and 6.6 percent of the first-round votes city-wide, they were at 12.0 and 17.9 percent, respectively, in those districts where they enrolled candidates. With more adept and timelier organization, the Russophile and moderate blocs, especially an upgraded rendition of the latter, in which Gorbachevian Communists such as Prokof'yev and Bryachikhin would have been natural kingpins, would have given Democratic Russia much more of a tussle, in all likelihood by biting into the uncommitted vote.[57]

In the runoff, Democratic Russia, to its credit, won 45.6 percent of the valid ballots. This, however, was with 46.5 percent of the registered combatants, and with a 6 percent drop in turnout signifying a sag in voter interest. The uncommitted candidates rather than the decimated right and center were again the principal competition. Hewing to disjointed and personalistic strategies, independents still reeled in 34.5 percent of the votes and 32.7 percent of the seats settled March 18. Straight negative votes declined almost 6 percent in the runoff. One explanation, volunteered to me by several knowledgeable Muscovites, is that many of the naysayers in the first round, unwilling to jump on the left's bandwagon yet leery of the alternatives, became abstainers in the runoff and helped Democratic Russia augment its vote share. The theory is plausible, but unverifiable with the extant data.

A generalization about Soviet democratization consonant with the Moscow election returns is that rules matter. If, say, the election had been decided by the unadorned plurality ("first past the post") criteria applied in most American

56. On number of candidates, the following figures for the left slate are illustrative. In the 264 districts with a single Democratic Russia candidate, the high and low vote shares for the left were 8.8 and 81.2 percent, respectively (mean of the scores 31.4, standard deviation 11.7). In the 128 districts with two left candidates, the range was from 15.8 to 86.1 percent; in the 25 districts with three left candidates, it was 18.3 to 72.5 percent.

57. In one rayon, Sevastopol'skiy, where the center was well organized (but the right was not particularly so), center and right together marginally outpolled the left in the first round.

and British elections, all 498 seats would have been awarded March 4 and the left slate would have come out with an enhanced majority.[58] If, by contrast, the axioms had been those of the grand historical alternative to the simple plurality (proportional representation, which links the assignment of seats to the contenders' share of the popular vote), Democratic Russia would be but the largest minority in a new Moscow Soviet; a majority of seats would be occupied by deputies elected as independents.[59] The future evolution of proto-parties in the USSR in and between elections will necessarily be strongly influenced by electoral procedures.[60] So germane will they be that it will be strange if a voice in writing the rulebook does not prove to be one of the cardinal stakes in the politics of political change.

THE CORRELATES OF SUCCESS

The most fascinating question to be asked about any authentic election is not which side came out on top—a glance at the returns will tell that story—but under what conditions its delegates and others did well or poorly. To obtain a clearer picture of this for the Moscow election, I resort to a convenient and proven instrument of quantitative analysis, "ordinary least squares" regression. That method, in brief, tests for statistical relationships between a specified dependent variable and a plurality of independent variables hypothesized to influence variation in it. Its use is restricted here to the first round of the election, thereby summarizing efficiently and doing so when the starting crew of candidates was intact.

The appropriate dependent variable in the regression is the performance of the left slate, the ultimate winner of the election. Our chief interest is in the left corporately rather than in its members, so the data are properly analyzed by city electoral district, not by isolated contender. The best yardstick of performance is the amalgamated vote share of all Democratic Russia candidates in the given district.

One auspicious avenue of inquiry, for which regression is well-tailored, is to delve into which characteristics of the candidates themselves are calibrated with success. Here a complication arises from the multiplicity of nominees, which would not be found in the archetypal Western election, contested by mature political parties. How, for example, does one tap the role of the gender of left candidates if in some districts Democratic Russia had both men and women on its ticket? A related problem is that most of the personal attributes presented in the official compilations render into categorical (nominal) variables, not continuous variables.

58. With a simple plurality required to win, no turnout requirement, and affirmative votes (no straight negatives), the left would have won 314 seats, the right 8, the center bloc 21, and unendorsed candidates 155.

59. Assuming that the straight negative votes had been proportionately allocated among the groups of candidates, pure proportional representation would have awarded 36.8 percent of the seats to the left, 3.9 percent to the right, 8.0 percent to the center slate, and 51.4 percent to the independents.

60. See the classic discussion in Duverger (1964, pp. 207–255).

Anyone can calculate the mean age of two or three candidates, but what is to be done with their occupation or affiliation with the CPSU?

On the second issue, age, being continuous, is the one vital statistic that poses no problem. Gender was coded as a dummy "woman" variable ("1" for women, "0" for men). After experimentation with more elaborate schemes, the CPSU and rayon-of-residence indicators, too, were collapsed into dummy variables.[61] In an attempt to manipulate occupation as a single, continuous variable, all candidates' work was ranked according to an eleven-point prestige scale.[62] Additionally, I recoded each of the groups, the discrete occupations, and bundles of them, as dummies—for example, "military" ("1" for military officers, "0" for all others).

All these values having been generated, there was no design impediment to averaging them in districts in which the left slate had more than one candidate. Thus Democratic Russia "womanness" would be entered as 1.0 in a district where the left nominated one woman (or several women), as 0.75 where it chose three women and one man, as 0.5 for one woman and one man, and so forth. As a check, I also logged in candidate characteristics as dummy variables of the type "present in district/not present in district," assigning the value "1" when one or more candidates on the left slate possessed the attribute and the value "0" when no candidate had it. This approach was invariably futile, prompting the conclusion that, although (as shall be seen) there is predictive power in the proportions among the candidates on the ballot, the voters were not inspired by the mere presence or non-presence of a person exhibiting one trait or another.

As a streamlining assumption, all non-left candidates (right, center, and slateless) were blended into a composite "other" category. For each district, they were coded by the same principles as the left candidates.

Finally, I incorporated the quantitative information that could be gleaned on the voters and the sections of the city in which they lived. In the best of all worlds, we would know more about this piece of the puzzle than is discernible in this instance. But several clues as to the social base of the Democratic Russia coalition do emerge from the available data.

Table 8 summarizes the results of the regression analysis. The coefficients in the second column indicate the amount of movement in the dependent variable (displayed here as a percentage) that goes with a controlled, one-unit rise in the value of the explanatory variable in the first column.

Characteristics of the District Contest

The first pair of substantive coefficients establish the straightforward point that the left's strength varied with the number of candidates it and its opponents

---

61. For CPSU affiliation, candidate members of the party and members of the Komsomol were grouped with full members of the CPSU. For rayon of residence, adjacent rayons were considered as ordinary "other" rayons. The regression was also run with the variables uncollapsed, with no improvement in explanatory power.

62. The categories employed are the same and in the same order as the major occupational groups in Tables 4 and 5.

Table 8. *Regression Coefficients for Left Slate's Percentage of Valid First-Round Votes*[a]

Variable	Coefficient[b]
Intercept	29.78 (3.62)
Characteristics of district contest	
Number of left candidates	8.47 (0.74)
Number of other candidates	−2.05 (0.23)
Characteristics of left candidates	
Age	−0.17 (0.06)
Woman	−5.52 (1.48)
Resident of rayon	8.14 (1.38)
Occupation	
Health professional	8.90 (3.71)
Military or police officer	6.52 (2.84)
Media/arts figure	5.63 (2.60)
Leader of cooperative	−6.80 (3.44)
Manager in production sector	−7.00 (3.01)
Characteristics of other candidates	
Occupation	
Komsomol official	30.49 (8.35)
Researcher in Academy of Sciences	15.45 (7.03)
Trade union official	15.01 (5.94)
Blue-collar worker	−7.47 (4.32)
Military or police officer	−11.03 (3.80)
Characteristics of district	
Cooperative housing	
(percent of dwelling space cooperatively owned)	0.22 (0.12)
Books in public libraries (millions per capita)	0.99 (0.22)
Foreign-language schools	
(per 1,000 school-age children)	−0.15 (0.07)

Standard error of the regression in 9.92.

a. $N = 420$ (excludes 76 districts in which there was no left candidate and 2 in which there was no other candidate).

b. Numbers in parentheses are standard errors of the coefficients.

marshaled in the arena. Its share of the ballots increased by more than 8 percent (plus or minus about 0.7 percent) for every Democratic Russia candidate over one in the district and declined by about one-quarter as much for every surplus non-Democratic Russia candidate. This lack of a fixed ceiling for left votes comports well with the semi-structured character of the election. Not a few Muscovites seem to have approached the election open to being romanced by the left, but with their hearts not yet set on it. The more times they were serenaded, and perhaps the more improvisations they heard on the melody, the more likely they were to consent.

Another facet of the competition was the voting turnout in the district, which in the first round ranged from 48.8 percent to 82.8 percent. Turnout had no impact on the dependent variable.

Characteristics of the Left Candidates

The largest set of statistically significant coefficients represented traits of the left nominees. To begin with, the left bloc did better when it ran candidates who were younger in age. There was a coupling in voters' minds, it would appear, between relative youth and the iconoclasm and vigor that Democratic Russia sought to exude. The contribution of this variable was modest. The expected vote share of the left candidates in a district went up by 0.17 percent for every year subtracted from their average age, or by 1.7 percent per decade.

The evidence is compelling about a gender effect. A Democratic Russia district ticket composed entirely of women would on average have received a 5.52 percent lower vote share than an equivalent team of men (plus or minus 1.48 percent). A 30-year-old female leftist thus had no more electoral muscle than a 63-year-old male. The gender bias of the voters put women radicals at double jeopardy, since so few women were nominated for deputy in the first place (and fewer of the left's total than for either the right or center bloc). There is no hard information on whether male and female voters were equally jaundiced toward women running for the left.

The left's chances of success were more affected by its candidates' place of residence than by their gender. The premium accruing to a nominee residing in the city rayon in which he or she was seeking office was 8.14 percent of the popular vote. One reason homebodies prospered, one assumes, is that they had better intelligence about contiguous electoral districts and were better equipped to mesh the left's program with local needs and controversies. By the same token, some citizens would have been more warmly inclined toward friends, neighbors, or near-neighbors than toward complete strangers.

It is intriguing that affiliation with the CPSU was not correlated with the left's candidate's voting allure. A left candidate who belonged to the party or its youth branch stood to get no more and no less of the votes than if he were not affiliated with the Communist Party. The real and somewhat perplexing news is the absence of a negative effect. What with Democratic Russia's outrage at much of what the CPSU had stood for since 1917, would progressive voters not have read the Democratic Russia platform as a charge to vote against all Communists? Some may have done so—but the temptation could not have been pushed too far for the simple reason that many of the most eloquent of the Democratic Russia activists themselves were still in early 1990 members of the CPSU. Turning thumbs down on all Communists would have meant spurning half of Democratic Russia's own slate, beginning with Popov and Stankevich.

Far from lashing out blindly at all those linked to the CPSU, left-leaning voters cheered some and eschewed others. By March 18, 280 members and affiliates of the CPSU had been elected, of whom 134 were on the left slate. Democratic Russia's Communists made up 47.5 percent of its caucus and 47.9 percent of all Communists in the new soviet.

The only indicator available of the socioeconomic status of the candidates is their occupation. When left nominees were ranked according to a comprehensive, vertical scale of occupational prestige, the regression turned up no covariation whatsoever with vote share. There was no selection for or against left candidates on the basis of the relative status of the jobs they held.[63]

When the focus is in on specific occupations and groups of them, the usual result is similarly neutral. The professors and scientists who made up the largest Democratic Russia group, for example, were not more or less apt to earn the voters' approbation than leftists with more plebeian backgrounds. Surprisingly, the electors evinced no more sensitivity, pro or con, to the livelihoods of the core public administrators in the left bloc, or to most of the subgroups among them.

One might have surmised, as both impressionistic Western overviews and wistful comments by Soviet functionaries have had it, that the populace has been flagellating all echelons of the bureaucracy wholesale at the polls. The Moscow election connotes otherwise. Radical reformers within the official structures, like Chairman Gonchar of Baumanskiy rayon (who comfortably won his district in the first round) and First Secretary Kapustin of Krasnogvardeyskiy rayon (who prevailed with a handsome majority in the runoff), may have been tarnished in the eyes of some voters by their entanglement with the *nomenklatura*. But counter to this seems to have flowed the same sort of admiration of the courage of intra-elite avatars of change that made Boris Yel'tsin a folk hero a year or two before.

The regression did furnish significant regression coefficients for five subgroups represented on the left slate. A position as a physician or other health care professional, a military or police officer, or in the communications media and arts levitated vote share pronouncedly upward, while work in a cooperative or in factory or other production management depressed it sharply. Although the rationale would seem to be different in each case, the overall effect is to show the messiness of voters' perceptions and of the resultant relationship between occupation and electability.

It might well have been public anxiety over environmental and health questions, and appreciation of the management skills nurtured in the financially strapped health sector, that gave medical personnel a leg up. Visibility and recognition alone may be enough to account for the greater popularity of the communication and arts figures.

Concerning the cooperatives, the left bloc's pro-market stance augured well for them and for other forms of non-state enterprise, and by electing Democratic Russia Moscow was in theory opting for further accommodation of the private sector. Yet this did not keep Muscovites from the inconsistency of demonstrating disapproval of real-life left candidates who had toiled in this sector—

---

63. I devised the eleven-point categorization on the basis of the Soviet sociological literature on stratification, conversations with Western specialists, and my own experience in the USSR. I tested a number of different classifications, but found the scale in every case to be unviable as an explanatory variable.

presumably because of disgust at the ethics of some current cooperatives, but possibly also out of lingering anxiety about the market even among persons willing to vote for marketization in the abstract. This is not to say that the electorate was any more charitable toward executives from the material production firms that are the hub of the unreformed Soviet economy. Such individuals did more wretchedly than any other job grouping on the left slate.

Army and police officers ranked only after health professionals in exceeding Democratic Russia's baseline vote. What this is arguably a tribute to is again the ambivalence within the left's constituency. Deciding upon a military or police professional on the radical slate was a neat way of balancing acquiescence in profound change with affirmation of certain of the collectivist and statist values of the old regime. Honest products of the most command-oriented of Soviet institutions, to this way of thinking, would be among the best qualified to pull Moscow and the country out of the rut of the "command-administrative system."

Characteristics of the Other Candidates

Of the characteristics of the non-Democratic Russia candidates in the election, the failure to hatch significant coefficients for every non-occupational characteristic is more than a little mysterious. One can see why voters would have been no less likely to ignore a non-left candidate's participation in the CPSU than a left candidate's. But why would they have responded to the age, gender, and place of residence of the left candidates, and yet not to the selfsame features of the non-leftists? The incongruity seems to mean that, depending on their dispositions toward radical change, citizens saw left-wing and other candidates through quite different binoculars.

The Institute of Sociology survey found that Moscow voters, who in 1989 rated incorruptibility and moral strength as the most desirable qualities in a candidate, now gravitated toward competence (*kompetentnost'*), the knack of grasping public problems and crafting viable solutions (*Moskovskaya pravda*, February 3, 1990, p. 2). Be that as it may: competence was found to insinuate one thing to someone wanting full-fledged Westernization and another to the person preferring less of an overhaul or none at all. Voters looking for a standpat deputy might reasonably be indifferent to qualities such as youthfulness and maleness that, rightly or wrongly, tend to be bracketed in Russian culture (and in the value systems of many societies) with action and change. And they could logically have underplayed the residential variable. To the extent that sharing a neighborhood or district welds a bond of trust, one may speculate that it would be of greater importance to voters who expect politicians to perpetrate fundamental change than to those shopping for agile managers of the status quo.

With respect to occupation, scaled job prestige was as lame a predictor of the left's vote share when run as an attribute of the non-Democratic Russia candidates as when tested for Democratic Russia's own fold. Nor was other-candidate membership in most of the bounded categories and subcategories of employment correlated with the left's success. Again, it is of note that the electorate displayed no blanket bias against (or for) core public administrators, entered this time as right, center, or unendorsed candidates. Yuriy Prokof'yev and Mayor Valeriy T. Saykin, both runoff victors in their districts, were but the most senior of 60 core administrators, among whom were 13 CPSU secretaries, elected to the city council.[64]

The regression did yield significant coefficients for five occupational subgroups among the non-left candidates. The left bloc could count itself lucky to face candidates from three white-collar subgroups, none of whose members had either drawn or repelled votes when enlisted by Democratic Russia. It is unclear why researchers in the institutes of the Academy of Sciences, the most highly regarded corner of the scientific establishment, were one of the pariah groups. Conceivably, they ran afoul of a preconception on the part of some voters that intellectuals ought to be liberal in their politics. The dramatically high coefficients for functionaries of the trade unions and Komsomol must reflect the unflattering public reputation of these two organizations. While voters did not take out their frustrations against the CPSU apparatus, they did against a pair of ancillary elites that many see as having all of the defects and none of the virtures of the party organs.

On the positive side, blue-collar workers running under other banners independently siphoned votes away from the left, whereas they had engendered no vote bonus for the left when they ran with its blessing. Military and police officers, on the other hand, were magnets for votes no matter which opinions they represented. They inflated the left's vote share if harnessed by the left (see above), but deflated the left's share, and by a higher percentage at the margin, when aligned against Democratic Russia. The army, regular police, and KGB, it is fair to say, give evidence here of an institutional aura singularly amenable to manipulation on behalf of both radical and non-radical programs, albeit more readily the latter.[65]

Characteristics of the District

The insight into the election that would undoubtedly be of the widest and most lasting applicability pertains to the voters, as distinct from the contestants. What, we badly want to understand, were the fault lines in the Moscow elec-

64. Prokof'yev drew 43.3 percent in the first round against two other candidates in district 388, defeating a Democratic Russia candidate in the runoff with 69.6 percent of the final vote. In district 150 (Krasnogvardeyskiy rayon), Saykin finished first of three candidates in the first round with 43.7 percent. When the runnerup (a left nominee) withdrew from the runoff, Saykin ran unopposed and won with 62.2 percent of the vote. The CPSU administrators elected included two of four *gorkom* secretaries in this group, five of twenty-four *raykom* first secretaries, and six at lower grades.

65. Twenty-nine of the 60 non-Democratic Russia administrators elected were army, regular police, or KGB officers.

torate? Which portions of it were behind candidates of various stripes? Did communities and coalitions of interests transect the seams between segments and strata of the populace?

Ideally, systematic data about voter alignments would be collected from individuals. In Western elections, political sociologists routinely conduct exit polls, interrogating voters about their personal backgrounds (ethnicity, occupation, partisan affiliation, and the like) along with how they have voted. Information from the two domains then is collated into a picture of group divisions in the election.

No such individual-level data are available for Moscow in 1990. Unless one is content to rely on anecdotes alone, it is necessary to ply other sources for inferences about persons and groups. The one tenable approach—sometimes used in other countries as a second best to survey results—is to mine existent information aggregated by territory. This strategy makes sense only insofar as: (1) the indicators at hand may be construed to bear some causal relation to political behavior; (2) the relevant social groups are segregated by territory; (3) the unit boundaries for the social indicators concur with those for voting returns; and (4) the number of areas for which there are both social and voting statistics is large.

World governments have spawned reams of territory-specific statistics since the coming of the modern population census in the seventeenth century, and the Soviet regime has been no exception. This information is more abundant for Moscow, which has it own statistical annual, than for any other center in the USSR. Regrettably, it is less than optimal for election analysis in several key respects.

The biggest hindrance, it goes without saying, has been the suppression of facts on political grounds. Most detrimental has been the paucity of data concerning what everywhere are taken as the correlates (education, occupation, income) of social class, the principal axis of political cleavage in most industrial societies. Either all such information has been withheld for Soviet regions and cities, or it has been kept secret for territorial parcels within them. The dearth has been mitigated some for Moscow by the heightened candor about social policy indicators in the Gorbachev era. These partially illuminate living conditions in different parts of the metropolitan area; with imagination, some will serve as imperfect proxies of social composition.

Further manipulation of the data is constrained by three other considerations. First, Russian and Soviet urban neighborhoods and districts, for a bounty of reasons that cannot be elaborated here, have been more heterogeneous in their makeup than most Western counterparts. Although there is some spatial differentiation of the social potpourri in Moscow, it is less acute than it would be if market pricing of housing, municipal fragmentation, and other causes had facilitated geographic separation of the classes. Second, all the quantitative information recorded up to now is constituted by city rayon, an administrative vessel which in the 1989 census had an average of 260,000 residents. Many of Moscow's rayons (mean area 32 square kilometers) encompass subzones with disparate histories and amalgams of economic uses. The final point is the disjunction between the rayons and the 15 times more numerous electoral districts. Even in the most favorable case, rayon-level data adduced into district-level analysis will inevitably contain measurement errors.

Real though these caveats are, they are not so severe as to obviate the exercise. Accordingly, I input eighteen district (rayon) characteristics in the regression as independent variables. One was a dummy variable for geographic centrality (coded as "1" for the thirteen inner rayons). Three were sociodemographic variables, giving the proportion of the population female, of pension age, and having been convicted of a crime the preceding year. Fourteen were yardsticks of public policy or its results, roughly capturing the state of provision in health care, schooling, housing, retail and consumer services, recreation, and environmental protection.[66]

The centrality measure, the sociodemographic variables, and most of the policy indicators were useless as predictors of the left bloc's vote share. It made no difference to Democratic Russia's success whether the electoral district was near the city center or in a more suburban location or whether women, retired persons, or criminals were overrepresented in the rayons' population. Nor did it matter if the rayon was a "have" or a "have-not" in terms of social services, housing supply, and most amenities.

The last three lines of Table 8 show significant coefficients for just three territorially arrayed variables, having to do with cooperative housing, public libraries, and schools functioning in foreign languages. As it turns out, however, all three converge on a single conclusion—the strong influence of Democratic Russia in what again may casually be labeled the urban middle class.

Cooperatively financed housing construction, dormant in Moscow and the USSR from the 1930s until the early 1960s, took wing under Nikita Khrushchev. Despite a sag in production after 1970, 9.7 percent of dwelling space in Moscow in 1989 was in cooperative apartments. While slightly more cramped than state-owned flats, they can be obtained relatively quickly and tend to be better maintained. The applicant has had to have a large nest egg of cash (customarily 40 percent of the value of the apartment) for down payment. The last circumstance, in particular, has deterred less savings-oriented blue-collar workers and helped skew the building cooperatives toward a professional, managerial, and academic clientele. Cooperative buildings are found mostly toward the edge

66. These were the policy indicators: hospital beds per capita; day care spots per preschool child; all classroom spaces and foreign-language schools per child of school age; square meters of housing per capita; proportion of the population in joint occupancy (communal) housing and in cooperative apartments; square meters of food and nonfood stores per capita; proportion of food sales in alcoholic beverages; seats in public dining outlets and cinemas, and books in public libraries, all per capita; and tons of air pollutants emitted from stationary sources per square kilometer. All data are for 1989 except for day care, cinemas, and air emissions, which are for 1988. Most of these and the other indicators were taken from *Moskva v tsifrakh 1989* (1989). Information about age groups, crime, housing structure, and liquor sales is from the data set *Sistema kompleksnoy otsenki sostoyaniya sotsial'no-ekonomicheskogo razvitiya Moskvy i yeyo administrativnykh rayonov*, prepared by the Central Mathematical Economics Institute. Printouts were kindly made available to me by Professor Vladimir Treml.

of Moscow, densest in the southwest quadrant, where in 1989 they comprised 22.6 percent of net housing in Cheremushkinskiy rayon and 17.5 percent in Gagarinskiy. Both of these boroughs are home to thousands of research personnel from Moscow University and the think tanks in the area.

Public libraries are best stocked in the older rayons of Moscow, being largest in proportion to the population in Baumanskiy, Krasnopresnenskiy, Frunzenskiy, and Leninskiy rayons. It is not idle speculation to associate books with readers, and these parts of the city core do indeed have clusters of writers, artists, and other mainstays of the creative intelligentsia. Most of the city's theaters, publishing houses, and intellectuals' clubs are located here. So it is fitting—making allowance for the defection of some intellectuals to the Russophiles—that Democratic Russia's liberal program would find resonance in electoral districts with these characteristics.

The elementary and secondary schools in which English, German, or some other foreign tongue is the language of instruction have a rather different connotation in Moscow. It has long been said in private—and there was some public confirmation of this during Yel'tsin's fleeting reign in the Moscow CPSU apparatus—that these enriched-curriculum schools cater to the offspring of the Soviet political and administrative elite, and that they are thus sited in proximity to housing projects in which large numbers of state and party officials live. While not all pupils in these schools have been from well-connected families, it is not unreasonable to assume that an unrepresentative portion of them have been.[67] Again, there is a significant correlation, this time a negative one, between per capita provision and the left slate's vote share. The most that can be said is that the intuitive explanation—that members and dependents of the power elite were as hostile to Democratic Russia as the struggling professionals in the cooperatives and the writers and artists were enamored of Democratic Russia—is not inconsistent with the evidence.

CONCLUSIONS

The new Russian left's triumph in the Moscow election is history. The sworn-in Moscow council chose Gavriil Popov over Aleksey Bryanchikhin as its head April 20, 1990, and Sergey Stankevich and Nikolay Gonchar are his top lieutenants. Popov, Stankevich, and about one-quarter of the Democratic Russia caucus have turned in their CPSU cards since July. They are again sailing uncharted waters, now those of government under conditions of stupefying uncertainty about the institutions and social forces surrounding them.

In dissecting the Moscow and similar contests, we should not feel torn between a focus on elite "superstructure" and one on popular "base." Without question, elites do matter, and not just masses. There would have been no Bolshevik Revolution without Bolsheviks. A democratic revolution in the con-

67. There were 88 foreign-language schools in 1989. Four rayons (Krasnogvardeyskiy, Solntsevskiy, Sovetskiy, and Zelenograd) had no schools, and the largest number (eight) was found in Krasnopresnenskiy rayon.

temporary USSR would be unthinkable without democrats and, as the left slate in Moscow demonstrates, without democrats who know what they are about. Democratization would not be making the inroads it has if anti-democrats had greater elan and ingenuity than they have shown to date.

At the same time, there is an architecture to the decisions Soviet voters make, and it must be gauged and probed by the best tools social science provides. Soviet electors, if Moscow's are any guide, are often finicky about candidates' demographic and other attributes. More important, there is evidence of regularity in the apportionment of support for contending programs among social groups. Only a battery of survey and other research will begin to clarify that terrain. If a Russian and Soviet middle class is in fact coming of age, we must be far better briefed than we are today about its dimensions and internal dynamics and about how these match up to the aspirations of other strata. If the Russian and other citizens of the Soviet Union are henceforth going to select their leaders through voting, the need for a political sociology of elections and post-election governance is so urgent that it should be an organizing and funding priority for Soviet studies as a whole.

Afterword

Western attention has recently been grabbed by Gorbachev's attempts to stabilize the Soviet economic and political scene by fortifying executive power and making strong use of police and other control instruments. It is of interest that elements of this approach have made an appearance in the city of Moscow, which after the 1990 election was hailed as a citadel of democratic values.

The radical-controlled Moscow Soviet has since last spring adopted a series of ringing declarations on sale of the housing stock to tenants, privatization of 16,000 small trade and service enterprises, protection of the metropolitan environment, and other good things. These resolutions, however, remain largely on paper. Legislators were unable to reach agreement on the composition of an *ispolkom* (executive committee) of senior civic administrators until January 17, 1991, nine months after they took office. Democratic Russia's caucus has been riven by infighting and is often tactless in dealings with other groups. Associates of Gavriil Popov on the presidium speak with undisguised contempt about the agitational proclivities of the corps of deputies. A number of the rayon soviets—21 of which were taken over by supporters of Democratic Russia as a result of the election—have been embroiled in conflict with city hall, in several cases after declaring their "sovereignty" over rayon territory. And there are signs of a backlash against fractious democrats among the electorate.

Popov, for his part, has written an open letter to the city soviet and the populace announcing the need to overhaul local institutions "whose internal frictions are holding up the very best decisions at the same time as the disintegration of the economy continues" (*Moskovskaya pravda*, January 16, 1991, p. 2). He is now for creation of a strong, directly elected Moscow mayoralty.

He cites the experience of some American cities, but clearly has in mind the precedent of the establishment of the USSR presidency in 1990. Popov wants the plenum of the Moscow Soviet turned into a checking organ, meeting only once a year; most policy is to be made by a "municipal council" selected by the full soviet, by the *ispolkom*, and by the mayor himself, who is to be surrounded by advisory councils and to have the right to veto council decisions. The rayon soviets are to be degraded to purely consultative bodies.

Implementation of these proposals would bring Moscow closer in certain respects to the governmental structure of a large United States city. Popov's plan probably makes good sense as a streamlining device, as a way of giving hope of delivery of concrete benefits to Democratic Russia supporters, and as a way of calming the fears among disorder of more conservative voters, who may very well have gained in strength since the spring of 1990.

The unanswerable question at the present time is whether it will be possible under crisis conditions to combine political restructuring and administrative rationalization with the commitment to greater openness and responsiveness in government. The Soviet people, Gorbachev insisted when he first espoused political reform in 1987, must "learn democracy." The early experience of Moscow suggests how complex and arduous that education will be.

REFERENCES

Duverger, Maurice, *Political Parties*, Barbara and Robert North, translators. London: Methuen, 1964.

Fainsod, Merle, *How Russia Is Ruled*, revised ed. Cambridge, Mass.: Harvard University Press, 1963.

Friedgut, Theodore H., *Political Participation in the USSR*. Princeton, N.J.: Princeton University Press, 1976, Chapter 2.

Hahn, Jeffrey W., *Soviet Grassroots: Citizen Participation in Local Soviet Government*. Princeton, N.J.: Princeton University Press, 1988.

Hough, Jerry F., "Party Saturation in the Soviet Union," in Jerry F. Hough, *The Soviet Union and Social Science Theory*. Cambridge, Mass.: Harvard University Press, 1977, 125–139.

Hough, Jerry F., and Merle Fainsod, *How the Soviet Union Is Governed*. Cambridge, Mass.: Harvard University Press, 1979, 305–312.

Moskva v tsifrakh 1989 (Moscow in Figures 1989). Moscow: Finansy i statistika, 1989.

Mote, Max E., *Soviet Local and Republic Elections*. Stanford, Calif.: Hoover Institution, 1965.

Popov, Gavriil, "Za chto golosuyet Rossiya (What Russia Is Voting For)," *Ogonyok*, 10:4–7, March 1990.

"Sozdan izbiratel'nyy blok 'Demokraticheskaya Rossiya' (Democratic Russia Voters' Bloc Created)," *Ogonyok*, 6:17–18, 1990.

Stankevich, S., and M. Shneyder, *Rekomendatsii po taktike kandidatov demokraticheskogo bloka i ikh komand v izbiratel'noy kampanii 1989–90 gg (Recommendations on Tactics of Candidates of the Democratic Bloc and Their Campaign Teams* *in the 1989–1990 Election Campaign)*. Moscow: Informtsentr Moskovskogo Narodnogo Fronta, 1989 (but no date specified).

"Za politiku narodnogo soglasiya i Rossiyskogo vozrozhdeniya (In Favor of a Policy of Social Harmony and Russian Rebirth)," *Literaturnaya Rossiya*, 52:2–3, December 29, 1989.

Zakon Rossiyskoy Sovetskoy Federativnoy Sotsialisticheskoy Respubliki o vyborakh narodnykh deputatov mestnykh sovetov narodnykh deputatov RSFSR (Law of the Russian Soviet Federated Socialist Republic on Elections of People's Deputies of Local Congresses of People's Deputies of the RSFSR). Moscow: Sovetskaya Rossiya, 1989.

Part IV

Mikhail Gorbachev as Leader

Mikhail Gorbachev as Leader: An Introduction

Peter H. Solomon, Jr.

THIS SECTION presents a series of appreciations of the leadership of Mikhail Gorbachev, written in 1990 and 1991. The assessment of a leader is far from a simple task, especially when he is still in office. Anyone undertaking this challenge soon confronts hard questions. By what standard should one judge a leader? By what he accomplishes or how? By the legacy he leaves behind or the skill he shows while at the helm? Or both? Another issue is how to assess a leader in midstream, before his term in office is over and the impact of his stewardship known. Inevitably this particular exercise calls for predictions about events in the future. And prediction, more than any other kind of analysis, reflects the assumptions and biases of its makers.

The articles that follow reflect differing perspectives on the proper criteria of assessing a leader (or at least on their relative weight). They also differ in the scenarios for the future that their authors think likely. Not surprisingly, therefore, the writers disagree in their evaluations of Gorbachev as well.

In the lead article George Breslauer starts by recognizing the special character of the leadership of Gorbachev. Gorbachev is not an ordinary leader, but a leader attempting to transform his country. This fact, Breslauer contends, should dictate how one sets out to assess him. To begin, it suggests a special standard of evaluation which includes both leadership and the results of leadership. For Breslauer a "transformational leader" achieves success when he develops and maintains support for fundamental change and effects change that makes his government or economy stronger and more effective. Gorbachev's status as transformational leader also suggests to Breslauer the utility of examining his stewardship in the light of studies of transitions from authoritarianism to democracy and the generalizations that this literature has produced.

Studies of regime transitions in the past suggest, Breslauer discovers, that the leader of a transformation must act as a political navigator, who, while pursuing grand goals, pays close attention to the management of political forces, new social groups and old elites alike. Above all the leader must employ tactics that prevent significant social groups from forming an alignment against him.

This tactical goal may require frequent changes in policy (two steps forward, one step back) and shifting alliances with right and left.

On the strategic as opposed to the tactical level, the leader of a political transformation must destroy old institutions while creating new ones (always dangerous because of the potential vacuum) and at the same time begin breathing new attitudes, even traditions, among the public. Rarely, Breslauer observes, does the same leader see this process through to completion.

In the light of such generalizations about the leaders of successful regime transitions, George Breslauer concludes, Mikhail Gorbachev has performed admirably. On the tactical level he has maneuvered with a sure hand, paying heed to the political implications of his actions, and on the strategic level he has accomplished the task of destroying old institutions while cushioning the repercussions. These accomplishments lead Breslauer to judge Gorbachev "a brilliant and indispensable transitional leader" at least for the first five years of his rule.

At the same time, Breslauer remains keenly aware that the ultimate test of Gorbachev's leadership will lie in what his leadership accomplishes. Whether he goes down in history as a "transforming" leader or a "tragic" one will depend upon what happens in the USSR in the years to come, and Breslauer provides the reader with a useful outline of the possibilities.

What makes Breslauer's article most valuable is that it offers a framework for the evaluation of both Gorbachev and his successors who will preside over later phases of the transformation of the USSR. Readers should note, however, that Breslauer's scheme is based upon the literature on transitions of *regimes* (usually from authoritarianism toward democracy). Regime transition in the USSR is complicated by two additional factors: (1) the simultaneous pursuit of a transition from an administered to a market economy; and (2) the undertaking of these two transitions in a multinational empire. To my knowledge, no previous successful transition to democracy has involved either of these "complications."

In fact, these complications help to explain the crises in the USSR during the second half of 1990 and the political stalemate surrounding their resolution. Gorbachev the leader was forced to confront the rapid disintegration of the centrally administered economy, separatist challenges, and the erosion of the authority of all-Union government over which he presided. In the economy, neo-feudal and premarket relations (especially barter) became widespread, and in the polity a multiplicity of competing centers of power and authority (center, republics, and local governments) emerged.

The authors of the next three essays shared the task of assessing the leadership of Gorbachev in the context of these developments. The editors of *Soviet Economy* asked them to address a deceptively narrow question: "Has Gorbachev's leadership outlived its usefulness?"

Peter Reddaway argues that Gorbachev will not be able to handle the crisis of authority of 1990 and has indeed outlived his usefulness. Reddaway finds the seeds of Gorbachev's current dilemmas in weakness that he displayed in the past. For Reddaway, Gorbachev was not the great navigator that Breslauer pictures, but rather a prisoner of old views. Gorbachev started reform in the Soviet Union, Reddaway continues, merely to make socialism work, and then pushed, against his better instincts and with much resistance in 1989–1990, to adopt radical reforms, such as privatizing the economy and establishing a multi-party system and confederation. Confused and conflicted, Gorbachev has shown in 1990–1991 "growing indecisiveness and erratic behavior," for example, by failing to submit his initial candidacy for president to popular election (when he would have won) or drawing back after an extensive flirtation from adopting the Shatalin plan for privatizing the economy.

To Reddaway, Gorbachev's biggest problem is that he cannot regain personal stature now that the central government over which presides has lost its authority. Reddaway concludes that Gorbachev has had his hour on the stage and has no more contributions to make.

Archie Brown agrees with Reddaway that in 1990–1991 Gorbachev faces a difficult situation, but Brown is unwilling to dismiss Gorbachev's role in the future. The reason is Brown's positive evaluation of Gorbachev's record in the past. Far from being a prisoner of old ideas, Gorbachev, in Brown's view, showed himself to be a flexible leader, constantly changing with the times. The radicalization of Gorbachev's policies in 1989 showed a striking capacity to adapt and revealed Gorbachev as a true pragmatist. Yes, Brown admits, Gorbachev remained attached to "socialism," but he redefined the term many times, to the point where he lost the support even of some socialist reformers (like Kurashvili). Gorbachev also showed a capacity for institutional innovation both in developing the Presidency (designed to give his leadership a legal basis; see Solomon, 1990) and in working toward a Union Treaty that shifts much power to the republics.

Archie Brown joins George Breslauer in stressing that transitions are by their nature long, difficult, and rarely smooth. Against this background, Brown gives Gorbachev high marks for managing the transition to a mixed political system (authoritarian and pluralist) and starting movement toward a mixed economy as well.

The Soviet historian Andranik Migranyan also views current events in a long-term perspective, specifically through the prism of his own theory of history. European history suggests to Migranyan that the development of democracies requires a social base, usually intermediate groups like entrepreneurs and a small middle class. Since groups of this kind emerged in Europe with the market economy, Migranyan inferred that in the USSR as well, the development of a market economy should precede democratization. Without economic revolution and the creation of a middle class, the only feasible political change in the USSR would be a shift from totalitarianism to authoritarianism (Migranyan, 1990).

For Migranyan, therefore, Gorbachev made a serious error in launching democratization so soon. This error in sequence had the terrible consequence of releasing centrifugal forces (such as separatist movements) and undermining political authority, especially of the central government. In 1991 and beyond Gorbachev's only function, Migranyan predicts, will be to preside over the shift of power to the republics, and his task will be keeping that process peaceful.

In another contribution to the discussion, completed in the spring of 1991, Jerry F. Hough tries to rebut the negative appraisals of Gorbachev, on the part not only of Reddaway and Migranyan but also, implicitly, of commentators elsewhere, such as Seweryn Bialer, Aurel Braun and Richard Day, and Robert Kaiser (Bialer, 1990; Braun and Day, 1990; Kaiser, 1991). Hough joins Breslauer and Brown in viewing political transitions as inherently rocky and requiring flexibility from their leaders. But Hough goes further than the others in assigning to Gorbachev the vision and capacity to anticipate most of the bumps in the road, including the virulent outbreak of ethnic separatist sentiments.

For Hough, Gorbachev represents the master political tactician, always concerned with the implications of his politics for his support and with the cultivation of his political resources. While Hough admits that he cannot know the motives of Gorbachev, he expresses resentment at the attempt by others to depict the leader as flailing and his policies as mere reactions to events. To counter such readings of Gorbachev's decisions and at the same time stretch the minds of readers, Hough insists that we recognize the possibility that the intricate, multistaged shift of power from party to governmental institutions (undertaken in 1988–1990) followed a Gorbachevian design, and that even the crisis atmosphere of 1990 was created by Gorbachev on purpose to isolate his opponents.

Hough goes on to argue that while Gorbachev holds masterfully to the center of the political spectrum, that spectrum itself has moved steadily leftward. Gorbachev became a radical reformer (though not a total revolutionary), a position from which he has yet to deviate. Gorbachev's alliance late in 1990 with conservative forces was in Hough's view a tactical step, intended to restore order, stabilize the economy, and recapture popular support in preparation for the next round of radical reform.

For Hough, like Breslauer, the leader of a political transformation must display exceptional political skill, if only to navigate the rough waters that he has produced and maintain or re-create support from society and its elites.

A similar emphasis on political skills is found in the classic study of the leadership of American presidents *Presidential Power*, by Richard Neustadt. Neustadt found that successful presidents (like Harry Truman) managed to add to their political resources by gaining both the respect of fellow politicians and popularity with the pubic at large (Neustadt, 1980). While Gorbachev succeeded on these counts during his first years in office, by 1990–1991 he had lost much of his professional reputation and popular following alike.

Breslauer, Hough, and Brown think that Gorbachev can make a recovery; Reddaway and Migranyan think not.

In his response to the discussion engendered by his article, Breslauer spells out further differences, both methodological and substantive, among the participants. In particular, he draws out his differences with Hough, in the process demonstrating that analysts can reach optimistic conclusions for very different reasons.

In the long run, though, the evaluation of Gorbachev by historians will depend, as Breslauer argues, not only on his skills as a leader transforming his country but also on the outcome of his efforts. The litmus test will be what happens in the USSR in the next few decades, well after Gorbachev himself has left the political stage.

References

Bialer, Seweryn, "The Last Soviet Communist," *U.S. News and World Report,* October 8, 1990, pp. 53–54.

Braun, Aurel, and Richard Day, "Gorbachevian Contradictions," *Problems of Communism,* May–June 1990, pp. 51–71.

Kaiser, Robert, "Gorbachev: Triumph and Failure," *Foreign Affairs,* Spring 1991.

Migranyan, Andranik, "The Long Road to a European Home," *Soviet Law and Government,* 29, 3:62–98, Winter 1990–1991.

Neustadt, Richard, *Presidential Power: The Politics of Leadership from FDR to Carter,* enlarged ed., New York: John Wiley, 1980.

Solomon, Peter H., Jr., "Gorbachev's Legal Revolution," *Canadian Business Law Journal,* 17, 2:184–185, 1990.

CHAPTER 14

Evaluating Gorbachev as Leader

George W. Breslauer

In March 1990, Mikhail Gorbachev had been General Secretary of the CPSU, and recognized leader of the country, for five years. In light of that, scholars, publicists, and journalists have begun to evaluate his leadership (M. Goldman, 1990; Hough, 1989; Hough, 1989–1990; *Newsweek*, June 4, 1990; Bonner, 1990). Most previous literature on Gorbachev had sought to fathom his leadership strategy, explain his ascendancy within Soviet politics, or predict whether or not his reforms can succeed. Evaluating the quality of his leadership was the next logical step.

THE NORMATIVE VERSUS THE ANALYTIC

That step is a risky one, for evaluation is both a normative and an analytic exercise, and it is always risky to mix the two. For example, those who dislike what Gorbachev has done often bring great passion to their negative evaluations; conversely, those who favor the values Gorbachev has tried to advance often bring equal passion to their positive evaluations. *Time* magazine may proclaim Gorbachev its "Man of the Decade," even as Soviet reactionaries damn his Westernization of the country and Soviet freemarketeers damn his continued commitment to "socialism." Both ends of the Soviet political spectrum express dismay that Gorbachev is so much admired abroad, yet so little admired at home. When the debate hinges solely on acceptance or rejection of the material and ideal values being advanced, it need not detain us long. It is not amenable to resolution through the marshaling of evidence.[1]

The analytic side of the exercise is more interesting and more challenging, for it allows us to take values as given and come to terms with the deeper

First published in *Soviet Economy*, 1989, 5, 4, pp. 299–340. The author would like to thank the Carnegie Corporation of New York for its support of the larger project on which this article is based. He would also like to thank Brian Sanders for comments on an earlier draft of this article.

1. As Hoffmann (1967, p. 113) puts it: "a man who is a hero to my neighbor may be a calamity to me."

counterfactual: what was the alternative? How much more "accomplishment" (i.e., change along specified value dimensions) could we have expected from any other Soviet leader in a period of five years? Leadership cannot be evaluated without some conception of its flip-side: opportunity. If the challenge is so great as to be impossible to achieve, then, by definition, no amount of brilliant leadership can overcome the constraints. Under these circumstances, there would be no opportunity to exploit. As Doig and Hargrove (1987, p. 14) conclude: "the favorable match of skill to task must be reinforced by favorable historical conditions if there is to be significant achievement." On the other hand, if the challenge was a simple one, or if existing social and political forces would have forced through the changes we have witnessed in any case, then the leader can hardly be credited with being an "event-making man" (Hook, 1943, p. 154).

Thus, the quality of leadership can only be evaluated relative to one's conception of the magnitude of the task, the magnitude and mutability of the constraints on change, and the magnitude of the divergence from the traditional, and currently available, skills and mentality required to carry out the task in the face of those constraints. In sum, to what extent was the exercise of leadership, and of the leadership strategy adopted by the person in question, a necessary (albeit not sufficient) condition for realizing the results witnessed to date?[2]

ESTABLISHING BASELINES FOR EVALUATION

This question sensitizes us to a related methodological concern: the baseline for judging accomplishment. Should we focus on the extent to which the current situation diverges along several value-dimensions from the situation five years earlier? Or should we focus instead (or in addition) on the extent to which the current situation falls short of our (or the leader's) vision of the desired future?

If the past is our baseline, and if we postpone the problem of determining Gorbachev's distinctive contribution to the outcome, it is easy to sum up what has changed in the past five years. This is the least taxing approach to evaluation, and one that predominates in public discourse. Domestically, we have witnessed: (1) desacralization of the Brezhnevite political-economic order, including the official principles and mind-set that underpinned it: the leading role of the party; the "community of peoples"; pride in the system's achievements; optimism about state socialism's potential; commitment to class struggle abroad; and a national security phobia that justified a repressive, militarized regime;

2. "Leadership" is a tricky concept to define. Burns (1978, p. 2) points out that "a recent study turned up 130 definitions of the term." As I employ the concept, it refers to a subcategory of the phenomenon—"transformational leadership" (see Burns, 1978, Part III)—that is most appropriate to the tasks facing Gorbachev. As I use the term, leadership of this kind seeks, through non-tyrannical means, to mobilize and institutionalize support for fundamental change in the structure and culture of a unit (in our case, a state). Evaluation of the quality of leadership must additionally posit that such change succeeds in improving the ability of the unit to deal with environmental threats to its survival and vitality.

(2) legitimation in principle of movement in the direction of a market-driven economic order, a multi-party system, and the right to secede from the Union; (3) changes in policy and structure that have greatly decentralized political initiative, have created more open and competitive political arenas, have moved far toward disenfranchising the nomenklatura, and have swept radical majorities into power in the governmental councils of major cities; (4) changes in economic policy that have allowed the emergence of a legal private sector (the "cooperatives") that has recently burgeoned and currently employs more than 4.6 million citizens; (5) changes in cultural policy, and in policy toward dissent, emigration, travel, religion, and association that have vastly increased the amount of political freedom within the Soviet Union; (6) changes in foreign policy that have opened the USSR to Westernizing political, cultural, and economic influences; (7) changes in foreign policy that have substantially reduced or eliminated Soviet imperial control in Europe, the magnitude of the Soviet military threat, and the expansionism of Soviet Third World policy, including withdrawal of Soviet troops from Afghanistan; and (8) changes in the institutions and processes of central decision making that have reduced the power and access of many constituencies that were central to the Brezhnevite political order (the regional party apparatus, the ministries, and the military, in particular).

If one accords primary responsibility for these changes to Gorbachev's leadership (both his initiatives and his unwillingness to suppress initiatives from within society), and if one's approach to evaluation requires that one share attachment to the values advanced, then the man would receive very high marks, both for the direction, magnitude, and breadth of the changes and for the speed with which they have taken place. Perhaps only revolutions from below have historically accomplished more in a shorter period of time.

Using the same methodology, however, one could specify how much has not changed, or has changed for the worse by a short-term humanitarian scale of values: (1) a doleful consumer situation that is perhaps worse than it was in 1985; (2) an economy that is experiencing accelerating negative growth of national income, that is ridden by a huge budgetary deficit and monetary overhang, and that suffers from potentially explosive repressed inflation; (3) widespread intercommunal violence in the southern republics; (4) a sharp rise in the incidence of violent crime throughout the country; (5) growing despair within the population and a crisis of public confidence in the reform process; and (6) continued Soviet military involvement in the Third World. If one believes that these phenomena are reprehensible and collectively outweigh what has been accomplished (either normatively or because one sees their consequences as likely to unravel gains in other realms), and if one attributes these shortfalls to Gorbachev's preferences or myopia, then the man would receive relatively low marks.[3]

3. As Bonner (1990, p. 15) writes: "I would fully share the feelings of the West [adulation of Gorbachev—GWB], were it not for other actions of Gorbachev which overshadowed his positive moves."

If we take as our baseline not the past but the vision of a future new order (be it our own or the leader's), our evaluation of Gorbachev, or of any leader, is likely to be quite different. The easy variant of this approach is simply to measure the shortfall between our preferred vision of a stable democratic polity, a tolerable federation or confederation, and a prosperous marketized economy, on the one hand, and current reality, on the other. By this mechanical standard, Gorbachev has failed—or at least has so far to go that his ability to close the gap between reality and vision must be questioned. Yet, by this very standard, one must return to an issue discussed above: the limits of the possible. It is quite likely that simultaneous democratization and marketization of a Leninist polity and a militarized command economy, set within a huge multinational empire, at a time of economic depression, labor unrest, and both ethnic and ecological militancy is an impossible task. Indeed, even accomplishing the first two elements of this equation without the additional qualifications would be historically unprecedented. If this vision is intrinsically impossible to achieve in the Soviet context, then Gorbachev can hardly be faulted for failing to accomplish the impossible. He can, however, perhaps be faulted as quixotic for believing (if he did) that he could, and for trying to do so.[4]

Assuming that this is an impossible challenge, our conception of the alternative possibilities and opportunities could drive our evaluation of Gorbachev's leadership. Within given constraints, different leaders can deal differently with the challenge. The quality of leadership can in that case determine the alternatives to complete success. One set of criteria in this vein is causal, historical, and counterfactual: how much of his agenda has he accomplished, and to what extent is he (causally) responsible for what was accomplished? Would alternative leadership strategies have achieved *more than* Gorbachev achieved in these five years—either by fulfilling more in the way of positive goals, or by accomplishing what he has with less discontent and instability? Were alternative leadership strategies available to him, intellectually and politically?

Another set of criteria is future-oriented and developmental in perspective: has he managed to make *further* progress toward these varied goals more easily achievable? Has he made it very difficult to reverse the accomplishments and to reverse the tide toward further accomplishment? Or, alternatively, has he instead created conditions that make likely a descent into civil war, anarchy, or fascism, and an attendant end to hopes for further reform?[5]

---

4. In an especially poignant passage, Doder and Branson (1990, p. 304) quote a close adviser of Gorbachev: "I know we can't succeed. But when I get in front of that warm and charming man [i.e., Gorbachev—GWB] who wants so much to do something for the country, I have no heart to tell him that we can't succeed." On the other hand, it is important to bear in mind that unprecedented outcomes are not necessarily impossible of achievement (though it helps to have advisers who believe in the feasibility of the project). Also, it may not be possible for social scientists to specify what is intrinsically impossible in social action that does not defy physical principles.

5. The last clause is an important qualification. Leadership policies that result in periods of anarchy or civil war do not always tarnish the evaluation of a leader (for example, Abraham Lincoln, Vladimir Lenin). In some cases, violent confrontation may be necessary to achieve the kinds of dramatic social transformations envisioned. This will become an important consideration as we proceed with our analysis. For the moment, we are dubbing "failure" for Gorbachev a violent scenario that decisively reverses the reform process for a long period of time.

Evaluating the quality of leadership requires us to engage in historical judgments on which the evidence is often thin or contradictory. It also requires us to defend controversial theoretical claims. This is so with respect to both the counterfactual-historical criteria and the future-oriented developmental criteria. To some extent, counterfactual argumentation is based on existing empirical evidence about what happened and why. But to some degree it is always based, implicitly or explicitly, on theories derived from the observation of trends in analogous situations. Since a counterfactual assertion in the social sciences can never be proven with certainty—given our inability to rerun history with controls—we can only fill in the missing data points by deduction from our understanding of relevant tendencies in analogous situations (what historians refer to as bridging the gaps with "historical covering laws") (Fearon, 1990; Breslauer and Tetlock, 1991).

As for future-oriented developmental criteria, these are determined in part by one's empirical assessment of current conditions in the USSR: is it "too late" to restore order? Is the economy on the verge of collapse? Is the society on the verge of anarchy? Has the "center" of the political spectrum disappeared? Has there occurred a total loss of legitimacy of leaders and institutions?

But the application of developmental criteria of evaluation is in large part also determined by one's theoretical perspective on what it would take to democratize a Leninist multiethnic empire and to marketize a militarized command economy. In part, then, one's evaluation of Gorbachev's leadership performance will be driven by one's *theory of transition* from a Soviet-type system (and empire) to a marketized democracy, which in turn will inform one's conception of the leadership strategies appropriate to the task. Given the unprecedented character of the task, one's theory of transition will derive from conclusions drawn about workable leadership strategies in analogous, though far from identical, milieux.

The unavoidable theoretical components within each set of criteria sensitize us to another dilemma of leadership evaluation: its indeterminate or inconclusive character. The future may reveal whose analyses of the desperation of the *current* situation in the USSR were correct (contrast M. Goldman, 1990, Reddaway, 1989a, 1989b, 1990, and "Z," 1990, with Parker, 1990, Gustafson, 1990, and Hough, 1989). The future may also increase our information base for counterfactual analysis, as sources and archives become more accessible. Then too, the future will presumably improve our theories about the reformability of Soviet-type systems, if the East Europeans navigate (or shipwreck) the passage more quickly than do the Soviets, under more propitious ethnic, cultural, and international circumstances. The future may additionally change our perspective on the long-run fate of things that, in the short-run, may have misleadingly appeared to be "successes" or "failures."[6]

---

6. Consider, for example, current reevaluations of the presidency of Dwight Eisenhower, and of the European vision of Charles de Gaulle. In this vein, Marshall D. Shulman (*The New York Times Book Review*, June 17,

In the case of Gorbachev, of course, only the future will tell us more about his personal fate and the fate of his policies. For, in this case, we are seeking to evaluate a leader in midstream. If he is overthrown and the country reverts to a prolonged period of counterreform, he will probably go down in history as a tragic figure. He may be praised for having attempted to destroy the Leninist system, or for having gotten away with as much as he did for as long as he did. But the first judgment would be based on purely normative grounds, while the second takes a very limited view of accomplishment. In either case, he would hardly go down in history as a success.

On the other hand, with or without Gorbachev, if the country experiences a zig-zagged process of "rolling reform" (two steps forward, one step back), which builds upon Gorbachev's foundations and eventually consolidates a transition to a market democracy, then he will probably be looked upon very favorably by historians who believe that the original constraints on change were great, requiring exceptionally skilled leadership to circumvent. Of course, if he survives and presides over a relatively smooth breakthrough toward marketization of the economy, democratization of the polity, and partial dissolution of the empire (whether or not he is around to consolidate these gains), he will surely go down in history as "the man of the century." The divide between positive and negative evaluations, then, appears to hinge on whether the reform process proves to be irreversible. This too we can only know with hindsight.

Given these uncertainties, we might be tempted to abandon the task of leadership evaluation. That would be unwise. Historians do not abandon their craft because the evidence is inconclusive; they seek to make the best of what they have, and to present their conclusions as tentative and always subject to future revision. Moreover, no matter how indeterminate the exercise, people will go on evaluating leaders, for better or for worse, and their evaluations will sometimes feed back into the political process itself. How Yelena Bonner (1990), Boris Yel'tsin (1990), or Andranik Migranyan (1989) evaluate Gorbachev can have a political impact. How Western scholars, politicians, and journalists evaluate Gorbachev can also have political implications, by affecting Gorbachev's image abroad, and by helping to shape the calculus of American leaders in dealing with him. And this, in turn, can affect the prospects for Gorbachev's success or failure. Thus, abandoning leadership evaluation because of its inconclusiveness or indeterminacy is to abandon scholarship. And abandoning it because of its normative components and possible political impact would constitute an unnecessary act of scholarly abdication.

GORBACHEV: EVENT-MAKING MAN?

In his classic *The Hero in History*, Sidney Hook (1943, p. 153) defines the "hero" as "the individual to whom we can justifiably attribute preponderant

---

1990, p. 5) quotes Dean Acheson: "Sometimes it is only in retrospect and in the light of how things work out that you can distinguish stubbornness from determination."

influence in determining an issue or event whose consequences would have been profoundly different if he had not acted as he did.'' A subcategory of the concept is the "event-making man," who accomplishes this as a result of his "outstanding capacities of intelligence, will, and character rather than of accidents of position" (*ibid.*, p. 154). Transformational leaders, then, are event-making men (or women) whose exceptional abilities allow them to overcome constraints on changing the structure and culture of a unit in ways that improve the unit's ability to survive and thrive in a changing environment. Beginning with a retrospective analysis of what Gorbachev has accomplished to date, the question that concerns us is whether Gorbachev has been an event-making man during the past five years. The answer appears to be "yes."

Social determinism can hardly explain the changes we have witnessed. The social, political, economic, and international forces supportive of *perestroyka, glasnost'*, democratization, and "new thinking" in foreign policy constitute factors that encouraged and facilitated the changes. Indeed, they were necessary conditions for the changes in policy to be enacted, implemented, and sustained.[7] But they were not sufficient conditions. The relationship between "social forces" and socio-political change was mediated by leadership.

Gorbachev's leadership was active and initiatory in the first years after he had consolidated his power (1986–1988). He intervened repeatedly to let the *glasnost'* genie out of the bottle, to encourage social forces to attack the bureaucrats, to hold off the forces of backlash (as reflected, for example, in the Nina Andreyeva letter in *Sovetskaya Rossiya* on March 13, 1988), to recall Andrey Sakharov from exile, to release political prisoners, and to force through a democratization program that began the process of transferring power from the party to the soviets. It was Gorbachev whose doctrinal pronouncements encouraged or tolerated *public* desacralization of the Brezhnevite order. This led social forces to believe that fundamental change was not only desirable and necessary (which many of them had probably believed already), but possible as well (a necessary condition for the development of a revolutionary consciousness [Wolpe, 1970]), while discouraging recalcitrant bureaucrats from thinking that they could hold back the tide.

It was Gorbachev who apparently took the lead on matters of foreign policy, often surprising his domestic audiences with announcements of Soviet concessions on nuclear and conventional arms control, making the fundamental decision to cut losses in Afghanistan, and later pulling the rug from under conservative East European elites by withdrawing the Soviet guarantee of protection against revolutionary forces. It was Gorbachev who articulated a vision of a post–Cold War world, Soviet integration into the European cultural, political, and economic orders, and demilitarization of foreign policy that became the bases for

---

7. For arguments that emphasize social forces as determinants of the origins and irreversibility of reform, see Lewin (1988), Hough (1990), Starr (1988), and Ruble (1990); for further analysis of forces pushing for and against the success of reform, see Breslauer (1990).

both planning and legitimizing his turnabouts in both domestic and foreign policy.

To be sure, once sufficiently emboldened and organized, social forces pushed to further radicalize Gorbachev's policies. By 1988–1989, it is fair to say, Gorbachev had become a leader who was frequently reacting to degrees of radicalization he had not anticipated, desired, or controlled, such as the political resurrection of Boris Yel'tsin, the Baltic and Transcaucasian secessionist movements, intercommunal violence in the southern republics, the Inter-Regional Group within the Congress of People's Deputies, coal miners' strikes in Siberia, the Ukraine, and the Far North, as well as demands for abrogation of the "leading role of the party" in both the Soviet Union and Eastern Europe.

But in the face of this society-driven radicalization, Gorbachev had a choice. He could have allied with conservative forces to "draw the line" and enforce strict limits. Instead, with the exception of intercommunal violence, he typically made a virtue of necessity, resisting the temptation to use force, often allying with more radical forces, using tactical surprise to further consolidate his power at the top, and purging or holding at bay those who would have preferred to use such radicalization as justification for reversing or halting the reform process. In this "second," more reactive phase of his leadership, Gorbachev was event-making principally in his ability to prevent the use of state-directed violence against the radicalizing tide. A tragic exception to this trend occurred in Tbilisi in April 1989.

MISSED OPPORTUNITIES?

Of course, Gorbachev must also take responsibility for what has not been achieved during these years: an improvement of the economic situation and a radical reform of the economic system. The pace of economic reform has lagged far behind the pace of change in other realms of policy. Gorbachev has sponsored an assault on the old system of planning, and severely disrupted its operations, without yet putting in place an alternative system for coordinating the economy through market forces. The result is a situation of extreme economic disruption. For this reason, economists evaluating Gorbachev's leadership tend to arrive at conclusions that are, on balance, negative ones (M. Goldman, 1990).

The argument is straightforward: if Gorbachev had launched a real and forceful economic reform in 1985–1986, or if he had chosen to reform agriculture first, or if he had avoided a variety of mistaken policies in earlier years, the economy would not be in the mess it is in today. This counterfactual assertion may be a correct one (though it is not uncontroversial), but linking it to leadership evaluation involves a further logical step: one must argue not only the likely effectiveness of alternative strategies of reform but also their intellectual availability and their political feasibility at the time they should have been adopted. To what extent were Soviet leaders, and Gorbachev in particular, aware in earlier years of the need for such immediate, radical economic surgery? And if they or he were aware, to what extent did the party leader have the political capacity in 1985–1986 to force its enactment and implementation?

The evidence is ambiguous, but it suggests that Gorbachev was a convinced radical on matters of economic reform when he came to power. The careful kremlinology of Anders Åslund (1989) reveals his differences with others in the leadership at the time. The radicalism of his lengthy December 1984 speech to the Central Committee reveals that he had been influenced by the ideas of Tat'yana Zaslavskaya, and that he was putting himself forward as the candidate to succeed Chernenko on the basis of such a radical platform (Gorbachev, 1984). What's more, during 1985, reform economists who were directors of several institutes and whom Gorbachev had consulted regularly as Secretary of the Central Committee, forwarded to the Politburo programs of radical economic reform (Hewett, 1988, Chs. 6–7; Brown, 1990, pp. 186–188; Doder and Branson, 1990, p. 82). Even allowing for the inconclusiveness of the historical record, it seems more than likely that radical economic reform was intellectually available, and was defined by Gorbachev in principle as a *necessity* for progress, already during 1985–1986.

But was it politically feasible at the time? And if so, at what price? Although Gorbachev consolidated his power faster than any leader in Soviet history, he still had to deal with a challenge that faces any new Soviet leader: to expand his political machine within the bureaucracies, and build his political team within the Central Committee apparatus and the Politburo. In the meantime, he has to live with many powerful holdovers from the old regime who do not lose their positions just because the old party leader has died or been replaced. Even among the Andropovites who replaced Brezhnevites during 1985–1986, the dominant orientations were more technocratic or anti-corruption than radical reformist. It is entirely conceivable that Gorbachev did not push harder for economic reform in 1985–1986 because he was building his political base. This interpretation is substantially reinforced by accumulating evidence of the long-term institutionalization of conventions and norms that served as constraints on leadership initiative within policy-making bodies (Hodnett, 1982; Jones, 1987; Hauslohner, 1989; Breslauer, 1989; Rigby, 1990; Daniels, 1990; Miller, 1990). Of course, even when he began the push for economic reform in 1987, the measures were relatively modest, not compared to the past, but compared to the degree of radicalism required to turn the economy around. New laws on joint ventures, cooperatives, and the Law on the State Enterprise were radical departures, but they constituted a "foot-in-the-door" approach, one that delegitimized old values and justified in principle entirely new approaches to economic organization and the world economy. These policies were revised and, in most cases, made more radical in 1988–1989, but the crucial issues of price reform, privatization of property ownership, and demonopolization of the state sector have still not been tackled as of this writing (June 1990). One could argue, therefore, that the economy might be in better shape today had Gorbachev imposed a much more radical economic reform in 1987–1988—and that he bears responsibility for the failure to do so.

Even if one believes that radical economic reform was necessary and feasible at the time, and that an opportunity was missed, one still has to come to terms with the possibility that the Soviet population might not have tolerated the economic deprivations in the absence of the safety valves Gorbachev has offered them: truly competitive elections and opportunities for authentic political participation at all levels of the political system. And one has to confront the possibility that the Soviet leadership would not have tolerated across-the-board radicalism. We know that the leadership was sharply divided (Åslund, 1989; Doder and Branson, 1990). It is entirely conceivable that, in exchange for greater radicalism in economic policy, Gorbachev would have had to "trade off" some of his radicalism in foreign policy, defense policy, or policy toward cultural and political reform. This in turn could have undermined his efforts to transform the image of the USSR in the eyes of the Western world, which has been at the basis of his efforts to undermine the xenophobic forces resisting reform at home. Thus, both at the level of elite decision making (the Politburo), and at the level of popular tolerance, it is the interrelationship among issues that matters in constructing a counterfactual argument that Gorbachev could have accomplished more had he tried.[8]

During 1987–1988, Gorbachev was either forced to go slow on economic reform in exchange for a faster pace in other areas, or he chose to do so. If he chose to do so, and had the power to do otherwise, one could retrospectively blame him for lacking the vision, understanding, and strategy required by the economic conditions of the time, or retrospectively praise him for understanding the need for preparatory changes in politics and culture at home and abroad. The choice hinges on one's theoretical beliefs regarding the relationship among political, economic, and cultural change.

This last point is at the heart of current debates about appropriate strategies of transition. It is important to bear in mind that no consensus among specialists exists on this matter. There is disagreement about the workability (not just desirability) of varying mixes of equity and efficiency considerations in the setting of economic policy (Hewett, 1988; Kornai, 1990). There is disagreement as to the proper sequencing of marketization and democratization, with some specialists arguing that the two must proceed simultaneously in order to help break bureaucratic monopolies (thus preventing the development of a racket economy), and in order to build popular support and consensus during a period of disruption and privation (Kornai, 1990, Ch. 3; Comisso, 1988).[9] Other

8. For this reason, I am skeptical of the utility of attempts to evaluate the quality of Gorbachev's leadership in discrete realms of policy.

9. This raises the question of the success of China in pursuing economic marketization without political democratization. The argument would be that the Chinese experience was not transferable to the Soviet Union

specialists argue the opposite: that radical economic reform requires the concentration of political power (a "strong hand") or moral authority (a truly
charismatic leader), and that simultaneous political democratization will only
undermine economic marketization (Migranyan, 1989).

Another grouping of specialists agrees that democratization and marketization must proceed simultaneously, but disputes the forms that each of these
should take. Thus, Hankiss (1989) and Yanov (1977) have argued that marketization should be accompanied by a period of elitist ("bourgeois") democracy in order to first institutionalize the rights of managers, entrepreneurs, and
a middle-class dominated parliament. In contrast, Kagarlitsky (1990) disputes
the character of marketization, arguing that privatization of the Soviet economy
will be politically unacceptable in a period of rising labor militancy, and that
only municipalization of the means of production, along with mass democratization of local power structures, will allow labor to negotiate its own sacrifices,
thereby improving the economic situation while maintaining political stability.

Still others argue that the decisive component of a successful strategy must
be international: opening up of the economy to world market forces (Hough,
1988; Hough, 1990; Parker, 1990). To this Kagarlitsky (1990) replies that such
an opening will only lead to conditions of dependence, exploitation, and (relative) frustration ("Third Worldization"), creating social and political tensions
that will ultimately bring down both reform and democratization (see also Janos,
1989). Sometimes the Japanese strategy of the 1950s is recommended as an
alternative to excessive privatization and global integration (Schwartz, 1990).

None of these theories is incorrect on the face of it. It is sobering to recall
that development theorists in the 1950s wrote off both Japan and Italy as
hopeless cases.[10] *Especially* at a time when Polish "shock therapy" and the
virtues of privatization are the Zeitgeist of everyday discourse in parts of Eastern
Europe and the Soviet Union, we should be hesitant about conclusions based
on the self-evident superiority of one or the other theory.

Similar counterfactual and theoretical arguments can be made regarding
Gorbachev's handling of the ethnic crisis. Gorbachev may have been aware
that the nationality problem was the most intractable issue on the agenda of
Soviet politics (Hough, 1989/1990). But he was apparently not aware of the
depth of the secessionist and explosive potential lying just below the surface
(Lapidus, 1989). Nor did he anticipate how quickly or fully his policies of
glasnost' and democratization would release that potential. One could argue
that, had he called a constitutional convention and offered the opportunity of
a confederation or of an orderly, extended secession process to the leaders of
the Baltic republic in 1987–1988, rather than begrudgingly and reactively in
1989–1990, he would have avoided the current crisis that has arisen due to

---

because of the relative weakness of Chinese party and state bureaucracies after the Cultural Revolution and the
continuing hold of the tradition of decentralization and entrepreneurship in China.

    10. Personal communication from Professor Richard Ericson, Columbia University.

unilateral secessions.[11] Or one could argue that, had he raised the status of Nagorno-Karabakh to that of an autonomous republic when the crisis first began in 1987, he might have averted the current situation of full-scale civil war in the Caucasus.

These counterfactuals rest on the assumption that the issues were ever negotiable on more moderate terms. This assumption may be correct, but the claim is equally plausible that the logic of interaction among political democratization, *glasnost'*, economic reform, and the ethnic issue was inexorable in its reinforcement of centrifugal forces, given the depth of the yearning for independence in the Baltic States, the depth of interethnic hostilities in the Caucasus, and the inevitable disruption and deprivation caused by economic reform. If this is true, the same outcome would likely have materialized by varieties of paths. A different leadership strategy would have changed the path, not the result. On this set of issues, the argument is strongest that Gorbachev faced an impossible, and irreconcilable, combination of tasks. The burden of argument falls on those who claim that Gorbachev, or any other leader, can combine democratization and marketization with maintenance of the federation in its current boundaries. Indeed, jettisoning several republics, and renegotiating terms of association with the rest, may be prerequisites for realizing the combination of democratization and marketization that is apparently key to Gorbachev's long-term agenda. Philip Goldman (1990) may be correct when he argues that "the prospects for successful democratization of the RSFSR increase as the number of republics decreases."

If the theory underlying this viewpoint is correct (a matter to which I will return below), it has profound implications for our evaluation of Gorbachev's leadership. Recall the earlier point: the flip-side of leadership is opportunity. This theory argues that no opportunity existed; therefore, more skillful leadership would not have made a difference. Here the argument is different from that which governed the evaluation of Gorbachev's economic leadership. In the ethnic arena, the argument is that Gorbachev had the political leeway to do things differently, but faced a no-win situation (I have come across no argument that Gorbachev preferred a different strategy toward the minority republics in 1987–1988, but was hemmed in by competing preferences within the Politburo). Yet here, as in the economic arena, if one accepts a pessimistic theory about the nature of the situation, one can still criticize Gorbachev as quixotic for failing to appreciate the strength of the centrifugal ethnic forces he was facing and unleashing.

The "event-making" man not only makes a difference—a big difference— but does so because of his outstanding personal capacities. On this score, there does not appear to be very much controversy in the West or the East, although voices are heard increasingly that Gorbachev is not up to the task of leading

---

11. This hypothetical, of course, assumes he had the power to make such an offer.

the Soviet Union to a more radical future (*Newsweek*, June 4, 1990). Yet even those who criticize Gorbachev for failing now to become sufficiently radical view him as an unusual member of the Chernenko-led Politburo. No member of that Politburo has been portrayed as capable of seizing the initiative on socio-political and international issues the way Gorbachev eventually did. Gorbachev's intellectual capacity and flexibility, his ability to learn on the job, his powers of argumentation, charismatic appeal, serenity in the midst of social turmoil, faith that turbulence will "smooth out" in the long run (see Tiersky, 1990, p. 114; *Time* magazine, June 4, 1990, pp. 27–34), his "sustained," single-minded motivation . . . and irrepressible optimism,"[12] his energy, determination, and tactical political skill have been noted by observers and interlocutors alike (see Doder and Branson, 1990, pp. 31, 304, and *passim*).[13] By previous Soviet standards, as well as by comparative international standards, he stands out as a man of unusual leadership capacity. It seems incontestable that, social forces notwithstanding, had Gorbachev not been selected General Secretary after Chernenko's death, the destruction of the Brezhnevite political order, the creation and nurturing of new democratic institutions and practices, and the radical concessionary turn of Soviet foreign policy would not have taken place as they did in the 1980s.

Thus far, we have been dealing with the causal-historical criteria for evaluation, concluding that Gorbachev's innovations in the areas of cultural policy, political reform, and foreign policy were products of his initiative and his distinctive event-making capabilities. Our evaluation of his leadership in the areas of economic reform and nationalities policy is less laudatory, but also causally less clear-cut. In economics it hinges in part on one's estimation of how much political leeway Gorbachev enjoyed to act upon the programmatic recommendations of radical economists, and in part on one's theory of transition. In the ethnic realm, it hinges in part on one's theory regarding the ultimate compatibility of diverse objectives within Gorbachev's program, and in part on one's estimation of the extent to which his policies represented bold departures from a preexisting Politburo consensus.

Even if we make allowances for the uncertainties and constraints, Gorbachev's handling of the economic and ethnic issues appears unimpressive compared to his handling of the other issues. He has been an "event-making man" in the economic and ethnic realms only in ways that overlap and inter-

---

12. Doig and Hargrove (1987, p. 19) find this characteristic to be typical of successful leaders of the public bureaucracies they studied.

13. Gorbachev's pragmatism, determination, and high learning capacity come through most forcefully in the impressive, recent book by Doder and Branson (1990, especially pp. 31, 75, 106, 126–128, 157, 163, 218–219, 251, 277–280, 290, 332–333, 374–376, 386, 409). Henry Kissinger (1979, p. 54) has argued that "it is an illusion to believe that leaders gain in profundity while they gain experience. . . . The convictions that leaders have formed before reaching high office are the intellectual capital they will consume as long as they continue in office." The evolution of Gorbachev's thinking during his first five years in office challenges the applicability to his leadership of Kissinger's generalization. If that challenge is sustainable, it will strengthen a positive evalution of Gorbachev's leadership. Alternatively, one could argue that Gorbachev's "convictions" were fixed before he came to power, and that his learning has been largely "tactical" within the bounds of his earlier convictions.

connect with his innovations in other realms: through his public desacralization and partial destruction of the Brezhnevite political-economic and socio-political orders.[14] Perhaps that in itself makes him an event-maker, given the powerful political and ideological obstacles to radical reform of that entrenched system. But he has been unsuccessful thus far in building an alternative to that order for reintegrating the economy and restructuring interethnic relations. In these issue-areas (but not necessarily in the others), it is fair to say that he has thus far been a better destroyer than creator.

The operative words in the last sentence are "thus far." Causal-historical criteria of evaluation measure the extent of impact of the changes to date. But future-oriented, theoretical criteria of evaluation are equally if not more relevant to judging leadership in midstream. Once we concede that a great deal has been accomplished in five years, we must be modest in judging the implications of that which has not been accomplished. Do current shortfalls portend reversal of the reform process, or its coming agenda? Is severe social conflict an incubator of accelerated reform or a portent of disintegration and reaction? To what extent has Gorbachev's leadership created circumstances that "lock in" future development toward economic and political revival, and "lock out" the extreme alternatives of anarchy, civil war, or fascism? These are not simply empirical judgments about the current situation in the USSR. They are implicitly theoretical judgments about processes of transition. To assess these matters, we must therefore place still greater weight on theory and comparative analysis. The question then reduces to the broader issue: can Gorbachev's reforms succeed? Rather than tackle so huge an issue here (see Breslauer, 1990), I will instead inquire into comparative perspectives on Gorbachev's leadership strategy and tactics, to judge the appropriateness of that strategy for effecting the task of systemic transformation. A review of several bodies of literature suggests that Gorbachev's strategy and tactics of transition may be enlightened ones.

TRANSFORMATIONAL LEADERSHIP

Generalizations about "transformational leadership" can be found in the substantial literature on leadership in private corporations (Tichy and Devanna, 1986; Selznick, 1957), public bureaucracies (Doig and Hargrove, 1987), as well as nation-states (Burns, 1978). Transformational leadership is defined in a variety of ways by these authors. But typically it involves a process of fundamental revitalization in which the leader must anticipate future needs, perceive the incompatibility between emerging environmental demands and

14. The notion of public desacralization requires a word of explanation. One could argue that, for most of the Soviet population, the Brezhnevite order was not "sacred." That is probably true. The significance of Gorbachev's desacralization was that it *publicly* rejected the sacred, thereby stripping the apparat and the official classes of immunity from systemic criticism, and thereby also emboldening the intelligentsia and the masses to believe that such forceful criticism could now be safely advanced in public. In a Leninist polity, such public desacralization is a crucial political act, as Khrushchev's anti-Stalin campaign demonstrated at an earlier stage of Soviet reformist history.

current ordering principles, articulate an alternative vision, mobilize commitment to that vision, destroy the existing order, and put programs in place that
will result in the replacement of the existing order with one better suited to the
environmental demands of tomorrow.

Rare is the individual leader who is able to accomplish all of these things.
When studying single-task organizations, such as Chrysler Corporation, analysts expect more of a transformational leader than they do when they study
organizations with broader mandates (such as the Department of Housing and
Urban Development) or nation-states coping with systemic crises (such as
Franklin Roosevelt's leadership in the 1930s). The more contradictory, complex, and unprecedented the task, the more we make allowances for the inability
of any individual to master the requirements of cultural transformation, political
mobilization, and technical-organizational design simultaneously.

At the level of the nation-state, transformational leaders tend to be judged, not
by the extent to which they design organizations and programs that are *efficient*
in the *near-term*. Rather, they are judged by the extent to which they transform
cultural and political biases as preconditions for *effectively* changing the direction
of the nation, and sustaining that redirection over the *long-term*. Thus, although
FDR was given poor marks for the coherence of his administrative policies, his
characterization as a great leader derived from the perception that he had "put a
new face upon the social and political life of [the] country."[15] De Gaulle and
Churchill are not remembered, and dubbed heroic leaders, for their competence
in technical-organizational design, but for their capacity to transform a nation's
politics, preferences, biases, expectations, identities, or self-image, albeit within
the parameters of the ostensibly immutable constraints of the time.

The transformational leader, then, makes a difference of a deeper sociocultural
sort, which he simultaneously tries to institutionalize in new power relationships.
Indeed, a given sociocultural orientation may be compatible with a variety of
organizational-technical designs. For example, there are many variants of liberal
democracy, and many types of market economies, with varying degrees of state
regulation of the economy. However, unless sociocultural and prevailing political-
ideological biases are tolerant of the generic types, no amount of clever organizational design will be compatible with the culture. Conversely, when sociocultural
biases become tolerant or expectant of liberal democracy or market economies,
they may tend to "forgive" the inefficiencies or failures of particular organizational
designs and allow a continuing search for more efficient forms set within the new
paradigms. The critical question to ask of any transformational leader is whether
he has sufficiently transformed cultural biases, and sufficiently institutionalized
their expression in politics, to make the system highly resistant to backlash against
the new paradigms, should specific organizational forms prove to have been
designed poorly. As Schumpeter put it, the main task of the "entrepreneur" is to

15. This is what a former Supreme Court justice wrote to FDR in 1937 (quoted in Leuchtenburg, 1988,
p. 20).

"break up old, and create new, tradition" (Quoted in Doig and Hargrove, 1987, p. 11).

In some cases, the distinction between technical-organizational design and cultural transformation is a murky one. But that murkiness serves to reinforce the argument that cultural change is more important than organization charts in the long-term evolution of a system. For "organizations are more than instruments; they are themselves bundles of desires [that] encapsulate ways of life as well as modes of achievement. How, indeed, could people be persuaded to commit themselves to organizational life . . . unless the organizations themselves contain the ties that bind—their values legitimating their desired practices" (Browne and Wildavsky, 1984, p. 252).

Transformational leaders in complex, multi-task environments are not necessarily expected to possess a detailed strategy, much less a blueprint. Rather, they are expected to have a vision of a desirable alternative to the present order, a sufficiently coherent action plan with which to gain the needed political support for their leadership, and the ability to inspire followers and mobilize supporters. They know in which directions they want the country to move, and which directions they want it to avoid. They often have in their mind models to emulate and adapt, or rules of thumb to apply. Of course, they make operational links in advance between a non-operational vision and programmatic requirements. But, to repeat, they lack detailed blueprints. As Tichy and Devanna (1988, pp. 93, 94) relate:

> Many of our successful transformational leaders, like Franklin D. Roosevelt when he developed the New Deal, did not have a clear vision of where they wanted to take their organizations. Instead, like FDR, they engage in "planful opportunism," the process of capitalizing on changing circumstances. They take advantage of "windows of opportunity." . . . Planful opportunism is the ability to turn unpredictable events into building blocks of change.

Transformational leaders do not necessarily preside over the final achievement. In many cases, they initiate and elaborate the process, experience a failure, and give way to other leaders who consolidate or further elaborate their accomplishment.[16] But the measure of successful transformational leadership is whether it creates a climate and then institutions or processes for "expected and continuous change through learning" (Browne and Wildavsky, 1984, p. 239). The goal of transformational leadership is to "set firmly in place new programs and new strategies through which still further social invention may take place" (Doig and Hargrove, 1987, p. 18). For these reasons, transformational leaders typically speak "the language of evolution" rather than the "vocabulary of creation and completion" (Browne and Wildavsky, 1984, p. 234). Since in-

---

16. Recall that Churchill and de Gaulle both ended their political careers on a note of rejection or repudiation. What is more, Doig and Hargrove (1987) found the pattern of success followed by failure to be quite typical of the successful executives they studied.

stitutionalization of new directions and processes takes a long time, it is often impossible to determine in the short term whether the innovations sponsored by the transformational leader have as yet become "irreversible." That complicates the task of evaluating leadership performance in midstream, or even shortly after the retirement or death of the leader. But the important point is that the leader has used his vision, intellect, and charisma to set the country on a new path and to raise high the price of going back.

It is often the case that these leaders possess the vision to anticipate a crisis before others within the organization do so. When this happens, the imperative is to exploit "trigger events" to get others to "share his sense of urgency" (Tichy and Devanna, 1988, pp. 29 and 46). For "one of the most difficult transformation tasks is to create a sense of urgency before there is an emergency" (*ibid.*, p. 47).

Once the crisis is widely appreciated, the leader must diagnose the problem in ways that discredit, disintegrate, and ultimately destroy the old order. It is the mark of a transformational leader that he entertains the "leap of faith that destruction will result in rebirth" (*ibid.*, p. 28). In this task, conflict is the ally of the leader. He must stimulate conflict as a means of disengaging people from previous patterns of thought and action. Conflict helps to raise consciousness and redefine the calculus of public political behavior (Burns, 1978, pp. 36–41).

Of course, successful transformational leaders must also rebuild as they destroy. They must "provide people with support by helping replace past glories with future opportunities" (Tichy and Devanna, 1988, p. 32). Those opportunities may come in many forms: material aggrandizement; social mobility; political participation; political mobility; a rebirth of national pride and collective accomplishment; and so on. The provision of a new opportunity structure is part of the process of balancing transformation with identity and stability. For, while the literature on transformational leadership stresses the need to delegitimize and destroy the old order as a *precondition* for building a new one, that literature is also aware that destruction must not be total, and reconstruction must to some degree overlap with the task of destruction.

Therein lies the risk involved in finessing the transition. As March and Olsen (1989, p. 65) put it: "It is easier to produce change through shock than it is to control what new combination of institutions and practices will evolve from the shock." Hence, transformational leaders must avoid the perils of loss of control at the crucial turning point: "organizations that fail to regain their equilibrium after embarking on a change spin out of control and eventually destroy themselves" (Tichy and Devanna, 1988, p. 28). In the business world, this means bankruptcy and perhaps disappearance of the organization; in the real world of nation-states it means something short of that: civil war, military coups, prolonged ungovernability, social turmoil, fascism, and the like. Nation-states rarely "destroy themselves" and large economies rarely "collapse." [17]

17. The notion that economies the size of the Soviet's do not collapse is attributed to Vladimir Treml of Duke University, in Parker (1990, p. 68).

GORBACHEV AS TRANSFORMATIONAL LEADER

These generalizations are pertinent to our evaluation of Gorbachev. If one accepts the notion that cultural and political transformation are preconditions for sustained administrative-organizational transformation, then Gorbachev's strategy of proceeding slowly on economic reform as he moved quickly on *glasnost'*, political democratization, and foreign policy change appears defensible.[18] As Thomas Naylor (1988, pp. x, 181), one of Gorbachev's early boosters, argued:

> it is impossible to change the economic system of a country such as the Soviet Union without first coming to grips with the uniqueness of its culture . . . the attitudes, values, and customs of its people. . . . Some of those cultural mores include a penchant for military authority and secrecy; an aversion to risk; a lack of commitment to democratic principles; a distrust of markets and capitalism; corruption; an underdeveloped consumer sector; and underinvestment in human resources development.

Gorbachev has clearly used the resources of his offices to delegitimize the old order—both its institutional framework and the social values it allegedly protected: social egalitarianism; social security; stable prices; guaranteed employment at the present place of work; autarky; political docility; and insulation from the outside world's political, cultural, and economic influences. He has simultaneously acted to create new opportunities for entrepreneurial initiative, both political and economic: *glasnost'*, voluntary associations (the "informal organizations"), multiple-candidate elections, freer travel abroad, and the cooperatives.

He launched *perestroyka* by defining the situation of the USSR in the world as one that demanded emergency surgery, lest the country descend into second-class status (Gorbachev, 1984). And he has played upon unanticipated trigger events (Chernobyl'; Matthias Rust's Cessna landing in Red Square; the miners' strikes) both to purge members of the Old Guard and to dramatize the urgency of the need for cultural and institutional change. He has defined a tight connection between his foreign and domestic policies, harnessing forces in the international environment to further the cause of consciousness-raising within the USSR (see Breslauer, 1989b). In each case, this served organizational-technical ends; but in each case it also served more important goals of transforming identities.

Thus, by opening the Soviet economy to global competition, he not only

---

18. Indeed, whether or not he had the political elbow-room to proceed rapidly on all fronts in 1985–1987 (which I doubt), Gorbachev appears to have concluded that cultural change ("the human factor") was a prerequisite for successful economic reform: "We have to begin, first of all, with changes in our attitudes and psychology, with the style and method of work. . . . I have to tell you frankly that, if we do not change ourselves, I am deeply convinced there will be no changes in the economy and our social life" (Gorbachev speech, April 8, 1986, as quoted in Doder and Branson, 1990, p. 137).

increases pressure on Soviet managers and draws in foreign capital, but also forces elite and mass alike to define progress relative to the achievements of advanced capitalist countries, rather than relative to the Russian of Soviet past.[19] By opening the country to cultural Westernization, he not only reduces the political, scientific, and international costs of trying to insulate the country from the information revolution, but challenges the idea of Russian or Soviet "originality" (*samobytnost'*) that had underpinned both the Brezhnevite order and the xenophobic strains of Russian national consciousness. By working to reduce international threats to the USSR, he not only creates preconditions for lowering the defense budget, but also dilutes the national security phobia that had been used to justify the Brezhnevite political order. By repudiating class struggle abroad, and by emphasizing the priority of "all-human values," he not only defuses regional crises and paves the way for arms control and other forms of superpower cooperation, but undermines the rationale for the CPSU's continued monopoly on power and truth. Indeed, the extraordinary importance of ideas and ideology in Leninist systems makes it all the more imperative that transformative leaders first neutralize the legitimacy of the traditional political culture if they are to create the political space for new patterns of behavior and organization.

As successful transformational leaders must, Gorbachev has recognized that a precondition for fundamental change is the destruction of old identities, and tolerance of the social conflict that inevitably accompanies such a passage. He has used social and political conflict as occasions for educating citizenry and polity alike to the idea that there is no change without pain, and no democracy without conflict.[20] He has reacted to unanticipated levels of conflict (except for intercommunal violence, and the use of violence against state organs) by claiming them as proof that the old way of doing things was intolerable and, more important, was now capable of being changed. He has articulated a vision of the USSR as a "normal," modern country on the model of the social-democratic European welfare state, even as he has fudged the question of whether a market-based pluralist democracy is consistent with "socialism." He speaks the language of evolution, defining change (both at home and abroad) as a long-term process that requires acclimatization to continuous change. While he has not transformed the egalitarian envy of the mass publics, he has fostered

19. Sanders (1990) notes that on-the-ground introduction of competitors' products and symbols (such as the opening of McDonald's in Moscow) serves to focus the attention of Soviet managers and workers alike on both the object of emulation and the distance between that object and existing production processes in the Soviet Union. This is analogous to the strategy of some American automobile manufacturers in bringing models of Japanese automobiles into their factories to highlight the competition and legitimize changes in local production processes and organization. For the same reasons, Gorbachev has used television to broadcast images of Western living standards and of the progress of Chinese economic reforms (Doder and Branson, 1990, pp. 293, 363).

20. "Gorbachev was right in believing that national argument was the way to dispel national apathy and to focus attention on problem-solving. The people, he said, 'are emerging from a state of social apathy and indifference.' . . . The Russia of the spring and summer of 1988 was quite different from the Russia of the previous year. The country had come alive again, groping for its future" (Doder and Branson, 1990, pp. 317–318). One cause of this change was Gorbachev's decision to televise nationally the debates among Politburo and Central Committee members before and during the Party Conference of June 1988.

a widespread belief in pluralism and markets as the desirable and feasible alternatives to political oppression and economic stagnation.

Related to this concern for cultural transformation has been Gorbachev's effort to create a new legal culture that would depersonalize the legal institutions of the state, and thereby provide a foundation of stable expectations for the protection of person and property. Both Gorbachev's efforts to develop a new legal code, to foster a more independent judiciary, to transfer power from party organs to soviets at all levels, and to turn the soviets into parliamentary institutions that would generate legislation binding on all people push in this direction. These, among other things, are components of his professed commitment to a "law-based state" (*pravovoye gosudarstvo*) to replace the previous order based on arbitrary rule by party officials. Progress in this realm has been slower and less spectacular than in other areas of *glasnost'* and democratization. In part that reflects the nature of the task. Legal reform and institutionalization of new procedures are slow processes, wherever they take place. While much more could perhaps have been accomplished in five years, the institutionalization of a rule of law is not a reasonable expectation in that time frame. What has been accomplished, however, has been delegitimation of "rule by men," legitimation of the search for a procedurally predictable alternative, and practical disruption of party organs' ability to monopolize political initiative.

Gorbachev has been a transformational leader in foreign policy as well, and his basic strategy of "culture first" has been applied there as well. In addition to changing the assumptions underlying Soviet foreign policy in the Brezhnev era, he has sought to undermine the very culture of international relations during the Cold War: the dominant "realist" paradigm that emphasized the balancing of military power; the "enemy image" that fed worst-case planning and weapons procurement; and the "two-camps" mentality that defined superpower competition as a confrontational, zero-sum game. Instead, he has justified a concessionary Soviet foreign policy by propounding an idealist vision of international politics that seeks to transform the enemy image of the USSR into an image of a partner in solving all-human problems. His conviction appears to be that such a transformation in assumptions about the enemy is a prerequisite for ending the Cold War and thereby creating an international environment that would be genuinely supportive of his domestic transformational challenge.[21]

And yet, partly because of the ethnic and economic issues, Gorbachev has presided over a process that, according to some observers, may have brought the country to the abyss of chaos, coup, or worse. He has acted as if possessed of an "insane optimism" (Drane, 1990) that he could simultaneously transform the nation, the empire, *and* the international environment. Perhaps such a degree of optimism is a prerequisite for successful transformational leadership, given the magnitude of the task. Yet there is serious question as to whether he has

---

21. For his most recent statements, see Gorbachev's speeches in Stanford and San Francisco, California (*New York Times*, June 12, 1990). For a stimulating and skeptical interpretation of Gorbachev's "New Thinking," interpreted as a "Gramscian strategy of counter-hegemony," see Kubalkova and Cruikshank (1989).

balanced transformation with stability sufficiently to avoid the "spin out of control." Similarly, there is serious question as to whether he has transformed biases sufficiently to maintain the momentum of change in the face of backlash. Are we currently witnessing creative disruption or incipient anarchy and restoration? One's evaluation of Gorbachev's *strategy* of transformation will hinge on the answer to the questions about the future. That is a matter to which we will return later in this essay. But first, let us examine more closely his political *tactics*, in the light of recent literature on the tactical requirements for navigating a successful transition to democracy. Admittedly, some tactical prescriptions for managing politics during the democratization of an authoritarian regime may have to be reconsidered when applied to the simultaneous democratization and marketization of a Leninist empire. But an evaluation of Gorbachev's leadership in light of this recent literature nonetheless provides another basis for making initial judgments.

TRANSITIONS TO DEMOCRACY

The Western literature on transitions to democracy has gone through several stages. The "first generation" of that literature treated democratization as a process that depended for its success on social, cultural, and economic preconditions. Little or no attention was devoted to leadership, which implicitly was treated as a hopeless exercise in the absence of the socioeconomic and cultural prerequisites. The more recent literature, in contrast, is much less deterministic and pessimistic. Its optimism and voluntarism are based on a reexamination of the West European historical experience, and on observation of the recent successful transitions in Southern Europe (Spain, Portugal, Greece), Latin America, and (tentatively) East Asia (see Rustow, 1970; Dahl, 1989, Chs. 17–18; O'Donnell and Schmitter, 1986; O'Donnell, Schmitter, and Whitehead, 1986; DiPalma, 1990; DiPalma, 1991).

This body of literature takes many confining conditions as mutable and not as decisive obstacles to democratic breakthroughs and democratic consolidation, even though it does acknowledge that some conditions may frustrate even the most skillful leadership strategy.[22] It focuses on coalition-building strategies within the elites, and on strategies for creating "political space" for new publics being mobilized into politics by the collapse of authoritarian regimes. Hence, it is primarily interested in leadership as a factor that not only facilitates the

22. This is an important point, and one that bears on my earlier argument that simultaneous democratization and marketization of a Leninist multinational empire and command economy at a time of rising labor and ethnic militancy may well prove to be impossible. Rustow (1970), for example, while rejecting earlier claims that certain socio-economic conditions are prerequisites for successful democratization, nonetheless treats one confining condition as necessary: the definition of the national community being reformed, which is precisely what is lacking in the Soviet empire. Similarly, Przeworski (1986, p. 63), who writes in the same optimistic vein about the ability to construct democracies in diverse milieux, nonetheless claims that "it seems as if an almost complete docility and patience on the part of organized workers are needed for a democratic transformation to succeed." And Levine (1988, p. 389), who is not a member of the optimistic school, argues that inter-elite trust and a valued relationship between leaders and followers are necessary conditions for "pacts" and "garantismo" to regulate the transition. See also Lyday (1990).

democratic breakthrough and consolidation, but also guards against the ever-present threat of military coup and other forms of regression. A number of prescriptions for successful leadership tactics can be gleaned from this literature and applied as tests to the Gorbachev administration.

Prescription No. 1: attempt to discredit alternatives to the democratic path, in order to keep them less legitimate in the public and elite consciousness than is the prospective democratic outcome. As Przeworski (1986, pp. 51–52) puts it: "what matters for the stability of any regime is not the legitimacy of this particular system of domination but the presence or absence of preferable alternatives." From this standpoint, Gorbachev's strategy of desacralizing and delegitimizing the Brezhnevite social order, and of discrediting even the alleged accomplishments of Brezhnevism (the welfare-state and military security) makes tactical sense. Similarly, his penchant for arguing that "there is no alternative" to continuing along the reformist path constitutes good politics. His arguments that national security and Soviet competitiveness in the 21st century would be threatened by the failure to join the "modern" world, to become a "normal" country, and to "learn democracy" powerfully advance the message that hypothetical alternatives to *perestroyka* simply are not palatable, from either a livability or a national security standpoint.

Prescription No. 2: mobilize new social forces into politics that will ally with reformist forces within the establishment. This is precisely what *glasnost'* and democratization attempted to do, and apparently what they have accomplished. *Glasnost'* began as an effort to activate new social forces by encouraging them to speak out and engage in self-organization, in order to outflank conservative forces within the bureaucratic and political establishments. When Gorbachev unveiled this populist strategy in mid-1986 (Doder and Branson, 1990, pp. 140–141), he probably did not anticipate how far it would go, and it clearly went much further than he had hoped or suggested. But when faced with the consequences, he did not lead a backlash; rather, he generally accommodated himself to the tide, legitimized its "extremism" (thus making a virtue of necessity), moved himself to the "left" (radicalism) on the elite political spectrum, and sought to create new political institutions that would regulate the conflicts now made manifest. This was an important move. It sent out early signals of an attractive democratic game, in order to avoid the early disillusion so common during failed transitions (DiPalma, 1991; also DiPalma, 1990).

From this perspective, it was fortunate that Gorbachev's speech at the January 1987 plenum of the Central Committee called for multicandidate, secret elections and general pluralization of the political order. It was also fortunate that the June 1988 Party Conference, and subsequent meetings of the Congress of People's Deputies and the Supreme Soviet, could be viewed on national television, thus demystifying politics and allowing people to believe that political involvement might be rewarding. Gorbachev also was politically wise in helping to ensure that the elections of March 1989 were conducted reasonably fairly. In sum, Gorbachev simultaneously was mobilizing new social forces, discrediting the old political order, and creating new political institutions to regulate the conflict among the forces unleashed by his policies. This created new political space within which democratic oppositions could develop ties with moderates within the regime.

Prescription No. 3: create opportunities for the cooptation of leaders and activists of opposition groups into new political arenas in which they, and reformist members of the establishment, can pursue and learn the pragmatic and accommodative tactics of a democratic process. Creation of the Congress of People' Deputies, and the Supreme Soviet, along with the persistent transfer of more political authority from party organizations to regional soviets at all levels, have marked Gorbachev's political reform strategy since 1987–1988. At the most general level, these innovations have sought to maintain stability by expanding the opportunities for authentic political participation at a rate equal to or exceeding the rate of political mobilization engendered by *glasnost'*.[23] But at the specific level of inter-elite interaction, these institutions have proven to be arenas in which general issues of proceduralism, rule of law, parliamentary practice, and the like, have been forced increasingly to the fore. Although the path has been a rocky one, and littered with conflict, that is unsurprising in any democratic transition. What is significant is that the slow process of institutionalization has begun and gained momentum. A recent comparison of deputies' speeches at the first and subsequent convocations of the Congress of People's Deputies reveals a significant rise in procedural thinking among the deputies (Sergeyev and Parshin, 1990). Equally significant, respect for proceduralism has grown, not only among reformists, but also among fence-sitters and conservatives. As DiPalma (1990) has argued, when conservatives conclude that democratization is the only game in town, they can sometimes become very fast learners.

Prescription No. 4: strip the privileged corporate interests of the old regime of their political *immunity*, but give them enough protection against dispossession that they do not exit *en masse* and seek allies who would help them to violently reverse the democratization process. Democracy is a system based on certainty of procedures and uncertainty of outcomes (Przeworski, 1986). Brezhnevism was a system based on uncertainty of procedures (arbitrariness) and certainty of outcomes. Those whose immunity was guaranteed by the Brezhnev regime had to be both stripped of that immunity and given a sufficient stake in the new order that they would not resort to "breakdown games." The imperative is to "make institutionalized uncertainty palatable" (DiPalma, 1991, manuscript ch. 3, p. 7), or at least to make it sufficiently palatable that significant segments of the establishment are more willing to play along than to defect. The idea is that they will not only play the game, but will also come to learn and, eventually, value the new rules. It is imperative both to frighten

---

23. According to Huntington (1968), maintaining a balance between the rate of mobilization and the availability of opportunities for political participation is key to maintaining political stability.

the conservatives into believing that there is no choice but to join the new democratic game and to reassure conservatives that there is a place for them, protected by the leader, in that game.[24]

From these perspectives, Gorbachev's political tactics look wise. Desacralization of the Brezhnevite political order, abrogation of the Communist Party's constitutionally guaranteed monopoly, and mobilization into politics of anti-official social forces have effectively destroyed the political immunity of the Brezhnevite ruling class. At the same time, Gorbachev has distanced himself from *abolitionist* forces, and thereby maintained his ties with conservative establishment forces, through: (a) his unwillingness to attack the socioeconomic privileges of elites too quickly or fully; (b) his *honorable* retirement of many Politburo and Central Committee members; (c) his willingness to allow many conservative and reactionary forces at Central Committee plenums and meetings of the Congress of People's Deputies or Supreme Soviet to be heard on television and read in the newspapers; (d) his introduction of an electoral system that initially reserved significant proportions of seats to elitist designation by party, trade union, *komsomol*, and Academy of Sciences executive committees; and (e) his apparent alliance with segments of the KGB (on which more below). To many radicals in the Soviet Union and abroad, these concessions appeared to be unacceptable conservatism—evidence of Gorbachev's upbringing as an apparatchik. From the standpoint of those steeped in the comparative literature on transitions, however, it made sense.

At the same time, Gorbachev's deft use of crises (some manufactured, some not) to purge or marginalize conservatives in the leadership both disarmed forces of backlash and encouraged bandwagoning tendencies among the fence-sitters by maintaining high uncertainty about the chances of success if they bucked him. Instead of being discredited by crises, he has used them in ways that have allowed him to actually increase his authority.[25]

Prescription No. 5: disperse or neutralize the means of violent coercion. This is an imperative in all democratic transitions, though it is more urgent in the Third World than in the European Leninist world, where military subordination to the party has been quite strong. Nonetheless, during his first five years in office, Gorbachev worked to reduce the political status of the military within top-level decision-making arenas, to purge the military command, and to sharply expand the flow of information about military affairs. He has labored to create a benign international environment that would defuse xenophobic claims that one can never spend too much on defense. Indeed, as part of his

24. This power tactic is applicable to pluralist leadership more generally. Thus, writing about presidential power, Richard Neustadt (1960, p. 64) advises the leader "to induce as much uncertainty as possible about the consequences of ignoring what he wants. If he cannot make men think him bound to win, his need is to keep them from thinking they can cross him without risk, or that they can be sure what risks they run. At the same time (no mean feat), he needs to keep them from fearing lest he leave them in the lurch if they support him."

25. On the importance of creating incentives for bandwagoning by fence-sitters, see Breslauer (1989a). On the importance of using power in ways that simultaneously increase one's legitimacy as leader, see Neustadt (1960).

strategy for delegitimizing Brezhnev's foreign and domestic policies and institutions, he has discredited the use of force at home and abroad as an instrument of policy.

Yet, even as he has challenged military prerogatives, he has taken care to
avoid simultaneously confronting the KGB (Rahr, 1989, 1990; see also Alexiev,
1989; Knight, 1989; Reddaway, 1989; Tsypkin, 1989). Although he has purged
the party, ministerial, and military apparatuses, he has not purged the KGB
apparatus and top command. No large-scale organizational reform or dismantling has been imposed on the secret police. At the level of elite politics, the
KGB Chairman is a full member of the Politburo as of this writing, while the
Defense Minister is still only a candidate member. Although former KGB
Chairman Viktor Chebrikov was eventually dropped from the leadership, this
did not necessarily reflect a divorce between Gorbachev and the KGB.

While some KGB officials lament the excesses of *glasnost'* and democratization, they have not had to lament any lack of work to occupy their
organization. The KGB's functions under Gorbachev have actually expanded
in the areas of foreign intelligence and counterintelligence (especially economic), and in the struggles against official corruption, terrorism, narcotics
trafficking, and, especially, organized crime within the USSR. It is not
insignificant that these are precisely the areas in which Gorbachev can call
upon the "forces of rectitude" (the phrase is Ken Jowitt's) to perform tasks
that are congruent with popular values. The KGB's recent efforts to improve
its public image, and to avoid campaigns of retribution against it for past
crimes, are furthered by such congruence. It is entirely conceivable that,
for many members of the KGB command, this is a source of support for
Gorbachev that partially or fully offsets their ambivalence about the new
politics. In any case, it is clear that Gorbachev has consciously followed a
policy of deference to KGB institutional interests as a means of co-opting
and politically neutralizing its leadership.[26] The strategy may be a wise one.

Prescription No. 6: when stalemates appear, up the ante in order to increase
the perceived costs of regression. This prescription is based on Robert Dahl's
famous dictum that democratic breakthroughs hinge on keeping the perceived
price of repression higher than the perceived price of toleration. The issue is
not whether the current price of toleration is desirable or enjoyable; the issue
is whether it is perceived to be more tolerable than the price of a violent
backlash.[27]

---

26. Most recently, Gorbachev is reported to have stripped of his military rank and decorations a retired
KGB major general, Oleg Kalugin, who had publicly revealed details of his life as an operative and had lambasted
the KGB's current role in Soviet politics and society (see *The Washington Post*, July 1, 1990, pp. A1, A28).
In the same issue of *The Washington Post* (p. A30), KGB Maj. Gen. Aleksandr Razhivin speaks of his support
for the rehabilitation of Stalin's victims and his belief in the inevitability of a multi-party system, adding: "I
refuse to answer for Beria's crimes. Now there is a new generation in the KGB. These are completely new
people." Of course, others within the KGB have recently mobilized against the "excesses" of *glasnost'*,
democratization, and demilitarization (see Rahr, 1990).

27. Note the parallel here with Przeworski's (1986) theory of relativity regarding legitimacy. In each case—
mass legitimacy and elite toleration—the issue is not whether the situation is perceived to be "the best," or

On this score, Gorbachev has pursued a consistently successful strategy during his first half-decade as leader. He has been a ''radical centrist,'' seeking to keep the process moving to the ''left,'' while himself dominating, but protecting, the floating center of the political spectrum. By encouraging the activation of social forces pushing for more radical change, or by joining with those social forces when they have surprised him, Gorbachev could more easily argue that the price of restoring the status quo ante had become prohibitive.[28] And by encouraging the public expression of popular views that are so impatient for change, and so enraged by the privilege and corruption of the old order, Gorbachev could more credibly argue that any effort to restore the status quo ante, even if successful in the short run, would only postpone the day of reckoning (as Poland's Jaruzelski discovered in 1989). The higher the level of anti-establishment social activation, the higher the perceived price among conservatives of leading a backlash.[29] And yet, at the same time, Gorbachev's selective protection of moderate and conservative interests has allowed him to dominate the center of the political spectrum by increasing the perception of him among middle-of-the-roaders as their protector against radical disenfranchisement.

Finally, by creating avenues of authentic political participation for released social forces, Gorbachev has disarmed the forces of reactionary backlash by robbing them of an excuse to ''crush counter-revolution.'' Rather than allowing the development of a situation in which social forces might have engaged in anomic outbursts or acts of revolutionary violence, Gorbachev has pursued policies that at once raised the price of repression *and* lowered the price of toleration. In the process, he has dominated the center-left of the political spectrum by increasing the level of felt political *dependence* upon him of most radical reformers, moderate-leftists and middle-of-the-roaders alike. This accounts for the fact that so many reformers criticize Gorbachev's ''conservatism,'' yet fear the prospect of his replacement.

Prescription No. 7: harness forces in the international environment that will help to maintain the momentum of reform while also helping to raise the costs of retrogression. This is precisely what Gorbachev's ''New Political Thinking'' in foreign policy, his approach to foreign economic relations, and

---

even ''desirable,'' but whether it is perceived to be the ''least bad'' among the alternatives defined as realistically possible. Note also that, in each case, we are dealing with an assumption of reasonably rational calculation on the part of the actors involved. For a critique that emphasizes the passion and rage in the Soviet Union that make such rational calculation unlikely, see Lyday (1990).

28. Hough (1989) argues that Gorbachev has been following a conscious tactic of creating ''controlled chaos'' to justify the further radicalization of reform. I perceive important elements of this, especially in 1987–1988, but I suspect that Gorbachev has also been exercising ''planful opportunism'' in response to unanticipated levels of social radicalization in 1989–1990. A good example was his response to the miners' strikes of summer 1989.

29. ''Gorbachev was not a man to be underestimated; he was mastering a certain kind of power that his opponents did not fully understand, going public when traditional party men expected him to operate behind the scenes. He exercised power differently. When they refused to hear his arguments for political reform, he announced that he would convene a party conference to seek approval for the reforms'' (Doder and Branson, 1990, p. 192; see also p. 344).

his process of cultural Westernization have attempted to do. By opening the country to economic and cultural Westernization, including travel abroad, he has raised dramatically the price in popular tolerance of efforts to reestablish a closed society, while raising the prospective and actual benefits of openness. By defusing conflicts with wealthy adversaries, he has increased the chance of getting economic assistance for his program, while reducing the prospective cost of defense. As I have argued above, his concessionary foreign policies have sought both to cut losses and to transform the international system, so that foreign countries, companies, and publics would develop a perceived interest in adopting policies that favor the continuation of *perestroyka*.

Furthermore, progress in foreign policy realms is easier and quicker to achieve than is progress, especially economic progress, at home. By simultaneously adopting radical reform in both domestic and foreign policies, Gorbachev has expanded the number of issue-areas within which he can seize the initiative, maintain the momentum of his leadership, and keep prospective challengers off balance. By developing such popularity abroad, Gorbachev has been able to build his authority as a statesman to compensate for lack of economic progress at home. And by delivering on his promise to reduce tensions abroad, he has carved out a realm in which would-be challengers find it difficult to claim that they could do better than he.[30] Thus, just as his foreign policies are central to his strategy of domestic cultural and political transformation, so are they crucial to his tactics for simultaneously expanding his political authority and making *perestroyka* increasingly costly to reverse.

In sum, Gorbachev has gone far to fulfill many of the prescriptions of those scholars who have examined the lessons of success and failure in non-Leninist settings. His strategy comes close to meeting Myron Weiner's (1987, p. 866) pithy summary: "For those who seek democratization the lessons are these: mobilize large-scale non-violent opposition to the regime, seek support from the center and, if necessary, from the conservative right, restrain the left . . . , woo sections of the military, seek sympathetic coverage from the western media, and press the United States for support."

Yet, for many people, both in the Soviet Union and abroad, the current situation is alarming. They claim that, after five years, *perestroyka* is in crisis. Substantial liberalization and democratization have taken place, but a democratic "breakthrough" and consolidation have not been completed (Bunce, 1989). A paralysis of power, and a collapse of central governmental capacity to implement policy, has occurred. Radical economic reform remains on the

---

30. This is how Doder and Branson (1990, p. 210) characterize Grobachev's calculations in convoking a three-day meeting of international intellectual and social elites in Moscow in February 1987: "The occasion, as he fully realized, offered an opportunity to enhance his authority, not just in foreign politics but on the domestic front. His enemies, he knew, were lying in wait, ready to turn on him the moment he blundered on security moves or some other issue. But he was becoming increasingly confident in his diplomatic skills, regarded with respect in the West. He demonstrated to the bureaucracy that he was the day-to-day captain of Soviet foreign policy . . . His mastery of detail and the quality of his reflections on display before a glittering audience in the Grand Kremlin Palace proved that the Soviet leader was a forceful figure, commanding the respect of the outside world and thus deserving respect at home."

drawing boards, while leaders of both the party and the state debate heatedly the costs and the risks to be borne in the course of marketization. Minority republics are attempting to secede, defying Gorbachev's constitutionalized procedures and timetable. Russian nationalism has grown stronger and more articulate. The election of Boris Yel'tsin as President of the RSFSR Supreme Soviet has forced the issue of constitutional reform and republic rights. The Communist Party may be on the verge of a split, perhaps into as many as three parties. The international environment appears not to be fully cooperating, as German reunification within NATO threatens to dash Gorbachev's claim that he could transform the international system through conciliation. Is all this a sign that Gorbachev's leadership has run its course? Has he led his people out of Egypt, only to see them perish in the desert before reaching the Promised Land? Or is the current turmoil part of a necessarily disruptive passage, the results of which will become visible only during the coming decade? The answer to this question hinges as much on one's theory of transition as on one's reading of the facts of the current situation in the USSR.

GORBACHEV'S CONTRIBUTION: TRAGIC OR TRANSFORMATIONAL?

Table 1 correlates four images of the future of Soviet domestic evolution with three images of the future of Soviet foreign policy. One's image of where things are heading will obviously go far to determine one's midstream evaluation of Gorbachev's general contribution to either Russian or Soviet history. I have indicated in the cells those combinations that are likely to be judged by historians as either tragic or transformational.

One image of the Soviet future is apocalyptic: social turmoil, civil war, and the ascendancy of a fascist regime. Those who speak of "Weimar Russia" are inclined toward this viewpoint. They view changes introduced to date as highly reversible, though only at an enormously high price in blood and death. They perceive the current situation to be hopelessly polarized, with mass toleration at the breaking point. They claim that the political center, which Gorbachev has dominated up to now, has virtually disappeared. Among the masses, they perceive hopelessness and disillusionment with *perestroyka* and with Gorbachev. The economy and the polity are both collapsing. The ethnic situation is out of control. The only result of all this can be a fundamentalist restoration.

A second scenario for domestic evolution is sometimes labeled "Ottomanization." This scenario looks toward gradual disintegration of sociopolitical cohesion and a condition of chronic instability. It predicts swings back-and-forth between partially reformist regimes and military or party-based "junta" regimes. But it predicts no decisive democratic breakthrough. It views the situation in the Soviet Union as a stand-off among conflicting social forces and between a diverse but mobilized society and an establishment that still has an abundance of coercive resources at its disposal. The result will not be a return

Table 1. *Images of the Soviet Future (to the Year 2010)*[a]

Domestic evolution	Foreign Affairs		
	Expansionist	Isolationist	Collaborative
Fascism	① *Tragic*	② *Tragic*	③ *Incompatible*
Ungovernability; chronic instability	④ *Tragic*	⑤ *Tragic*	⑥ *Probably incompatible*
Zig-zag path to democratization, dismemberment, and marketization	⑦ *Probably incompatible*	⑧ *Transformational*	⑨ *Transformational*
"Smooth" democratization, dismemberment, and marketization	◯10 *Incompatible*	◯11 *Transformational*	◯12 *Transformational*

a. Numbered entries indicate evaluation of Gorbachev's role.

to Stalinism—the price would be too high—but neither will it be a victory for the forces of "modernity." Instead, the Soviet Union will slip into the pattern of chronic instability so typical of the Third World.

Fascism and Ottomanization are the pessimistic scenarios, though the first is more pessimistic than the second. Two optimistic scenarios envisage a rocky and a smooth road to eventual democratic and market breakthrough, accompanied in each case by Soviet elite acknowledgment that the empire cannot be sustained in its current boundaries. Optimism is based on a perception that the price of failing to reform and to allow self-determination (or to come back to them after a brief consolidative reaction) is simply too high in the modern world. Optimists perceive an actual or potential social base for pluralistic market systems in the USSR, and political, ideological, and international factors facilitating or determining the transition (for an overview, see Breslauer, 1990). The two optimistic scenarios differ from the pessimistic also in their empirical reading of the situation in the USSR today. Optimists are skeptical of the claim that the Soviet economy is collapsing. They acknowledge considerable polarization and dissillusionment, but not the disappearance (or irretrievability) of patience or hope, the collapse of the political center, or delegitimation of the reform process itself.

There are many degrees of optimism to be found among those who fall into this camp. Not surprisingly, Mikhail Gorbachev himself professes to be the most optimistic. As he stated in his March 15, 1990, Presidential inaugural address:

> The principal achievement of *perestroika* is democracy and *glasnost'*, and this is the decisive factor in the whole course of further reform. . . .
>
> Society had to go through all this. We were simply unprepared for sweeping changes, and even now we are still not quite ready for them. In a word, the preparatory phase was a truly indispensable one. . . . I understand how dramatic the situation is, how complicated and unusual the problems are, and how emotionally charged society is, but I do not see any grounds for panic, let alone for a change of policy. On the contrary, *perestroika* must obviously be radicalized. And I shall use my presidential powers above all to this end (Gorbachev, 1990, pp. 3, 6, 5).

Gorbachev also explained his theory of transition to the editors of *Time* magazine (June 4, 1990, pp. 28, 32):

> Perestroika has already awakened our people. They've changed. We have a different society now. We will never slip backward. There's still a question of whether the process will go slower or faster, whether it will be more or less painful. But we will certainly keep moving ahead. There might be certain zigzags along the way. That's unavoidable when a country is undergoing major changes. . . .
>
> Once the economic reform really gets under way and millions of people become aware of their places in the new order and pitch in vigorously, they'll become more optimistic and confident of their future.

Although he does not address the issue, Gorbachev presumably intends to complete the work he has finished, to preside over the second stage of *perestroyka*. If he does so, and succeeds in what he had proclaimed to be his goal, he will assuredly go down in history as one of the greatest leaders of modern times.

Most optimists are not as confident as Gorbachev that the process of democratization and marketization is irreversible. Yet they remain optimists because they perceive a social base for still further democratization, even as the regime tackles radical economic reform. And while they perceive potential sources of contradiction between political democratization and economic marketization (be it privatized or municipalized), they do not perceive a live option of choosing between the two, and view the two as capable of being mutually reinforcing.

An increasingly popular theory, developed by Andranik Migranyan (1989), combines a pessimistic perception of the current situation in the Soviet Union with an optimistic theory of leadership for avoiding the worst and eventually navigating the rocky path to a democratic market system. Migranyan argues that a transition from "totalitarianism" to "democracy" is impossible without going through a stage of "authoritarianism." The optimism of those who study the Spanish and Portuguese transitions, Migranyan argues, is a product of the authoritarian, not totalitarian, character of those regimes. The Soviet Union needs first to develop a civil society that is based upon a propertied class that will provide the social base for eventual democratization. Without this propertied class, democratic reforms will be easily reversed.

This theory of transition in turn determines Migranyan's evaluation of Gorbachev as leader. He criticizes Gorbachev for not having introduced economic reform before introducing political reform, so as to create a bourgeoisie that would make a democratization program viable. Having failed to do so, he now faces the fruits of his myopia: social turmoil. At worst, he will be swept away by a social catastrophe, consigned by history to a place next to Kerensky in the pantheon of leaders. At best, he still has an opportunity to correct the situation by establishing a Gaullist presidency, declaring martial law, and halting further disintegration of governmental authority. He should use his emergency powers to force through radical economic reform and to repress labor unrest that results therefrom. Eventually, he will be able to relax martial law, expand the social base of his regime by constructing a grand coalition that includes the new bourgeoisie, and further develop a constitutional order. Thus, Gorbachev has a choice: either perform the function of a Jaruzelski or be swept away by a "catastrophe."[31] If he successfully follows this advice, of course, he would be highly praised as a leader who overcame his earlier mistakes, learned on the job, and ultimately steered the Soviet Union from totalitarianism through authoritarianism to an elitist democracy.

The controversial assumption underlying Migranyan's historical counterfactual is that Gorbachev could have achieved economic reform earlier without an expansion of mass political participation, which others claim to be necessary to overcoming bureaucratic sabotage of any economic decentralization. The controversial assumption underlying his image of the current situation in the USSR is that the political center has disappeared, the population cannot "learn democracy," and the results of a prolonged stalemate will be a social and political explosion that will favor the fascists. Finally, the assumption underlying Migranyan's proposed scenario for the 1990s is that Gorbachev could

31. As Roman Szporluk once put it (personal communication), the Soviet leader could become a "Gorbazelski" or a "Gorbacescu"!

reassert governmental authority and use coercive powers without unleashing social anarchy, civil war, and a fascist restoration.[32]

In contrast, optimists who do not accept Migranyan's assumptions and prescriptions believe that democratization and marketization must proceed in tandem. Following the optimistic literature on transitions to democracy, they would urge upon Gorbachev a very different leadership strategy based upon a different theory of transition: simultaneous movement to the *left* on both political and economic reform. He must preside over the partial dismemberment of the Soviet Union, perhaps by calling a constitutional convention to negotiate secessions, minority rights within seceding units, and the terms of association among the republics that remain within the Union (be it a federation or confederation). He must radicalize his policies, continuously creating new coalitions to his *left*, uniting reformist establishment forces with radical opposition forces that are opposed to playing breakdown games (for example, the A. Sobchaks, G. Popovs, and B. Yel'tsins). He must use his powers to introduce a multiparty system within which competing *national* parties will foster alliances that cut across class and sectoral lines. And he must use those powers to create new national trade unions within which labor can negotiate through organized intermediaries that cut across sectoral and branch lines. Representatives of the national parties and national unions must also be brought into a grand coalition of center-left forces.

DiPalma's (1991) optimistic theory of transitions to democracy treats stalemates not necessarily as precursors of breakdown but instead as potential incubators of creative breakthroughs. Thus, stalemates typically result when the price of restoring the status quo ante is perceived to exceed the price of living with the new turbulence. Crisis, rather than portending breakdown or catastrophe, often becomes psychologically routine or at least more palatable than the price of backlash. But eventually, as stalemate makes stagnation appear dangerous to internal or national security, a majority of the elite comes to the conclusion that the price of living with continuing stalemate exceeds the price of forging a historic compromise that effects a democratizing breakout from the stalemate. From this perspective, stalemate can be creative, especially when society is perceived to be an asset, rather than, as in the pessimistic scenarios, its being typically perceived to be a liability due to its low level of "political culture."

Optimists may differ among themselves as to Gorbachev's role in this prospective radicalization of both economic and political reform. If one views him

---

32. DiPalma (1991) forcefully echoes Juan Linz in arguing that parliamentarism rather than presidentialism is crucial for sustaining the transition from authoritarianism to democracy, for it gives the broadest array of social forces a perception of representation in the policy-making process and, therefore, an incentive to transfer their loyalties to the democratic order. However, Migranyan implicitly rejects the applicability of this analogy by arguing that the contradictions between democratization and marketization, and the greater constraints on change posed by Leninist "totalitarianism," dictate a temporary combination of strong presidentialism and limited parliamentarism.

as a man who has a "great political gift . . . for compromise . . . but not for decisive radical action" (*The New York Times*, April 15, 1990), or as "a brilliant tactician in the increasingly irrelevant arena of Kremlin politics . . . [whose] understanding of Soviet society is incomplete . . . [and whose] vision of the future is both narrow and vague" (*Newsweek*, June 4, 1990, p. 18), one will be inclined to see the next radical stage as presided over by new leaders. In that case, one might gravitate to the conclusion that Gorbachev was a brilliant and indispensable transitional leader, whose capacity to destroy the old system without inducing civil war or fascism exceeded his ability to create a new system. But if he is superceded by more "enlightened" leaders who succeed in steering the country toward a marketized democracy, Gorbachev would still go down in history as the man who led the political and psychological breakthrough that made this transformation possible.

Of course, one's evaluation of Gorbachev's leadership will presumably be based on his foreign policy accomplishments as well. Table 1 suggests three directions for Soviet foreign policy in the future: an expansionist restoration; an enduring isolationist retrenchment; and collaborative internationalism. By Gorbachev's reckoning, only the last of these three would qualify as "success," since Soviet isolation, to his mind, would run counter to his goal of broader Soviet integration into the international order. By the reckoning of most Western observers, however, both the second and the third scenarios would be considered progressive, since they each imply an end to Leninist expansionism.

Certain combinations of domestic and foreign policy evolution are so incompatible, and hence unlikely, that we may rule them out prima facie. Cells 3 and 10 clearly fall into that category, while cells 6 and 7 arguably may also. We will therefore dispense with further consideration of them. If the "downstream" consequence of Gorbachev's great experiment is found in cells 1, 2, 4, or 5, his leadership will have failed on its own terms, as well as on the terms of most Western evaluators. He will be praised by historians for his intentions, but will be dubbed a tragic episode in Russian and Soviet history. If, on the other hand, the downstream consequence is found in any of cells 8, 9, 11, 12, Gorbachev's leadership will have succeeded on most of its own terms, as well as on the terms of most Western evaluators. He will then likely go down in history as a successful transformational leader, whether or not he presides over the christening of the edifice he helped to design.

CONCLUSION: IN PRAISE OF GORBACHEV'S LEADERSHIP STRATEGY

During his first five years in power, Gorbachev has been an event-making man, exercising unique leadership skills to break his country out of the preexisting order at home and abroad, and to begin the process of building alternative political and international orders. Although he has had social, political, and international allies in each of these endeavors, overcoming constraints and breaking logjams required from him enlightened acts of leadership. It is doubtful that anyone else in the leadership could have supplied them.

What is more, from a comparative perspective, his strategies and tactics of transformation appear to be enlightened as well. Focusing his attention on cultural transformation through desacralization of the old order, followed by legitimation of alternative assumptions about social, economic, and political life, accords with the thrust of much literature on transformational leadership. So does his creation of new institutions that both channel political activity into new arenas and stack the deck in favor of social groups which share his general vision of the country's future. Gorbachev's leadership deserves very high marks from those who approach leadership evaluation by emphasizing changes in structure and culture, rather than greater efficiency or short-term material accomplishments, in reaching conclusions. Rather than simply focusing on how much particular leaders are able to maximize gains within the game being played, an attempt to evaluate transformational leadership must consider the degree to which the leader has been able to restructure the very game itself to the *eventual* benefit of the unit he leads.

Adopting a political tactic of "radical centrism" also accords with the prescriptions advanced in recent literature on leadership strategies during transitions to democracy. By selectively appeasing or allying with conservative forces, while simultaneously raising the price of backlash, Gorbachev has been able to maintain the political initiative without inducing a conservative or reactionary coup. By releasing radical social forces, but providing them with democratic avenues of political participation, he has been able to keep up the momentum of reform, while reducing incentives for nihilism on the left and repression on the right. By fashioning a foreign policy that mobilizes international forces in support of *perestroyka*, he has increased the attractiveness of staying the course, while raising higher the price to be paid for a backlash.

Let me avoid being misunderstood. Whether Gorbachev's efforts have made reform irreversible remains to be seen; irreversibility is typically only knowable in retrospect, if even then. The guesses that observers put forth typically hinge in part on their perception of the degree of polarization, desperation, and incipient anarchy within Soviet politics and society today. Alternatively, those guesses hinge on observers' implicit theories of transition: assumptions about the types and degrees of disruption that are necessary but containable in the course of democratizing and marketizing a Leninist multinational empire.

Yet, on both empirical and theoretical grounds, both optimists and pessimists should avoid stating their positions too forcefully. The state of public and elite opinion in the USSR today is in evolution and is poorly understood: existing studies have not tapped into attitudes toward "least bad" solutions, or into the relationship between attitudes and behavior. As for theory, while it provides useful, transferable propositions, it remains the case that the task facing the Soviet leadership is unprecedented. This could mean that it is impossible; or it could mean that we have yet to develop a theory of transition that specifies the necessary components of a successful strategy. In this essay, I have sought to indicate why Gorbachev's strategy and tactics have worked to this point, and why the popular claim that they have exhausted their utility should be questioned. I am not prepared to write off their continued capacity to navigate the transition, or Gorbachev's capacity to revise his tactics should radical centrism no longer prove appropriate to the evolving situation.

AFTERWORD: THE 28TH CONGRESS OF THE CPSU

This paper was completed before the 28th Congress met in Moscow during the first two weeks of July 1990. However, *Soviet Economy's* publication schedule allowed the addition of a "last-minute" section, based solely on newspaper accounts of the proceedings.[33]

Although the Congress yielded mixed results for the progress of *perestroyka*, it did provide a demonstration of Gorbachev's radical centrist tactic in action. The delegate selection process had been dominated by regional party machines, yielding a Congress that was far more conservative than the party membership as a whole. As a result, during the first days of debate, Gorbachev and his reformist allies were subjected to widespread, frequent, and harsh criticism, while Yegor Ligachev led the conservative charge. When viewed in light of the reactionary tide that had dominated the Congress of the RSFSR Communist Party in June 1990, it appeared that Gorbachev might be forced to abandon his plans to restructure the party's leading organs. It even appeared that he could be forced out as General Secretary, or be forced to share power with a hard-line Deputy. At a minimum, it appeared that hardliners would consolidate their power to obstruct Gorbachev and *perestroyka*.

Yet, by the end of the Congress, Gorbachev had stemmed and reversed the conservative tide. He was overwhelmingly re-elected as General Secretary, and his chosen candidate, Vladimir A. Ivashko, trounced Yegor Ligachev for the Deputy position. The Politburo was totally reconstituted, expanded to include the First Secretary of every republic, plus a series of political nonentities. Yegor Ligachev retired to Siberia after failing to win even re-election to the Central Committee, which was expanded to a total of more than 400 members, most of them middle-of-the-roaders.

These changes greatly strengthened Gorbachev's hand in dealing with the leading party organs. The new Politburo is now a marginalized policy-making body. Without leaders of state, military, or police bureaucracies represented on it, the Politburo is no longer an oligarchy of elites that can pretend to dictate policy in all sectors, or that can easily force Gorbachev to subject himself to the discipline of a lowest-common-denominator consensus-building process. With a trusted deputy in charge of day-to-day party affairs, Gorbachev can concentrate on affairs of state, confident that the Politburo cannot become

---

33. The issue of *Soviet Economy* in which this essay appeared went to press on July 19, 1990.

either a unified or an assertive force. Finally, by having himself elected General Secretary by the Party Congress, not the Central Committee, Gorbachev established the precedent that he would not be held accountable for his performance to the Central Committee. The net result of these changes was to make the leading party organs less of a threat to, or constraint on, the General Secretary, and to encourage bandwagoning tendencies among the uncommitted.

At the same time, Gorbachev appeased conservatism by refusing to abolish democratic centralism, to disband party cells in the workplace, army, and police, or to accede to other such demands of the Democratic Platform, a radical faction within the CPSU and Congress. The result was that Boris Yel'tsin, and many radical deputies, including the mayors of Moscow and Leningrad, withdrew from the CPSU in order to challenge the party order from without.

Gorbachev had apparently hoped to avoid the defection of the radicals. His tactic of radical centrism called for neutralizing or purging the orthodox Leninists, as represented and rallied by Ligachev, moving the center-of-gravity of the party to the center-left, and encouraging the radical left to believe that he would use his new powers to the benefit of radicalizing reforms. He succeeded on the first two scores, but lost the radicals in the process. Yet, if there really existed a threat that the anti-reform forces would dominate this Congress, then the first two purposes were more important to Gorbachev than the third.

As for the substance of policy, this Congress reflected a struggle among three major organizational tendencies within the party. One tendency, represented by Ligachev, was willing to fight to maintain the *monopolistic* position of the party in society, economy, and polity. A second tendency, represented by Yel'tsin, was *abolitionist*, demanding that the party abdicate its leading role, politically and organizationally, by dissolving party cells in non-political institutions and by ceding the party's organizational resources. Gorbachev adopted the centrist position—anti-monopolistic *and* anti-abolitionist. As he put it: "The question of whether there should or should not be party organizations at enterprises can be answered very simply: there should be. This naturally fully applies to members of other parties" (*The New York Times*, July 3, 1990, p. A5). Gorbachev was calling for the party to adopt a *competitive* posture, and for the population to decide which organizations to join. Let society decide, seemed to be his message.

In both his opening and closing speeches, and in shorter statements in between, Gorbachev played upon the dominant fears of conservative and uncommitted Congress delegates: that society would decide against them, and deal with them accordingly, in the absence of successful reform. He presented himself as the sole indispensable leader who could steer the party and country away from such a fate. When delegates threatened a vote of no confidence in the leadership, Gorbachev warned them that such a rebellion could so divide the party that it would never recover: "If you want to bury the party, to divide the party, just continue this way. But think seriously about it" (*The New York Times*, July 8, 1990, p. 4). And when wrapping up his re-election as General

Secretary, he made clear his demand that the party allow radicalization of reform. The only real choice lay between demonopolization and marginalization: "The party's success depends on whether it realizes that this is already a different society. Otherwise it will be marginalized by other forces . . ." (*The Wall Street Journal*, July 11, 1990, p. A10). He called on them to "put an end to this monopoly forever" (*The New York Times*, July 11, 1990, p. A6). This posture apparently created a bandwagoning effect among Congress delegates, who apparently more feared a marginalized future without Gorbachev than a radicalized, competitive future with him at the helm.

For radical democratizers within the party, the fear of staying inside the party apparently exceeded the fear of being isolated from the party's organizational resources. This has led many Western journalists to conclude that Gorbachev's tactical intra-party victory will eventually give way to a strategic defeat for Gorbachev and the CPSU. Defection of the party's left-wing will reinforce popular perceptions of the party as an increasingly irrelevant institution (*The New York Times*, July 15, 1990, p. E3; *The Pittsburgh Press*, July 15, 1990, p. A4). Perhaps this conclusion will prove to be a correct one. Or perhaps, if Gorbachev keeps pushing the party to the left, and stabilizes the economic situation while radicalizing reform and permitting the development of multiparty pluralism, he will avoid both economic and political collapse.

Final Comment. Following the optimistic theories of transition discussed above, I conclude that Gorbachev must keep moving to the "left." If he uses his new-found power simply to consolidate a center-right coalition, he will purchase neither order nor progress. But judging from recent events, this appears not to be his intention. Despite the defection of the radicals, he did move the party away from the right at the 28th Congress, leading one exultant delegate to proclaim: "The monster of conservatism has been slain!" (*The Pittsburgh Press*, July 15, 1990, p. A4). And in his first Presidential decree following the Congress, he ordered demonopolization of the broadcast media (*The Washington Post*, July 16, 1990, p. A1). But Gorbachev also ordered Kremlin adjudication of local disputes over media control. How he handles this and analogous struggles over access to the party's organizational resources will be an important indicator of the depth of his desire and ability to force demonopolization and a truly competitive multi-party system. And this in turn may help to determine whether Gorbachev's strategy of transformation proves to be a success.

REFERENCES

Alexiev, Alex, "Commentary [on Rahr]," *Radio Liberty Report on the USSR*, 1, 51:20–22, December 22, 1989.

Åslund, Anders, *Gorbachev's Struggle for Economic Reform.* Ithaca, N.Y.: Cornell University Press, 1989.

Bonner, Yelena, "On Gorbachev," *The New York Review of Books*, 37, 8:14–17, May 17, 1990.

Breslauer, George W., "Thinking About the Soviet Future," in George W. Breslauer, ed., *Can Gorbachev's Reforms Succeed?* Berkeley, Calif: Center for Slavic and East European Studies, University of California at Berkeley, 1990.

———, "From Brezhnev to Gorbachev: Ends and Means of Soviet Leadership Selection," in Raymond C. Taras, ed., *Leadership Change in Communist States*. Boston: Unwin, Hyman, 1989a.

———, "Linking Gorbachev's Domestic and Foreign Policies," *Journal of International Affairs*, 2:267–282, 1989b.

Breslauer, George W., and Philip Tetlock, "Introduction," in George W. Breslauer and Philip Tetlock, eds., *Learning in U.S. and Soviet Foreign Policy*, forthcoming, 1991.

Brown, Archie, "Power and Policy in a Time of Leadership Transition, 1981–1988," in Archie Brown, ed., *Political Leadership in the Soviet Union*. Bloomington: Indiana University Press, 1990.

Browne, Angela, and Aaron Wildavsky, "Implementation as Exploration (1983)," in Jeffrey L. Pressman and Aaron Wildavsky, eds., *Implementation*, third edition, expanded. Berkeley: University of California Press, 1984.

Bunce, Valerie, "The Transition from State Socialism to Liberal Democracy," typescript, Evanston, Illinois, October 1989.

Burns, James McGregor, *Leadership*. New York: Harper and Row, 1978.

Comisso, Ellen, "The Political Conditions of Economic Reform in Socialism," typescript, San Diego, California, April 1988.

Dahl, Robert, *Democracy and Its Critics*. New Haven, Conn: Yale University Press, 1989.

Daniels, Robert V., "Political Processes and Generational Change," in Archie Brown, ed., *Political Leadership in the Soviet Union*. Bloomington: Indiana University Press, 1990.

DiPalma, Giuseppe, *To Craft Democracies* (forthcoming) University of California Press, 1991.

———, "Transitions: Puzzles and Surprises From West to East," paper presented at Conference of Europeanists, Washington, D.C., March 23–25, 1990.

Doder, Dusko, and Louis Branson, *Gorbachev: Heretic in the Kremlin*. New York: Viking, 1990.

Doig, Jameson W., and Erwin C. Hargrove, eds., *Leadership and Innovation*. Baltimore: Johns Hopkins University Press, 1967.

Drane, Melanie, "Can Gorbachev's Reforms Succeed?" seminar paper, Berkeley, Calif.: May 1990.

Fearon, James D., "Counterfactuals and Hypothesis Testing in Political Science," paper prepared for presentation at the American Political Science Association Meetings, San Francisco, August 30–September 2, 1990.

Goldman, Marshall I., "Gorbachev the Economist," *Foreign Affairs*, 2:28–44, 1990.

Goldman, Philip, "Some Thoughts on the Question 'Can Gorbachev's Reforms Succeed?' " Seminar paper, Berkeley, California, May 1990.

Gorbachev, Mikhail S., *Zhivoye tvorchestvo naroda* (The Living Creativity of the People). Moscow: Politizdat, 1984.

———, *Speech by USSR President Mikhail Gorbachev*. Moscow: Novosti, 1990.

Gustafson, Thane, "The Road to Anarchy?" *Sovset*, January 31, 1990.

Hankiss, Elemer, *East European Alternatives: Are There Any?* manuscript, Budapest, Hungary, September 1988.

Hauslohner, Peter, "Politics Before Gorbachev: DeStalinization and the Roots of Reform," in Seweryn Bialer, ed., *Politics, Society, and Nationality Inside Gorbachev's Russia.* Boulder, Colo.: Westview, 1989.

Hewett, Ed A., *Reforming the Soviet Economy.* Washington, D.C.: Brookings Institution, 1988.

Hodnett, Grey, "The Pattern of Leadership Politics," in Seweryn Bialer, ed., *The Domestic Context of Soviet Foreign Policy.* Boulder, Colo.: Westview Press, 1982.

Hoffmann, Stanley, "Heroic Leadership: The Case of Modern France," in Lewis J. Edinger, ed., *Political Leadership in Industrialized Societies.* New York: John Wiley & Sons, 1967.

Hook, Sidney, *The Hero in History.* Boston: Beacon Press, 1943.

Hough, Jerry F., *Opening Up the Soviet Economy.* Washington, D.C.: Brookings Institution, 1988.

——, *Russia and the West: Gorbachev and the Politics of Reform,* second edition. New York: Simon and Schuster, 1990.

——, "The Politics of Successful Economic Reform," *Soviet Economy,* 5, 1:3–46, 1989.

——, "Gorbachev's Politics," *Foreign Affairs,* 68, 5:26–41, 1989–1991.

Huntington, Samuel, *Political Order in Changing Societies.* New Haven, Conn.: Yale University Press, 1968.

Janos, Andrew C., "Social Theory and the Dynamics of Political Change in Communist Societies," typescript, Berkeley, California, 1989.

Jones, Ellen, "Committee Decision-Making in the Soviet Union," *World Politics,* 36, 2:165–188, 1984.

Kagarlitskiy, Boris, *The Dialectic of Change.* London: Verso, 1990.

Kissinger, Henry, *White House Years.* Boston: Little-Brown, 1979.

Knight, Amy, "Commentary [on Rahr]," *Radio Liberty Report on the USSR,* 1, 51:22–24, December 22, 1989.

Kornai, Janos, *The Road to a Free Economy.* New York: Norton, 1990.

Kubalkova, V., and A. A. Cruickshank, *Thinking New About Soviet "New Thinking."* Berkeley, Calif.: Institute of International Studies, University of California at Berkeley, 1989.

Lapidus, Gail W., "Gorbachev and the 'National Question': Restructuring the Soviet Federation," *Soviet Economy,* 5, 3:201–250, 1989.

Leuchtenberg, William E., "Franklin D. Roosevelt: The First Modern President," in Fred I. Greenstein, ed., *Leadership in the Modern Presidency.* Cambridge, Mass.: Harvard University Press, 1988.

Levine, Daniel H., "Paradigm Lost: Dependence to Democracy," *World Politics,* 40, 3:377–394, 1988.

Lewin, Moshe, *The Gorbachev Phenomenon.* Berkeley, Calif.: University of California Press, 1988.

Lyday, Corbin, "The Gorbachev Interregnum and Multiethnicity: A Soviet Time of Troubles," seminar paper, Berkeley, California, May 1990.

March, James G., and Johan P. Olsen, *Rediscovering Institutions: The Organizational Basis of Politics.* New York: The Free Press, 1989.

Migranyan, A., "Dolgiy put'k yevropeyskomu domu" (The Long Road to the European Home), *Novyy Mir,* 7:166–184, 1989.

Miller, John H., "Putting Clients in Place: The Role of Patronage and Cooption into the Soviet Leadership," in Archie Brown, ed., *Political Leadership in the Soviet Union.* Bloomington: Indiana University Press, 1990.

Naylor, Thomas, *The Gorbachev Strategy.* Lexington, Mass.: Lexington Books, 1988.

Neustadt, Richard, *Presidential Power.* New York: John Wiley & Sons, 1960.

Newsweek, "Why Is He a Failure?" (cover story) June 4, 1990.

O'Donnell, Guillermo, and Philippe C. Schmitter, *Transitions from Authoritarian Rule: Tentative Conclusions about Uncertain Democracies.* Baltimore: Johns Hopkins University Press, 1986.

O'Donnell, Guillermo, Philippe C. Schmitter, and Laurence Whitehead, eds., *Transitions from Authoritarian Rule: Comparative Perspectives.* Baltimore: Johns Hopkins University Press, 1986.

Parker, Richard, "Inside the 'Collapsing' Soviet Economy," *The Atlantic Monthly,* 4:68–80, June 1990.

Przeworski, Adam, "Some Problems in the Study of the Transition to Democracy," in Guillermo O'Donnell, Philippe C. Schmitter, and Laurence Whitehead, eds., *Transitions from Authoritarian Rule: Comparative Perspectives.* Baltimore: Johns Hopkins University Press, 1986.

Rahr, Alexander, "Gorbachev and the Post-Chebrikov KGB," *Radio Liberty Report on the USSR,* 1, 51:16–20, December 22, 1989.

Reddaway, Peter, "Is the Soviet Union on the Road to Anarchy?" *Washington Post,* August 20, 1989a, p. B1.

———, "Life After Gorbachev: The Soviets' Grim Future," *Washington Post,* November 26, 1989b, p. C1.

———, "Commentary [on Rahr]," *Radio Liberty Report on the USSR,* 1, 51:24–27, December 22, 1989c.

———, "The Road to Anarchy Revisited," *Sovset,* April 24, 1990.

Rigby, T. H., "The Soviet Political Executive, 1917–1986," in Archie Brown, ed., *Political Leadership in the Soviet Union.* Bloomington: Indiana University Press, 1990.

Ruble, Blair, "The Soviet Union's Quiet Revolution," in George W. Breslauer, ed., *Can Gorbachev's Reforms Succeed?* Berkeley: Center for Slavic and East European Studies, University of California at Berkeley, 1990.

Rustow, Dankwart, "Transitions to Democracy," *Comparative Politics,* 2:337–363, 1970.

Sanders, Brian, "The Path to Change: Managing the Process of Transformation," seminar paper, Berkeley, California, May 1990.

Schwartz, Andrew, "Japanese Neomercantilism: An Agenda for Soviet Development?" seminar paper, Berkeley, California, May 1990.

Selznick, Philip, *Leadership in Administration.* New York: Harper and Row, 1957.

Sergeyev, Viktor, and Pavel Parshin, "Process-Oriented and Procedural Thinking as Reflected in Political Texts," paper presented at Third U.S.-Soviet Workshop on "Models and Concepts of Interdependence Between Nations," Berkeley, California, January 26–29, 1990.

Starr, S. Frederick, "The Changing Nature of Change in the USSR," in Seweryn Bialer and Michael Mandelbaum, eds., *Gorbachev's Russia and American Foreign Policy.* Boulder, Colo.: Westview, 1988.

Tichy, Noel M., and Mary Anne Devanna, *The Transformational Leader*. New York: John Wiley & Sons, 1986.

Tiersky, Ronald, "Perestroika and Beyond," *Problems of Communism*, 39, 2:109–114, 1990.

Tsypkin, Mikhail, "Commentary [on Rahr]," *Radio Liberty Report on the USSR*, 1, 51:27–30, December 22, 1990.

Weiner, Myron, "Empirical Democratic Theory and the Transition from Authoritarianism to Democracy," *PS*, 10, 3:861–866, 1987.

Wolpe, H., "Some Problems Concerning Revolutionary Consciousness," in Ralph Miliband and John Saville, eds., *The Socialist Register 1970*. London: The Merlin Press, 1970, pp. 251–280.

Yanov, Alexander, *Detente After Brezhnev*. Berkeley, Calif.: Institute of International Studies, University of California at Berkeley, 1977.

Yel'tsin, Boris, *Against the Grain*. New York: Summit Books, 1990.

"Z" (anonymous), "To the Stalin Mausoleum," *Daedalus*, 119, 1:295–344, 1990.

CHAPTER 15

The Quality of Gorbachev's Leadership

Peter Reddaway

GEORGE BRESLAUER'S article on Gorbachev's leadership qualities (Breslauer, 1989) is an extremely stimulating, formidably argued matching of theory against practice. Its many fruits deserve a longer response than can be given here. If he had written it in early 1989 rather than so much later in 1990,[1] I would have been impressed and persuaded by almost all his points, rather than by just many of them. As it is, I believe that Gorbachev's vision of the future has increasingly proved uninspiring or off-target to many Soviet people, and, combined with certain apparent mistakes on his part, has led to a crippling and irreversible decline in his authority. This makes impossible, in my view, the kind of continuing success of his leadership that Breslauer thinks plausible. Although disagreement with Bresaluer is not the structural focus of this essay, an attempt is made here to marshal selected arguments supporting conclusions which Breslauer's paper tended to deflate.

GORBACHEV IN HISTORICAL PERSPECTIVE

If Gorbachev were voluntarily to relinquish the presidency in the near future, he would probably still receive good marks from historians—first for the dazzling skill with which (as Breslauer rightly demonstrates) he has undermined party rule, the "administrative-command system," and the traditional political culture, without (until things changed in the fall of 1990) provoking a sharp conservative backlash, and second for opening up the system to new political and economic forces. For historians may well judge that conducting a relatively peaceful transition from totalitarianism to democracy and the market was *in*

First published in *Soviet Economy*, 1990, 6, 2, pp. 125–140. This essay, as well as the following ones by Archie Brown and Andranik Migranyan were written independently of each other, in response to the query "has Gorbachev's leadership outlived its usefulness?" [Eds.]

1. The material was updated just prior to publication in August 1990. It appeared, however, in the last issue of the 1989 volume of *Soviet Economy*.

itself an impossible task, let alone one which could be achieved from start to finish under a single leader.[2]

After all, profound upheavals such as the French revolution of the late 18th century, the Russian revolution of 1917–1921, or the Iranian revolution of the late 1970s, produce, perhaps invariably, a degree of turnover in the revolutionary leadership, especially early on. Thus, even if Gorbachev leaves the stage sometime soon, historians may be impressed by the *longevity* of his tenure—and attribute it primarily to the leadership skills that Breslauer documents. He has, after all, already survived for nearly two years since his "revolution from above" began to slip out of his control, under pressure first from the incipient revolution from below and later from the conservative reaction which both these revolutions provoked.

The current danger, as I shall argue, is that Gorbachev may, despite his now minimal domestic authority, cling to office by trying to use his declining and increasingly uncertain power before it becomes *completely* unusable. This could all too easily slow down, sabotage, halt, or even reverse urgently needed economic reform, and could also increase the already serious danger of major domestic strife or even civil war.

But whether or not Gorbachev clings to office, an important question posed by Breslauer remains: What are the criteria for judging a transition to be successful? Would it be a success if, by the year 2000, Russia (with or without the Ukraine and Belorussia) had embraced democracy and the market, but, in the meanwhile, civil war had killed a million people? Historians might reckon that such a tragedy could have been avoided if, for example, in the early years, Gorbachev's leadership strategy had been less (or, alternatively, more) radical. Or they might conclude that his strategy was probably the best one possible, and any other would only have led to even more deaths. The purpose of this brief paragraph is only to stress, somewhat more than Breslauer does, the importance of historical perspective for arriving at solid, rather than tentative, interim judgments about the quality of Gorbachev's leadership.

At the root of Gorbachev's aforementioned mistakes, in my view, is the political conditioning he received as a young apparatchik in the USSR of Khrushchev's time. This led him to believe, with Khrushchev, that if one trusted the people, loosened political controls, increased incentives, created opportunities for political participation, strove for social justice, and conducted a more peaceful foreign policy, the people would be grateful, would work harder, would overcome bureaucratic resistance to their newly released creativity, and would "make socialism work" rather than challenge it by supporting nationalism, regionalism, anti-communism, or multi-party democracy. Both leaders failed (or did not want) to see that within Soviet society lay the seeds of potential anti-Russian and anti-communist resolutions. Doubtless Gorbachev

---

2. On the day that Gorbachev's compromise program for economic reform was approved by the USSR Supreme Soviet, Leonid Abalkin expressed the view at a press conference that "to create a real market . . . will require at least ten years, perhaps an entire generation" (*The Washington Post*, October 20, 1990, p. A1).

had more of an inkling of this than Khrushchev, since he could not be completely unaware of the public appearance and growth of these seeds, i.e., of dissident movements, from the mid-1960s until the temporary suppression of most of them in the early 1980s. Such an inkling may help to account for the notable "schizophrenic" but characteristic swings in his rhetoric between supreme optimism about the success of *perestroyka* and increasingly frequent anxiety that *perestroyka* is threatened from various quarters by "disaster," "catastrophe," or "civil war."

GORBACHEV'S VISION: A CRITICAL APPRAISAL

In any case, for a transformational leader to be successful, he needs, as Breslauer suggests, to have charisma, or at least a broad and compelling vision of where he is leading his people. In the USSR, unlike abroad, Gorbachev has never in my opinion had significant charismatic appeal.[3] But he has had a broad vision which, from January 1987 and for about three years, he expounded repeatedly and at length. This vision has understandably had much appeal in the West, especially to people of social democratic orientation. But its appeal in the USSR is less broad, and has declined with the passage of time as it has come to seem increasingly utopian or off-target, or both.

Gorbachev's vision of those three years focused on an entity which has scarcely existed in an organic sense, namely the "Soviet people." It posited the following: (a) a strong central government; (b) limited powers for the republics; (c) an economy based on market socialism, with strong regulation from the center, an enlarged but still small private sector, and harder work from everyone; (d) a polity much more flexible and open than before, based on the rule of law (*pravoporyadok*), but still controlled by a Communist Party which would remain the only party permitted to function freely in the political arena; (e) greatly expanded freedom of expression and association, but with limits still imposed on the mass media (*glasnost'*); (f) social justice for all; and (g) a peaceful, conciliatory foreign policy which would permit the defense budget to be steadily reduced.

Apart from the last component, which has been successfully pursued and has met with popular approval and only limited resistance from military leaders and hard-liners, all the other components of this vision have proved to be either problematic or unpopular. The broad reason for this is that as *glasnost'* progressively articulated what previously had been more sensed emotionally than understood by the mind, namely the seemingly comprehensive failures and brutality of the entire system, most of the main features of that system consciously became increasingly repugnant. Thus extreme centralism, big gov-

---

3. Breslauer seems to disagree on this point. My view is that working people were at first either cautiously supportive of him or skeptical because he sounded like a better educated, though not necessarily otherwise better, version of Khrushchev. Their opinion of him has clearly worsened in the last two years. Relatively few educated people seem to have been captivated by him, as opposed to appreciating and supporting many of his policies.

ernment, Russification, the Communist Party, the KGB, Marxism-Leninism, official trade unions, even Lenin and the military, have for many become objects of distaste and revulsion. Conversely, their opposites have become increasingly, if sometimes irrationally, attractive—decentralization, small government, nationalism, regionalism, political pluralism, the right to strike, isolationism, even tsarism and pacifism. Most of this has diverged sharply from Gorbachev's vision. In addition, few people have wanted to work harder, as inflation has gathered pace and the economic future has darkened, and social justice has remained largely on paper.

None of this might have been so serious if Gorbachev had been adroit to the degree Breslauer suggests at redefining goals and norms as events unfolded. However, on the big confrontational issues of 1989–1990—the mounting demands for confederalism, a multi-party system, disestablishment of the Communist Party, and radically privatizing economic reform—Gorbachev was at first strongly and on principle opposed, and only gave way slowly, grudgingly, and in most cases partially or (as on economic reform) highly ambiguously. All this has made his vision uncertain and therefore ineffective.

Part of his motivation in this growing reluctance to redefine goals has clearly been, as Breslauer shows, his desire to continue to bring the traditional party-state apparatus along in his wake, moving unhappily but steadily to the left, i.e., his desire to neutralize its political power if he cannot reform it. But another part has been what Bialer (1990, p. 53) calls the "strategic rigidity" and "commitment to basic ideological 'truths' " that exist beneath his flexibility. And yet another part may be his desire to maintain viable relations with the powerful organizations—the party, military, KGB, and MVD—which he might decide to call on in a future attempt to save his own political skin.

In any case, while his vision was clear in seeing the need for cultural change at the start, he has not been able to adjust easily to the outcomes of that change. And while he has succeeded in breaking up the old traditions of government, he has not met the Schumpeter-Breslauer prescription about creating "new tradition." He has found this task much harder than that of allowing the progressive removal of political controls and presiding over what often seems, especially to Soviet conservatives, to be *samotyok*, or the spontaneous unfolding of social processes. Indeed, he has clearly been uneasy about some of the destruction of the old culture, and his vision of the future has differed greatly from that of the more dynamic social forces.

All this helps to account for the growing indecisiveness and erratic behavior which Bialer and others have observed in Gorbachev over the last year. Instead of focusing on his mistakes and weaknesses and devising bold new strategies to overcome them, he has either vacillated or acted much too late. When chided for this, he has insisted on the need for patience in finding political solutions, but also indicated that he will use a big stick if all else fails.

Thus, for example, he eventually rejected the advice of those who thought it important for him to obtain a popular mandate and thereby strong authority as President. By the time he took this decision, early in 1990, his popularity rating was too low for success at the polls to be probable. On the nationalities issue, where he has admitted being taken by surprise by the strength of ethnic nationalism, he did not learn from his disastrous equivocation over the Nagorno-Karabakh crisis in early 1988 that the only hope in dealing with something as volatile as nationalist passions is—as Yuriy Afanas'yev and Andrey Sakharov urged in 1988—to act decisively and get out ahead of the nationalists by sponsoring a new union treaty *early* (e.g., Supporters, 1988). Instead, Gorbachev did not realize how much the Russians' imperial urge was waning, and got serious about a new treaty only in mid-1990. By this time various republics, provoked rather than intimidated by his temporary blockade of Lithuania in the spring, were already bolting through the stable door. With sovereignty an ever more popular code word for complete or near-complete independence, Gorbachev's chances of getting their agreement to anything more than a weak, unstable confederation or commonwealth had become small.

The one chance of perhaps doing better than this lay in the so-called Shatalin Plan for radical economic reform, since this had extensive input and at least a considerable measure of support from the republics. But despite the rapidly deteriorating economic situation, despite the public clamor for decisive measures, despite seeming to endorse Shatalin's plan in public, despite the unanimous view of leading economists that compromise between this plan and the governmental Ryzhkov-Abalkin Plan would spell economic chaos, in October 1990 Gorbachev once again opted for a vacillating middle path.[4] Evidently the right had stood behind Ryzhkov when he said he would resign if his plan were not adopted or taken into account, and Gorbachev felt too weak to face his resignation. Apparently he feared both the blows to his remaining authority which would be sure to be inflicted by the Supreme Soviet when he tried to replace Ryzhkov's government with new ministers,[5] and also the danger that

4. This compromise was duly criticized by thirteen economic advisors, including Stanislav Shatalin and Nikolay Petrakov, in an open letter in *Komsomol'skaya pravda*, November 4, 1990. The compromise may also have resulted in part from Gorbachev's strong antipathy to private property. This has been little noticed in the West, where he is often thought to favor transition to a capitalist market. His belief in market socialism, a system which has worked badly in the few countries where it has been tried, is well documented by Allen Kroncher (1990). Later, in a speech to legislative deputies from the military, Gorbachev dwelt at some length on his commitment to socialism. Speaking dismissively about private property, he declared: "Staying within the framework of the socialist choice [of October 1917], we shall be promoting collective, social forms of property. And I see that such is the mood of people" (*Sovetskaya Rossiya*, November 15, 1990, p. 3). In the same speech Gorbachev casually revealed that he had just sent some economic instructions not only to government bodies, but also to party organizations. Apparently he did not notice that he had thereby violated a basic aspect of his policy of separating the party from economic administration. All this makes it understandable that the strongly conservative Ivan Polozkov, head of the Russian Communist Party, should, in a major report (*Sovetskaya Rossiya*, November 16, 1990, p. 2), express support for Gorbachev's economic reform program. This was because the program's goal was to create "a regulated market economy of socialist type" and had nothing to do with capitalism.

5. This explanation is supported by a statement of his associate, Aleksandr Yakovlev, in a long interview in *Die Welt*, November 19, 1990, p. 15 (translated in *Foreign Broadcast Information Service: Daily Report: Soviet Union*, November 20, 1990, pp. 52–55). Such an attempt, Yakovlev said, would result in "a tough, protracted process in the Supreme Soviet" (p. 54).

the entire operation would provide opportunities for deputies and retiring ministers (and the media) to place the blame for failures on himself. This could have led to calls for his own resignation.[6]

A COMMENT ON MIGRANYAN

Before moving on from a discussion on Gorbachev's mistakes, a brief comment on Andranik Migranyan's (1989) analysis of Gorbachev's first few years is in order. In the abstract, I agree with him that it would probably have been much better to have achieved, as a first stage, a radical marketing reform and only a limited shift toward democracy. Legislatures without strong representation of autonomous interests (farmers, trade unionists, businessmen, professional people, etc.), as Aleksandr Tsipko (1990) has also pointed out, will inevitably lack cohesion and be too easily swayed by populist passions. However, Breslauer is certainly correct to question whether radical economic reform was politically feasible in the early Gorbachev years, given the strong anti-market forces in the Politburo and Central Committee, which it probably would have been impossible to dislodge or override.

By contrast, Migranyan's second assumption—that the political center has eroded, that the people cannot assimilate democracy fast enough, and that a prolonged stalemate would lead to social explosions which will favor the forces of reaction—strikes me as reasonable. But his third assumption—that Gorbachev can still successfully reassert central authority and force through economic reform by adopting authoritarian methods—seems much more implausible in November 1990 than it must have seemed in early 1989, when Migranyan was writing, even though Gorbachev has in the meantime persuaded the legislature to give him the power (on paper) to act in this way.[7] This point is elaborated below.

GORBACHEV'S EVAPORATING SUPPORT

I have several interrelated reasons for believing it implausible that Gorbachev could reassert his authority. First, Gorbachev's popular authority, i.e., popular approval of him (as measured by the All-Union Center for the Study of Public Opinion), has sunk from 52 percent in December 1989 to 21 percent in October 1990 (*Moscow News*, No. 45, November 18–25, 1990, p. 7). Second, the conditions of daily life—not much discussed by Breslauer, partly on the reasonable grounds that their deterioration does not *necessarily* compromise either

6. This line of explanation was taken even further by the main author of Gorbachev's compromise program, Abel Aganbegyan. Asked in an interview why Gorbachev had suddenly rejected the Shatalin program, he said: "I think he thought it would mean the end of our administration" (*The Washington Post*, November 25, 1990, p. C2).

7. Igor Klyamkin (1990) takes a similar view, believing that in all likelihood authoritarian rule will be needed to maintain political stability while marketization reforms are forced through. Without it, the unemployed and the marginally employed (*marginaly*) would be successfully exploited by populist politicians.

Gorbachev's leadership or an eventually successful transition—have deteriorated very rapidly in the last year or two. Shortages and rationing of goods, social aggression, crime, bloody ethnic clashes, administrative chaos, bewilderment as to where authority lies, real anxiety about the future—all these phenomena have become progressively more acute.

If there were still hope, rather than deep anxiety, none of this might be critical. But for most citizens Gorbachev no longer provides hope. Indeed many of those who constitute his 21 percent support base may do so not because they really approve of his performance, but more because they are fearful of the unknown future: What may follow may well be even worse. Bialer (1990) is almost certainly right: Gorbachev is probably becoming, if he has not already become, part of the problem, not part of the solution. And seemingly he cannot escape. Maneuver as he may, too many people put most of the blame for their dashed hopes of *perestroyka* on him. Hence his plummeting popularity.

More dangerous for him still has been the incipient collapse of support for him in the now enlarged polity, a polity in which passions have grown steadily more intense and the main institutions of the center have lost almost all their authority. Gorbachev has been commendably frank about what, in a speech of November 16, he called the "vacuum" and the "paralysis" of power. Whenever he issues decrees, he said, "debates begin: 'What sort of decree is this? Do we have to carry it out, or not?' " To this he commented in disgust: "This way we'll never get an executive that functions properly" (*Izvestiya*, November 17, 1990, p. 2). While most of the pervasive ignoring of presidential decrees has been silent in nature, in some cases it has not. For example, A. Gorbunovs, Chairman of the Latvian Supreme Council, rejected the authority of such decrees, and explained: "I am not subordinate to the President, since it was not the President who appointed me. I was elected by the republic's Supreme Council, and evidently it will . . . determine my future" (TASS, November 16, 1990).

The all-Union legislature, too, had, by fall 1990, become almost impotent. Its laws were not implemented; the President had persuaded it to hand over many of its powers to him, especially those regarding the economy and law and order; and its very legitimacy was disappearing, as relatively freely elected legislatures were voted in by now sovereign republics.[8] The Supreme Soviet even failed by a wide time margin to observe the Constitution and rotate its membership on time, i.e., to replace 20 percent of its members with new representatives from the Congress of People's Deputies.[9]

At lower levels, too, most political institutions either lost authority or became impotent, including the Moscow and Leningrad city soviets,[10] which both have

8. On all this see the interview with an influential USSR deputy, Yuriy Ryzhov, in *Moscow News*, No. 44, November 11–18, 1990, p. 7. Ryzhov believes the Union legislature "has already played its role," and "now it's time to move on."

9. See the scathing article about this by Yelena Bonner (1990).

10. On the role of radical democrats in paralyzing power in the Leningrad city soviet, see Andrey Chernov (1990).

a majority of democratic deputies. As Moscow's Mayor Gavriil Popov said, "The fact that 'democrats' are in power does not mean that they wield any power. I essentially have no real power. I don't command anything. I cannot provide a building, I can't ensure protection for privately run shops. I can't do a lot of things" (*The Washington Post*, November 25, 1990, p. A20). The reasons for this paralysis of power throughout the country have been obstructionism by central government ministries, sabotage and de facto usurpation of power by Communist Party organizations, conflicting laws, and, in some places like Leningrad, extreme behavior by radical democrats.

Within this increasingly angry, frustrated, and dislocated polity, then, it is scarcely surprising that patience with the President has been wearing thin.

MOUNTING PRESSURES FROM THE RIGHT

On the right, conservative Leninists increasingly view Gorbachev as having passively allowed an anti-communist revolution to begin. With his authority so low and the likelihood of him effectively restoring order now apparently minimal, they are fast losing faith in his ability to protect them from the volatile wrath of the people.[11] Many conservative Russian nationalists and military leaders are angered even more by Gorbachev's failure to halt the trend toward dismemberment of the country.[12]

Thus, the divided right has been gradually developing some cohesion, basing itself ideologically on the writings of such publicists as Karem Rash (Tsypkin, 1990a) and the editor of *Soviet Literature*, Aleksander Prokhanov. The latter, often dubbed "the nightingale of the General Staff," sums up much of his diagnosis of the situation in this passage from a recent essay. For the first time in world history, he writes, "a state is collapsing not as a result of external blows, plague, or elemental disasters, but as a result of deliberate actions by leaders, who received their authority from structures devised by themselves. It's not important what moves them—a Herostratus complex,[13] catastrophic incompetence, or service to interests alien to the fatherland. They will go down in history. For millennia they will be praised abroad and damned in the fatherland. The king of *perestroyka* is naked, blindingly naked, and the tailors sewing his morning dress are packing their bags" (Prokhanov, 1990, p. 7).

11. On Revolution Day in 1990, for example, several hundred hard-line communists infiltrated the official parade in Moscow and displayed banners with slogans like "Anti-communist Gorbachev—Get Out of the Communist Party!" (*The Washington Post*, November 8, 1990, p. A64).

12. For evidence of pervasive military anger with Gorbachev, see the report of his meeting with 1,100 military deputies in *Krasnaya zvezda*, November 16, 1990. Also, the mysterious military maneuvers near Moscow in September, which have caused a long furor in the press, suggest to me contingency planning for some sort of intervention. See especially the letter from Deputy S. Shatalov in *Sovetskaya Rossiya*, October 21, 1990.

13. Herostratus was the Greek who burned down the temple of Artemides in Ephesus in order to immortalize his own name.

A more moderate ideologist of the right, the novelist Valentin Rasputin, was appointed to the Presidential Council, but this muzzled him only to some extent. He still lamented in an interview, for example: "The inert powerlessness of the authorities leads to people losing their last remnants of faith and hope. The wooliness and feebleness of the actions of those from whom they await definite decisions and actions—this is one of the main causes of the present situation" (*Moskovskaya pravda*, October 21, 1990, p. 2).

The main political threat that Gorbachev has felt from the right has come from the military conservatives. The Russian Communist Party is conservative and hostile to him, but as yet only a potential threat, since it is young and still forming its identity. The most direct flexing of its muscles to date came in the report by First Secretary Polozkov to its expanded Central Committee plenum of November 1990. In this the party called on Gorbachev "to take the most decisive measures to create order in the country. If the dystrophy of authority should go still further, then we will be compelled to review our attitude to the actions of the center" (*Sovetskaya Rossiya*, November 16, 1990, p. 2).

Evidently more worrying to Gorbachev than this, though potentially connected to it, has been the growing militancy of respected military leaders like his personal advisor and former Chief of the General Staff, Sergey Akhromeyev. Akhromeyev argued at length in a recent article that while the military would act internally only on the orders of the Supreme Soviet and the President, "in the summer of 1990 a united offensive of the destructive forces [of separatists and capitalists] began against all-Union state and public structures. Thereby an offensive began also against our federated state with the aim of dismembering it, and against our socialist system with the aim of destroying it. Today this is not seen only by people who do not want to see it." This passage led directly into his final sentence—a call for immediate action: "The time has come actively and decisively, within the framework of our Constitution, to defend our federated socialist state, the cause of our lives, and the future of our children" (*Sovetskaya Rossiya*, November 14, 1990, p. 6).

Akhromeyev would appear to be acting on behalf of many military leaders and to be exerting strong pressure on Gorbachev to declare presidential or martial law, all from a politically loyal position. At the same time the Soyuz faction in the all-Union legislature, which claims that over 500 deputies belong to it, has become the base from which other military officers like its chairman V. Alksnis and N. Petrushenko (see *Izvestiya*, November 24, 1990, p. 1) have pushed for the same thing by more confrontational and threatening means. Thus Lieutenant-Colonel Alksnis gave a lengthy interview to *Sovetskaya Rossiya* (November 21, 1990, p. 1) demanding that Gorbachev declare presidential rule in the republics. Also, if he failed to assert his authority within a month, Alksnis said he would press for Gorbachev's resignation. What must worry

Gorbachev is that this direct challenge to him has not to date met with strong, high-level rebuttals. Hence his heightened concern in November 1990 to be very solicitous to the military.[14]

Gorbachev seems, in fact, to be increasingly concerned about possible direct military intervention in politics. Apparently this has strengthened his resolve to try to overcome the political and economic crisis by using authoritarian methods. If he rules forcefully by decree, as he seemed to be calculating in late November, he will be able to appease the military and use them in the ways *he* wants, and will not have to share political authority with them. It will be presidential rule, not martial law. And if presidential rule does not work, he will have martial law "in reserve" as a last resort.

This is the strategy suggested to me by Gorbachev's proposals of November 17 for the further strengthening of presidential and executive power, by the closely related resolution "On the Situation in the Country" adopted by the Supreme Soviet on November 23, and by the draft Union Treaty published the next day. Later Gorbachev said he was confident that in the end all the republics would sign the treaty: "Even those who are most vocal in condemning it today won't be able to change anything." He described its opponents as demagogues: "Even if they are in power, they are all frightened of holding a referendum."[15] These words built on his much tougher approach to the republics, especially the Baltic ones, since the early fall.[16] They were also aimed at intimidating the republics, whose declarations of sovereignty he had still not recognized, into signing temporary agreements with the Union government within a month, as a step toward their eventual signing of the treaty.

As for Gorbachev's proposals to further strengthen his own powers, these involve subordinating all major executive bodies directly to himself and reducing the restraining powers of the legislature to almost nothing. Some liberals were at first misled by the abolition of the Council of Ministers, which entailed the subsequent resignation of its chairman, Ryzhkov. But others noted that since Gorbachev had been implementing what was virtually Ryzhkov's reform program since early October, it was very unlikely that he would now launch a serious assault on the tacitly vindicated, still flourishing ministries.[17] More broadly, the bolder commentators criticized Gorbachev's proposals wholesale, especially for their vagueness of purpose. This, they implied, was designed to conceal his systematic preparations for

14. See, for example, his speeches of November 16 and 17, both in *Izvestiya*, November 17, 1990. However, in the latter speech (p. 2), he rebuked Alksnis for claiming that he had "lost the army." Evidently this rebuke provoked Alksnis's threat to demand his resignation. Presidential measures to increase the military's security in the minority republics were announced on November 27.

15. *RFE/RL Daily Report*, No. 225, November 28, 1990, p. 3, citing TASS and *The Washington Post* of November 27.

16. Aleksandr Yakovlev (1990) took a much more benign view of the republics in an interview (see note 5). Everything would depend on "how many powers the republics are willing to cede." This would determine what sort of all-Union institutions were needed. The Kremlin might "find out that we no longer need any government at all" (p. 54).

17. See Igor Klyamkin in *Moscow News*, No. 47, December 2–9, 1990, p. 4.

authoritarian rule, which could, in one writer's view, take the country "towards its ultimate ruin."[18]

Gorbachev showed great irritation at this criticism. In a rambling speech he accused one columnist, Pavel Voshchanov, of having written his article in response to "an order—an order from certain forces." Spelling out his conspiracy theory further, he went on: "Let us not avoid this—there are forces which do not want to normalize the situation in the country." "Certain people" were accusing him of exploiting the situation to try to set up a "dictatorship." "Let us be vigilant, let us be vigilant, comrades!" (*Izvestiya*, November 23, 1990, p. 1; *FBIS*, No. 227, November 26, 1990, pp. 26–27).[19]

This speech confirmed that Gorbachev's theory, unless it sees conspiracies on *both* left and right, focuses on the left. His previous reference to a conspiracy against him had been ambiguous. In the same speech in which he rebuked Lieutenant-Colonel Alksnis for attacking him, he said: "Maybe someone wants to discredit the President; that would be a gift to those who want to dislodge the main forces in the leadership of the country and the republics. I see this both at the republican level, and at the local, and at the Union levels. It is done consistently, as if according to a program or the scheduled timetable of a building job. I even wonder where it comes from, from what committee? Or group. Probably the group that's connected with timetables" (*Izvestiya*, November 17, 1990, p. 2). At the start of this cryptic passage Gorbachev may be referring to the likes of Alksnis. Then, apparently, he accuses such people of playing into the hands of Boris Yel'tsin and the leftist conspiracy.

THE UNEASY LEFT

The left, meanwhile, having implored Gorbachev to join it in a coalition, finds it probably cannot afford to go on courting him much longer, because then it would start sharing responsibility with him in the people's eyes for the all-round deterioration in their lives. Not surprisingly, therefore, it has issued its first strong call for him either to join it and help push through rapid economic and democratic reform, or else resign.[20]

The key figure for Gorbachev on the left has been Boris Yel'tsin. After his election in May 1990 as president of the RSFSR, the chances that Gorbachev and he could cooperate adequately, if not well, seemed quite good. But in the early fall came Gorbachev's watershed, when he was compelled by the Shatalin Plan to choose *either* radical economic reform, confederalism, and democracy (the first

18. Stepan Kiselyov, in *Moscow News*, No. 47, December 2–9, 1990, p. 5. Other commentators writing in a similar vein were L. Telen and A. Gel'man in *ibid.*, pp. 4–5, and S. Sokolov and P. Voshchanov in *Komsomol'skaya pravda*, November 23, 1990, pp. 1–2.

19. The speech was only briefly reported in the main press, presumably because it rambled and was at times hardly coherent.

20. Letter of T. Zaslavskaya, E. Klimov, P. Bunich, Yu. Afanas'yev and 18 others in *Moskovskiye novosti*, No. 46, November 18, 1990.

required the second and third), *or* weak economic reform, limited federalism, and authoritarianism. Earlier he had always quietly kept the option of authoritarianism open, but had distinguished himself from his predecessors by not being paranoid about criticism and opposition, by generally remaining calm as unfavorable processes unfolded, and by maintaining a ban, in most circumstances, on repressive police measures. In 1989 all this became harder for him as opposition grew. And when he digested the political implications of the Shatalin program in September 1990 he feared the democratic commitment, the possible fragmentation of the country, the acceptance of private property, and the loss of the authoritarian option which it would entail. So he rejected Shatalin's plan.

But Yel'tsin already had embraced the plan and all its implications. So, although both men continued to feel the need for each other, real cooperation became impossible. Since neither wanted to be blamed for this, or to play into the hands of the right by quarrelling, they kept their mutual criticisms low-key in tone, and on November 11 had a long private meeting. But Yel'tsin was quick to see that Gorbachev's proposals on executive power of November 17 were pro-center and anti-republics (*The Washington Post*, November 22, 1990, p. A62). Also, doubtlessly knowing that opinion surveys had found public attitudes to be negative about Gorbachev's assumption of extra powers in September 1990 (Vyzov and Gurevich, 1990, p. 1), Yel'tsin suggested that his request for still more powers should be put to the people in a referendum. This caused Gorbachev to accuse Yel'tsin of trying to fan the differences between them, even though they were "80 percent in agreement" (*The Washington Post*, November 24, 1990, p. A18). Yel'tsin was later conciliatory, saying that continued confrontation between them was "unacceptable" (*ibid.*, November 28, 1990, p. A27).

However, Yel'tsin needs Gorbachev to give the RSFSR control over its resources, but Gorbachev rejects this as dangerous Shatalinism. And Gorbachev needs Yel'tsin's support to avoid becoming a captive of the right; but Yel'tsin cannot give it, for this would mean surrendering his political credo and losing all credibility with his electorate. Meanwhile, the RSFSR has been busy investing its paper declaration of sovereignty with some reality by making economic, political, and diplomatic deals with other republics, sending its delegations abroad, setting up its own agencies, and trying to assert at least veto power over the activities of the many federal institutions on its territory. Its conclusion of a full-scale treaty with the Ukraine was a particularly impressive event, with Yel'tsin showing in a powerful and moving speech that his administration means what it says about sovereignty and the equality of nations (*Foreign Broadcast Information Service: Daily Report: Soviet Union*, November 21, 1990, pp. 72–78).

GORBACHEV'S OPTIONS

Thus, unless Gorbachev summons all his courage and embraces the left, he appears trapped. If the left breaks with him, it could perhaps (and despite its fears of its own increasing impotence) use the power that Yel'tsin (with an approval rating still around 50 percent) has over "the street" to organize demonstrations which would force his resignation. But if he at last heeds the right's calls to impose presidential or martial law he would face other hazards. The military, KGB,[21] and MVD are sufficiently divided politically that they might refuse to obey some of his orders. Here lie the seeds of civil war. Also, the right distrusts him so deeply that it might not keep him in power for long, once he was its captive.

The danger now, then, is that Gorbachev will either turn right, despite the obvious danger that this could provoke civil war, or, less likely, go on maneuvering in the vanishing political center, using his skill at infighting to ward off both left and right. In the latter case the trend toward *mnogovlastiye* (many [competing] powers)[22] and anarchy would accelerate, as Moscow and the republics, notably the RSFSR, fought more and more for control over economic institutions, police, natural resources, taxation, military draft, and so on, in the now widely denounced "war of laws," a war which shows that little solid progress toward the rule of law has yet been made.[23]

If, however, Gorbachev were to embrace the left, and then to step down soon as President, the optimistic scenario would have him replaced by a president who would persuade as many republics as possible to adopt an updated version of the Shatalin Plan, then assist them to implement it, each under a "strong and tough" (*sil'nyy i zhestkiy*) leadership of the sort Shatalin believes (in tune with the approach of Migranyan and Klyamkin) that his plan requires.[24]

Even under these circumstances, though, longer-term dangers in abundance would remain, which could easily threaten or derail the process of transition. In general terms the main danger would probably be that radical reform would be sufficiently sabotaged by conservative forces and popular culture and that a reactionary coalition based on an ideology of conservative Russian nationalism and primitive welfare socialism would gather strength.[25] This coalition, the embryo of which can be seen already, would consist of the following:

(1) a new unemployed or semi-employed *Lumpenproletariat*, created by marketization;

21. See Tsypkin (1990b). See also a remarkable letter of dissent from four serving KGB officers in *Komsomol'skaya pravda*, October 10, 1990, p. 2.

22. See an especially forceful denunciation of the paralysis caused by *mnogovlastiye* by Sergey Alekseyev, chairman of the USSR Constitutional Oversight Committee, in *Literaturnaya gazeta*, No. 44, October 31, 1990, p. 1. For his equally strong argument that only speedy and wholesale privatization of property can "avert the developing ferocious struggle between the Union and the republics over the dividing up of state property," see *Moskovskiye novosti*, No. 42, October 21, 1990, p. 6.

23. Gorbachev's frequent exhortations that this pervasive "legal nihilism" must stop have had a tragic quality about them, as did the empty prescription with which Aleksandr Yakovlev (*loc. cit.*, p. 53) concluded his frank analysis of this profound problem: "Democracy presupposes, above all, fulfillment of the law. But we do not yet have any real laws that would correspond to the building of democracy. That is a deficiency. One of our country's leading politicians said that the Russian laws are characterized by the fact that they are not observed. This state of affairs must be ended." Such exhortations are spoken as though they could be implemented by extra willpower and administrative action.

24. *Meeting Report* (Vol. VII, No. 1) of the Kennan Institute, summarizing Shatalin's address to the Institute, October 2, 1990.

25. Prokhanov in his above-quoted article argues the need, if Russia is to survive, for a coalition between the Russian patriotic movement and the only major political organization which shares many of its concerns, the Russian Communist Party.

(2) a strong Leninist contingent from the old Party-state apparatus;

(3) conservatives from the military, KGB, and MVD;

(4) people from military units returning, humiliated, to bad housing from Eastern Europe; and

(5) disgruntled Russian colonists (possibly millions of them) escaping to Russia from the anti-Russian nationalism of the republics in a militant right-wing mood similar to that of the *pieds noirs* returning to France from Algeria around 1960.

Such a coalition could accuse the left of massive failure with a "non-Russian" reform. It could then take power, either at the polls or through a coup. Civil war all too easily could result.

CONCLUDING NOTE

In conclusion, let me try to sum up Gorbachev's central dilemma, then quote the suggestive thoughts of a historian, General Dmitriy Volkogonov, about Gorbachev's leadership to date. Gorbachev is a leader who has ever less real authority in the eyes of the Soviet polity and people, has no hope of recouping any, and is facing deepening problems of an economic, constitutional, and social nature which could only be turned around by a leader with very great authority. At the same time he possesses so much formal authority that he is widely described as having "taken all power on himself," he has military leaders demanding that he take drastic action to restore order, and he has some cover from foreign criticism, because the West would probably react mildly to a declaration of the presidential rule for which he is apparently preparing, so as not to lose his support in the worldwide coalition against Iraq. A declaration of presidential rule could easily be rationalized by him as the only way to salvage reform from chaos. But under a leader of minimal authority, repression of either a systematic or stop-go variety would almost certainly produce more chaos and much more death.

General Volkogonov's analysis is less focused on the present. Stressing his respect for Gorbachev "as a person," he made these main points in a speech to the RSFSR Supreme Soviet.[26] Gorbachev, he said, "has played a large, historic role in the collapse of the totalitarian system, both in our country and in the countries of Eastern Europe. If, though, we are honest, he did not so much play a role, did not so much do things—he did not hinder the process. Did not hinder, because the system itself had come to the point of breakdown, of collapse. This too was very praiseworthy, but we should not say that he foresaw it."

Volkogonov went on: "The President, unfortunately, does not have new

26. The speech was delivered on October 25 and extracted in the new RSFSR newspaper *Rossiya*, No. 1, November 1990, p. 2.

ideas. Put in front of yourself 10 to 15 of the President's speeches. They are all similar: Without fail each of them speaks of a decisive stage, of a decisive phase, of new approaches, about the necessity to move forward. But there are no new ideas. This is very sad. I have to say that the absence of new ideas illuminates very well that indecisiveness, that marking of time, those attempts at innumerable compromises which, in the final analysis, always come out to the right of center.''

Volkogonov believes that Gorbachev "does not possess the capacity for vision . . . yet today a man of vision is exactly what is needed. Right now the first fundamentally great decision we've approached in five and a half years is the market. . . . How much indecision, how much delay and procrastination! If two years ago we had prepared for this gradually, we would now already be on our feet.''

Volkogonov's criticism of Gorbachev is not, he says, a prelude to any "radical" suggestions: "I would simply like to recall from history that a person who tries to accommodate everyone may, in the end, not accommodate anyone.''

REFERENCES

Breslauer, George, "Evaluating Gorbachev as Leader," *Soviet Economy*, 5, 4:299–340, October–December 1989.

Bialer, Seweryn, "The Last Soviet Communist," *U.S. News and World Report*, October 8, 1990, pp. 53–54.

Bonner, Yelena, "Zakon—ne vorota, mozhno i ob'yekhat' (The Law Is Not a Gate—It Can Be Circumvented)," *Moskovskiye novosti*, No. 43, October 28, 1990, p. 11.

Chernov, Andrey, "In Favor of the 'Strong Hand'," *Moscow News*, No. 41, October 21–28, 1990.

Klyamkin, Igor, interview in *Moskovskiy komsomolets*, June 7, 1990.

"Supporters and Opponents of *Perestroyka*: The Second Joint *Soviet Economy* Roundtable," *Soviet Economy*, 4, 4:275–318, October–December 1988.

Kroncher, Allen, "What Sort of Market Does Gorbachev Want?" *Soviet Analyst*, 19, 21:4–6, October 1990.

Migranyan, Andranik, "Dolgiy put' k yevropeyskomu domu (The Long Road to the European Home)," *Novyy mir*, 7:166–184, 1989.

Prokhanov, Aleksandr, "Ideologiya vyzhivaniya (The Ideology of Survival)," *Nash sovremennik*, 9:3–9, 1990.

Tsipko, Aleksandr, lecture at George Washington University, Washington, D.C., November 1, 1990.

Tsypkin, Mikhail, "Karem Rash: An Ideologist of Military Power," *Radio Liberty Report on the USSR*, 2, 31:8–11, August 1990a.

Tsypkin, Mikhail, "A Split in the KGB?" *Radio Liberty Report on the USSR*, 2, 39:6–9, September 1990b.

Vyzov, L., and G. Gurevich, "O doverii soyuznomu rukovodstvu (On Trusting All-Union Leadership)," *Argumenty i fakty*, 42:1, October 1990.

CHAPTER 16

Gorbachev's Leadership: Another View

Archie Brown

SOME OF those who were slow in the first place to realize that Gorbachev was a serious and radical reformer have been quick to write him off when his popularity in the Soviet Union went into decline and problems mounted. I would not wish to deny that the gravity of the Soviet Union's economic situation, the bitterness of some of the inter-ethnic tensions and—not least—the problem of conflicting institutional claims to legitimate power and authority[1] have brought the country closer to crisis than any time within the past five years. It is clear, too, that there are big dangers ahead for Gorbachev, although salutory to recall that he has surmounted a great many already.

It would, of course, be a quite astounding political feat if Gorbachev were to lead the Soviet Union all the way from the highly authoritarian, unreformed system that he inherited and of which he had been a part—with its command economy and monist polity[2]—through the transition period and into pluralist democracy and a market economy. The impressive example of King Juan Carlos—to whom Gorbachev himself has referred, admiringly, as "a kind of guarantor of political stability" (*Moscow Television Service in Russian*, 1530 GMT, October 27, 1990)—is not a close parallel. Quite apart from the fact that no transformation of the economic system remotely comparable to that needed in the Soviet Union was involved in Spain, the King was and is head of state, not chief executive. As a constitutional monarch, he has borne nothing like Gorbachev's direct responsibility for policy as well as for procedure as

First published in *Soviet Economy*, 1990, 6, 2, pp. 141–154. The author wishes to thank the British Academy and the Economic and Social Research Council of the U.K. for grants which have facilitated his research on this and related topics, and which have funded study visits to the Soviet Union. [Eds.]

1. The prominent academic lawyer, Sergey Alekseyev, who is also Chairman of the Committee for Supervision of the Constitution of the USSR, has written recently that "any program of economic reform is doomed to failure if there is no resolution of the political problem of multiplicity of powers *(mnogovlastiye)* taking shape among us" (Alekseyev, 1990). Alekseyev is not advocating an end to political pluralism but greater jurisdictional clarity.

2. Albeit "*imperfectly* monist" (my italics), as Gordon Skilling noted long ago (Skilling, 1966, p. 449).

chief executive in the period of transition to what is already becoming a qualitatively different system.[3]

I do, however, take the view that if any politician anywhere can pull off the remarkable feat of presiding over such an entire transition, it will be Gorbachev. No one in Eastern Europe has succeeded in doing it, but then no Communist leader there was the initiator of change to the extent that Gorbachev has been.[4] There are Western newspaper commentators (not least in the United States) who have moved unobtrusively from saying that nothing of substance has changed or is likely to change in the Soviet Union to arguing that pretty well everything has changed and little thanks to Gorbachev who is now an irrelevance, along with the Communist Party. More serious studies lead, however, to an altogether more positive evaluation of the part played by Gorbachev, of which George Breslauer's analysis, reprinted here in Chapter 14, provides an excellent example (Breslauer, 1989; see also Bialer, 1989; Brown, 1989a; Hough, 1990a; Rigby, 1990; and White, 1990).

Jerry Hough, though, goes too far in his most recent major article when he portrays some of the unintended consequences of liberalization as an integral part of Gorbachev's long-term strategy. I find it hard to accept that in order "to demonstrate to the Russians that total democratization would lead to the disintegration of the country" Gorbachev deliberately took the "basic decision . . . to let unrest in the republics—especially the smaller ones—go to an extreme" (Hough, 1990b, p. 655). And although, like Jerry Hough, I believe that it is still, to say the least, premature to write off Gorbachev, I am less ready than Hough to assume that Gorbachev has nothing to fear from the conservative Communist "right" and only a little more to worry about on the radical "left" (Hough, 1990b).[5]

Before examining briefly the dangers to Gorbachev from both "right" and "left," it is worth emphasizing that many of his supposedly more radical critics, including Boris Yel'tsin, are not any more radical by disposition or intellectual conviction than he is, although by temperament they may be more impulsive.

---

3. Gorbachev was the *de facto* chief executive in the Soviet Union but not head of state from March 11, 1985, to October 1, 1988. Since then he has been the head of executive *and* head of state, succeeding Gromyko in the latter (at that time mainly honorific) post. The title and scope of the office of head of state changed, however, in each successive year from 1988 to 1990. In October 1988 Gorbachev became Chairman of the Presidium of the Supreme Soviet, in May 1989 Chairman of the Supreme Soviet, in March 1990 President (*Prezident*) of the USSR.

4. That is not to assume that the transition will be a smooth one or even that there may not be backtracking. While the old system could never again be what it was—for the knowledge and political experience gained by Soviet citizens in the last few years cannot be taken away—it is, as I shall go on to suggest, too early to rule out completely the possibility of authoritarian alternatives to Soviet democratization and pluralization.

5. This difference of emphasis is notwithstanding the fact that at a conference on the Soviet Union and East-West relations attended by European and American academics, diplomats and journalists, plus a sprinkling of politicians a month or two before Chernenko died, Hough and I were in a minority of two in arguing independently that when—rather than if—Gorbachev succeeded Chernenko serious reform and change would occur in the Soviet Union, especially once Gorbachev had consolidated his power, which we gave reasons for saying would happen unusually quickly. That made little impact on the conventional wisdom of the time and place. Summing up the proceedings, the Chairman said: "Well, at least we know one thing. The *Soviet Union* isn't going to change!"

The main difference between their position and Gorbachev's derives from their having been either in opposition or carrying less comprehensive responsibilities than Gorbachev over the past few years. They enjoy the luxury of being untainted by the gap between expectations and results. Gavriil Popov, indeed, has recently suggested that the radicals on the Moscow City Soviet should resign their posts if they cannot soon effect the changes their electors hoped for, rather than themselves become discredited as non-deliverers (Popov, 1990). The disadvantages of incumbency have become increasingly evident; Yel'tsin quite clearly owes much of his popularity to his anti-establishment stance.

PRESSURE FROM THE "RIGHT"

Gorbachev, in contrast, has had to weigh in the balance the conflicting views of a greater variety of institutional interests and public constituencies than have any of his critics. Among these are several on the "right." Oppositionists can now criticize the military or the KGB and, in turn (in what is just as remarkable a change), shrug off the criticisms of the latter. But Gorbachev, who has impinged more upon the traditional interests of the military and the KGB than any Soviet in the past half-century,[6] cannot discount the possibility of an alliance between party conservatives, Russian nationalists, and senior military officers. KGB participation in such an alliance could also not be ruled out, since both their budget and record have been under attack and it is part of the logic of democratization and liberalization of Soviet society that their role should be a much more minor one than it has been in the past.[7]

Aleksandr Prokhanov, the Soviet writer closest to the military, has recently emphasized the great importance of the relationship between what he calls the "national-patriotic movement" and the Communist Party of the Russian republic, led by Ivan Poloz'kov, arguing that the *Rossiyskaya kompartiya* and the "patriotic movement" must cling together in order to prevent their destruction by the "liberals" (cited by Kazutin, 1990, p. 7).

A coalition embracing a large part of the Communist Party apparatus in Russia, senior military (and possibly KGB) officers, and Russian nationalists is a potential threat which could become an actual one for Gorbachev and the proponents of enlightened change if shortages give way to hunger and there is further breakdown of law and order in the Russian republic. Lately he has

6. I would not wish to extend the generalization back any further, for Stalin, after all, executed a large proportion of the senior officer corps in the late 1930s. Khrushchev also in a number of ways dealt blows to the military and the KGB, but recent Soviet revelations on the fall of Khrushchev do not show the military playing any significant part in Khrushchev's removal, although the KGB leadership was on the side of the anti-Khrushchev plotters.

7. The Shatalin Plan—a 238-page document entitled *Transition to the Market: Conception and Program*—proposed a 10 percent cut in the budget of the Ministry of Defense and a 20 percent reduction of the budget of the KGB (as well as a 70–80 percent cut in expenditure on aid to foreign countries) (*Perekhod*, 1990, p. 87). Pressures from the army and the KGB appear to have been among the several important reasons why Gorbachev's attitude toward the document was ambivalent and why he did not give it his comprehensive endorsement, even though in essence he accepted many of the arguments of the Shatalin group. For an illuminating discussion of the Shatalin Plan, see Hewett (1990–1991).

made several attempts to solidify his relations both with the military and the security forces.

On November 13, 1990, he had a meeting with military deputies from soviets in different republics, at which, however, he was given a hostile reception; on November 27, with the obvious backing of Gorbachev, the Defense Minister, Marshal Dmitriy Yazov, informed the Soviet public in a televised address that soldiers would use force to defend both themselves and their installations in any republic in which they came under attack, and they would seize power, water, and food installations if local authorities attempted to cut off their supplies. Having already involved the KGB (and also reinstated workers' committees) in the task of combating thefts from shops and black-marketeering, Gorbachev went on to entrust the KGB with the supervision of distribution of food and medical aid beginning to reach the Soviet Union by the planeload (especially from Germany). Gorbachev no doubt shares the public concern that otherwise much of it would disappear from the backs of lorries long before it reached its destination (*Moscow Domestic Service in Russian*, 1600 GMT, November 13, 1990; *Izvestiya*, November 15, 1990, p. 2; *The New York Times*, November 28, 1990, pp. A1 and A5).

Gorbachev has complained, not unreasonably, that he is being held responsible for a "paralysis of power" and accused at the same time of attempting to "turn in another direction, that of dictatorship" (*BBC Summary of World Broadcasts: Soviet Union*/09312 C/1/2, November 26, 1990). In his most dramatic concession so far to those whose primary concern is with what they see as the "paralysis of power"—most notably, the military and the security forces—Gorbachev, on December 2, 1990, appointed as Minister of Interior the 53-year-old Boris Pugo, until then head of the Party Control Committee and previously Chairman of the KGB and subsequently party First Secretary in Latvia, and appointed the 47-year-old General Boris Gromov, formerly commander of Soviet troops in Afghanistan and a political hard-liner, as First Deputy Minister (*The New York Times*, December 3, 1990, p. A4).

In so doing Gorbachev has taken a calculated risk. He may be trying to coopt Gromov before his enemies succeed in doing so, and the appointment is doubtless intended as a sop to the military and all those who have jumped on the law-and-order bandwagon. The risk lies in the fact that Gorbachev has at a stroke turned the military man, Gromov, who has given a few worrying signals of seeing himself as a national savior (Brown, 1989b, pp. 495–496; Foye, 1990, pp. 1–2) into a politician who can now legitimately aspire to the highest political office, as he could not constitutionally have done from his recent post as commander of the Kiev Military District.

Of course, there *is* a problem of deteriorating order in the Soviet Union and it will be interesting to see what Pugo and Gromov do to combat it. But Gorbachev would be taking a leap in the dark if he were to increase unduly his dependence on the army or the security forces as instruments of rule (Brown, 1990). On the one hand, he would be putting at risk the residual gratitude and goodwill of the liberals and the radical democrats, which has not been entirely dissipated. Even the radical deputy, Yuriy Vlasov—the weightlifter-turned-writer who caused such a stir at the First Congress of People's Deputies with his televised attack on the KGB—remarked in an interview as recently as October 1990 in one of Russia's new newspapers that he believed in Gorbachev and "only with Gorbachev do I associate movement forward" (Vlasov, 1990). On the other hand, if Gorbachev becomes too beholden to the military, the generals will be likely to seek a more influential voice in political decision making and, given the traumatic changes they have endured over the past two years, they are unlikely wholly to trust him. Indeed, the greater the role the army plays in any new Soviet leadership coalition, the less likely it is that the coalition will continue to be headed by Gorbachev.

In the meantime, Ivan Poloz'kov has been busily creating a Central Committee apparatus of like-minded people for the Communist Party of the RSFSR, and the Central Committee annex off Kuybyshev Street is likely soon to be vacated by the reduced all-Union Central Committee staff to make way for Poloz'kov's men. It is also quite possible that the Russian Communist Party will gain control of *Pravda* from the all-Union party. The present editor, Ivan Frolov, is very much a Gorbachev man, but he is under attack from some of his own staff as well as from the Russian Communist Party. If, as some allege, the Communist Party has already become an irrelevance in the Soviet Union, perhaps none of this matters. But if one considers the country as a whole and the Russian republic in particular, the fact is that so far there is no other political organization or party which has such a wide network of institutional bases and potential for wielding power in association with those prepared to back them with coercive force.

THE CHALLENGE FROM THE "LEFT"

If I am correct in suggesting that it is still premature to rule out the threat to Gorbachev from those whose opposition is from a more conservative standpoint, what of the challenge from those who espouse a more radical position? Of these, Yel'tsin has by far the broadest support. He has a personality which appeals to many Russians, he appears decisive whereas Gorbachev is increasingly portrayed as indecisive,[8] and, above all, he has the advantage of being free of responsibility for the conduct of economic policy in recent years. The stark fact is that only a minority of Soviet citizens are enjoying a higher standard of living than they did under Brezhnev—if that term is employed in the conventional way to refer only to economic well-being and to exclude all consideration of the far-reaching extension of political liberties.

The potential threat Yel'tsin can pose to Gorbachev is discernible from the draft Constitution of the RSFSR produced by the working group of the Con-

---

8. This portrayal is not totally without justification and yet is not entirely fair, for Gorbachev has had a real political need to retain room for maneuver and to keep a variety of options open.

stitutional Commission on October 19, 1990, but not yet published in the mass media or presented to the legislature of the Russian republic for approval.[9] This document is a remarkably liberal one which represents a complete break with anything which can meaningfully be called the Soviet system. It was described to me in Moscow recently by one of its critics as "an entirely bourgeois liberal constitution." One might quibble about "bourgeois," but otherwise the statement is no more than the truth. The political language is comprehensively unsoviet and draws from both Western and pre-revolutionary Russian political experience. Thus, for example, not only does the Congress of People's Deputies disappear but so does anything called a Supreme Soviet. The legislature is renamed "Parliament" with the pre-revolutionary terminology "State Duma" in parentheses (*Parlament/Gosudarstvennaya duma/*) *(Konstitutsiya Rossiyskoy Federatsii: Proyekt*, 1990, pp. 28 and 37).

The danger for Gorbachev if Yel'tsin remains more of an opponent than an ally lies in the section of the draft Constitution on the Presidency. At present Yel'tsin is only Chairman of the Supreme Soviet of the RSFSR with limited powers. The new post is called "President of the Russian Federation" and it not only greatly extends the executive power of its holder in comparison with the Chairmanship of the Supreme Soviet but stipulates the election of the President "by the citizens of the Russian federation" for a period of four years with the possibility of that person being re-elected for not more than one more four-year term of office (*Konstitutsiya: proyekt*, 1990, p. 34). Once the Constitution has been adopted by the Supreme Soviet of the RSFSR (no doubt with some amendments to the existing draft which indeed already offers variants in a number of its articles), it is to be expected that elections will follow before long—perhaps in the spring of 1991.[10] That immediately raises the distinct possibility of Boris Yel'tsin—rather than Gorbachev who would not be a contender—becoming the first leader of Russia in the whole of Russian history to be popularly elected. If their periodic attempts to work together had ended in failure and the relationship of Gorbachev and Yel'tsin was at that time adversarial rather than co-operative, such an outcome would put Gorbachev in a difficult position indeed. Given that he was elected indirectly by a legislature which itself was chosen in imperfectly democratic elections (however great an advance they undoubtedly were over the sham elections of the unreformed Soviet system), could Gorbachev reasonably expect his decrees to carry more authority in Russia than the decisions of Yel'tsin?

The conclusion I would draw is that Gorbachev still needs an alliance with Yel'tsin and the forces he represents more than he has publicly acknowledged. But some might (and do) argue that Yel'tsin does not need Gorbachev. The

---

9. I received the copy of the 65-page draft which I cite in this article from a deputy of the Supreme Soviet of the RSFSR in Moscow in late October 1990.

10. That was how it appeared in late 1990. By February 1991, it no longer looked at all certain that the forces pushing Gorbachev in a more conservative direction were ready to accept a more overtly liberal alternative to him. It had become far from clear that democratic elections in the Russian republic would or could take place in 1991.

President of the USSR could, after all, come under increasing pressure to take the risk he did not run in 1990 and be virtually forced to attempt to establish a greater legitimacy for his rule by holding an all-Union presidential election. Since a week is now a long time in Soviet politics, it would be foolhardy indeed to predict the result of a hypothetical election at some uncertain future date. It would be even more rash, though, to assume that Yel'tsin, if he were to choose to contest such an election, could not win it.

Does this then mean that Yel'tsin, who is not lacking in personal ambition, has no reason to seek a co-operative relationship with Gorbachev? I think not. Much will depend not only on Gorbachev's established ability to get out of tight corners but on Yel'tsin's choice between his short-term and long-term political interests and on his perception of what is for the greater good of his country. There is no way in which the transition to a market economy can be rendered painless, and there is great political need for a broadly based coalition of those who are in favor of such a major change of direction. The more authoritarian coalition (discussed above) which could be put together as an alternative to Gorbachev is not the sort of alliance whose interests and convictions would push it in the direction of marketizing the economy. That is one reason why, if it came to power, it would have no real solutions to offer. If, however, Yel'tsin became the *de facto* chief executive of Russia or of the whole Soviet Union, and had lost the support of Gorbachev and of the centrist forces whose loyalty he could command, and if Yel'tsin tried to marketize the Soviet economy in the face of the opposition of what is now called "the military-ideological complex" (Abuladze et al., 1990, p. 4) and a polarized public opinion, he would begin to learn what Gorbachev has been up against. It is very questionable whether Yel'tsin's authority—in isolation from and in opposition to Gorbachev—would last long enough to enable him to stabilize the currency and make the necessary economic changes in the Soviet Union. Those changes, we should bear in mind, would initially impose still greater hardship on Yel'tsin's supporters than they are suffering at present.

It has been a commonplace among Soviet social scientists to point to the good fortune of the Polish government in having a legitimacy which their Soviet counterpart lacked. This, it was said, enabled them to introduce the kind of shock therapy which the Soviet economy also required but which was too alarming in its potential political consequences for their political leadership to contemplate. Yet November 28, 1990, saw the resignation of Tadeusz Mazowiecki as Polish Prime Minister after he had been beaten into third place (with only 18 percent of the votes) in the Presidential election, losing not only to Lech Walesa but to the outsider Walesa dubbed "the man from Mars," the émigré Stanislaw Tymiński. It is never easy to make austerity measures popular and next to impossible in the Soviet Union when the populace is being asked for the umpteenth time in the course of seventy years to make sacrifices now for the sake of a better future. To persuade people that this time it might be true is precisely why as broad as possible a coalition of those who believe in the realistic possibility of such a future is needed.

GORBACHEV'S POLITICS

That is one reason why I cannot agree with Seweryn Bialer when he argues that increasingly Gorbachev "is a problem rather than a solution" (Bialer, 1990, p. 54). Gorbachev by himself does not, of course, constitute a solution, but his political acumen and international authority remain vital assets for those who wish to transform the Soviet polity and economy. That prestige, which is in decline but nevertheless higher outside the Soviet Union than in it, may yet be translated into substantial Western assistance for the Soviet transition—at the point when a significant number of Western governments are convinced, as the Germans are already, that they will be helping a transition to a market economy and giving political pluralism a chance to take hold rather than offering a lifeline to the defenders of the old Soviet system. Bialer's view of Gorbachev as a problem derives partly from his belief that while Gorbachev is "not doctrinaire," nevertheless "his commitment to *basic* ideological 'truths' is deep and profound—it is internalized, it is in his mind and soul and it constitutes the only comprehensive frame of reference for his thinking on political, social and, particularly, economic issues" (Bialer, 1990, p. 53).

Gorbachev's thinking still contains elements of the old as well as the new, but—in sharp contrast with Bialer—I see virtually no end to his pragmatism. Gorbachev naturally continues to think of himself as a socialist, but the meaning he imparts to the concept of socialism has changed so radically over the years that he is now a more enthusiastic advocate of the market than many Western European democratic politicians who have held office in post-war governments. In expressing support for a "mixed economy" he is using the standard language of social democracy, even though as leader (still) of the Communist Party he has to try to distinguish his position from that of social democrats. There is little left that is distinctively *Communist* about Gorbachev's socialism and, given the extent to which his views have developed, it would be interesting to know what are the "*basic* ideological 'truths' " which are engraved on his mind and soul. The many scholars and journalists who have been rash enough from 1985 onward to tell us what Gorbachev could *never* accept might do well to ponder the fate of their previous predictions rather than set new limits to Gorbachev's own intellectual restructuring and new standards of radicalism for him to attain.

There are, of course, growing numbers of radicals in the Soviet Union today who believe that Gorbachev has reached the limits of his usefulness in the process of transforming the Soviet system into a functioning democracy and market economy. There are others who, while accepting that any such trans-action will inevitably be a long and difficult haul, believe that they must put pressure on Gorbachev for speedier and more decisive action both on market-ization and the granting of sovereignty to the union republics.[11] They are concerned also to provide countervailing pressures on Gorbachev to those of the ministerial network and the "military-ideological complex."[12]

MODERNIZATION OR TRANSFORMATION

On the other side, however, are many critics who believe that Gorbachev has gone beyond the *modernization* of the system and has undermined its foundations. Not all of them are people who accepted uncritically the old order. Indeed, one of the boldest reformers of the later Brezhnev years as well as of the early period of *perestroyka*, Boris Kurashvili, of the Institute of State and Law in Moscow, published an article in *Pravda* recently which views the main thrust of Gorbachev's economic policy (notwithstanding its zigs and zags) as being toward the embracing of capitalism (Kurashvili, 1990a). Kurashvili ob-jects also to the way older notions of "right" and "left" have been turned on their heads, so that the stronger a person's support for privatization in the Soviet Union, the more of a left-winger he is considered to be. In his most recent book, which went to press in April 1990, Kurashvili—who was one of the earliest advocates in print of a multi-party system as well as of a market economy in the Soviet Union—regarded a split in the Communist Party of the Soviet Union as being both "inescapable and useful." He envisaged the formation of a party of democratic socialism, which would support a competitive party system and would be for the market, but within the framework of new reforms of public, rather than private, ownership; of a *right*-of-center Social Democratic Party, with which orientation he associates Aleksandr Yakovlev, Gavriil Popov, and Yuriy Afanas'yev; and of an "orthodox moderate-*left* Communist Party" espousing policies such as those favored by Yegor Ligachev. At the time his book went to press the author saw Gorbachev as the leader with the best prospects of forming what in Kurashvili's terms (as distinct from those now prevailing in the Soviet Union) would be "an optimal for *perestroyka* left-of-center tendency, a party of democratic socialism." But he was already con-cerned about Gorbachev's willingness to abandon the principle of public own-

11. This is the position of most of the signatories of an open letter by "the founders of *Moscow News*," i.e., those who have founded it anew in 1990 as a wholly independent weekly newspaper (Abuladze et al., 1990, pp. 1, 4). They make, *inter alia*, a strong plea for "a stable political partnership between Mikhail Gorbachev and Boris Yel'tsin" *ibid.*, p. 1), although elsewhere a number of them have expressed strong criticism of Gorbachev for what they see as vacillation and indecisiveness. Even in the open letter, they go so far as to say that Gorbachev should either take decisive action (of a liberal tendency) or resign his office as President (*ibid.*, p. 4). The authors include, beside the film director, Tengiz Abuladze (whose name comes first alpha-betically), such prominent reformers of varying degrees of radicalism as Ales' Adamovich, Yevgeniy Ambart-sumov, Yuriy Afanas'yev, Oleg Bogomolov, Aleksandr Gel'man, Elem Klimov, Yuriy Levada, Andrey Nuykin, Vyacheslav Shostakovskiy, Galina Starovoytova, Vladimir Tikhonov, and Tat'yana Zaslavskaya.

12. The authors of the open letter cited in note 11, writing in mid-November, argue that "the present Council of Ministers is, as a matter of fact, a cabinet of departmental monopolies, operating at the command of the military-ideological complex" (Abuladze et al., 1990, p. 4).

ership and so suggests as an alternative leader Boris Gidaspov (the Leningrad party first secretary) or "a figure of his type" (Kurashvili, 1990b).

Kurashvili, as a genuine reformer of socialist convictions,[13] is now making statements which could lead him to be mistakenly identified as a conservative Communist, even though his starting-point is a very different one. Thus, both in his 1990 book and in his recent *Pravda* article, Kurashvili expresses concern that there is an attempt to return the Soviet Union to capitalism, albeit one sometimes shrouded in socialist or otherwise obfuscatory phraseology. He regards the talk about "contemporary civilization" as a euphemism for capitalism and argues that what is needed is "destatization without privatization" (*razgosudarstvleniye bez privatizatsii*) (Kurashvili, 1990a, p. 4). To press on toward capitalism is, he holds, a recipe for "civil war and, most probably, a return to authoritarian socialism" (Kurashvili, 1990b, p. 5). In his *Pravda* article[14] Kurashvili (1990a) sees three forces in Soviet politics—conservatives, modernizers of socialism, and liquidators of socialism. From his standpoint (although this is implicitly rather than explicitly stated in his *Pravda* contribution) Gorbachev has moved from being a modernizer of socialism to being a would-be liquidator of it.

Views such as those of Kurashvili are not as unrepresentative of Soviet society as a whole as their relative neglect in the West might suggest. Opinion is very divided on privatization and if Gorbachev is not going fast enough in this area for some, he has already moved too far for others. If he is now being criticized from many different points of the Soviet political spectrum, this is not primarily because of his irresolution, still less incompetence, but because of the sheer difficulty of changing a system far more deeply entrenched than any of the East European ones (whose transitions are also turning out to be not entirely painless). In many ways he has behaved more like a Western politician (and an unusually skilled one at that) than a Soviet leader, although he also wielded the traditional levers of power with extraordinary skill in order to renew entirely the composition of the Brezhnev-Andropov Politburo he inherited, before downgrading that institution drastically this year. It is Gorbachev's responsiveness to different bodies of opinion and to diverse (and conflicting) institutional interests, his wheeling and dealing, and his tactical flexibility while moving in a basically liberal direction—one step back has frequently been followed by two steps forward—which have so impressed Western politicians who recognize a master of their art, one operating in an infinitely tougher

13. His work was praised by Tat'yana Zaslavskaya in her famous leaked Novosibirsk seminar paper of 1983 (Zaslavskaya, 1984).

14. Publication of Kurashvili's article was at first refused, and then delayed, by the editor, Ivan Frolov. Authors who write critically about privatization found it difficult in 1990 to publish such views not only in newspapers at the most liberal end of the Soviet political spectrum but also in papers supportive of Gorbachev. This they interpreted as further evidence of Gorbachev's conversion to belief in the desirability of a substantial measure of privatization. It is, of course, common to find anti-privatization articles in the pages of newspapers and journals controlled by Gorbachev's hard-line opponents, whether Russian nationalists or old-style Communists.

environment and facing problems which make their own pale almost into insignificance.

INSTITUTIONAL INNOVATION

There *are* no straightforward solutions to the problems of transforming the Soviet Union's political and economic system and the relations among its hundred and more nationalities. The draft of the Union Treaty published on November 24 falls far short of what will be acceptable to the titular nationalities of a number of Soviet republics, but what is acceptable to those dominant nationalities is often quite unacceptable to national minorities within their borders. The document (*Pravda*, November 24, 1990, p. 3) contains many of the features of a genuinely federal system, including some which were crucially absent from the Soviet Union in the past, such as a Constitutional Court to resolve disputes between republics or between them and the center which cannot be reconciled politically.

One institutional innovation, the elevation to a central policy-making role of the Council of the Federation—which for some, but not all, republics may be too little too late—represents a third remarkable change in the character of collective decision making in the Soviet Union in the course of a single year. At the beginning of 1990 the Politburo was still *de facto* the highest collective policy-making body in the country. Its power ebbed after the creation of the Presidency and the Presidential Council and especially after the 28th Congress of the CPSU, when such leading office-holders as the Foreign Minister, the Chairman of Gosplan, the Chairman of the KGB and the Minister of Defense ceased to be Politburo members and that body reverted to being the highest executive committee of the Communist Party rather than of the country.

The fact that the Presidential Council was appointed by the President on his own initiative could be seen as a considerable strengthening of Gorbachev's power, for promotion to the Politburo had been by a process of collective co-option, in which Gorbachev had to carry his colleagues with him in making appointments. To change the entire composition of the Politburo within five and a half years was a remarkable achievement, but it was, nevertheless, a constrained power of appointment in comparison with that normally wielded by Presidents and prime ministers in Western systems and constrained in a way in which the choice of members of the Presidential Council of the USSR was not.

It is, then, on the face of it, striking that in November 1990 Gorbachev abolished the Presidential Council and that in the draft Union Treaty he proposes making the Council of the Federation—a body first created in March 1990, but hitherto inferior in standing to the Presidential Council—into the chief collective decision-making institution within the state. For this, once again, takes the power of appointment out of Gorbachev's hands—as well as, in contrast with Politburo promotions, that of the party oligarchy—and hands it to the electorates of the union republics. According to Article 14 of the draft Union Treaty the Council of the Federation will be led by the President and will consist of the presidents of the republics (who, in turn, will have been elected either directly by the citizenry or indirectly by the legislatures of their republics) and the Vice-President. Even the latter is to be elected—at the same time as the President of the USSR.

Whether, of course, the Council of the Federation in reality will turn out to be a viable body remains to be seen, as does the question of its relations with the cabinet of ministers which is to replace the Council of Ministers. How different that body (with its prime minister [*Prem'yer Ministr*], rather than Chairman of the Council of Ministers) will be from its predecessor is also something which only time will tell. Gorbachev has borrowed eclectically from Western terminology and institutional example, particularly the Fifth French Republic and the United States. An example of the latter influence is his decision to set up a body analogous to the National Security Council. In addition to these new institutional arrangements, Gorbachev has his recently acquired powers to rule by decree.

NEW COMPLEXITIES

None of this provides any guarantee that decrees and laws emanating from the all-Union organs in Moscow will be obeyed throughout the country or even *in* Moscow where the problem of *mnogovlastiye*[15] is a serious one. The Supreme Soviet of the USSR has been pulling in one direction and the Supreme Soviet of the RSFSR in another. There are similar differences between the Central Committee of the CPSU and the Central Committee of the Russian Communist Party, between the Moscow City Soviet and the Moscow Communist Party organization, and between the President of the USSR and the Chairman of the Supreme Soviet of the Russian republic. To all of these may soon be added differences between the Council of the Federation and the cabinet of ministers, unless the latter body is more responsive to the President's wishes than was the old Council of Ministers (which is presumably Gorbachev's hope).

The Soviet system in its operational principles used to be a relatively simple one. It has now become enormously complex and political outcomes far less predictable. Ideological polarization and competing nationalisms mean that there is not the kind of value consensus which would provide sure foundations for either a fully functioning democracy or a market economy. While Gorbachev's position is indeed vulnerable to attack from both "right" and "left" (however defined), most of his difficulties are a reflection of the magnitude of the tasks of transforming the Soviet system. A more unambiguous commitment at an earlier stage of his leadership to the economic policies and political changes

15. See note 2.

he espouses today would almost certainly have led to his overthrow and the restoration of an altogether more familiar type of Communist system.

Given the ideological inheritance and prevailing power structures, given ethnic and cultural diversity so great that different peoples in the Soviet Union might be living almost in different centuries, the achievements of Gorbachev between 1985 and 1990 are likely in longer historical perspective to bulk far larger than the failures. From being a highly authoritarian system which represented the very model of orthodox Communism, the Soviet Union has become a mixed political system—containing both authoritarian and pluralist elements—and is moving in the direction of creating a mixed economy and, however haltingly, a market one. Whether Gorbachev will regain the support of his Soviet contemporaries—and not just the respect of the West and posterity—probably still depends above all on how quickly people see tangible economic results.

Gorbachev's political demise has been proclaimed many times already and each such announcement has proved to be a considerable exaggeration. His position is now under serious threat, but it would probably still be rash to predict he will soon depart from the political scene. More surely, it would be an illusion to imagine that the task of transforming the Soviet system would become any easier if he did.

REFERENCES

Abuladze, Tengiz et al., "Strana ustala zhdat' (The Country Is Tired of Waiting)," *Moskovskiye novosti*, 46:1, 4, November 18, 1990.

Aleskeyev, S., "Narastayushcheye mnogovlastiye (A Growing Multiplicity of Powers) *Literaturnaya gazeta*, October 31, 1990, p. 1.

Bialer, Seweryn, "The Changing Soviet Political System," in Seweryn Bialer, ed., *Politics, Society, and Nationality Inside Gorbachev's Russia*. Boulder, Colo.: Westview Press, 1989.

———, "The Last Soviet Communist," *U.S. News and World Report*, October 8, 1990, pp. 53–54.

Breslauer, George W., "Evaluating Gorbachev as Leader," *Soviet Economy*, 5, 4:299–340, October–December 1989.

Brown, Archie, ed., *Political Leadership in the Soviet Union*. London: Macmillan and Bloomington: Indiana University Press, 1989a.

———, "Political Change in the Soviet Union," *World Policy Journal*, 6, 3:469–501, 1989b.

———, "Selling Hard to Save the Soviet Union," *Newsday*, November 29, 1990, p. 2.

Foye, Stephen, "Rumblings in the Soviet Armed Forces," *Radio Liberty Report on the USSR*, 2, 11:1–3, March 16, 1990.

Hewett, Ed A., "The New Soviet Plan," *Foreign Affairs*, 69, 5:146–166, 1990–1991.

Hough, Jerry F., *Russia and the West* (revised and updated edition). New York: Touchstone, 1990a.

———, "Gorbachev's Endgame," *World Policy Journal*, 7, 4:639–672, 1990b.

Kazutin, Dmitriy, "Ionych vstupayet v RKP? (Will Ionych Join the RCP?)," *Moskovskiye novosti,* 46:7, November 18, 1990.

Konstitutsiya (osnovnoy zakon) Rossiyskoy federatsii: proyekt rabochey gruppy i gruppy ekspertov konstitutsionnoy komissii RSFSR (Constitution [Basic Law] of the Russian Federation: the Draft of the Working Group and Group of Experts of the RSFSR Constitutional Commission). Moscow, October 1990.

Kurashvili, B. P., "Pravyye i levyye, ili gde iskat' optimal'nyy put' v ekonomike? (Right and Left, or Where to find the Optimal Path in the Economy?)," *Pravda,* October 4, 1990a, pp. 3–4.

Kurashvili, B. P., *Strana na rasput'ye . . . (Poteri i perspektivy perestroyki) (The Country at the Crossroads . . . [Losses and Prospects of Perestroyka]).* Moscow: Yuridicheskaya literatura, 1990b.

Perekhod k rynku. Chast' 1. Kontseptsiya i Programma (The Transition to the Market: Part 1. Concept and Program). Moscow: Arkhangel'skoye, August 1990.

Popov, Gavriil, "The Times Are Getting Tougher," interview by Yegor Yakovlev, *Moscow News* (English language edition), 42:7, October 28–November 4, 1990.

Rigby, T. H., *The Changing Soviet System.* Aldershot, England: Edward Elgar, 1990.

Skilling, H. Gordon, "Interest Groups and Communist Politics," *World Politics,* 17, 3:435–451, 1966.

Vlasov, Yuriy, "Vot pochemy ya vyshel iz partii (That Is Why I Left the Party)," *7 s plyusom* (Moscow), 10:6, October 1990.

White, Stephen, *Gorbachev in Power.* Cambridge: Cambridge University Press, 1990.

Zaslavskaya, Tat'yana (anonymously), "The Novosibirsk Report," *Survey,* 28, 1:88–108, January 1984.

CHAPTER 17

Gorbachev's Leadership: A Soviet View

Andranik Migranyan

IN MANY respects, Gorbachev's leadership has indeed outlived its usefulness. This resulted from some fundamental mistakes and misconceptions built into his strategy of transition. Unfortunately, Mikhail Sergeyevich did not sufficiently understand the nature of the regime he was attempting to reform. That system, which is appropriately called "totalitarian," subordinated the individual to society, society to the state, and the state to the party. In this respect, the system differed importantly from traditional authoritarian regimes, such as Franco's Spain, in which society (and economy) were not entirely dominated by the state or party. As a result, in Spain, institutionalized material interests had already coalesced, and could form a basis for new establishment politics after Franco died. In contrast, in the Soviet Union, no such interest-coalescence had been allowed to occur (Migranyan, 1989). The first task for Gorbachev, therefore, should have been to institutionalize new interests, and new forms of interest group politics, *within* the state and, especially, the party. Only later should he have released broader social forces that would push for mass democratization.

This means that a properly sequenced strategy of transition from Soviet Leninism should have concentrated first on reforming the economy, only later on renegotiating the terms of interrepublic relations within the Union, and only last on mass democratization. Instead, Gorbachev proceeded in the reverse direction, pursuing political reform first. This had the consequence of releasing all centrifugal forces that, in response to their liberation from a suffocating regime, would seek alternative identities, both individual and collective, but without institutionalized forms of conflict resolution into which to channel their demands. The predictable consequence of this situation was a collapse of

First published in *Soviet Economy*, 1990, 6, pp. 155–159. The author has published extensively, in both the Soviet Union and the United States, about the requisites for a successful transition from totalitarianism to democracy. This essay was prepared for *Soviet Economy* in November 1990. It was written in response to the query "has Gorbachev's leadership outlived its usefulness?" as were the essays by Peter Reddaway and Archie Brown above—all submitted independently of each other. [Eds.]

governmental authority throughout the country, rather than a transformation of the system into a more institutionalized, democratic polity and market economy.

THE COLLAPSE OF AUTHORITY

That process has accelerated during the second half of 1990. First, the institutional center of the USSR has collapsed. Declarations of sovereignty by almost all republics have made the Lithuanian model more the rule than the exception. Popular fronts and movements have captured or besieged local and republican governments in almost every region outside of Central Asia. The central government, or Gorbachev himself, issue decrees that are simply ignored by those "required" to implement them in the locales. Even the army, which is one of the few powerful institutions still fighting for the integrity of the centralized state, finds its unity disintegrating and its regulations being defied by the republics. For example, republican authorities increasingly refuse to enforce conscription. It is an irony of recent history that Gorbachev has acquired extraordinary presidential powers at a time when he is incapable of enforcing their implementation. He could implement them through raw force, but that would destroy his democratization program.

A second collapse is taking place within the RSFSR itself. Important provinces and territories within the Russian Republic are declaring sovereignty over the laws and natural resources within their boundaries. This is something that Boris Yel'tsin and his associates did not anticipate. Moreover, this trend toward fragmentation mirrors a broader collapse of power structures throughout the country. Within all but the smallest territories, component units are declaring their "sovereignty." Within cities, for example, districts (*rayony*) defy city authorities and declare "local control" over property, licensing, even airspace! In practice, this has typically meant that small units want to keep all the benefits of power while passing upward all the burdens and responsibilities of power. The result is municipal ungovernability.

A third form of collapse has been that of the center of the political spectrum in Moscow. Gorbachev's previous strategy of building unity and consensus through bridging the center and the left has become increasingly irrelevant, losing him the opportunity to lead a grand coalition. Much to the surprise of Gorbachev and his colleagues, the purge of conservatives at the 28th Party Congress left Gorbachev exposed at the right wing of the top-level political spectrum. Although the Party Congress was a great victory for democratic forces, in that it destroyed CPSU domination of the state and *de facto* federalized the party, the rate of change at the societal level was even greater. The growth of sentiment for radical change at the mass level proceeded so rapidly that Gorbachev has come to be perceived as conservative, that is, as part of the problem, precisely *because* the Ligachevs no longer stand to his "right" within the leadership.

What should he have done to prevent this? He should have abandoned the party, rather than trying to revitalize or reform it. He should have effectively disbanded the party for its association with crimes and nationalized the property of the CPSU. He should have encouraged the establishment of formal opposition parties and given them easy access to organizational and media resources. And he should have established a nationwide "Presidential Party" within which left-center "grand coalitions" could have been set up throughout the country. Instead, Gorbachev left the CPSU in possession of formidable organizational and financial resources with which it retains the power to frustrate both democratization and marketization. This ensures the perpetuation of stalemate and the further identification of Gorbachev as part of the problem.

GORBACHEV'S OPTIONS

I fear that this stalemate could shortly result in a backlash. Popular support for the democrats has been based largely on a negative idea: negation of the Communists. And democratic forces have neither the executive authority, the experience, nor the power to combat CPSU obstruction of efforts to solve by radical means the economic problems the country faces. There is already evidence that the democratic forces in charge of many governmental councils are turning on each other. Should the masses turn against the democrats, conservative groups, nationalists, and military figures could coalesce and seek to impose a "national socialism." If the army disintegrates, this could result in the Lebanonization of the Soviet Union. If the army holds together, it could result in Nazification.

This bleak scenario can be prevented—it is by no means foreordained. The army is far from a unified institution, and its leaders know that they lack an alternative program for dealing with the country's problems effectively. I do not believe, therefore, that a military coup is at present much of a possibility in the USSR. Moreover, the masses (especially, but not only, in the minority republics), even if they reject the democrats, are not likely to tolerate the reestablishment of a terroristic regime. Nonetheless, the improbable is not necessarily the impossible. The pessimistic scenario must be taken seriously.

Gorbachev, I believe, can play an important role in preventing it. In this respect, Gorbachev's leadership is still needed—his "train has not left the station." To exercise that leadership, however, he must come to terms with the following conclusions that he has not yet shown a sufficient inclination to accept:

First and foremost, Gorbachev must acknowledge that the republics, not the center, currently have the power and legitimacy to run affairs within their territories. He should not resist that process. On the contrary, he should *smooth* and *facilitate* it. He should establish a coordinative committee, headed by himself, that would negotiate the terms of dissolution. His recent proposal to elevate the Council of the Federation to the status of a Presidential cabinet, replacing the Presidential Council, is a step in this direction (*Izvestiya*, November 18, 1990). It provides an institutional format within which Gorbachev could facilitate devolution. However, it will be crucial to see how Gorbachev conducts politics within the Council of the Federation. If he plays power politics that attempts to maintain a strong center, and does not accept the partial dissolution of the Soviet Union, he will prolong the current stalemate and potentially foster a right-wing backlash. But if he uses the Council as an arena for negotiating the terms of dissolution (however partial) or confederation, he could perform a positive historical function.

Second, Gorbachev continues to have an important role to play in *blocking* conservatives and reactionaries at the top. His tactical political skills are needed to prevent the coalescence of a reactionary coalition that might seek to turn back the clock. This would happen only at the price of immense bloodshed and the burying of democratization. Gorbachev retains a pivotal tactical-political role in holding off a violent backlash. To be sure, this is a negative function (preventing regression), but it is no less vital to the success of a transition.

And *third*, Gorbachev has an important role to play in preventing extreme radicalism from unleashing a civil war. Gorbachev must prevent a "Nuremberg" mentality from prevailing among democratic forces. The best way to do this is to disband the CPSU, so that party officials can melt into society and avoid lynchings and nationwide retribution. Similarly, he must prevent revenge taking violent form against the KGB and the army, for this too could unleash the forces of violent backlash. As we know from transitions elsewhere, when the opposition adopts violence as its tactic, the democratic transition is sacrificed, and civil war or backlash regimes ensue.

Gorbachev has a tactical advantage in performing the second and the third of these roles. For the two complement each other. His ability to prevent a Nuremberg atmosphere from taking concrete form also increases the sense of dependency on him among conservative forces within the establishment. And that facilitates the task of blocking their coalescence and ascendance as an anti-reform coalition.

Even if Gorbachev fulfills these functions, the country will still face the daunting consequences of his misguided strategy of transition. Centrifugal forces within the republics will remain so strong, and governmental authority so weak, that overcoming entrenched opposition to marketization will remain an urgent item on the agenda. This will have to be done within a context of unleashed democratic forces within many of the republics. Now that Gorbachev has allowed democratization to precede economic reform, the country is faced with a new situation. It is no longer possible to reverse the sequence. One must instead devise a strategy of transition that might make the best of a bad situation.

In this connection, I would not abandon my earlier argument (Migranyan, 1989) that strong leadership is needed to push through marketizing reforms that would create an organized social and political base for institutionalized, democratic politics. I would simply transfer the locus of application of that argument to the republican levels. This will be difficult to accomplish, given the released populist forces throughout the country. Perhaps only strong but charismatic leaders within each republic will be both powerful and legitimate enough to carry this off. Those leaders would not necessarily be liberal-democrats; in some cases, they might override democratic institutions, creating common cause with "the people" against existing institutions and processes. But that is the price that will have to be paid if the transition is to succeed. Gorbachev must facilitate the transition to this outcome, even though it would largely nullify his own authority. In other words, his leadership is still needed to create the conditions for his own irrelevance.[1]

REFERENCES

Migranyan, Andranik, "Dol'giy put' k yevropeyskomu domu (The Long Road to the European Home)," *Novyy mir*, 7:166–184, 1989.

---

1. In December 1990, after this article was written, Andranik Migranyan was quoted as saying that "an all-out confrontation between [the] center and republics might result in removal not just of the nationalist forces, but also [threaten] Gorbachev himself. It might create a climate in which the moderates would be swept away by extremists" (*The Washington Post*, December 24, 1990, p. A10).

CHAPTER 18

Understanding Gorbachev: The Importance of Politics

Jerry F. Hough

MIKHAIL GORBACHEV has fascinated Americans from the day that they first became conscious of him during his trip to Great Britain in December 1984, when Margaret Thatcher proclaimed him a man with whom it was possible to do business. For a specialist of the party apparatus, he had been fascinating even earlier. He had stood out as the only graduate of Moscow University and the only lawyer among the *obkom* first secretaries of the RSFSR, as the youngest official among the voting members of the party's Central Committee of 1971, and then as a Politburo member who was 24 years younger than the average of the other members when he was elected.[1]

But if Mikhail Gorbachev has fascinated us, he has also seemed mysterious. Never has a figure who has been so well-known and studied for so long surprised so many observers so consistently.

In our minds, he changed from a man with a "profoundly nonliberal attitude" who could not favor reform because he did not use the word *reforma* (Bialer and Afferica, 1985, pp. 611–613, 619–622; 1986) into a veritable Andrey Sakharov who was trying to "transfer power from an unredeemable Communist Party to a revamped hierarchy of popularly elected Soviets" (Reddaway, 1989). Then he seemed to change again into an irrelevant "Dowager Empress of China" who could not prevent Boris Yel'tsin from introducing the 500-day plan at his will ("Z," 1990)—and most recently into either a totalitarian dictator or a prisoner of the army or the KGB.

We do not need yet another debate about Gorbachev's strategy and power position in 1991. Evaluation of his leadership is even more difficult now than it was before. How does one evaluate a leader if one scholar is quite convinced that Gorbachev was simply being reactive in 1988–1989 (Breslauer, 1989),

---

First published in *Soviet Economy*, 1991, 7, 2, pp. 89–109. [Eds.]
1. He was also fascinating enough for me to spend considerable time reading *Stavropol'skaya Pravda* in Moscow in 1978 and 1979. For a debate on the importance of such factors as education, see Coffman and Klecheski (1982, pp. 199–200), and Hough (1982, p. 43).

while another (Hough, 1989a) is convinced that he was following a Machiavellian strategy during these very years? Above all, how can one evaluate Gorbachev's leadership until one sees how it turns out—at least learns whether he survives the next few years and whether reform goes forward or not?

We would do better to step back and analyze ourselves. Why have we analysts been so consistently wrong?

Part of the answer is that our friends in the Soviet Union are radicals, and many of us consciously avoid making analyses that could be used against them. Accepting any political analysis that they offer solves this problem, but their analysis has constantly shifted. Scholars play many roles—indulging in journalism, policy analysis, and forecasting (which I call "astrology")—but in their scholarly role, they should inform their own society. If our friends are so weak that they can be hurt by our analysis, they are in deep trouble. Scholars should look at competing predictions and assumptions of the past and try to determine which have been right and which wrong, so that they can reconsider them and learn. This kind of learning process has been conspicuous by its absence in Sovietology during the last six years. We need to apply the basics of our discipline if we are to understand the 1990s better than we did the 1980s.

RECOGNIZING THE EXISTENCE OF POLITICS

In the past, Americans twitted Soviet ideologists for talking about the dominance of the economic factor and economic classes in political life. Instead, we argued, the success of the Bolsheviks in transforming the Soviet Union in accordance with their ideology disproved what that ideology said about the primacy of economics and the secondary nature of politics.

But Americans themselves have always had the greatest difficulty in understanding and even recognizing politics in the Soviet Union, except for a few dramatic conflicts within the party Politburo. Even at the Politburo and immediate sub-Politburo level, we did not recognize differences between Stalinists (e.g., Vyacheslav Molotov and Lazar Kaganovich), let alone the liberal character of the policy advice of a man such as Andrey Vyshinskiy. In the Khrushchev period, we treated Frol Kozlov and Mikhail Suslov as Khrushchev's enemies rather than his political allies, and under Brezhnev we were oblivious to the politics raging in the Politburo on the question of growth versus social justice and did not notice when Yuriy Andropov took over Andrey Kirilenko's political machine (Hough, 1990a, pp. 60–62, 144–146).

We collectively were no more successful in comprehending the peculiar relationship between social forces and policy in the Soviet Union. In the 1960s, Alfred Meyer correctly wrote:

> In dealing with the Communist world, our notions of what a political system is or does have been suspended. For describing that world, we have used concepts and models reserved for it alone or for it and a few other

systems considered inimical. Thus one might almost say that the Communist world was analyzed outside the framework of comparative political science. Or else we used one set of concepts for Communist countries and another for the rest of the world. Most American political scientists would reject the elitist models of Pareto, Mosca, and Michels and would criticize a sociologist like Mills for seeking to apply them to the United States. Yet have not most studies of the Communist world described Communist states in the crudest Paretan terms as the rule of self-appointed elites striving to perpetuate themselves and structuring the entire system to this purpose? And I stress the crudeness of these interpretations, which neglect most of the subtleties and sophistication of both Mosca and Pareto (Meyer, 1967).

In the 1960s and 1970s, a group of scholars tried to analyze the complex politics among bureaucratic officials and civil servants with different interests and perspectives—and indirectly, the politics among the respective social forces represented by the bureaucratic actors. They also looked at the efforts of various types of intellectuals to change the priority of values and the paradigms which shaped policy choices. In retrospect, this work was describing the participatory politics that slowly undermined the social support for the old economic and social system and created the so-called new thinking adopted by the leadership after 1985.

Nevertheless, the effort to describe Soviet politics in these terms had almost no influence on American scholarly thinking. Even while Soviet intellectuals were participating very effectively in the political process, if with a time lag, they developed a concept of the Soviet system that denied the impact of any meaningful politics other than efforts to organize the popular overthrow of the ruling class. Westerners basically adopted this Soviet intellectual vision (both those who emigrated and those we met in Moscow), so they too[2] continued to see a Soviet political system that was basically devoid of politics.

Marxism-Leninism had insisted that Western countries were dominated by those who owned the means of production and that Western governments were little more than the tools of the ruling class. Soviet intellectuals followed the lead of the Yugoslav dissident Milovan Djilas, and earlier of Leon Trotsky in applying this Marxist-Leninist analysis to the Soviet Union. This revised version of Marxism-Leninism described the managers of means of production—the bureaucrats—as a united and all-powerful ruling class, but in this version the political leadership remained just as powerless as Western governments had been depicted in the past. The managers of the means of production could not evolve in a progressive direction any more than the bourgeoisie of Marx and Lenin. The only hope for progress was revolution by "civil society," the new word for "proletariat," although it now referred, of course, to a different social class.

This image of an immutable and privileged bureaucratic class, a powerless

---

2. For two books that show Soviet scholars using their "professional" analysis of the outside world as a covert method of supporting change in the USSR and hence engaging in effective political participation, see Rozman (1985) and Hough (1986b).

political leader, and the possibility of change only through a revolutionary overthrow of the ruling class has permeated our thinking about Mikhail Gorbachev. He has been described as riding a tiger, as a man on a surfboard, as a cork on a raging river. He has been the "superstructure," to use Marxist language. He has never been given any credit for ideas of his own. At first, it was thought that he was a creature and representative of the bureaucratic class, but then many began to think—or to talk as if they thought—that he may cross over to the new revolutionary class. But once he created democratic institutions, he was treated as a tragic figure who had fulfilled his role and who was to be discarded as no longer relevant. Finally in the winter of 1990–1991, he somehow had, voluntarily or involuntarily, become the prisoner of the old ruling class, especially the military and police components within it.

I contended in the 1980s, as in the 1970s, that the Soviet Union could not be understood if one did not recognize that it has a politics—and a politics that would be quite recognizable by a Western politician who understood Soviet institutions, the levers of power embodied in them, the interests of the major social forces, and their relative strength at a particular time.

I have also argued that dogmatic Marxism-Leninism is as poor a tool for understanding the Soviet Union as it is the United States. There is no united, privileged, bureaucratic ruling class in the Soviet Union. Soviet bureaucrats are the most underprivileged managerial stratum in the world, and they are divided by the same kind of occupational, institutional, regional, ethnic, and age cleavages found in the West. Politics centers on conflicts among those with the different interests suggested by these cleavages in the managerial stratum and in the population as a whole. It also consists in the efforts by politicians to take advantage of—and manipulate—these conflicts in one way or another.

A skilled leader must understand the levers of power in his society's political system. He must have a strategy for seizing control of—or modifying—those levers by building a majority coalition among those whose influence derives from them. He must neutralize those who might defeat him and his program "extraconstitutionally"—that is, by means other than the control of the recognized levers of power. Scholars must try to understand this process, but it is not easy. Dissimulation is one of the key techniques in consolidation of power, and it can mislead scholars as well as those it is designed to disarm.

The titles of many of my articles have reflected these assumptions: "Gorbachev's Strategy," "The Politics of Successful Economic Reform," "Gorbachev's Politics," and "Gorbachev's Endgame" (Hough, 1985, 1989a, 1989b, 1990c). I have repeatedly insisted that Gorbachev was being misinterpreted because we were not thinking of him as a normal politician and were not examining the imperatives of his political situation.[3]

---

3. The following, for example, is from an article I wrote for *The Washington Post* in response to a 1988 editorial that depicted Gorbachev as embodying "Brezhnevism without Brezhnev" because he had not spelled out a detailed economic reform plan (*The Washington Post*, March 5, 1986, p. A18): "Americans have great

The degree to which Gorbachev has, indeed, had a strategy and the degree to which he has simply reacted to events is deeply controversial. Clearly the Soviet leader cannot have foreseen everything. But just as clearly he cannot have been as naive or short-sighted as many seem to have believed.

Consider, for example, the nationality question. Two of the most sophisticated Armenians in Moscow (Abel Aganbegyan and Yuriy Arutyunyan) have said privately that they wrote memoranda to Gorbachev warning about the situation in Nagorno-Karabakh, but that they themselves were surprised that the emotions were so deep and the violence so long-lasting. One would not expect Gorbachev to be more prescient. Yet those who think that Gorbachev did not understand that the nationality question was explosive should ask themselves why he permitted no debate of the issue prior to 1988.[4]

Given more, those who think Gorbachev naive should ask themselves why Gorbachev, who very much wanted the Pope to visit Moscow in the summer of 1988 for the celebration of the 1000th anniversary of the introduction of Christianity into Russia, categorically refused the one condition the Pope made in the winter of 1987–1988—a visit to Lithuania?[5] Clearly, as perceived at the time, Gorbachev feared that the Pope's visit would stir up unrest in Lithuania. Is it really credible that a few months later, in the summer of 1988, he believed that he could permit an independent party (the Popular Front) in Lithuania, allow the public discussion of the Hitler-Stalin Pact and the conquest of Lithuania of 1939 and 1940, and establish free competitive elections in this context without the most extreme results?

We need to give a lot of thought to the history of the last six years, including some very serious research. An understanding that politics matters and that Gorbachev is a politician—and not just a politician playing coalition politics within the Politburo—is the first step in that effort.

THE CONSOLIDATION OF POWER

When we analyze Republican and Democratic national conventions, we are not misled by the rhetoric of the candidates or the delegates. We know that votes and the convention rules matter and that, regardless of who makes the finest speeches, a candidate who has a majority of committed delegates is certain to win. We know that we must understand institutional arrangements

---

difficulties in thinking of Soviet leaders as politicians . . . President Reagan is widely hailed as a peculiarly successful leader. [He did not] give the details of his program in the 1980 campaign or in his speeches after becoming president. . . . When President Carter got involved in details it was said that this was a flaw. Why should Gorbachev lay out all the details? He wants to rule for 15 years. Let others work out the details and get blamed if they don't work out quite right. His job is to say there will be radical reform and to accumulate the power to ensure that it will be done'' (Hough, 1986a).

4. The Central Committee journal, *Kommunist*, did not have a single article on the subject until October 1988. Two articles were published in *Kommunist*, No. 15 (October) 1988: Korteyeva et al. (1988) and Zeymal' (1988).

5. *The New York Times* reported that the Pope was not invited specifically because of his demand to visit Lithuania (*The New York Times*, Jan. 3, 1988, part IV, p. 2).

if we are to understand the acquisition of power. We know that we must understand the strategy that contenders use to acquire power within these institutional arrangements.

Of course, we must understand the real arrangements, not merely the formal ones. We must understand the unwritten constitution that underlies British politics, and we must realize that the Queen of England does not really have powers formally accorded her. But each of these institutional arrangements has its rules for the acquisition of power, which we need to understand. And, of course, we must always be aware of the possibility of revolution—acquisition of power by extraconstitutional means—and must have some sense of the conditions in which this is possible and impossible.

We have become extraordinarily insensitive to institutions in the Soviet Union. In other countries, the unwritten constitution gives power to the military and defines how future rulers compete for power. The Soviet unwritten constitution put decision-making power in the party Central Committee and Politburo. An older generation of scholars strongly emphasized the "organizational factor" in Stalin's rise to power, but a younger generation tended to be revisionist on this point. The political stability under Leonid Brezhnev left little reason for scholars to think about the institutional mechanisms through which power was acquired or maintained during his long reign. And the Soviet intellectuals on whom we have come to rely have understood nothing about intraparty mechanisms. They have talked about the resistance of "bureaucrats" or "the party apparatus" to Gorbachev and about his need to create democratic institutions to circumvent them, but they have had no detailed sense of how the bureaucracy and party apparatus are organized and how they interrelate.

One thing is absolutely certain: Gorbachev understood the mechanisms of power in the Soviet system extremely well, and he set out to gain control of them in a very determined and even ruthless way. Some may argue that Gorbachev took excessive risks in overcoming opposition to himself within the existing system and that he unleashed forces that he could not control. In my opinion, this notion is not accurate, but at least it is plausible. What cannot be plausibly argued or assumed is that Gorbachev was not deeply conscious of the requirements of a consolidation of power within the existing system and not deeply concerned about taking the required steps. Over the decades, my most abiding scholarly interest has been the structure of power in the party and the relationships of cadres policy to it. I have followed these questions with meticulous care, and Gorbachev's sophistication in this realm, often at the most detailed level, has always struck me as extraordinarily impressive.

Yet we in the West have seldom thought through Gorbachev's problems and strategy in this most simple area. We, along with Soviet intellectuals, have said, on the one hand, that the Russian people are security-oriented and afraid of economic reform, but on the other, that Gorbachev had to give the people the vote in order to overcome resistance to economic reform. At each stage, Gorbachev's propagandists described his moves in a way that would seem plausible to the intelligentsia and would manipulate their attitudes in the desired direction. A great many observers both in the Soviet Union and the United States were taken in.

Any serious student of the structure of power in the Soviet Union before the summer of 1990 would have focused on the role of the Central Committee—the plenum of the Central Committee, as Soviets would express it. Although Westerners often said incorrectly that the Politburo was the focus of power in the old system, the only institution that could elect or replace a General Secretary—or any Politburo member—was the Central Committee. Whoever controlled a majority of the voting members of the Central Committee controlled the Politburo and the rest of the political system. Normally the loyalty of the Central Committee to the General Secretary was taken for granted by any potential challenger and, therefore, not tested, but a General Secretary who did not continually worry about that loyalty courted the fate that befell Nikita Khrushchev in October 1964.

It was obvious from the beginning that Mikhail Gorbachev would not have been elected General Secretary if he had had to rely on the Politburo, and Yegor Ligachev confirmed in 1988 that Gorbachev's election depended on officials who sat on the Central Committee rather than the Politburo in March 1985. Yuriy Andropov had come to head the Kirilenko machine within the Communist Party, and these were the men with whom Gorbachev allied himself to gain his majority within the Central Committee. Ligachev had worked in the Bureau of the Central Committee for the RSFSR under Kirilenko from 1962 to 1965, and the first deputy head of the cadres department had been Kirilenko's personal assistant. Viktor Chebrikov and Vladmir Shcherbitskiy had come from Kirilenko's base of power in Dnepropetrovsk and Nikolay Ryzhkov and Boris Yel'tsin from his base of power in Sverdlovsk (Hough, 1990a).

The Central Committee that elected Gorbachev was composed of the 300-odd top officials of the Soviet Union in 1981, and clearly neither Gorbachev nor radical market reform had unanimous support within it. Almost all of Gorbachev's behavior in 1985 and early 1986 can be attributed to the character of the Central Committee at the time and by his knowledge that a new one would be elected at the 27th Party Congress in March 1986. He retired members of the old Central Committee as fast as he dared (40 percent of the voting membership had been retired or seriously demoted by the time of the Congress), but he took no radical action that might provoke a majority into repudiating him.

Those who think that Gorbachev made a mistake with his "acceleration" and discipline-oriented economic program of 1985 simply do not understand his problems. The program was certainly not ideal from an economic point of view, but Gorbachev had other concerns. There is no reason to assume that the program represented his actual economic thinking at the time. Indeed, the direction of his thinking was more accurately suggested by such vague comments as the one he made to the editors of *Time* magazine in August 1985. He said he was contemplating "truly grandiose plans in the domestic sphere." (*Time*, Sept. 9, 1985, p. 29). But aside from short-term political considerations, there was a lot to be said for giving "acceleration" a chance, in order to build support for more radical reform when it failed.

The great strength of the General Secretary always rested on his ability to control the appointment of regional first secretaries, for they in turn controlled the selection of delegates to the Party Congress that elected the Central Committee. This "circular flow of power" was crucial for every General Secretary from Stalin to Gorbachev. The weakness of the position of the General Secretary after 1961 was that the members of the Central Committee, who were the top central and regional officials of the country, could be replaced on the committee only once every five years. Even if a General Secretary removed an official who sat on the Central Committee—or seriously offended him with some policy—that official continued to be a Central Committee voting member until the next Party Congress. If a General Secretary planned a large-scale personnel change, the number of lame ducks on the Central Committee could rise dangerously high. For example, by the late spring of 1988, the proportion of lame ducks among the voting members was approaching 20 percent, with the next Party Congress not expected until March 1991.

Gorbachev clearly was aware of this problem and eager to do something about it. In February 1987, he announced a Party Conference for the summer of 1988. As a close adviser, Ivan Frolov said privately in March 1987, there was no reason to take this step except to make changes in the Central Committee membership, as had been done in Party Conferences under Stalin. When a draft version of new party rules was published in May 1988 (presumably a preparatory step for their enactment at the forthcoming Party Conference), it included a provision giving Party Conferences the right to make a "partial" change among the Central Committee members. Then a decision was made—when and how is uncertain—that revision of the party rules would have to wait until the next Party Congress; no change in Central Committee membership occurred at the conference. The following April, however, Gorbachev solved his immediate problem with the Central Committee by inducing (or coercing) 74 of the retired members to leave the Central Committee "voluntarily."

CHANGING THE MECHANISMS OF POWER

At some point Gorbachev decided to make a fundamental change in the mechanisms of power in the Soviet Union. He decided to eliminate the threat of his removal by the Central Committee by taking that power away from it altogether. In October 1988, he introduced a change in the constitution to change the post of chairman of the Presidium of the Supreme Soviet to that of chairman of the Supreme Soviet, elected by a Congress of People's Deputies that was partly elected by popular vote in competitive elections. Gorbachev assumed the new top governmental post in addition to his party job. In practice, this made it virtually impossible for the Central Committee to remove him from his government post and therefore, from his post of General Secretary (Hough, 1989a).

In 1990 he went much further. The party rules enacted at the 28th Party Congress went well beyond those suggested two years earlier at the time of the 19th conference. Now the General Secretary was to be elected at the Party Congress itself, not by the Central Committee, and the Politburo was to be composed largely of ex officio members, not removable by the Central Committee (the General Secretary, Deputy General Secretary, and the first secretaries of the union republics). The power to approve (and often make) personnel change in the government—the power of *nomenklatura*—was taken away from the Central Committee and local party organs. Through a series of rumors and leaks to the Western press, Gorbachev threatened to abandon the Communist Party altogether if the Politburo and Central Committee did not give up their policy-making powers over him.[6]

From this perspective—and to be sure, others may be valid—the removal of Article 6 of the Soviet Constitution[7] and the introduction of meaningful legislative elections were not really aimed at overcoming general bureaucratic and apparatchik resistance to economic reform. Instead, these moves were intended to prevent high bureaucrats and party officials with seats on the Central Committee from removing the General Secretary from power, perhaps because he was too much of a reformer, perhaps for other reasons.

We must examine many of the events of 1990 and 1991 through this prism. I am not certain when Gorbachev decided to end the power of the Central Committee and Politburo and to rest his main base of power on a governmental post. In February 1987, he said that "some comrades" favored the election of regional party secretaries. I understood that this step would make the Central Committee even more dangerous for a General Secretary and would destroy his base of power within it. I assumed that the term "some comrades" referred to opponents of Gorbachev who were seeking to democratize the system.[8]

Perhaps I was wrong in my 1987–1989 interpretations. Gorbachev may have already been planning to eliminate the dominant role of the leading party organs and could have been dissembling until it was too late for the old Politburo and Central Committee to protect themselves. Or perhaps Gorbachev only changed his plans in 1988 and 1989 as he encountered difficulties in working his will at the 19th Party Conference. Or he may have concluded from events in Central Europe and from the 1989 and 1990 elections that it was dangerous to leave

---

6. This argument is made in Hough (1990c, pp. 656–662).

7. Article 6 stipulated that the Communist Party was the "leading and guiding force" in Soviet society. [Eds.]

8. This interpretation was found in a number of places, including Hough (1989a), reprinted in this volume.

himself irrevocably tied to the fate of the Communist Party—and to allow his continuation in the government post after 1994 to depend on the character of the Congress of People's Deputies at that time.

But whatever the timing of Gorbachev's decision, it was well under way in 1990. Already in the summer of 1989, Nikolay Ryzhkov had said that the old mechanisms of power were no longer effective, and the Kirghiz party first secretary had complained that "someone" seemed deliberately to be discrediting the Communist Party (*Pravda*, July 21, 1989, p. 2). I argued at the time, first in the pages of *Soviet Economy* and then in the pages of *Foreign Affairs*, that Gorbachev was deliberately stimulating national unrest and a sense of disorder to produce public demand for a strong leader and for order. He was also intent, I wrote, on convincing the Russian people that support for the radicals and real democracy would lead to the breakup of the Union. I contended that, just as Stalin created an artificial war scare in 1927 to set the stage for his final consolidation of power, so Gorbachev was creating an artificial (or at least exaggerated) sense of chaos in 1990 for the same purpose.

> As a result of the decades of censorship, many Russians apparently were unaware of the depth of national feeling in the non-Russian areas. Gorbachev, in my view, has deliberately given extremists in small and safe Estonia their heads, has deliberately allowed the safe Armenian-Azerbaijani conflict to work itself out, and has permitted media coverage of these events (not to mention emotional debate in the Congress of People's Deputies about them) so that the Russians vividly understand the centrifugal forces in the country. . . . If the glue of the system among the Russians is the fear of the breakup of the country, the general secretary needs to ensure that nationality policy stirs up the non-Russians enough to remind everyone (including the non-Russians) that excessive democratization could mean civil war (Hough, 1989a, pp. 39, 41).

But if Gorbachev was to move his base of power from the Central Committee to the presidency, then it was essential to endow the presidency with the kind of powers that the General Secretary had—but without any danger of being removed, at least until 1995. That, in my opinion, is what he was doing.

The logical outcome of this analysis was very clear. Once Gorbachev had used the chaos to accumulate emergency power, then it was in his interest to try to end the chaos.

> Just as Stalin turned against the right when it no longer served his purpose, one should not assume that Gorbachev will not turn against the radical intelligentsia, the radical non-Russian nationalists, or against electoral mechanisms if they come to seem counterproductive to him. If this happens, of course, Gorbachev's propagandists will say that "poor" Gorbachev has been defeated by the conservatives, and those with a rosy view of the Soviet leader in the U.S. will, as before, echo that line. We should not be fooled.

Anarchy comes from the inability to apply force successfully, not from its successful application (Hough, 1989a, p. 38).

I see absolutely no reason to consider that analysis incorrect. It is still premature to evaluate Gorbachev's success as a leader in this respect. I doubt that he has unleashed forces that will escape his control, but it is a possibility that we should examine before making a final judgment about him. We should not, however, evaluate Gorbachev's leadership on the basis of mistaken assumptions about his strategy that are held by our Bukharinite friends in the Soviet Union. That, it seems to me, is the weakness of the Breslauer article (Breslauer, 1989).

1917 OR 1929?

When leading radicals, including Boris Yel'tsin, quit the Communist Party after the 28th Party Congress, they naturally described Mikhail Gorbachev as a man who had served a useful historical role but was now being overtaken by events. They argued that if he did not accept the Shatalin 500-day plan, which deprived the central government of all financial powers, the republics would enact it over his objections. Gorbachev, they said, had become irrelevant and powerless. When Gorbachev showed in the late fall and the winter of 1990–1991 that he still did have some of the "teeth of iron" that Andrey Gromyko had mentioned in 1985, they said the president had either become conservative or the captive of conservative forces such as the army or the KGB. *Perestroyka* was dead, they said; but, fortunately, the use of force would simply provoke more resistance, and revolution was not only possible, but likely. The year 1991, they suggested, was as revolutionary as 1917.

Many Westerners accepted this line of analysis, but it seems to me that it should be treated with extreme skepticism.

First, the picture of Gorbachev being painted in the winter of 1990–1991, in my view, was simply wrong. Language was used—or misused—in a way that created a very inaccurate impression. Originally people distinguished between *glasnost'* (essentially greater freedom of speech), *demokratizatsiya* (democratization of political institutions), and *perestroyka* (economic reform). They used the word *reforma* to mean radical reform of the existing system, not a revolution that would replace it with a Western political and economic system.

By 1990, however, the radicals were using the word *perestroyka* to mean the introduction from above of a free market and full democracy—and perhaps even toleration of the breakup of the Soviet Union. The word "reform" was being used to mean a revolutionary introduction of the Western political and economic system. The word "reformers" came to mean "conservatives." It was reminiscent of the late 1960s, when the extremists on the American left called both Lyndon Johnson and Richard Nixon fascists.

In fact, a serious analysis of Mikhail Gorbachev must be based on a serious use of language. The political spectrum to the right of the radicals includes a broad range of people. On the far right are extreme reactionaries who opposed even Leonid Brezhnev because of his policy of détente with the West. Many of the noisiest Soviet "conservatives" to whom we pay too much attention are actually of this type. Then come the moderate reactionaries who would only like to return the Soviet Union to the Brezhnev period. My impression is that the number of such advocates is small among the politically significant elements of the population. Next on the spectrum are the moderate reformers—those who favored most of the reforms of the 1985–1988 period (*glasnost'*, an opening to the West, cooperatives, and so forth). They would even approve a cautious extension of these reforms, but oppose many of the changes of 1988– 1990 (competitive elections with non-Communist candidates, toleration of na- tionalist dissent, movement toward a major recognition of private property). This group of moderate reformers includes men like Yegor Ligachev and Ni- kolay Ryzhkov. Then come more radical reformers such as Valentin Pavlov, the current prime minister, and Mikhail Gorbachev.

Gorbachev favors a very substantial introduction of market mechanisms into the Soviet Union—*radical* reform, but he does not favor a revolution to in- troduce the American economic system through shock treatment. Gorbachev favors a continuation and expansion of the opening to the West, as well as the type of liberalization that is implied by *glasnost'*, but he does not favor full Western democracy. He supports major decentralization of power to the re- publics (and to the provinces within the large republics), but not the breakup of the Soviet Union. That does not mean, however, that he has abandoned radical reform. It simply means that he has never been a radical revolutionary.

Nothing that happened in Lithuania should have been a surprise to anyone, and there was no basis for the hypothesis that the army was forcing Gorbachev to reverse his policy. When Gorbachev plunged into the crowds in Lithuania a year ago, he promised his listeners 'real federalism," but, as *The Washington Post*'s David Remnick reported at the time, Gorbachev spoke in a "menacing tone." "Today I am your friend," he said, "But if you choose to go another way, then I will do everything I can to show you are leading people to a dead end." His liberal adviser, Aleksandr Yakovlev, warned then of an unacceptable "domino effect" if the Baltics seceded. Gorbachev held out a vague hope for secession to the Lithuanians if they followed constitutional procedures, but these procedures were so forbidding that Lithuanian president Landsbergis properly dismissed the idea as "a propaganda trap" and an "absurd deceit" (*The Washington Post*, Jan. 13, 1990, pp. 1, 16).

By November 1990, Gorbachev had come close to repudiating the possibility of constitutional secession. "Disintegration and separation cannot happen in our country, simply under any circumstances." And he made this rather men- acing statement: "Whether we like it or not, our fate is already sealed. If we start splitting, there will be . . . a dreadful war." But at the same time,

Gorbachev was more fervent than ever in support of real federalism, saying "We favor profound changes in our Union, first and foremost by way of a distribution of powers" (*Pravda*, Dec. 1, 1990, p. 4).

In effect, Gorbachev was consistent in using a combination of carrots and sticks in the republics to try to separate the moderates and radicals. If you push for independence and revolution, he warns implicitly, you risk economic pressure and even troops. But if you work within the system, he has said explicitly, you will enjoy great individual freedom, and your republic will have autonomy.

Gorbachev today is what he has always been—a modernizing, Westernizing czar such as Kemal Ataturk was in Turkey, Lee Kuan Yew was in Singapore, and many Third World rulers in countries like Taiwan and South Korea. His so-called move to the right is actually an abandonment of the radical revolutionaries, who have now served their purpose for him in the transformation of ideology and in the legitimization of dictatorial power for himself. He acted not because of army pressure, but to recapture popular support. He was not losing his last bastion of support, as some argued, but rejecting—and scapegoating—those who had cost him popular support.

Anyone who sees him as a tragic, transitional figure because he will not introduce a Western political and economic system has little sense of history. Washington and Jefferson were slaveholders; Lincoln was ambivalent about the abolition of slavery; and Franklin D. Roosevelt took only the first steps toward establishing a massive social safety net. Great figures in history are ambiguous; they initiate great changes rather than finish them off.

The second flaw in the Soviet radicals' assumption that the Soviet Union is now revolutionary—and that it may even be disintegrating as a country—contradicts all that we know about revolution and national integration throughout the world.

The belief that the Soviet Union will disintegrate and that some of the republics will gain independence in this decade is the one based on the least comparative perspective. When one ethnic group controls an ethnic group in another country, eventually the dominant group always seems ready to give up its control. Soviet policy in Central Europe, for example, confirms a pattern observed many times in the last 50 years.

But when one ethnic group controls another within the same country, the dominant group almost never yields control voluntarily. Until now, the only instances in which dominated groups have gained full independence have been when a foreign army has supported the independence struggle or when power collapses in the capital, usually because of defeat in war. The Austro-Hungarian Empire is a typical example. The Soviet Union is hardly the last empire in the sense that one ethnic group controls others within its borders. Virtually every Asian and African country represents such an empire. In the postwar period, there have been hundreds of secessionist movements in these countries, but only one has been successful—Bangladesh, where the intervention of the Indian army was decisive (Horowitz, 1985, p. 272).

Basically revolution cannot be successful if military units fire on the demonstrators, unless the latter are able to mobilize a stronger military counterforce. Troops of one ethnic group can usually be trusted to fire on members of another ethnic group who are trying to break up a country. Future developments in countries such as Yugoslavia, Canada, and Czechoslovakia may compel us to modify this generalization; if so, the precedent would probably still not be relevant to the Soviet Union for at least ten or fifteen years.

No one expected that Soviet troops would fail to fire on insurgents in Poland, Hungary, or Czechoslovakia. Soviet troop behavior in places such as Georgia and Lithuania suggests that Gorbachev's problem is not to persuade the troops to fire, but to restrain them from acting too rashly. If over 40 million Moslems were in revolt and had guerrilla bands supplied with foreign arms in the mountains, the Soviet military would face serious difficulties. But a military force that kept 35 million Poles under control is not going to have problems with 3 million Lithuanians. Indeed, the most striking fact about the actions in Lithuania and Latvia in January 1991 was the tiny size of the Soviet military units that were needed—in one case a company, in the other a battalion.

Mass revolution by members of a country's dominant ethnic group has a better chance of success because troops of that ethnic group may refuse to fire on their own. The Communist leaders in Poland, Hungary, and Czechoslovakia who knew that they could count on Russian troops to keep them in power clearly felt that their own young troops would not prove reliable.

THE YOUNG AND THE MILITARY

In general, young men between the ages of 15 and 22 are the only group that throws rocks at troops, joins guerrilla movements, or faces tanks in sufficient numbers or with sufficient persistence. Even then, they are almost never successful if the army fires at them. Revolution is successful only when the same factors that brought the young men into the streets affect the 18-, 19-, and 20-year-olds in the military.[9]

In the Soviet Union, one fact on which all observers agree is that young people are politically passive. Ask Russian friends if their college students are ready to face tanks, and they look at you as if you are insane. At Moscow University, it is reported, some first-year students arrive politically oriented, but by the third and fourth year they have become "pragmatic." In the spring of 1990, Moscow University students came in large numbers to hear speeches by such radicals as Moscow Mayor Gavriil Popov, but by the winter of 1990–1991 the turnout was sparse. At the Moscow Historical-Archive Institute, where

---

9. When a country is poor, the army is usually composed of poorly educated peasants and may have little in common with elite urban student demonstrators; but as a country industrializes, the soldiers become more urbanized and better educated—and more similar in background to demonstrators (Hough, 1990a, pp. 52–54).

the radical Yuriy Afanas'yev is the rector, no more than about 10 percent of the students are said to support his views.

There is a consensus among Soviet professors about the reason for their students' political passivity. Students either leave school to go to work in the new cooperatives, or they study economics in preparation for such careers. This is a crucial point for Americans to understand. Soviet citizens over 55 have reason to be terrified that the inflation associated with economic reform will nullify their unindexed pensions. Young people, by contrast—at least those with ambition and talent who are capable of organizing opposition—will benefit enormously from economic reform. They are getting a real chance at a privileged life.

We must understand clearly the meaning of the young people's political passivity. If the students of Moscow University and Leningrad University are not revolutionary, then Moscow and Leningrad are not revolutionary. Indeed, because of the crucial role of youth in revolution, economic reform is not a cause of revolution, but the antidote to it. The only way that Gorbachev could provoke a revolt would be to throttle economic reform and frustrate the only "dangerous" group in society. There is no evidence that he is so reckless.

Only one other group besides young people can carry out a successful revolution against a leader; the military. Many now warn of the possibility of a military coup against Gorbachev; but that fear is based either on a desire to mobilize support for Gorbachev or an idealized view of him as a leader forced to take the steps he took in January 1991.

In fact, the Soviet military has every reason to support Gorbachev. While the top officials were unhappy over the loss of Eastern Europe and the unification of Germany, they know that those events eliminated NATO as a significant military threat. Their fears about the disintegration of the Soviet Union lead them to much greater concern about Islamic fundamentalism in Central Asia than about extremism in the tiny Baltic republics. In the long run, they fear China. Gorbachev has brought the United States into alliance against these short-term and long-term dangers from the south.

In addition, the Pentagon solidified Soviet military support for economic reform by showing visiting Soviet generals the best American military technology. Their purpose was to persuade the Soviet officers that their forces could not defeat the United States. But a side effect was to convince the Soviet military that a drastic improvement in civilian high-technology industries such as computers and electronics was vital for defense. If conservatives in the Soviet military ever had any doubt about the need for economic reform, the quick American victory over Iraq must have convinced them that an improvement in Soviet technology was essential to ensure a potent military force in the 21st century.

By all indications, Gorbachev's strategy now is to satisfy the Russians, including the military, by taking whatever steps are necessary to keep the Union together, while insisting that decentralization is necessary for social peace. Indeed, the clause on decentralization in the March 1991 referendum on the Union was included not simply to facilitate a "yes" vote, but to commit the Russian population to decentralization.[10]

He will move ahead with economic reform. The conservative complaints about a market economy refer to one that involves the adoption of the Polish shock treatment and rapid privatization of heavy industry.[11]

The decentralization of power to the republics is an inherent part of the economic reform. This policy is based both on political and economic calculation. Decisions on the details of economic reform usually create a no-win situation for politicians, and Gorbachev is glad to leave the responsibility to local politicians. Who wants to vote to cut food subsidies or raise taxes to pay for them? Presidents Reagan and Bush understood that if the central government cut taxes, then state government would have to raise them to maintain services. As a consequence, presidents and congressmen are re-elected and state governors often defeated. Gorbachev has the same strategy.

The events of March and April need to be understood in these terms. The American press was filled with stories about Gorbachev's precarious position, about the possibility of revolt in the face of price increases, and about a string of victories for Yel'tsin and the radicals. In fact, Yel'tsin and the radicals suffered a series of defeats. Gorbachev won the March referendum that they had turned into a referendum on him, carrying even Moscow and Leningrad. Emergency power was not, as reported, decentralized to Yel'tsin alone, but to Yel'tsin, the RSFSR Supreme Soviet, and the Presidium of the RSFSR Supreme Soviet together—and the latter two institutions are more conservative than the Congress of People's Deputies, with which Yel'tsin had been dealing. A report appeared that a group of Communist deputies had defected to Yel'tsin, giving him control of the Russian parliament; but when the list of these deputies was published, it turned out that their voting record had already been more radical than Yel'tsin's.[12]

Most important of all, the demonstrations and strikes that were organized to protest the sales tax of March 1 and the price rise of early April failed. The radicals, despairing of their ability to win within a parliamentary framework, had hoped that they could use the economic discontent and the price increases to produce the kind of popular uprising that occurred in Poland in 1980, when meat prices were raised there. The radicals failed, and Yel'tsin's acceptance

10. See the discussion in Slider (1991).

11. Oleg Ozherel'yev, Gorbachev's new advisor on economic reform who replaced Nikolay Petrakov, confirmed this understanding (*Financial Times*, March 27, 1991, p. 1).

12. Regina Smyth of Duke University has constructed a radical-conservative scale for legislators of the RSFSR Congress of People's Deputies on the basis of 24 key roll-call votes. In this study (in which 0 was the most conservative and 100 the radical), the average deputy received a score of 55.6 and Yel'tsin had a score of 71. The average score of the 95 Communists who endorsed him in March was 77, which meant that the great majority of them were among the 400–450 deputies who had been part of Yel'tsin's minority group throughout the Congress (Smyth, 1990).

of the anti-crisis program represented a recognition of that fact. Gorbachev was delighted to transfer the coal mines to the republics, because now they will have to deal with the problem of raising taxes for subsidies.[13] He is happy to cede them a great deal of authority as long as macroeconomic power remains in the hands of the central government. If historical analogies are to be used, 1991 is far more like 1929—the year Stalin completed his consolidation of power and launched his great transformation of Soviet society.

Those who think that Gorbachev has been in any more danger the last few years than Stalin was between 1926 and 1929 should ponder recent events. Clearly, Soviet leaders were aware for a long time of the need to raise the price of goods such as meat and bread, but they were afraid to do so, lest they produce a reaction similar to that in Poland in 1980. The issue, however, was raised twice in one year; in the spring of 1990 by Nikolay Ryzhkov and then in March 1991. The first instance was timed—quite unnecessarily—to coincide with Yel'tsin's struggle to be elected chairman of the RSFSR Supreme Soviet. The second was timed—again unnecessarily—to coincide with a special session of the RSFSR Congress considering Yel'tsin's leadership. That is, in both cases Gorbachev deliberately created a situation that would benefit Yel'tsin on an issue that many thought very dangerous. Gorbachev believed that the situation was totally under control, and he thought that he could use Yel'tsin rather than be used by him.

Legislative elections are scheduled for 1994 and presidential elections for 1995. They are more dangerous, for the middle-aged and elderly have a disproportioniately greater power than young people in elections. Gorbachev wants to be able to say in 1994 and 1995, "Remember how bad 1990 was? You gave me great powers. Are you better off then you were four years ago?" He wants the memories of 1990 to be as exaggerated as possible. He wants his electoral opponents to be identified with even greater market freedom than he is, with disorder, and with the breakup of the USSR, so that he can command the electoral center.

I believe that Gorbachev's position will be very strong in the mid-1990s. The most rebellious republics may not formally recognize Soviet hegemony, but as they are compelled to make real decisions on economic reform and management to their republics, they will de facto remain part of the country. The agricultural and services reform that worked in China and Hungary should work in the Soviet Union. Industrial reform will be much more difficult, but that is not Gorbachev's immediate worry. The Communist Party has an excellent chance to become a dominant electoral party in the Slavic areas on the model of Mexico's Institutional Revolutionary Party or Japan's Liberal Democratic Party for the rest of this century. A democratic politician cannot simultaneously

13. The transfer of coal mines to the republics, as recently announced (*The New York Times*, May 7, 1991, pp. A1, A7), had been part of the Gorbachev plan of the fall 1990 that had been developed in response to the Shatalin Plan.

play at revolution and command the electoral center as the Soviet radicals are attempting, and their strategy almost surely redounds to the benefit of the Communists.

Of course, if Gorbachev cannot produce results before 1995, all bets are off. But even then the establishment of martial law is more probable than Gorbachev's acceptance of an electoral defeat. In any event, the extreme-case scenarios of an overthrow of Gorbachev in 1995 will come only shortly before the overthrow of George Bush in 1996, at the latest. In political life, the four years until 1995 are a long time, and it is time to stop fretting about the "tragic" Gorbachev and use the next few years to achieve what we can.

CONCLUSION

Political science departments have often professed a scorn for "area specialists" and expressed a preference for political theorists and comparativists. But the hiring practices of the major departments have belied their words. Moreover, the scholars and books that gain the most respect are the ones with a pronounced area specialization.

The crucial issue is the way in which the area is studied. The understanding of the area must extend to a minutely detailed level, and as the scholar ages, it must grow in scope; but the area must also be understood in the perspective of world experience. For example, the old literature on national character describes virtually all pre-industrial peoples in similar terms—not unlike the literature on Russian political culture. But the literature on the impact of industrialization, urbanization, and education of peoples around the world makes it apparent that Russian political culture is likely to change as well.

Similarly, the world has had great experience with ethnicity, with revolution, and with democratization. As in Russia in 1917, that experience shows that the role of the army is crucial: Will the soldiers fire on demonstrators or not? If one talks with Moscow radicals caught up in the emotion of the moment, it is easy to see revolution imminent; if one looks at the experience of the world, however, one is reminded of the dangers of romanticism on this point, especially when soldiers are asked to fire on those of different ethnic background.

There also should not be any romanticism about democratization. The experience of the West is that this process takes well over a century after it begins in earnest, and Latin America is confirming the West European experience. There are many intermediate points on the spectrum between pure democracy and pure authoritarianism—many systems with virtually dictatorial rulers and with legislatures and competitive elections.

Least of all should there be romanticism about local majorities, especially local ethnic majorities. The experience of white-black relations in the American South for a century after the Civil War is far more typical than one would like. One may believe that the central government—say a Supreme Court—should not intervene to overturn decisions by local majorities that deny the display or sale of "obscene" books or art, that impose school prayers in the schools, that establish segregated classrooms, that prevent women from having abortions. But a serious analysis cannot overlook the fact that the United States and Western Europe do not have pure democracy, but constitutional democracy, and constitutional democracy contains an inherent conflict between the rights of the majority and the rights of the individual. It is not sophisticated to denounce as conservatives people in the Soviet Union who share the American fear of absolute power for local majorities and who want the American combination of both democracy and constitutional guarantees for the individual.

The great shortcoming of Soviet intellectuals is that they were educated within the tradition of a dogmatic Marxism-Leninism that grossly neglected political and ethnic factors in society. The newspapers they read completely censored discussion of Soviet domestic politics and democratic theory and described revolution and ethnic conflict abroad in the most tendentious terms. The strength of liberal education in the West is that it emphasizes the importance of a multiplicity of factors in human history and encourages exposure to a broad range of world experience. We have had too little faith in what our social scientists have learned about politics, revolution, and ethnicity in the world, and we have had too much faith in the judgment of those who were educated and lived in a closed society with a dogmatic ideology. By denying our own intellectual tradition and theories, we have made one mistake after another analyzing Gorbachev and Soviet society in the 1980s. We will understand the Soviet Union of the 1990s only if we return to our intellectual roots.

REFERENCES

Bialer, Seweryn, and Joan Afferica, "The Genesis of Gorbachev's World," *Foreign Affairs*, 64, 3:605–644, 1985.

———, "Gorbachev's Preference for Technocrats," *The New York Times*, February 11, 1986, p. 31.

Breslauer, George, "Evaluating Gorbachev as Leader," *Soviet Economy*, 5, 4:299–340, October–December 1989.

Coffman, Richard, and Michael Klecheski, "The 26th Party Congress Conference: The Soviet Union in a Time of Uncertainty," in Seweryn Bialer and Thane Gustafson, eds., *Russia at the Crossroads: The 26th Congress of the CPSU*. London: George Allen & Unwin, 1982.

Horowitz, Donald L., *Ethnic Groups in Conflict*. Berkeley: University of California Press, 1985.

Hough, Jerry F., "Changes in Soviet Elite Composition," in Seweryn Bialer and Thane Gustafson, eds, *Russia at the Crossroads: The 26th Congress of the CPSU*. London: George Allen & Unwin, 1982, pp. 39–64.

———, "Gorbachev's Strategy," *Foreign Affairs*, 64, 1:33–55, 1985.

———, "Something Will Change in the Soviet Union," *The Washington Post*, March 15, 1986a, p. A21.

————, *The Struggle for the Third World: Soviet Debates and American Options.* Washington, D.C.: Brookings Institution, 1986b.

————, "The Politics of Successful Economic Reform," *Soviet Economy*, 5, 1:3–46, January–March 1989a.

————, "Gorbachev's Politics," *Foreign Affairs*, 68, 5:26–41, 1989b/1990.

————, *Russia and the West: Gorbachev and the Politics of Reform*, Second ed. New York: Simon & Schuster, 1990a.

————, "The Logic of Collective Action and the Pattern of Revolutionary Behavior," *Journal of Soviet Nationalities*, 1, 2:34–65, Summer 1990b.

————, "Gorbachev's Endgame," *World Policy Journal*, 7, 4:639–670, Fall 1990c.

Koroteyeva, V., A. Perepelkin, and O. Shkaratan, "Ot byurokraticheskogo tsentralizma k ekonomicheskoy integratsii suverennykh respublik (From Bureaucratic Centralism to the Economic Integration of Sovereign Republics)," *Kommunist*, 15:22–23, October 1988.

Meyer, Alfred G., "The Comparative Study of Communist Political Systems," *Slavic Review*, 26, 1:3–12, March 1967.

Reddaway, Peter, "Is the Soviet Union on the Road to Anarchy?" *The Washington Post*, August 29, 1989, p. B1.

Rozman, Gilbert, *A Mirror for Socialism: Soviet Criticisms of China*, Princeton, N.J.: Princeton University Press, 1985.

Slider, Darrell, "The First 'National' Referendum and the Referenda in the Republics," *Journal of Soviet Nationalities*, 2, 1, Spring 1991.

Smyth, Regina A., "Ideology vs. Regional Cleavage: Do the Radicals Control the RSFSR Parliament?" *Journal of Soviet Nationalities*, I, 3, Fall 1990.

"Z" (anonymous), "The Soviet Union Has Ceased to Exist," *The New York Times*, August 31, 1990, p. 27.

Zeymal', K., "Narodnosti i ikh yazyki pri sotsializme (Nationalities and Their Languages Under Socialism)," *Kommunist*, 15:64–72, October 1988.

CHAPTER 19

Gorbachev: Diverse Perspectives

George W. Breslauer

IN MY article initiating this discussion, I argued that Gorbachev had wrought immense positive changes on the Soviet political, social, and foreign policy landscapes.[1] I depicted him as an "event-making man" who had induced or forced these changes through a strategy of transforming culture and politics before economics, and through a political tactic of "radical centrism." The strategy called for destroying the old system, and the public consciousness that had permitted it to survive, while constructing new channels of authentic political participation. The tactic entailed dominating the center of the political spectrum, playing the left and the right off against each other, and taking initiatives to keep the center of the spectrum moving to the left (i.e., in the direction of marketization and democratization), but doing so in a way that would not cause despair among the forces of coercion. I argued that comparative political science literature on transformative leadership justifies such an initial strategic focus on culture and politics, while the comparative political science literature on transitions to democracy justifies a tactic of radical centrism.

In an Afterword written two days after the 28th Congress of the CPSU (July 1990), I suggested that, following the prescriptions implicit in these bodies of literature, Gorbachev would be well advised to keep moving to the left, and to forge a workable compromise with the Yel'tsin forces, to keep the process of transition from stalling more than temporarily. This assumed, however, that Gorbachev would and could simultaneously or subsequently appease those forces on the right that might be tempted to employ extraconstitutional means to stop the transition process. I concluded that Gorbachev had performed brilliantly as a leader, and indicated my skepticism of claims that his strategy and tactics had exhausted their utility. Nonetheless, in a complex, 4×3 chart, I outlined twelve conceivable, and eight possible, scenarios for the long-term Soviet future, with four of the eight constituting historical "failure" for Gorbachev in eventually achieving democ-

First published in *Soviet Economy*, 1991, 7, 2, pp. 110–120. Selectively updated, July 1991.
1. The article (Breslauer, 1989) constitutes Chapter 14 of this volume.

ratization and marketization, and four of the eight constituting historical "success." I left open the possibility that, in longer historical perspective, Gorbachev's leadership might yet be evaluated a tragic failure.

In Fall 1990, it became increasingly clear that the gap between Gorbachev and the Yel'tsin-led forces was not going to be bridged or reduced so easily. The degree of radicalization on the left exceeded the lengths to which Gorbachev was willing to go, while personal animosities and political passions reduced the willingness of the far-left forces to compromise. Gorbachev rejected the Shatalin Plan for rapid marketization, privatization, and confederalization of the Soviet system. Subsequently, he endorsed a military crackdown in Lithuania and Latvia, a KGB crackdown on economic speculation, new restrictions on *glasnost'* in the print and electronic media, and personnel changes that strengthened political forces seeking to circumscribe political freedoms. These and other such actions created a perception among most Western analysts that Gorbachev was "moving to the right."

Peter Reddaway (1990) analyzed the early months of this trend, and anticipated some of its subsequent features. His identification of changes in personnel, mood, and political assertiveness to the right of Gorbachev led him to conclude that other important shifts were probably in the offing. He argued, therefore, that, while he could agree with much of my analysis of Gorbachev's first five years in power, the subsequent evolution of events led him to conclude that Gorbachev was likely soon to be proven a tragic figure, and that his project was about to fail. Archie Brown (1990) demurred from Reddaway's conclusion, while conceding that right-wing forces and tendencies were becoming visibly stronger. Andranik Migranyan (1990), in turn, argued that Gorbachev could not reconstitute the political "center," but could use his continuing political strength to ease the transition to a confederal system.

Recent events, I believe, reinforce the conditional optimism expressed by Archie Brown and myself. Because we did not view Gorbachev as either a prisoner or a spiritual ally of extreme right-wing forces, we would be inclined to treat the period, October 1990 to April 1991, as a stalemate, during which both the right and the left were able to frustrate the realization of their antagonists' goals. What happened in April–May 1991, then, would be interpreted as a progressive breakout from that stalemate. As suggested by the theories I had used in my article, that stalemate was broken only when the costs of either repression or continued deadlock appeared to outweigh the costs of mutual compromise. The miners' strikes may have played a crucial role in forcing that calculation onto Gorbachev and his allies, while political mobilization on the right,and Gorbachev's demonstrated willingness to accommodate right-wing forces, may have been decisive in changing calculations on the left. Boris Yel'tsin's landslide victory in the June 1991 election for President of the Russian Republic must have reinforced Gorbachev's decision to move again to the left, and facilitated his defeat of a right-wing challenge later that month. By mid-July 1991, a truce, and a series of compromises, had been forged between

Gorbachev and the radicals, including Gorbachev's tacit endorsement of the creation of a new, left-wing political party to challenge the CPSU. The compromises may not hold, and new stalemates may appear. Hence, there is no point in declarations of vindication, much less victory, by either optimistic or pessimistic analysts. Yet it is worthwhile to analyze the assumptions underlying divergent analyses.

JERRY HOUGH'S CRITIQUE

Jerry Hough's (1991) critique takes issue, to varying degrees, with all the previous contributors to this discussion. His perspective is nicely reflected in his analysis of events since October 1990. In Hough's view, Gorbachev moved to the right of his own free will, in order to jettison the Yel'tsin forces and put an end to the disorder he had intentionally stimulated during 1988–1990. Hence, this was not a period of "stalemate," and it was not broken by a "compromise" in April/May 1991. Rather, Gorbachev emerged victorious and the Yel'tsin forces conceded defeat. Now Gorbachev will get on with the task he has always embraced: that of ruling like a dictator over a process of transition to a marketized economy and a federal system.

But Hough's article is more than simply a dissenting portrayal of Gorbachev's power and principles. It is also a hard-hitting critique of Sovietologists who disagree with him. Thus, Reddaway's predictions had been based upon several images and assumptions that Hough for some reason attributes to the entire Sovietological profession. Reddaway saw Gorbachev as a political captive of right-wing forces, with little political autonomy to turn the tide, and with very little popular support. Reddaway's analysis treated much of Soviet officialdom as a ruling bureaucracy, the privileges of which would be threatened by further appeasement of the Yel'tsin-led forces on the left.[2] The author also claimed that Soviet society is in a pre-revolutionary situation, with the only stabilizing alternative to civil war, anarchy, mass revolution, or Russite fascism being the bureaucracy's acquiescence in privatization of the economy, democratization of the political system, and shrinkage *cum* confederalization of the Union. The burden of Jerry Hough's article is to debunk these images and assumptions, and to discredit the authors who adhere to them.

Hough's article brings together several *types* of claims. One type concerns the allegedly myopic intellectual history of Sovietology. A second concerns the nature of Gorbachev's actual political strategy and acumen. A third concerns the workability of Gorbachev's transition strategy. And a fourth type (to which much less attention is given) concerns the requisites of leadership evaluation as an intellectual task. Although I share with Jerry Hough an urge to distance myself from many of Reddaway's assumptions, and while I agree with many

2. On the other hand, he also perceived differences of interest within the organizations comprising officialdom: "The military, KGB, and MVD are sufficiently divided politically that they might refuse to obey some of his orders" (Reddaway, 1990, p. 137).

specific points in Hough's article, I also find myself uncomfortable with many of the alternative perspectives he advances. Hence, I will pay considerable attention to Jerry Hough's analysis, and shall address each of the types of claims in the order just indicated.

THE STATE OF THE ART

After reading the preceding chapter an impression is gained that the Sovietological profession is guilty of the sin of collective misjudgment. According to Jerry Hough, it has gotten it all wrong during the past six years.[3] As I read his charge, Hough identifies seven maladies afflicting Sovietologists: (1) a poor prediction record; (2) incorrect specification of Gorbachev's goals, values, strategy, and political acumen; (3) logical inconsistency in the evolution of characterizations of Gorbachev; (4) misunderstanding of the nature and developmental dynamics of Soviet society and politics; (5) misperception of the current distribution of attitudes within Soviet society and politics; (6) lack of theoretical and comparative sophistication; and (7) a motivated bias not to learn from mistakes, in order to continue assisting "radical," revolutionary," or "Bukharinite" friends in Moscow.

Hough asks us to adopt a differentiated view of Soviet society and politics, yet simultaneously depicts the Sovietological profession as a monolith. There may be many individuals[4] who are "guilty" of some of these charges, and there may even be some who are "guilty" of all of them. Without even conducting research on the matter, I am certain that most American specialists on the USSR are "innocent" of simultaneous infection by the *entirety* of this complex syndrome. Can the above, blanket charges be documented? Quite likely, some investigators would be especially curious and eager to track the methodology for documenting hidden, or even conscious, motives (charge No. 7).

Some of Jerry Hough's specific charges, in my opinion, are not defensible, such as the claim that Gorbachev "has never been given any credit for ideas of his own." Others are easy foils or straw men, such as the argument that Gorbachev "cannot have been as naive or shortsighted as many seem to have believed." Still others are simply questionable, such as the claim that Hough's work on participation in the USSR in the 1960s and 1970s "had almost no influence on American scholarly thinking": what was the "totalitarianism versus pluralism" debate that dominated the field in the 1970s all about?[5] And

3. On this score, the language in the paper is more difficult to live with than misleading. Jerry Hough points out that *he* was usually correct, but then writes about and addresses the profession (of which, of course, he is a distinguished member) as the "we" who had it all wrong.

4. It is not clear to me whether Hough's targets encompass scholars, journalists, newspaper editorial writers, American politicians, or all of these.

5. Hough is more correct in his claim that few scholars viewed the pluralization under Brezhnev as presaging elite-initiated radical reform after Brezhnev. Most scholars used their evidence of debates and influence to make a point about the nature of politics under Brezhnev, rather than a point about the impact of modernization and its implications for the future. To the extent that they reflected on the future, they saw debates as presaging either the creation of more dissidents or the development of a political base for "moderate reform" after Brezhnev. Furthermore, only one extremist wing among Sovietologists treated politics as meaningful only if it was based

still others are plausible, yet controversial, such as his eclectic use of selected bodies of comparative literature to buttress specific arguments (a point to which I will return below).

GORBACHEV'S VALUES AND STRATEGY

Turning attention now to the specification of Gorbachev's strategy and goals, the credibility of Jerry Hough's claims increases dramatically, in part because they are more nuanced, and in part because he has marshaled, here and elsewhere, a formidable body of circumstantial evidence to support his perspective. For example, Sovietologists have debated whether Gorbachev learned from the experience of 1985–1986 that more radical reform was required, or whether he understood this all along and was consolidating his power before launching a program he had worked out well in advance. I myself have wavered between these positions, but have been increasingly persuaded by Hough's accumulating evidence, as well as by other information that has become available.[6]

I also find persuasive Hough's account of Gorbachev's power consolidation strategy. And I am partial to his conceptualization of the political spectrum as populated by extreme and moderate reactionaries, moderate and radical reformers, and revolutionaries, though it is important to bear in mind that the Soviet revolutionaries in question are of the Vaclav Havel variety, and do not espouse violent revolution (a point that is important to bear in mind when using social scientific theories of revolution to predict their effectiveness or their fate). I also agree that Gorbachev's recent strategy has aimed at driving a wedge between the separatists and the "moderates" in the minority republics.

Hough and I part company again, however, regarding the specification of Gorbachev's "non-negotiables." Interestingly, on this score Hough stands closer to Peter Reddaway's than to Archie Brown's position. In Hough's view, Gorbachev is a "modernizing, Westernizing czar" such as ruled the Newly Industrializing Countries (henceforth NICs, such as Singapore, Taiwan, and South Korea) in the 1950s through 1970s. Gorbachev, according to Hough, would be more likely to declare martial law than to accept electoral defeat. He will never accept the withdrawal of any republic from the USSR, even by constitutional means. To buttress his case, Hough advances a continuity thesis consistent with his political explanation of 1985–1986: Gorbachev has always been a radical reformer, but has never been a revolutionary.

In contrast, Archie Brown refuses to embrace a specific definition of Gor-

---

on "efforts to organize the popular overthrow of the ruling class" (Hough, 1991, p. 91). For conflicting Sovietological perspectives on what the post-Brezhnev era would hold, see Breslauer (1978), Wesson (1980, *passim.*), Byrnes (1983, *passim.*), and Colton (1984).

6. For example, Boris Yel'tsin, 1990, p. 127, claims that the anti-alcohol campaign was launched in 1985 at *Ligachev's* initiative, not Gorbachev's. For my endorsement of the "political," rather than "learning" explanation for Gorbachev's apparent conservatism on economic issues, see Breslauer (1989, pp. 307–308). Nonetheless, it remains to be determined to what extent Gorbachev's understanding of Soviet nationalities problems predated 1987–1988. Hough (1991) presents some useful new data in support of a political explanation, but it seems to me that the debate remains inconclusive.

bachev's limits, arguing that the man has evolved pragmatically over time and proved willing to accept degrees of democratization he did not earlier anticipate. This adaptation is consistent with the framework I advanced in my earlier article. In the face of hard choices, Gorbachev decided that the costs of repression (both the internal and the international costs) exceeded the costs of tolerance, and subsequently made a virtue of necessity by endorsing the radicalization as "learning democracy." It would be surprising were he not subsequently to have internalized, at least partially, the values and beliefs he espoused to justify his adaptations. This is precisely one pattern of elite adaptation that has been highlighted in recent comparative political science literature on transitions to democracy among late-democratizers.

Hough may nonetheless prove to be correct about Gorbachev's limits; time will tell. But when we look back, it will be important that our criteria for evaluation are clear. Hough's argument that Gorbachev will never countenance "full Western democracy" is too underspecified to serve as such a criterion. And Hough's claim that Gorbachev will not tolerate Polish-style "shock therapy" for the economy constitutes a position on tactics that does not spell the difference between a radical and a revolutionary.

ON THE EFFECTIVENESS OF GORBACHEV'S STRATEGY

Let us turn now to Jerry Hough's claims about the effectiveness of Gorbachev's strategy. As Hough sees it, Gorbachev remains firmly in control, and is in no danger of either revolution or military coup. This argument is a striking contrast to Reddaway's, and I find myself somewhat closer to Hough than to Reddaway on this score. It seems to me that Gorbachev has indeed rigged the political process to a point that it would be very difficult to dislodge him by constitutional means. However, violent revolution is not the only means by which public pressure can topple a leader or a regime, as the examples of East Europe demonstrate. Ungovernability caused by prolonged wildcat strikes, a collapse of morale within the elite, elite efforts to buy off popular discontent by sacrificing the current leader—these are all time-honored means by which leaders can fall. Perhaps because Hough, in this article at least, depreciates the relative importance of ideas (other than nationalism) in the maintenance of elite morale and cohesion, and perhaps because he assumes that limited economic reform will quickly buy off popular discontent, he gives little or no credence to these scenarios.

I too, if forced to bet, would wager on Gorbachev's political longevity, but for different reasons. I do not share Reddaway's or Migranyan's perception that the center has collapsed in Soviet politics. I still view Gorbachev as an indispensable liaison and mediator, whose political power and radical centrism offset backlash tendencies, force compromises on extremists to the left, and create bandwagoning incentives for the many fence-sitters. Gorbachev's recent victories within the Central Committee and USSR Supreme Soviet, and his compromise "at the dacha" with nine republic presidents, along with Boris Yel'tsin's conciliatory rhetoric of May–July 1991, suggest that Gorbachev enjoys more political autonomy than was indicated by Reddaway's analysis. I agree with Hough's contention that heavy reliance on statements by Yel'tsin's allies as barometers of Soviet elite and public opinion (a feature of Reddaway's article) is a misguided research strategy.

Hough concedes that Gorbachev may fail, but considers success to be the better wager. He bets that the separatist republics will calm down and accept their fate, in the awareness that Russians will shoot them down if they press for independence. Meanwhile, Gorbachev will rule like a czar over a quasi-democracy in which legislatures are very weak, and in which a conservative Russian population will view Gorbachev as a laudable centrist. All this will be accepted by the Russians because agricultural and service reforms will improve both the consumer situation and, more important yet, the opportunities for upward social mobility. The Communist Party, he argues, may even become a dominant party in Slavic areas on the Mexican or Japanese models "for the rest of this century."

This is certainly an optimistic scenario, from the standpoint of those who either depreciate democratic values, believe that Russia is not ready for multi-party democracy, or believe (as did Migranyan) that an authoritarian phase of historical development is required before a "totalitarian" Soviet regime can develop a market economy and a social class with a propertied stake in further democratization. Hough seems to endorse Migranyan's perspective when he argues that European democratization took more than a century and that there are no shortcuts. Perhaps this will prove to be the case, but it is worth bearing in mind that numerous schools of thought exist among "comparative political scientists" regarding the prerequisites for democratization.

ON THE USE OF COMPARATIVE ANALYSIS

Some of Jerry Hough's generalizations about revolutions and secession strike me as sound points. However, at a deeper level, I do not quite know what to make of Hough's use of comparative analogs. His optimistic picture of where the USSR will be for the remainder of this century is based upon an eclectic invocation of disparate comparative referents. When measuring power in the Soviet system, we are asked to think of British politics and of American party conventions. When thinking about the stability of multi-ethnic states, we are told to treat the Soviet Union as analogous to a Third World empire (African or Asian). When pondering Gorbachev as a "modernizing czar," we are urged to think of the East Asian NICs as our referent. When considering the electoral appeal of the CPSU in Slavic republics, we are told to focus our minds on Mexico and Japan. When thinking about the social base for reform in the USSR, we are told to recognize the universal impact of social modernization in creating an educated, sophisticated middle class.

But when thinking about the *Russian* middle class, we are told to think of them as ethnic Russians and material acquisitives first and foremost, not as latent democrats whose conscience would be violated, and political behavior affected, by having Russian troops sent regularly to shoot down separatists, or by having their elections canceled.

There may be a coherence here, but I cannot define it. Each specific point has a plausibility to it, but the sum total does not add up. Hough is depicting a relatively smooth path (my term, not his) to marketization and eventual democratization, without reducing the territorial size of the current Union. In my earlier article, I defined that as a least likely scenario. Perhaps that skepticism derives from my greater emphasis on three factors that Hough's analysis underplays: (1) elite self-legitimation and the role of ideas in maintaining elite cohesion and morale; (2) the impact of international incentives and sanctions on Soviet elite calculations; and (3) the experiences of 1989–1990 in Eastern Europe, where the issue was not violent revolution (on which matters Hough's comparative generalizations are sound), but rather a situation of diminished governability, loss of legitimacy, splits in the elite, and selective or complete abdication.

I am not claiming that the USSR is heading toward a 1989. Russian nationalism may indeed mute expressions of political defiance, the young middle class may aspire largely to become economic entrepreneurs, and the CPSU may prove able to maintain selectively its organizational and electoral dominance in *rural* areas of the Russian Republic (as has been the case in rural Bulgaria, Rumania, Albania, and Serbia). But, if all this comes to pass, my guess is that it will be a highly unstable equilibrium, with its further evolution highly unpredictable. Because of this inherent unpredictability, I find myself torn between the projection of my hopes (a zig-zag path to marketization, democratization, and partial dismemberment) and the projection of my fears (Ottomanization and extreme backlash).

Based upon my reading of the comparativist literature on leadership, I have been impressed by the apparent correspondence between Gorbachev's behavior and what is called for in cases of transformative leadership. Beyond that, however, no existing body of literature can tell us what will produce a progressive and stable equilibrium in a situation such as that in which the Soviets find themselves. Indeed, no grounded theories can demonstrate that such equilibrium is even within the realm of possibility.

ON LEADERSHIP EVALUATION

The final issue on which Jerry Hough advances claims is the task of leadership evaluation. On this score, he takes issue with me in three respects. First, he argues that since we disagree about the degree to which Gorbachev was being reactive (as opposed to Machiavellian) during 1988–1989, it is impossible to evaluate Gorbachev's leadership. Second, and related to the first, he argues that I "evaluate the quality of Gorbachev's leadership on the basis of mistaken assumptions about his strategy that are held by our Bukharinite friends in the Soviet Union.'' Third, he contends that leadership evaluation in midstream is inappropriate; we should first see whether Gorbachev survives the next few years and whether reform goes forward or not.

I have already addressed the third objection in my earlier article. Midstream analysis is not inappropriate, only limiting, as I indicated by leaving open the question of whether Gorbachev would ultimately be judged by historians to have been a tragic or a transformational leader. Yet, in Gorbachev's case, a partial, highly positive, retrospective evaluation is in order, given the striking changes he has brought about at home and abroad.

As for Hough's first objection, I simply disagree. Whether Gorbachev was being reactive or initiatory in 1988–1989, what counted was the choice he made in his response to events, not whether he anticipated or instigated them. True, if he actually instigated them, he might be dubbed even more politically adroit than we might otherwise assume. But the general task of leadership evaluation ultimately hinges on values, results, and responses. Evaluations of Franklin Delano Roosevelt, Charles DeGaulle, and Winston Churchill do not hinge on these leaders' synoptic capacities.

As to whether we can engage in leadership evaluation without detailed specification of the leader's strategy, I am of two minds. On the one hand, it is surely necessary to know what a leader was trying to do if one wants to evaluate his skill at accomplishing it. On the other hand, I am not convinced that leadership evaluation necessarily requires one to take the leader's goals as one's standard for evaluation. By that method (and to reduce things to absurdity), if one argues that Leonid Brezhnev merely wanted to stay in power until he died, Brezhnev's leadership was a great success.

But success on the leader's own terms is different from success as a "transformative leader" or an "event-making man." Gorbachev has been an "event-making man" in both domestic and foreign affairs because he has destroyed the old system and begun a process of transformation in a direction that is well captured by the processual phrases, "marketization," "democratization," and "federalization" (if not, "decolonization"), whether or not he possessed mixed motives in fostering processes of *de facto* democratization. How far he goes down each of these paths remains to be seen, but I see little reason to doubt the aptness of the concepts for characterizing the process of transition he has nurtured.

Furthermore, thinking of things in this way alerts one also to the contradictions among these processes, and to the skill (or lack thereof) with which Gorbachev handles those contradictions. True, the task is unprecedented, and is not likely to proceed smoothly. But because I perceive Gorbachev's radical centrism not to have exhausted its utility for dealing with those contradictions, I share Archie Brown's conclusion that we should not write off Gorbachev's ability to keep the transition process on track without sacrificing the democratization project. And because I believe that Gorbachev would be neither inclined nor able to stuff the democratization genie very far back into the bottle, I choose to evaluate him on the basis of his ability to cope with all these tasks, not just economic reform and federalization. On this score, I would accord him very high marks for services already rendered, and leave to future historians the task of judging his "ultimate" success.

CONCLUSION

It strikes me that this extended discussion has been useful in highlighting diverse approaches to the task of leadership evaluation. Whether one chooses to adopt Gorbachev's values and program, or those of his more radical opponents, as one's standard, one can employ any of three *time-spans* for judging his contribution: retrospective; near-term future; and long-term future. A retrospective approach (what has he accomplished in six years?) can yield a positive evaluation if one is impressed by how much he has transformed since 1985 and if one believes that destroying the ideological and organizational power of the old system was a prerequisite for progress. Alternatively, a retrospective evaluation can be negative if, like Migranyan, one argues that Gorbachev has missed opportunities to embrace a strategy likely to make democratization irreversible.[7]

A future-oriented approach can be linked to retrospective evaluation (as in Migranyan's argument) or can be explicitly of the "wait-and-see" variety. In this discussion we have seen two types of wait-and-see argument. One focuses on the near-term, and is adopted by Reddaway and Hough. Reddaway's suggestion that Gorbachev's leadership has run its course, and is about to give way to a right-wing reaction, portends a negative near-term evaluation. Hough's suggestion that Gorbachev will soon push through radical economic reform that will stabilize the country portends a positive near-term evaluation.[8]

The second type of wait-and-see argument takes a long-term perspective on the processes of transformation now in train. This is an approach I outlined in the chart in my earlier article. Unless one adheres dogmatically to a theory of history which forecasts the outcome of these processes, one must leave open the possibility that Gorbachev's leadership will ultimately be judged either tragic or transformational. Yet one can simultaneously engage in retrospective evaluation of Gorbachev's accomplishments to date. A positive evaluation of those accomplishments is only inconsistent with an eventual, negative evaluation of Gorbachev's ultimate historical accomplishments if one believes that, in his first six years, Gorbachev irretrievably lost opportunities to set his country on the correct path.

7. On the other hand, there is an unresolved tension within Migranyan's articles as to whether the path of democratization is recoverable. This mirrors a major intellectual challenge for social science: to define conditions that spell the difference between missed opportunities and (irretrievably) lost opportunities.

8. Hough makes explicit his preferred temporal approach to evaluation by arguing that we suspend judgments about the quality of Gorbachev's leadership "until one sees how it turns out—at least to learn whether he survives the next few years and whether reform goes forward or not."

REFERENCES

Breslauer, George W., *Five Images of the Soviet Future: A Critical Review and Synthesis.* Berkeley, Calif.: University of California, Institute of International Studies, 1978.

————, "Evaluating Gorbachev as Leader," *Soviet Economy,* 5, 4:299–340, October–December 1989.

Brown, Archie, "Gorbachev's Leadership: Another View," *Soviet Economy,* 6, 2:141–154, April–June 1990.

Byrnes, Robert, ed., *After Brezhnev: The Sources of Soviet Conduct in the 1980s.* Bloomington: Indiana University Press, 1983.

Colton, Timothy, *The Dilemma of Reform in the Soviet Union,* first edition. New York: Council on Foreign Relations, 1984.

Hough, Jerry F., "Understanding Gorbachev: The Importance of Politics," *Soviet Economy,* 7, 2:89–109, April–June 1991.

Migranyan, A., "Dolgiy put' k yevropeyskomu domu" (The Long Road to the European Home), *Novvy Mir,* 7:166–184, 1989.

————, "Gorbachev's Leadership: A Soviet View," *Soviet Economy,* 6, 2:155–159, April–June 1990.

Reddaway, Peter, "The Quality of Gorbachev's Leadership," *Soviet Economy,* 6, 2:125–154, April–June 1990.

Wesson, Robert, ed., *The Soviet Union: Looking to the 1980s.* Stanford, Calif.: Hoover Institution Press, 1980.

Yel'tsin, Boris, *Against the Grain.* New York: Summit Books, 1990.

Part V

Epilogue

Half Measures

Yevgeniy Yevtushenko

Half measures can kill when on the brink of precipices,
chafing in terror at the bit,
we strain and sweat and foam because we cannot
jump just halfway across.

Blind is the one who but half sees the chasm,
and half recoils because he lost his way,
half mutineer and half suppressor
of the rebellion he has spawned.

Semi-effective semi-actions push the half-people
back to the half-rear,
the half satiated ones are but half hungry,
and those half free—are half enslaved.

Half fearful, halfway on the rampage . . .
a bit of this and yet a half of that,

a timid party-line towing "Robin Hood"
half walking to a semi-guillotine.

Lost is the opposition's firmness.
Swashbuckling with a wispy sword,

The Russian-language original first appeared in print in *Ogonyok* (Ivanidze, 1990, p. 29); an earlier version of the English-language translation by Alexis N. Obolensky and Victor H. Winston had appeared elsewhere (Hewett; *The New York Times*, February 7, 1990, p. A25; Gore, 1990). The poem was composed, recited, and then written down at a private dinner in Moscow on January 16, 1990. At the dinner table, in addition to Yevgeniy Yevtushenko, were Senator Albert Gore, Jr., Leon Fuerth, Victor H. Winston, Inter-Regional Group leader and current mayor of Moscow Gavriil Popov, and *Ogonyok's* Vitaliy Korotich and Lev Gushchin (Hewett). [Eds.]

one cannot be a half-guard with the cardinal,
and simultaneously half a king's musketeer.

There is no semi-fatherland,
nor can we fathom semi-conscience;
half freedom is the trek to jail,
and saving our fatherland halfway
would fail at bay.

REFERENCES

Gore, Albert, Jr., "Yevgeny Yevtushenko," *Congressional Record*, 136, 11:S1062, February 8, 1990.

Hewett, Ed A., "Editorial Periscope," *Soviet Economy*, 5, 2:104–106.

Ivanidze, Vladimir, "Karabakh, bol' moya . . . (Karabakh, My Pain . . .)," *Ogonyok*, 4(3261):26–29, January 1990.

Chronology of Noteworthy Events, March 11, 1985–July 11, 1991

1985

March

11 Mikhail S. Gorbachev is named General Secretary of the Communist Party of the Soviet Union (CPSU).

12 U.S.-USSR negotiations on nuclear and space arms begin in Geneva.

17 Soviet diplomat defects to U.S. from post in New Delhi.

18 *Pravda* articles encouraging new forms of CPSU management accelerate campaign against corruption and inefficiency.

24 Soviet soldier kills U.S. officer in Potsdam, East Germany. U.S. retaliates by expelling USSR military attaché from Washington, D.C.

April

7 Gorbachev announces unilateral, six-month freeze on deployment of intermediate-range nuclear missiles in Europe.

8 Gorbachev's new emphasis on increased economic production is voiced at meeting of the Central Committee (CC) of CPSU.

16 Andrey Sakharov's hunger strikes begin in Gorkiy.

17 USSR announces unilateral nuclear test moratorium set to begin in August.

18 Local governments are ordered to take steps to promote expanded production of high-quality goods and services.

23 Leadership changes are announced at CC CPSU Plenum. KGB head Viktor Chebrikov and CC CPSU Secretaries Nikolay Ryzhkov and Yegor Ligachev are promoted to full Politburo membership; Minister of Defense Sergey Sokolov is named candidate member.

26 Warsaw Treaty Organization (WTO) is renewed for 20 years.

May

15 Gorbachev's speech during visit to Leningrad demonstrates new style of leadership.

17 Decrees are issued to control production, sale, and consumption of alcohol.

20 U.S. Navy officer John Walker is arrested by FBI for attempting to sell classified documents to USSR. Arrest of three accomplices follows shortly thereafter.

21 New bilateral U.S.-USSR trade agreement is announced.

27 Gorbachev calls Geneva talks "fruitless," pointing to plans for Strategic Defense Initiative (SDI) as obstacle to arms agreement.

June

11 Gorbachev addresses CC proposing new economic program to promote efficiency.

14 USSR expels U.S. diplomat for espionage.

18 U.S. cancels annual meeting of U.S.-USSR naval officers to protest Potsdam killing.

18–19 U.S. and USSR negotiations in Washington, D.C., focus on Afghanistan.

23 Gorbachev's popularity is in evidence during visit to Kiev.

July

1 Grigoriy Romanov is compelled to retire from Politburo at CC CPSU Plenum. Promotions include Eduard Shevardnadze, who becomes full member, and Lev Zaykov and Boris Yel'tsin, who gain positions in CPSU Secretariat.

2 USSR Supreme Soviet (VS) approves Andrey Gromyko as chairman of its Presidium. Eduard Shevardnadze replaces Gromyko as Foreign Minister.

10 USSR and China sign trade agreement.

12 Measures expanding decisionmaking power of enterprises in 1986 are decreed by CC and Council of Ministers (CM).

16 Second round of U.S.-USSR arms talks ends in Geneva.

August

1 Gorbachev is named head of Defense Council.

6 USSR institutes five-month unilateral moratorium on nuclear testing.

21 U.S. accuses USSR of using carcinogenic powder to track movements of diplomats.

26 Anti-alcohol campaign is stepped up. CM issues resolution to raise prices of alcoholic beverages.

26 Gorbachev criticizes U.S. anti-Soviet rhetoric in *Time* magazine interview.

September

4 USSR urges U.S. to cancel planned antisatellite test and threatens to void Soviet commitment to a two-year deployment ban.

10 Gorbachev proposes a chemical weapons–free zone in central Europe.

12 Britain expels 25 Soviet diplomats for espionage, which prompts a series of retaliatory expulsions during the following week.

19 U.S.-USSR nuclear and space weapons negotiations resume in Geneva.

26 U.S. reveals defection of KGB agent Vitaliy Yurchenko.

27 Nikolay Tikhonov is replaced by Nikolay Ryzhkov as chairman of CM.

30 USSR proposes a 50 percent reduction in long-range weapons.

October

2–6 Gorbachev visits France and proposes arms agreements with France and Britain which bypass U.S.

9 *Pravda* publishes long-term economic program emphasizing production of consumer goods and services.

15 Nikolay Talyzin becomes candidate member of Politburo.

23 USSR proposes freeze on intermediate-range missile deployments.

24 Andrey Sakharov ends series of hunger strikes in Gorkiy after Yelena Bonner receives permission to travel abroad.

26 Draft of revised program of the CPSU (first new program since 1961) is published in *Pravda*.

27 USSR proposes to halt construction of radar at Krasnoyarsk, predicating offer on reduction of U.S. radar installations in Britain and Greenland.

November

4 Vitaliy Yurchenko alleges kidnapping by CIA and departs days later for USSR.

7 Geneva arms talks adjourn.

19 Gorbachev's first summit meeting with U.S. President begins in Geneva.

21 Summit ends, yielding agreements with President Ronald Reagan on air safety, resumption of athletic, cultural, educational, and scientific exchanges, and accord on environmental protection.

23 Five ministries and a committee are merged to form the *Gosagroprom* to oversee agricultural production.

25 Former National Security Agency specialist Ronald Pelton is arrested by FBI for espionage on behalf of USSR.

December

7 Incidence of AIDS in USSR is officially acknowledged.

24 Boris Yel'tsin becomes first secretary of the Moscow *Gorkom*, replacing Viktor Grishin.

29 USSR denies alleged violations of Antiballistic Missile (ABM) and Strategic Arms Limitation Talks II (SALT II) treaties.

1986

January

1 Exchange of New Year's greetings between Gorbachev and Reagan is televised in USSR.

15 Gorbachev proposes elimination of nuclear weapons by the end of decade, and extends nuclear testing moratorium for additional three months. Shevardnadze begins first visit to Japan.

16 Fourth round of nuclear and space arms negotiations opens in Geneva.

February

8 Gorbachev's pronouncements in *L'Humanité* include negative references to Andrey Sakharov, and dismiss Stalinism as "concept" that slanders USSR.

11 Anatoly Shcharansky crosses to West Berlin in East-West exchange of prisoners.

18 Politburo member Viktor Grishin is compelled to retire.

25 Twenty-seventh Congress of CPSU, marked by Gorbachev's call for economic reform and sweeping personnel changes in CC, opens in Moscow. Politburo members Boris Ponomarev and Vasiliy Kuznetsov are retired. Lev Zaykov is promoted to full membership, and Yuriy Solov'yev and Nikolay Slyun'kov become candidate members.

March

3 Andrey Sakharov's letter to Gorbachev is officially acknowledged.

7 U.S. orders limits on personnel in USSR, Ukrainian, and Belorussian missions to UN, which prompts diplomatic protest.

10 Two U.S. warships steam to waters within six miles of Soviet Black Sea coast in defiance of declared twelve-mile limit.

13 Gorbachev proposes indefinite nuclear test moratorium in exchange for moratorium on testing by U.S.

15 Gorbachev encourages mass-media officials to criticize bureaucracy in CPSU.

April

1 Three-day protest demonstrations by university students begin in Yakutsk.

10 TASS announces intent to resume nuclear testing after second U.S. test in 1986.

24 Anticommunist poems by Nikolay Gumilev are published for the first time in USSR.

26 Reactor at Chernobyl' nuclear power plant explodes. Authorities make first announcement about the accident four days later.

29 USSR requests assistance from West Germany and Sweden to combat Chernobyl' fire.

29 Commercial flights between U.S. and USSR resume after eight-year interruption.

May

8 Fifth round of U.S.-USSR arms control negotiations begins in Geneva.

14 Gorbachev proposes four-point program to strengthen the International Atomic Energy Agency in a televised speech prompted by Chernobyl'. USSR nuclear testing moratorium is extended to August 6.

15–17 Elem Klimov becomes first secretary of the Union of Filmmakers, which prompts subsequent release of previously banned films.

20 USSR announces replacement of Anatoliy F. Dobrynin by Yuriy V. Dubinin as ambassador to U.S.

28 CC and CM decree measures to thwart incomes in second economy.

29 USSR negotiators in Geneva offer arms reduction proposals in exchange for U.S. adherence to strict interpretation of ABM treaty for 15 to 20 years.

June

10–11 WTO summit in Budapest adopts proposal for reducing NATO-WTO forces by 100,000 to 150,000 men within two years.

16 CC CPSU Plenum adopts draft of Twelfth Five-Year Plan for 1986–1990.

18–19 Fifth session of VS enacts legislation on economic and social development.

July

18 Gorbachev meets former President Richard Nixon in Moscow.

22 U.S. and USSR arms negotiators hold special session of Standing Consultative Committee in Geneva to discuss U.S. threat to abrogate SALT II.

25 President Reagan offers to delay SDI deployment.

28 Gorbachev's major foreign policy speech in Vladivostok advances five-point plan for regional cooperation in Asia, offers to withdraw six military regiments from Afghanistan, and proposes improved relations with China.

31 Seven-day negotiating session in Geneva on verification of underground nuclear tests comes to end.

August

5 U.S. and USSR announce program of 13 educational, scientific, and cultural exchanges.

18 Gorbachev announces extension of nuclear testing moratorium until end of 1986.

19 Foreign sector of economy is reorganized to encourage joint ventures with Council for Mutual Economic Assistance (CMEA) and Western firms.

20 Cancellation of river diversion projects is announced.

23 Soviet UN employee Gennadiy F. Zakharov is arrested by FBI for espionage.

28 Measures for improvement of wage and salary scales are introduced.

30 U.S. journalist Nicholas S. Daniloff is detained in Moscow for alleged espionage.

September

5–8 President Reagan demands Daniloff's release, terming arrest and indictment on September 7 an "outrage."

12 Zakharov and Daniloff are released and placed in custody of their embassies, pending trial.

17 U.S. orders 25 members of USSR UN mission to leave or face expulsion.

18 Sixth round of arms control talks opens in Geneva. U.S. proposes medium-range missile limit of 200, with only 100 to be deployed within range of Europe.

18 Gorbachev rejects Reagan's demand for Daniloff's release.

19 Shevardnadze meets with Reagan to discuss Daniloff and arms control, and proposes summit meeting in Iceland.

29 USSR drops charges and releases Daniloff.

30 Daniloff arrives in U.S. Zakharov is released after pleading no contest, while USSR agrees to release dissidents Yuriy Orlov and his wife.

30 U.S. and USSR announce forthcoming summit meeting in Reykjavik, Iceland.

October

11–12 Gorbachev's second summit meeting, in Reykjavik, which focused on arms reduction, fails to yield agreement because of U.S. position on SDI research.

15 U.S.-USSR arms talks resume in Geneva.

16 Model statute on cooperatives is decreed by CC and CM.

19 Five U.S. diplomats are ordered to leave the USSR.

21 Order to 55 Soviet diplomats to leave the U.S. is followed by the expulsion of 5 additional U.S. diplomats and the withdrawal of Soviet service personnel from U.S. consulates in Moscow and Leningrad.

22 Gorbachev's television address accuses U.S. of misrepresenting Soviet proposals at Reykjavik.

November

4 Conference on Security and Cooperation in Europe opens in Vienna to review 1975 Helsinki accords on human rights.

7 USSR announces grounds for acceptance of applications to emigrate.

8 Vyacheslav M. Molotov dies.

10 Gorbachev attends meeting of CMEA leaders in Moscow.

15 New measures to streamline quality control in production are promoted by Gorbachev at CC CPSU Plenum.

19 VS considers legislation allowing private entrepreneurs to manufacture selected consumer goods and provide basic services.

21 Law authorizing entrepreneurial economic activities by individuals is enacted.

December

5 USSR qualifies adherence to SALT II treaty obligations after U.S. deployment of B-52 armed with cruise missiles.

16 Politburo member and Kazakhstan CP head Dinmukhamed A. Kunayev is compelled to relinquish party post to Gennadiy Kolbin (an ethnic Russian). Several hundred students participate in anti-Russian protest riots in Alma-Ata during following two days.

16 Gorbachev telephones Andrey Sakharov in Gorkiy to initiate his return from exile. Sakharov's meeting with Academy of Sciences President Guriy I. Marchuk follows.

18 USSR announces intent to end nuclear testing moratorium after a test planned by U.S.

23 Andrey Sakharov and Yelena Bonner leave Gorkiy and return to Moscow.

29 Fifty Soviet émigrés return to Moscow from U.S.

1987

January

1 Quality control under *Gospriyemka* is introduced in inspection of output of selected industrial enterprises.

6 Boris Pasternak's Nobel Prize for literature is openly disclosed for the first time in USSR.

8 Viktor Chebrikov's involvement in miscarriage of justice by KGB is made public.

10 U.S. Marine Clayton Lonetree is detained after confessing security violations involving KGB agents in Moscow.

13 Decrees regulating activities of joint ventures are promulgated by CC and CM.

15 U.S. Department of Commerce lifts control on exports of oil-drilling equipment to USSR.

15 U.S.-USSR talks on strategic and medium-range nuclear missiles resume in Geneva.

27–28 CC CPSU Plenum during which Gorbachev accuses CPSU of stagnation and calls for secret balloting with multiple candidates for government positions and affiliated delegates. Dinmukhamed Kunayev leaves Politburo; Aleksandr Yakovlev becomes candidate member. Anatoliy Luk'yanov and Nikolay Slyun'kov are elected to CC Secretariat.

February

3 Brezhnev's son-in-law, Yuriy Churbanov, is arrested for alleged corruption.

8 Daily protests begin in Moscow in support of Jewish dissident Yosif Begun.

10 USSR announces release of 140 political prisoners (the largest release of such detainees since 1956).

12 Dissidents and supporters demonstrating in Moscow are assaulted by plainclothes security police.

12 Decree on local cooperatives is promulgated by CM.

14–16 USSR hosts international peace and disarmament forum. Andrey Sakharov participates in proceedings, voicing appeal for democracy.

25 Gorbachev addresses labor union convention, declaring that "democratization" is not synonymous with abandonment of socialism.

26 USSR conducts first nuclear test in 18 months, ending moratorium.

28 Gorbachev offers agreement to eliminate intermediate-range nuclear missiles in Europe.

March

6 Yegor Ligachev voices opposition to criticism of CPSU's accomplishments prior to *perestroyka*.

12 First cooperative café opens in Moscow.

13 Anatoliy Rybakov's book *Children of the Arbat* is excerpted in weekly publication.

14 Dinmukhamed Kunayev is placed under investigation for gross violations of CPSU standards.

24 Second Marine guard is arrested at U.S. embassy in Moscow.

26 A state building trust, operating under new experimental *khozraschet* system, is dissolved in first bankruptcy in USSR since 1920.

31 Yakovlev encourages *glasnost'* during meeting with journalists and media administrators.

April

2 France expels three Soviet diplomats on charges of espionage. Two French businessmen are expelled from the USSR two days later.

6 Two members of Congress inspect partially completed new U.S. embassy building in Moscow and find its security "fully compromised."

10 During visit to Prague, Gorbachev proposes to limit USSR's nuclear arsenal and destroy all chemical weapons.

11 Start of USSR troop withdrawal from Mongolia is announced.

13–15 U.S. Secretary of State George P. Shultz's visit to Moscow yields agreement to share data from unmanned space probes.

30 U.S. Secretary of Agriculture announces USSR's intended purchase of 4 million metric tons of subsidized wheat.

May

1 Law legalizing work for profit in selected consumer goods and service establishments is in force.

6 Members of antisemitic *Pamyat'* demonstrate in Moscow.

16 Successful launching of the new 100-ton *Energia* rocket is announced.

23 USSR stops jamming Voice of America transmissions for the first time since 1980, but continues interference with Radio Liberty and Radio Free Europe.

29 West German teenager Mathias Rust is arrested after landing a light aircraft in Red Square near the Kremlin.

29 Gorbachev and WTO heads of state call for direct negotiations with NATO on conventional and tactical nuclear weapons.

30 Defense Minister Sergey Sokolov is discharged and replaced by Dimitriy Yazov. Also purged is the commander of air defenses, Aleksandr Koldunov.

June

21 Multicandidate elections for local soviets take place in selected areas.

25–26 CC CPSU Plenum endorses Gorbachev's plan for partial dismantling of central economic control and price subsidies and adopts *Osnovnyye polozheniya* to guide reforms through 1991. Sergey Sokolov is removed from Politburo and replaced by Aleksandr Yakovlev. Nikolay Slyun'kov and Viktor Nikonov are promoted to full Politburo membership; Yazov becomes candidate member. Gorbachev calls for an All-Union CPSU conference (first since 1941) to be held in June 1988.

July

1 Law expanding autonomy of enterprises replaces 1965 statute following session of VS focused on economic reform.

6 Tatars begin three-week protest vigil in Moscow, demanding autonomous homeland in Crimea. Police clash with hundreds of protestors two days later.

12 Soviet consular delegation arrives in Israel.

15 Vladimir Shcherbitskiy survives purge of Ukrainian CP.

17 Six laws restructuring prices, banking, TsSU (to become *Goskomstat*), *Gosplan*, *Minfin*, and industrial ministries are enacted.

22 Gorbachev proposes global elimination of all intermediate-range nuclear missiles.

August

11 USSR confirms deployment of world's first rail-mobile missile.

11 U.S. and USSR agree in Geneva to a system of compulsory "challenge inspections" of chemical weapons facilities.

16 First markets regulated by new private business laws begin selling consumer goods in Moscow.

23 Crowds demonstrate in Vilnius, Riga, and Tallinn, marking the anniversary of the 1939 Nonaggression Pact between Germany and USSR.

September

1 New guidelines regulating rallies and demonstrations in Moscow, but banning all gatherings in Red Square, are introduced.

8 Three U.S. Congressmen visiting USSR are taken on surprise visit of Krasnoyarsk radar facility.

15 Shevardnadze's meeting with Secretary Shultz in Washington leads to tentative agreement on Intermediate-Range Nuclear Forces (INF) treaty.

24 Politburo authorizes individuals and cooperatives to operate small shops and kiosks.

29 Ignoring U.S. objections, USSR test-launches ICBM, which lands 500 miles northwest of Hawaii.

29 Gorbachev reappears on TV, ending absence from public view since mid-August.

30 Decree mandates *khozraschet* in scientific organizations.

October

21 Boris Yel'tsin addresses CC CPSU, attacking Ligachev for delay of reform, and Geydar Aliyev announces retirement from Politburo citing poor health.

23 Gorbachev's meeting with Shultz in Moscow leads to Reagan's announced consent (on October 30) to forthcoming summit meeting.

November

2 Gorbachev's speech commemorating 70th anniversary of the Bolshevik Revolution denounces Stalin and notes contributions of Nikolay Bukharin.

9 U.S.-USSR talks on banning underground nuclear testing open in Geneva.

11 Boris Yel'tsin is dismissed from leadership of Moscow *Gorkom* and replaced by Lev Zaykov.

18 Yel'tsin is relegated to deputy directorship of State Committee for Construction.
19 Chemical weapons storage facility at Tooele, Utah, is visited by Soviet delegation under terms of "challenge inspection" agreement.
22 Shevardnadze's meeting with Shultz in Geneva yields agreement on resident observers at former INF production sites and short-notice on-site inspections of former deployment sites.
30 Gorbachev's interview on U.S. television highlights proposal for 50 percent reduction in strategic nuclear arms.
30 During trip to France, Ligachev alleges authority to chair meetings of CC.

December

6 *Moscow News* publishes Nikolay Bukharin's denunciation of Stalin.
7 Gorbachev's third summit meeting and first trip to U.S. begins in Washington, D.C. Discussions with Reagan include consideration of troop withdrawal from Afghanistan.
10 End of summit yields treaty mandating destruction of about 2,600 INF missiles and mutual verification of installations for 13 years.
10 Andrey Sakharov's pronouncements on Human Rights Day deplore continued incarceration of political prisoners, but note the release of hundreds during 1987.
18 Soviet UN diplomat Mikhail Katov is expelled from U.S. for espionage.
26 USSR discloses information on its 50,000-ton chemical weapons stockpile.

1988

January

1 Law on the State Enterprise goes into effect.
11 Gorbachev's meeting with Czechoslovak leaders is followed by call for change in Eastern Europe.
12 *Novyy Mir* begins serialization of Pasternak's *Doctor Zhivago*.

February

5 USSR Supreme Court rehabilitates Nikolay Bukharin and Alexey Rykov.
6 Nikolay Talyzin is criticized for failing to implement economic reforms and is replaced as head of *Gosplan* by Yuriy Maslyukov.
8 Gorbachev proposes to terminate Soviet military presence in Afghanistan by mid-March of 1989.
11 Armenians demonstrate in the Nagorno-Karabakh region of Azerbaijan demanding its reunification with Armenia.
12 Two U.S. Navy ships are damaged by Soviet ships in purportedly Soviet territorial waters in the Black Sea.
18 Boris Yel'tsin is removed as candidate member of Politburo during two-day CC CPSU Plenum.
20 Mass demonstrations to protest Nagorno-Karabakh take place in Armenia.

26 Gorbachev calls for restoration of order after demonstrations in Yerevan.

27 USSR removes 30 medium-range missiles and five launchers from base in East Germany.

28 More than 30 Armenians die in Sumgait during ethnic rioting and pogrom by Azerbaijanis.

March

13 *Sovietskaya Rossiya* publishes letter by Nina Andreyeva defending Stalin and attacking *glasnost'* and *perestroyka*.

16 Gorbachev's speech in Belgrade blames Stalin for conflict with Tito.

16–17 Defense Secretary Frank Carlucci and Dimitriy Yazov meet in Bern for disarmament talks.

23 USSR VS obstructs transfer of territory from Azerbaijan to Armenia.

25 General strike to compel transfer of Nagorno-Karabakh to Armenia begins in Stepanakert.

26 Military and KGB troops prevent scheduled mass demonstration in Yerevan calling for unification of Nagorno-Karabakh with Armenia.

April

5 *Pravda* prints article critical of Nina Andreyeva's letter in *Sovietskaya Rossiya*.

6 Firm decision to commence withdrawal of Soviet troops from Afghanistan is reached during Gorbachev's meeting with Najibullah in Tashkent.

8 Geneva accords on Afghanistan are announced.

10 Easter services are televised for the first time in USSR.

14 Geneva accords on settlement of Afghanistan war are signed.

19 CPSU's ideological secretaryship is temporarily shifted to Aleksandr Yakovlev after Ligachev is reprimanded for support of Andreyeva's letter.

May

3–4 *Pravda* and *Izvestiya* denounce *Solidarność* and Polish labor strikes.

7 More than 100 dissidents meet in Moscow to form independent political party "Democratic Forum." Five members are arrested after forum announces opposition to CPSU and its intention to field candidates against CPSU.

11 *Literaturnaya Gazeta* prints selections from George Orwell's *1984*.

15 First military contingents return to USSR from Afghanistan.

21 New leadership of CP is installed in Armenia and Azerbaijan in attempt to control conflict.

26 Law on cooperatives is enacted by VS.

27 Soviet record on human rights is criticized by President Reagan in Helsinki.

29 Fourth summit meeting involving Reagan and Gorbachev begins in Moscow.

31 Moscow State University students are addressed by Reagan.

June

1 INF treaty ratification is formalized, and nine agreements covering arms control, nuclear power research, transportation, student exchanges, and fisheries are signed by Reagan and Gorbachev, marking end of Moscow summit.

5–12 With full state support, Russian Orthodox Church celebrates 1,000th anniversary of Christianity in Russia.

13 USSR Supreme Court voids sentences of Grigoriy Zinov'yev, Lev Kamenev, and over thirty other prominent individuals purged by Stalin.

15 Supreme Soviet of Armenian SSR passes resolution urging reunification with Nagorno-Karabakh.

20 Government of Estonian SSR officially recognizes The People's Front of Estonia.

28 Nineteenth All-Union Conference of the CPSU, the first since 1941, opens in Moscow. Gorbachev proposes restructuring of government into a system with national legislature and elected president. Other reform proposals include limits on CPSU interference in the economy, tenure of ranking officials, enhanced authority for local soviets, and multicandidate elections.

July

1 CPSU Conference ends, approving support for legal reform, democratization, greater independence for national regions, and limits on bureaucracy.

2 First inspections by Soviet representatives under terms of INF treaty take place in California.

4 General strike breaks out in Armenia. Hundreds of demonstrators confront troops and police at Yerevan airport in following days.

8 More than 200,000 demonstrate in Yerevan to commemorate deaths in airport clash.

11 Chief of Staff Sergey Akhromeyev is received by President Reagan at White House.

11 Gorbachev begins six-day visit to Poland.

12 Legislature of Nagorno-Karabakh votes to secede from Azerbaijan and join Armenian SSR.

15–16 Gorbachev and WTO leaders call for moratorium on nuclear testing and chemical weapons. Resolution ends Gorbachev's visit to Poland, which was marked by denunciation of Stalin's deportation of Poles.

28 Israeli consular delegation arrives in Moscow.

29 Gorbachev announces new political and economic reform initiatives at CC CPSU Plenum.

August

3 Release of Mathias Rust from jail reflects warming relations with West Germany.

15 Secret protocols detailing 1939 pact between Germany and USSR are printed in Estonian newspaper.

17 Nuclear test in Nevada is observed by participating Soviet scientists.

September

- 5 Yuriy Churbanov's corruption trial begins in Moscow.
- 30 Yegor Ligachev is removed from secretaryship of ideology and relegated to agriculture at CC CPSU Plenum. Vadim Medvedev ascends to both ideology and propaganda portfolios. Andrey Gromyko is retired as President, Anatoliy Dobrynin replaced by Aleksandr Yakovlev as Secretary of Foreign Affairs, and Viktor Chebrikov moved to secretaryship of legal affairs. Gromyko and Solomentsev are retired and two candidate members replaced by three new ones at the Politburo.

October

- 1 VS confirms Gorbachev as President, Anatoliy Luk'yanov as Vice President, and Vladimir Kryuchkov as KGB Chairman, replacing Chebrikov.
- 20 Andrey Sakharov is elected to Presidium of Academy of Sciences.
- 25 Four prominent leaders of Uzbekistan CP are arrested on charges of corruption.
- 26 Helmut Kohl's speech detailing visit to Moscow reinforces efforts to warm relations between West Germany and USSR.
- 27 Finance Minister Boris Gostev announces 58-billion-dollar deficit for 1988.

November

- 6 Andrey Sakharov departs for first trip abroad.
- 16 Estonian Supreme Soviet amends republic's constitution to give officials right to ignore USSR laws that conflict with Estonia's.
- 22 Eight are killed and 126 wounded in ethnic violence in Baku and other cities in Azerbaijan.
- 26 Presidium of the USSR nullifies Estonia's disregard of USSR laws.
- 27 Gorbachev denounces regional nationalism.
- 28 VS convenes in Moscow.

December

- 1 VS approves Gorbachev's plan to transform it into two-chamber legislature, comprising Congress of People's Deputies, or CPD (with 1,500 elected members out of 2,250), and lower house (new Supreme Soviet), and limits the Presidency to two five-year terms.
- 1–2 Airplane hijacked in Ordzhonikidze is flown to Israel, but returned with arrested hijackers the next day.
- 2 CM decree accords state enterprises and cooperatives rights to trade with foreign entities.
- 5 Estonian Supreme Soviet sustains its constitutional amendment on supremacy of Estonian laws.
- 6 Gorbachev addresses UN General Assembly in New York, announcing reduction of Soviet military force by 500,000 men and deployment in Europe by 10,000 tanks, 8,500 artillery pieces, and 800 combat aircraft. Meeting with Reagan and President-elect George Bush follows.

7 Earthquake registering 6.9 on Richter scale devastates Armenia, destroying town of Spitak and severely damaging other settlements. More than 25,000 are killed and tens of thousands injured.

7 Chief of Staff and Deputy Prime Minister Sergey Akhromeyev is retired.

8 Gorbachev cuts short visit to New York to return to Moscow and visit Armenia.

9 Emergency aid from U.S. for victims of Armenian earthquake begins to arrive.

13 Radar sites violating ABM treaty are dismantled near Moscow and Gomel'.

29 Brezhnev and Chernenko are dishonored by removal of their names from all towns and institutions in USSR.

30 Churbanov receives twelve-year prison sentence.

1989

January

6 Politburo approves economic austerity measures to reduce level of state investment, impose price controls on cooperatives, adjust compensation of state-employed workers to productivity, and streamline distribution of stockpiled merchandise.

6 Gorbachev meets with Andrey Sakharov and representatives of the intelligentsia.

12 Presidium of VS opposes transfer of Nagorno-Karabakh to Armenia.

18 New language law is enacted in Estonia.

18 Academy of Sciences excludes Andrey Sakharov from list of candidates to CPD.

26 New language law is enacted in Lithuania.

February

2 Yel'tsin calls for open parliamentary elections.

3 Prospective withdrawal of Soviet troops from Czechoslovakia is announced in Prague.

15 Last contingents of Soviet troops leave Afghanistan.

25 More than 50 nationalists are arrested in Tbilisi during a 15,000-strong demonstration to mark 68th anniversary of Soviet annexation of Georgia.

March

2 Mutual and Balanced Force Reduction (MBFR) talks in Vienna end.

5 More than 5,000 supporters of Yel'tsin demonstrate in Moscow.

6 Shevardnadze presents disarmament proposal at Conventional Forces in Europe (CFE) talks involving NATO and WTO members.

12 CM decree breaks up *Gosagroprom* and allows individual farmers and groups to lease land.

16 CC CPSU establishes special commission to investigate Yel'tsin on charges of violating discipline by calling for open parliamentary elections in February.

18 Abkhazian separatists voice demands for autonomy.

19 More than 10,000 supporters march in Moscow to protest Yel'tsin's persecution.

24 Gorbachev voices opposition to interventions in WTO countries' affairs during Moscow meeting with Hungarian Premier Grosz.

26 Nationwide multicandidate elections are held for 1,500 seats in the CPD. Most CPSU candidates, including Leningrad's Yuriy Solov'yev, are defeated. Yel'tsin wins Moscow at-large seat with 89 percent of the vote. Popular fronts in Baltic republics win by impressive majorities.

29 Gorbachev rationalizes defeat of CPSU candidates and denies need for multiparty system.

30 Ministry of Defense announces exemption of university students from military service.

April

3 Gorbachev journeys to Cuba.

5–7 Gorbachev visits Great Britain.

7 Soviet nuclear submarine with 42 crew members catches fire and sinks off Norway.

9 Violence in Georgia leads to clash with troops, dispersing 10,000 nationalist demonstrators in Tbilisi, killing 20, and wounding more than 200 participants. Poison gas is in use.

14 Georgian CP leader Dzhumber Patiashvili is replaced by KGB chief Givi Gumbaridze.

21 Academy of Sciences yields one of its reserved seats in CPD to Andrey Sakharov.

25 Removal of 1,000 tanks, in first stage of unilateral Soviet withdrawal of 10,000 tanks and 50,000 troops from Eastern Europe, begins in Hungary.

25 Retirement of 72 CC CPSU members, 24 candidate members, and 12 members of its Auditing Commission is announced. Retirees include Nikolay Tikhonov, Geydar Aliyev, and Sergey Sokolov.

May

2 President Bush approves subsidized sale of 1.5 million tons of wheat to USSR.

4 New language law is enacted in Latvia.

10 U.S. Secretary of State James Baker visits Moscow to discuss resumption of Strategic Arms Reduction Talks (START).

11 Gorbachev informs Baker of unilateral removal of 500 nuclear warheads and proposes asymmetrical reductions of conventional forces in Europe.

14 Gorbachev's visit to Beijing prompts demonstrations in support of democracy in China.

18 Supreme Soviet of Lithuanian SSR declares sovereignty of Lithuania and amends the republican constitution.

18 Estonian legislation declares the republic's sovereignty.

25 Live television coverage of first CPD begins and continues for 13 days. Gorbachev's majority exceeds 95 percent in secret ballot for the presidency.

26 Deputies elect 542 members to the new bicameral VS.

27 Yel'tsin finishes 12th in contest for 11 seats in Soviet of Nationalities reserved for RSFSR.

29 Yel'tsin's supporters threaten national strike, whereupon Gorbachev rules that one seat in Soviet of Nationalities may be relinquished. This prompts Yel'tsin's election by acclamation after deputy from Siberia steps down.

30 Gorbachev delivers presidential acceptance speech, making first disclosure of defense spending ($128 billion) for 1989.

31 Yel'tsin addresses CPD, calling for limit on CPSU powers.

June

3 First session of the new USSR VS opens in Moscow.

3–4 Ethnic Meskhetians are attacked by Uzbek mobs in Fergana. Forty Meskhetians and ten Uzbeks are killed. Security forces restore order after rioting spreads to Kokand and other localities, doubling death toll within ten days.

6 Ryzhkov discloses government deficit (6.2 percent of GNP) and cost of Afghan war ($70 billion).

8 Representatives from Baltic republics stage walkout at CPD.

9 Gorbachev, Sakharov, and Ryzhkov address final session of first CPD.

12–14 Gorbachev visits West Germany, setting stage for elimination of Berlin Wall in November.

19 START and space weapons negotiations resume in Geneva.

21 Nursultan Nazarbayev becomes First Secretary of Kazakh CP, replacing Genadiy Kolbin.

26 Emergency reactor in Soviet submarine submerged near Norway shuts down.

26 Live TV coverage of VS proceedings is discontinued.

27 Six of Ryzhkov's 57 nominees to CM are rejected by VS.

July

1 Ethnic violence is termed "enormous danger" and threat to *perestroyka* in Gorbachev's nationally televised speech.

4–7 Gorbachev visits France and addresses Council of Europe.

7–8 Gorbachev's speech at annual WTO meeting in Bucharest calls for "tolerance" among allies. Closing communiqué recognizes "different models" of socialism.

10 Coal miners in Siberian town of Mezhdurechensk go on strike, protesting working conditions, poor wages, housing and medical care, and shortage of consumer goods.

11 Coal industry minister Mikhail Shchadov addresses miners. Strike spreads across the Kuzbas during the week.

13 Strike with political overtones begins in Vorkuta coal basin.

15 Gorbachev's letter to President François Mitterrand informs summit of industrial nations in Paris of enhanced interest in Soviet integration in global economy.

15 Coal miners in Makeyevka in Donbas begin strike.

16 Gorbachev appoints commission headed by Nikolay Slyun'kov to investigate coal miners' grievances and negotiate a settlement.

17 Negotiations between Slyun'kov's committee and striking miners move forward.

18 Gorbachev addresses CC CPSU, calling attention to popular loss of confidence in CPSU and threatening to purge opponents of *perestroyka*. Ligachev denounces multiparty democracy and unrestricted press.

19–20 Coal miners' strike spreads to Pavlodar and Karaganda in Kazakhstan.

21 Strikes end in Kuzbas and Vorkuta coal basins.

23 Gorbachev voices support for strikers' demands.

25 Miners at Donbass and Karaganda return to work.

27 VS passes resolution supporting Lithuanian and Estonian moves toward free-market economic systems.

29 Latvian legislation declares the republic's sovereignty.

30 Andrey Sakharov and several hundred members of CPD meet to form Inter-Regional Group of deputies to be headed by Sakharov, Yel'tsin, Yuriy Afanas'yev, Gavriil Popov, and Academician Viktor Palm of Estonia.

August

2–3 Laws reforming taxation of cooperatives and state enterprises are enacted.

8 Estonian Supreme Soviet sets residency requirements for voting and holding office, prompting a strike by members of the ethnic Russian minority.

11 USSR Ministry of Justice declares new Estonian laws unconstitutional.

17 Politburo supports limited economic autonomy for constituent republics, reserving jurisdiction over foreign affairs, defense, and internal security for federal government.

18 Aleksandr Yakovlev discloses existence of six secret protocols detailing the 1939 pact between Germany and USSR on the division of Poland and annexation of Baltic states.

22 Lithuanian Supreme Soviet declares the annexation by USSR in 1940 illegal.

23 Fiftieth anniversary of the 1939 nonaggression pact is marked by massive demonstrations and 400-mile-long human chain from Tallinn to Vilnius, formed by more than one million residents of Baltic republics.

24 New language law is enacted in Kirghizia.

28 New language law is enacted in Moldavia.

September

8 Ukrainian nationalist movement Rukh holds first meeting in Kiev, attended by more than 1,000 delegates. Resolutions call for removal of First Secretary of Ukrainian CP Vladimir Shcherbitskiy and transformation of USSR into "confederation" of autonomous republics.

9 Yel'tsin arrives in New York for eight-day speaking tour of U.S.

12 Yel'tsin meets briefly with President Bush.

18 *Pravda* reprints Italian press article detailing Yel'tsin's purported excesses during U.S. visit.

19   Gorbachev condemns republican separatists at CC CPSU Plenum focused on nationalities and sets next CPSU congress for October 1990.

20   Vladimir Shcherbitskiy, Viktor Chebrikov, Viktor Nikonov, and candidate members Talyzin and Solov'yev are removed from the Politburo; Vladimir Kryuchkov and Yuriy Maslyukov are promoted to full membership, and Boris Pugo and Yevgeniy Primakov to candidate membership.

21   Gorbachev's concessions on ABM Treaty and radar station at Krasnoyarsk are communicated to President Bush during Shevardnadze's visit to U.S.

23   Shevardnadze and Baker sign "understandings" in Jackson Hole, Wyoming, regarding exchange of information on strategic and chemical weapons and nuclear tests.

23   Gorbachev and British Prime Minister Margaret Thatcher meet in Moscow.

25   VS begins its second session.

28   Shcherbitskiy is removed from leadership of Ukrainian CP.

October

1   Defense Minister Yazov begins six-day visit to U.S.

6   U.S. Secretary of Defense Richard B. Cheney meets Yazov at the Pentagon.

6   Gorbachev's visit to East Berlin, where he urges reforms in a speech marking the 40th anniversary of East Germany, leads to demonstrations and subsequent retirement of Erich Honecker (on October 18).

7   U.S. Federal Reserve Chairman Alan Greenspan begins Moscow visit to facilitate development of market-oriented financial institutions in USSR.

9   VS approves decree granting the right to strike (first time since the Bolshevik Revolution). Legislation excludes workers in transportation, communications, defense, electric power, coal mining, and oil and gas sectors.

13   Gorbachev denounces *Ogonyok* and demands resignation of *Argumenty i Fakty's* editor Vladislav Starkov.

16   Secretary Baker voices support for *perestroyka* and offers U.S. advisors on economic affairs.

20–21   Coalition of Russian nationalist, anti-Western, and populist deputies meeting in Tyumen' issues programmatic declaration.

21   New language law is enacted in Uzbekistan.

23   Shevardnadze criticizes invasion of Afghanistan and admits violation of ABM Treaty by the Krasnoyarsk radar station.

24   Nationalist deputies of CPD convene founding meeting of *Rossiya*.

26   Gradual dissolution of WTO and NATO is proposed by Shevardnadze at WTO foreign ministers meeting in Warsaw.

27   Right of WTO states to political independence is endorsed by Shevardnadze after meeting with Prime Minister Tadeusz Mazowiecki of Poland.

27   Most miners in Vorkuta defy new restrictive legislation by staging a one-day strike.

28 New language law is enacted in the Ukraine.

November

4 Kryuchkov's TV interview discloses abuses of KGB during Stalin's reign.
9 Opening of Berlin Wall marks final stage of East European separation from USSR.
13 Motion to debate the CPSU's leading role in society is defeated by three-vote majority.
14 Gorbachev attacks West for "exporting capitalism" to Eastern Europe.
23 Legislation on leasing is enacted by VS.
27 VS grants economic autonomy to Baltic republics, decrees reform measures for environmental protection, and adopts draft law prohibiting censorship.
30 Gorbachev's concept of a "Common European Home" is enunciated during visit to Rome.

December

1 Ukrainian officials announce intent to recognize and register congregations of Catholic (Uniate) church.
1 Gorbachev meets with Pope John Paul II at the Vatican.
2–3 Gorbachev attends first summit with President Bush near Malta. No major disarmament or trade agreements are signed, but leaders express satisfaction with meetings during concluding joint news conference.
4 During WTO meeting in Moscow, Gorbachev and leaders of East Germany, Bulgaria, Hungary, and Poland issue statement condemning 1968 invasion of Czechoslovakia.
6 Lithuanian Supreme Soviet overwhelmingly votes to abolish CPSU's political monopoly and, the next day, to legalize opposition parties.
7 Russian-language edition of Solzhenitsyn's *Gulag Archipelago* is published and distributed.
8 Gorbachev counteracts conservative criticism at CC CPSU meeting by threatening to resign.
8 *Pravda* article suggests possibility of removal from the Constitution of Article Six, which assigns leading role in society to CPSU.
10 Inter-Regional Group cancels plans for two-hour general strike in support of debate to eliminate Article Six.
12 Gorbachev tells opening session of second CPD that efforts to repeal Article Six from the Constitution are premature, and wins relatively narrow majority vote to postpone the debate.
14 Andrey Sakharov dies of a heart attack in Moscow. Gorbachev leads citizenry in tribute as Sakharov's body lies in state at the Academy of Sciences.
16 CPD approves Ryzhkov's economic plan and abolishes system of automatic seat allotments to CPSU and other organizations.
18 USSR and European Community (EC) sign ten-year commercial agreement in Brussels.

19 CPD approves proposals that delay price and other elements of economic reform. Inter-Regional Group's effort to mount a vote of nonconfidence is decisively defeated.

20 Lithuanian CP overwhelmingly votes to break with CPSU.

20 Gorbachev and Prime Minister Marian Calfa meet in Moscow and agree to commence negotiations on Soviet troop withdrawal from Czechoslovakia.

23 Gorbachev voices support for new government of Romania following Nicolae Ceauşescu's capture by armed forces supporting the popular uprising.

24 CPD votes to condemn the nonaggression pact of 1939.

25–26 Emergency CC CPSU meeting to address split of Lithuanian CP prompts plan for Gorbachev's personal intervention.

27 More than 40,000 Lithuanians demonstrate in Vilnius in support of the splinter CP.

28 Latvian Supreme Soviet votes to delete references to CPSU's "leading role" from republic's constitution.

31 Azerbaijani riot near Iranian frontier prompts destruction of stations along border.

1990

January

3 Troops are dispatched to suppress Azerbaijani rioting.

4 Western press reporters are forbidden to cover riots in Azerbaijan.

11 Gorbachev visits Vilnius to persuade Lithuanian CP leader Algirdas Brazauskas to rescind break with CPSU, and denounces quest for Lithuanian independence while 250,000 hold nationalist rally in Vilnius.

11 Armenian legislature asserts right to veto USSR laws.

13–14 Anti-Armenian pogroms in Azerbaijan result in about 30 killings.

15 Demonstrators in Moldavia demand reunification with Romania.

15 Brazauskas is elected President of Lithuanian Supreme Soviet two days after Gorbachev's unsuccessful visit.

15 Gorbachev declares state of emergency in Azerbaijan, and approves airlift of 11,000 troops to restore order.

20 Soviet forces enter Baku. Official death toll reaches 93 within next three days. Azerbaijani Popular Front members are rounded up after a blockade of Baku harbor directed by the nationalists.

February

4 More than 300,000 pro-democracy demonstrators march in Moscow after opening of CC CPSU Plenum.

7 CC supports removal of Article Six from the Constitution.

9 Gorbachev and Shevardnadze meet with Secretary Baker in Moscow to discuss troop limits in Europe.

10 Gorbachev meets in Moscow with Chancellor Helmut Kohl, who announces qualified Soviet consent to German reunification.

11 Foreign ministers of NATO and WTO meet in Ottawa to discuss U.S. proposal for "open skies" aerial surveillance.

12 Official death toll reaches 18 after rioting breaks out in Dushanbe following rumors that Armenian refugees in Tadzhikistan are receiving preferential housing.

13 USSR, U.S., Britain, France, and the two Germanys agree in Ottawa to an arrangement ("four plus two") for negotiations on German reunification.

24 Lithuanian Sajudis, led by Vitautas Landsbergis, wins in multiparty elections for legislative and local offices.

25 Pro-democracy demonstrators march in more than 30 cities throughout the USSR.

26 USSR and Czechoslovakia sign agreement on phased withdrawal of all Soviet troops by July 1991.

27 Presidential powers are expanded in draft law adopted by VS.

28 VS enacts law on land ownership.

March

4 Yel'tsin is elected to RSFSR VS in nonpartisan elections for local and legislative offices in the Ukraine, Belorussia, and RSFSR.

4 Elections in Lithuania yield nationalist control of republican Supreme Soviet (90 of 141 deputies).

6 Gorbachev voices opposition to a united Germany's membership in NATO.

6 Legislation on ownership of property in USSR is refined.

9 Georgian Supreme Soviet passes resolution condemning forced incorporation of the republic in 1921.

11 Landsbergis becomes President of Lithuania after republican Supreme Soviet votes (124 to 6) to declare independence from USSR. Gorbachev calls vote "illegitimate and invalid."

11 Soviet troops begin withdrawal from Hungary.

13 Third CPD convenes in Moscow, voting to repeal Article Six of the Constitution and approve new office of Executive President.

15 Gorbachev is elected to new Presidency (by vote of 1,329 to 495).

15 USSR establishes limited diplomatic relations with Roman Catholic church.

18 Democratic opposition groups win runoff elections for control of Moscow, Leningrad, and Kiev city councils. Democratic Russia wins one-third of seats in VS of RSFSR.

19 Lithuanian parliament forms noncommunist coalition government headed by Kazimiera Prunskiene.

19 Gorbachev's televised address emphasizes opposition to control of industrial plants by new Lithuanian authorities.

21 Gorbachev issues decree banning distribution of firearms and ordering the surrender of all firearms in Lithuania to USSR Ministry of Internal Affairs. Lithuanian military deserters are ordered to return to their units or face arrest.

22 USSR military convoys roll through Vilnius.

23 Western diplomats are ordered to leave Lithuania within twelve hours.

24 Gorbachev commences appointments to sixteen-member Presidential Council.
25 USSR paratroopers seize headquarters of Lithuanian CP.
27 Vilnius hospital is raided, and 23 Lithuanian deserters are detained by paratroopers.
28 Landsbergis calls for talks with Gorbachev.
30 Estonian parliament votes to declare republic in state of "transition" to independence.
31 Gorbachev broadcasts demand for "immediate annulment" of Lithuanian declaration of independence.

April

2 Yakovlev meets with Lithuanian delegation in Moscow.
2 Estonian parliament voids USSR legislation on secession of republics.
9 USSR Deputy Premier Leonid Abalkin outlines economic reform proposal, which includes destatization, unemployment benefits, privatization, and measures to introduce new fiscal and monetary policies and infrastructure.
10 USSR VS enacts law regulating economic relations between federal authorities and constituent and autonomous republics.
11 Estonian parliament votes to obstruct USSR's conscription of Estonian citizens.
13 Massacre of Polish officers at Katyn' forest by NKVD is officially admitted for the first time in USSR.
13 Gorbachev decrees annulment of identity cards for citizens of Lithuania, threatening retaliatory embargo and energy blockade.
18 Lithuanian parliament offers brief moratorium on new laws prompted by declaration of independence.
19 Oil and gas pipelines to Lithuania are shut off, which prompts gas rationing in the republic and retaliatory obstruction of natural gas transfers to Kaliningrad.
19 Yuriy Afanas'yev resigns from CPSU.
24 Landsbergis compares U.S. reluctance to intervene with appeasement of Hitler in Munich.
24 Nikolay Petrakov rationalizes Gorbachev's opposition to Polish-style "shock treatment" for reform of the Soviet economy.
25 U.S. and USSR agree to a 5,000-ton limit on chemical weapons stockpiles.

May

1 Independent and unofficial organizations are permitted to participate in May Day parade in Moscow.
4 Latvian Supreme Soviet declares independence from USSR after unspecified period of transition.
12 VS draft law prohibits public insults directed at Gorbachev, mandating jail sentences for offenders.
14 Gorbachev issues decree voiding Latvian and Lithuanian attempts to secede from USSR.
15 Secretary Baker visits Moscow to discuss forthcoming summit meeting.

16 First RSFSR CPD opens in Moscow.
16 Lithuanian government agrees to suspend laws relating to independence (but not the declaration).
17 Gorbachev meets with Premier Prunskiene in Moscow.
24 Gorbachev tells Lithuanian officials that secession may be considered in 1992 if declaration of independence is suspended.
24 USSR VS considers Ryzhkov's economic reform proposal, which includes severe austerity measures and substantial price increases.
25 Gorbachev rules out "shock therapy" in economic reform proposals.
27 USSR troops kill six civilians in Yerevan, which leads to 23 additional killings in subsequent antigovernment demonstrations in Armenia.
29 Yel'tsin defeats Aleksandr Vlasov on fourth ballot in electoral contest for chairmanship of RSFSR VS.
30 Moldavia recognizes Lithuania as sovereign state.
30 USSR VS revises law on pensions.
31 Gorbachev's second summit with President Bush begins in Washington, D.C.

June

1 Yel'tsin meets with Lithuanian President Landsbergis in Moscow.
2 Gorbachev and Bush meet at Camp David, Maryland, after signing agreements on chemical and strategic weapons.
4 Gorbachev meets President Roh Tae-Woo in San Francisco, and announces normalization of relations between USSR and South Korea.
4 Uzbek residents of Osh riot after authorities limit allocation of new housing to citizens of Kirghizia.
4 USSR VS amends law on enterprises.
5 State of emergency in and around Osh is declared, after rioting leads to 11 killings.
5 Shevardnadze announces USSR's unilateral removal of tactical nuclear weapons from Europe at ministerial meeting of Commission on Security and Cooperation in Europe (CSCE) in Copenhagen.
6 Rioting spreads to Frunze and leads to sealed border between Uzbekistan and Kirghizia.
7 WTO leaders in Warsaw declare end to view of West as "ideological enemy."
8 Russian republic declares sovereignty over its territory and natural resources.
12 Gorbachev proposes transitional "associate membership" in WTO for former East German troops.
12 USSR VS enacts law on freedom of press.
13 Rioting in Kirghizia yields death toll of 148.
13 USSR VS gives Gorbachev power to institute economic reforms by decree.
14 USSR VS enacts law on taxation of enterprises but rejects proposal to triple bread prices.
19 RSFSR members of CPSU convene conference in Moscow.
20 RSFSR CP independent of CPSU is formally established.

20 Uzbekistan declares sovereignty.
21 Moldavia declares sovereignty.
23 Conservative Ivan K. Polozkov becomes leader of RSFSR CP.
29 Lithuanian Supreme Council agrees to moratorium on declaration of independence, which prompts end of economic embargo three days later.

July

2 Twenty-eighth Congress of CPSU convenes in Moscow.
3 Gorbachev calls for regulated market economy and faces Ligachev's sharp criticism for excessive radicalism.
6 Yel'tsin addresses 28th Congress, calling for drastic reform of CPSU.
6 Gorbachev receives invitation to visit NATO headquarters in Brussels.
9 Congress approves expanded Politburo to include representatives from all USSR republics.
10 Gorbachev is reelected General Secretary of CPSU.
11 Vladimir A. Ivashko defeats Ligachev in elections for Deputy General Secretaryship of CPSU.
12 Yel'tsin is nominated to CC of CPSU.
13 Following Yel'tsin's lead, Moscow and Leningrad mayors Popov and Sobchak resign from CPSU.
13 Congress of CPSU adjourns after electing new CC, which excludes Ligachev, Yakovlev, and Medvedev, who also lose positions on CPSU Secretariat. Ligachev announces intent to retire.
14 CC CPSU elects new 24-member Politburo, and eliminates "candidate" status.
15 CPSU loses monopoly on radio and television broadcasts.
16 Gorbachev and Kohl meet in Zheleznovodsk, where they announce agreement to allow reunified Germany to join NATO, while Soviet forces remain in Germany's eastern part for three to four years.
16 The Ukraine declares sovereignty of the republic.
25 Gorbachev's presidential decree orders ethnic militants throughout USSR to disarm within 15 days. Action by security forces is threatened.
30 Negotiations between federal and republican representatives to draft a new union treaty begin in Moscow. Baltic republics refuse to participate.

August

1 Gorbachev and Yel'tsin agree to cooperate on approach to economic reform.
2 Gorbachev announces formation of working group of economists headed by Presidential Councillor Stanislav Shatalin.
2 Shevardnadze announces USSR's intent to discontinue production of SS-24 rail-mobile ballistic missile after meeting with Baker in Irkutsk.
3 USSR and U.S. issue joint statement condemning the invasion of Kuwait by Iraq.
10 RSFSR Presidium reaffirms ownership of republic's natural resources.
11 Gorbachev extends deadline for disarmament of nationalists.
13 Gorbachev's decree rehabilitates all victims of Stalinism.

15 RSFSR and Lithuania conclude agreement on trade and economic cooperation.
15 Gorbachev's decree restores USSR citizenship to Solzhenitsyn and other dissident intellectuals forced to emigrate after the 1960s.
17 Gorbachev's speech voices support for decisive measures against Iraq.
22 Turkmenistan declares its sovereignty.
23 Armenia declares independence.
23 Gorbachev denounces RSFSR's declaration on natural resources.
24 Tadzhikistan declares sovereignty of the republic.
27 UN is assured of USSR's resolve to "observe the regime of sanctions" against Iraq.
29 Gorbachev and Yel'tsin meet for two days in Moscow to discuss relations with republics and the adoption of the "Shatalin Plan" for economic reform.

September

1 USSR VS begins to consider rival economic plans proffered by Ryzhkov and by Shatalin.
1 Yel'tsin demands Ryzhkov's resignation.
5 Gorbachev meets with Iraqi Foreign Minister Tariq Aziz in Moscow.
9 President Bush meets Gorbachev in Helsinki to discuss Persian Gulf crisis. Joint statement recognizes Soviet role in Israeli-Arab peace efforts.
11 Ryzhkov denounces the Shatalin Plan, threatening to resign if adopted reforms prove too radical. Gorbachev announces preference for Shatalin's approach.
12 Representatives of U.S., USSR, Britain, France, and the Germanys meet in Moscow to sign treaty ending "four powers" rights and responsibilities in Germany. Treaty sets 1994 for USSR troop withdrawal from Germany's eastern part, where stationing of Western troops will be forbidden.
13 Shevardnadze and West German Foreign Minister Hans-Dietrich Genscher sign friendship treaty between USSR and Germany.
14 Gorbachev proposes the "Presidential Plan," drafted by Academician Abel Aganbegyan, which is an alternative to the Ryzhkov and Shatalin plans.
17 USSR and Saudi Arabia reestablish diplomatic relations.
18 *Komsomol'skaya Pravda* prints Alexander Solzhenitsyn's "How to Revitalize Russia."
21 Gorbachev requests emergency powers from VS to issue presidential decrees on wages, prices, and "law and order" issues during unspecified period of transition.
24 USSR VS grants Gorbachev new powers through March 1992, endorses his proposal for a "conciliation committee" seeking a compromise between the Shatalin and Ryzhkov plans, and enacts law on measures to stabilize the economy.
26 VS approves new law facilitating religious education in schools.

26 Yazov denies rumored link between military exercises and purported conspiracy to seize power.

27 Gorbachev exercises new powers by issuing emergency decree demanding fulfillment of contractual deliveries to the state.

30 Shevardnadze suggests Soviet participation in military action against Iraq if authorized by UN.

30 USSR establishes formal diplomatic relations with South Korea.

30 Agreement on opening of consulates in Moscow and Tel Aviv is reached between USSR and Israel.

October

 1 USSR VS overwhelmingly votes to guarantee freedom of religious observance.

 2 Student protesters demanding progress on Ukrainian sovereignty establish tent city in Kiev.

 3 Shevardnadze and Baker announce tentative agreement on Conventional Forces in Europe Treaty after meeting in New York.

 9 RSFSR VS authorizes implementation of the Shatalin Plan in the republic.

 9 USSR VS adopts law granting equal status to all political parties, but retaining CPSU cell organizations in the armed forces.

13 Poland and the Ukraine sign agreement establishing diplomatic relations between "sovereign states."

15 Gorbachev is awarded Nobel Peace Prize.

16 Gorbachev presents "Presidential Plan" for economic restructuring to USSR VS. Yel'tsin and Shatalin voice their opposition.

18–19 Yevgeniy Primakov visits Washington, D.C., to discuss Persian gulf crisis with President Bush.

19 USSR VS approves Gorbachev's plan and decrees guidelines for economic stabilization and transition to market economy.

20 Opposition party, Democratic Russia, holds first congress in Moscow.

24 USSR VS denies the right of republics to supersede federal laws. Russian and Ukrainian soviets oppose the federal legislation.

25 Supreme Soviet of Kazakhstan declares sovereignty of the republic.

26 Coal miners in Donetsk inaugurate first nationwide independent labor union.

26 Gorbachev, exercising emergency powers, issues decrees allowing foreign citizens to operate wholly owned subsidiaries and lease land, devalues the ruble, increases interest rates, and allows citizens of the USSR to invest in enterprises.

26 Gorbachev meets Prime Minister Felipe Gonzáles in Madrid.

26 Moldavia declares state of emergency to thwart attempts by Gagauz minority to gain independence.

28 Parliamentary elections in Georgia, with all parties supporting independence, produce majority vote for "Georgia Round Table."

28 USSR Ministry of Interior Affairs dispatches troops to Moldavia to forestall violence.

29 Gorbachev and President Mitterrand sign treaty of friendship and cooperation in France.

31 Shatalin Plan is adopted by RSFSR VS.

November

2 Ethnic violence in Dubossary, Moldavia, results in six killings.

2 Gorbachev's decree forces enterprises to surrender 40 percent of hard-currency earnings to federal government.

9 Gorbachev visits Kohl in Bonn to sign nonaggression and friendship agreements and accord on Soviet troop withdrawal from eastern part of Germany.

13 Yel'tsin claims Gorbachev's consent to "coalition government of national unity."

13 Gorbachev promotes republican sovereignty within "federal framework" in speech addressing the military.

16 Gorbachev addresses emergency session of USSR VS, accusing unidentified adversaries of efforts to discredit him.

17 USSR VS approves Gorbachev's reorganization proposal creating a new Federation Council comprising the heads of 15 republics, establishing new position of Vice President, and eliminating the Presidential Council.

17–18 Gorbachev visits Italy, where he meets with Pope John Paul II and Premier Guilio Andreotti.

19 Yel'tsin denounces Gorbachev's government reorganization plan as effort to increase presidential power at the expense of republican autonomy.

19 Second CSCE summit in Paris affords NATO and WTO leaders opportunity to sign CFE Treaty limiting each alliance to 20,000 battle tanks and artillery and to 30,000 armored vehicles, 6,800 aircraft, and 2,000 combat helicopters.

19 President Bush fails to secure Gorbachev's public support for use of force in Persian Gulf during meeting in Paris.

21 CSCE heads sign Charter of Paris for New Europe.

23 Gorbachev proposes new Union Treaty to govern federal government's relations with republics, allowing republican control of territory, economic affairs, and natural resources, but retaining preeminence of federal over republican laws and control of military and foreign affairs.

27 Dimitriy Yazov informs television audience of Gorbachev's orders to defend military installations, monuments, and servicemen in rebellious republics.

29 USSR votes in UN Security Council to authorize use of force against Iraq.

30 RSFSR legislature approves principle of private ownership of land.

December

1 Joint session of parliamentary delegations from Lithuania, Latvia, and Estonia is held in Vilnius.

1 Municipal authorities institute food rationing in Leningrad.

2   Boris Pugo is named Minister of Internal Affairs, replacing the relatively liberal Vadim Bakatin.

3   Private ownership of land in RSFSR is legalized by republican VS.

4   VS grants Gorbachev new executive powers to facilitate transition to market economy.

10   USSR VS enacts laws on trade union and investment activities.

10   Shevardnadze requests U.S. food aid during meeting with Baker in Houston, Texas.

11   Kryuchkov pledges fight against "anti-Communist forces" obstructing central authorities in USSR.

12   President Bush announces approval of one-billion-dollar federal loan guarantee to allow food sales to USSR, and expresses support for Soviet ties with World Bank and IMF.

12   State of emergency is declared in South Ossetian Autonomous Oblast.

12   Kirghizia declares sovereignty.

13   Shevardnadze visits Turkey to discuss Persian Gulf crisis.

13   Gorbachev meets South Korean President Roh in Moscow.

17   Gorbachev addresses fourth CPD in Moscow, demanding a popular referendum on the proposed new union treaty in each constituent republic.

20   Shevardnadze announces surprise resignation in speech before CPD, warning of approaching dictatorship. Congress votes to reaffirm course of USSR foreign policy after Shevardnadze agrees to serve until VS approves his departure.

22   Kryuchkov attacks Western involvement in Soviet economic affairs as attempt to gain strategic information.

24   CPD votes to approve Gorbachev's proposal to vest added autonomy in constituent republics of the federation and adopts resolution on priority measures to overcome political and economic crisis.

24   Moldavian authorities receive Gorbachev's order to rescind republican laws conflicting with USSR legislation.

25   Subordination of Cabinet Minister to USSR President and new post of Vice President are approved, but Gorbachev's proposal to create Supreme State Inspectorate is rejected by CPD.

25   CPD mandates nationwide referenda on Union Treaty and on private ownership of land.

26   Gorbachev nominates Gennadiy I. Yanayev as Vice President and facilitates his election on a second ballot the next day.

26   Nikolay Ryzhkov is hospitalized after suffering a heart attack.

27   RSFSR parliament votes to contribute less than one-tenth of the 250 billion rubles requested for USSR federal budget.

28   Popular TV show *Vzglyad* is banned by Chairman of the State Committee on Radio and TV Leonid Kravchenko.

29   Secret decree on joint army-police patrols and presidential decree on 5 percent sales tax covering consumer goods and services are enacted.

30   Moldavia heads off direct confrontation with USSR by agreeing to reconsider contradictory republican laws.

1991

January

1 Drastic increases in wholesale prices are instituted.

1 Emergency curfew in Dushanbe is lifted but state of emergency in Tadzhikistan remains in effect.

2 Interior Affairs Ministry troops (OMON) surround Lithuanian CPSU headquarters in Vilnius, and sieze newspaper publishing plant in Riga.

3 Federation Council approves an economic agreement between the republics for 1991.

4 Soviet freighter with military cargo is stopped in Red Sea by patrols enforcing embargo against Iraq.

5 Gorbachev issues decree to distribute farmland to individuals and cooperatives, but makes no mention of private ownership.

7 Defense Ministry officials announce planned enforcement of the draft by airborne units in the Baltic and other rebellious republics.

7 Presidential decree orders removal of Georgian police forces from South Ossetia.

8 Prunskiene meets Gorbachev in Moscow in an effort to alleviate continuing conflict.

9 OMON troops surround TV tower in Vilnius in show of support for anti-Lithuanian demonstrators.

10 Gorbachev informs Lithuanian authorities that imposition of presidential rule in Lithuania is under consideration.

11 State Committee on Radio and TV attempts to expand control of news media by confiscating the Interfax news agency's equipment.

11–13 OMON troops storm several buildings in Vilnius after Lithuanian National Salvation Committee announces intent to control the republic.

13 Takeover of Lithuanian radio and TV center results in 14 killings, which prompts U.S. protest suggesting possible cancellation of scheduled summit meeting, reconsideration of agricultural credits, and curtailment of medical and technical aid.

14 Gorbachev denies knowledge of decision to use force in Vilnius.

14 Valentin Pavlov becomes Prime Minister of USSR.

15 Aleksandr Bessmertnykh ascends to post of Foreign Minister.

15 USSR VS enacts new law on employment.

16 USSR and Germany sign agreement for construction of housing for troops returning from Germany's eastern part.

16 USSR VS sets March 17 as date for national referendum on preservation of USSR as an integral state.

19 Petrakov resigns post of economic advisor to Gorbachev.

19 Gorbachev contacts leaders of the alliance against Iraq, urging restraint in Persian Gulf crisis.

20 OMON troops attack republican Interior Ministry in Riga, killing four Latvians.

20 More than 100,000 opponents of CPSU participate in Moscow demonstrations organized by popular liberal movements and political parties. Yuriy Afanas'yev condemns "bloody attack" in the Baltics.

21 RSFSR VS begins debate on Gorbachev's leadership.

22 Gorbachev expresses condolences to families of killed Lithuanians and Latvians, but blames republican leaderships.

22 Gorbachev decrees a monetary reform requiring exchange and removal from circulation of 50- and 100-ruble notes and limiting cash withdrawals from personal deposits.

24 Efforts to censor Gorbachev fail to secure majority in RSFSR VS.

24 Defense Ministry spokesman denies assistance to Iraq from Soviet military advisors.

24 Leading Soviet cultural figures protest censorship of TV.

25 Moscow's municipal council announces plan to ration meat, grains, and vodka on March 1.

26 Gorbachev issues decree allowing police and KGB wide-ranging search and seizure rights in investigating corruption.

26 Founding conference of Congress of Democratic Forces, comprising 46 independent political parties, opens in Kharkov.

27–28 Foreign Minister Aleksandr Bessmertnykh discusses Lithuania and Persian Gulf crisis with President Bush and Secretary Baker in Washington, D.C.

30 Boris Pugo announces the withdrawal of all added airborne units from Baltic republics.

30 CC CPSU Plenum debates economic and political crisis.

30 Reactionary political group *Yedinstvo* proposes Gorbachev's replacement as General Secretary of CPSU by Nina Andreyeva.

February

1 Joint police-army patrols are introduced in major cities.

8 Kryuchkov announces replacement of First Deputy Chairman of KGB Filip Bobkov by Viktor Grushko.

9 Overwhelming vote of residents favors Lithuanian independence.

12 Pavlov defends monetary reform involving 50- and 100-ruble notes as measure against international bankers' conspiracy to precipitate hyperinflation in USSR.

12 Viktor Grushko accuses CIA of increasing espionage in USSR.

12 Yevgeniy Primakov delivers Gorbachev's message to Saddam Hussein in Baghdad.

15 Vladimir Yegorov and Oleg Ozherel'yev become aides to Gorbachev.

15 Yevgeniy Primakov visits Tokyo to discuss Gorbachev's planned visit to Japan.

16 Three EC foreign ministers discuss Persian Gulf with Gorbachev in Moscow.

16 Yel'tsin's interview on CNN voices sharp criticism of Gorbachev for alleged pursuit of personal dictatorship.

18 Gorbachev presents four-point peace plan for the Persian Gulf to Iraqi ministers Tariq Aziz and Saadoun Hammadi in Moscow.

18 USSR VS meets to open fifth session, expected to last until June.

19 Yel'tsin's television interview elicits call for Gorbachev's immediate resignation.

20 USSR VS approves resolution denouncing Yel'tsin's televised attack on Gorbachev.

20 Pavlov presents draft law on new Cabinet of Ministers to USSR VS.

21 Tariq Aziz returns to Moscow with Iraq's answer to Gorbachev's peace initiative.

21 Bessmertnykh attends Council of Europe meeting in Madrid.

22 Pavlov outlines plan to dismantle *Gosplan*.

22 About 400,000 supporters of Democratic Russia attend rally near the Kremlin.

25 WTO agrees to disband its military structures by March 31, 1991.

25 Gorbachev submits a list of 23 candidates for newly created Cabinet of Ministers for VS approval. Kryuchkov and Yazov are to join Bessmertnykh and Pugo as prominent members of the cabinet.

25 USSR VS adopts resolution to reaffirm the prospective March referendum on preservation of the Union.

26 Delegations from Baltic republics participate in meeting of Nordic Council of Copenhagen.

26–28 Gorbachev visits Belorussia. Speeches warn of possible civil war, accuse Yel'tsin of divergence from *perestroyka*, term relations with U.S. as "fragile," urge CPSU to form a centrist coalition, and stress need for renovation.

28 USSR VS Chairman Anatoliy Luk'yanov attributes cease-fire in the Persian Gulf to Gorbachev's diplomatic initiative.

March

1 USSR VS enacts law on hard currency, providing a foreign exchange market for foreign and domestic firms.

1 Widespread warning strikes begin at coal mines in Donbas, Kazakhstan, and Vorkuta.

2 Georgian Supreme Soviet forwards direct appeal to UN to investigate conflict in South Ossetia.

3 Plebiscites for independence yield support of 79 percent of Estonian and 87.5 percent of Latvian voters.

4 USSR VS ratifies "Two-Plus-Four" Treaty on German unification.

4 British Prime Minister John Major meets representatives of Baltic republics in Moscow. Meeting with Gorbachev follows.

6 Federation Council approves draft of Union Treaty granting republican governments broad powers.

6 USSR VS enacts law establishing municipal militias and allowing CPSU cells in police departments.

7 USSR VS approves Yanayev, Pavlov, Bessmertnykh, Pugo, Kryuchkov, Yazov, Primakov, and Bakatin, nominated by Gorbachev to the new Security Council.

9 Yel'tsin declares "war" on federal leadership, disputing Gorbachev's statement that RSFSR will sign Union Treaty.

9 Revised draft of Union Treaty is published in *Izvestiya*.

10 Massive demonstration in Moscow is addressed by Afanas'yev, Popov, and other supporters of Yel'tsin.

10–12 Strikers in spreading strike of coal miners meet Yel'tsin in Moscow but fail to secure access to Gorbachev.

11 Gorbachev meets Turkish President Turgut Özal in Moscow.

12 Georgian Supreme Soviet extends state of emergency in South Ossetia.

13–15 Following meeting with Yel'tsin, Özal visits Kiev, Alma-Ata, and Baku for talks with republican leaders.

15–16 Baker meets Gorbachev and Bessmertnykh in Moscow. Meetings with representatives of Baltic republics, Georgia, and Armenia follow.

16 Bessmertnykh proposes six-point plan with limitation on arms exports to the Middle East.

16 Pavlov and Israeli Prime Minister Yitzhak Shamir meet in London.

16–17 Ethnic confrontation in South Ossetia prompts several killings.

17 Nationwide referendum on the preservation of USSR takes place despite refusal of Baltic, Armenian, Georgian, and Moldavian governments to participate. More than 76 percent endorse the federation. In a parallel referendum, about 70 percent favor directly elected presidency of RSFSR.

17–18 Gorbachev and Bessmertnykh meet Genscher in Moscow to discuss withdrawal of troops, aid to ethnic Germans, and return of Erich Honecker to Germany.

19 Gorbachev issues presidential decree on reform of retail prices, transportation tariffs, and social security.

19 First Soviet study of the 1943 Katyn' massacre of Polish officers by NKVD is published in Moscow.

19–21 Strike spreads to several hundred coal mines, involving Gorbachev, Pavlov, and Nazarbayev in efforts to avert crisis.

21–25 Fighting between Georgians and Ossetians continues to intensify in South Ossetia.

25 USSR CM bans street rallies in Moscow until April 15.

28 Extraordinary session of RSFSR CPD opens in Moscow. During the following week, Yel'tsin survives threatened vote of no confidence, gains right to rule by decree as chairman of VS, and secures tentative date in July for direct presidential election.

31 Bessmertnykh arrives in Beijing to discuss border dispute with China.

31 Military structure of WTO is dissolved.

31 Referendum on Georgian independence yields nearly unanimous vote of support.

April

2 Senior economic officials disclose mounting first-quarter budget deficit, warning Gorbachev of approaching economic ''catastrophe.''

2 Richard Nixon meets Gorbachev in Moscow.

2 Retail price increases go into effect on wide range of foodstuffs and consumer goods.

2 Yel'tsin and Silayev are accused by *Sovetskaya Rossiya* of transacting illicit business with Westerners.

5 Gorbachev exempts additional goods from 5 percent sales tax to lessen impact of price increases.

6 RSFSR appoints Moscow Chief of Police, defying Gorbachev's decree.

6–7 Representatives of Baltic states, Armenia, Georgia, and Moldavia meet in Kishinev to discuss cooperation on efforts to gain independence.

7 Easter services in Moscow are broadcast live on Soviet TV.

8 Gorbachev issues decree on emergency measures to resolve deteriorating crisis in agriculture.

9 Gorbachev announces one-year "anti-crisis" program at Federation Council meeting, calling for transition to free market prices, privatization, and reduced defense spending.

9 Gorbachev appoints Viktor Komplektov as ambassador to U.S.

9 Georgian Supreme Soviet proclaims republic's independence.

9 USSR troops begin withdrawal from Poland.

12 Union of Journalists expels Leonid Kravchenko for reinstituting censorship of TV.

13 Leaders of coal miners call for general strike to force political change in USSR.

14 Zviad Gamsakhurdia is elected by Georgian Supreme Soviet to five-year presidency of the republic.

15 Yel'tsin begins three-day visit to France, which includes brief meeting with Mitterrand.

16 Gorbachev arrives in Japan for first visit ever by a leader of USSR.

17 Strikers at largest coal mine in USSR win pledge to eliminate federal and institute RSFSR jurisdiction over mine property and administration.

17–19 Gorbachev addresses Japanese parliament, appealing for investments. Meeting with Prime Minister Toshiki Kaifu ends without resolution of Kurile Islands dispute, except for agreement to accelerate work on World War II peace treaty.

20 Gorbachev and South Korea's President Roh meet on the island of Cheju.

20 *Soyuz* fraction of USSR VS deputies convenes second congress, calling for imposition of state of emergency and rejection of draft Union Treaty.

21 First interparliamentary conference of democratic representatives from constituent republics convenes in Moscow.

22 Supreme Soviet of Kirghizia votes to reject draft Union Treaty.

22 Gorbachev joins Pavlov in ceremonies marking anniversary of Lenin's birth.

23 USSR VS issues decree supporting Pavlov's "anti-crisis" program, which includes ban on strikes.

23 Gorbachev and representatives of nine republics, including Yel'tsin, sign agreement supporting legislative approval of new Union Treaty and Constitution, and affirming right of Baltic republics, Moldavia, Armenia, and Georgia to reject the Treaty.

23 Gorbachev issues presidential decree voiding Armenian legislature's nationalization of CP assets.

23 Strike in Belorussia intensifies. Demands for economic and political change include removal of CPSU committees from factories and sale of CPSU assets.

25 Gorbachev threatens to resign at CC CPSU Plenum in response to blame for current crisis. General Mikhail Sarkov and heads of Moldavian and Kirghizian CP are appointed to Politburo.

25 Gorbachev commemorates fifth anniversary of the disaster at Chernobyl'.

25 RSFSR VS sets rules for election of RSFSR President.

26 Massive one-hour strike to protest worsening living conditions takes place in RSFSR.

29 Yel'tsin meets leaders of striking coal miners in Novokuznetsk.

29 Destructive earthquake registering 7.2 on Richter scale devastates Georgia, killing more than 100 people.

30 USSR gains observer status on one of GATT's committees.

May

1 Yel'tsin pledges to transfer control of Kuzbas mines to RSFSR.

1 Relatively austere May Day parade in Moscow reflects political change and economic crisis.

2 Yazov begins first trip ever by Soviet Defense Minister to China.

3 Gorbachev convenes Moscow meeting between Chairman Levon Ter-Petrossyan and President Ayaz Mutalibov in effort to abate ongoing Armenian-Azerbaijani conflict, with recent killings exceeding 50 people.

5 Yel'tsin and Kryuchkov agree to create RSFSR KGB with duties to be delineated after ratification of Union Treaty.

6 First Deputy Prime Ministers Doguzhiyev of USSR and Skokov of RSFSR sign agreement for transfer of mines in Kuzbas, Komi, and Rostov to RSFSR jurisdiction.

6 USSR enacts law to compensate victims of the Chernobyl' disaster.

6 Shevardnadze begins tour of U.S., including meeting with Bush.

6 Gorbachev's meeting with Mitterrand at dacha near Moscow is detailed at press conference.

7 Appointment of six advisors to Gorbachev is announced. List comprises Vice President of Council of Nationalities Boris Oleynik, Director of IMEMO Vladlen Martynov, economists Leonid Abalkin and Yuriy Yaremenko, and Vice Presidents of Academy of Sciences Vladimir Kudryavtsev and Yuriy Osipyan.

7 Ryzhkov enters race for RSFSR presidency.

8 Landsbergis and Prime Ministers Godmanis of Latvia and Savisaar of Estonia meet with President Bush in Washington, D.C.

8 Intensified conflict in South Ossetia yields additional killings.

8 Mutalibov rules out talks with Armenia to end conflict.

8–9 Bessmertnykh begins tour of Middle East, visiting President Hafez Al-Assad in Damascus and King Hussein in Amman.

9 Strike of coal miners in Kuzbas basin subsides.

9 USSR troops deployed in Armenia and Azerbaijan are accorded wider range of authority to cope with heavy fighting in the region.

10 Members of Stalinist and antisemitic *Yedinstvo* demonstrate in Moscow in support of General Al'bert Makashov's candidacy in elections for presidency of RSFSR.

10 Bessmertnykh meets Prime Minister Shamir in Jerusalem on first visit to Israel by a Foreign Minister of USSR.

11 Yel'tsin declares alliance with Gorbachev in effort to avert disintegration and economic collapse of USSR.

11 Campaign for RSFSR presidency intensifies, with Vadim Bakatin and Kemerovo Obkom Chairman Aman-Gel'dy Tuleyev joining the race.

12 *Soyuz* announces support of Ryzhkov's candidacy for RSFSR presidency.

12 Bessmertnykh meets Egyptian President Hosni Mubarak and Secretary Baker in Cairo.

12 Gorbachev meets Yel'tsin and chairmen of the Supreme Soviets of 14 of RSFSR's 16 autonomous republics to discuss Union Treaty and issues of sovereignty. Tatarstan refuses to endorse treaty.

13 USSR VS fails to approve draft law on emigration.

13 Gorbachev issues decree to enhance output of raw materials by offering producers a range of incentives within "special regime" in key sectors of the economy.

13–14 Bessmertnykh's Middle East tour includes second meeting with Baker in Cairo, opening of new USSR embassy and talks with King Fahd in Riyadh, and return to Damascus to brief Assad on prospects of proposed talks with Israel.

14 Crime statistics reported by USSR Ministry of Internal Affairs indicate increase to highest level since World War II.

15 Gorbachev meets Chinese Communist Party First Secretary Jiang Zemin, arriving for five-day visit to USSR.

16 Gorbachev signs decree banning railway strikes and work stoppages in energy and other key industrial sectors.

16 Vladimir Shcherbakov defeats Stepan Sitaryan in VS vote for post of Deputy Prime Minister of USSR.

18 *Pravda* announces prospective replacement of five-ruble notes.

18 Deportation of Armenians from Nagorno-Karabakh prompts appeals for UN intervention.

20 USSR VS votes to delay implementation of new emigration law until beginning of 1993 and to institute sanctions against wildcat strikes.

21 President Bush meets Chief of Staff General Mikhail Moyseyev in Washington, D.C.

21 Anniversary of Andrey Sakharov's birth is marked by five-day international conference in Moscow, attended by Gorbachev and Yel'tsin.

21 Fourth session of RSFSR VS opens in Moscow to approve law on executive presidency of the republic.

21 Report of the International Atomic Energy Agency presented at four-day conference in Vienna minimizes impact of Chernobyl' disaster on health of Soviet population, which prompts objections from Ukrainian and Belorussian participants.

22 Gorbachev meets Prime Minister Andreotti in Moscow.

22 USSR VS adopts first consumer rights law in Soviet history.

23 Stock exchange, first founded by Peter the Great, reopens in Leningrad.

24 Gorbachev and heads of most constituent and autonomous republics meet in Novo-Ogarevo on Union Treaty, agreeing that new union should be a federation. Yel'tsin alleges agreement to change "socialist" to "sovereign" in USSR's name but notes discord on taxation, local defense, and ownership of mineral resources.

24 Attacks on Latvian and Lithuanian border posts by OMON military units controlled by USSR Ministry of Internal Affairs intensify, which prompts protest from presidents of Baltic republics.

25 Delegates from popular movements in Baltic republics, Moldavia, Armenia, and Georgia set up coordinating body to facilitate independence.

26 Zviad Gamsakhurdia wins Georgian presidency by majority vote of 86.5 percent in first contested popular election of republican leader in USSR.

27 Margaret Thatcher meets Gorbachev and addresses students in Moscow.

29 Chairman of USSR VS Anatoliy Luk'yanov urges West to invite Gorbachev to summit of "group of seven" industrial nations, mentioning 30-billion-dollar annual aid as desired goal.

29 Port of Kaliningrad, off-limits since 1945, is reopened to foreign shipping.

29 Gorbachev begins working visit to Kazakhstan.

29 Nearly 200 Soviet soldiers apply for political asylum in Germany.

29 Secretary Baker gives cautious assessment of reform plan outlined to members of Congress, the World Bank, and the IMF by Yevgeniy Primakov and Grigoriy Yavlinskiy in Washington, D.C.

30 Erich Honecker alleges grant of political asylum from USSR.

June

1 Pugo blames Lithuanian leadership for January killings in Vilnius, following announced intent by USSR Prosecutor General to institute criminal proceedings against OMON.

4 Robert Strauss is nominated as nineteenth U.S. ambassador to USSR.

5 Gorbachev's Nobel Prize acceptance speech defends *perestroyka* as best opportunity for world peace.

6 Yevgeniy Primakov reiterates request for Western support for ruble convertibility and anti-inflation measures, but denies need for massive financial aid.

7 Delegations led by Bessmertnykh and Baker fail to resolve differences over START.

8 Defense Ministry denies allegations by members of RSFSR CPD of Soviet troop participation in Persian Gulf war.

10 *Pravda* attacks Yel'tsin on eve of election.

11 Gorbachev's spokesman voices "definitely positive" reaction to Robert Strauss's prospective ambassadorship.

11 U.S. grants $1.5 billion in credits for food sales to USSR.

12 Yel'tsin, Ryzhkov, Bakatin, and leader of the Liberal-Democratic Party, Vladimir Zhirinovskiy, compete in first popular election for RSFSR presidency.

12 Municipal elections produce over 60 percent majority vote for Popov in Moscow.

12 Sobchak wins over 70 percent of the vote in municipal elections in Leningrad; majority opts to change city's name to St. Petersburg.

13 Preliminary vote count confirms Yel'tsin's election as President of RSFSR by majority vote exceeding 60 percent.

13 Prime Minister Major invites Gorbachev to London for July talks with "group of seven" leaders.

13 The Islamic Soviet-Saudi International Commercial Bank, first in USSR with equal foreign partnership, opens in Alma-Ata.

17 Pavlov requests emergency powers at session of USSR CPD.

17 Yavlinskiy presents tentative plan of Soviet and Harvard economists to Gorbachev. Pavlov dismisses the plan as "pretty piece of paper."

17 Kryuchkov's address to closed session of USSR CPD alleges Western efforts to undermine USSR.

18 In Berlin, Baker outlines limited Western measures to assist economic reform in USSR.

18 Yel'tsin departs for visit to U.S.

19 Yel'tsin meets U.S. legislators in Washington, D.C., requesting measures to promote trade with Russian republic.

19 Last contingent of Soviet troops stationed in Hungary departs for USSR.

20 Yel'tsin meets President Bush, who reaffirms support for Gorbachev.

20 Gorbachev announces intent to merge the Yavlinskiy-Harvard plan with "anti-crisis" program, denying disagreement with Pavlov.

21 Yel'tsin's speech at New York University alleges understanding with U.S. regarding parallel relations with USSR federal and RSFSR republican authorities.

23 "Group of seven" meeting agrees in principle to offer USSR associate membership in IMF.

24 Last contingent of Soviet troops stationed in Czechoslovakia departs for USSR.

25 Gorbachev discusses "grand bargain" reform proposal with Grigoriy Yavlinskiy and Graham Allison of Harvard.

26 OMON troops raid telephone center in Vilnius, shutting down communications for two hours.

29 Investigation of Shevardnadze and Yakovlev by CPSU's Control Commission is announced.

July

1 USSR VS overwhelmingly approves legislation covering destatization of enterprises and other state-owned properties.

2 Gorbachev voices encouragement to newly formed Democratic Reform Movement, spearheaded by Shevardnadze, supported by Aleksandr Yakovlev, and favored by RSFSR Vice President Aleksandr Rutskoy and Prime Minister Ivan Silayev, municipal leaders Popov and Sobchak, military-industrial executive Arkadiy Vol'skiy, former presidential economic advisors Petrakov and Shatalin, and media liberals Fyodor Burlatskiy and Yegor Yakovlev.

 3 *Pravda* prints Gorbachev's sharp criticism of CPSU.
 3 Shevardnadze notifies CPSU of intent to resign membership.
 3 Economic program prepared for Gorbachev's presentation to "group of seven" leaders in London is alleged by Pavlov not to differ from the "anti-crisis" program.
 4 Yel'tsin voices approval of Democratic Reform Movement.
 4 Shevardnadze's resignation from CPSU is announced.
 5 USSR VS broadens legislation of privatization and foreign investment.
 5 Gorbachev and Kohl, at dacha near Kiev, discuss forthcoming meeting of "group of seven."
 8 After meeting at Novo-Ogarevo, Yel'tsin and other leaders of "nine-plus-one" republics declare support for Gorbachev's forthcoming presentation to "group of seven" leaders in London.
10 Bessmertnykh and General Moyseyev lead delegation of disarmament experts for meetings in Washington, D.C.
11 President Bush discusses with Bessmertnykh prospects for concluding negotiations on strategic nuclear weapons pact.

Name
Index

Abalkin, Leonid I., 4, 83, 132, 175, 210,
271–272, 276, 281–282, 432, 435, 520,
532
Abdramanov, Dinmukhamed, 304
Abramov, Fyodor, 156–158, 183
Abuladze, Tengiz, 452, 454, 458
Abushayev, Vladimir K., 353–354
Acheson, Dean, 395
Adamovich, Ales', 268, 454
Afanas'yev, Vladimir S., 334, 344
Afanas'yev, Yuriy N., 43, 60, 139, 140,
151, 279, 435, 441, 454, 478, 515,
520, 527, 529
Afferica, Joan, 465
Aganbegyan, Abel G., 71, 81, 83, 175,
436, 469, 523
Akhmatova, Anna, 154
Akhromeyev, Sergey F., 439, 510, 512
Alekseyev, Sergey, 446, 458
Alexander I, Tsar, 129
Alexiev, Alex, 413, 426
Aliyev, Geydar A., 5, 248, 507, 513
Alksnis, Viktor, 439, 440–441
Allison, Graham, 535
Ambartsumov, Yevgeniy A., 454
Anchishkin, Aleksandr I., 83
Andreotti, Guilio, 525, 533
Andrews, Josephine, 326
Andreyev-Rayevskiy, Aleksey, 183
Andreyeva, Nina, 167, 278, 396, 509,
528
Andrle, Vladimir, 290, 324
Andropov, Yuriy N., 3–6, 12–17, 65–
66, 71–72, 75, 79–80, 122, 136, 159,
253, 455, 466, 471

Anfimov, Oleg G., 272
Anisimov, Yevgeniy, 192, 234
Antonov, Mikhail, 164, 170, 173–175,
179, 183
Antosenkov, Yevgeniy, 54
Apenchenko, Yuriy, 324
Arbatov, Georgiy A., 116, 132
Arutyunov, Sergey, 198
Arutyunyan, Yuriy Y., 199, 234, 496
Asaris, G. K., 207
Åslund, Anders, 318, 324, 398, 426
Assad, Hafez al–, 532–533
Astaf'yev, Viktor, 158, 160, 162, 167,
183
Astrakhantsev, Aleksandr, 160, 183
Ataturk, Kemal, 477
Avaliani, Teymuraz, 308, 310
Avelichev, Aleksandr, 108, 139, 151
Aziz, Tariq, 523, 528–529

Baganov, I., 310
Bagramov, Eduard A., 234
Bahry, Donna, 208, 234
Bakatin, Vadim V., 273, 287, 526, 529,
533–534
Baker, James A., III, 513, 516, 518, 520,
522, 524, 526, 528, 530, 533–535
Baklanov, Grigoriy, 162, 170–171
Balashov, Yevgeniy B., 356–357
Batalin, Yuriy P., 54, 59–60
Batkin, Leonid M., 108, 139–140
Bauer, Otto, 223
Baygushev, Aleksandr, 164, 183
Begun, Vladimir, 168
Begun, Yosif, 505

537

Beissinger, Mark R., 33, 60
Belousov, B. M., 271–272, 274
Belousov, Igor S., 271–272
Belov, Vasiliy, 156, 158, 160, 162, 176–177, 183
Belyayev, Albert, 162
Benediktov, Ivan, 172, 183
Bessmertnykh, Aleksandr A., 527–530, 532–534, 536
Bialer, Seweryn, 9, 35, 60, 388–389, 434, 445, 447, 453, 465, 483
Biryukova, Aleksandra P., 272
Blatt, Joshua, 326
Bobkov, Filip D., 528
Bobrovnikov, Yuriy, 310
Bocharov, A., 155, 178, 183
Bogantseva, Irina V., 354
Bogomolov, Oleg T., 83, 175, 454
Bondarev, Yuriy, 118, 122, 158, 162, 167, 169–170, 179
Bonner, Yelena G., 108–109, 139–152, 392, 395, 426, 437, 445, 501, 504
Boyko, Aleksey, 301
Braginskiy, Aleksandr P., 354
Braun, Aurel, 388–389
Brazaukas, Algirdas, 225, 518
Breslauer, George W., 31, 35, 60, 241–245, 287, 324, 385–434, 436, 445, 447, 465, 475, 483, 485–495
Brezhnev, Leonid I., 5, 8, 11–13, 15–18, 28, 30, 35, 37–38, 42–43, 45, 48, 54, 56–58, 66, 68–69, 71–72, 74–76, 82–83, 85, 88, 95, 98, 100, 107, 113, 136, 138, 141, 153, 155, 158–159, 162, 171, 197, 200–201, 216–217, 220, 233, 248–249, 271, 273, 280, 289, 409, 412–413, 454–455, 466, 468, 470, 475, 476, 488, 493, 505, 512
Brinton, Clarence C., 276, 286
Bromley, Yulyan V., 194, 223, 234
Bronshteyn, M. L., 208
Brown, Archie, 387, 389, 398, 427, 431, 446–460, 486, 489, 493, 495
Brown, Demming, 155, 183
Browne, Angela, 405, 427
Brudny, Yitzhak M., 110, 153–189, 193, 233–234
Brummel, Igor, 305
Bryachikhin, Aleksey M., 358–359, 368, 378
Bryukhanov, Viktor, 28
Budyka, Aleksandr D., 75

Bukharin, Nikolay I., 163–164, 167–168, 173–175, 507–508
Bulin, Yevgeniy, 171, 184
Bunce, Valerie, 416, 427
Bunich, Pavel G., 83, 139, 441
Burlatskiy, Fyodor M., 113, 268, 536
Burns, James McGregor, 391, 403, 406, 427
Bush, George, 18, 480, 482, 511, 513, 516–517, 521, 523–526, 528, 532–533, 535–536
Bushin, Vladimir, 164, 171, 184
Bushnell, John, 37, 60
Busygin, Mikhail I., 274
Bykov, Nikolay, 85, 89
Bykov, Valeriy A., 273
Byrnes, Robert F., 488, 495

Calfa, Marian, 518
Cameron, David R., 31
Carlucci, Frank C., 509
Carter, Brian, 31
Carter, Jimmy, 469
Catherine the Great, 129
Ceaușescu, Nicolae, 518
Chabanov, A., 270
Chagall, Marc, 163
Chalmayev, Viktor, 157, 184
Chazov, Yevgeniy I., 273
Chebrikov, Viktor M., 26, 135, 196, 228, 248, 285, 414, 471, 499, 505, 511, 516
Cheney, Richard B., 516
Chepelev, N. M., 253
Chernenko, Konstantin V., 3–6, 11–14, 16–18, 65, 72, 74, 80, 159, 248, 253, 278, 398, 401–402, 447, 512
Chernov, Andrey, 437, 445
Chernyak, Volodymyr, 313
Chernykh, Yevgeniy, 168, 184
Chevrov, S. P., 274
Chichik, Yuriy M., 262
Chirkin, Albert, 171, 184
Chirskov, Vladimir G., 272
Chistyakov, V., 171, 184
Chivilikhin, Vladimir, 157, 184
Churbanov, Yuriy, 505, 511–512
Churchill, Winston, 279, 404–405, 493
Coffman, Richard, 465, 483
Cohen, Stephen F., 86, 89, 108–109, 139–152, 155, 184
Colton, Patricia, 326
Colton, Timothy J., 8–9, 65–91, 101, 107–111, 243–245, 326–381, 488, 495

Comisso, Ellen, 399, 427
Condee, Nancy, 91
Conner, Walter D., 35, 42, 60
Cumings, Bruce, 287

Dahl, Robert, 410, 414, 427
Daniels, Robert V., 250, 398, 427
Daniloff, Nicholas, 503–504
Darst, Robert G., 160, 184
Dashkevich, Ivan, 310, 324
Davis, Angela, 280
Davletova, L. Ye., 274
Day, Richard, 388
De Gaulle, Charles, 394, 404–405, 493
Demichev, Pyotr N., 75, 162
Dimidov, V., 297
DiPalma, Giuseppe, 410–412, 420–421, 427
Djilas, Milovan, 467
Dobrynin, Anatoliy F., 502, 511
Doder, Dusko, 278, 393, 398–399, 407–408, 411, 415, 416, 427
Doguzhiyev, V. Kh., 271–272, 532
Doig, Jameson W., 391, 402–405, 427
Dolgikh, Vladimir I., 253
Doronin, Anatoliy, 164, 184
Dorosh, Yefim, 184
Dostoyevsky, Fyodor M., 158
Drane, Melanie, 409, 427
Drobizhev, Sergey, 190
Dubinin, Yuriy V., 502
Dubrovina, Elida, 165, 184
Dunayev, Mikhail, 164, 184
Dunlop, John B., 159, 184
Durasov, Vladimir A., 274
Duverger, Maurice, 346, 369, 380
Dzhafarli, T. M., 33, 60
Dzyuba, Ivan, 234

Edel'man, Natan, 129
Eisenhower, Dwight D., 394
Elizabeth II, Queen, 470
Ericson, Richard, 400

Fahd, King, 533
Fainsod, Merle, 326, 380
Fearon, James D., 394, 427
Fed, Nikolay, 184
Federov, Svyatoslav V., 116
Federov, V., 292, 324
Feshbach, Murray, 37, 60, 91
Filimonov, L. I., 273
Fitzpatrick, Sheila 281, 286

Fomenko, Aleksandr, 184
Foye, Stephen, 234, 449, 458
Franco, Francisco, 460
Freeman, Adair, 286
Friedgut, Theodore, 299, 312, 320, 324, 326, 380
Frolov, Ivan, 450, 472
Fuerth, Leon, 497

Gabrielyants, G. A., 272
Gamsakhurdia, Zviad, 531, 534
Garden, Patricia, 156, 184
Gayer, Ye. A., 264
Gefenider, Vladimir E., 366
Gellert, Natalya, 221
Gel'man, Aleksandr, 108, 139, 441, 454
Genscher, Hans-Dietrich, 523, 530
Gerashchenko, Viktor V., 273
Gidaspov, Boris V., 252, 255, 261, 455
Gidwitz, Betsy, 37, 60
Gintner, Yu. 0., 199, 234
Giriyenko, Andrey N., 285
Girnius, Saulius, 235
Gladkiy, Ivan, 54
Glinkin, Pavel, 185
Glotov, Vladimir V., 108, 129–130, 139, 151–152
Goble, Paul, 99, 101, 233, 235
Godmanis, Ivars, 532
Godson, Joseph, 324
Golden, Miriam, 31
Goldman, Marshall, 390, 427
Goldman, Philip, 190, 401, 427
Golik, Yuriy, 301
Golikov, V., 310, 318
Gonchar, Nikolay N., 350, 373, 378
Gonzáles, Felipe, 524
Gorbachev, Mikhail S., 3–18, 20, 23–26, 28, 30, 32, 37–39, 41–46, 48–53, 55–61, 65, 67–69, 71–85, 87–89, 91–92, 100–101, 107, 109, 111–126, 128, 132–138, 140–144, 146–153, 159–164, 166, 170, 174, 176–177, 181, 190, 194–197, 199, 201, 204–205, 217, 220, 227–233, 241–244, 246–256, 258–259, 264–285, 290, 296, 299–302, 304–305, 308, 314, 317, 320, 323, 326–329, 335, 344, 346, 350, 356, 376, 379–380, 385–403, 406–458, 460–466, 468–481, 483, 485–494, 499–536
Gorbachev, Vyacheslav, 162, 185
Gorbunov, A. V., 203, 437

Gordon, Leonid, 292, 297, 310, 313, 320–321, 324
Gore, Albert, Jr., 497–498
Gostev, Boris I., 81, 511
Gramov, Marat G., 274
Granick, David, 31, 37, 60
Greenspan, Alan, 516
Gribov, V. G., 274
Griboyedov, Aleksandr, 129
Grishin, Viktor V., 5, 14, 55, 74, 248, 501–502
Gromov, Boris V., 287, 449
Gromyko, Andrey A., 5, 14, 16–17, 59, 74, 107, 124, 132–133, 134, 136, 138, 248, 262, 274, 278, 475, 500, 511
Grossman, Gregory, 37, 60, 122–123, 130
Grossman, Vasiliy, 145, 151, 172
Grósz, Károly, 513
Grushko, Viktor F., 528
Guboglo, M., 222, 235
Gudirov, I., 306
Gudkov, Lev, 178, 185
Gumbaridze, Givi, 513
Gumilev, Nikolay, 502
Gunko, Boris, 171, 185
Gusev, Vladimir K., 272
Gushchin, Lev N., 497
Gusman, Yuliy S., 354
Gustafson, Thane, 9, 108, 112–131, 158, 185, 427

Hahn, Jeffrey W., 242, 326, 380
Hammadi, Saadoun, 528
Hamman, Henry, 71, 89
Hankiss, Elemer, 427
Hanson, Philip, 89, 290, 325
Hauslohner, Peter A., 7–8, 31–64, 91, 98, 100, 102, 158, 185, 289, 324, 398, 427, 498
Havel, Vaclav, 489
Heinemeier, Meredith M., 50, 61
Herzen, Alexander, 129
Hewett, Ed A., 6, 91, 108–109, 112–131, 139–152, 398–399, 427, 448, 498
Hitler, Adolf, 469, 520
Hodnett, Grey, 200, 235, 398, 427
Hoffmann, Stanley, 390, 428
Holloway, David, 218, 235
Honecker, Erich, 516, 530, 534
Hook, Sidney, 428
Horelick, Arnold, 16, 18
Horowitz, Donald L., 477, 483
Hosking, Geoffrey, 155, 185

Hough, Jerry F., 3, 9, 55, 61, 94, 102, 108, 118–120, 128–130, 132–138, 243, 245–286, 341–342, 380, 388–390, 396, 400, 415, 428, 447, 465–484, 487, 488–492, 494–495
Huntington, Samuel, 412, 428
Hurenko, Stanislav, 29
Hussein, King, 532
Hussein, Saddam, 528
Hyland, William G., 4–5, 11–18, 148, 150–151

Isayev, A. S., 273
Ivanidze, Vladimir, 498
Ivanov, Anatoliy, 157, 168–169, 185
Ivanov, Ivan D., 66, 89
Ivanov, Viktor, 169, 185
Ivashko, Vladimir A., 28, 30, 522
Izrael', Yuriy A., 273

James, Daniel, 324
Janos, Andrew C., 428
Jaruzielski, Wojciech, 415, 420
Jefferson, Thomas, 477
John-Paul II, Pope, 460, 517, 525
Johnson, Lyndon B., 143, 475
Jones, Ellen, 235, 398, 428
Jowitt, Kenneth, 129–130, 158, 185
Joyce, John, 151
Juan Carlos, King, 446

Kadar, Janos, 68
Kaganovich, Lazar M., 168, 466
Kagarlitskiy, Boris, 400, 428
Kahan, Arcadius, 95, 102
Kaifu, Toshiki, 531
Kaiser, Robert G., 388–389
Kalashnikov, Vladimir I., 46–47, 274
Kallas, Siim, 208, 235
Kalugin, Oleg, 414
Kamenev, Lev B., 510
Kamentsev, Vladimir M., 274
Kamshalov, Aleksandr I., 273
Kapustin, Aleksandr F., 350
Kapustin, Ye. I., 38, 61
Karakeyev, K. K., 201, 235
Karamzin, Nikolay, 129
Karpets, Vladimir, 164, 185
Katov, Mikhail, 508
Katushev, Konstantin F., 272
Kazakevich, D. M., 42, 61
Kazakov, Leonid, 55

Kazintsev, Aleksandr, 164, 173, 175, 179, 185
Kaziyev, Bagautdin, 185
Kazutin, Dmitriy, 448, 459
Kennedy, John F., 18, 143
Kerensky, Alexander, 420
Khallik, K., 202, 235
Khatyushin, Valeriy, 164, 171, 185
Khlevnyuk, Oleg, 117, 130
Khomyakov, Aleksandr, 254
Khramov, Sergey, 310
Khromilina, Z. I., 283
Khrushchev, Nikita S., 5–6, 12–14, 18, 20, 35, 43, 54, 57–59, 83–84, 91, 100, 113, 119, 138, 146, 153, 155–156, 167–168, 172, 200, 219, 248, 377, 403, 432–433, 448, 466, 471
Khukhry, A., 170, 186
Kiernan, Brendan, 287
King, Gary, 326
Kionka, Riina, 225, 235
Kirichenko, Vadim N., 13, 274
Kirilenko, Andrey P., 13, 136, 466, 471
Kirkpatrick, Jeane, 149
Kiselev, Viktor, 142, 151
Kiselyov, Stepan, 441
Kislinskaya, L., 130
Kislyuk, M., 309, 320
Kissinger, Henry, 402, 428
Klimov, Elem, 162, 502
Klopov, Ye. V., 91, 96, 102
Klyamkin, Igor, 108, 139, 436, 440, 443, 445
Klyuchevskiy, Vasiliy O., 142
Knight, Amy, 413
Kochetov, Vsevolod, 155
Kohl, Helmut, 511, 518, 525, 536
Koksanov, I. V., 271, 273
Kolbin, Gennadiy V., 81, 504, 514
Koldunov, Aleksandr, 506
Kolesnikov, Vladislav G., 271–272
Kolpakov, Serafim V., 273
Komarov, Yu. T., 270
Komozin, A. N., 61
Komplektov, Viktor G., 531
Kon, Igor, 98
Konarev, Nikolay S., 273–274
Kondrat'yev, Nikolay D., 174–175
Konotop, Vasiliy, 172, 186
Konovalov, V. F., 271, 273
Koreyeva, V., 469, 484
Kornai, Janos, 71, 89, 125, 130, 399, 428
Koroteyeva, V., 194, 235

Korotich, Vitaliy A., 108, 118, 122–123, 139, 151, 162, 171, 497
Korsakov, I. A., 261
Kosolapov, Richard, 180
Kostakov, Vladimir G., 43, 46, 61
Kosygin, Aleksey N., 12, 14, 67, 82, 275
Kotlyar, Nikolay I., 272
Kovalenin, A. V., 165–166, 185
Kovalev, Andrey N., 366
Kozhinov, Vadim, 158–159, 165–166, 169, 171, 173, 174, 185
Kozlov, Frol R., 13–14
Kozlov, V., 192, 220, 223, 235–236
Kravchenko, Leonid, 526, 531
Krivosheyev, V., 84
Kroncher, Allen, 435, 445
Kryuchkov, Vladimir A., 274, 285, 511, 516–517, 526, 528–529, 532, 535
Kryzhkov, V. B., 267
Kubalkova, V., 409, 428
Kudryavtsev, Vladimir N., 532
Kugul'tinov, David, 221, 236
Kuleshov, V., 185
Kulikov, Ye. V., 28
Kulov, Yevgeniy G., 28
Kunayev, Dinmukhamed A., 5, 74–75, 134, 248, 504–505
Kunyayev, Stanislav, 167, 173–174, 179, 181, 186
Kuptsov, V. A., 82
Kurashvili, Boris P., 387, 454–455, 459
Kutyryev, B. P., 49, 61–62
Kuzmin, Apollon, 161, 165–166, 186
Kuznetsov, Vasiliy V., 502

Landsbergis, Vitautas, 519–521, 532
Lane, David, 98, 102, 289, 324
Lanshchikov, Anatoliy, 170, 173, 186
Lapchenko, Boris, 165–166, 186
Lapidus, Gail W., 35, 62, 91, 110, 190–237, 400, 428
Lapin, V., 171, 186
Laqueur, Walter, 166, 186
Latsis, Otto, 45, 62, 142, 151
Laverov, Nikolay P., 272–273
Lavrov, Kiril, 162
Lee Yew Kuan, 477
Legasov, Valeriy, 29, 37
Lemayev, Nikolay V., 272
Lenin, Vladimir I., 3, 85, 129, 136, 148, 158, 173–174, 190, 196, 198–202, 223, 230–231, 250, 255, 316, 335, 393, 434, 467, 531

Leuchtenberg, William E., 428
Levada, Yuriy, 454
Levine, Daniel H., 410, 428
Levine, Herbert S., 67
Levinson, Aleksey, 294, 307, 324
Levy, Marion J., 91, 102
Lewin, Moshe, 428
Lewis, Philippa, 155, 186
Ligachev, Yegor K., 5, 23, 26, 46–47,
   77, 89, 107–108, 115, 118–122, 124,
   134–135, 137, 167–168, 170, 176, 194,
   226, 228, 247–248, 252–253, 264, 269–
   270, 275–276, 279, 424–425, 461, 471,
   476, 489, 499, 505, 507–509, 511, 515,
   522
Likhachev, Dmitriy, 114, 164
Likhonosov, Viktor, 156, 186
Lincoln, Abraham, 393, 489
Linz, Juan, 420
Lipski, Jan J., 308, 324
Lisenkov, Anatoliy, 164, 186
Livshits, R., 37, 40, 62
Lobanov, Mikhail, 187
Logunov, Anatoliy, 116
Lomonosov, Vladimir, 54
Lonetree, Clayton, 505
Loshchenkov, Fedor, 115
Lowe, David, 155, 187
Lugovoy, E., 187
Luk'yanov, Anatoliy I., 133, 505, 511,
   529, 534
Lushnikov, Vladimir, 301
Lyashko, Aleksandr, 20
Lyday, Corbin, 410, 414, 428
Lysenko, Valentin, 307, 310–311
Lyubomudrov, Mark, 160, 164, 187

Maguire, Robert A., 187
Major, John, 529, 535
Makashov, Al'bert, 532
Makashova, N., 299, 324, 329
Maksimov, Yuriy P., 265
Maksimova, N. K., 59, 62
Malakov, Mikhail, 167–168, 187
Malenkov, Georgiy M., 14
Malyayev, V., 116–117, 130
Malyshev, Vadim M., 274
Manayenkov, Yuriy A., 285
Mann, Dawn, 117, 130, 258, 286
Manyakin, S. I., 75
Mao Tse–tung, 15, 18
March, James G., 406, 428
Marchuk, Guriy I., 115, 504

Markova, Yekaterina, 164, 187
Marples, David R., 7, 9, 19, 20, 22–24,
   29–30, 293, 324
Martynov, Vladlen, 156, 532
Marx, Karl, 3, 17, 190, 467
Masaliyev, Absamat, 283
Maslov, A., 203, 236
Maslova, Inga S., 55, 62
Maslyukov, Yuriy D., 207, 271–273, 285,
   508, 516
Massell, Gregory, 139
Matveyets, G., 187
Matveyev, Viktor M., 354
Mazowiecki, Tadeusz, 452, 516
Mazurov, Kirill T., 43
McAuley, Alastair, 98, 102
McGuire, James M., 287, 325
Medvedev, Grigoriy, 21–23, 30
Medvedev, Vadim A., 196, 207, 275,
   511
Medvedev, Zhores A., 6, 7, 10, 19–30,
   122, 130
Medvedeva, O., 43
Mehnert, Klaus, 187
Mekhlis, Lev Z., 172
Mel'nikov, Aleksandr G., 264
Mel'nikov, V. I., 273–274
Menshikova, T., 193, 236
Meshkov, A. G., 28
Meyer, Alfred G., 484
Micklin, Philip P., 160, 187
Migranyan, Andranik, 387–389, 395, 400,
   419–420, 428, 431, 436, 443, 445, 460–
   464, 486, 490–491, 494–495
Mihalisko, Kathleen, 29–30
Mikhal'chenko, Aleksandr I., 273
Mikhaylov, Oleg, 157, 187
Miller, John H., 398, 428
Miloserdnyy, A. K., 270
Mironov, E., 303
Mitchell, Alison, 287
Mitterrand, François, 514, 525, 531–532
Mohammed the Prophet, 129
Molotov, Vyacheslav M., 14, 466, 504
Moore, Barrington, 129, 131
Morton, Henry W., 102
Mostovoy, Pavel I., 272–273
Mostovshchikov, S., 122, 131
Mote, Max E., 380
Moyseyev, Mikhail A., 265, 533, 536
Mozhayev, Boris, 156, 164, 187
Mubarak, Hosni, 533
Mukhametsyanov, Aklim K., 270

Mukomel', V., 192, 236
Muksinov, I., 199
Murakhovskiy, Vsevolod S., 75
Mustafin, Dmitriy, 187
Mutalibov, Ayaz N., 532

Nabokov, Vladimir, 163
Najibullah, 509
Naylor, Thomas, 407, 428
Nazarbayev, Nursultan A., 514, 530
Nemchinov, Vladimir S., 73
Nenarokov, A. P., 236
Nenashev, Mikhail F., 274
Neustadt, Richard, 388–389, 412–413, 428
Nikitin, Ye. V., 52, 236, 272
Nikitinskiy, V. I., 36, 62
Nikonov, Anatoliy, 157
Nikonov, Viktor P., 75, 90, 275, 285, 506, 516
Nixon, Richard M., 475, 503, 530
Nuykin, Andrey, 454

O'Donnell, Guillermo, 317, 325, 410, 429
Obolenskiy, V. V., 85
Obolensky, Alexis N., 497
Ofer, Gur, 108
Ogarkov, Nikolay V., 13, 16
Oleynik, Boris, 532
Orlov, Yuriy, 504
Orwell, George, 509
Osipenko, O. V., 131
Osipyan, Yuriy A., 532
Ovechkin, Valentin, 156
Özal, Turgut, 530
Ozherel'yev, Oleg, 480, 528

Padunov, Vladimir, 91
Paliyevskiy, Pyotr, 157, 187
Palm, Viktor, 515
Panichev, Nikolay A., 273
Parker, Richard, 400, 429
Paskara, P., 236
Pasternak, Boris, 164, 505, 508
Patiashvili, Dzhumber, 513
Pavlov, Valentin S., 273, 476, 527–531, 535–536
Pavshentsev, A. Yu., 253
Pelton, Ronald, 501
Perón, Juan, 322
Pervyshin, Erlen K., 271, 273
Peter the Great, 129, 533

Petrakov, Nikolay Ya., 434, 480, 520, 527, 536
Petro, Nikolay N., 160, 187
Petrov, S. B., 261
Petrov, Vladimir, 162
Petrushenko, N., 439
Pigalev, Vadim, 161, 187
Pisarev, Yuriy, 187
Polad-Zade, Polad A., 274
Polozkov, Ivan K., 439, 448, 450, 522
Ponomarev, Boris N., 502
Popov, Gavriil K., 38, 49, 62, 114, 116–117, 244, 279, 344, 346, 349, 350–351, 372, 378–379, 380, 421, 438, 448, 454, 478, 515, 522, 529, 535–536
Pravda, Alex, 62, 95–97, 102, 325
Primakov, Yevgeniy M., 116, 285, 516, 524, 528–529, 534
Prokhanov, Aleksandr, 167, 190, 193, 236, 438, 443, 445, 448
Prokof'yev, Yuriy A., 343–346, 358, 368, 375
Proskurin, Pyotr, 158
Prunskiene, D. P., 270
Prunskiene, Kazimiera, 519, 521, 527
Pryor, Frederic L., 34, 62
Przeworski, Adam, 410, 412, 414, 429
Pstygo, Ivan, 168–169
Pugin, Nikolay A., 272
Pugo, Boris K., 285, 287, 449, 516, 526, 528, 529, 534
Pushkin, Aleksandr, 129, 140
Pylypchuk, Volodymyr, 313

Rahr, Alexander, 413, 429
Rakitskiy, Boris, 312, 321
Rash, Karem, 438
Rasputin, Valentin, 157–158, 160, 162, 170–171, 176–177, 188
Razhivin, Aleksandr, 414
Razumovskiy, Georgiy P., 115, 133–134, 253–254, 259
Reagan, Ronald, 11, 16–18, 24, 68, 118, 469, 480, 501, 503, 507–511
Reddaway, Peter, 108, 120, 131, 139, 277–278, 286, 386–389, 413, 429, 431–445, 460, 465, 484, 486–487, 489–490, 494–495
Redlikh, R., 290, 325
Reese, Tony, 190
Remnick, David, 476
Renner, Karl, 223
Rigby, T. H., 398, 429, 447, 459

Rimashevskaya, Natal'ya, 35, 42, 62
Rockwell, Richard, 91
Rogacheva, Nellya N., 354
Rogovin, V. Z., 38, 62
Romanov, Grigoriy V., 5, 13–14, 17, 74, 248, 500
Roosevelt, Franklin D., 73, 143, 404–405, 477, 493
Rozenova, Lira I., 274
Rozman, Gilbert, 467, 484
Rubin, V., 311, 325
Ruble, Blair A., 8–9, 31, 36, 55, 63, 91–103, 245, 262, 286, 289, 325, 396, 429
Rumer, Boris, 236
Rumyantsev, Oleg, 318
Rusak, Nikolay I., 273
Rust, Mathias, 407, 506, 510
Rustkoy, Aleksandr, 536
Rustow, Dankwart, 410, 429
Rutland, Peter, 243–245, 287–325
Ryabev, Lev D., 66, 271–272, 300, 302, 309
Rybakov, Anatoliy, 167, 505
Rykov, Aleksey I., 508
Ryzhkov, Nikolay I., 5, 23, 25, 65, 76–77, 81, 83, 123–124, 131, 196, 211, 223, 255, 257, 264, 269–272, 274–276, 278, 293, 300–301, 305–306, 309, 314, 323, 435, 440, 471, 474, 476, 481, 499–500, 514, 517, 521, 523, 526, 532–534
Ryzhov, Yuriy, 437

Sagdeyev, Roal'd Z., 116, 269
Sakalauskas, Vitautas, 218
Sakharov, A. N., 157, 188
Sakharov, Andrey D., 3, 7, 9–10, 108–110, 113, 139–152, 222, 260, 266, 269, 279, 285, 306, 348, 396, 435, 465, 499, 501–502, 504–505, 508, 511–515, 517, 533
Salutskiy, Anatoliy, 171, 180–181, 188, 320
Samolis, T., 47
Samsonov, A. S., 257
Sanders, Brian, 390, 407, 429
Sarkov, Mikhail, 532
Savisaar, Edgar, 532
Saykin, Valeriy T., 375
Schumpeter, Joseph A., 404, 434
Schwartz, Andrew, 429
Selyunin, Vasiliy I., 85, 90, 167

Selznick, Philip, 403
Semanov, Sergey, 157, 188
Semenov, Georgiy, 158
Semenov, Yuriy K., 273
Senchagov, Vyacheslav K., 273
Sergeyev, Aleksey, 164, 180, 188
Sergeyev, Viktor, 412, 429
Serov, V. M., 273
Shabad, Steven, 108, 139
Shabad, Theodore, 6, 151
Shakhnazarov, Georgiy K., 133
Shalayev, Stepan A., 52, 55, 63, 296–297
Shamir, Yitzhak, 530, 533
Shasharin, Gennadiy A., 28
Shatalin, Stanislav S., 59, 63, 111, 435–436, 441–443, 448, 475, 480, 486, 523–525, 536
Shatrov, Mikhail, 114, 167
Shauro, Vasiliy, 161
Shchadov, Mikhail I., 272, 297–298, 307, 514
Shcharansky, Anatoly, 502
Shchekochikhin, Yuriy, 123, 131, 179
Shcherbakov, Vladimir I., 273, 304, 533
Shcherbina, Boris Ye., 20, 23
Shcherbitskiy, Vladimir V., 5, 14, 20, 23, 26, 28–30, 74, 248, 264, 507, 515–516
Shekhova, Lyudmila T., 354
Shelepin, Aleksandr N., 55
Shêlest, Petr Ye., 28
Shevardnadze, Eduard A., 5, 255, 273, 283, 285, 287, 317, 500–501, 503, 507–508, 512, 516, 518, 521–524, 526, 532, 535–536
Shevtsov, Ivan, 164, 169, 188
Shibayev, Aleksey, 55
Shimko, V. I., 271, 273
Shipler, David K., 139
Shirokov, Andrey V., 361
Shiropayev, Aleksey, 188
Shishkin, O. N., 271–272
Shkabardnya, Mikhail S., 274
Shkaratan, O. I., 212, 236
Shlyapentokh, Vladimir, 91
Shmelev, Nikolay P., 72, 83–85, 90, 114, 139, 164, 175, 266, 282
Shostakovskiy, Vyacheslav, 454
Shtromas, A., 236
Shukshin, Vasiliy, 158
Shulman, Marshall D., 394
Shultz, George P., 506–508

Shustkov, L. V., 265
Shutkin, V., 346
Silayev, Ivan S., 271–272, 530, 536
Simonov, Konstantin, 155
Sitaryan, Stepan A., 533
Skilling, Gordon, 446, 459
Skokov, Yuriy, 532
Slavetskiy, Vladimir, 188
Slavskiy, Ye. P., 66
Slider, Darrell, 50–51, 63, 260, 479, 484
Slyun'kov, Nikolay N., 75, 77–78, 81, 83, 297–298, 502, 505–506, 515
Smyth, Regina, 480, 484
Snetkov, Boris, 265
Sobchak, Anatoliy A., 244, 421, 522, 535–536
Sofronov, Anatoliy, 162
Sokolov, Pavel N., 331
Sokolov, Sergey L., 441, 499, 506, 513
Solchanyk, Roman, 29–30
Solnick, Steven, 326
Solomentsev, Mikhail S., 5, 14, 135, 248, 274, 511
Solomon, Peter H., 385–389
Soloukhin, Vladimir, 158, 173
Solov'yev, Boris, 252, 255, 264
Solov'yev, Yuriy P., 260, 285, 502, 513, 516
Solzhenitsyn, Alexander, 188, 517, 523
Sorokin, M. I., 265
Spechler, Dina R., 188
Srebnyy, Mikhail, 294
Stakhanov, Aleksey, 291
Stalin, Josef V., 12–15, 18–19, 41, 44, 66, 74, 84–85, 98, 110, 121, 133, 142, 145, 154–156, 161, 163, 170–174, 196, 199–200, 202–203, 205, 219–221, 223, 229, 237, 247, 249, 278, 280, 344, 414, 448, 469–470, 472, 474, 507–510, 517
Stankevich, Sergey, 244, 346, 348–349, 365, 372, 378, 380
Starkov, Vladislav, 516
Starovoytova, Galina, 222, 454
Starr, S. Frederick, 91, 396, 429
Stevenson, Irene, 287
Strauss, Robert S., 534
Stroyev, Yegor S., 285
Suleymanov, Olzhas, 117
Surovtsev, Yuriy, 188
Suslov, Mikhail A., 12, 155, 158–159, 466
Swayze, Harold, 154, 188

Sychev, Vyacheslav V., 273
Systsov, Appolon S., 271–272
Szporluk, Roman, 237, 420

Tae-Woo, Roh, 521, 526, 531
Talyzin, Nikolay V., 65, 77, 79, 83, 285, 501, 508, 516
Tatu, Michel, 119, 120, 128–129, 131
Taubman, Philip, 71, 247
Teague, Elizabeth, 37, 42, 45, 51, 63, 286, 290, 325
Tedstrom, John, 207, 237
Telen, L., 441
Telyatnikov, Leonid P., 21
Ter-Petrossyan, Levon A., 532
Terekh, Kondrat Z., 273
Tespin, A. I., 63
Thatcher, Margaret, 4, 17, 285, 309, 465, 516, 534
Thorne, Ludmilla, 303, 305, 310–311, 313, 325
Thornton, Judith, 20, 26, 30
Tichy, Noel M., 403, 405–406, 429
Tiersky, Ronald, 402, 429
Tikhonov, Nikolay A., 5, 74, 248, 275, 306, 500, 513
Tikhonov, Vladimir I., 454
Tishkov, V. A., 194, 222, 237
Tolstykh, Boris L., 273
Toome, Indrek, 218
Trakin, Nikolay I., 349
Trehub, Aaron, 38, 63
Treml, Vladimir G., 37, 63, 377, 406
Trevor, Margaret, 326
Troitskiy, E., 176, 188
Trotsky, Leon, 14, 163, 167, 173–174, 467
Troyepolskiy, Gavriil, 158
Tsipko, Aleksandr S., 436, 445
Tsypkin, Mikhail, 413, 429, 438, 443, 445
Tucker, Robert C., 143
Tuleyev, Aman–Gel'dy, 533
Tvardovskiy, Aleksandr, 157
Tymiński, Stanislaw, 452

Ugolov, Fyodor, 165–166, 188
Usmanov, Gumer M., 285
Ustinov, Dmitriy F., 17, 74, 248

Vaganov, S., 43, 63
Valijas, Vaino, 198
Vanous, Jan, 108–109

Varennikov, Valentin, 265
Vasinskiy, Aleksandr, 87
Velichko, Vladimir M., 273
Vikulov, Sergey, 157, 179
Vilchek, L. Sh., 156, 188
Vlasov, Aleksandr V., 521
Vlasov, Yuriy, 450, 459
Volkogonov, Dmitriy, 444, 445
Volkov, Aleksandr N., 54, 272
Vol'mer, Yuriy M., 273
Volodin, E., 190, 193, 237
Vol'skiy, Arkadiy I., 536
Voronin, Lev A., 271–272, 297
Voronov, Yuriy, 162
Voronskiy, Aleksandr, 154
Vorontsov, N. N., 273
Vorotnikov, Vitaliy I., 5, 7, 26, 248, 260, 287
Voschanov, Pavel, 441
Voynovich, Vladimir, 172
Voznesensky, Andrey Y., 188–189
Vyshinskiy, Andrey Y., 466
Vyzhutovich, Valeriy, 152
Vyzov, L., 445

Walder, Andrew, 91, 100, 102, 129, 130–131
Walesa, Lech, 277, 452
Walker, John, 500
Wallace, George, 277
Weber, Max, 129, 131
Weiner, Myron, 416, 430
Wesson, Robert, 488, 495
White, Stephen, 35, 38, 64, 447, 459
Wimbush, S. E., 237
Winston, Victor H., 3–10, 108, 112–131, 139–152, 497
Wolpe, H., 430

Xiaoping, Deng 63, 81, 136

Yagodin, Gennadiy A., 116, 273
Yakovlev, Aleksandr N., 6, 8, 75, 77–78, 118, 121, 124, 161, 168, 206, 247, 253, 435, 440, 443, 454, 476, 505–506, 509, 511, 515, 520, 535–536
Yakovlev, Vitaliy F., 162, 172, 273
Yakovlev, Yegor, 536
Yakushev, Vladimir, 180
Yanayev, Gennadiy I., 323, 526, 529

Yanov, Alexander, 156, 175, 189, 400, 429
Yanowitch, Murray, 100, 102
Yaremenko, Yuriy V., 532
Yarin, Venyamin, 180–181, 233
Yashin, Aleksandr, 156, 189
Yavlinskiy, Grigoriy A., 534–535
Yazov, Dmitriy T., 217, 219, 265, 272, 449, 506, 509, 516, 524–525, 529, 532
Yefimov, Nikolay I., 273
Yegorov, Vladimir, 528
Yekimov, Boris, 164
Yel'tsin, Boris N., 4, 5, 81, 107, 111, 122, 132, 134–135, 177, 242, 244, 247, 251–252, 259, 261, 263, 265, 267, 274, 279, 283, 314, 317, 323, 334, 343, 346–347, 373, 395, 397, 416, 421, 424–425, 430, 461, 465, 471, 475, 480–481, 485–487, 489–490, 495, 500–501, 507–508, 512–516, 519, 521–525, 528–536
Yemchenko, F., 310
Yemel'yanov, Ivan Y., 28
Yeretennikov, Gennadiy A., 28
Yevtushenko, Yevgeniy, 14, 114, 497–498
Yurchenko, Vitaliy S., 500–501

Zakharov, Gennadiy F., 503–504
Zakharov, Vasiliy G., 162, 274
Zalygin, Sergey, 156–157, 160, 162, 164, 189, 274
Zaslavskaya, Tat'yana I., 3, 33, 37–39, 42, 46, 49, 58–59, 64, 85–86, 90–91, 102–103, 114, 318, 325, 398, 441, 454–455, 459
Zaykov, Lev N., 51, 75, 77, 255–257, 264–265, 269, 343–344, 500, 502, 507
Zdravomyslov, A., 317, 319, 325
Zekulin, Gleb, 155, 189
Zelenevskiy, V., 189
Zemin, Jiang, 533
Zhdanov, Andrey A., 154
Zhirinovskiy, Vladimir, 534
Zhitnukhin, Anatoliy, 189
Zhukov, Dmitriy, 13, 157, 189
Zinov'yev, Grigoriy Y., 510
Zoshchenko, Mikhail, 154
Zotov, V., 237

Subject
Index

Abkhazia, 191–192, 205, 219, 513

Academia (Soviet), 115–116, 196, 250, 342, 352, 357, 373, 377, 478, 507, 511. *See also* Intelligentsia

Academia (Western), 4, 8, 139, 466. *See also* Sovietology

Academy of Medical Sciences, 165

Academy of Pedagogical Sciences, 354

Academy of Sciences, 28, 139, 293, 532; Congress of People's Deputies and, 260, 512–513; economics branch of, 83; elections and, 339, 375, 413; institutes of, 7, 31, 38, 116, 203, 292, 321, 346; president of, 115; RSFSR and, 182, 356; Sakharov and, 260, 512–513, 517; Ukrainian, 313

Adygey Autonomous Oblast, 259

Adzharia, 205

Afghanistan, 17–18, 217, 265, 279, 343, 392, 396, 449, 500, 503, 508–509, 512, 516

Africa, 477, 491

Agriculture, 75, 262, 531; bureaucracy in, 56, 80, 274; coal mines and, 303; cooperatives and, 45, 72; CPSU leaders and, 77, 256, 275; elections and, 258–259, 261, 263; family farming in, 46, 174; Gorbachev's secretaryship of, 48, 69, 71; individually owned farmland, 527; investment in, 158, 270, 275; *kolkhozy*, 81, 147; market prices and, 66; productivity of, 71, 92; professionals in, 48, 256; reform in, 4, 83, 94, 133, 136, 162, 182, 281, 397, 481,

491; *sovkhozy*, 80; Stalin's legacy to, 155–156; workforce in, 95, 137

AIDS, 501

Air defense, 134, 506

Air safety, 501

Alcoholism, 37, 43, 66, 85, 158, 165–166

Aleuts, 220

Algeria, 444

Alma-Ata, 9, 99, 109, 191, 199, 504, 535

Altayskiy Kray (Altay), 261–262

American "leftists," 109, 149

Anti-alcohol campaign, 3, 5, 48, 162, 165–166, 168, 170, 177, 489, 499–500

Anti-Americanism, 121

Anti-communist demonstrations, 527. *See also* Demonstrations

Anti-cosmopolitan campaign, 174

Anti-crisis program *(1991)*, 531, 535–536

Anti-Lithuanian demonstrations, 527

Anti-nuclear movement, 29, 30

Anti-Semitism, 114, 160–161, 167–169, 172, 174, 192. *See also* Pamyat'

Anti-Stalinism, 155, 157, 162, 172, 403.

Antiballistic Missile Treaty (ABM), 501–502, 512, 516

Apparatchiks, 33, 121, 314, 343, 413, 432, 473. *See also inter alia* Communist Party

Architectural landmarks, preservation of, 156, 158–159, 345, 355–356

Arctic, 26, 294

Argentina, 321–322

Armenia, 133–134, 191, 203, 253, 266, 279, 469, 474, 530–531; conflict with

Azerbaijan and, 109, 191, 203, 224, 266, 279, 474, 532; demographic composition of, 220; earthquake in, 269, 276, 512; elections and, 133; independence of, 523, 534; legislation in, 518; Nagorno-Karabakh and, 469, 508–510, 512; nationalism in, 111, 191; refugees, 519, 533; violence in, 521
Arms control, 11, 16–17, 396, 408, 502–504, 510, 525. *See also* Disarmament
Article Six. *See* Constitution of USSR
Arts, 87, 97, 171, 193, 339, 350, 352, 355, 357, 371, 373, 378
Asia, 477, 491, 503
Association of Russian Artists, 355
Astrakhan', 115
Auditing Commission of CPSU, 75, 513
Austerity, 521. *See also* Ryzhkov program
Austro-Hungarian Empire, 477
Austro-Marxists, 223
Authoritarianism, 179, 191, 194, 294, 324, 326, 385–387, 410, 419–420, 436, 440–442, 446–447, 452, 458, 460, 482, 491
Automobile production, 48–49
Autonomization, 202
Autonomous regions, 200–201, 205, 221
Autonomous republics, 205, 221, 400, 520, 533
Azerbaijan, 133–134, 253; conflict with Armenia and, 109, 191, 203, 224, 266, 279, 474, 532; demographic composition of, 220; language policy, 212; military service in, 218; Nagorno-Karabakh and, 508–510; nationalism in, 191; unemployment in, 192; violence in, 511, 518

Baku, 511, 518
Baltic Military District, 218
Baltic republics, 212, 215, 217–218, 270, 530–532; Chernobyl' and, 30; discrimination against Russians in, 175, 181, 221; economic reform and, 210–212; elections and, 260, 267, 513; informal groups in, 215; language policy and, 212; legal status of, 193, 204; military intervention in, 254, 479; nationalist movement in, 109, 176, 179, 191, 212, 227–228, 246, 284, 401; republic militias and, 218; secession of, 279, 397, 400, 476, 534; strikes in, 290; Union Treaty and, 440

Bangladesh, 477
Banking system, 53, 73, 122, 357
Bankruptcy, 73, 506
Barter system, 284, 386
Bashkir ASSR, 137, 192, 205, 219
Beijing, 513, 530
Belgium, 214
Belorussia, 43, 77, 80, 285, 311, 432, 502, 529; Chernobyl' and, 7, 24, 27–28, 30, 315; demographic composition of, 220; elections in, 519; strike in, 531
Berlin Wall, 514, 517
Bern, 509
Birobidzhan. *See* Jews
Black Hundreds, 166
Black market, 45, 282, 449
Black Sea, 502, 508
Bloc of Social-Patriotic Movements of Russia, 182, 233, 355–357
Blue collar workers, 47, 97; conservatism of, 86, 88; elections and, 340–342, 352, 371, 375; housing of, 377; skill of, 96; wages of, 35–36, 39, 48–49, 54. *See also* Workers
Bolshevik party, 73, 156, 166, 326, 378, 466
Bolshevik Revolution, 4, 11, 127, 148, 378, 507, 516
Bonn, 525
Bourgeoisie, 168, 321, 400, 420, 451, 467
Bragino, 27
Bread prices, 521
Brezhnev era, 5, 12–13, 56, 68, 113, 129, 402, 468; appointments of, 115; attacks on, 83, 391–392, 396, 411, 413; censorship and, 66, 141; CPSU leadership and, 249, 466; cooperatives and, 45; ethnic relations and, 197, 216, 233; foreign policy and, 409, 413; Gorbachev's attitude toward, 69, 396, 408, 411, 413; military and, 217; nostalgia for, 476; reform in, 12, 488; republics and, 200–201; Russian nationalism and, 159; social contract of, 100, 289; social policy of, 8, 98, 421; stability of, 95, 124; stagnation and, 12, 107; thick journals and, 153, 155, 158
Brigade system, 46, 50, 54–55, 79, 81, 263
Brookings Institution, 108, 112
Brussels, 517, 522

Budget, state, 109, 285, 290, 319, 392, 511, 526; deficit, 514, 530

Bulgaria, 492, 571

Bureau for Social Development, 56

Bureaucracy, 8, 12, 56, 65, 68, 70, 81, 124–125, 165, 175, 196, 283, 292, 342, 467, 502, 510; attacks on, 132–133, 147, 262, 373, 396; Chernobyl' and, 22; conservatism of, 120, 246, 411; corruption of, 122–123, 356; diminished authority of, 101, 142, 399; distribution network and, 318–319; Gorbachev and, 324, 398, 416; privileges of, 78, 80, 276, 467, 487; resistance of, 40, 52–53, 58, 78–80, 82, 84–85, 88, 119, 121, 146, 211, 228, 270, 302, 320, 324, 420, 432, 470, 473; trade unions and, 303–304, 313, 357. *See also inter alia* Communist Party; Ministries

Cabinet of Ministers, 529

Cadres department, 132–133, 172, 181, 199, 215, 470–471. *See also* Central Committee

Canada, 214, 477, 519

Capitalism, 3, 17, 32, 34, 57, 68, 148, 321–322, 345, 348, 407, 435, 454–455

Caucasus, 12, 212, 220, 265; anti-Russian movement in, 176, 181; interethnic violence in, 192, 195, 228, 317, 401; military service and, 216; nationalism and, 175, 179; secession and, 179, 397; strikes in, 290

Censorship, 7, 140, 142, 279, 348, 474, 483, 517, 531

Center for the Study of the Worker's Movement, 310, 321

Central America, 18

Central Asia, 209, 265, 282, 461; economic sovereignty in, 211; health problems in, 208; Islamic fundamentalism in, 479; interethnic violence in, 191–192, 195, 228; language policy in, 212, 216–217; military service and, 216; nationalism in, 317; river diversion project and, 160, 355

Central Committee of the CPSU (CC), 16, 72, 78, 84, 107, 115, 126, 150, 196, 199, 202, 226, 262, 280, 353, 398, 471, 522; agriculture and, 270; attacks on, 275; cadres department of, 132–133, 172, 199, 470–471; conservatism and, 268; dead souls of, 113, 249; elections and, 223, 343; Gorbachev and, 118, 135, 248, 269, 281, 465, 474, 490, 504, 517; journal of, 192, 282, 469; joint ventures and, 505; lame ducks in, 108, 113, 135, 138, 249–250, 264, 472; media and, 408; membership changes in, 5, 28, 65–66, 108, 113, 116–117, 126, 134–138, 161, 247–249, 251, 282, 413, 424, 471, 513; multiparty system and, 190; powers of, 134, 258, 320, 470; removal of Yel'tsin, 251–252, 283; resistance of, 119, 436; restructuring of, 125, 133; Russian bureau in, 205, 231; Russian nationalism and, 159; second economy and, 502; thick journals and, 154. *See also* Communist Party; Party congresses; Party plenums

Central Economic Mathematical Institute (TsEMI), 83, 321

Central Europe, 473, 477

Central Intelligence Agency (CIA), 270, 357, 501, 528

Central planning. *See* Planned economy

Central Trade Union Council (VTsSPS), 39, 53–57, 304

Centralism, Soviet state and, 40, 190–191, 201–202, 227, 230, 232–233, 392, 433

Centrist coalition, 529

Charismatic leadership, 59, 129–130, 400, 433, 464

Chechen-Ingush ASSR, 192, 200, 220, 249

Chelyabinsk, 137, 256

Chemical waste, 182

Chemical weapons, 500, 506–508, 510, 516, 520–521

Chernobyl' nuclear disaster, 6, 8, 19–30, 315, 407, 502, 533; contamination, 7, 20, 24, 27–28; coverup and, 7; evacuation, 7, 21–24, 27–28; fifth anniversary of, 6, 532; IAEA report, 29; Kiev May Day parade, 7, 23, 26; media coverage, 6, 21, 23–26, 29–30; nuclear energy policy and, 19, 26, 29–30; official reaction to, 6–7, 20, 22–26; political implications of, 28–30; radioactivity, 21–25, 27–29; reactor design, 19, 22, 29

Child welfare, 43

China, 18, 136, 138, 465; agricultural reforms, 81, 481; Communist Party of, 250, 256; economic reform in, 14–15, 68, 88, 208, 399, 407; Gorbachev's visit to, 513; nationalities and, 211; regional protectionism and, 127; relations with USSR, 500, 503, 530, 532–533

Chistka (purge), 5, 506

Chita, 137, 257

Christian-Democratic party, 224

Christianity, 1,000th anniversary of, 469, 510

Churches: preservation of, 156, 355; destruction of, 168–169

Cinema, 171

Civil liberties, 348

Civil society, 287, 321, 420, 467

Civil war (*1917–1921*), 81, 169, 173; (*1990s*), 403, 406, 420–421, 432–433, 443–444, 455, 463, 474, 487, 529

Class struggle, 281, 391, 408

Clienteleism, 129

Coal industry, 266, 274, 290–291, 294, 302, 309; investment in, 292; labor productivity and, 292–293; accident rate in, 293; republics and, 480; wages in, 514

Coal miners, 271, 284, 287, 323; privileges of, 291; solidarity of, 291; education level of, 292; wages of, 291–294, 298, 311

Coal miners' strikes; 7, 256, 265, 269, 277, 284–285, 290, 293, 321, 397, 407, 415, 486, 514–515, 530–532; aftermath of, 301–315; beginnings of, 294–296; demands of, 294, 296–299, 306, 313, 319; economic autonomy and, 297–299, 301–303, 305, 308–309; government concessions to, 297–300, 302; historic impact of, 315–320; leaders of, 292, 306, 308; management and, 296; new union and, 290, 313–314; official union and, 294, 296–297, 303–305, 308, 310–312; Resolution *608* and, 302–303, 305–306, 309–310, 312, 314; right to strike, 516; spread of, 299–301; strike committees and, 295, 298–300, 303–306, 308, 310, 312

Cold War, 109, 148, 150, 151, 280, 396, 409

Collective leadership, 8, 456

Collectivization, 155, 167–169, 172–174

Colonialism, 356

Command economy, 67, 172–173, 191, 318, 393, 446; CPSU and, 124; marketization of, 394, 410. See also Planned economy

Command-administrative system, 201, 206, 220, 231, 431

Commissions: on Ideology, 196; on Questions of Interethnic Relations, 196; on Security and Cooperation in Europe (CSCE), 521, 525

Committees: for the Supervision of the Constitution of USSR, 446; on *Glasnost'* and Rights and Appeals of Citizens, 249; on Legislation, Law, and Order, 304; on People's Control, 253; on Radio and TV, 526–527

Communal violence, 192, 195, 233, 511, 513, 518, 521, 524–525, 527

Communications, right to strike in, 516

Communist ideology, 155, 211, 231, 323, 341, 408, 509, 511; advocates of, 44, 51, 439, 443, 466; attacks on, 45; Bukharin and, 174; Gorbachev and, 45, 51, 56, 83, 403, 434, 453; military-ideological complex, 452, 454; role of, 12, 154, 458, 494; shaping of, 5, 77, 159, 275. *See also* Leninism; Marxism-Leninism

Communist Party of the Soviet Union (CPSU), 7, 15, 28, 32, 101, 206, 222, 501, 509, 524, 531; apparatus of, 15, 33, 81, 120, 124–126, 128, 132–134, 162–163, 254, 310, 334, 448, 465, 470, 511; attacks on, 160, 224, 474, 536; attitudes toward reform, 32–33, 147, 279, 434, 438; Brezhnev and, 12; democratization of, 47, 125–126, 253–254; discipline, 172, 267, 270, 356; elections and, 256–266, 326–327, 330, 334, 336, 338–339, 341–344, 348, 350–354, 357, 359, 370–371, 375, 512; federalism and, 227, 232; fragmentation of, 223–227, 231, 416, 454; future of, 481, 491–492; Gorbachev and, 3, 4, 11, 71, 144, 206, 253, 277, 390, 435, 453, 462–463, 473; hegemony of, 322–33, 481; ideological secretaryship of, 509, 511; leading role of, 32, 108, 120, 125, 301, 391, 397, 425, 433, 460, 517; local, 81, 120, 124–125, 133, 196, 223–224, 293–294, 296, 305, 473; loss of power, 34, 322, 396, 431, 447, 474, 514; miners' strikes and, 314, 316;

monopoly of power, 32, 40, 190, 226, 320–321, 335, 408, 413, 425; nationality policy of, 196, 232; party-state apparatus, 46, 68, 91, 133, 136, 142, 144, 146, 268, 289, 317, 321, 434–444; personnel changes in, 126, 136–137, 407; privileges of, 415; property of, 313; reform of, 15, 132, 134; regional, 250–256, 261, 269, 473; resignations from, 317, 378, 426, 475, 520, 522, 536; resistance of, 320; rules of, 249, 251–252, 258, 268, 472–473; tenure of office in, 125–126; violation of standards of, 505; workplace and, 288, 294, 424–425. See also inter alia Central Committee; General Secretaryship of the CPSU; *Gorkoms; Obkoms;* Party congresses; Party plenums; Politburo; *Raykom*

Computerization, 66

Concentration camps, 174

Confederation, 393; of republics, 193, 211, 227, 230, 387, 400, 421, 434, 435, 441, 463, 486, 487

Congress of Democratic Forces, 528

Congress of People's Deputies (CPD), 343–344, 355, 397, 411–413, 437, 450–451, 473, 480, 514, 535; Article Six and, 517; candidates' occupations and, 263; coverage of, 474; CPSU members in, 257; Credentials Committee of, 252; economic reform and, 518; elections to, 110, 144, 193, 203–204, 211, 223–224, 247, 252, 256–272, 277, 279, 285, 513; "Moscow Group," 266; Persian Gulf and, 534; radicals and, 266–267; Russian nationalism and, 176–177; Supreme Soviet and, 267, 472

Conscientious objectors, 218

Conservative movements. See also inter alia Interfront; Rossiya; Soyuz; United Front of Russian Workers; *Yedinstvo*

Constituent Assembly, 326

Constitution of RSFSR, 450–451

Constitution of USSR, 268, 420, 439, 531; Article Six and, 301, 305–307, 312, 314, 320, 335, 473, 517–519; collapse of, 111, 444; demands for change in, 288, 297, 348, 416, 421; draft amendments to, 109; head of state and, 144; reform of, 107, 134, 143–145, 196, 203, 472, 511; republics and, 200;

Russian state institutions and, 231; secession and, 476; violations of, 144

Constitutional democracy, 482–483

Constitutional monarchy, 446

Constitutional Oversight Committee, 230

Constitutions: (*1918*), 219; (*1936*), 336; (*1977*), 200–201, 203, 219

Construction industry, 56, 250, 255–256; employment in, 95

Consumer goods, 313, 526, 530; coal industry and, 291, 293; distribution of, 319, 359; prices and, 86; private markets and, 100, 507; quality of, 44; sector; 34, 42; shortages of, 283, 293, 437, 448; strikes and, 514; subsidies for, 37; supply of, 42, 66, 101, 172, 293, 299, 491

Consumer rights law, 533

Consumption, 34, 38, 42, 49, 58. See also Food

Control Commission of the CPSU, 535

Conventional Forces in Europe (CFE) Treaty, 512, 524–525

Cooperatives, 179, 373, 476; agriculture and, 45, 72, 527; corruption in, 122–123; expansion of, 43, 142, 392, 407, 478; foreign trade and, 66, 511; laws on, 123, 398, 504–505, 509; legitimacy of, 45; restrictions on, 80, 180; service sector and, 46; small-scale industry, 45; state chartered, 32; taxation of, 515; unpopularity of, 176–177; wages and, 284

Cooperators' Union, 307

Corruption, 45, 160, 171; Brezhnev era and, 129, 415; bribe taking, 122–123; bureaucracy and, 122–123, 356; campaign against, 4, 13, 66, 71, 75, 81, 121, 398, 414, 499; exposure of, 121, 147, 309; removal from CPSU for, 134, 249; trials for, 504, 511–512

Council for Mutual Economic Assistance (CMEA), 503–504

Council of Europe, 514, 529

Council of Ministers, 81, 207–208, 270–271, 274, 353, 454; abolition of, 440, 457; bureaus of, 56, 73, 79–80; chairmanship of, 136, 223; commissions of, 68, 77, 115; decrees of, 502, 504–505, 512; Presidium of, 65–66, 272

Council of Nationalities, 143, 177, 200, 258, 259, 261, 263, 264, 267, 532

Council of the Federation. See Federation Council

Council of the Union, 143, 258–259, 267
Credit system, 53
Crime, 392, 437, 533. *See also* Organized
    crime
Crimean Tatars, 192, 200, 205, 220–221,
    507
Cuba, 513
Cultural affairs, 97, 99, 114, 355, 528;
    exchange programs and, 501, 503;
    Gorbachev and, 177, 402, 409, 434,
    485; liberalization in, 49, 77, 84, 160,
    162–163; nationalities and, 145, 191,
    193, 196, 198, 220, 223, 230; plural-
    ism in, 163–164, 176, 215; politics and,
    142, 258; reform and, 87, 227, 318–
    319, 392, 399, 402, 404, 407–409, 422,
    434, 485; Russia and, 165, 170–171,
    174, 176; Suslov and, 155; Yakovlev
    and, 161–162; Zhdanov and, 154. *See
    also* Arts; Literature
Currency reform, 84, 182, 209, 283, 452
Czechoslovakia, 169, 477–478, 508, 512,
    517–519, 535

Daily newspapers, 27, 87, 122, 158, 163,
    167, 180, 213, 261–262, 450, 454–
    455, 499, 501, 509, 517, 523, 533,
    536
Day care, 289
De-Stalinization, 12, 14, 142, 168, 200,
    234
Decembrists, 161
Decentralization, 72–73; economic re-
    form and, 31–32, 42, 58, 81, 121, 141,
    195, 206, 293, 318, 323, 420; Kosygin
    reform and, 67; political reform and,
    110, 146, 148, 195, 203, 208, 232,
    234, 392, 434, 476, 479–480
Defense Council, 268, 343, 500
Defense industry, 264, 271; right to strike
    in, 516
Defense policy, 12, 356, 408, 399, 413;
    jurisdiction over, 515; spending and,
    154, 531
Democracy, 109, 140, 279, 335, 404; de-
    nouncement of, 515; Gorbachev and,
    268, 408, 423, 441–442, 474; insti-
    tutions of, 51, 468; introduction of, 109,
    139, 191, 321, 348, 359, 380, 385–
    386, 394–395, 402, 410, 412, 419–
    421, 431, 436, 446, 460–461, 463, 470,
    475, 485, 490; legal reform and, 443;
    perestroyka and, 144, 419; resistance

to, 285, 323, 407, 457, 474. *See also*
    Democratization
Democratic Forum, 509
Democratic party (Soviet), 311
Democratic platform, 424
Democratic Reform Movement, 536
Democratic Union, 296, 307
Democratization, 56, 133, 190, 199, 208,
    412, 417, 482, 491, 505; CPSU and,
    125–126, 253–254, 473; economic re-
    form and, 53, 58, 387, 393, 399–401,
    410, 419, 423; Gorbachev and, 53, 87,
    246, 277, 388, 419, 461, 489, 493–
    494; military and, 217; nationality pol-
    icy and, 234, 394, 423, 474; *nomenkla-
    tura* and, 142, 277; *1988* legislation
    and, 148; opposition to 51, 164, 194,
    314, 379, 414, 462–463; political, 87,
    124, 207, 220, 232, 303, 342, 368,
    379, 393, 395–396, 400–401, 406, 409–
    410, 418, 447–448, 485–487, 492;
    public participation in, 50, 142, 202,
    258, 416; republics and, 208; social
    policy and, 49, 411, 419–420, 460,
    491; support for, 412; workplace and,
    49–54, 56, 142
Demokraticheskaya Rossiya (Democratic
    Russia), 111, 311, 327, 348, 355–357,
    379, 386, 527, 529; Congress of, 524;
    creation of, 349; elections and, 350–
    351, 353–354, 361–363, 365–366, 368–
    375, 377–378, 519
Demokraticheskiy Trud (Democratic La-
    bor), 308
Demonopolization, 398, 425, 426
Demonstrations, 196, 228, 269, 281, 519;
    anti-military, 218; coverage of, 285;
    failure of, 480; in Moscow, 314, 507,
    512–513; restrictions on, 144, 530;
    Russian minorities and, 205, 213
Deregulation. *See* Economic reform
Destatization, 520, 535
Détente, 12, 16, 475
Dictatorship, 482, 528; of CPSU, 40, 326;
    Gorbachev and, 441, 449, 477; She-
    vardnadze's resignation and, 317
Diplomats, expulsion of, 499–500, 503–
    504, 506, 508, 519
Disarmament, 181, 499–501, 505, 509,
    511, 536. *See also* Arms control
Dissent, 87, 392; repression of, 34
Dissidents, 216, 504–505, 509, 523

Distribution network, 42, 100, 318, 449; inefficiency of, 319
Dnepropetrovsk, 123, 471; mafia of, 74
Dnieper, 19, 30
Donbas coal basin, 288; living conditions in, 293; miners' strike and, 299–300, 302, 311–313, 514–515, 529; production of, 291
Donetsk, 123, 292, 296, 300–301, 303, 307, 310, 312–313, 524
Draft, 443; resistance to, 218, 461
Drugs, 163, 414
Dual power (*1917*), 308
Dushanbe, 519, 527

Earthquakes, 269, 276, 512, 532
East Asia, 410, 491
East Germany, 221, 232, 259, 265, 499, 509, 516–517, 521
Easter services, 509, 531
Eastern Europe, 167, 169, 277, 444, 508; democratization in, 3, 190; communism's collapse in, 18, 225–226, 287, 317, 362, 396–397, 479, 490, 492, 517; economies of, 33–34, 86; reform of, 394, 400, 447, 455; Soviet withdrawal from, 513
Ecology. *See* Environmentalism
Economic and Social Research Council, 446
Economic growth, 34, 38, 58, 65, 71–72; decline in, 31, 41; imbalances in, 33
Economic reform, 69, 88, 124, 134, 180, 397, 406, 432, 502, 522, 528; advocates of, 86, 89, 206, 233, 314, 479; austerity measures in, 512; chaos in, 4; Chernenko and, 13; CPSU and, 15, 81, 113; deregulation in, 32–33, 41; Gorbachev and, 5, 14, 42–50, 67, 69, 72, 87, 108, 174, 247, 278, 281, 398, 402, 406–407, 421, 436, 441–442, 463, 468, 493, 521; implementation of, 8, 77, 91, 133, 140, 146, 172, 276, 399–400, 419–420, 446, 460; opposition to, 31, 44, 78–79, 127, 164, 173, 182–183, 256, 269–270, 446, 470, 473; private enterprise and, 66, 68, 392, 434; "radical," 32, 42, 53, 57–58, 75, 164, 182, 233, 314, 399–400, 416, 435–436, 441, 494; republics and, 210–212, 285, 481; savings, 283; Shatalin Plan and, 435, 441; "shock treatment" for, 476, 520–521; trade and, 53, 283; Western as-

sistance to, 535. *See also inter alia Perestroyka*
Economic sociology, 39
Economic statistics, 66
Economists, 82–83, 196; as advisors, 516, 527
Education, 48, 66, 94, 97, 181, 263, 277, 377–378; exchanges with U.S., 501, 503; freedom of choice and, 43; increase in, 39, 92–93, 96, 98–99; language policy and, 212
Egalitarianism, 31, 34, 38, 41, 57, 86, 277, 342, 407–408
Egypt, 417, 533
Election to Moscow *Gorsoviet (1990)*, 326–381; campaigning, 332–334, 344, 353; candidates and, 327, 330–332, 336, 338–343, 355–357, 359, 361, 371–375; centrist bloc, 357–361, 368; CPSU and, 343–346, 353; electoral commissions, 333–336, 349; electoral districts, 328–329; left-wing bloc, 346–354; nominations for, 331–334, 349–350; results of, 337, 361, 369; right-wing bloc, 354–357, 362, 368; runoff in, 336–338, 361, 368; voting procedures, 335–337, 371; women candidates, 339–343, 371–372
Elections, 108, 125, 137, 142, 147, 224–226, 251–256, 278, 309, 316, 323, 399, 411, 413, 492; Congress of People's Deputies (*1989*), 144, 177, 223, 256–266, 269, 327; CPSU and, 125–126; legislative (*1994*), 481; municipal, 535; Nineteenth Party Conference (*1988*), 114–116, 251, 510, 512–513; pre-*1990*, 366; presidency (*1995*), 481; presidency of RSFSR (*1990*), 441, 451; presidency of USSR (*1990*), 519; propaganda and, 326, 345; of republic leadership, 534; RSFSR Supreme Soviet chairmanship (*1990*), 521
Electoral system, 9, 472, 474, 491; introduction of, 469, 473; multicandidates, 9, 87, 111, 115, 125, 142, 326–327, 407, 411, 476, 505–506; multiparty, 85, 132, 144, 190, 224, 226, 279, 287, 343, 348, 387, 391, 414, 421, 426, 432, 434, 454, 491; new electoral law, 143; power of recall, 125; reform of, 50, 327; secret ballot, 9, 114–115, 125, 505
Electric power industry, 7; right to strike in, 516

Elites, 66, 158, 373, 375, 385, 407, 423; Brezhnev and, 56, 488; bureaucratic, 101; collapse of, 490, 492; education and, 93–94; intellectual, 37, 99, 154–155, 159, 162; local, 201, 213, 215, 294, 306; military, 217; miners' strikes and, 294, 306; national, 9, 95, 99, 101, 301; nationality policy and, 212–213, 215, 233; party, 170–171; political, 8, 37, 143, 148, 155, 167–168, 175–177, 233, 249, 276, 326, 378, 399, 413–414, 424; professional, 99; reform and, 45–46, 50, 72, 161, 249, 388, 400, 410–412, 418, 488; republic, 200, 202, 221, 231; social contract and, 35, 38

Emancipation of serfs, 84

Emergency powers, 144, 420, 474, 489

Emigration, 392, 504; law on, 533

Employment, 39, 54, 95, 289; family, 43; individual, 43, 45, 47, 55; job placement bureaus, 43, 54; job security and, 34, 38, 43, 289, 407; legal protection and, 43, 289; mobility, 43; redundancy, 43, 46, 57, 127, 146, 289

Energy sector, 7, 19, 56, 314; Lithuanian blockade, 520. *See also* Coal industry; Oil and gas industry

Engineers, 47, 49, 81, 97, 340, 342, 350, 352, 357; CPSU leaders and, 256; "proletarian," 292

Enlightened monarchy, 109, 140

Enterprise councils, 51–52, 56

Enterprises, 142, 168, 175, 500; accountability of, 58, 71, 82; bankruptcy and, 73; CPSU and, 129, 310; destatization of, 535; earnings of 45, 314; ethnic tensions and, 207; foreign trade and, 511; independence of, 52–53, 66, 71, 75, 80, 206, 210, 269, 302, 379; law on the state (*1987*), 51–53, 67–68, 73, 75–76, 88, 269–270, 289, 506, 508; regulation of, 54, 121, 127; republic control over, 201, 209, 211, 228; taxation of, 209, 515, 521

Entrepreneurship, 84, 175, 387, 400, 404, 407, 492

Environmental protection, 517

Environmentalism, 266, 373, 377, 379, 393, 501; Chernobyl' and, 7; ecological disasters and, 262, 274, 354; economic development and, 175, 207, 230; informal groups and, 347; intelligentsia and, 271; miners' strikes and, 297; na-

tionalist movements and, 156, 158–160, 220, 355; republics and, 208–209, 211

Eskimos, 220

Espionage, 500–501, 503–504

Estonia, 109, 111, 133, 211, 224, 253, 277, 279, 474, 510, 520, 525; Communist Party of, 198, 225; currency reform in, 209; demographic composition of, 220; economic autonomy and, 208–209; ethnic Russians in, 175, 191, 207, 515; independence of 529; military service in, 218; nationalist movement in, 176, 510; parliament of, 225; sovereignty of, 513; Supreme Soviet of, 209, 511, 515; women, 218

Ethnography, 196–198

Ethnonationalism, 192–193, 217

European Community, 517, 528

Exchange rates, 282

Executive presidency, 519

Expansionism, 147, 392

Exports, 49, 504

Factories, 147, 330; CPSU leaders and, 256; directors of, 263; shut down of, 146; social benefits in, 319. *See also* Enterprises

Far East, 220, 259, 261, 265

Fascism, 403, 406, 417–418, 420–421, 487

Federalism, 393, 401, 421, 442, 456, 476, 487, 493; restructuring of system, 191, 194–195, 199, 202–206, 212, 228–229, 232–233; structure of USSR, 191–193, 199–201, 205, 222, 226–227, 231, 279, 356; Lenin's views on, 200, 202, 230–232

Federation Council, 206, 456–457, 462, 525, 527, 531

Fergana Valley, 192, 514

Filmmakers Union, 9, 162, 502

Finland, 330

Fisheries, 510

Five-Year plans, 66, 79, 82, 98, 143, 255, 282, 284–285

Food: credits for purchases, 534; distribution and, 449; factories and, 319; imports of, 37; miners' strikes and, 289, 293–295; *1982* Food Program, 48; prices of, 42; rationing of, 283, 294, 319, 437, 525, 528; supply crisis, 172, 270, 311, 359; U.S. aid, 526

Foreign aid (Soviet), 448

Foreign currency. *See* Hard currency

Foreign Ministry, 500, 527, 533

Foreign policy, 12, 124, 204, 234, 407, 417; Brezhnev and, 16; changes in, 11, 392, 396, 402, 415; control of, 230–231; CPSU and, 511; East-West relations, 4, 109, 447; Gorbachev and, 15, 138, 149, 406, 409, 413, 415–416, 422, 432–433, 485, 493; *perestroyka* and, 109, 234, 423; Shevardnadze's resignation and, 526. *See also inter alia* Disarmament; Soviet American relations; Summit meetings

Foreign trade, 49, 66, 209, 504

Fragmentation, 321–322, 442, 461; CPSU and, 223–226. *See also* Communist Party

France, 444, 457, 501, 506, 508, 514, 519, 521, 523, 525, 531–532

Free economic zones, 182

Freedom of assembly, 144, 433

Freedom of speech, 7, 433

Freemasons, 163, 169

Gagauz, 219, 221, 524

GATT, 532

General Secretaryship of the CPSU, 14, 78, 80, 86, 118–119, 126, 136, 248–251, 254, 280–283, 308, 471–474, 499, 522; Andropov and, 71; Gorbachev and, 3, 11, 16, 38, 42, 44, 48, 50, 73–75, 134, 148, 153, 199, 253, 278, 308, 390, 402, 424, 425; removal of, 268, 473. *See also* Central Committee; Communist Party; Party congresses; Party plenums; Politburo

Geneva, 11, 16–17, 499–504, 507, 509, 514

Geneva Convention, 218

Georgia, 109, 111, 139, 160, 253, 266, 278; Abkhazians in, 191, 205; demonstrations in, 512; demographic composition of, 220; earthquake in, 532; elections in, 524; forced incorporation of, 519; independence of, 531, 534; military service and, 218; separatism and, 227; South Ossetians in, 191; Supreme Soviet of, 530; violence in, 513

Germany, 16, 129, 163, 169, 449, 454, 479, 515, 518, 525, 527, 536; Berlin, 535; troop withdrawal from, 530; unification of, 417, 519, 522–523, 529

Gerontocratic governance, 4

GKES (State Commission on Foreign Economic Relations), 66

GKNT (State Committee on Science and Technology), 80

Glasnost', 88, 132, 216, 275; bureaucracy and, 119, 124, 277, 303, 411; campaign for, 44, 49, 100, 195, 380; Chernobyl' and, 7; conception of, 142, 475; consequences of, 110, 141, 150, 190, 201, 232, 285, 400–401, 412, 419; defenders of, 81, 139, 396; Gorbachev and, 128, 147, 400, 406–407, 476; labor movement and, 295; media and, 66, 433; military and, 217; opposition to, 118, 124, 153, 161–162, 164, 166–170, 194, 228, 414, 509; origins of, 6, 411; restrictions on, 486

GNP, 33, 37, 514

Gomel', 26, 512

Gorkiy, 137, 170, 499, 501, 504

Gorkom (municipal committee of the CPSU), 117, 251, 257, 259, 261, 277, 344, 345

Gosagroprom (State Agro-Industrial Committee), 56, 65, 270, 501, 512

Goskomgidromet (State Committee for Meteorology), 21

Goskomstat (State Committee for Statistics), 507

Goskomtrud (State Committee on Labor and Social Problems), 36, 39–40, 43, 49, 53–55, 57; conservatism of, 54; history of, 53–54

Goskomtsen (State Committee on Prices), 53, 80, 271

Gosplan (State Planning Committee), 43, 53, 68, 73, 77–80, 83, 122, 167, 207, 254, 270, 285, 456, 507–508, 529

Gospriyemka (state quality inspection system), 79, 290, 505

Gossnab (State Committee for Material and Technical Supply), 79, 302

Gosstandart (State Committee for Standards), 79

Gosstroy (State Committee for Construction), 508

Gosteleradio (State Committee on Radio and TV), 527

Great Britain. *See* United Kingdom

Greece, 410

Green Party, 224

Greenland, 501

"Group of Seven," 534–536

Gulags, 174, 294, 517

Hard currency, 283, 302, 354, 525, 529
Harvard University, 535
Health care, 7, 47–48, 97, 354, 373, 377,
  449
Hegelian philosophy, 316
Helsinki, 504, 509, 523
Hereditary monarchy, 129
Hitler-Stalin pact. See Molotov-Ribben-
  trop pact
Homosexuality, 170, 171
Housing, 345, 354, 377–378; cost of, 42;
  expansion of, 100, 208, 379; factories
  and, 319; shortages of, 55, 86, 207,
  293, 444; subsidies for, 37; trade unions
  and, 289, 311
"Human factor," 51, 407
Human rights, 139, 220, 223, 228, 231,
  504, 508–509
Hungary, 15, 88, 169, 208, 232, 478,
  481, 503, 513, 517, 519, 535; eco-
  nomic reforms in, 13, 68
Hunger strike, 499, 501

Iceland, 503–504
Incomes, 8, 34, 36, 42–43, 182; distri-
  bution of, 66, 277; nonlabor, 32, 42,
  45, 47, 59; unearned, 71, 75, 87
India, 172, 214, 477, 499
Individual rights and freedoms, 43, 74
Industrial relations before *perestroyka*,
  288–291
Industrialization, 19, 40, 94, 167, 173
Industry, 66, 71, 77, 101, 262–263, 276,
  281, 319, 481
Inflation, 283, 290, 304, 392, 434, 479,
  528, 534
Informal groups, 166, 223–224, 228, 317,
  355, 407
Institutes: Economics, 38, 83; Economics
  and Organization of Industrial Production (IEiOPP), 83; Economics of the
  World Socialist System (IEMSS), 83;
  Ethnography, 195; Marxism-Leninism, 196, 202; Sociological Research,
  86; Sociology, 362, 374; Space Research, 116; State and Law, 7, 31, 203,
  454; the USA and Canada, 83, 116,
  139; World Economy and International
  Relations (IMEMO), 175, 532; World
  History, 346

Institutionalization, 56, 404, 460; economic reform and, 42, 58; political reform and, 460–461; problems of, 53,
  322, 405, 409, 412; social contract and,
  36, 44, 50; social policy and, 58, 422;
  workers' movement and, 301, 316
Intelligentsia, 8, 84, 140, 179, 220, 246,
  250, 254, 257, 265, 269, 277–280, 308,
  378, 467; CPSU and, 173, 341; coal
  miners and, 311, 318; environmentalism and, 271; Gorbachev and, 119, 122,
  128–129, 162, 268, 512; Jewish, 174;
  liberal-reformist, 157, 163–164, 168,
  171–172, 176, 227, 474; media and,
  193; nineteenth century, 150; non-Russian, 212; reform and, 89, 140–141,
  470; Russian nationalist, 110, 158, 167,
  170, 180–181, 192; technical, 39, 41,
  47, 350; thick journals and, 154; weaknesses of, 160, 483. *See also* Academia
  (Soviet); Professionals
Inter-Regional Group, 181, 227, 279, 346,
  348, 355, 397, 497, 515, 517
Intercontinental ballistic missiles (ICBMs),
  507
Interest rates, 524
Interfax, 527
Interfront, 221, 225
Intermediate-range nuclear forces (INF),
  507–508, 510
International Atomic Energy Agency
  (IAEA), 7, 29, 502, 533
International Monetary Fund (IMF), 526,
  534–535
International Research and Exchanges
  Board (IREX), 31, 287
Internationalism, 190, 198
Investment, 33, 210, 283, 290; civilian
  sector and, 66; coal industry and, 293;
  legislation on, 536. *See also* Economic
  reform; Joint ventures
Iran, 518
Iraq, 444, 479, 522–525, 527–529
Irkutsk, 137, 522
Islamic fundamentalism, 479
Israel, 108, 506, 510, 523–524, 530, 533
Italy, 92–93, 95, 400, 516–517, 525, 533
Ivanovo Oblast, 265

Japan, 18, 24, 147, 400, 407, 481, 491,
  501, 528, 531
Jews, 160–161, 163, 165, 167–169, 172–
  174; associations, 215; Birobidzhan,

205; dissidents, 502, 505. *See also* Anti-Semitism
Joint ventures, 66, 148, 170, 182, 356, 398, 503; law on (*1987*), 9, 133, 504

Kaliningrad, 260, 534
Kalmyks, 200, 220–221
Karachay-Cherkes Autonomous Oblast, 258
Karaganda, 303, 515
Karelia, 260–261, 269
Katyn' forest massacre, 520, 530
Kazakh Writers Union, 117
Kazakhstan, 88, 221, 278, 301, 315, 515, 529; corruption in, 134; demographic composition of, 220; political appointments in, 74, 81, 253; riots in, 109, 260, 504, 514; sovereignty of, 524
Kazan', 80
Kemerovo, 137, 256, 264, 292, 295, 298, 309, 533
KGB, 285, 336, 375, 434, 444, 505, 513, 528; abuses of, 517; Andropov and, 13; attacks on, 450, 463; chairmanship of, 414, 456, 499, 511; depolitisization of, 313, 348; elections and, 339, 350; fight against crime and, 449, 486; Gorbachev and, 248, 280, 413, 443, 449, 475, 487; increased authority of, 322; workers' unrest and, 289
Khozraschet, 50, 71, 146, 196, 206, 208–209, 506–507
Khrushchev era, 5, 12–14, 54, 100, 113, 153, 155, 200, 219, 432
Kiev, 7, 20–23, 26–27, 30, 123, 261, 264, 317, 449, 500, 524, 536
Kirghizia, 220, 253, 283, 474, 515, 521, 526, 531–532
Kirov, 137
Kishinev, 213, 531
Kokand, 514
Kolkhozy. *See* Agriculture
Komi ASSR, 132, 137, 262, 292, 294, 305–306, 532
Komsomol, 156, 178, 258, 317, 339, 341, 350, 353, 370–371, 375, 413
Konfederatsiya Truda (Confederation of Labor), 310
Korean minority, 220
Kosygin reform program, 12, 46, 67, 82
Krasnaya nov', 154
Krasnodar, 53, 115, 134, 254, 259, 262, 264

Krasnoyarsk, 137, 501, 507, 516
Kremlin, 4, 12, 14–15, 23, 72, 74–76, 78, 84, 161, 346, 421, 426, 440, 506, 529. *See also* Moscow
Kuban', 260
Kulikovo Field, *600*th anniversary of battle, 158
Kurchatov Institute of Atomic Energy, 29
Kurgan, 137
Kurile Islands, 531
Kursk, 27
Kuwait, 522
Kuybyshev, 115, 136, 137
Kuzbas coal basin, 265, 288, 294, 301, 314, 514; living conditions in, 293; mine transfer and, 532; miners' strike in, 257, 294–299, 308–310, 312, 319, 514; production of, 291–292; workers' committee of, 318, 320
Kyshtym, 24

L'vov, 123, 264
Labor force, 31, 43, 37–38, 40, 54, 91, 95, 100, 266, 289; bureaucracy in, 40; discipline and, 37; militancy of, 400; productivity of, 292. *See also* Workers
Labor law, violations of, 37, 40
Labor unions, first independent, 524; convention of, 505. *See also* Trade unions
Land ownership, 519, 525–526
Language laws, 512, 515–516
Language policy, 176, 193, 196, 201, 212–216, 221, 227
Latin America, 410, 482
Latvia, 79, 111, 203, 209, 220, 224, 437, 449, 478, 525; Communist Party of, 206; CPSU and, 518; demographic composition of, 220; Gorbachev on, 528; independence of, 529; military intervention in, 486; military service in, 218; Russians in, 191, 205, 207; secession of, 520; sovereignty of, 515; Supreme Soviet of, 209, 218; violence in, 527
Law and order, 228, 437, 448–449. *See also* Legal reform
Law on Laboring Collectives (*1983*), 51, 54–55
Law on the State Enterprise. *See* Enterprises
Leadership, 47, 51, 55, 66, 99, 101, 155, 206, 224, 260, 289, 326, 388, 412, 414, 463; Brezhnev and, 12; bureau-

cracy and, 82, 85; Chernenko and, 4; collective, 16, 68, 70, 74–75, 91, 280; CPSU and, 33, 37, 80, 88, 133, 194–195, 223, 226, 256, 261, 278, 283, 286; debate on, 528; evaluation of, 394–395, 419, 492–494; Gorbachev and, 3–4, 13, 15, 18, 44, 58–59, 65, 135, 138, 143, 146–147, 150–151, 159, 204, 228, 232–233, 247, 255, 279, 387, 390, 392–393, 397–398, 401–402, 410, 413, 416, 420–421, 425, 431–432, 444, 455, 460, 462, 464–466, 469, 474, 486, 494; Ligachev and, 168; nationalities problem and, 192–195, 204, 216, 221, 225, 229, 232; political, 74–78, 82, 84, 91, 155, 290–291; Soviet, 8, 17, 31–32, 44, 108, 133, 136, 146, 148, 159, 204, 228, 232–233, 387, 390, 399, 413, 423, 450, 461, 467; top leader, 69–74; transformational, 385, 386, 389, 391, 396, 403–410, 422, 433, 485, 492–494; Yel'tsin and, 260. *See also* Communist Party; Politburo
League for Spiritual Rebirth of the Fatherland, 355
Leasing, 514, 517, 524
Lebanon, 462
Legal Affairs Commission, 196
Legal nihilism, 443
Legal reform, 66, 68, 71, 87, 124–125, 142, 194–195, 387, 409, 437–438, 443, 461, 518; independent judiciary, 408
Legal scholars, 196, 203; training of, 122
Legitimacy, 408–409, 411, 414, 452; of CPSU, 194; elections and, 326; leadership and, 31; of political authority, 31–32; of Soviet state, 191, 289, 394
Lenin Prize, 158
Leningrad, 48, 77, 127, 255, 310, 438, 455, 479; corruption in, 123; elections and, 252, 254, 261–262, 265, 317, 348, 480, 535; employment in, 97; *gorkom* of, 259, 261, 437; rationing in, 525; Russian nationalism and, 180; stock exchange in, 533; U.S. consulate in, 504; wage reforms and, 49
Leningrad University, 479
Leninism, 6, 129–130, 190, 196, 227, 356, 393–395, 403, 408, 410, 413, 420, 422–423, 425, 438, 444, 460. *See also* Communist ideology; Marxism-Leninism
Liberal-Democratic party, 534

Liberalization: calls for, 321; culture and, 49, 162–163; elections and, 327; Gorbachev and, 447, 476; intellectual, 88; process of, 190, 416; television and, 163
Liberals. *See inter alia* Nineteenth Conference *(1988)*
Libraries, 378
Likhachev Auto Works, 259, 263, 354
Lipetsk, 285
Lishniye lyudi (Griboyedov's superfluous people), 129
Literary criticism, 157, 164
Literature: *Children of the Arbat*, 505; *Day of Judgment*, 169; *Diktat*, 210, 309; *Doctor Zhivago*, 164, 508; *Everything Lies Ahead*, 160; *Fire*, 160; *Forever Flowing*, 145; *Gulag Archipelago*, 517; *Life and Adventures of Ivan Chonkin*, 172; *Life and Fate*, 172; *Parting of the Ways*, 160; *October, 1916*, 179. *See also* Village prose
Literaturnaya gazeta, 113, 122–123
Literaturnaya Rossiya, 355–356
Lithuania, 206, 222, 232, 267, 523, 525, 527; annexation of, 204, 469, 515; autonomy of, 111, 209, 226, 229, 461, 476; blockade of, 435; Communist Party of, 176, 224–225, 253, 518, 520; demographic composition of, 220; elections in, 519; energy blockade, 520; ethnic Russians and, 213, 224–225; Gorbachev and 476, 528; language policy, 176; military intervention in, 478, 486; military service in, 218; nationalism and, 111; Poles in, 191, 219, 221, 224–225; secession of, 520; sovereignty of, 513; supremacy of laws of, 204; Supreme Soviet and, 515; Supreme Soviet of, 204, 209, 218; suspension of laws and, 521
Living standards, 34, 41, 209, 276–277, 289–290, 298–299, 319
London, 4, 13, 535–536
Lubyanka prison, 123

Machine building, 56, 80
Mafia, 121, 123, 356
Management, 80, 255–256, 262, 319, 377, 467–468; autonomy of, 53, 67, 82; coal miners' strikes and, 294, 296; decentralization of, 146, 318; elections and, 52, 88, 258, 339–342, 352, 371, 373;

mid-level, 39; pressures on, 66, 407; reform of, 67, 71, 76, 79, 86; trade unions, 289; wages and, 48; workers and, 51, 289–290. *See also* Enterprises

Mari ASSR, 137

Market economy, 68, 76, 88, 100, 143, 190, 436; advocates of, 206, 318, 348; democratization and, 400, 410, 420; economic reform and, 31–32, 42, 142, 210, 475; Gorbachev and, 290, 320, 408, 435, 454, 476, 481, 486–487; Lenin and, 174; opposition to, 182, 233, 287, 304, 318–319, 374, 457, 462, 471, 480; Russian nationalists and, 172–173, 323; transition to, 73, 86, 142, 175, 182, 256, 314, 386–387, 392–395, 399, 410, 416–421, 423, 431–432, 435–436, 445–446, 452–453, 458, 461, 485–487, 491–493, 524; unemployment and, 443. *See also* Economic reform

Market socialism, 175, 433, 435

Marxism, 6, 17, 67, 86, 308, 318, 322, 356, 467

Marxism-Leninism, 3, 148, 158, 196, 202, 434, 467–468, 483. *See also* Leninism

Maslyukov Commission, 204, 207, 228

May Day parades, 7, 23, 26, 520, 532

Media (Soviet), 55, 65, 68, 75, 79, 115, 120, 143, 271, 327, 450–451, 455; anticorruption campaign and, 121–122; anti-Semitism and, 167; Chernobyl' and, 6, 23–24, 29–30; coal miners' strikes and, 294, 296, 300, 306, 310, 316; election coverage and, 338, 346, 349, 351, 354, 359, 361; *glasnost'* and, 45, 66, 163, 193, 413, 433, 474, 506; Gorbachev and, 3, 278, 390, 436; independence of, 426, 454; nationalities question and, 195–196, 200, 212, 247, 279; *perestroyka* and, 140–142, 147–148; political candidates from, 339, 342, 350, 352, 357, 373; reform and, 59, 162–163; regional newspapers, 158, 163, 180, 293, 305, 309, 312, 346, 359; reproaches of, 118, 166, 169–170, 194, 441; restrictions on, 483, 486; social policy and, 35–36; *Tass*, 292. *See also* Daily newspapers; Television

Media (Western), 14, 69, 277, 307, 416, 426, 447, 466, 473, 480, 488, 501, 516, 518; Chernobyl' and, 6, 29; CNN, 528; Gorbachev's succession and, 4; magazines, 4, 29, 108, 119–120, 139, 390, 419, 471, 474; *Reuters*, 292. *See also Time* magazine

Memorial Society, 145, 172–173

Meskhetian Turks, 220–221, 514

Mexico, 481, 491

Mezhdurechensk, 294–297, 305, 307, 309, 514

Middle class, 49, 179, 379, 387, 400, 491–492

Middle East, 527, 532–533; arms exports to, 530

Military, 147, 322, 407, 462; in Afghanistan, 279; airlift of, 518; applications for asylum, 534; Central Committee and, 250; Chernobyl' and, 21–23; conscription in Estonia, 520; CPSU cells in, 524; defenders of, 179, 181, 356; defense of installations, 525; defense spending, 148, 275, 281; draft enforcement by, 527; draft evasion, 219; economic reform and, 13; elections and, 263, 265, 268, 357; ethnic tensions and, 193, 205, 217, 486; exercises, 524; Gorbachev and, 135–136, 413, 433–434, 438, 440, 443, 448–450, 465, 468, 475, 477, 479; language problems in, 216–217; national units and, 200, 218; nationality policy and, 111, 191, 216–219, 227, 254, 438; opposition to, 269, 313, 448; preservation of order by, 439, 444, 461; reliability of, 478, 482, 487; Third World and, 392; veterans' organization, 43; withdrawal of, 513, 518–519, 523, 525, 528. *See inter alia* Ministry of Defense

Military-ideological complex, 452, 454

Military-industrial complex, 228, 275, 344

Mineral resources ownership, 534

Minfin (Ministry of Finance), 53, 79, 507

Ministries, 121, 127, 142, 227, 270, 280, 304, 317, 322, 392, 440, 454; economic, 206, 211; federal, 53, 209–210, 220; industrial, 79, 207; list of 272–273; local control of, 209; purges in, 413; resistance of, 438

Ministry of Atomic Energy and Industry, 7, 23

Ministry of Coal, 293

Ministry of Communications, 271

Ministry of Defense, 134, 356, 448, 506, 513, 527–528, 532, 534

Ministry of Electric Power, 28

Ministry of Finance. *See Minfin*

Ministry of Health, 22, 27
Ministry of Heavy and Transport Machine Building, 79
Ministry of Interior Affairs (MVD), 179, 322, 339, 443–444, 487, 519, 524, 526–527, 533–534. *See also* OMON
Ministry of Justice, 515
Ministry of Medium Machine Building, 22–23, 28, 66
Ministry of Power and Electrification, 22
Ministry of the Automobile Industry, 79
Ministry of the Communications Media Industry, 271
Minsk, 27
Missiles: deployment of, 16, 499, 504, 507, 509; production of, 522
Modernization, 66, 84, 121, 197, 454, 477, 488–489, 491
Moldavia, 213–214, 220, 224, 515, 518, 521, 530–531; Communist Party of, 532; conflict of laws in, 526; demographic composition of, 220; Gagauz in, 219, 221; independence of, 534; language policy, 213–214; Popular Front of, 213; Russians in, 191, 205; sovereignty of, 522; Supreme Soviet of, 214; violence in, 524–525
Molodaya gvardiya, 110, 153, 155–156, 164, 167–169, 171–173, 175–176, 179; anti-Semitism in, 169; circulation of, 153, 177–178, 180; Russian nationalism, 156–157, 159, 163–164
Molotov-Ribbentrop pact, 193, 469, 506, 510, 515, 518
Mongolia, 506
Moscow, 7, 23, 29, 38–39, 49, 69, 83, 108–110, 115, 139–140, 144, 176, 181, 196, 203, 215, 218, 223, 227, 264, 287, 292, 297, 305, 314, 319, 416, 423, 438, 451, 454, 469; cooperatives in, 284; corruption in, 123; daily newspapers of, 118, 162–163, 331, 346, 349, 359, 508; demonstrations in, 518, 529; elections in, 177, 255, 259, 261, 265, 267, 326–381, 480; employment and, 97; intelligentsia of, 171–172, 265, 280; May Day parade in, 532; mayor of, 478, 497; McDonalds in, 407; municipal elections in, 535; opposition movements in, 311–312, 317, 479; rationing in, 210, 528; as RSFSR capital, 182; Sakharov's return to, 3, 9; as seat of power, 4, 11, 18, 21–22, 71, 75–

76, 82, 114, 141, 147, 190–191, 195, 204, 208, 211, 221–222, 224–225, 260, 262, 266, 285, 294, 308–310, 313, 443; strikes in, 307, 315; U.S. consulate in, 504; Yel'tsin and, 5, 81, 252, 259
Moscow Association of Voters, 347, 349
Moscow Cooperative Institute, 84
Moscow *Gorkom*, 5, 107, 114, 127, 252, 254, 257, 343, 457, 501, 507
Moscow *Gorsoviet*, 330, 344, 347, 353, 359, 372, 378–380, 437, 448, 457
Moscow Popular Front, 347, 349
Moscow State Institute of Historical Archives, 139
Moscow State University, 116, 123, 179, 346, 349, 378, 465, 478–479, 509
Moslem population, 216, 478
Mosyr', 27
Multinational system, 190, 194, 197, 227, 232, 267, 386, 393–394, 423
Munich, 69, 520
Municipal militia, 529
Mutual and balanced force reduction (MBFR), 512
MVD. See Ministry of Interior Affairs

Nagorno Karabakh, 109, 145, 167, 191, 203, 205, 224, 232, 252, 266–267, 400, 435, 469, 508, 510, 512, 533
Nanay, 263
Narkomtrud, 36
Narodnoye Soglasiye (Social Harmony), 355
Nash sovremennik, 110, 153, 155, 157–59, 162–173, 175, 179, 181; anti-Semitism in, 160–161, 169; circulation of, 151, 157–159, 178, 180; Russian nationalism, 157, 159–160, 164, 180; environmentalism, 160; Russophobia and, 176
National income, 122, 392
National minorities: demands of, 192, 219, 223, 456; Gorbachev and, 220; internal migration of, 207–208, 212; Lenin and, 203; rights of, 231, 421; Russians as, 191, 194, 205, 207, 212–215, 221–222, 444
National security, 392, 408, 411, 457
Nationalism. *See inter alia* Russian nationalism
Nationalities (non-Russian), 9, 99, 110, 145–146, 190–234, 285; anti-Russian demonstrations, 191–192, 444; ethnic

relations and, 195, 197–199, 215, 403, 418, 491; ethnic unrest and, 6, 109, 134, 191–192, 194–195, 208, 213, 216, 223, 228, 230, 233, 290, 388, 393, 400–401, 410, 434, 446 435, 456, 469; Gorbachev and, 432, 489; language rights and, 193, 212–216; national question and, 197, 223, 233; punished peoples and, 205, 220–221. *See also* National minorities; Nationality policy; Republics

Nationalities Forum (Tallinn), 215

Nationality policy, CPSU and, 232; debate over, 193–195, 199, 229, 233; deportations and, 229; Gorbachev and, 228, 282, 402, 474; history of, 196–197, 200

Nationalization, CPSU assets, 531

NATO, 417, 479, 503, 506, 516, 518–519, 522, 525

Natural resources, 111, 220, 230, 442–443, 461, 522–523, 525

Neotraditionalism, 129–130

NEP, 115, 173–174

Neva dam, 262

New Deal, 67, 73, 143, 405

"New thinking," 109, 149–150, 197–198, 396, 409, 415, 467

New York, 515, 535

Newly Industrializing Countries (NICs), 489

Newspapers. *See* Daily newspapers

Nicaragua, 17

Nineteenth Conference of the CPSU (*1988*), 109, 118–119, 121–122, 124–127, 132, 136, 168–169, 203, 211, 242, 248, 262, 408, 411, 472–473, 510; Central Committee and, 134–135, 249–250; conservatism at, 114, 116; delegate selection, 107–108, 112–116, 133, 251, 344; Gorbachev's objectives, 107, 112–114, 134–135; liberals at, 115, 117; *1941* party conference and, 113, 117; results of, 135–138; Russian nationalism and, 169–170; voting irregularities at, 115–116

NKVD, 174, 520

Nobel Prize, 3, 504, 524, 534

Nomenklatura, 142, 146, 251, 271, 334, 373, 392

Nordic Council, 529

Novo-Ogarevo, 526, 534

Novocherkassk, 289

Novosibirsk, 38, 49–50, 54–55, 83, 85, 136–137, 261, 292–293, 297, 309–310, 455, 532

Novyy Mir, 153, 155–157, 160, 162, 164, 177–178, 508; anti-Stalinism of, 155; Russian nationalism and, 155–156; village prose and, 155–157

Novyy Uzen', 192

Nuclear power, 179, 355, 510. *See also* Chernobyl'

Nuclear waste, 182

Nuclear weapons, 506–508; disarmament negotiations, 499, 505–508, 521, 536; manufacturing, 66; removal of, 513; submarine, 513; testing, 500–505, 507, 510, 516

Nüremberg, 463

Obkom (oblast committee of CPSU), 117, 126–127, 136, 248, 251–254, 256–258, 260–264, 268, 295, 303, 312, 315, 465; elections to CPSU conference, 114, 116–117; first secretaries, 115; soviets and, 119, 128

Odessa, 123

OFT. *See* United Front of Russian Workers

Ogonyok, 118, 122, 129, 139, 162, 163, 170, 171, 173, 351, 497, 516

Oil and gas industry, 315, 520; right to strike in, 516

"Old guard," 13–14, 16

OMON, 527, 534–535

Omsk, 137, 261

"Open skies," 518

Ordzhonikidze, 511

Orel, 285

Orenburg, 82, 137, 256

Organized crime, 122–123, 414

Osh, 521

Osnovnyye polozheniya, 506

Ottoman Empire, 129, 418, 492

Palace of Congresses, 116

Palestine, 357

Pamyat', 114, 166–167, 169, 171, 224, 307, 506

Panama, 357

Paris, 514, 525

Party congresses, 72, 134–135, 137–138, 225, 249, 253–254, 282, 472; *20th* (*February 1956*), 230; *27th* (*February 1986*), 5, 7, 18, 26, 37, 43–46, 51,

55, 67, 124, 161, 253, 281, 471, 502;
28th (July 1990), 108, 249–250, 308,
423–426, 456, 461, 473, 475, 485, 522
Party plenums: *(March 1985)*, 59, 499;
(July 1985), 500; *(June 1986)*, 503;
(November 1986), 504; *(January 1987)*,
9, 47, 50–53, 56, 83, 250–252, 505;
(June 1987), 8–9, 67, 76–77, 208, 506;
(February 1988), 508; *(July 1988)*, 510;
(September 1988), 511; *(September
1989)*, 195, 214–215, 221, 229, 516;
(February 1990), 518; *(January 1991)*,
528; *(April 1991)*, 532
Pavlodar, 515
Peasantry, 94, 155–158, 165, 173–174,
250, 259, 262–263
Pechora Basin, 288, 294
Pensions, 43, 289, 303, 311, 479, 521
Penza, 123, 260
People's Control Committee, 75
People's Front. *See* Popular Front
Perestroyka, 91, 247, 251, 285, 359, 438,
454; advocates of, 86, 92, 139, 161–
162, 396, 416, 423; American perceptions of, 148–151; conception of, 59,
109, 120–121, 128, 140–143, 202, 316,
475; consequences of, 60, 98, 147, 190,
419; divergence from, 529; ethnic violence and, 514; expectations for, 85,
101, 380, 418; "from below," 296,
320–322; Gorbachev and, 8, 53, 67,
71–72, 91, 107, 112, 126, 144, 163,
195, 246, 407, 411, 433, 437; local
government and, 303; nationality policy and, 111, 145, 194, 234; opposition
to, 56, 92, 113, 118–119, 121, 124,
139, 145–146, 153, 164, 166–170, 300,
345, 355, 424, 509; origins of, 144;
republics and, 208; Ryzhkov and, 81,
270. *See inter alia* Economic reform
Perm', 123, 136–137, 256
Peronism, 321–322
Persian Gulf, 523–529, 534
Petrograd, 127
Planned economy, 40, 319; coal mines
and, 299, 302, 308; deficiencies of,
290, 317; disintegration of, 317, 386,
397; dissatisfaction with, 206; maintenance of, 32–33; plan fulfillment and,
289, 292; transition to market and, 73,
342, 386. *See also inter alia* Command
economy; Five-Year plans; *Gosplan*
Plebiscite, 529

Plenums of the Central Committee of
CPSU. *See* Party plenums
Pluralism, 412; cultural, 163–164, 173,
176, 215; ethnic, 198; market economy
and, 418; opposition to, 110; political,
142, 193, 287, 320, 387, 408, 411,
434, 446–447, 453, 458; totalitarianism vs., 488
Poetry, 171, 173, 497, 502
Pogroms, 509, 518
Poison gas, 513
Poland, 17, 55, 232, 246, 277, 285, 289,
292, 304, 307–308, 317, 323, 357, 400,
415, 452, 478, 480–481, 509–510, 515–
517, 524, 531
Police, 529, 531
Police-army patrols, 526, 528
Polish Association (Vilnius), 214
Politburo, 4, 13, 71, 74, 76, 86, 114,
154, 206, 254, 264, 284, 343, 356,
402, 408, 512; administration of, 14,
16, 275; anti-alcohol campaign and, 165;
Brezhnev and, 280, 455; Chernenko
and, 81; Chernobyl' and, 6, 7, 20, 24,
26, 28; composition of, 285, 414, 473;
conservatism and, 75, 120, 136; CPSU
conference and, 117–118; economic
reform and, 80, 82, 398, 436; elections
and, 125–126, 134, 252, 260, 265; expansion of, 522; language policy and,
216; members of, 79, 107, 115, 260;
membership change, 5, 8, 75, 134, 170,
250, 413, 499–502, 504–508, 511, 516;
miners' strikes and, 297, 315; nationality policy and, 196; political skills of,
255; powers of, 258, 399, 470–471;
republics and, 207, 225, 253, 401; resistance of, 119, 247, 269–270, 281–
282; river diversion project and, 160;
trade unions and, 56; *28th* Congress
and, 424; weakening of, 241, 320, 456;
Yakovlev and, 77, 161; Yel'tsin and,
107, 251–252
Political asylum, 534
Political contract, 158–159, 161–162
Political economy, 39, 59, 99–100
Political parties, 334, 421, 454, 462;
Moscow elections and, 348–349; post-
revolutionary, 154, 322, 326; prere-
volutionary, 153. *See also inter alia*
Democratic Russia; Electoral system
Political prisoners, 396, 505, 508
Political rights, 33, 43, 194

Popular Front, 227–228, 461; of Baltic republics, 109, 260, 513; elections and, 144; of Estonia, 225, 510; of Lithuania, 469; of Moldavia, 213; Moscow and, 347, 349; Russia and, 307
Populism, 58, 411, 436, 464
Portugal, 410, 419
Potsdam, 499–500
Power, consolidation of, 7, 13–14, 108, 133–135, 246–256, 270, 280–281, 285, 320, 396–398, 447, 469–470, 474, 481, 489. *See also* Leadership
Prague, 506, 512
Pravovoye gosudarstvo, 409. *See also* *Rechsstaat*
Presidency of RSFSR, 532, 534–535
Presidency of USSR, 511, 533; creation of, 320, 380, 456; elections and, 312, 314, 387, 457; emergency decree and, 524; Gorbachev and, 268, 387, 419–420, 426, 431, 435, 438, 447, 461, 474; imposition of rule of, 527; powers of, 519, 526; presidential law and, 439–440, 443–444; public insults to, 520; republics and, 437
Presidential Council, 206, 233, 439, 456, 462, 520, 525
Presidential Plan (*1990*), 523–524
Presidential Security Council, 529
Press, freedom of, 521
Prices, 80, 179, 523, 527; central control of, 40, 58, 512; coal, 299, 318; Congress of People's Deputies and, 518; fuel, 314; increase of, 521, 530; market, 66, 319; reform of, 42, 45–46, 53, 55, 73, 86, 209, 282, 284, 398; retail, 305; stability of, 34, 407; subsidies and, 73, 506; wholesale, 285. *See also* Economic reform
Primary party organizations (PPOs) 114, 117, 125–126, 193, 251, 255–256
Pripyat', 22–23, 30
Privatization, 68, 111, 142, 379, 387, 398, 400, 433–434, 443, 454–455, 480, 486–487, 520, 531, 536; law on private firms (*1986*), 68, 504
Productivity, 34, 51, 147, 208–209, 212, 512; decline in, 33, 37; wages and, 67, 79
Professional'no-Obshchestvennyy Soyuz (Professional and Social Union), 308
Professionals, 9, 37, 39, 48–49, 97, 100, 212, 263, 342, 373–374, 377–378, 436; in agriculture, 48; incomes of, 47–48; social status of, 47, 58; women as, 9, 95, 98–99. *See also* Academia (Soviet); Intelligentsia; White collar workers; Yuppies (Soviet)
Proletariat, 291–292, 467
Property, 278, 345, 347–348, 359, 462, 519; class distinction and, 420, 491; legal reform and, 408; local control over, 461; nationalization of, 313; ownership by republics, 211, 230, 443; private, 182, 356, 435, 442, 476; privatization and, 398, 443; public ownership of, 32, 454; state, 45, 71, 73
Prosecutor general, 534
Prostitution, 163
Protectionism, 127, 210
Public Committee to Save the Volga, 355
Pugwash Conference, 139
Punished peoples, 192
Purges (*1930s*), 85, 173, 280, 510

Radical centrism, 423–425, 485, 490, 493
Railway strikes, ban on, 533
Rationing, 283, 294, 319, 437, 525
Raw materials, 182, 522
Raykom (raion committee of the CPSU), 251, 259
Rearmament, 12
Rechsstaat, 125
Red Square, 134, 407, 506–507. *See also* Moscow
Referendum (*March 1991*), 480, 526–527, 529–530
Refugees, 191
Regional Workers Committee (RWC), 309–310, 312–313, 318, 320
Rehabilitation: of Bukharin, 163–164, 167–168; of Stalin's victims, 414; of Trotsky, 163
Religion, 317, 392; education and, 523; freedom of, 348; Islamic fundamentalism, 18; observance of, 524. *See also* Russian Orthodox Church; Uniate Church
Republics: autonomy and, 109, 193–194, 200–201, 203, 205, 207–208, 210, 230, 232, 285, 317, 416, 433, 440, 454, 461, 476–477; economic sovereignty of, 206–209, 211, 227, 231; elections and, 133, 144; federalism and, 199, 231, 421; governance of, 101; military and, 218, 449; relations among, 182,

211–212, 215, 460; relationship to center, 199–200, 203–204, 207, 212, 230, 386; secession of, 110, 145, 401, 435, 481, 489, 491; Shatalin Plan and, 435, 475; state property and, 443; Union Treaty and, 387, 456–457; unrest in, 392, 397, 447. *See also* Confederation; Federalism
Resource allocation, 193, 201, 211
Restructuring. *See Perestroyka*
Riga, 207, 506, 527
Risk-taking, 44, 148, 407. *See also* Entrepreneurship
River diversion project, 84, 160, 165, 172, 355, 503
Rock music, 160, 162–164, 168, 170–171
Roman Catholic Church, 519
Romania, 492, 514, 518
Rossiya club, 181, 233, 355, 356, 516. *See also* Bloc of Social-Patriotic Movements of Russia
Rostov, 87, 532
RSFSR, 255, 284, 335, 401, 514; Central Committee for, 471; Communist Party of, 231, 439, 443, 448, 450, 457, 521–522; Congress of People's Deputies of, 480–481, 521; cooperation with Lithuania, 523; corruption in, 123; Democratic Russia and, 111, 327–328; demographic composition of, 220; draft constitution of, 450–451; election law and, 330–332, 334, 353, 359; elections in, 260–261, 317, 338, 346, 349–350, 359, 492, 519, 530; federalism and, 202; fragmentation of, 461; Gorbachev and, 302, 465; *Gosplan* of, 254; national institutions of, 181–182, 203–205, 231, 356; national resources of, 443, 461; presidency of, 441, 451; rationing in, 210; Russian nationalism and, 233, 355; sovereignty of 323, 442, 521; Supreme Court of, 267; Supreme Soviet of, 111, 177, 181, 303, 317, 328, 416, 444, 451, 457, 480–481, 533; trade with U.S., 535; Volga Germans and, 221
RSFSR Writers Union, 160, 162–163, 170, 173, 179, 181, 320, 355
Ruble: banknote withdrawals, 528, 533; convertibility of, 534; devaluation of, 524
Rukh, 515

Rule of law, 32, 129–130, 136, 409, 412, 433, 443
Russian language, 193, 212–216
Russian literature, 154–155. *See also* Literature; Village prose
Russian nationalism, 118, 155–170, 172, 174–175, 179–181, 183, 192, 202, 204, 231, 233, 323, 355–357, 416, 438, 443, 448, 455, 492, 516; conservative, 110, 156, 162, 166, 173, 178; liberal, 110, 156–157, 160, 162, 164; neo-Stalinists, 157, 162, 164, 167; popularity of, 177–178; preservation of USSR and, 176, 192; radical slavophiles, 110, 157–158, 161–162, 164, 166, 169–170, 173, 178; thick journals and, 155–156
Russian Orthodox Church, 157, 355, 510
Russian Popular Front, 307
Russian revolution: from above, 129; *1917* and, 156, 173, 432, 482; *70th* anniversary of, 251. *See also* Bolshevik party
Russians: in Baltic republics, 175, 179, 191, 205, 207, 213, 224–225, 515; demographic trends, 175, 216; language requirements for, 176; as national minority, 194, 212–215, 221–222, 444
Russification, 28, 203, 212, 285, 434
Russophobia, 176
Ryabev Commission, 300, 309
Ryazan', 170
Ryzhkov program (1990), 435, 517, 523

Sajudis (Lithuanian National Front), 176, 224–225, 519
Sakhalin, 115
Sales tax, 526, 530
Saratov, 221, 254
Saudi Arabia, 523, 533; joint venture bank with, 535
Scandinavia, 211, 529
Scientific community. See Academia (Soviet)
Scientific exchanges, 501, 503
Scientific Research Institute of Labor, 53
Secession, 145, 182, 224, 230, 279, 386, 388, 416, 439, 477, 491; of Baltic republics, 176, 179, 191, 204, 212, 227–228, 397, 476; Caucasus and, 179, 227, 397; Gorbachev and, 400, 416, 421, 489; language laws and, 214; right of, 192, 200, 203, 339; Stalin and, 202
Second economy, 37, 502

Secretariat of Central Committee of the CPSU, 65, 69, 74–75, 77, 81
Security Council. *See* Presidential Security Council
Self-determination, 192, 202–203, 207, 222, 418
Senior citizens, 353; organization of, 43
Services, 66, 86, 99–101, 481, 491, 526; employment in, 35–36, 38, 95
Sex: education, 171; maturation, 98
Shadow economy, 122, 182
Shatalin Plan, 111, 387, 435–436, 441–443, 448, 475, 480, 486, 522–525
Siberia, 13, 54, 220, 514; coal mines in, 292, 294, 299, 308, 397; elections in, 256–257, 261; Ligachev and, 137, 264, 424; nuclear power and, 26; river diversion project, 160, 355; workers in, 265
Singapore, 477, 489
Slavophiles, 161, 177
Slyun'kov Commission, 297–298
Sochi, 139
Social contract, 8, 35–39, 41, 44, 57, 100, 158, 289–290; benefits of, 35, 44; cost of, 37, 41; dealignment of, 37–42; definition of, 35; economic reform and, 58; institutionalization of, 36, 44, 50; support for, 36
Social Democracy, 453–454
Social groups, 468; conflicts of, 9, 58, 101, 408, 420; influence of, 385, 391, 396, 411, 466; mobility and, 86, 100, 491
Social policy, changes in, 14, 33–34, 39, 91; crisis in, 38; defense of, 40, 53; economic reform and, 41, 179, 466; Gorbachev and, 8, 42, 44, 47, 56–58, 415, 422, 432; political reform and, 43, 51
Social security, 530
Socialism, 3, 9, 32, 34, 45, 73, 76, 79, 83–84, 142, 168, 171, 173, 197, 223, 291, 322, 348, 354, 387, 390–391, 408, 432, 435, 439, 443, 453, 455, 505, 514. *See also* Communist ideology; Leninism; Marxism
Sociology, 38, 91, 98
Solidarność (Solidarity), 56, 285, 292, 304, 307, 323, 509
South Africa, 317
South Korea, 317, 477, 489, 521, 524, 526, 531; airline disaster, 16

South Ossetian Autonomous Oblast, 191, 526–527, 529–530, 532
Sovetskaya Rossiya, 180–181, 396, 509, 530
Soviet Economy, 6–7, 9, 30, 63, 89, 101–102, 107–111, 138–139, 184–185, 187, 234, 245, 286, 324, 386, 423, 428, 445, 458, 474, 483, 495
Soviet of Nationalities, 514. *See also* Council of Nationalities
Soviet-American relations, 4, 11, 15, 17–18, 148–149, 279, 416, 479, 499–502, 504. *See also inter alia* Foreign policy; Strategic policy; Summit meetings; Superpowers; United States
Sovietology, 66, 183, 216; Chernobyl' and, 7; coal miners and, 290, 320; CPSU and, 32, 77, 118, 136, 248, 250, 268; criticism of, 285, 466–467, 471, 475, 482–483, 487; defense of, 488; economic reform and, 40, 67; elections and, 327, 373; Gorbachev and, 280, 395, 398, 422, 489; nationality question and, 109; *perestroyka* and, 148, 158; Western commentators and, 5, 9, 42, 51, 55, 108, 149, 193, 246, 264, 288, 486
Soviets, 449; authority of, 142, 322, 396, 408, 412; Bolshevik revolution and, 127, 321; CPSU and, 119, 124, 126–128, 133, 266, 268; elections and, 142, 180, 310, 312–313, 338, 465, 506; Lenin's vision of, 208, 335; local level, 125–126, 133, 147, 207, 261–262, 264, 300, 305, 308–309, 312, 317, 319, 328, 339, 347, 379; reform of, 117, 277, 301, 303; republic, 309, 312–313, 317
Sovkhozy. *See* Agriculture
Soyuz faction, 4, 439, 531, 533
Space flights, 506
Spain, 214, 410, 419, 446, 460, 524, 529
Speculators, 59
Spitak, 512
St. Petersburg name change, 535
Stagnation, 12, 67, 107, 197, 285, 316, 408. *See also* Brezhnev era
Stakhanovite movement, 48
Stalin Prize, 174
Stalingrad, 163, 221
Stalinism, 12, 14–15, 40–41, 73, 83, 109–110, 140–142, 154, 167–169, 171–175, 177, 192, 207, 219–220, 228, 247, 418, 466; defense of, 509; denunciations of,

507–508; excesses of, 121, 226; rehabilitation of victims, 510, 522; as Western concept, 501
Standard of living, 182, 317, 319, 450
Star Wars, 12, 17, 130. *See also* Strategic Defense Initiative (SDI)
State Committee for Material Reserves, 115
State Committee for Safety, 28
State Committee on Public Education, 116
State Committees, list of, 273–274
State Duma, 451
State Industrial Inspectorate Commission (State Industrial Atomic Inspectorate), 29
Statism, 32, 140–142, 321, 374
Stavropol', 12, 69, 75, 115, 123, 137, 258–259, 264, 278
Stepanakert, 509
Stock exchange, 533
Strategic arms limitation talks (SALT), 501, 503–504
Strategic arms reduction talks (START), 513–514, 534, 536
Strategic Defense Initiative (SDI), 500, 503–504
Strategic policy, 11, 18, 147
Strikes, 196, 213, 215, 221–222, 246, 277, 281, 285, 288–290, 314–317, 324, 434, 480, 490, 514; ban on, 531; living conditions and, 532. *See also* Coal miners' strikes
Students, 179, 534; demonstrations of, 502, 504; exchange of, 510; tent city and, 524
Subsidiaries, foreign owned, 524
Subsidies, 182, 193, 209, 211, 356, 480; coal industry and, 302; consumer goods, 37; economic reform and, 32; food, 37; housing, 37; transportation, 37; wheat purchase, 506, 513
Succession to power: Andropov, 12; Chernenko, 12; Gorbachev, 13–15, 18
Sumgait, 509
Summit meetings, 118, 148; Geneva (*1985*), 11, 18, 501; Reykjavik (*1986*), 503–504; Washington, D.C. (*1987*), 9, 507–508; Moscow (*1988*), 509–510; Malta (*1989*), 517; Washington, D.C. (*1990*), 521; other U.S.-USSR presidential meetings, 511, 523, 525, 534–536

Superpowers, 11–12, 167, 172, 408–409; relation between, 16–18. *See also* Soviet-American relations
Supply system, 133, 285, 293, 302. *See also* Distribution network; *Gossnab*
Supreme Court (USSR), 43, 267, 508, 510
Supreme Soviet of USSR, 249, 258, 303, 306, 457; cabinet confirmation by, 270, 274–275; chairmanship of, 136, 267–269, 275, 447, 451, 472, 500; conservative members of, 181; economic reform and, 432; elections to, 114, 257, 264, 267; Gorbachev and, 254, 277, 283, 412, 435, 440; Inter-Regional Group and, 227; legislation, 503–504, 506, 512, 514; legislative power of, 144, 262–263; member rotation in, 437; military and, 439; nuclear energy and, 26; property and, 211; reform of, 200; republics and, 207, 209, 212; *Rossiya* Club and, 355; Russian nationalism and, 177; Ryzhkov and, 276; secession and, 204; sessions of, 28, 76, 127, 143; television and, 217, 301, 411, 413; trade unions and, 304; workers and, 180
Svedlovsk, 137, 180, 256, 471
Sweden, 6, 23, 26, 502
Syndicalism, 318

Tadzhikistan, 92, 192, 220, 519, 523, 527
Taiwan, 477, 489
Tallinn, 191, 207, 215, 506, 515
Tambov, 123, 260
Tashkent, 509
Tatar ASSR, 137, 205, 285, 533
Taxation, 32, 177, 182, 209, 443, 480, 515, 534; evasion of, 122
Tbilisi, 191, 205, 217, 228, 266, 397, 512–513
Teachers, 47–48
Television, 17, 252, 300, 356, 407; censorship of, 531; Congress of People's Deputies and, 266, 411, 450, 513; CPSU's monopoly and, 522; criticism of, 164; *glasnost'* and, 107, 217, 246, 285, 301, 408; Gorbachev on, 507–508; liberalization of, 163; Lithuania and, 519; nationality question and, 195; party conference and, 121, 127, 132; Supreme Soviet and, 514; *Vremya*, 154;

Vzglyad, 526; Yel'tsin on, 528–529. *See also* Media (Soviet)

Temperance Society, 258

Territorial homelands, 192

Terror, 155, 168, 172–174, 249, 462

"Thaw," Gorbachev's, 66, 83–84

Thick journals, 110, 153–155, 177. *See also Molodaya gvardiya; Nash sovremennik; Novyy Mir*

Third World, 356, 392, 400, 418, 477, 491

Three Mile Island, 24

Time magazine, 390, 419, 471, 500

Tiraspol', 213

Tomsk, 137, 168, 256, 264

Totalitarianism, 129, 387, 419–420, 431, 444, 460, 465, 488, 491

Trade Unions, 57, 307, 436; attempts to organize, 37; Congress (*17th*) of, 55; Congress (*18th*) of, 52, 56; elections and, 339, 341, 350, 353, 357, 371; enterprise councils and, 52, 56; guaranteed seats of, 258, 413; independent, 290, 313–314, 318, 421; influence of, 55, 288, 321–322; legislation on, 526; public opinion of, 39, 289, 375, 434; resistance of, 40, 51, 56; Russian nationalism and, 110, 180; social benefits and, 289; social contract and, 36; Western model of, 320; Yel'tsin and, 279. *See also* Coal miners' strikes; Central Trade Union Council

Transportation, 37, 95, 509, 530; right to strike in, 516

Travel, 392, 407, 415

Tsarist tradition, 140, 156, 173, 299, 326, 434

Tselinograd, 221

Turkestan, 265

Turkey, 477, 526, 530

Turkmenistan, 220, 523

Twelfth Five-Year Plan (*1986–1990*), 5, 18–19, 26, 43, 503

Tyumen', 137, 181–182, 256, 292, 315, 516

Udmurt ASSR, 137

Ukraine, 29, 179, 253–255, 285, 294, 397, 432, 502, 517, 524; Chernobyl' and, 7, 19, 24, 28, 30; Communist Party of, 515–516; demographic composition of, 220; elections in, 260, 264, 519; government of, 23; inter-republic migrations and, 207; inter-republic negotiations and, 111, 442; national composition of, 220; nationalism and, 28, 312; parliament of, 20, 213; Secretariat of, 253–255; sovereignty of, 522. *See also* Donbas coal basin; Kiev

Ukrainian Popular Front (*Rukh*), 215

Ul'yanovsk, 137

Unemployment, 57, 72, 192, 290, 319, 436, 443, 520. *See also* Employment

Uniate Church, 517

Union of Kuzbas Workers, 309, 311

Union of Theater Workers, 162

Union Treaty, 111, 387, 435, 440, 456–457, 490, 522, 525–526, 529, 531–534

United Front of Russian Workers (OFT), 110, 180–181, 233

United Kingdom, 6, 25, 67, 369, 446, 470, 500–502, 512, 516, 519, 523; Gorbachev's *1984* visit, 4, 13, 16–17, 465

United Nations, 502–503, 511, 524–525, 529, 533

United States, 4, 9, 68, 92–93, 116, 121, 266, 277–278, 280, 308, 407, 460, 465, 468; agricultural credits, 527; ambassadorship to USSR, 534; Chernenko and, 16; Cold War and, 148, 150; Congress of, 507; consulates in USSR, 504; credits for food, 534; Department of Agriculture, 506; Department of Commerce, 505; economic advisors, 516; embassy in Moscow, 503, 506; FBI, 501, 503; Federal Reserve, 516; food aid, 526; medical aid, 527; National Security Agency, 501; Navy, 500, 508; Pentagon, 516; perceptions of *perestroyka* and, 109, 149; political system of, 144, 222, 256, 262, 369, 457, 482–483; San Francisco, 521; Social Science Research Council, 8, 112; Sovietology and, 280, 466, 471, 474, 478; trade with RSFSR, 535; trade with USSR, 500. *See also inter alia* Disarmament; Soviet-American relations; Summit meetings

United Toilers' Front of Russia, 355

United Workers' Front, 307, 320

Urals, 24, 26, 137, 256, 261, 264–265

Urbanization, 92–94, 98–99

Uskoreniye, 3, 5, 65, 471

USSR State Prize for Literature, 158

USSR Writers Union, 115, 167
Uzbekistan, 122–123, 191–192, 220, 253, 511, 514, 516; rioting in, 521; sovereignty of, 522

Vatican, 469, 517, 525
Verkhovnyy Sovet (VS). *See* Supreme Soviet
Veterans, 43, 258, 319
Vice-presidency of USSR, 457, 511, 526
Vienna, 29, 504, 533
Village prose, 155–157, 160, 179
Vilnius, 214, 506, 515, 518–520, 525, 527, 534–535
Vladivostok, 503
Volga Germans, 192, 200, 220–221; aid to, 530
Volga River, 355
Volgograd, 221
Vorkuta coal basin, 288; miners' strike and, 300–302, 304–308, 514–516, 529; production of, 291; worker-manager relations, 294
Voronezh, 87, 260
Vremya. See Television
VTsSPS. *See* Central Trade Union Council
Vzglyad. See Television

Wages, 34, 37, 48, 120, 319, 503, 523; administration of, 39, 53–54, 86, 100, 289; coal miners and, 291–294, 298, 311; cuts in, 290; decentralization and, 58; differentials in, 43–44, 54–55, 66; egalitarianism and, 38; productivity and, 79; reform of, 35–36, 48–50, 282; worker unrest and, 288, 307
"War of laws," 443, 461
Warsaw, 323, 516, 521
Warsaw Treaty Organization (WTO), 499, 502–503, 506, 513–514, 516, 518, 521, 525, 529–530
Washington, D.C., 11, 16, 112
Weberian theory, 129
West Germany, 221, 271, 502, 506, 510–511, 514, 523
Western Europe, 16, 211, 320, 348, 354, 387, 392, 396, 408, 410, 453, 482
Westernization, 129; advocates of, 111, 157, 374; bureaucracy and, 119; Gor-

bachev and, 278, 408, 415, 477, 489; opposition to, 161–162, 170–171, 355, 390; *perestroyka* and, 162, 164, 171; reform and, 174, 348, 392.
White collar workers, 50; elections and, 340, 342, 352, 375; public participation of, 88; social policy and, 35–36, 96; wages of, 49, 97; women as, 98
Wildcat strikes, 533
Women, 49, 101, 160, 259; committees of, 43, 218, 258; earnings of, 98; elections and, 339–343, 352, 370–372; paraprofessional, 9, 95; professional, 9, 95, 98–99;
Workers, 9, 97, 179, 407; elections and, 250, 258–259, 263; Gorbachev and, 47, 58, 433; management and, 51, 86, 282, 289–290, 296; organization of, 287–288, 301, 303–305, 307, 309–311, 315–323, 449; prices and, 284; reform and, 49, 89, 321; social mobility of, 96; Supreme Soviet and, 262; unemployment of, 43, 60; unrest and, 37, 40, 100, 246, 287–288, 291, 301, 314–315; wages of, 8, 44–45, 48, 55, 59. *See also* Blue collar workers; Coal miners' strikes; Labor force
Working middle class, 95–98, 101
World Bank, 526, 534
World War I, 85
World War II, 93, 171, 213, 220
Writers, 69, 75, 78, 84–85, 155–158, 179, 339, 341, 378

Yakutia, 6, 219, 502
Yaroslavl', 115, 123
Yavlinskiy-Harvard plan, 535
Yedinstvo (Unity), 181, 221, 355, 528, 532
Yel'sk, 27
Yerevan', 509–510, 521
Young Communist League. *See* Komsomol
Youth, 192, 478–479
Yugoslavia, 125, 172, 211, 318, 467, 477, 509
Yuppies (Soviet), 8–9, 47, 98

Zheleznovodsk, 522
Zionism, 169, 357